THE TURBULENT YEARS

by the same author

LONDON LINES
I HAVE NO GUN BUT I CAN SPIT
UNAUTHORIZED VERSIONS: POEMS AND THEIR PARODIES
THE FABER BOOK OF ENGLISH HISTORY IN VERSE
THE FABER BOOK OF CONSERVATISM

The Turbulent Years

My Life in Politics

KENNETH BAKER

faber and faber

LONDON · BOSTON

To Mary and our children

First published in 1993
by Faber and Faber Limited
3 Queen Square London WCIN 3AU

Photoset by Parker Typesetting Service, Leicester
Printed in England by Clays Ltd, St Ives plc

© Kenneth Baker, 1993

Kenneth Baker is hereby identified as author of this work in
accordance with Section 77 of the Copyright, Designs and
Patents Act 1988.

A CIP record for this book
is available from the British Library

ISBN 0-571-17077-3

2 4 6 8 10 9 7 5 3 1

Contents

List of Illustrations

Preface

'To disentangle confusion and illustrate obscurity'

– Dr Johnson

The 1980s were turbulent years not just for me but also for the country. I was a Minister from 1981 and a member of the Cabinet from 1985, responsible for some of the most controversial and significant policies of the Thatcher years. I sometimes think we forget just how controversial some of these policies actually were.

As Industry Minister, I fought for three years against bitter opposition to privatize British Telecom, and BT is now generally regarded as one of the greatest successes of privatization. It paved the way for privatization of the other utilities, and as Environment Secretary I announced the commitment to privatize the water industry. This was condemned as selling off the family silver but, as I explain, if it had not happened then the vital capital programmes of that great industry would by now have been slashed by the Treasury.

The abolition of the Greater London Council and the Inner London Education Authority were also controversial, but today few call for their return. As Education Secretary, the education reforms I introduced in 1986–88 were angrily opposed by the vested interests of Britain's education establishment, though many classroom teachers welcomed them. Controversy still rumbles on about some aspects of these reforms, such as testing, but a general consensus has developed that these reforms were intrinsically necessary and on the right lines.

As Party Chairman, I was at the heart of the events that led to the decline and fall of Margaret Thatcher. This episode will be much written about, not least by herself. But what I have tried to do is to set out the flow of events as I witnessed them.

Finally, as Home Secretary, I had to fight hard in the face of opposition from the European Community in order to retain Britain's right to control her own frontiers.

xi

These years were certainly turbulent and controversial, and I was not surprised that I found myself the target of much criticism. However, that is the lot of most senior politicians. My wife, Mary, who has been for me a constant source of help and advice throughout my political life, has always said that there are two requirements for political success – rude health and a thick skin. I have been lucky to have both. Lucky too to have had the chance of serving a great Prime Minister, Margaret Thatcher, and making a positive contribution to the successes of the 1980s – a decade which I think will increasingly be looked back upon as one of the pivotal periods in British history this century.

I have found that writing an autobiography is a fascinating business. Although the impressions and views that I formed of people, places and events have not changed very much over the years, when I set about re-creating the actual flow of events of which I was part then impressions proved a poor guide. Because memory plays tricks with the past, events are sometimes remembered only in part, or in a jumbled order which misleads the writer when assessing their relevance. I didn't keep a diary for every day of my life, but I did so for those times when I was engaged in important and exciting events which I felt should be recorded – the high days and the holy days. Drawing upon these records has been invaluable. First it ensured that the events about which I write in this book did take place in the sequence I report them and that memory had not transposed them to the wrong day, week, month or even year. Second, a diary brings back to life the drama and excitement felt at the time. Most diarists are too keen to commit to posterity their own self-justifying views. While it may be important to know and record these, I found that some of the most fascinating records I kept were the views and comments of those I met.

Some very personal things have been said to me by two of the Prime Ministers I have served – Ted Heath and Margaret Thatcher. Since some of these things were clearly said in confidence, I have respected this. Both Prime Ministers said many other things to me, when we were alone or in the presence of others, where clearly they did not expect that same degree of confidence to be extended. So I have been as frank in my record of these turbulent years as is consistent with trust. I have no doubt that an elected politician who has been involved in major political changes as I have been repays a debt to the public and to posterity by setting down his account of what he saw, what he heard, and how he saw events happen.

Dr Johnson was once reproached for being too frank in his criticism of the Government of the day. In his magisterial reply, infinitely more eloquent than anything I could express, he set out the guiding principle which I have followed:

The time is now come in which every Englishman expects to be informed of the national affairs, and in which he has a right to have that expectation gratified. For whatever may be urged by Ministers, or those whom vanity or interest make the followers of Ministers, concerning the necessity of confidence in our governors, and the presumption of prying with profane eyes into the recesses of policy, it is evident that this reverence can be claimed only by counsels yet unexecuted, and projects suspended in deliberation. But when a design has ended in miscarriage or success, when every eye and every ear is witness to general discontent or general satisfaction, it is then a proper time to disentangle confusion and illustrate obscurity, to show by what causes every event was produced, and in what effects it is likely to terminate; to lay down with distinct particularity what rumour always huddles in general exclamations, or perplexes by undigested narratives; to show whence happiness or calamity is derived, and whence it may be expected, and honestly to lay before the people what inquiry can gather of the past, and conjecture can estimate of the future.

I would like to give my thanks to many people – principally Mary and our children, who have stood up so well to the demands of my life in politics. I was lucky to have had three such supportive friends in John Lee, Alistair Burt, and Steve Norris as my Parliamentary Private Secretaries during most of my ministerial career. I was also fortunate to have two outstandingly able, eloquent and wise political advisers, Peter Davies and Tony Kerpel. I would like especially to thank Tony for the help he has given me in writing this book. He was at my side for many of the events and has been a valuable source of recall and accuracy. I would also like to thank my excellent, hard-working, good-humoured and ever patient secretary, Kathy Hubbard.

I would like to put on the record my appreciation and gratitude to all my Departmental Private Secretaries for their loyalty and the long hours they devoted, and also thank all those civil servants in the various Departments where I have served for their work in helping me to shape Government policies.

Finally, I would like to thank all those people in Acton, St Marylebone and the Mole Valley who supported me and voted for me on many occasions and gave me the great honour of representing them in the House of Commons. Without their electoral support I would have had no opportunity to play my part in the Turbulent Years.

CHAPTER I

Early Years

*Family – School – National Service – Oxford – Business
and Marriage*

Anyone who has pursued a political career is often asked when they first became interested in politics. There is no easy answer, because for me – and I suspect for most others – there was no one single moment or event which led to the vital decision. An interest in and a commitment to politics depends upon a wide range of influences including family background, education, experience, friends, ideas, ambition, and a desire to help other people. It was my grandfather, Edward Baker, who first made me conscious of the political world, though he was not a particularly political person. In the late 1940s he had retired from his job as a manager at Newport Docks and came to live with us in Twickenham. As our house there had three bedrooms, with one for my parents and one for my older sister Dodie, I shared my bedroom with him for four years. I came to love and respect him greatly.

My grandfather told me many stories about the exciting industrial struggles in the docks at Newport during the late nineteenth and early twentieth century, but he had no bitterness or any feelings of class hatred. He had a sturdy, independent view of life, believing very much that people should pull themselves up by their own efforts. At the same time he had a strong conviction that one had a duty to help those who had fallen into difficulties. He used to sing to me many of the old music hall songs, and one in particular about Disraeli, whom he looked upon as a bit of a card.

My grandfather was a remarkable person. He had left school at the age of twelve in 1882, when his father, a carpenter, simply walked out one day after telling his wife he was off to America to seek his fame and fortune. Once this was done, he intended to send for her and the children. My great-grandfather left behind a young family of five children with no means of support, and so my great-grandmother took in washing while my grandfather, the younger son, went out to earn money

money for his mother and sisters. He started with various jobs in a bakery, working twelve or fourteen hours a day, and he then found work at Newport Docks as a coal trimmer. Newport was at that time a busy coaling port that shipped much of the anthracite mined in the Welsh Valleys, and my grandfather was to work in the docks for sixty-two years. His job was to be at the dockside when a ship arrived, and help to load the coal and trim the balance of the cargo – on his wedding certificate he is described as a coal trimmer. At that time labourers were hired by the day for as little money as the shipowners could get away with. My grandfather became involved with the dockers' union, and as he could write with a beautiful copperplate hand – his mother had seen to that – he became secretary of the local branch of the Dock, Wharf, Riverside and General Workers' Union and kept their minutes.

The hours were long and the wages low. It was the normal practice to work shifts of thirty-six hours, and a man earning £4 a week had a very good job. I remember my grandfather saying, 'We all lived within easy reach of the docks, and although working hours were long we were very happy. We worked in groups of eleven and shared our work and pleasures. Usually the men would call for one another on their way to work, and their wives were all friendly with one another, like their menfolk.' The pleasures before the First World War were simple. 'We would hire a hall for dancing or gymnastics and all the equipment would be bought by the men themselves, and as a real treat a docker's family would hire a four-horse brake for a day's outing.'

Edward Baker was an active trade unionist in those early days of that great movement. Ben Tillett, the dockers' leader, used to visit his house down in the docks, and he even met Keir Hardie. He was asked to stand as a Member of Parliament in the interests of the new Labour Party, but since MPs got no salary he simply could not afford it, for by that time he was married and had two children.

He was a kind and very gentle man who always thought the best of people. There was one person, however, whom he could never forgive, and that was his own father, who eventually returned one day from America as penniless as the day he left. He walked in the door and said to his wife, Mary, 'I've come home, can I have a cup of tea please.' She accepted him back. A handsome man, he certainly had ideas well above his station and his friends called him 'The General'. The story grew, and he did nothing to suppress it, that he had made a lot of money and bought land in Chicago which he had subsequently lost gambling. At any rate for a penniless carpenter he lived well, and the only photograph we have of him shows him in evening dress. He was a good craftsman and we still have one of the tables that he made. He was largely self-taught and had committed to memory many speeches from Shakespeare's plays, which he loved to recite. He died early this century from throat cancer whilst sitting quietly in his chair.

My grandfather had by then become a popular figure in the docks. He bought a house in Milman Street for £100. During the First World War he collected money for the families of dockers who had been called up and were injured or killed in action. Many families in Newport were kept from starvation and misery through his work, and in 1918 he was presented with a hand-painted illuminated address by the dockers as a token of their gratitude for the work he had done for their families. I am proud to have this hanging on our wall at home.

In 1899 Edward had married an Irish girl, Margaret Desmond, whose family – like so many others – had left Ireland in the 1880s and 1890s to find work. Margaret was strikingly beautiful and had trained to be a teacher at a college in Wandsworth. I still have her annotated copy of *Hamlet* from her student days. She was a strong and determined character, and when one of my grandfather's nieces, Ada, was also left behind by parents who sailed off to America to find their fortune – which they actually did in Chicago – Margaret took in Ada and brought her up as one of the family. That was how families lived in those days. My father told me that when Margaret died unexpectedly young in 1917, there was a huge funeral in Newport and her coffin was carried through the streets on the shoulders of friends and mourners.

Such was the trust in my grandfather by both employers and workers at the docks that he finally became a manager of the port during the Second World War. He had a remarkable influence upon me, instilling through the example of his life the importance of serving others. I believe that his disenchantment with the Labour Party dated from the time when Jimmy Thomas came to Newport to try to settle a strike. Although he failed, he claimed credit later when it was settled. My grandfather became pretty disenchanted with politics of that sort. I think that he probably ended up voting Conservative, but we rarely discussed current political issues.

His son, my father, had left school at sixteen and joined the Civil Service as a clerk in the Post Office, which meant moving to West

Kensington and taking digs in London. He was determined to make the most of his chances, as the Baker-Desmond desire for self-improvement was very strong in him. From his meagre earnings he bought books which I still have, among them a collection of Tennyson's poems, and he must have felt very proud when he purchased his first leather-bound volume of poetry. He continued his education by studying at home, where he took exams to become a chartered secretary and a certified accountant.

My father had that love of literature which is a thread passed from generation to generation in our family. He started to read Dickens, whose books became his abiding love. He used to read aloud to my sister and myself, and we'd talk of the various characters as if they were family friends just about to come through the door. When I was ten, my father gave me an illustrated copy of *A Christmas Carol*, which I still cherish. Both my wife, Mary, a graduate in English, and I have tried to pass on to our children this love of literature, because the English language is the most valuable asset our nation has. It needs to be cherished, used well, kept in good order, and passed on in good shape. It gladdens us that all our children, like ourselves, seem to spend more time reading books than watching television.

After the war ended in 1918, my father returned to Newport to work at the Board of Trade, where he met my mother, Amanda Harries. She also had an Irish mother and her father was also a Welsh dock worker. I only met him a couple of times. He was a big bluff man who towards the end of his life had a stroke. When he started to come around from it he spoke only in Welsh, which he had last used as a boy, and his family could not understand him. My mother, Amanda, was one of the kindest people I ever knew. I never heard her speak ill of anyone in her life – she was always looking for the good things in others – and she was hardly ever angry with either my sister or myself. She was devoted to her family, very proud of her house, and her simple goodness made us a happy and united family.

When my mother and father married in 1927, my father bought a semi-detached house in the better part of Newport, and I was born there in 1934. Few mothers entered hospital in those days. When my father's promotion took him to London in 1939 he sold the house for less in cash than he had paid for it, a result of the deflation of the 1930s.

We then lived in Twickenham for a year, and my first real memories stem from that time, and the outbreak of war. The radio was crucially important, and I remember hearing tunes like 'Run, Rabbit, Run', 'Who Do You Think You're Kidding, Mr Hitler?' and 'Hang Out the Washing on the Siegfried Line'. I also recall putting sandbags around the windows of our downstairs lavatory, since my mother took Dodie and me to sleep there during the bombing raids. Some nights we were taken down in blankets by a neighbour to sleep in his underground shelter. I remember listening in a hushed group to Churchill speaking on the radio. I was too young to understand much more than that he was a good Englishman protecting us from more bombs and the villains called 'Hitler the Hun' and 'Musso the Wop' who featured in the *Dandy* and the *Beano*.

In the middle of the Blitz my father's office moved to Liverpool. We were evacuated to Southport to join him, and it was there that I was really brought up. We lived in a flat at Number 70 The Promenade, right on the seafront at the end of the Marine Lake, looking out on those vast stretches of sand which the sea only covers about three times a year. It became one huge playground and I walked many miles over it, taking care to avoid the treacherous sinking sands found in the Ribble estuary, and which we were told had swallowed up whole shrimping carts in Victorian times.

During the war we had double summertime, which meant that the clocks were put forward two hours. Like many children who lived during these times I have memories of long, sunny summer evenings, light until well past ten o'clock, when we would sit up late to watch the glorious sunsets over the Irish Sea. I went to the nearest local primary school, Holy Trinity, and walked the mile to get there with my sister. It was a small Victorian red-brick school with a yard enclosed by a high wall, and no playing field. The school prided itself on good old-fashioned education – learning tables by heart, spelling tests, books to be taken home and poems to be recited – but the closest we came to primary science was to go on a walk, cut down some pussywillow and then draw it.

In 1986 I was holding a constituency surgery in Dorking when a small elderly lady called Kathleen Renn came to see me. She asked whether I was the same Kenneth Baker who had been at Holy Trinity School during the War. When I said 'Yes', she replied that she had taught me. I did indeed remember her when she had then been Miss Makin, a young teacher with black hair who had helped me with spelling and English. I was delighted when, a little later as Education Secretary, I was able to take her with me on a nostalgic visit to our old school, a visit which evoked happy memories for us both.

The War dominated everything. At night we heard the bombers over Liverpool and sometimes over Preston. After these attacks my mother would take us by train to Liverpool to see the damage, and the miraculous survival of the Liver birds. At school, wounded soldiers from the infirmary on the sea front would come to tell us about their experiences. We sang patriotic songs like 'There'll Always Be an England', and worked hard to sell National Savings stamps for the war effort. When victory was in sight we had a great tableau in which I was one of the supporters of Britannia. I remember passing one of the bandstands in Southport in 1941 where a vicar was taking a service in which every single verse of 'Onward Christian Soldiers' was being sung with great enthusiasm. In 1945 at the same bandstand I heard 'Deep in the Heart of Texas', for by the end of the war American soldiers had suddenly appeared in Southport. They were popular, since they held huge bonfire parties on the sands where they gave as presents to children small packets of powdered soup, which I had never tasted before.

This was a very happy time for me. The main entertainments were the radio and cinema. I tried to get home early from school to listen to the plays which started at 4.30 p.m., just before Children's Hour, and were often thrillers like the Sherlock Holmes or Father Brown stories. 'Saturday Night Theatre', the main play of the week, was eagerly awaited and listened to by millions. My sister used to get the weekly magazine, *The Picturegoer*, a sepia-tinted journal with the latest news of the films and their stars. We went to the pictures a lot – it was the time of Charles Laughton as Captain Bligh, James Mason as 'The Man in Grey', and Margaret Lockwood as 'The Wicked Lady'. When I later moved to the King George V Grammar School in Southport the whole school was taken to see Laurence Olivier's *Henry V*, a film which to me was sheer magic.

In the winter, when we could not play on the sands, my father, sister and I would set off on a Sunday afternoon for a long walk around the town. We would try and pass as many of the twelve cinemas as possible so that we could look at the black and white photographs of scenes from the films which were posted up outside. One of my closest friends at Holy Trinity was the son of the manager of the Palladium Cinema in Lord Street. He was a special friend because he could smuggle us in to the final half-hour of the afternoon film. I soon became an expert in film endings.

I remember very clearly going to the theatre, rather than to a panto-mime, for the first time. My parents took my sister and me to see a play about the Scarlet Pimpernel at a theatre in Liverpool. I think the theatre was called The Crane. I can still see in my mind's eye the first scene set in a French inn near Calais where the Scarlet Pimpernel, pursued by the agents of Robespierre, was hiding some aristocrats he had saved from the guillotine in Paris. Would the packet boat arrive in time? I remem-ber the lazy, grubby waiter at the inn being greeted with laughter as he spat on a plate and wiped it on his greasy apron. I can clearly recall these scenes. Although the actors were not famous, the producer unknown, the sets a bit shaky and the props rather tawdry, to me it was still magic. I simply adored the theatre and asked to go as often as possible. Even today I still experience a thrill of anticipation every time I sit in a theatre and the curtain goes up.

In 1946, after we had returned to Twickenham, my parents would take my sister and me to the Richmond Theatre to see the regular repertory company which changed its production every two weeks. We would go on Monday evenings, since the 4/6d tickets cost less on that day. We would walk over the Chertsey Bridge and then across Rich-mond Green to that lovely little theatre, now thankfully saved from closure. There we saw plays by Somerset Maugham, Priestley, Shaw, Terence Rattigan, Sheridan, and ones that have virtually now been forgotten like *The Shop at Sly Corner* and *Edwin, My Son*.

The only political event I can recall from those far-off Southport days was the General Election of 1945 and the lively campaign run by the local Liberal candidate, whose name was Bob Martin. His genuine claim to fame was that his family firm produced the famous 'Bob Martin' dog powders. His opponent, the Tory incumbent, was one of the old school, a member of the Hudson Soap family. Bob Martin failed to win – my first experience of Liberal disappointment.

School

Back in Twickenham after the War, I won a place at Hampton Grammar School, a fine, traditional grammar school that has since become independent. It was there that I started to learn Latin and French, and I was introduced to the serious study of Shakespeare when we read in class *Henry IV*, Part I. One day a boy whose name also happened to be Baker left to go to St Paul's, a school of which I had barely heard. I must have mentioned this to my father, for some time later he asked me whether I would like to go there as well. He applied on my behalf and I went for an interview to the great Victorian red-brick building in Hammersmith which has, alas, since been demolished, though I imagine we would not make that same mistake again. I was seen by one of the legendary Pauline teachers, A. B. Cook, and asked to write an essay and answer some maths problems. I was then offered a place.

I was very surprised at this translation. I think it was part of my father's continual desire to do the best for his children, and I was very grateful to him for this. As a middle-ranking civil servant it was also a very substantial financial sacrifice for him to pay the school fees. We lived modestly, did not own a car at that time, and never went out to restaurants or took holidays abroad. Both of my parents shared the attitude that wealth and material things were less important than giving opportunities to my sister and myself. My sister Dodie also lived at home sometimes helping me with my homework. She went on from her grammar school to art college.

St Paul's, founded in 1509, was the London school to which the rising middle classes, particularly merchants, had over the centuries sent their sons. Its whole ethos was built on effort, competition and achievement. It maintained exceptionally high academic standards and provided an excellent education for the strivers. One of the school's greatest features has been its attitude to religious tolerance, which was insisted upon by its founder, John Colet, in 1509. In the Humanist tradition he decreed that the school should provide free education for 153 scholars – for that was the number of fishes in the miraculous draft – of all colours, creeds and races. As a result, many Jewish families chose St Paul's, which brought to it the talents of the Jewish people, while latterly the school has attracted many Indian, African and Chinese pupils. St Paul's was much more cosmopolitan and metropolitan than most other independent public schools.

I was lucky to come under the spell of two outstanding teachers: P. D. Whiting for history, and C. P. Longland for English. P. D. Whiting was almost totally bald, and his strong bull-like physique commanded respect from his pupils. Dedicated to the study of history, he had become an acknowledged expert in Byzantine coins and was a moving spirit behind the Historical Association, a group of devoted amateur historians. He invited notable historians to speak at the school, and I remember going to hear R. H. Tawney lecture at the London School of

Economics about the profits made by Army and Navy contractors in the reign of Charles I. P. D. Whiting took us out on Saturdays, rather unusually for schools in those days, to places like Audley End, Porchester Castle and the oldest Saxon church in East Anglia. In these ways he made history interesting and compelling. He became an institution at St Paul's, having many years earlier taught Max Beloff, and later Karl Leyser, who was to become one of the Chichele Professors at All Souls. After my generation, at least another twenty years of Paulines benefited from Whiting's enthusiasm. He was also good at getting his pupils into Oxford and Cambridge, and I have little doubt that my acceptance at Magdalen College, Oxford, where Karl Leyser was the Senior Dean, was very much due to P. D. Whiting.

My English teacher, C. P. Longland, had the great gift of enthusing his pupils by infecting them with a love of literature. We studied Shakespeare in that thorough textual way which meant one really had to know the play backwards. Greater understanding led to greater enjoyment, and I still think this is the best way to teach Shakespeare, but it requires gifted and well-educated teachers. It was C. P. Longland who introduced me to the work of G. K. Chesterton, himself an Old Pauline. I remember him reading the following passage from one of Chesterton's essays. It is a brilliant piece of writing which in two sentences, by the clever use of words, images and assonance, sums up the contrasting natures of France and England:

It requires long years of plenitude and quiet, the slow growth of great parks, the seasoning of oaken beams, the dark enrichment of red wine in cellars and in inns, all the leisure and life of England through many centuries to produce at last the generous and genial fruit of English snobbishness. And it requires battery and barricade, songs in the streets and ragged men dead for an idea to produce and justify the terrible flower of French indecency.

I decided to read more Chesterton and went off to Foyles, where I bought a first edition of a book of his essays for 3/6d. I just had to have it even though it meant I did not have enough money to take the 73 bus back from Oxford Street to Richmond. And so I walked back from Charing Cross Road to our house in Twickenham, a very good way to get to know the streets of London. I had picked up the bug of book collecting and I have not stopped since.

I have only collected those writers whom I have enjoyed reading, but I do like to buy, when I can afford to, the first editions of their works.

When I began collecting books one could buy a Dickens first edition for about two guineas. Today, depending upon their condition and the type of binding, they start at £60 and can go up to £1,000. One of my pleasures today is to try and spot the great writers and poets of the future.

Collecting, like any other passion, requires thorough determination. When I made ministerial visits out of London I insisted, much to the chagrin of civil servants who largely look upon their Ministers as machines that exist only to do what the Department wants, that I had to visit the local secondhand bookshop. All my Private Secretaries became familiar with *Skoobs Directory of Antiquarian Booksellers*. I am glad to say that some of the civil servants who accompanied me also started to buy books.

St Paul's believed in keeping the bodies as well as the minds of its boys active and busy. There was a long lunch-break of two hours when every boy had to do some sport – rugby, cricket, squash, swimming and even boxing. Each year, every boy at the school had to enter the Green Cup, which meant having to box for at least three rounds. This is now thought too barbaric and has been stopped. Although I cannot say I liked it, and some boys faced it with fear, the annual boxing competition did create a sort of manly camaraderie which it is all too easy to sneer at. Various interest groups also met in the lunch-hour and John Adair, one of my closest friends who was later to become the Professor of Leadership Studies at Surrey University, and I founded the Historical Society. We also debated furiously, first at the Chesterton Society named after that delightful and polemical writer, and then in the Eighth Form at the Union Debating Society. John arranged many debates with other schools, and back in 1952 and 1953 he organized the first school debating contests, which have developed into the annual Observer Mace competition.

Around this time I began to take an interest in current affairs and politics. My father was not particularly partisan but I do remember his explaining to me the austerity Budgets of Stafford Cripps. In those postwar years of rationing, when each year I queued up to get ration books for such basic things as bread, everything seemed to be pretty bleak and I could see little advantage in Socialism if after five years of peace we still had rationing. By 1951 I felt the Attlee Government had very largely run its course and I was glad there was a change. Some of my friends at school were Socialists; if I was anything at that time it was rather more Liberal or Conservative.

These were the days when every young man was called up at eighteen and had to do National Service for two years. We prepared for this at St Paul's by becoming members of the Combined Cadet Force, which virtually every boy joined. We went to school in uniform on Mondays, and paraded in the afternoon. There were annual camps and field days, when we marched over Hammersmith Suspension Bridge, remembering to break step, on our way to exercises on Barnes Common and Richmond Park. There was no grumbling, just the recognition that this had to be done, and that St Paul's might as well train its young to be leaders who could get officers' commissions.

National Service

After I had been offered a place to study history at Magdalen College, Oxford, I decided like most of my generation to do my National Service first. After medical examinations my call-up papers arrived and I reported to the Barracks of the Middlesex Regiment in Mill Hill, having first been sent a single ticket to get there together with a postal order for my first week's wages, which amounted to 28 shillings. After ten weeks of square-bashing, floor-scrubbing, endless bulling of boots and blancoing of webbing, I asked to be transferred from the Infantry to the Royal Artillery, which I considered marginally more cerebral. I went to the Mons Officer Cadet School at Aldershot, and after being commissioned as a Second Lieutenant I went out to the Suez Canal Zone to join the 181 Independent Light Battery.

I enjoyed my National Service because it was the first time I had been away from home and that was good in itself. I learnt the crucial importance of teamwork, from the Commanding Officer at the top, right down to the latest recruit. I had instilled into me a responsibility for the lives of others. I also came to respect the professionalism of the well trained, disciplined Army mind, which did not depend upon great flights of imagination but rather upon the steadiness and thoroughness of well established drills and procedures. The British Army was not, and is not, good at producing the reckless bravura of a Prince Rupert or the splendid individuality of a Lawrence of Arabia, but it does produce loyal, reliable, well disciplined officers who are conscious of their duty and proudly and professionally fulfil it. Above all, its strength depends upon the non-commissioned ranks, Corporals, Sergeants, and particularly Sergeant-Majors. Later when I worked in industry I reflected that one of the failures of many companies was that they did not have that essential layer of management equivalent to the senior non-commissioned officer upon which much of the success of the British Army depends.

In 1953 and 1954, Britain's task in policing the Canal Zone was to keep the Suez Canal open as a major trade route to the East, and generally keep peace in the area. This was just eight years after the war, and Britain still had a major role as an international peacekeeper – a role that we would eventually be unable to afford. In Egypt King Farouk had just been deposed by General Neguib, and a certain young nationalist, Colonel Nasser, was about to take over from Neguib. One of Nasser's demands was that the 60,000 British soldiers, sailors and airmen should leave the Canal Zone, where we were still technically on 'active service' and very much an occupying army. Anthony Eden, the Foreign Secretary in Winston Churchill's second administration, began to negotiate a withdrawal and many of the Army and RAF camps were transferred from the Canal Zone to Cyprus in order to maintain the British military presence in the Eastern Mediterranean.

In those early days of Egyptian nationalism, pressure upon the British forces was very considerable. A Major Salem used to visit the main Egyptian towns of Port Said, Ismailia and Suez making fiery speeches from the back of a lorry. He would get so agitated that he would dance with anger, and thus became known as the 'Dancing Major'. We were made to feel that we were unjustly oppressing this part of the world and that we should get out at once. If any Egyptians were killed in accidents such as being knocked down by an Army truck, then the nationalists vowed to kill five British soldiers in revenge, which they invariably did within a week. This was my first experience of dealing with terrorists, and it brought home to me the insuperable difficulty of an army occupying a country where it had no allies or friends to support it. I was reading some Sydney Smith at the time, and somewhere he says 'an occupying army only controls the square yard around the sentry box'. I can confirm this maxim.

Unlike some of my comrades, I found the dry heat of Egypt agreeable. We lived in tents without any air-conditioning, slept under mosquito nets and kept our water cold in porous clay jugs. I was impressed at the sheer adaptability of British soldiers and the way they coped and remained cheerful in unusual circumstances. We were all in this together. Ultimately it is that spirit of loyalty and comradeship which holds any army and indeed any country together. That was the abiding lesson which I took with me from my National Service.

I spent about eighteen months halfway along the Canal on the banks of the Sweet Water Lake – a great geographical misnomer, as it was an open sewer – as a member of 181 Independent Light Battery. We were equipped with large 4.2-inch mortars which had a range of up to 3,000 yards and were very effective for the immediate support of infantry. As they had fixed firing pins and were barrel-loaded, they could deliver a heavy barrage more quickly than other pieces of artillery. The Infantry had a smaller 3-inch mortar and the Americans had one of 150 millimetres. Some of these smaller weapons had been sent to Turkey, which then passed them on to Libya, whose soldiers did not know how to use them, so in 1954 I was posted to Tripoli as a lonely mortar instructor to the Libyan Army.

Libya was then ruled by the very old King Idris, who had failed to produce a son and heir. He had a rather cheerful elderly wife who occasionally appeared with him in public, which was unusual in the Arab world. Although they seemed to be very happy together, a young Egyptian Princess was found for him as a second wife to see if he could produce an heir. Idris' mind, however, was apparently on less conjugal matters, for he spent much of his time praying at the tomb of his father in the desert. All this uncertainty about whether there would or would not be a royal succession allowed the seeds of later revolt to be sown.

Libya, where oil had not yet been discovered, was a poor country with a narrow fertile coastal belt where the farms were well managed, often by Italians. It had been an Italian colony before the war, and in more distant times had been the granary for the Roman Empire. It was a peaceful happy country whose main export apart from food was sponges. I was attached for three months to the British Army Headquarters Mess in Tripoli, where I found a strange post-colonial atmosphere. Most importance was attached to arranging polo matches in the evening sun. I spent most of my time, however, with the Libyan Army and my excellent Palestinian interpreter, Sergeant Muhandes. Together we managed to train two troops of Libyans to fire the mortars, and we left them a training manual in Arabic. It was a bit of a toytown army, and I don't recall meeting the young officer who was later to take over his country and plague the world with his support of international terrorism.

Whilst in Libya I had to rely rather more on my own devices. I had two books with me, *Richard II* and Mill's *Essay on Liberty*. This was my library, and both works gave me much scope for reflection. *Richard II* is one of Shakespeare's most political plays, for it deals with the very heart of politics, which is the acquisition, exercise and forfeiture of power. Indeed Enoch Powell believes that the historical plays of Shakespeare show such a profound understanding of the nature of politics that they could not have been written by just one man but by several, and one of those must have been an active politician at the Court of Elizabeth I. Fanciful as this notion is, certainly the play made me think about the political process. It was a happy accident that I also had Mill's seminal essay on the nature and extent of political liberty, and I remember walking along the beautiful and utterly isolated coast near Tripoli turning over in my mind the great questions of how much power the state should have over individuals and how that power required to be justified and organized. This was all pretty theoretical for a young mortar instructor, but I was able to contrast it with my experience of the ordered life of the Army, where individual liberty was restricted for a common purpose. While I was convinced that the best way for any society to function was to give as much freedom as possible to the individual, there seemed to me to be natural limits upon the extent of that freedom. It was this that made me more of a Conservative than a Liberal.

Oxford

Following the end of my National Service in 1955, I took up my place at Oxford. I was the first member of my family to go to any university, let alone Oxford, which soon cast its seductive charm over me. At Magdalen, the most beautiful of all the colleges, I was lucky to study history under four distinguished tutors. There was the ex-Pauline, Karl Leyser, a Medievalist, and John Stoye, who taught about the eighteenth century. The doyen was K. B. McFarlane, who had transformed Medieval Studies with his work on 'bastard feudalism'. He was a tall retiring figure with his head leaning to one side, and during tutorials he stroked a Siamese cat on his lap. He was so meticulous over historical facts that he actually wrote very little, which was disappointing for both his students and fellow historians. I remember Tom Boase, the President of Magdalen, saying that he had asked McFarlane to check the details of a booklet which the College had prepared to celebrate the 500th anniversary of its foundation in 1458. When the booklet was returned, he was surprised to find that McFarlane had made two corrections on every line.

Finally, I studied under A. J. P. Taylor, the great iconoclast. He used to sit curled up in his chair like a pixie, with a Lowry behind him and another cat in his lap, and mischievously destroy his students' assumptions. He gave his famous lectures, which he later repeated for the BBC, at nine o'clock on Wednesday mornings in the Examination Schools in The High. When asked why he didn't start later he replied, 'If I spoke at eleven o'clock, there would be no hall large enough in Oxford to hold my audience.' He used to walk briskly into the room and speak for an hour without notes whatever the subject – the First World War, the Russian Revolution, or Dissent in Foreign Policy. He had clear heroes and villains, and condemned Churchill as a war strategist because of his responsibility for the Gallipoli landing of the First World War and the Anzio landing of the Second. Taylor dubbed both of these events as 'cigar butt strategy' saying, 'The statesmen of the world would gather in front of a large map of the world with cigar butts in their hands, and then point at a place with their cigar butts saying, "Let us go there"'. He was a wonderfully stimulating man who had a penchant for outsiders like Charles James Fox, 'the first leader of the Opposition', or Lloyd George, 'the greatest Prime Minister of this century'.

My major regret about Oxford is that I didn't study enough to do better than a Second, but I had been diverted by the University's other charms. I have always enjoyed the theatre, although I never felt moved to work in it. The closest I came was during my time at Oxford, when I volunteered to become the stage manager for a Magdalen College production of *Antony and Cleopatra* which was to be put on at the little Elizabethan theatre at Abingdon. Antony was played by Alan Garner, a bearded and intense undergraduate who kept a diary in Egyptian hieroglyphics. He fascinated me with stories about Shakespeare's 'Dark Lady of the Sonnets', for he lived at Alderley Edge in Cheshire, where Mary Fitton, the Dark Lady, had also come from. Alan has since become celebrated as one of Britain's most imaginative authors of children's books, receiving the ultimate accolade of having his work recommended for inclusion in the National Curriculum!

Enobarbus was played by Dudley Moore, an organ scholar at Magdalen, and even then a cheerful, witty and irrepressible figure. He had one of the best speeches in the play, describing Cleopatra in her barge, and spoke it beautifully. A close friend of mine, Kevin Garry, played the

Old Soothsayer who at the end of the play has one of the most memorable lines in a piece studded with wonderful poetry: 'A woman is a dish for the gods, if the devil dress her not.' Kevin has spent his career in international news reporting, becoming the deputy head of Reuters. Jeremy Wolfenden, the gifted editor of *Isis* who alas was to die young, played Pompey, and Michael Welbourne, who was to pursue a gifted academic career, played Caesar. All these talented people were marshalled together by the undergraduate producer, Anthony Price, who made a great impression upon them and me. I had rarely seen someone who was in such total command of a situation. He knew exactly what he wanted and imposed his will and interpretation of the play upon the company of amateur actors and actresses. His view was startlingly original, for in his production all of Antony's supporters were the goodies and wore Roman dress, whereas Caesar's supporters were the baddies wearing modern service dress. Cleopatra was cast not as a flighty young girl but as a middle-aged matron having a last fling.

My job was really quite simple – to ensure that the actors turned up on time for the rehearsals and the show, that the props were in the right place, and in particular that there was an asp in the basket. With such a dominating and demanding director I provided the still centre of calm, and very often I was upbraided by Anthony for my placid approach. Calm, however, was just what that production needed to make sure it opened at all. Some of the performances had unscripted moments of hilarity. In the famous death scene, one of Cleopatra's handmaidens, Charmian, who was played by Fiona O'Neill, Ian Fleming's stepdaughter, dies just before Cleopatra. As the stage at Abingdon was so small, very often her bare foot would extend behind the scenery. When this happened, the stagehands would tickle her foot with a feather, which added a new challenge to her interpretation of this most tragic scene. Although I enjoyed helping in this production, I decided that a career on the boards was not for me. I found politics much more compelling, and anyway the element of theatre is not exactly absent from it.

My wife, Mary, starred in many productions when she was at university, and we still go to the theatre as much as we can. Several times during the stressful years of the 1980s, when I was a Cabinet Minister, we escaped to see wonderful plays. The theatre is one of the great glories of London and should be treasured and supported. The funding of the National Theatre and the Royal Shakespeare Company is one of the rare instances when the Government has got it right and backed winners. This is money well spent, and governments should not be parsimonious when it comes to funding the performing arts.

I was, by now, actively involved in Conservative politics at the University. At that time there was a splendid figure, Mrs Stella Gatehouse, the wife of a North Oxfordshire vicar, who used to come to a little garret near Carfax once a week to give speaking lessons to aspiring Conservative undergraduate politicians. All of my contemporaries who later went into national politics – Paul Channon, Toby Jessel, George Gardiner, Alan Haselhurst, Andrew Rowe, Tony Newton – passed through her hands. She gave many stuttering and embarrassed young students the confidence to get up on their feet and speak to an audience. She was our 'Mother Courage', well turned out, handbag at the ready, cigarette about to be lit, and with a deep chuckle. She was full of kindness and encouragement. Through her we organized speaking teams to go out to meetings in Oxfordshire and the Home Counties, and we toured more far-flung Labour areas during vacations. Four of us took an open van up to Durham for a week to speak in market squares, at the railway works and in works canteens. All this was good experience and real fun, and I decided then that I would become active in politics when I came down.

Many politicians of the first rank came to speak at Oxford. I went to hear Anthony Eden, the Prime Minister, speak before the Suez Crisis and found him woodenly boring; Enoch Powell came as a junior Housing Minister to defend the repeal of the Rent Acts; Harold Macmillan returned as Prime Minister to unveil a bust of himself in the Union building and moved his student audience with his reminiscences of the lost generation who died in the trenches in the First World War. Chips Channon, whose son Paul was President of the Oxford University Conservative Association, brought Rab Butler to speak in an attempt to revive Rab's popularity after Suez. As part of a student delegation from Oxford I attended the famous 1957 Brighton Party Conference when Quintin Hailsham rang his Chairman's bell to revive the Party's fortunes. Politics had entered my blood.

The most famous of the Oxford undergraduate activities was the Oxford Union Debating Society, and I only spoke in the Union during my second year, becoming its Secretary in my final term. The Union still has one of the most demanding audiences. Several of the leading Conservatives who came down to speak, such as Harry Hylton-Foster, later to become the Speaker of the House of Commons, said they never spoke as undergraduates in the Union as they found it far too forbidding. The most eloquent and witty undergraduate speaker in my time was undoubtedly Brian Walden, who seemed destined then to be a future Labour Prime Minister.

One night in 1957 I had dinner with Clement Attlee and his wife when he came to speak at the Union. I was struck by his modesty. Compared with today, his arrival as a former Prime Minister was low-key. His wife drove him in their old car, and the first thing we had to do was find a place where it could be parked without incurring a fine. In the debate, Attlee defended the House of Lords in his characteristically direct way, saying, 'In my experience the House of Lords works rather well. Leave it alone.'

The event that occasioned the greatest passion during my time at Oxford was the Suez invasion in 1956. Edward Boyle resigned from the Government and came to speak with great dignity to a packed meeting of Conservatives. He was heard with respect but the Oxford University Conservative Association overwhelmingly supported the Government, though after a stormy meeting on a Sunday afternoon there were some resignations from Committee members opposed to the Suez invasion. Having served in Egypt, I had no doubt that the Egyptians could perfectly well operate the Canal efficiently and so the argument that the Egyptians were not competent to run the Canal was absurd. However, I supported the Suez action because its purpose was to ensure that the Suez Canal remained an open international waterway. Under Nasser it was quite possible that an Egyptian-controlled Canal would, for political reasons, deny access to other countries in the Middle East.

Britain and France were acting to insert a crowbar into the trap that was closing around Israel. Any military action by us had to be quick and effective, but rarely had an operation of this sort been so badly planned and executed. America was clearly not going to support what they saw, and what I also felt, as being an imperial last fling, but after British troops had been committed I believed there was a clear duty to support our country.

Oxford was deeply divided, and for a fortnight everything else was forgotten. There were large marches and rallies both for and against the Government. I remember walking up The High with Brian Walden, who said 'This will finish Eden.' He was right. He also said, 'The Tories will lose the next election.' He was wrong. I took a £10 bet with him, a vast sum in those days, that the Tories would win the next election. After we came down in 1958 our ways separated, and even though we met again frequently in the House of Commons and in television studios I fear that I have not yet been paid, but then I have never reminded him of our student wager.

The other great international event of that year was the Soviet invasion of Hungary. I remember sitting in the early evening gloom, in one of the ground-floor rooms of the cloisters at Magdalen, listening with friends to the last tragic and moving appeal on the radio from Imre Nagy begging for help as Soviet tanks moved into Budapest. This was an act of brutal Soviet imperialism and it showed me that the only way of defeating this evil system was by being stronger than they were.

Business and Marriage

My immediate personal concern, however, was how to earn a living. I didn't relish entering the Civil Service, and that was a disappointment to my father. Instead I applied to Shell and was offered a graduate training post at £750 a year, a great improvement upon the money I had received as a Lieutenant in the Gunners, which was about £250 a year. I found I didn't much like working for a large company, and after two years decided that I wanted to work for a smaller operation. I joined the Chairman of Aquascutum, Gerald Abrahams, as his Personal Assistant and learnt a great deal about the clothing industry from him, especially how to manage companies and the crucial importance of proper management accounting. This allowed me after three years to join Minster Trust, a city investment trust then being run by Peter Cannon. He had a very enlightened approach in that Minster invested on a long-term basis in British industrial companies. If these ran into trouble then Peter stood by them and pulled them around.

Peter Cannon became my guide and mentor, and after a few months he appointed me, at the age of thirty-two, as Managing Director of a public company in the clothing industry, supplying Marks and Spencer. The company had been losing money, so I had been given a challenge. I enjoyed tackling the problems of running a group of factories, planning new product lines, cutting back overheads and having both to close and open factories. I liked to go into a factory at seven o'clock in the morning to see how it was being run and what was in the post, and I really enjoyed getting completely involved in the business. Within eighteen months we had turned a loss into a profit and started to expand by buying other businesses.

By then the most important event in my life had taken place. In the spring of 1962, at the age of twenty-eight, I had met Mary Muir at the engagement party of Nicky Fairbairn, whom Mary knew from Edinburgh, and Elizabeth Mackay whom I knew from Oxford. I was immediately attracted to Mary, who was much more beautiful, interesting and lively than any girl I had ever known. She also had a spectacular car. It was an old Triumph Roadster convertible whose number plate began with the initials FUN. After that evening, Mary gave me a lift home in her car and the die was cast. We fell in love and became engaged a few months later at Nicky and Elizabeth's wedding in Edinburgh.

Marrying Mary was simply the best thing that has happened to me, and the fact that we have lived happily together for over thirty years and have enjoyed a close family life with our three children is a great credit to her. Throughout my career Mary has been a steadying influence, for politics is a hectic and busy world which creates unique pressures, and involves crises and difficult decisions. There is also a steady stream of derision and criticism, and to cope with all of that one needs the stability of a happy family life. When we met, Mary was teaching a remedial class in one of the first comprehensive schools in London, and she was to go on teaching until our second child was born.

Before meeting Mary, I had never visited Scotland. Indeed, like most English people, I had little knowledge of its character and culture and scant appreciation of its beauty. I came to like Scotland even more after we decided to spend our honeymoon touring the Highlands, and have now visited Scotland so many times that it has become a second home. Mary has ensured that our children, who have all been educated at Scottish universities, are aware and proud of their ancestry. It has certainly given me an awareness of the unique nature of the United Kingdom, for I was born in Wales, lived much of my life in England, had two Irish grandmothers, and married a Scot. Hence I have never had any doubt at all about the importance of the unity of the United Kingdom. I have also learnt to stop using the word 'English' to describe something which is really British.

After leaving Oxford I kept my hand in politically by serving on a Ward Committee of the Twickenham Conservative Association and became involved in all the activities of canvassing, membership drives, and running fêtes. I decided that I wanted to do more, and in 1960 I was elected as a councillor to Twickenham Borough Council. I made a note that the costs of running my first campaign amounted to £44.2.6d. Those were the days. Being a councillor is a useful experience for anyone who wants to become an MP. It is not just the experience of debating in the council chamber, or learning the give and take necessary in working with political colleagues, or realizing how difficult it is to meet the demands of the local electorate who want good services and low rates; it is also a constant reminder that the purpose of political power is to improve the lot of ordinary people. Before the local government reorganization of 1964, Twickenham was served by its own separate small Borough Council, which worked well. It was my first appreciation of Edmund Burke's 'little platoons' working better than large battalions. I held my council seat for two years and then lost it to a Liberal – my first taste of the downside as well as the upside of politics.

CHAPTER 2

Into Politics

Poplar 1964 – Acton 1966–70 –
St Marylebone 1970 – Parliamentary Secretary to the
Civil Service Department 1972–74 – The Fall of Ted –
Opposition 1974–79

In 1962 Geoffrey Howe, whom I had got to know through London politics, told me that Poplar, a safe Labour seat in the East End, was looking for a Conservative Parliamentary candidate and he suggested that I should put my name forward. I jumped at the opportunity, although I had not previously taken the trouble to apply to be on the candidates list at Conservative Central Office. My priority at this time was to establish a business career before attempting to enter the House of Commons.

The headquarters of the Poplar Conservative Association was in a semi-detached Victorian house, Number 151 Bow Road, next to Poplar Town Hall. This house, which has since been demolished, had a considerable importance for the Conservative Party since it was here that the little band who later formed themselves into the Bow Group met to discuss political ideas. Those early Bow Group members, led by Geoffrey Howe and Leon Brittan, held these meetings deep in the heart of the impoverished East End and rededicated themselves to the Disraelian concept of one-nation Toryism.

I was courting Mary, who was a little surprised, to say the least, that I wanted to fight Poplar, but I was adopted in 1963 and together we worked the constituency hard for the months leading up to the 1964 election. There were more Tory voters than I had expected, many being the traditional patriotic working-class supporters whom Lord Randolph Churchill and Disraeli had attracted to the Tory cause. We spent many happy evenings canvassing in Bow, Poplar and the Isle of Dogs, together with any friends we could dragoon to help the handful of elderly ladies who ran the Conservative Association. Mary never felt any qualms about climbing up and down the staircases of tower blocks on her own and rattling the letterboxes of flats. We felt quite safe and encountered no hostility on the doorsteps, but at times we met a good deal of surprise that Tories were actually knocking on the doors in Dockland. I remember calling on one flat and meeting a burly docker wearing a singlet and lathered up for his evening shave. As I gave him my arguments for voting Conservative, he looked at me rather quizzically and said, 'Mate, what have I got to conserve?' The people were warm and friendly and Mary and I enjoyed many cups of tea in the houses and flats of Poplar.

My Labour opponent was Ian Mikardo, seeking to return to the House of Commons after being beaten at Reading by Peter Emery, who had himself once fought Poplar. Ian treated me kindly and rather indulgently, for in such a safe Labour seat there was no advantage in an experienced old pro, whom I remembered making a very funny speech at the Oxford Union, savaging a young opponent on his first outing.

Thirty years ago the East End was still scarred by many empty council-owned bombsites which were inadequately protected by corrugated-iron sheets. Peter Black, who had fought Poplar in the 1950s and was a Conservative GLC councillor, formed a Housing Association whose purpose was to build new houses on these sites. These were the early days of the Housing Association movement and we asked Poplar Council to sell some of their sites to this Association to help the homeless. The Council refused to release even one. This was my first taste of the dog-in-the-manger attitude of the socialism practised by Labour councils. They believed the Council should be a monopoly provider of housing in the area and did not want anybody else to act upon their own initiative or with their own money. I got very angry with this dogmatic attitude as it was not bringing any benefit to the people of Poplar. The Labour councillors had a vendetta against the middle classes, whom they didn't want playing any role in the area. The Council's deliberate policy of creating a single-stratum society of thorough greyness, dullness and mediocrity made me more determined to defeat Socialism and all its works.

At the election in October 1964 I managed to reduce the Labour majority in Poplar, rather against the trend of that election which marked the end of thirteen years of Conservative rule. On election night at about 9 p.m. the heavens opened and we got soaked to the skin. We took refuge in a pub called The Gun on the Isle of Dogs, and while we were in there we heard a news flash on the radio that Khrushchev had fallen from power in the Soviet Union. If this event had taken place just twenty-four hours earlier, and the electorate had realized that we were moving into dangerous and uncertain times, then they might have decided to stick with Sir Alec Douglas-Home as Prime Minister, for he was much more experienced in foreign affairs than his challenger, Harold Wilson. Chance plays a crucial element in political success and failure.

Acton 1966–70

Poplar was my first taste of a Parliamentary political campaign. I decided next time to have a shot at a more winnable seat, but I knew that I was unlikely to be adopted for a safe one. Mary and I also agreed that I would not seek to be a candidate in any constituency more than twenty miles from our home base in London. This led to some quite difficult decisions, because safe Conservative seats tended to be in country areas and in those days these constituencies usually expected 'the wife and children' to make their life and home in the constituency while the MP spent the week in London. Mary said she had not married me in order to live separate lives. She was adamant on this issue. The result is that for most of our married life we have been able to have breakfast together as a family every day, and I could generally take the children to school when they were young, and often get back briefly around their bedtime.

In 1965 I applied for the marginal seat of Acton as Philip Holland, who had lost it in 1964, had moved on to a safe one. It was possible that with a bit of luck and a strong following wind it could be won back. Conservative selection procedures for Parliamentary candidates are elaborate and unpredictable, although I cannot complain because I have appeared before only four selection committees and was selected in each case. Each constituency is different: one will be looking for a good local MP to represent its interests, and another will be looking for a potential Minister. But the actual process of determination is a bit of a lottery. One certain favourite lost because he assured the selection committee in an old and famous Home Counties town that he intended to 'put them on the map', whereas they thought that they were not only on it already but right at its centre. Another front runner for a large rural seat in Suffolk was rejected when he admitted that he didn't drive. He was disliked by the outgoing Tory MP, a wily old fox who was determined to stop him. The MP persuaded the selection committee to ask each candidate the apparently harmless question as to whether they had a clean driving licence. The reply revealed that this candidate had no licence at all, which meant that he was obviously going to have difficulty in getting around a large rural seat. It was a case of, 'Damn his principles, can he drive?'

Wives are expected to accompany husband candidates and to undergo their own visual appraisal by the Women's Committee. This applies to husbands of female candidates too. There was a time when wives were asked to say a few words or answer questions – Elspeth Howe had to do this when Geoffrey was adopted for Reigate, and Mary was asked a question at Acton. But now this has been quite rightly stopped. On the whole, selection committees like to adopt a family man, and some unmarried candidates would sometimes acquire a girlfriend or boy-friend, as decorative or homely as they thought the Committee required, and an engagement might or might not follow the selection.

At my Acton selection meeting in 1965 I felt certain I had lost because, after I had made a powerful attack upon Harold Wilson and George Brown, I was asked by a heavy crew-cut man at the back of the hall whether I supported flogging and hanging. He turned out to be a prison officer at Wormwood Scrubs, which was right on the border of the constituency. I explained why I opposed both, in spite of the fact that about 300 prison officers actually lived in Acton and many votes turned on the issue in this marginal seat. I wasn't even prepared to agree to the retention of hanging for the killing of police or prison officers.

After I had given my reply there was an uneasy silence. Then suddenly someone jumped up and said that this question should not be asked of any candidate, whereupon a fierce debate broke out among the sixty members of the Selection Committee, culminating in a motion of 'no confidence' in the chair. I was so amazed and embarrassed to have caused such an uproar that I offered to withdraw my nomination, as this was clearly such a key issue for the Association. They were shocked by my offer but it did mean the whole debate was rather sheepishly concluded. The family had quarrelled in public and they were rather ashamed. They asked me not to withdraw and settled down to ask questions about rates and housing.

When I joined the other candidates I found that they had been asked the same question and had all opted for keeping capital punishment for the murder of prison and police officers. I felt certain that one of them, Michael Shersby, who was later to become the MP for Uxbridge, would win. I was therefore very surprised when the President came in and said that I had been selected. I learnt from this episode that it is always better to stand up and defend what you believe in, even if it is unpopular, rather than advocate something which you don't believe in just to get applause. To the credit of the Party workers in Acton they never raised this issue with me again. Indeed the prison officer who asked the question became one of my staunchest supporters. The Association knew my views and I knew theirs, but it never stopped us from working closely together and becoming good friends for many years.

Harold Wilson timed the 1966 election brilliantly, for the Labour Government had been in power just long enough to show what it could do, but not long enough to be blamed for its mistakes. In Acton, Labour increased its majority but I decided not to look around for a safe Shire seat. Mary and I had come to like Acton and had made many friends through the camaraderie of campaigning in a marginal seat. My decision to stick with the constituency was vindicated, albeit in tragic circumstances. In October 1967, the sitting Labour Member of Parliament, Bernard Floud, committed suicide. I had found him to be a charming if rather retiring person who would have been happier, I suspect, as a don. He had been very depressed following the death of his wife from a slow debilitating illness, but there were rumours of other deeper reasons why he had taken his own life. Just before the General Election in 1966 I had received a dossier in a plain envelope alleging that Floud had been involved in the Burgess/Maclean spy ring since his Cambridge days. The anonymous dossier was a scrappy collection of innuendoes and unsupported allegations and I told my agent, Ron Hollis, to destroy it as I was not going to play that sort of game. The rumour that Bernard Floud had been the Fifth Man in the spy ring continued to run for many years although recent revelations prove that he was not. His son, Professor Roderick Floud of London University, loyally defended his father's reputation and I was glad to have seen it vindicated.

At the time of Bernard Floud's suicide in October 1967 I was the Managing Director of a public quoted company which I had brought back from the edge of bankruptcy into profitability. I now had to decide, literally overnight, whether I would stand in the forthcoming by-election, which we were most likely to win because of Labour's unpopularity. I went to talk to my mentor, Peter Cannon, the Managing Director of Minster Trust, who said that I must do what I really wanted to do. Perhaps anticipating my decision he said he would be willing to let me remain a Board member of the company after I was elected while he searched for a new Managing Director.

This notion appealed to me because I have always believed that MPs benefit from having outside interests in addition to their constituency responsibilities. While constituency duties must always come first, and be discharged conscientiously and fully, MPs should also bring to the House of Commons a continuing experience of the world outside politics. The added depth of outside experience, and the supplementary income, help an MP both to relate to life outside Westminster and to withstand the pressures that may from time to time be applied by the Whips' Office.

Back in 1967 the salary of an MP was just over £3,000, and MPs had to buy the paper, stamps and envelopes for their constituency correspondence as well as pay for their own telephone calls. Since Mary and I also had a mortgage and two young children to support, finance had to be a consideration. Nevertheless, I decided to stand again for Parliament, and politics rather than business was to be the dominant part of my life for the next twenty five years. But the move into full-time politics was also a wrench, because I had enjoyed working in industry and building a successful team.

Labour tried to postpone the day of reckoning for as long as possible and did not move the writ for the by-election for nearly six months, hoping that delay would bring about a recovery in the Government's fortunes. But quite the reverse happened as things just got worse. This electoral gerrymandering by Harold Wilson also proved very unpopular and led to an informal agreement between the parties that future by-elections had to take place within three months of a vacancy occurring.

The March 1968 Acton by-election, together with three other by-elections on the same day, could not have come at a better time for the Tories. Harold Wilson was at the very lowest point of his popularity, and during the three weeks of our campaign the Government's woes boiled over. George Brown, the Deputy Leader of the Labour Party, launched the Labour campaign in Acton but during its course he resigned. Roy Jenkins, the Chancellor of the Exchequer, introduced a Budget which raised taxes by the prodigious sum of £900 million. There was a run on the pound and Jenkins had to rush to Bonn to cobble together a package to support it which he then announced to the House of Commons in the middle of the night. All the banks closed for three days. With that background any Tory candidate would have won Acton.

While the result of most by-elections rests on the national standing of the Government, I did introduce one local issue when I opposed the wholesale demolition of several rows of small Victorian terraced houses which were due to be replaced by high-rise tower blocks. I was accused by Labour of wanting to turn the clock back, and my campaign for preservation was described as being 'quaintly eccentric'. This was just a few months before the explosion at the Ronan Point tower block in East London which brought home to many people the architectural and social disasters we had been creating.

I was helped in my campaign by a new young member of the Conservative Research Department, Chris Patten, a heavy smoker with a tendency to plumpness, very bright and with a flair for fluent composition. He sat quietly in a corner of the office and soon became very popular with the Acton workers. Every day Chris briefed me on the national issues and prepared punchy press statements for me. We became friends, and when the campaign was over I presented him with a first edition of George Orwell's *Road to Wigan Pier*, as I thought that politically it would be right up his street. It was.

On Thursday 31 March I was elected with a swing of 15 per cent and the other three by-elections on that day saw the return of Dudley Smith, the election of Keith Speed, and the capture of one of Labour's safest seats, Dudley, with an even bigger swing. Two of those four Conservative victors were later to lose their seats in the 1970 General Election which put Harold Wilson out of office and Ted Heath into Number 10. The fact is that by-elections are only snapshots of the electorate's mood at a specific time, and wider political conclusions should never be drawn from them. But in March 1968 it did seem like the beginning of the end for Harold Wilson.

It is very exciting to become a Member of Parliament, and my mother and father were extraordinarily proud. I was equally proud when they came to watch me from the Strangers Gallery in the House of Commons just a few weeks before my father died. Mary was rather apprehensive about how the balance between politics, business and family life would work out. In April I made my maiden speech on the Second Reading of the Finance Bill, for there is no point in a new backbencher hanging around and waiting. I quoted Robert Graves to describe the Wilson/Jenkins economic mess as 'in the midst of life we are in debt, here to pay and gone to borrow'. After I had finished speaking I went into the Smoking Room where Iain Macleod, then the Shadow Chancellor, was sitting in the chair which Churchill is supposed to have used. His arm immediately shot up, he beckoned me over, and offered me his congratulations and a whisky. Over drinks, he invited me to become the newest and most junior member of his Treasury Opposition team.

I was lucky to be asked to serve on the Finance Bill Committee. This was the first occasion that the Bill was being dealt with upstairs in Committee rather than on the floor of the House, and it was a valuable and memorable initiation into the detailed work of Parliament. Roy Jenkins, the Chancellor, rarely came to the Committee but Iain hardly left it, sitting hunched up in his chair on the right of the front row. We sat through several nights, and while some of the younger members would slip away for a snooze on a sofa Iain did not. Even though he was uncomfortable, tired and in pain, he would sit through the night. It was inspiring leadership. When Roy Jenkins appeared, he would sit directly opposite Iain two yards away. Within a few minutes of Jenkins' arrival Iain would find a reason to intervene in the debate and then lash him with withering sarcasm. Iain could not stand Roy Jenkins, who he thought represented the worst element of the soft Left. He once said to me, 'The trouble with Roy is that he has sold out to the Duchesses and the drawing-rooms of Belgravia.'

However, Iain did respect and like Harold Lever, another Treasury Minister, who was rich enough actually to have a drawing-room in Belgravia and yet was much franker about his Socialism. Like Iain, Harold was a world-class bridge player and a witty and engaging speaker. When he married for the third time he invited many Labour MPs to a party where he said that on meeting his wife they could exchange only a few words in French. The MPs' eyes lit up as they demanded to know these saucy words, whereupon Harold told them, 'Christian Dior, Cartier, Hermès and Chanel.' When Harold Lever talked of the poor it was, in George Orwell's phrase, rather like listening 'to a choir sing in a jeweller's shop'.

I learnt some very good political lessons from Iain. Roy Jenkins was increasing the tax on slot machines, in particular those which took sixpenny and shilling coins. Iain wanted to oppose this and insisted that the Conservative amendments to this proposal should simply refer to 'penny machines on piers'. Terence Higgins, the MP for Worthing and one of Iain's lieutenants, patiently tried to explain that we needed much broader amendments to cover those machines in town amusement arcades. But Iain's acute political judgement recognized that as far as the public were concerned it was better to focus on 'Penny machines on piers. That's what everybody remembers, that's what they understand, that's where we can defeat Labour.' How right he was.

Iain was the best speaker I ever heard in the House of Commons. Like Michael Foot he never needed notes, having a photographic memory which must have been invaluable to him when earning his living as a professional bridge player. He also had a capacity to coin memorable and devastating phrases. One night he attacked the Department of Economic Affairs, one of Wilson's dafter creations, saying, 'There are four Ministers in this Department and I defy anyone in the House to name them all.' The Secretary of State was Peter Shore, one of Wilson's protégés, and Iain went on, 'It is a disgrace that the Prime Minister should provide a mink-lined kennel for his favourite poodle.' On another occasion, looking at the whole of the Government Frontbench including Wilson, Callaghan and Jenkins, Iain spat out, 'Look at them all. As Shakespeare said, 'Small choice amongst rotten apples". '

Those who worked closely with Iain Macleod revered him, but he left no significant written work incorporating his philosophy and ideas. At one dinner where I heard him speak he said, in reply to a question, 'I am an old-fashioned Tory, not a Conservative.' Iain inspired people with his personality and by his physical presence. He believed passionately in the social agenda of caring Conservatism and was an eloquent spokesman for the disadvantaged, disabled and poor. But he had a strong belief in the virtue of lower taxation. When I rather cheekily introduced a Ten Minute Rule Bill to reduce income tax to 25 pence in the pound he told me that this was his target for cutting income tax. After my defeat at Acton in the 1970 General Election Iain kindly regretted my absence from the House when he made his first and only speech as Chancellor of the Exchequer. His premature death, just three weeks later, robbed the Conservative Party of a charismatic and shrewd standard-bearer.

I found it was more fun to be a backbench MP in Opposition than in Government. We enjoyed good sport tilting at Harold Wilson. But one forgets how good Wilson himself was at Question Time, brushing off Ted Heath and scoring off that wonderful old Tory buffoon Walter Bromley-Davenport. In 1969 it seemed that we were going to sweep Labour from power, but during the first six months of 1970 Wilson bounced back and steered Labour ahead in the opinion polls. This was helped by a regular procession of Labour Ministers coming to the House almost every day to announce increased public expenditure. When

Richard Crossman, the Leader of the House, announced extra money for London Zoo, Iain Macleod commented acidly, 'They haven't even forgotten the monkeys.'

I developed an interest in other issues, in particular the potential misuse of computers in our society. Having used computers in business I knew how powerful and pervasive they could be. In 1969 I introduced as a private Member the Data Surveillance bill, the first attempt to protect statutorily personal information held on individuals by large computer systems. My Bill did not get very far but its principles were later enshrined in the Conservative Government's own Data Protection Act.

When Harold Wilson called a General Election in June 1970 he was confident that Labour would win. A week before polling day Labour led the Conservatives by 12 points and Wilson, travelling on the train back to Liverpool, spoke to assembled journalists about his new ministerial team. Ted Heath had been written off as a loser. But on the Monday before polling day Conservative MPs and candidates in west London were summoned to a great rally at two o'clock in the afternoon on Hounslow Heath. It was a scorching hot day and we were in our shirt-sleeves to welcome Ted, who arrived standing in an open-topped Land-Rover. He was a man transformed. He had just been given the overseas trade figures showing a huge deficit and he used them to flay the Government's supposed economic recovery. It was this lunchtime rally which marked the turning-point of the election.

On Thursday the Conservative Party won with an overall majority of thirty seats, but I was defeated. In spite of assiduously nursing the constituency with a dedicated team of volunteers, I could not stop it returning to its traditional Labour colours and I lost the seat to Nigel Spearing. The result was not a total surprise, for after fighting three elections in Acton over the space of five years we had very accurate canvassing returns showing how people voted, and in 1970 we actually predicted the exact swing against us compared with 1967. Nonetheless it is very depressing to lose a seat when the rest of your Party unexpectedly wins power. There was, however, a great compensation, for Mary had given birth to our third child, a boy, just two days before. Now without a Parliamentary seat, I was very grateful that Peter Cannon had allowed me to retain my business involvement, particularly as in 1970 we had moved house from Twickenham to Pimlico, where we were to live for the next twenty-three years.

The object of this move was to be as near to Westminster as we could afford, and in those days that meant Pimlico. We were very lucky to find a whole house. At last I had a room which could house my library, and in the centre of it we put a huge piece of 6' × 8' blockboard covered with bright yellow fablon. This rested on four filing cabinets, creating a double desk for us both. Mary and I could work anywhere, even with the constant interruptions of family life – the children running around, music playing or the television on. Although later we divided our desks and moved them to two interconnecting rooms we always managed to resist the temptation of establishing a study for me. Too many Ministers' lives are crammed with evenings spent alone, working on their red boxes and ministerial papers. Indeed that side of a Minister's life has become far too burdensome over the years. If Margaret Thatcher was ever told by her staff that some of her Ministers were not getting through their boxes as quickly as they should – and that sort of news always got back to Number 10 – then she would give her Cabinet a little homily about the virtues of application.

St Marylebone 1970

The first by-election after the 1970 General Election was caused by Quintin Hogg's re-elevation to the peerage as Lord Chancellor. Quintin had given up his hereditary peerage in 1963 to stand as a possible Leader for the Conservative Party, and was returned as the MP for St Marylebone in a by-election. There was now a vacancy for his seat, and I applied for it along with around 450 other hopefuls, including Douglas Hurd, Ted Heath's Political Secretary, and John Cope, the personal assistant to the Party Chairman, Peter Thomas. The three contestants chosen for the final selection meeting were Ross McWhirter, Douglas Hurd and myself. I suspect that the word may have gone out from Central Office and Number 10 that it would be rather good if Douglas were adopted. If so, it did him no favours and probably sank his chances.

After we had made our speeches and answered questions the three of us with our wives tried to pass the time casually. Sir Louis Gluckstein, an immensely tall and stooped courtly figure who had himself been an MP, was then the president of the Association. He came through the door, went up to Douglas, took him by the hand and rather surprisingly announced to him that I had been adopted. I could see from Douglas' face that this was a cruel moment. He must have thought that as Louis approached him first then he was the lucky man. Later I discovered why I had won. It wasn't because I had been more eloquent, more witty or dealt with the questions more convincingly. It was because Mary, rather bored with the two-hour wait, had wandered around the building, found some of the Women's Committee washing up the cups and offered to help. Later the Women's Chairman, Pam Bevington, told us that this was what clinched my selection.

There was a very low turnout in the by-election and the majority fell from 9,000 to 6,000, but this actually represented a 1.8 per cent swing to the Tories and proved that the best opportunity a Government has of winning a by-election is in the immediate aftermath of a General Election.

On my return to the House, Paul Bryan, who was Minister of State at the Department of Employment, asked me to be his Parliamentary Private Secretary, the first unpaid rung on the ministerial ladder. The Department of Employment was in the eye of the storm, since it was carrying through a major Bill to reform industrial relations involving strike ballots and cooling-off periods.

Parliamentary Secretary to the Civil Service Department
1972–74

In March 1972 Mary and I were at the cottage in Dorset that we had bought as a bolt hole a few years earlier, giving a drinks party for a few friends and neighbours, when the telephone rang and I was told it was the Prime Minister. Our only telephone was in the sitting-room, where people were milling around and chattering loudly. I could hardly hear what Ted was saying and had to keep asking him to repeat himself. He offered me the post of Parliamentary Under-Secretary at the Civil Service Department, a position previously held by David Howell, who had been moved to the Northern Ireland Office a week earlier. Most people had not expected the post to be filled, and so this was a pleasant surprise.

The Civil Service Department had been created by Harold Wilson following the Fulton Report in 1968, in order to improve the management of the Civil Service. The head of the Department was that mandarin of mandarins and a close confidant of Ted Heath, Sir William Armstrong. When I arrived at the Department a few days later I found that David Howell's office had been appropriated by him. Furthermore,

David's private office staff had been disbanded and his furniture distributed around the Department. I was offered a much smaller office, which I declined, saying that I wanted not only William's old office but the furniture as well. Since both William and the Department clearly felt there was no need for a junior Minister I decided to establish my position from day one.

William had also moved quickly to dispose of the services of David Howell's political adviser, Mark Schreiber, who had worked on the reform of Government with David and Ted up to the 1970 election. Political advisers were looked upon in those days as unnecessary outsiders – grit in the well-oiled machine. I certainly wanted Mark at my side, and so I asked the Prime Minister to allow me to keep him. Much to William's chagrin, he agreed.

My Cabinet boss was George Jellicoe, who was also Leader of the House of Lords, and I much enjoyed working for him. George was a born leader, and it was a great pity there was no war going on somewhere where he could lead his country to victory. A year later, in 1973, Profumo-type rumours circulated in London linking Ministers' names with call-girls. George's name came up, together with that of Tony Lambton, a junior Defence Minister. Ted, who was much more sensitive about these sorts of allegations than Margaret Thatcher was to be, decided that both would have to go. The press hounded George wherever he appeared, and on the night before his resignation, having smelt blood, they massed in great numbers to pursue him. George went with his wife to speak at a large Naval dinner in the Great Hall at Greenwich in honour of his father, the famous Admiral. He knew that it was going to be the last public event of his ministerial career, but he carried it off with great style. It was a superbly defiant gesture which I shall always remember.

The purpose of the Civil Service Department was to improve the efficiency of public administration, and it was presumably the inspiration for Jim Hacker's Department in 'Yes Minister'. I was also handed the task of fulfilling a 1970 Manifesto pledge to cut the size of the Civil Service, for all we had managed to do was just to stop it rising even further. George asked me to urge Ministers in other Departments to cut numbers, but I soon found that not one was remotely interested in doing this. Each Department behaved like a great feudal army, jealously guarding its own territory, marching to its own tunes, training its own officials, and confident in the knowledge that its ministerial officers would change every couple of years.

My ministerial visits were greeted in most Departments with a mixture of boredom and annoyance. When I called on the junior Minister at the Foreign Office, Tony Kershaw, to persuade him to reduce the number of diplomatic staff, the meeting was interrupted by the Permanent Secretary at the Foreign Office, Sir Denis Greenhill. He entered the room carrying a red box which he placed on a table and slowly proceeded to open, taking from it a document seemingly printed on parchment. He held this reverently and addressing himself to me said, 'This is a minute from the Foreign Secretary, and I have been instructed by the Foreign Secretary to make the following comments . . .' Put very simply, the message to me was 'get stuffed'. However, it was conveyed with such style and formality that I realized I was dealing with one of the great Departments of State.

During this apprenticeship as a junior Minister I learnt a lot about the internal workings of Whitehall, and was actually quite glad to sit at the feet of William Armstrong, who had an encyclopaedic memory. In 1973 we were going through a rough patch, so Ted appointed Geoffrey Johnson-Smith, a Sussex MP who had also been a television presenter, to improve the image of the Government. Geoffrey was attached to the Cabinet Office, which was regarded as being at the heart of things. On the morning he arrived, William arranged a briefing meeting which I attended. Without recourse to a single note, William recounted the history of every Minister of Communications who had been appointed since the mid-1930s and explained why each one had failed. It was a *tour de force*, and I could quite see how Ted had come to rely upon this man in moments of crisis. Indeed that relationship had become so close that William was openly referred to as 'the Deputy Prime Minister', and I found he spent much of his time at Number 10.

The most important decision that Ted Heath's Government made in its four years was that to join the Common Market, which took effect on 1 January 1973. I actually had much greater sympathy with the idea of the European Free Trade Association (EFTA), which Reggie Maudling had promoted very strongly in the 1950s. However, the six major European countries were creating a Common Market and it was essential that British industry and commerce should not be denied access to that market. I supported entry for two reasons. First, Britain should be in the Common Market for commercial and trading purposes. Second, membership would minimize the chance of a future war between the countries of Europe. I was never in the ranks of the Europhiles who looked forward to a federal Europe, and indeed the arguments that Ted used were predominantly those of British economic self-interest. There was certainly no talk of a United States of Europe, or increasing the powers of the Community's central institutions at the expense of individual nations. It is for taking Britain into the European Economic Community that Ted will be primarily remembered.

On the other hand Ted got the management of the domestic economy disastrously wrong. In 1972 inflation, fuelled by high wage demands, was rising sharply and the Government was searching for ways to contain it. In the early summer I attended a seminar at Chequers summoned by the head of the Think Tank, Victor Rothschild. In a debate about the economy, Reggie Maudling the Home Secretary favoured statutory intervention, while others, like Tony Barber the Chancellor, were more hesitant. However, Ted was really shaping economic policy himself, together with a small group of senior civil servants which included William Armstrong, Douglas Allen – the Permanent Secretary at the Treasury, and Sir Frank Figgures – the head of the National Economic Development Office (NEDO). On 6 November 1972 Ted announced that there would be a standstill on prices, rents, dividends and pay for a temporary period, together with a change in the law to make this regulation permanent.

A few Tories, notably Enoch Powell and Nick Ridley, opposed this policy vehemently. Others, like Margaret Thatcher, Keith Joseph, John Nott and myself, suppressed any misgivings in the hope that it would work in the short term. I was the junior Minister appointed to serve in the winter of 1972–73 on the Counter Inflation Bill which set up the instruments of the statutory policy – the Price Commission and the Pay Board. The Ministers in charge of this policy were Maurice Macmillan, who had only the sketchiest understanding of it, Patrick Jenkin and myself. We were faced with an Opposition Frontbench consisting of Tony Benn, Reg Prentice and Peter Shore, reinforced by Brian Walden on Labour's Backbench. Firing behind us, and frequently upon us, from the Tory Backbenches were John Biffen, Nick Ridley and Peter Tapsell.

The debates in the Committee Stage of this Bill went to the very heart of economic policy. The central issue was whether it was better to leave the economy as free as possible and subject mainly to market forces, or whether the Government should intervene directly to control decisions made by businesses and trade unions. The Conservatives, in a complete role-reversal, were now advocating one of the most rigid regimes of supervision and control which had ever been proposed. While we were debating one of the central clauses of the Bill, which established sweeping interventionist powers, Brian Walden sent across a note to me saying, 'Just wait until we get our hands on Clause 12. We are much better Socialists than you are.'

In 1973 and 1974 I was involved as a junior Minister in implementing this Prices and Incomes policy. What it came down to was that on a Friday afternoon a small group of Ministers would meet in the Treasury under the chairmanship of Terence Higgins, the Financial Secretary, to determine such matters as the rates of pay for plumbers, new tariffs for taxis, the increase in rents for furnished flats as opposed to unfurnished flats, whether wage increases could be allowed for genuine promotions and what were genuine promotions, and whether price increases could be allowed if these led to increased investment. It is impossible to regulate a free economy in this way. The policy was buttressed by tripartite meetings between the Government, the CBI and the trade unions which were supposed to produce a national consensus. All of this was dignified by the word 'corporatism' and announced to the world in a series of press conferences at Lancaster House, presided over by Ted Heath with William Armstrong sitting at his right hand on the platform. Anyone involved in trying to run this policy would never attempt it again. Enoch Powell was its greatest critic. In a series of brilliant speeches he demolished its intellectual basis and predicted that it would lead to a head-on conflict between organized labour and the Government. He was right. In the second miners' strike this is exactly what happened.

The Fall of Ted

At the end of the Parliamentary session in the summer of 1973, Ted Heath summed up the Government's position with the rosy analysis that we only faced 'the problems of success'. But on 6 October Egypt invaded Israel during Yom Kippur and transformed the political and economic situation of Western Europe. The West was faced with the disruption of its oil supplies from the Middle East. The United States had a degree of oil self-sufficiency but Europe was not so fortunate. Moreover, as Britain had low stocks of coal we were soon plunged into an energy crisis. All this added to the Government's economic difficulties. Tony Barber, the Chancellor of the Exchequer, increased interest rates to 13 per cent and called for special deposits from the clearing banks. The October trade deficit rose to £300 million, which was the highest it had ever been. A State of Emergency was declared in November, there were restrictions on the use of electricity, and by Christmas Peter Walker had issued petrol coupons. On 1 January 1974 a three-day working week was introduced across the country to preserve energy supplies.

The Government, by now into 'Stage Three' of its ill-fated statutory prices and incomes policy, wanted to ensure that the miners agreed to a wage settlement within government guidelines. In July 1973 there had been a secret meeting in the garden of Number 10 between Ted Heath, William Armstrong and Joe Gormley of the National Union of Mineworkers. Gormley had said he would be able to deliver a settlement if the miners were considered as a special case. The basic wage increase for workers across the country was 9 per cent but the miners were offered 13 per cent on the basis of their dangerous occupation and the 'unsocial hours' they worked. Even so, Gormley could not deliver an agreement and the more militant miners' leader, Mick McGahey, called for a 'go slow' as a prelude to a full strike. Ted Heath, having little confidence in his Employment Secretary, Maurice Macmillan, was in effect conducting these negotiations himself until in December he called back Willie Whitelaw from Northern Ireland to replace Maurice.

When Parliament resumed on 9 January 1974 it was clear that the Government was boxed into a corner. At a meeting of the 1922 Conservative Backbench Committee there were many calls for an immediate General Election, including one from Dan Awdry, the MP for Chippenham and a Shire MP respected as one of the steady men at the centre of the Party. Marcus Sieff, the Chairman of Marks and Spencer, told me that the Government had about three weeks before the economy got into real trouble. There was now a growing national mood for matters to be brought to a head and for the Government to take a grip. One way was for it to get a renewed mandate through a General Election. On 10 January John Nott, then a Treasury Minister, told me that he was urging his colleagues to hold an election on 31 January or possibly 7 February. February 14th would be too late. John was particularly concerned about deflationary measures that would be necessary to defend the pound. That week I spoke at two political meetings in London and Nottingham, and at both of these the local Conservative Associations called for an immediate General Election. Private opinion polls taken for the Party indicated that we could win a General Election if one was called very quickly.

But over the weekend senior Ministers decided to continue their efforts to reach agreement with the unions. The Whips Office was divided 6:7 on whether there should be an election at all – a fact which particularly impressed Ted, who himself had been a former Chief Whip. On 14 January William Armstrong told me he had advised Ted that there were another three or four weeks left to make up his mind, just the type of advice Ted wanted to hear. I saw Ted the same day and urged him to make a quick decision, as did those close to him like Tim Kitson, his PPS, and Douglas Hurd, his Political Secretary. As each day passed, the ability to play the key card of a snap election, one of the few advantages a Prime Minister possesses, was being eroded.

Further meetings with the TUC were arranged at which Hugh Scanlon and Len Murray said that if there was a special deal for the miners they would do whatever they could to stop it setting a benchmark for other groups of workers. But this was a pledge which TUC leaders simply could not deliver. The result of all these delays was that a General Election could not now be held on 31 January or 7 February.

At the next meeting of the 1922 Committee, Angus Maude led the demand for an immediate election, and opinion among the Party's backbenchers had now shifted to 70:30 in favour of this. Humphrey Atkins, the Chief Whip, wanted an immediate decision from Ted, and Jim Prior had a blazing row with Ted when he tried to persuade him personally to hold the election quickly. Ted believed, however, that he could talk the miners into an agreement on their wage settlement. Tim Kitson told me Ted was worried that a snap election would lead to a very large Tory majority, and that this would be more damaging to his policies than a small majority. That week's Cabinet did not discuss an election. Margaret Thatcher told me that she favoured an immediate election, but Ted was dithering probably because he did not relish the prospect of losing both of his official homes. Enoch Powell, who had predicted a head-on conflict between Government and unions, said that Ted was mentally and emotionally unstable. However, it wasn't Ted who cracked.

On 1 February William Armstrong, the Cabinet Secretary, had a nervous breakdown and had to be led away from a meeting of civil servants, uttering obscenities. By then it was clear that all this talking was leading nowhere and precious days had been lost. It was only at

Prime Minister's Questions on 5 February that Ted spoke of the 'flouting of the will of Parliament', which was greeted with a sharp intake of breath around the Chamber. He announced a General Election two days later on 7 February.

The February 1974 election was one of the worst campaigns I ever experienced. The Pay Board leaked figures damaging to the Government and helpful to the miners' case. Campbell Adamson, the Director-General of the CBI, torpedoed the Government by calling for the repeal of the Industrial Relations Act. Enoch Powell, who had resigned his seat, urged Tories to vote Labour because of Ted Heath's commitment to the EEC. To cap it all, the monthly trade deficit was huge. Conservative Central Office had been lulled into complacency by favourable opinion polls indicating a Tory lead of up to 11 points. The actual election result was disastrous. Although neither of the main parties received an overall majority, the Conservatives now had 297 seats compared with Labour's 301. A Labour lead of four had replaced a Conservative lead of thirty-five. Because the Conservatives had actually received more votes, although not seats, than Labour, Ted tried to do a deal with Jeremy Thorpe, Leader of the Liberal party. When this effort failed it was clear to everyone that the Conservative Government could not continue. An election called to resolve the issue of 'Who governs Britain?' had given an equivocal verdict which went against Ted.

Opposition 1974–79

Harold Wilson was surprised to be back in Number 10. Rumours were circulating about various property deals done by a brother of Marcia Williams, his political secretary, involving the reclamation of slag heaps, and quite unwittingly I helped to bring this out into the open. On 5 April 1974, I intervened at Prime Minister's Question Time to praise Eddie Milne, the Labour MP for Blyth, who had spoken out in the wake of the Poulson affair against scandalous profits made by property speculators. In his reply Wilson accused me of smearing him, as it was perfectly reasonable to reclaim slag heaps. I was amazed that the Prime Minister should use my rather harmless question to bring this issue to a head himself, and it was to dog him for several months.

After his election defeat Ted put together a new team for what might be a short-lived period of Opposition. Willie Whitelaw became Chairman of the Party and Michael Wolff, one of Ted's closest advisers and speech writers, was appointed to run Central Office. Tim Kitson, the MP for Richmond who had been Ted's Parliamentary Private Secretary since 1970 and with whom I had spent many hours playing bridge during all night sessions, asked me if I would help Ted by joining him as a second PPS. Most of my friends, including Paul Bryan, advised me to say 'no', for Ted was likely to lose again in any snap election which Harold Wilson might spring. I saw no reason to dissent from this analysis but nonetheless I felt that since the Leader of the Party had asked for my personal help then I would give it. Ted had made me a junior Minister and I felt that I owed him my support, even though it might have been, as someone said at the time, 'a rare example of a rising politician joining a sinking ship'.

I did what I could to help by getting Ted to spend more time with Conservative backbenchers, for as Prime Minister he had not cosseted his Parliamentary colleagues. As a PPS I attended meetings of the Shadow Cabinet which soon turned to the important issue of what the Conservative strategy should be. At a meeting on 3 May 1974, Alec Douglas-Home argued that we should 'return to base' by appealing to regional loyalties and extending home ownership. Peter Walker developed this with a radical proposal to transfer all council houses and flats to their tenants free of charge. I thought this was socially desirable, imaginative and politically shrewd, but it was generally felt to be a step too far, and instead we committed ourselves to selling council houses and flats with generous discounts. Willie Whitelaw wanted a greater commitment to more effective industrial relations laws, but in view of the bruising time we had just had he said these should not be too detailed.

The most interesting debate was between Ted Heath and Keith Joseph on incomes policy. Keith, supported by Margaret Thatcher and Geoffrey Howe, wanted the Shadow Cabinet to bring in experts on monetarism who would explore alternatives to the policies which had failed when we were in office. Ted, supported by Peter Walker and Ian Gilmour, was very cool about this. Most of the others remained silent. It was agreed that there would be a meeting with economists later in the year, but the beginning of the debate within the Tory Party about the whole future of economic policy and monetarism had begun.

Keith Joseph developed his economic ideas during the rest of the summer. Presumably he felt unencumbered by his own record as a compassionate and high-spending Secretary of State for Social Services.

In September he circulated to the Shadow Cabinet a speech he intended to make in Preston which condemned prices and incomes policy as 'a weasel phrase', called for a return to sound money and bluntly said, 'Monetary control is a pre-essential for everything else we need and want to do.' Keith was right, but most of the Shadow Cabinet were still tied to the policies they had followed when in government. Ted was particularly sensitive about Keith's rejection of the immediate past and was emotionally hurt and annoyed by it. At one meeting he said to him, 'Your analysis of the Government's record has left me heartbroken' – a term I'd never heard him use before. Some colleagues around the table tried to persuade Keith not to deliver his Preston speech while others suggested changes. Finally Ted and Keith had a meeting for an hour and a half to discuss the speech together. Keith modified some of his phraseology but not his conclusions. He delivered the speech on 5 September, and it was this speech which persuaded Margaret Thatcher that a wholly new approach to economic policy was necessary.

During this time I saw rather more of Margaret Thatcher in action. I had not come across her very much while she was Education Secretary, apart from taking a delegation to meet her about saving St Marylebone Grammar School, which she did. I had first met her in the late 1960s when we travelled together on the train – a rare experience for her – to Norwich to take part in an Anglia TV programme. She was by herself and was busy with her papers, carefully preparing what she was going to say. The only comment I can recall from that journey was when I mentioned Julian Amery rather favourably and she responded tartly, 'I don't think that the future of the Conservative party lies with Julian Amery.' It would have required a person with an exceptional gift of foresight to have seen that it was going to lie with my travelling companion.

After the February 1974 defeat, Ted appointed Robert Carr as Shadow Chancellor, and to beef up the attacks on Labour he appointed Margaret as Robert's deputy. She made the most of this with some good debating speeches in the House, and it could be argued that in this way Ted laid the foundations of his own defeat.

At this time Ted was advocating a coalition Government. In June, speaking to the Parliamentary press gallery, he called for a Government of National Unity, a theme which owed a lot to Ian Gilmour. The theory behind it was that a coalition Government would defuse Harold Wilson's charge that another Tory Government would bring back the three-day week. National Unity became the core of our election strategy in October 1974 – an election I never believed we had a chance of winning, and indeed we did not. On 10 October Labour was returned with 319 seats, an overall majority of three, while the Conservatives dropped to 277 seats, a loss of twenty.

At eleven o'clock on the morning after our defeat, I went round to Ted's house in Wilton Street, where I found him still in his pyjamas and dressing-gown. Tim Kitson told me that he had advised Ted to stand down but Toby Aldington, who had also seen Ted that morning, had offered the opposite advice. Ted was very silent and gloomy as I gave him what I thought was the good advice that, 'You had better resign now as Leader if you don't want to be hurt. There are many people in the Party who are out to destroy you – the malicious, the malcontents, the sacked, the ignored and overlooked are all blaming you. Too many fair-weather friends. Central Office is deeply divided and the old guard are openly attacking you. Even someone with your resilience is going to be hurt.' Ted listened, but I realized my message was not getting through to him.

Later that evening Mary and I gave a dinner party for Ted to which we invited Toby Aldington, Peter Carrington, Michael Wolff, Douglas Hurd and William Waldegrave, so that Ted was amongst friends. But I sensed then that he was determined to go on being Party Leader. As Toby accompanied Ted to his car he said to me, 'Ted is too truculent and too aggressive to give in.' Over the weekend Ted stayed with Toby and spoke to Francis Pym, who encouraged him to stay. Ted told me on the Sunday, 'Francis seems to be one of the few who are talking sense at the moment.'

I was surprised that Ted still wanted to continue as Party Leader. He had fought four General Elections, winning one and losing three. The next election would be more than four years away, and it was clear that the Conservative Party would have to change significantly those policies which we had followed in Government. A growing number of MPs and members of the Shadow Cabinet were already demanding this change. It was going to be a very difficult situation to handle for someone who was so prickly about any criticism of his record as Prime Minister. But by the end of the weekend it was clear that Ted had decided he would go on because, amongst other things, he had to 'save the Party from extremism'.

I told Ted on Monday that if his decision was to remain as Party

Leader then the one thing he must do to secure his re-election was to put his name forward immediately. However, he refused to do this and put off the decision for some months. Jack Weatherill, who was then a Conservative Whip and later to become Speaker, told me that a majority of the Parliamentary Party were determined to have a change of leader in the New Year. Jack felt the best strategy for Ted would have been to obtain a unanimous request from the Executive of the 1922 Committee for him to continue as Leader. However, the Chairman of the 1922 Committee, Edward du Cann, and some of the other members of its Executive who met in Edward's City office in Milk Street, and who were later dubbed 'The Milk Street Mafia', decided otherwise.

Keith Joseph was widely talked of as an alternative candidate, but Ted felt he would beat him. It was late in the day, after Keith had made clear he did not want to stand as Leader, that Margaret Thatcher announced her candidacy. Tim Kitson headed Ted's campaign, and together we did what we could to rally wavering Conservative MPs. Margaret's team, led by Airey Neave, ran a clever and subtle campaign, and she was particularly active in seeing individual MPs. When Ted too adopted this tactic it was rather like being summoned to the Head-master's study: one knew one was there for a purpose, it was rather uncomfortable, and the sooner it was over the better.

I was with Ted in the Leader of the Opposition's room in the House of Commons (it has now become the Home Secretary's office), when Tim Kitson brought in the result of the first leadership election ballot. Ted was sitting on the sofa at the window. He looked crestfallen as it became clear that he had been beaten in the first round. Although Margaret had not received the necessary overall majority on the first ballot, she had won 130 votes to Ted's 119. Ted decided to withdraw straightaway, and with calm dignity he drew up in his own hand his resignation statement. As I left Ted's office I passed Reggie Mandling uncharacteristically rushing down the corridor and muttering, 'The Party's taken leave of its senses. This is a black day.'

Ted was shattered. He had never believed the Party would turn on him in this way. The following night he spoke at a large dinner for my constituents in the House of Commons. He was cheered loudly, for like many Conservative Associations they were instinctively loyal to the Party Leader and remembered the good days when he had nursed the Party back to a winning position in the late 1960s. Ted thanked me for my loyal support and said that his active life in politics was not over. He said, 'The health of the Conservative Party is not good. We cannot build the future of our Party by denigrating its recent past. We must look after all our fellow citizens and not just one class.' He added presciently, 'Our future lies in Europe. That is what is at stake.'

Ted could never believe that Margaret Thatcher was anything other than a temporary bird of passage. Their post-1975 relationship has been tragic, and Ted could never forgive her for standing against him and defeating him. The fact that Margaret was a woman made it worse. Ted could not stand her personally and he came to loathe her policies, looking upon Thatcherism as an aberration, and taking considerable satisfaction from her own fall from the Party leadership in 1990.

I had grown fond of Ted while serving as his PPS. He was passionately concerned to ensure that his policies were fair and just. He had been seduced into believing that the interventionist policies he turned to in mid-term were going to work, whereas they actually wrecked his Government. If Ted had continued as leader then the tensions between the various views in the Party would have put enormous strains upon its unity. But I do not believe this was the central issue in the 1975 leadership election. The Parliamentary Party got rid of Ted because he was a loser.

I tried to dissuade Ted from going to the Blackpool Party Conference in 1975 and even wrote from France, where we were on holiday, urging him not to attend. This was the first occasion on which Ted established the alternative Court of malcontents whom he entertained during Party Conference time. His friends in the media loved it because he was quite open about accusing the group around Margaret of 'going for me'. As for Keith and Margaret herself, they were 'traitors'. All these phrases were immediately and lovingly reported and actually did Ted no good at all.

Just as Ted's services were no longer required, neither were mine. I did not expect to be offered any post in the new Shadow Cabinet, even though I had been punctilious in ensuring that Ted's team did not attack Margaret personally during the leadership election. After all, the Party had to pull together after the election whatever the outcome. I returned to the Backbenches and to business, where I remained for another seven years.

During this period, one of the most interesting Parliamentary duties I undertook was to serve on the Procedure Committee of the House of Commons, which was then considering major reforms. That great

Parliamentarian, Enoch Powell, now representing the Northern Ireland seat of South Down as an Ulster Unionist, was also a member and for four years we enjoyed some fascinating debates about the nature of our constitution and the procedures of the House of Commons. It was this Committee which recommended the establishment of the Departmental Select Committees which have done more to enhance the power, position and influence of MPs than anything else since the War. We also gallantly tried to stop the proceedings of the House at 10 p.m. but failed totally.

I also became Chairman of the Hansard Society, which is an All-Party Parliamentary Group promoting an understanding of British Parliamentary democracy. I wanted to get over to young people the significance of Westminster and how important it was that they should be interested and involved in the process of democracy. To that end I persuaded the National Westminster Bank and other companies to fund sixth-form conferences to be addressed by leading figures from each of the Parties. These conferences were very popular, and I remember one huge meeting in the Methodist Central Hall attended by nearly 1,000 sixth-formers who were addressed by a fairly new young MP whose name was Neil Kinnock. I was impressed by the rapport he established with his audience and how he moved them with an eloquent, passionate commitment to Socialism. This age group was always his best audience.

The art of political communication has always fascinated me. A politician uniquely has the opportunity, and indeed the duty, to speak out on issues – and I mean literally to speak. He or she stands up in front of an audience or sits in television and radio studios being interviewed. Politicians engage in the art of persuasion, persuading hundreds, thousands or even millions of people of the rightness of their views. A politician's personal power of persuasion is crucial. The rotund oratory of the past no longer compels. The great speeches of Churchill are moving but they are 'historical'. Political speeches today have to be pithy, and must encapsulate a message in a few words for the television 'soundbite'. It is sad that most politicians today lack the ability or time personally to craft memorable speeches and instead resort to whole teams of speech writers.

I spread my wings in the mid-1970s by writing for the *Guardian*, the *Times*, the *Daily Telegraph* and the tabloids. I was pleased when the *Guardian* printed my first article, which satirized the idea of dog licensing and a national corps of dog wardens. (Ten years later, as

Environment Secretary, I was to abolish the dog licence.) I covered a wide range of subjects – the Inner London Education Authority, small business, tax reform, training for the unemployed, splitting the Treasury into two Departments, and the need to level the tilted chessboard on which employers and employees fought out their industrial disputes. In 1976, I forecast that:

The present Government is likely to be the last Government in Britain that has an overall Socialist majority in the House of Commons committed to carrying out a Socialist programme.

For the most part these contributions went unnoticed by my elders and betters. But it was great fun to write them. I had to go out and sell them to editors, as few backbenchers are rung up and asked to write anything. I learned that one had to go out into the market place and blow one's own trumpet.

The article of mine which has been most reprinted – and this was a salutary lesson – was not about a major political issue at all. It appeared in the *Daily Telegraph* and argued that Gilbert and Sullivan's operetta *Iolanthe* was a clever political pastiche: the Queen of the Fairies was really Victoria; the Lord Chancellor was Gladstone; Joseph Chamberlain and Charles Dilke were the 'ravenous hordes who all came aboard at Sloane Square and South Kensington Stations'; Sergeant Willis was John Brown; and Strephon was Lord Randolph Churchill. The article even occasioned some correspondence from historians in the letter columns of the *Daily Telegraph*. Every so often, I get a letter from an amateur operatic society asking for my permission to republish the piece in their programme of *Iolanthe*. Such is fame.

Another article which is occasionally reprinted is one on book-collecting that I wrote for the *Times*. Victor Rothschild, whom I had first met at Chequers when he was head of the Think Tank under Ted Heath and busy reminding Cabinet Ministers how ineffective they were in achieving their objectives, was a great collector of eighteenth-century books. I believe he gave his collection of the first editions of Swift and Pope to his university college. Rothschild was a polymath: a scientist, a businessman, fascinated with the mechanics and mentality of gambling – on which he produced the best report since the war, while owing to his family background he was a connoisseur of grand premier cru, which he generously offered to his guests.

Writing in the *Times*, Victor argued that buying eighteenth-century books had not been as good an investment as buying shares. I countered by asserting that if he had bought nineteenth- and twentieth-century rare books he would have comfortably beaten the *Financial Times* index. We shared a love of books, and we also happened to share the same barber. Although Victor was almost bald, each morning he would walk over from his house overlooking St James's Park to be shaved, a wonderful eighteenth-century trait. We would pass messages to each other via our barber.

The other interest I started in the late Seventies was the compilation of an anthology of satirical poetry. One of the most popular anthologies since the War had been Lord Wavell's *Other Men's Flowers*, compiled when he was Commander-in-Chief of the armies in Egypt and India. I was much impressed with the wide range of Wavell's poetic interest, and in particular I was fascinated by one section which he called 'Hymns of Hate'. Over the years I put aside various satirical poems. The English language is particularly rich in satirical poetry, with fine writing by Dryden, Swift and Pope as well as the late Victorian poets, Browning and Kipling, and that tradition continued well into the twentieth century.

I persuaded Eyre Methuen to publish this collection, and was lucky in having the advice of Geoffrey Strachan, their Managing Director, in producing this my first book, entitled *I Have No Gun But I Can Spit*. I followed the book with four other anthologies, one on the poetry of London called *London Lines*, then *English History in Verse*, which appeared on the bestseller lists, another on poetic parodies called *Unauthorized Versions*, and, in May 1993, *The Faber Book of Conservatism*.

Producing these books has given me a very great deal of pleasure. It is important that politicians, even busy politicians like Ministers, should not spend their entire lives preoccupied with ministerial work, red boxes, and the pressing problems of the day. While this is expected of them, and they must do it, they should also find time to do something different. I think it was Churchill who said he always liked to have 'a book on the go', and I must say that I have found the same pleasure in doing that. It took me out of myself and reminded me of the fact that what seemed to be so demanding and preoccupying day by day should be seen against the much broader background of developments over the centuries which lie behind us.

In 1976, Jim Prior, Margaret's Shadow Employment Secretary, asked me to join his team to fight Michael Foot's Dock Work Regulation Bill. This enshrined the dock workers' monopoly to work not only in ports but also within a five-mile zone around each coastal and tidal waterway dock. I quickly appreciated that the way to destroy this measure was to focus on the five-mile zone, and in committee I persuaded Labour's Employment Secretary, the hapless Albert Booth, to produce maps with the zone drawn on them. This produced some amusing absurdities, since one of the five-miles zones included within it Doncaster Race Course. From that moment the Bill was doomed. On 27 May the Labour Government's majority for this Bill fell to just one vote, but later when Brian Walden and John Mackintosh refused to support it the Bill had to be emasculated.

A few days after that dramatic vote, Norman Lamont, the MP for Kingston upon Thames, and I set off for an official visit to Hong Kong and China. We had only just got there when the Deputy Chief Whip, John Stradling Thomas, telephoned to say that we might have to return to Westminster as Margaret had tabled a motion of no confidence in the government. This was going to be debated on 9 June and it looked as though we were going to win. Norman and I pointed out that this was highly unlikely, as the Liberals would rally to the support of Labour in order to maintain the Lib/Lab coalition. We went on to China, and were visiting a remote cooperative fruit farm in the Canton province when a young man ran up to us and rather unexpectedly said we were wanted on the telephone. We returned to the headquarters hut and located the telephone, which was of the wind-up type last seen in Europe in the 1920s. The call was from the Ambassador in Peking saying that the Chief Whip had contacted him to ask us to return at once.

We were very fed up and went on to Shanghai, where we found Julian Amery and his wife sitting in the guest house having a splendid break-fast of bacon and eggs washed down by a bottle of Mou Tai, the Chinese sake. Julian had been swanning around South China with one of his old military friends, a Chinese general from the War, when he had also been asked to return. All three of us decided that we had no intention of returning, and I was chosen to pass this information to the Chief Whip. However, Julian's wife, Katie, who was the daughter of Harold Mac-millan, gave us a stern lecture on duty and loyalty and said we had to return. In desperation I telephoned Stradling Thomas, who assured me that we were going to defeat the Government and that Margaret had specifically asked us to come back for the vote.

When I put the telephone down there was a polite knock at the door and our Chinese hosts asked if there was anything they could do to help. Their telephone tapping had been very effective, but they were still bemused by British Parliamentary practice. Although it was the monsoon period, when China Airways did not always fly, we managed to reach Peking and boarded another flight to London. Norman and I were woken up during the flight by Julian, who had taken the sensible precaution of bringing his own supplies of Mou Tai. We were somewhere over the Himalayas on a brilliant moonlit night and Julian told us to look out of the window for we were just flying over Gilgit. Displaying a fine sense of imperial history, he said, 'Do you realize that Gilgit was the point at which the three great Empires – the British, the Russian, and the Chinese – met? That was where the Great Game was played.'

Julian was a good man to have as a travelling companion, for later that night we were marooned for four hours in the sweltering heat of Islamabad airport. As we tried to find an air-conditioned room – for it was rumoured that the airport had one – we got lost and asked an old man sweeping the floor where this room was. The sweeper replied by asking our names, and when he heard Julian's he went down on his knees reverentially saying, 'Amery Sahib, Amery Sahib.' He thought Julian was a reincarnation of his father, Leo, who had been the Secretary of State for India during the War. The old man then led us ceremoniously to the air-conditioned room. We were eventually met at Heathrow by the Tory whip, Spencer Le Marchant, who brought with him a bottle of champagne to accompany the news that the Opposition had now decided they could not win this critical vote but it was very good of us to have come back.

James Callaghan, who had succeeded Harold Wilson as Leader of the Labour party and Prime Minister, decided after these cliffhanging votes in 1976 that he could not govern with a Labour majority alone. He therefore created the Lib/Lab pact with David Steel which kept him in power until 1979. During the winter of 1979 the organized trade union movement decided to take on Callaghan just as they had taken on Harold Wilson and Ted Heath. The Winter of Discontent destroyed any remaining public confidence in the Labour Government. It also marked the beginning of the end of the old-fashioned Labour party, dominated by the trade unions. The seeds of the later split when the Social Democrats left to form their own Party had been lying dormant for some time, but during that winter they germinated.

The crisis that led to Callaghan's defeat came when the Scottish Nationalists decided to desert him over the issue of devolution. On 28 March 1979, the House of Commons debated a motion of no confidence in the government tabled by the Conservative Opposition and the Scottish Nationalists. It was a day of high drama. Margaret entered the Chamber to cheers at 3.15 p.m., wearing a light grey suit, a white blouse, and a long floppy tie. She looked very crisp and was heard in complete silence as she made four points: tax was too high; trade unions were too powerful; the rule of law was being flouted; and the state was too powerful. She said, 'We are a nation on the sidelines.' However, it was the Labour backbenchers who shouted, 'More, more,' when she sat down. Eric Heffer called out to Jim Callaghan as he began to speak, 'Be kind, Jim.' Callaghan made a good debating speech saying, 'When Mrs Thatcher discovered that the Scottish Nationalists and the Liberals were prepared to vote against the Government she tabled a motion of no confidence. She had the courage of their convictions.' Turning to the Scottish Nationalists, Callaghan used that much quoted phrase, 'It's like turkeys voting for an early Christmas.'

There was great uncertainty throughout the day about the vote. I went over to the Norman Shaw offices to have a drink with Ted Heath and Tim Kitson. Ted was very gloomy, saying that Callaghan would never have been able to make the speech he did if Margaret had not disowned the period of his premiership from 1970 to 1974. This continuous rejection of his record hurt him more than anything else. Ted predicted that the Tories would lose that night, and would also lose the next election whenever it came. At dinner in Pratt's the same evening all the old High Tories thought that we were going to lose the no confidence motion by one vote. In the wind-up speeches back in the House, Willie Whitelaw was bluff and stuck closely to his notes. Michael Foot's reply was quite brilliant, with a superb attack on the Liberals and contempt for David Steel, whom he dismissed as 'the boy David sheltering behind the Scottish Nationalist shield'.

As we went through the lobby, Margaret was standing with Humphrey Atkins, her Chief Whip, who was apologizing in the belief that we had lost by one vote. We returned to the Chamber looking rather crestfallen while the Labour benches looked very cheerful. Adam Butler, one of Margaret's PPSs, came into the Chamber and told us the vote was tied, but a Labour Whip who followed him looked very confident. Margaret was looking very dejected when suddenly Tony Berry, who had been counting in the Labour Lobby, appeared from behind the Speaker's Chair and held up his thumb. We couldn't believe it. Spencer Le Marchant holding the teller's slip stepped up to the table and read out, 'Ayes 311 – Noes 310.'

The no confidence motion had been carried. Callaghan rose very coolly and said he would recommend to the Queen that Parliament should be dissolved. This of course meant a General Election. We filed out of the Chamber to the refrain of Labour Members defiantly singing 'The Red Flag'.

The General Election campaign of 1979 began with tragedy. Airey Neave, one of Margaret's closest colleagues and the man likely to become her Northern Ireland Secretary, was murdered by a car-bomb planted by Irish terrorists. The subsequent Conservative campaign was the first in which the Party quite deliberately made a pitch for the C2 voters, aspiring skilled manual workers who had seen their wage differentials squeezed under Labour and for whom the Conservative Manifesto pledges of lower taxes, the sale of council houses and reform of trade union law was a potent mixture. Gordon Reece, the Conservative Party's Director of Publicity, used the tabloid press and 'soft' television programmes to expose Margaret to this new target audience.

Saatchi and Saatchi, who had made a big impact with their 1978 poster campaign, which included the famous shot of a dole queue over which was the slogan 'Labour Isn't Working', ran extensive advertising in the popular press in addition to posters. They hit hard at Labour with an updated version of their best poster, which now read 'Labour Still Isn't Working'. Conservative Party political broadcasts featured news film of the Winter of Discontent, reminding voters of the way the Labour Government had been powerless in the face of trade union obduracy. The Conservative campaign, it has to be admitted, was more about stirring resentment at the Labour Government and motivating voters to turf it out than getting people to vote positively for the Conservative alternative.

One also tends to forget that all through the election, although the Conservatives held their lead over Labour, Jim Callaghan's personal ratings were actually higher than Margaret's. However, the Labour Government's days were over. As Callaghan himself later said, 'There are times, perhaps once every thirty years, when there is a sea change in politics. It then does not matter what you say or what you do . . . I suspect there is now such a sea change – and it is for Mrs Thatcher.' On

3 May, the Conservatives won 339 seats to Labour's 269, a majority of forty-three and the highest number of Conservative MPs returned since 1959. Britain not only had a Conservative Government again, it also had its first woman Prime Minister.

CHAPTER 3

Joining the Government

Writing the Job Specification – Minister for Information
Technology – The New Technology – The Falkland Islands

On Friday, 4 May 1979, Margaret Thatcher entered Downing Street
with the prayer of St Francis on her lips. I waited with a little hope,
but not much more, for a call from Number 10. It did not come.
Several friends rang up and sympathized. Norman Lamont felt very
peeved that he was only offered a Parliamentary Under-Secretary's job
at Energy after he had been Keith Joseph's second-in-command and
said, 'Keith has let me down.' Peter Morrison, the Whip, rang up to
commiserate, but he must have known I had not been left out as an
oversight. I think I was still not forgiven for my support of Ted back
in 1975. This was confirmed when Ted rang me up and said, 'I'm very
sorry. It's all my fault, and I'm to blame.'

However, it is the lot of most MPs not to be offered ministerial
office, and so it is pointless being fed up or bitter. I rang Michael
Jopling, the Chief Whip, and rather cheekily asked to propose or
second the Loyal Address to the Queen's Speech which starts the
Parliamentary session. This is an important occasion at the beginning
of each new Parliament, particularly as a new era was opening. I also
wanted to show my old friends, and the new MPs, that I was still
around.

It was as usual a packed House, doubly significant for the fact that it
was going to be Margaret's first speech as Prime Minister and the first
debate broadcast by the BBC. The proposer, the old and faithful MP
for Newcastle, Bill Elliott, and the seconder were expected to be short
and witty. I'd remembered speeches by John Nott and Neil Kinnock
which were both witty although only one was short. I much enjoyed
making mine. I reminded the House that the Conservative Party was a
bird with a right wing and a left wing, but like a bird its brains were in
the middle. However, what this speech is remembered for is my advice
to new Conservative MPs: if they wanted to get on, they would have to

find a foothold 'in the narrow strip of land that lies between sycophancy and rebellion'.

Thirteen years later, after I had left the Government of my own accord, I asked the then Chief Whip, Richard Ryder, if I could propose the Loyal Address for the new Parliament in 1992. I liked the idea of beginning and rounding off this period with these two speeches from the Backbenches. In May 1992, I reminded the new, ambitious and eager Tory MPs that many hours of boredom and making speeches in an empty Chamber lay ahead of them and, 'they will meet the Parliamentary twins, Humdrum and Humbug. If they can endure Humdrum and occasionally engage in Humbug they will be the darling of the Whips Office. No post will be beyond their grasp.'

The proposer and seconder of the Loyal Address were invited to the eve-of-session dinner at Number 10. There was a little ceremony on these occasions which began with Margaret shouting out, 'Bar the doors,' whereupon all the doors to the room were shut. Then the Cabinet Secretary read out the Queen's Speech. The Speaker was invited and was the only person present unaware of the contents, which had been cleared by Ministers in the weeks before. After the dinner several Ministers came up and said it was a disgrace that I was not in the Government – a small consolation. As I was leaving, Margaret took me to one side and said, 'I'm sorry, I'll try to fit you in next time.' But if she had really wanted to include me in her first Government she could have done it then.

However, it is no good any young politician going off to sulk in his tent. I was intrigued with the broadcasting of the House and saw the potential of making our debates more widely understood – just as Hansard had opened up Parliament to the literate reading classes, broadcasting would open it up to the listening classes. I persuaded Capital Radio, the very successful London pop music station, whose audience of young people had probably hardly heard of Parliament (and what they did know made them deeply suspicious), to allow me to make a five-minute programme which went out every Friday evening at 7.30 p.m. incorporating the highlights of the week. It was called 'Party Pieces' and was a success from the start. I persuaded the experienced radio presenter, Ed Boyle, to help me with the technical side, which was quite new to me. Later we invited Graham Tope, a Liberal MP, and Chris Price, a Labour MP, to do some of the programmes in order to create a balance. Chris later lost his seat and became the successful

Director of Leeds Polytechnic. 'Party Pieces' still continues with a variety of MP presenters.

It was great fun doing this. There was always a serious content, usually the issue of the week, but it was spiced up with the liveliness of Westminster. I wanted to catch listeners' ears in five minutes and show that what was going on in Westminster was of importance to them.

The radio public who were hearing the proceedings of the House of Commons for the first time were shocked by the background noise, the cat-calling and the irreverence, particularly at Prime Minister's Question Time. Parliament seemed like a noisy rabble. This never bothers MPs themselves. Put three or four hundred men and women together in a small space for a short time, let them loose at the Government with direct questions aimed at belittling Ministers, throw in a good pinch of anger, indignation and wit, and you get a good lively show. If you wanted solemnity, respectful silence and acres of boredom then all you had to do was to visit any Parliament in the Eastern bloc, where dissent was stifled and noise unknown. 'Annoyed of Tunbridge Wells', 'Appalled of Lincoln' and 'Disgusted of Dagenham' all had to learn that noise meant freedom.

I also remained active on the Backbenches and continued as a Member of the 1922 Executive. In the 1970s I had established a reputation as one of the scourges of the Inner London Education Authority, and Mark Carlisle, the Education Secretary, asked me to do a report on the ILEA's future which I cover in chapter 10.

I was also involved in policy work on the economic regeneration of London. I headed a group set up by the Centre for Policy Studies, the think-tank established by Keith Joseph in 1975 to work on the philosophical justification of Conservatism and the fashioning of new policies. The study group produced a paper called *The Developing Docklands*, which I presented to a packed meeting of the CPS chaired by Margaret. We advocated an Urban Development Corporation as well as Enterprise Zones, though we were disappointed that only 10 per cent of Docklands was to be covered by a Zone. We were reinforcing the ideas that Michael Heseltine, the Environment Secretary, and Geoffrey Howe, the Chancellor, were working on. We felt strongly that the key to redeveloping Docklands was private development, which would increase the value of the land and in turn promote more development. But infrastructure investment was also needed, and the Group strongly advocated the completion of the trunk road network.

As a backbencher, I was also able to continue my business interests, particularly with Logica, in the field of information technology. The Government had little understanding of the significance of the micro-chip revolution which was about to transform society. There was another industrial revolution actually in the process of happening, and it was essential that we were not left trailing behind America and Japan. In 1980, I set out an industrial strategy in a series of articles and speeches and specifically in a speech setting out a ten-point programme (see Appendix 1). I called for the appointment of a Minister for Information Technology and a comprehensive programme to develop hardware and software in the UK, to promote British products overseas, to expand research and development, and to increase training and education in the new IT skills.

I sent my strategy paper to several Ministers, campaigned strongly for it to be accepted, and persuaded Margaret Thatcher to visit Logica, Britain's most lively and energetic software company, to see for herself the potential for information handling. That was at the time when you had to explain to most people just what software was. Margaret's visit clearly made an impact, for in January 1981 she appointed me to the Department of Trade and Industry with the title of Minister of State for Industry and Information Technology. This was the first time that a Minister had actually written out his own job specification before being appointed.

Minister for Information Technology

One of the problems was explaining to people exactly what Information Technology was. Sometimes I was introduced as the Minister for Information and sometimes as the Minister for Technology. In fact my concern was with the science and application of information accumulation, transfer and acquisition, particularly by electronic means. More simply it was knowledge at work. My message was that the Wealth of Information was just as important as the Wealth of Nations. The *Financial Times* had a competition to define Information Technology and the winning entry read: 'Information Technology is the modern method of getting to know as much about your business as your grandfather knew about his.' A limerick was also submitted in this competition:

> Ken was a man of few airs
> And when Maggie answered his prayers
> She said with apology
> Try Information Technology
> They've already used Administrative Affairs.

The 1981 reshuffle was Margaret's first. It was dubbed 'the night of the long hatpin'. Norman St John-Stevas was sacked for irreverence. His amusing quips about the Blessed Margaret, the Leaderene, and Little Niglet were assiduously repeated to Number 10. Angus Maude and Reg Prentice left of their own volition. John Patten and John MacGregor joined the Government as junior Ministers.

The Government was in a very rocky position. The recession was biting deep. Many factories were closing each month and manufacturing industry was being slaughtered by high interest rates and an overvalued £. One commentator said 'Baker has boarded the *Titanic* only to discover that he has been given a reserve seat in one of the lifeboats.'

My Secretary of State at the Department of Trade and Industry was Keith Joseph. He was beleaguered and only too glad that someone was going to take off his shoulders responsibility for the new industries. He left me completely alone to get on with my job, but rightly concerned himself with the broad strategies of ending the Post Office mail monopoly and British Telecom's telecommunication monopoly. We saw eye to eye, and I found him one of the best Secretaries of State to work with.

This was the low point of the Thatcher years. There had been a bitterly unpopular Budget, unemployment was rising, factories were closing at a record rate, and when I visited Yorkshire or Lancashire the DTI official who met me at the station usually gave me a list of factories which were closing that very day. The Cabinet was openly divided, the SDP racing ahead, Margaret Thatcher was dismissed as a one-term Prime Minister, and there was talk of a leadership challenge in October. So desperate was Number 10 that at the DTI we had to devise a package of industrial support which she could announce in a censure debate in the House of Commons. The depths had been plumbed.

When a factory was closed in a constituency Margaret had agreed to see the local MPs from whichever Party. This was a formidable obligation for her, and I had to sit in on several of these interviews. She took careful notes in each case and asked me to follow up certain issues. But in the summer of 1981 she was very tired and harassed because the

Government was under pressure due to the depth of the recession. She never doubted that what she was doing was right, but she did feel cornered and that the press was unfairly hostile. After one meeting with the Labour MP for Goole she asked me to stay behind. She showed me a letter of praise from George Thomas about her speech at the opening of John Wesley House. She was amazed that the press had carpingly selected her comment that Wesley's mother had 'an iron will', and said, 'I had read four books about Wesley, why did they select that?' I thought the answer was rather obvious.

During that summer, on the occasions when I saw her she seemed embattled against the world. In July 1981 Francis Pym, Lynda Chalker, Richard Luce and I dined together. Francis was very gloomy, saying, 'It's already too late. We must be guided by the interests of our Party. Is it more damaging to fight with her or to change leaders? That's finely balanced.' This sort of talk was very prevalent in the summer of 1981.

The New Technology

As the new Minister for Information Technology, I was convinced that we, as a country, had to coordinate our activities to cope with the microchip revolution. We had been brilliantly inventive. Britain had won sixty-one Nobel Prizes, a record surpassed only by the USA, although per head of population our success rate was twice that of America. But we rarely benefited financially and economically from this. A Scotsman, Logie Baird, had been among the first to develop television, and he used to demonstrate his work in a small room in Soho which is now a restaurant. Yet America and Japan dominated the television industry. It was particularly galling that the first working computer had been developed at Manchester University, but by 1981 we had just one British company, ICL, and that was hanging on by its teeth. We had also invented liquid crystals, though other countries were capitalizing on this better than the UK.

The microchip moreover was to affect not just the technological and electronic industries but every industry in the country, through revolutionizing the processing of information, the design of its products and the control of the manufacturing process. The working habits and conditions of tens of millions of workers were to be affected whether they were in banks, factories or in retail shops.

The French Government in 1978 had identified 'Télématique' as a crucially important area and it provided substantial funding to French companies; the European Commissioner for Industry had focused upon 'Informatique' and was planning to devote research and development funds to it; and in Japan MITI had initiated a programme to develop semiconductors so that America should not dominate the world markets. Compared to all this, Britain's effort was fragmented and disjointed. The Labour Government had started a modest programme of micro-electronics support which was aimed at persuading people to use the new technologies and to provide training for them.

In fashioning a new set of policies to deal with this challenge, I was helped first by Michael Marshall, and then by John Butcher, as the junior Ministers at the DTI. John brought his own private experience of the computer industry and I found his practical and down-to-earth advice invaluable. Deciding first that we should provide more money for micro-electronics applications and research and development, we increased the support from £100 million in 1979–80 to £350 million in 1983–84. Neither of my Secretaries of State, Keith Joseph and Patrick Jenkin, demurred, in fact they were willing to find this money from other parts of the Department. Less than a quarter of the Department's budget went on the new technologies: three-quarters went on things like regional aid for the older industries.

We introduced a new scheme that channelled £25 million to support fibre optics and optic-electronics. These British inventions were major technological breakthroughs, and I was keen that Britain should not lose out on them. We provided £10 million for a robotics programme to encourage small companies with grants of up to 50 per cent to use the new technology to control machines and to improve their productivity. Industry simply had to move quickly to ensure that it remained in business at all. My message to British businesses was very simple: 'Automate or liquidate.' I managed to find £6 million for companies to buy and use the new systems of computer-assisted design and manufacture – CADCAM – that were then beginning to appear. This was in addition to the £28 million we were providing for flexibility manufacturing systems.

We soon found that the polytechnics and colleges of further education did not have the most up-to-date equipment in CADCAM, so we provided them with it. I also wanted to encourage businesses to use micro-electronic technology in their offices. One or two large companies like Esso and BP had created electronic offices with managers having data terminals on their desks. Now this is quite common, but it was exceptionally rare in the early 1980s. We therefore launched an Office of the Future scheme in which money was provided for twelve projects to show both the private and public sector how office work should be reorganized by using the new equipment that was just coming on to the market – word processors and faxes were still novel inventions at that time.

The money that we spent on all these schemes was catalytic. It was meant to bring about change. Where we could we benefited British companies in both hardware and software to give them the chance to build up sufficient strength to allow them to compete overseas. We were one of the leading countries in the development of software – we still are.

The most significant programme that I introduced was in April 1981, and I even managed to persuade the Prime Minister to launch it herself. Its object was to get a microcomputer into every secondary school. Over half our schools did not have any sort of computer. We identified two computers – the BBC Acorn, made in Cambridge, and the Research Machine, made in Oxford. If schools bought either of these then we would meet 50 per cent of the cost. It was an offer they couldn't refuse.

It was extremely disappointing that the Department of Education was lukewarm about the 'Micros in Schools' initiative. They resented another Department interfering in 'their schools', and every obstacle was put in the way – there weren't enough teachers, or there wasn't enough software, so I had to provide support for both of these. Within a few months 1,000 schools had applied for a computer, and manufacturing them became a problem. As soon as every secondary school had at least one we opened up the offer to primary schools as well. Having seen young children become fascinated with the interplay of keyboard and screen and also seen them acquire operating skills so quickly, I was persuaded that computers could assist learning, particularly in basic numeracy and literacy. Children had to learn keyboard skills at school, since whatever they were to do in life they were going to come into contact with the microchip. We have to train the young people of today for the jobs of tomorrow. Now, in a primary school there are usually half a dozen computers and there are scores or hundreds in a secondary school. We do have a world lead in computing in the classroom. In 1983 when the Queen visited Delhi I persuaded the Foreign Office and the

Palace to arrange for her to give as a gift to the President, not the usual silver salver, but some Acorn computers for schools.

Early in 1981, having read a report in a Sunday newspaper, I went to visit a computer training centre in Hammersmith which had been set up by Chris Webb, who is now the Director of Education in Islington. It provided keyboard training for sixteen- to twenty-one-year olds who had usually lost out on their education. Most of the students did not have a job, having left school with no qualifications or possibly with one or two CSEs. The majority of the trainees were black. What I found were motivated and dedicated young people learning a skill that would get them a job. Because it involved electronics and computers it also enhanced their status and self-respect. The students hadn't got much out of their eleven years of free state education, but this centre gave them a chance to catch up.

I was so impressed with this concept and with Webb's vision that I persuaded Keith to use it as a model for a national network of Information Technology Centres (ITeCs). Margaret too was enthused, and as part of the industrial package she assembled in July 1981 – at the depth of the recession – she announced support for twenty ITeCs. Michael Heseltine asked for two ITeCs in Liverpool to help him in his plan to regenerate that riot-torn city. These were very successful, and by 1983 there were 55 ITeCs training 1,500 young people, with plans to expand to 150 centres training 5,000. Some of them also spawned new equipment and business ventures. Most of them were in the inner cities.

I was hamstrung by the slowness and reluctance of the DES to take any initiatives on technological education. They fought shy of influencing the curriculum, for this was left to individual schools and the LEAs. In March 1982 at Southampton University I called for a new programme of training and technical skills. In the CPC lecture at the Party Conference, I argued that these skills would create more jobs than they threatened. I was delighted therefore when David Young, who had been appointed Head of the Manpower Services Commission, proposed to provide £100 million for technical and vocational training in schools. This initiative was known as TVEI. It allowed teachers in schools to provide special courses for fourteen- to sixteen-year-olds in practical technological training, and was particularly directed at those who were bored with the last two years of state education and likely to drop out. The classes that David and I visited were full of motivated youngsters who were discovering the relevance of education and the importance of learning and training.

I wanted to go further, and in 1984 I started with Henry Chilver, the Vice-Chancellor of the Cranfield Institute of Technology, to plan a new high-tech college or university. Again, the DES was very suspicious. Even with Keith Joseph's prompting they were reluctant to take on a new funding obligation for a new university, although I was prepared to raise a lot of money from industry for this. The scheme never really got off the ground in the way that I envisaged, though one of its fruits was to enhance and expand Cranfield's expertise in this area.

The opportunities in the micro-electronics industries were immense, and it was essential that British industry did not lose out. The industry had some visionaries and far-sighted people but there were also some who were defensive of their own established positions, reluctant to invest significantly in R&D and always looking for protection. I believed we must seek partners overseas, and I was particularly impressed with Japanese companies, as their technology was outstanding and innovative.

When advising Logica and other companies, I had visited Japan several times in the 1970s. Difficult as it might be, I felt British IT companies would benefit by close working relationships with the Japanese. I was particularly impressed with the Fujitsu plant on the slopes of Mount Fuji, where their technology, efficiency and dedication were outstanding. This was one of the reasons why I asked Robb Wilmott, who had been appointed the Managing Director of ICL in the rescue package of 1981, to cooperate with the Japanese. He needed no persuading. I also dispatched to Japan in 1982 a team of officials and businessmen to assess the state of Japanese technology. They came back with proposals that led to the Alvey Programme of additional research into the faster and more powerful British computers of the 1990s. Over a five-year period £350 million was committed by the Government, industry and universities. This was a breakthrough to get companies which were vigorous competitors in the market to pool some of their basic research.

Research was the key, but it was very expensive and most other countries around the world provided generous state assistance. We increased our resources in research, for electronics, for computing and IT, through the Alvey Programme, and the first European Research Programme, known as 'Esprit'. This allowed companies, universities, and research institutes to work together across national boundaries on technological developments.

There were also the new techniques of viewdata and teletext which Britain had pioneered. There were three different standards – French, British and American – and we tried very hard to get the British standard adopted around the world. I even made an official visit to Las Vegas – the last British Minister to do so had been Geoffrey Rippon – not to gamble but to promote British viewdata at the international radio and communications exhibition which is held there annually. I was, however, successful in persuading New Zealand to take Prestel rather than the French Antiope system, after the French had been shown to be cheating with a video tape whereas I had risked an on-line demonstration in the Rotary Club near One-Tree Hill in Auckland!

In all of this I was acting partially as a missionary for the new technologies. It was essential that Britain should focus on them as they were to be as important in changing society as had been the early inventions of the Industrial Revolution in the eighteenth century. We had to dispel the mentality of holding up change by getting a man to walk in front of a motor car carrying a red flag – the procedure which Parliament had insisted upon when the car first appeared. People had to understand the job opportunities that the new technologies would bring. If we didn't adapt and use them then we would have to settle for economic decline and permanently high levels of unemployment. I particularly wanted to appeal to the young, because they knew more about the new technology than their parents.

All this was brought together in 1982, which was designated as Information Technology year. There were thousands of events around the country and we even had a special Post Office stamp commissioned. We ended the year with a large conference in the Barbican addressed by Margaret.

Margaret had become an enthusiast for the new technologies and had given me a free hand to get on with all these programmes. I prepared a speech for her to give at the conference, and most Prime Ministers would have simply accepted it with some tinkering from the Number 10 staff. Not at all. I was summoned to Number 10 one afternoon at four o'clock and we went through it line by line. Then up to her flat with Robin Butler, her Private Secretary, Brian Unwin, a Cabinet official who had been appointed to coordinate IT and who was later to become Chairman of Customs and Excise, and John Vereker, one of the Number 10 staff and a favoured son who was later to become a Deputy Secretary at Education, to write and rewrite as she served us with dinner

– shepherd's pie cooked by herself. She bustled around setting an extra place and filling up the plates. She also opened a huge box of chocolates. During the supper she commented that Elspeth Howe's kitchen at Number 11 was better and more spacious, and added, 'We must do something about that after the Election.'

She was determined to make this speech as good as possible, much more political and with a strong emphasis on the private sector. At one stage she called for the collected verse of Kipling, as she wanted to quote from 'The Secret of the Machines'. I forbore to remind her of his line, 'the female of the species is more deadly than the male'. Margaret liked technological issues, and one never forgot that she had trained as a chemist. The drafting session went on and on in the sitting-room of her flat, and by the early hours she had taken off her shoes and had a whisky. It was a remarkable evening. Six hours totally devoted to working on her speech with no other Government business being done and no interruptions. Margaret really worked hard at getting her speeches right. As we left exhausted in the early hours, three red boxes were delivered. Her night's work was about to begin.

The Falkland Islands

Every schoolboy knew that the Falkland Islands were part of the British Empire because they issued stamps which had the King and Queen's head on them. But exactly where they were, who lived on them, and what happened there, was known only to the few hundred islanders themselves, geographers and possibly a few historians who remembered that Dr Johnson wrote an essay about them.

All this was to change in March 1982. After Argentina's leader, General Galtieri, launched a sea, air and land invasion to reclaim the Falklands, all the world came to hear of South Georgia, Port Stanley, Goose Green and Bluff Cove. A new word, 'yomping', was coined to describe the only way that British soldiers with their heavy packs could march over the sodden bogs that covered most of the islands. Galtieri's act of unprovoked aggression also transformed Margaret Thatcher from seeming to be an embattled, stubborn Prime Minister into a Warrior Queen.

It was an extraordinary crisis. Britain had been in discussion with Argentina over this disputed territory which the Argentinians called Las Malvinas. Nick Ridley, then a junior Foreign Office Minister, had been dispatched to the Falklands to dispose of the problem. He had devised an ingenious scheme to lease the islands back from the Argentinian Government, but when he tried to explain all this to the House of Commons the old Tory colonial Right, led by Bernard Braine, Julian Amery, John Biggs-Davison and Ian Gow, savaged the idea and claimed that we were betraying the Islanders. Peter Shore joined in from the Labour Frontbench, condemning Nick for dealing with Fascists.

The Foreign Office retired hurt. They had identified a potential source of trouble that soured relations between Britain, Argentina and other South American countries, and had thought they could shuffle off this remaining colonial obligation with very little bother. Having been baulked in the House of Commons, they then did little more. The Falklands' remote isolation was emphasized by the proposal of John Nott, the Defence Secretary, to withdraw the ice-breaking vessel, HMS *Endurance*, from the South Atlantic. But Peter Carrington as Foreign Secretary resisted this. When some scrap metal merchants encouraged by the Argentinian Government landed in South Georgia to see if they could scavenge for anything, the Foreign Office view of leaving *Endurance* in the South Atlantic was vindicated. But there were no plans to reinforce the Islands, or extend the runway of Port Stanley airport as a group led by Lord Shackleton had recommended.

On Friday 2 April I started the day with an early visit to Methuen, my publishers, to agree the marketing plans for my second anthology of poetry, *London Lines*. Then I went on to the House, since the payroll vote was needed on some measure.

There was a lot of gossip in the tearoom about a possible invasion, and Tristan Garel-Jones, then a backbench Member of Parliament, was particularly bellicose. At 11 a.m. Humphrey Atkins, who was the Lord Privy Seal and the member of the Cabinet who answered for the Foreign Office in the Commons, reported to the House that he had been in touch with the Governor of the Falklands just thirty minutes earlier but there was nothing new to report. As I left the Chamber at 11.30, I bumped into Richard Luce, the Minister of State ultimately responsible for the Falklands, behind the Speaker's Chair. He was worried, ashen and hurrying. He muttered, 'They've just landed.'

It so happened that I had arranged a lunch at Number 10 for the Prime Minister to meet four industrialists and four academics to discuss the training of technologists. I expected this lunch to be cancelled. Not at all. It went ahead and we joined the Prime Minister for drinks in the main drawing-room. She said, 'It now looks as if the Argentinians have landed. It's going to be logistically very difficult to send out a Fleet and to conduct a campaign 8,000 miles away. But we know our duty.'

Then on to lunch, and for the next hour the Falklands were forgotten and we were totally absorbed and immersed in technology training. Margaret then asked if we minded her leaving, saying as she rose, 'I must sort out rumour from fact.'

There was no sense of crisis at Number 10 and Margaret was very cool. Patrick Jenkin told me there had been a short Cabinet in the morning, and another on Saturday at which every member was asked to give his views on the sending of the Fleet. All agreed that it should go. Quintin Hailsham, ever mindful of constitutional proprieties, had insisted that these major decisions must be taken by the whole Cabinet and not left to ad hoc Committees.

There was still a great deal of confusion. One of the more reliable sources of information turned out to be a radio ham who reported that the Governor had been arrested and that the Islands had been seized. The House was summoned to sit on Saturday and the Prime Minister opened the debate. She was not at her best. She announced that a Fleet was being assembled and would sail on Monday to the Falklands with the clear purpose of recapturing them. 'Too late. Too late!' bawled Labour MPs. This was followed by a brilliant and devastating analysis by Michael Foot of the failure of diplomacy, intelligence and defence.

Labour's attitude to the whole Falklands affair was determined by two considerations. First, they hated Fascism and this was a Fascist invasion. Second, they did not want to make the same mistake that Gaitskell had made during Suez of attacking an operation in which British troops were engaged. So the most pacifist leader that Labour had had since George Lansbury had to support this most daring and dangerous military operation.

The debate in the House went badly for the Government. The most memorable intervention came from Enoch Powell who said:

The Prime Minister, shortly after she came into office, received a soubriquet as the 'Iron Lady'. It arose in the context of remarks which she made about defence against the Soviet Union and its allies; but there was no reason to suppose that the right hon. Lady did not welcome and, indeed, take pride in that description. In the next week or two this House, the nation and the right hon. Lady herself will learn of what metal she is made.

I felt that from that moment Margaret knew she had to go on right to the end.

The Defence Secretary, John Nott, wound up the debate but he misjudged the mood of the House by seeming too casual, and by the end of it you could see he was very depressed. He almost slunk out of the Chamber. In my view, it was at that moment he decided that whatever the outcome of the invasion he would leave politics. That was a pity. He had been a good Minister and was to speak very well in the House as the Falklands campaign developed. He was one of the wittiest speakers in the House, a strong defender of Thatcherite economics, who had actually refused to take a job under Ted Heath when I had pressed Ted to appoint him. He was an independent spirit. John has a delightful Yugoslav wife who spent much of her time looking after their daffodil farm in John's Cornish constituency. I was very sorry to see him leave politics, but he has had a successful career in the City since then.

All that, however, was for the future. That evening the Tory back-benchers summoned Peter Carrington and John Nott to appear before the party's Defence Committee. The backbenchers made it very clear to them that they thought the whole episode was a shambles and a national disgrace. In this feverish atmosphere there were rumours of impending resignations. Willie Whitelaw went around saying that Peter must be supported. Tim Kitson told me that he had spoken to Ted Heath, who was on one of his many visits to China, and Ted had said he was prepared to serve in the Government. That offer was not followed up. This crisis had to be handled by Margaret herself.

On Sunday, Mary and I spent a quiet day gardening at the Old Vicarage, but the weeding was interrupted with telephone calls. I spoke to Max Hastings, who was then working as a journalist on the *Evening Standard*. He told me that 'the whole expedition was madness', 'the game's not worth the candle' and 'the colonial Right of the Party is baying for blood and that's one of the most unpleasant scenes in British life'. Max was, however, to make his name in the Falklands. He joined the expedition, landed with the troops, filed vivid stories, and was the first journalist to march – complete with rucksack and walking stick – into Port Stanley. He later wrote a book on the Falklands with Simon Jenkins. One ended up editing the *Daily Telegraph* and the other the *Times*.

It is ironic that Max's later glittering journalistic success started with a great deal of dubiety on his part. He was not alone. Many were apprehensive, worried about the enormity of the task that lay ahead. Norman Lamont, then a Junior Minister at the Department of Energy, rang me on Sunday saying, 'We have gone out of our collective mind.' I had many conversations with Norman, who remained very apprehensive and uneasy for most of the time. I also remember Nick Ridley telling me over breakfast at 3 a.m. after a party that Tim and Susie Sainsbury gave for Tim's birthday in their country house, that the whole episode was mad – 'She is mad and will have to go.' War does odd things to people's judgement. For my part, although I believed it was a risky undertaking, I thought it right that British forces should be committed to recapturing the Falklands in the event of negotiations not succeeding.

On Sunday, strenuous efforts were made to prevent Peter Carrington from resigning. Willie Whitelaw and Michael Jopling, the Chief Whip, over lunch at Dorneywood – the country residence of the Home Secretary – persuaded him to stay his hand. Tony Royle, the Member for Richmond, told me that he had spoken to Peter late on Sunday and Peter said he intended to sleep on it and see what the papers said on Monday. The papers were vicious, particularly Andrew Alexander in the *Daily Mail*. And so, on Monday morning, Peter Carrington, Humphrey Atkins and Richard Luce all resigned. This was an honourable act. Peter felt that on a major area of policy, for which he was directly responsible, he had let the country down and left Britain in an embarrassing and difficult position. He was respected for his decision to resign, but he was also hurt by the reaction of Conservative MPs. He'd never made much effort to conceal his contempt for the wilder backbenchers – nor they for him. His resignation made the Prime Minister's position easier, since he provided Parliament with the scapegoat it demands on these occasions. But his departure meant that Margaret was deprived of one of the wisest and most experienced counsels around her.

It was one of the strange ironic accidents of British public life that on that morning the memorial service for Rab Butler was to be held in Westminster Abbey. The Prime Minister, Willie Whitelaw, Francis Pym and most of the Government attended in deep mourning. They listened to Peter Carrington reading a passage from the Book of Wisdom, and to an address which spoke of Rab's determination not to split the Tory Party in a moment of crisis. A Canon read Drake's prayer, 'Oh Lord God, when thou givest to thy servants to endeavour any great matter, grant us also to know that it is not the beginning, but the continuing of the same unto the end, until it be thoroughly finished, which yieldeth the true glory.' The Amens were said with a fervour that Rab would have relished.

I had walked over to the Abbey with Richard Luce, who had also resigned with Peter. He had loved his job in the Foreign Office, for coming from a diplomatic family it suited his temperament. Richard is tall and thin, walking with a slight stoop because of fairly constant pain in his back, and this gives him a most kindly and courteous air. Richard said, 'We'd been caught napping, I had to go.' But he was very worried about what would happen when Peter's calming advice was not available.

While we were sitting in the Abbey waiting for the family and friends of Rab to enter, Richard told me that earlier that morning, in his last act as a Minister, he had gone out to Northolt to welcome the returning Falklands Governor, Rex Hunt. When Richard told him that Peter was going to resign, the Governor burst into tears. On the Sunday morning, when it had become clear that Peter was to go, the outgoing Permanent Secretary at the Foreign Office, Michael Palliser, and the incoming one, Antony Acland, were also in tears. So the Foreign Office was facing the world blubbing. Lachrymosity triumphed over the stiff upper lip. It was just as well we had a Prime Minister whose tear glands were renowned for being dry.

On the Tuesday, the Prime Minister briefed all those Ministers not in the Cabinet. In spite of press reports that an Argentinian had passed information to the Foreign Office ten days before the invasion – Tom Trenchard, then a Minister of Defence, told me that the MoD knew on 29 March – the Prime Minister asserted vigorously that the first she had known of the possible invasion was Wednesday 31 March. By now she had really focused upon General Galtieri, whom she'd probably never heard of a few weeks earlier. 'We have got to beat him to make the world safe for democracy,' she said. She was very determined, saying, 'I remember when we lost the *George V* and when the British Fleet was destroyed in Scapa Flow. We have to accept risks.' This was to be the first of several such references to the Second World War I heard Margaret make over the years. I believe that her memory of the war years, when she was growing up, was a crucial part of her political attitude. She admired the resolution and patriotism of Churchill and absorbed something of his spirit into herself.

To Margaret, the expedition had become a crusade, but many had misgivings and anxieties. As I left the House of Commons I saw the very frail figure of Harold Macmillan being helped into a car from the door of the Prime Minister's entrance to the House. What advice had he given? Did Margaret remember that he was the one who pulled the rug from under Anthony Eden at the time of the Suez invasion and after British troops had become engaged?

For the next three weeks the Fleet sailed south. There were further debates in the House involving the Prime Minister and John Nott, who now spoke very much more confidently. Al Haig, the American Secretary of State, tried to get a peace initiative off the ground. The US was alarmed at the effect on South America of a British land invasion in their backyard. Haig shuttled between London and Buenos Aires but nothing came of it. The crisis overshadowed everything, and in the Cabinet Room maps of the Falklands were permanently pinned up on easels. On 25 April the British Fleet reached the Falklands and we captured South Georgia without loss of life.

All during the crisis cameras were massed outside Number 10. During this period, the Prime Minister had begun to develop the practice of going out and speaking to the assembled press. In America, the President personally takes press conferences in the White House, and the British equivalent has become the Downing Street impromptu. When news of the recapture of South Georgia arrived, Margaret went outside Number 10 with John Nott and stood by him as he delivered the glad tidings to the waiting media. But some reporters had the temerity to pass over the good news and shouted carpingly, 'What next?' Riled by this, Margaret, who had turned to go back indoors, returned to the reporters and famously admonished them in a high Biblical manner, saying 'Rejoice.' This triumphal answer was carried around the world. It was much closer to the sentiment of the nation than the hand-wringing of the BBC.

During all this time, we had been very strongly supported by David Owen of the new Social Democrat Party. But the support from Labour had got thinner, and a peace party had emerged led by Tony Benn. The Campaign for Nuclear Disarmament had also come out in its true pacifist colours and staged anti-war marches.

After the Prime Minister had made a statement on the recapture of South Georgia, Mary brought our children for dinner in the House. In the dining-room that night were Enoch Powell and his wife, and Tony Benn and his wife. Here were two ends of the political spectrum – both of these remarkable politicians with white faces, staring eyes, and the intensity of those fired by great passion.

As the campaign gathered pace, there were fewer doubters on our side. The mood in the Parliamentary Party was 'finish them off'. After South Georgia, the Labour Party started to distance itself from the Government and called for peace negotiations before an invasion of the Islands. James Callaghan argued for a naval blockade, and meeting me one night in a television studio he said bluntly, 'Starve them out.'

The poll rating of the Government had shot ahead to 43 per cent, with Labour trailing at 31 per cent and the SDP at 25 per cent. By the beginning of May we had started to bomb the Port Stanley runways. We had sunk the Argentine battlecruiser *Belgrano* but had lost HMS *Sheffield* to a missile attack. John Nott made a statement late at night to the House on 4 May and told Members that as many as thirty of our soldiers and sailors had been killed. The tally of casualties on the other side was much higher. Ian Mikardo sharply asked whether the Prime Minister was still rejoicing. A peace proposal by Francis Pym, the new Foreign Secretary, involving the Falkland Islanders determining their own future was rejected by Galtieri. The British forces landed, and after another month's fighting the Argentinians hoisted the white flag over Port Stanley on 14 June.

That evening I was dining at the British Embassy in Stockholm and all the Swedish guests warmly congratulated us on our victory. Even neutral Sweden could scarce forbear to cheer. It was one of the most remarkable naval and military operations since the War, and a great tribute to the professionalism and courage of our armed services. No one expected the Task Force to happen; no one believed that we would or could respond with such determination to the Argentinian aggression; and no one forecast such a speedy and decisive outcome.

The real victor was the Prime Minister. The Falklands episode brought out her best qualities – her determination to win against all the odds and in the teeth of most advice. She fought from her favourite position – back to the wall in a tight corner. The circumstances were quite unique. The difficulties were those of logistics and geography. But the reluctance of other countries to become involved meant that we could act speedily and without hindrance. Argentina was isolated, and the rest of the international community remained bystanders, although we did have US Defence Secretary Caspar Weinberger in our corner. It was for his help at this crucial hour that he later received the extraordinary accolade of an honorary Knighthood.

At Prime Minister's Question Time on 17 June, Enoch Powell rose and asked the following question:

Is the right hon. Lady aware that the report has now been received from the public analyst on a certain substance recently subjected to analysis and that I have obtained a copy of that report? It shows that the substance under test consisted of a ferrous matter of the highest quality, that it is of exceptional tensile strength, is highly resistant to wear and tear and to stress, and may be used with advantage for all national purposes?

The backbenchers only slowly realized that this was a generous tribute disguised in a convoluted Enochian joke, and for Enoch a joke is no laughing matter. The public analyst had tested the metal and found that it was the toughest steel. From now on 'The Iron Lady' became an unofficial title bestowed in admiration rather than sarcasm.

By transforming the spirit of the nation the Falklands War also transformed the spirit and fortunes of the Government. Economically we had been going through a very difficult period of high unemployment and industrial decline. There had been little to celebrate and a series of withdrawals from major sectors of industry. The Falklands campaign showed that by determination, resolution, good planning, courage, resourcefulness and character, the flow of events could be altered. At the Party Conference in October Margaret said:

I just want to say this, because it is true for all our people: the spirit of the South Atlantic was the spirit of Britain at her best. It has been said that we surprised the world, that British patriotism was rediscovered in those spring days. It was never really lost.

CHAPTER 4

British Telecom Privatization

Removing the Dead Hand of the British Treasury – Cable –
The Film Industry – Space

My first Parliamentary task was to complete the British Telecommunications Bill which was in Committee. Keith Joseph had decided in 1979 that the monopoly on the supply of services and equipment enjoyed by the national telecommunications and post industry should be ended. This was an important but relatively limited first step.

I had taken a close interest in telecommunications policy when I was elected in 1968 because it was a huge and rapidly growing area of economic activity. It had been state-controlled from the beginning, and few politicians were interested in it or realized its enormous potential, which was being held back by its state ownership. I served on the Standing Committee of the Post Office Bill 1969 – a measure introduced by John Stonehouse, then Postmaster General – which converted the old General Post Office from a Government Department into a nationalized industry. The Conservative Shadow Spokesman was Paul Bryan, and from that time he and I became close friends.

Paul was one of those Tory MPs who have almost disappeared from the scene – a country Member from Yorkshire, a farmer, who had won the DSO in the War. He had also been the officer commanding the War Office Selection Board which selects those who are to be commissioned. This gave him useful experience when he became the Vice-Chairman of the Party responsible for selecting candidates, since he could pick out a bad 'un better than most. In 1970 he became a Minister at the Department of Employment under Robert Carr and asked me to become his Parliamentary Private Secretary – the first rung on the ladder of preferment. Paul was uneasy at the Dispatch Box – he had served in the Whips' Office for far too long – and he left the Government after two years. He became an eminent backbencher whose shrewd and sound judgement counted for much. His deputy in the 1969 Bill was Ian Gilmour, whom Paul had assisted to get back into the House. Ian had lost his seat in Norfolk and had been turned down by several constituencies until Paul helped to find him a safe berth in Amersham.

In 1969 I had enjoyed the Committee Stage of the Bill, for I was allowed a very free hand. I moved amendments (which were not pursued) to split the Post Office into two parts, Telecommunications and Post; to introduce a proper share structure for the telecommunications side; and to sell shares in it to the public. These ideas – radical for their time – were indulged as the iconoclastic dreams of a new, young MP who should not be discouraged. The tolerant attitude was, 'Give him his head but not our support.' There is much more freedom to do this as a backbencher in Opposition than in Government. Selling off the telephone network in 1969 was an idea normally associated with a few right-wingers. It took sixteen years for this idea to be realized, and within twenty-two years even the Labour Party had dropped its policy to reverse it.

So in 1981 I came with enthusiasm to this task, for we were only really tinkering with the problem. I found a strong ally in the Department in David Young. Keith had appointed David, a solicitor whose previous experience had been in property and the Jewish training institution ORT, to be his Special Adviser at the Department of Trade and Industry. We became good friends as we found that we both wanted to reduce the Department's responsibilities and privatize the great nationalized industries which came under its wing. David didn't really think like a conventional politician. He had a wide-ranging lateral mind which was fertile with ideas. He fully earned the verdict which Margaret passed on him: 'David doesn't bring me problems, he brings me solutions.'

The Telecommunications Bill was essentially a paving measure which gave us powers to liberalize the telecommunications industry and to end its eighty-year-old monopoly. To achieve this, first BT's monopoly of equipment had to be ended. When it came to telephones it was a case of Ford's famous dictum, 'Any colour you want as long as it's black,' and there was a waiting list of 250,000 fed-up customers. We wanted to see shops in the High Street selling telephones and businesses being allowed to own their private networks, using them as they wanted rather than how BT determined. We set up an evaluation process separate from BT, which at that time had all the expertise and whose exhaustive examinations of equipment had become so stifling that only its favoured suppliers seemed to get through. New arrangements to end all this were announced in July, and by the end of the year we had set up a new body to approve telephone equipment. I also wanted to stimulate other companies to provide value-added services on the BT network such as electronic mail and other services combining networks and computers. A licensing system for this was established by the summer of 1981.

The Telecommunications Bill also had a small but important Clause, Number 76, to allow us to dispose of the Government's ownership of Cable and Wireless. This was the old operation which provided radio links with all the outlying parts of the British Empire, particularly the smaller colonies. Travelling the globe you would come across a radio mast with a small station manned by men in long khaki shorts – this was the traditional role of Cable and Wireless. Keith had appointed as its Chairman and Managing Director not some retired politician, for the chairmanship had become a sinecure for long and unimaginative service, but instead a businessman, Eric Sharp.

Eric had spent his life in the chemical industry with Monsanto, having started in the Civil Service in the office of the Government Chemist. Keith had come across him at the Centre for Policy Studies, which Eric had supported. He was to become one of the most successful business appointments made in the Thatcher years. Eric transformed Cable and Wireless from being a sleepy backwater into a major international telecommunications company. He saw the importance of Cable and Wireless taking telecommunications into China through Hong Kong. He provided a network in the Guandong province after an agreement had been signed between Margaret and the Prime Minister of China – a deal which Eric had brought about himself.

On 9 March 1981, less than two months after my appointment, I announced to the House that the Government intended to sell 49 per cent of Cable and Wireless to the public. This was the first of the really big privatizations. The advantages were clear: freedom from Government interference; access to private capital markets; commercial expansion across the world uninhibited by the British Government's views; and, above all, as I said to the House, 'Cable and Wireless will escape from the dead hand of the British Treasury.' Ian Mikardo said that this 'last remark will be filed for future reference.'

But BT was all-powerful, and it had to be exposed to real competition. The only way was to license another major network, and from the first days in office I worked to ensure that a licence could be given to Mercury, which was at that time a consortium of Cable and Wireless,

BP and Barclays. They planned to set up a figure-of-eight network linking the main towns across the country principally for business customers.

By July, the discussions with the Mercury consortium were continuing so successfully that we announced a licence would be issued to allow them to begin their big investment programme in 1983. Some of the shares of Cable and Wireless were sold in October 1981 at 168p and raised £181 million. Two further tranches were sold in 1983 and 1985, and the total proceeds to the Treasury were £1 billion. In all the talks I had with Treasury Ministers the only thing they were interested in was the proceeds that would go to the Exchequer. Nothing had to be done to interrupt that flow. When Cable and Wireless had been privatized I received the following cable from Eric Sharp: 'With reference to Item 3 in your brief of March 21st 1981 I am pleased to state in Field Marshal Montgomery's words to Churchill "Mission accomplished. Await further instructions"'. I replied in the following terms: 'Under your Chairmanship Cable and Wireless has escaped from the thraldom of the public sector. As Cicero said "Abiit, excessit, evasit, erupit, O Felix Mercury."' This roughly translated as 'O happy Mercury, he has left, he has escaped, he has broken away.'

The licence to allow Mercury to operate was exceptionally difficult to negotiate. We had to play the role of the honest broker, weighing up Mercury's desire for the easiest and cheapest access to BT's network with BT's concern that Cable and Wireless were just going to skim off the most profitable parts of the business. This would leave BT with the unprofitable task of providing little-used lines to the most remote parts of the country.

The Bill got its Third Reading on 2 April, but not before a night of drama when Ian Mikardo, Dennis Skinner and Bob Cryer had decided to run the official Opposition and cause us the maximum difficulty and embarrassment. It was the first time that the House had sat for twenty-five hours since 1979. This was good Opposition, for the morale of the Labour Party needed picking up after the defection of the SDP. Labour were rudderless and leaderless. Michael Foot was not to be seen anywhere. Through the long night of the debate, Margaret turned up on several occasions to vote. During all-night sittings Prime Ministers are told by their Number 10 staff to go to bed – 'You must keep up your strength for the key meeting in the morning with the Head of State who is passing through London (that is if he hasn't been deposed in his absence).' But Margaret knew it was more important to be seen staying up late with her backbenchers during the night to support key pieces of liberalizing legislation.

We sat through to breakfast, and then we sat through to lunch on the following day. As the debate had started on 1 April, under the great procedures of the House of Commons we had extended All Fools' Day into 2 April! Apart from calls of nature I didn't leave the Chamber at any time during the debate. John Lee, the MP for Pendle and my new PPS, provided me with a symbolic fresh daisy at breakfast and another at lunchtime. We eventually completed the Bill in the afternoon of the second day. Margaret sent me a charming letter, for she was good at thanking her lieutenants and did so more graciously than Ted had done.

Good as this Bill was, it was not enough and I wanted to go further – those 1969 amendments had to be carried. My ally was David Young. On Sunday 5 July 1981 he and I had supper with Keith at his house in Chelsea in order to persuade him to push ahead with the privatization of BT itself. I had prepared a paper setting out a timetable: a Bill by spring 1983; a Regulatory Authority which would police the market and promote competition; Mercury licensed in 1983 to provide the first tranche of competition; other service providers licensed for private networks; sale to the public in 1983–84; more competition to be provided from local cable companies by 1990–91. This was the strategy that was agreed at that meeting.

BT would benefit enormously from being privatized. As a Minister responsible for a nationalized industry, in this case BT, I had to approve its tariffs, its wage settlements, its investment programme, and its Board appointments. Ministers are not best suited to do this. We were blamed for every little service failure; blamed if tariffs went up; blamed for any shortfall in investment and blamed for any strike. I could not see any up-side at all. A business like BT should be run by businessmen and businesswomen, not second-guessed by Ministers who are birds of passage.

The Chairman of BT, Sir George Jefferson, who had been a senior manager in the defence industries, was very cooperative since he saw privatization as the way in which professional managers could run the business without always being checked by Ministers. He was irked by having to come and see me about quite trivial matters – the pensions of Board members – as well as major matters such as BT's investment programme.

On 22 July Keith and I took our proposals on Mercury to a Cabinet Committee chaired by Margaret, who was very enthusiastic. Willie Whitelaw, as Home Secretary, was rightly concerned for reasons of security about allowing any operators other than BT into the telecommunications business – a concern too of Peter Carrington. But, to his credit, Willie overcame traditional Home Office objections of this sort. I calmed some anxieties by forecasting that Mercury, by the year 1990, would probably only amount to 2 per cent of BT's revenues. In the event it turned out to be 7 per cent.

At this discussion I had two great advantages. First, a lot of this was technical and I was better briefed than the others around the table. Second, most of the other Ministers had no idea about the development of telecommunications other than vaguely believing it was a good thing and probably inevitable. Ministers come to these committees armed with departmental briefs which are only concerned with how the matter in question – the specific proposal – is going to affect their Department. In my experience, the best discussions at Cabinet Committee and Cabinet were when the Ministers did not open their briefs but turned their own minds to the issues that lay behind the details. I had taken the trouble before the meeting to square many of the departmental quibbles, and I tried to lift my colleagues' eyes to the broad landscape and the bright dawn that was breaking over it! This was an approach which tended to make the duller suspicious. But I had to get Mercury through that Cabinet Committee otherwise everything would be stalled.

The path to BT privatization was not to be easy. In 1981 we spent a lot of time trying, as an alternative to privatization in the short term, to devise a bond which BT could issue to raise cash for its investment programme. If such a bond could have been issued then one of the reasons for privatization would have disappeared. It became known as the 'Buzby Bond' after an annoying little bird which BT used in its TV commercials. I met Geoffrey Howe and Leon Brittan in July to see if a way could be found. The crux of the issue was that as it was a nationalized industry, whatever bond BT issued the Government would have to stand fully behind it, so it could not be significantly cheaper than gilt-edged borrowing. Moreover, the amount of the bond being discussed was about £150 million, whereas the capital expenditure of BT that year was £1.5 billion. It wouldn't have helped very much. Warburgs, the merchant bank, produced some ideas on profit-related bonds or preference shares, but all these instruments were unreal since the ownership of the company remained with the state and there was no real risk to the investor. I was glad that the search for this Eldorado failed, because it was taking our eye off the ball.

In the September 1981 reshuffle, Keith was moved to the Education Department and Patrick Jenkin took over at Trade and Industry. I had known Patrick from the early days of the Bow Group when he was part of Iain Macleod's team, and we had also been Ministers under Ted. Patrick was one of the most decent people in politics. He delegated to his Ministers, and backed them up whenever they were in trouble. He devoured red boxes and digested them more thoroughly than anybody I can recall. It was quite usual at a morning meeting for his driver to bring in the three or four red boxes of the previous night and for Patrick to take out from the bottom of one of them a brief of thirty or forty pages with underlining and comments on the very last page. He was absolutely straight, and at times this made him appear naïve and rather unworldly, but I would rather have had Patrick behind me in a tight corner than many of the other Ministers I have served.

I had to induct Patrick into our great strategy for BT. He was enthusiastic, but in presenting it to Margaret he never had that special relationship which Keith had with her. In her eyes, Patrick was always a late convert to the cause, and she was never quite certain that he would cherish the lamp which Keith had lit. By late 1981, BT privatization, which had not been mentioned in the 1979 Manifesto, had become official Government policy, and so we started to put in hand the preparations for a Bill. Margaret took a strong personal interest, as she wanted more liberalization before privatization. We had a splendid debate on this right in the middle of the Falklands Crisis on 22 April 1982.

We had to get Cabinet approval for the drafting of the Bill to turn BT into a public company; to remove its licensing and approval powers; and to set up a regulatory authority – Oftel. All this was needed prior to privatization. In spite of the Fleet approaching the Falklands, Margaret found time to focus on this domestic issue. She launched a spirited attack on BT and its monopolistic practices and overmanning – 'I want more liberalization before privatization'. As always, there was a grain of truth in what she was saying, and she had been very well briefed by goodness knows who. She wanted new money to go into new telecommunications systems and not into BT. She fought everyone like a tigress for an hour, landing broadsides on Patrick Jenkin, Nigel Lawson, Lord Cockfield and myself. Galtieri had no chance.

I explained to her patiently that the strategy behind our policy was to give Cable and Wireless a licence to establish the alternative network, Mercury. If we tried to set up small networks, or to break up BT into regional companies, then the privatization would have to be postponed for five to ten years. The only feasible policy was mine – namely to allow the other big telecommunications company in the UK to establish a competitive network, and within ten years to extend competition further through local cable companies and other service providers. Events have fully justified this policy. We had to get on or else nothing would have happened. Similar doctrinal arguments were to take place over British Rail, with the result that privatization and the benefits which would flow from it have been postponed for several years.

At last, in June 1982, the Cabinet agreed to the proposal to sell 51 per cent of BT and to set up a regulatory authority. I had wanted this decision three months earlier, because a big and complicated Bill introduced late in the year would not get through if there were an early election.

I had to fight hard to keep on course. George Jefferson, Eric Sharp and David Young were on my side, but this did not stop Margaret pursuing her own views very strongly. There was another sharp volley of fire in November, and on that occasion Arthur Cockfield, then Secretary of State for Trade, intervened over the issue of the role of the Monopolies and Mergers Commission and in my view very nearly derailed the whole scheme in that lugubriously unhelpful way for which he became famous.

On 29 November 1982, Patrick Jenkin introduced the Telecommunications Bill – the first denationalization of a major utility in the Thatcher years. To illustrate how demoralized the Labour Party had become even at that time, there were only twelve Opposition Members in the House during his speech. I was delighted that at last we had started the final lap of this race. The great principle had been accepted and the debates over the following months concentrated on less crucial matters such as the 999 Service, the survival of rural kiosks, the level of connection charges, and the funding of the pension scheme. Understandably, for some people these were not minor at all. Lobbies formed on each of these issues, and from time to time the Bill looked in danger from one pressure group or another.

In April 1983 there was a strike in the City of London by militant members of the Post Office Engineering Union which threatened to damage the City. There was a danger that the strike would spread to the rest of the country. It was a political strike, principally over interconnecting Mercury to the BT network, for the strikers demanded the withdrawal of the Bill and no Mercury. Michael Edwardes, who was then the Chairman of Mercury, demanded that Mercury must go ahead and must have full interconnect otherwise it would not be viable. There were all the ingredients for a major disruption of the telephone network on the eve of a possible election.

At a meeting in Number 10 on 26 April, Norman Tebbit urged no provocation of the POEU because it was 'a responsible union'. Geoffrey Howe did not want British Telecom to be let off the hook and he believed that they were using this episode to put pressure upon the Government. The Prime Minister was quite clear, saying, 'We mustn't give in, Mercury must have interconnect.' But the clear brief that I had was not to let this strike escalate into a major national stoppage. So we stood firm and the militants backed off. As Margaret said, 'I don't want any trouble. British Leyland has settled and a BT strike could close my options for an early election.' She looked out of the window and observed, 'The weather is not very warm, not voting weather yet.'

As the Bill was not completed in time for the General Election of June 1983, we had to reintroduce it in the new Parliament under the new Secretary of State, Cecil Parkinson. He too had to be inducted into the complexities of telecommunications policy. But by the time the Bill was ready for introduction, Cecil had resigned over the Sara Keays affair and I had my fourth Secretary of State, Norman Tebbit, who also had to be introduced to the great mysteries of telecommunications policy. When it came to Secretaries of State, I counted them in and I counted them out. All four were very different, but the one who undoubtedly had the greatest impact upon our policy was Keith Joseph. Keith was not a particularly good administrator, and he did not have the gentle art of carrying through a difficult and complicated political programme. But on economic matters he had a very clear vision of what needed to be done.

The extra competition for BT would not just come from Mercury. In 1981 George Jefferson had proposed to set up a cellular mobile telephone network on the megahertz frequencies that had become available. I was not prepared to hand over his new technology to a BT monopoly. So we decided, much to BT's chagrin, that there would be two operators and there would be a competition to allocate the second network. In addition, BT could hold only 50 per cent of the new Cellnet, with the other half being held by Securicor. The competition for the second network was won by Racal-Millicom, who set up Vodaphone.

Two players in the marketplace competing with each other drove the market forward more quickly than in any other European country, whose telephone systems remained firmly under state control. This brought great benefit to the UK in equipment manufacture and service supply, quite apart from providing customers across the country with what has become an almost indispensable tool of communication. The market had an enormous potential, and I urged Sir Ernest Harrison, the Chairman of Racal, to develop a really small handset for the pocket and purse. Then there would be a real mass market. Mobile phones had become so popular ten years later that in 1991 Norman Lamont, as Chancellor of the Exchequer, could not resist the temptation to tax them. It was just as well that the Treasury had not been allowed to stifle the development of mobile phones by introducing this tax earlier.

To regulate the overwhelming power of BT and the rest of the industry we needed a good regulator and a good system of regulation. Bryan Carsberg was the Arthur Andersen Professor of Accounting at the LSE, but he was not just a mere accountant. I liked his approach, and in 1983 I was so keen to get him that we tracked him down to a graduate economics school at the University of Omaha where he was giving an address at lunchtime. I telephoned him late at night from our house in Pimlico and offered him the job. He was very successful in encouraging the other players in this great industry and restraining BT, both in a realistic way – though BT now believes there should be a regulator for the regulators. Bryan went on to become the Director-General of the Office of Fair Trading.

After seeing in America their complicated and burdensome system of regulation, I was determined to have a simpler one. We appointed Stephen Littlechild, a young Professor at Birmingham University, to examine this. He came forward with a report which was the foundation of regulation in the telephone industry and became the model for the other regulatory regimes we were to set up. He rejected control by measuring the return on assets, which is the heart of the American system, in favour of one based upon prices related to the RPI. This led to the famous 'RPI minus X' formula which meant that the real cost of using a telephone has fallen over the last decade. It is a good deal for the customer and still allows BT and Mercury to make substantial profits.

Littlechild also made recommendations about the terms of interconnect – the price that new networks have to pay BT to gain access to its national network. BT jealously guarded this, since its most valuable assets were the wires going to every home and business in the country. The interconnect negotiations between BT and Mercury were tough and protracted. But without a successful outcome there would have been no Mercury.

It was also important to end BT's monopoly to provide the first instrument in every home, which they claimed was necessary on safety grounds. Again, Littlechild recommended the ending of this, and so in February 1983 we accepted all his recommendations but gave BT two years' grace since the senior management threatened to resign if it happened faster. The Labour Party opposed all this, as they did all the Bills and all the moves to greater competition and liberalization. Labour had no conception of the importance of this market and what had to be done to drive it forward. We now have the best telecommunications network and services in Europe, with British companies as lead players in the international scene finding opportunities and partners overseas. None of this could have happened if we had not pressed ahead so hard in the early 1980s.

When I embarked upon liberalization and particularly privatization in 1981 there were many faint-hearts – 'Don't go too far Kenneth; it will split the Party; rural MPs will lose out; you'll never get it through the House of Lords – too many business interests there that will be affected; British equipment manufacturers aren't up to coping with the opportunities that will be created; the POEU will strike and ruin the whole operation; the Labour Party will renationalize; even if you get past all these hurdles no one will eventually want to buy the shares.' But it was the old, old story – if you know you are right you must press on and win converts, and we did. The successful privatization of BT made possible all the other public utility sales of the 1980s. We showed it could be done and that the benefits to the country were enormous.

In the year after the 1983 Election, we prepared the sale of BT to the public and engaged the services of merchant bankers, lawyers, advertising agencies and PR firms to work on the prospectus. It was no easy matter, because the licences which were to be given to BT and Mercury would largely determine their basis of operation for many years to come. Ministers frequently had to resolve difficult disputes between BT and the rest of the industry. By the end of the Parliamentary session on 30 July 1984 I was able to make a full presentation to the Prime Minister of the flotation which was to take place a few months later. In the autumn of 1984, just after I had left to go to the Department of the Environment, 51 per cent of BT was successfully sold to the public. The issue was oversubscribed many times and the Treasury received £3.7 billion. Another tranche was sold in 1991 for a further £5 billion, and the final tranche in 1993. A new era had started.

Cable

Clearly I needed allies in the Government to promote the changes that had to come about. I persuaded Margaret to appoint five independent businessmen as IT advisers – they became known as the Information Technology Advisory Panel (ITAP). In addition to this, a unit was set up in the Cabinet Office to coordinate all the various issues that were coming to a head, and Brian Unwin was appointed to lead it. Without this support, I would have had a lonely and difficult time promoting technological change.

Towards the end of 1981 I came to realize the enormous potential of cable networks. In America I had seen cable developing principally as an entertainment media, led by soft-porn films and sport. But cable had a much greater potential than sleazy entertainment. A network, particularly if fibre optics were used, would be a network of communication for the entire country and as important in stimulating economic activity as the railways had been in the nineteenth century.

A huge range of services could be provided over such a network – home shopping, retrieval of information on train and air timetables, traffic holdups, weather conditions and the availability of hotel rooms; the payment of bills; the delivery of training courses; and voice telephony and document transmission. Combined with the new technologies of viewdata and teletext, digitized colour pictures could be transmitted of houses for sale or goods offered in a sales catalogue. All this was in addition to a larger number of entertainment channels. The extension of choice would drive this enterprise forward, and I felt it important to start talking up the possibilities of all this happening.

On 5 January 1982 I convened a large meeting of officials from all the various Departments to thrash out the issues involved. On 2 February I made a presentation to the Prime Minister, and on 25 February the

Economic Policy Committee of the Cabinet debated Cable and Direct Broadcasting from Satellite (DBS) for the first time. Michael Heseltine and Peter Walker supported this potential new development, though Willie Whitelaw and Francis Pym were apprehensive, principally because of its effect upon the BBC and ITV.

In March, ITAP produced a report which emphasized the huge employment gains in cabling Britain and advocated that it should be left to the private sector and should be put in hand at once, with the laying down of cable to start long before the next election. They estimated that the capital investment over a period of ten years would be £2–3 billion. At the annual conference of the Institute of Directors in March, held in the Albert Hall, I used all the latest big-screen and computer-controlled technologies to argue for this.

However, there were formidable obstacles. BT wanted to maintain its monopoly of the communications network and to extend it to television. BT had the technology and the ducts that led into every house in the country to allow them to do this. So, very early on, we decided to prevent BT's exclusive access and as an alternative strategy to allow the development of separate cable companies across the UK which would provide the same range of services that BT could provide.

The other problem was that the BBC and ITV feared the competition that would come from a proliferation of channels. I recall walking around the gardens of Leeds Castle in the spring of 1982 with George Howard, Chairman of the BBC, trying to allay his fears. George, who owned one of the great houses in the North, Castle Howard, had been appointed Chairman rather unexpectedly by his old friend Willie Whitelaw. His brightly coloured corduroy clothes and scarves soon became familiar to a wider audience. I liked his gentle geniality and respected his genuine concern about the effect that cable could have on the BBC. The Labour Party, not surprisingly, was against all of this. The old Socialist back-bencher, Frank Allaun, spoke for them all in a debate in November 1982 when he said, 'We have four channels and that's enough.'

Willie Whitelaw, as Home Secretary, appointed a Committee under Sir John Hunt, the recently retired Cabinet Secretary, to report on the regulatory regime for cable. Recognizing that it was going to happen, they opted for a regulatory authority with teeth. There were to be no political and religious channels. But they also came out against pay-per-view, a system which charged viewers to watch individual programmes.

In September I decided to take the whole debate to the Edinburgh International Film Festival. I was the first Minister to do this and no doubt probably the last. I argued the case strongly but came up against a barrage of criticism – cable would be full of American films; news and current affairs would be destroyed; just more soap for the masses; quality would go; we didn't have enough talent in the UK in the creative arts to fill up the expanding opportunities. So, Gresham's Law would operate and the bad would drive out the good: more was worse. George Howard even argued that cable would be socially divisive, as it would divorce town from country.

So here we had the entertainment industry – ITV in cahoots with the BBC, a duopoly – protecting its own privileged positions. At the same meeting Ted Turner, the pioneer of the CNN news channel in Atlanta, was given the bird. What I saw then was the British genius to institutionalize torpor. I fought back and arranged a seminar in November 1982 at Number 10 with fifty of the top business people from the computing, electronics and communications industries. The Prime Minister was keen, but I had to square the Home Office, which had responsibility for broadcasting and guarded this fiefdom jealously. I soon became convinced that broadcasting policy should not lie with the Home Office, since it was being driven forward by technological change and this was not the Home Office's strong card. When I was Home Secretary, I recommended in 1992 to Number 10 and to Sir Robin Butler, the Cabinet Secretary, that responsibility for broadcasting should be transferred from the Home Office to a new Department which should also be responsible for the Arts, Heritage and Sport.

Willie Whitelaw, to his great credit, recognized the inevitable. At the critical meeting on 18 November 1982, when the policy for cable was decided, I remember him saying, 'There could be no one more passionately and personally against the whole concept of cable TV than me. I hate the prospect. But I recognize that it will come and it will create jobs on a wide scale.' He had a difficult position that was not made any easier by a twenty–minute presentation from Brian Unwin at the beginning of the meeting. Through some oversight, Willie had not been told there was going to be this presentation, and he burst out in anger – 'Why wasn't I told? You all take me for granted.'

There was a very good debate about pay-per-view at this meeting. I argued that it could provide programmes for local sports, for ethnic minorities, and other specially made programmes for a wide variety of different interest groups. Willie was worried that cable TV would outbid the BBC and ITV for major sporting events. When Ferdinand Mount, Head of the Number 10 Policy Unit, said that TV had almost killed some sports like the Grand National, Willie intervened by saying that TV had saved golf, and he knew that because he had negotiated the terms when he was Chairman of the Royal and Ancient. Willie remained strongly against pay-per-view, arguing, 'We have an appalling relationship with the BBC, the worst of any government in recent times' (to which the Prime Minister nodded) 'and I have to take the brunt of that relationship. It is all very unpleasant and they have made it clear to me that pay-per-view is not acceptable.' 'That, Willie,' said the Prime Minister, 'is even worse than your first argument.' However, no decision was made on pay-per-view at that time, and it was left hanging in the air as a future possibility.

We also agreed that there would be no pornography channel, since there were some who felt that cable profitability depended upon soft-porn pornography. We had the strongest safeguards in Europe, but Margaret wanted them strengthened further. She insisted there would be no porn channel, saying, 'X-films are now going too far.' Tim Raison, stirred to protest, said, 'Some of the best films I have seen were X-films.' 'How can you believe that, Tim?' said Margaret, and continued with a sweet smile, 'I will add you to my list of Ministers who have said unfortunate things.' If such a list existed it must have by then included most of the Government. Others rallied to Tim's support since his view seemed quite sensible, and this prompted the Prime Minister to say, 'Some of the best films I've seen weren't X. *Gone with the Wind*, the best film ever made, wasn't an X.' It was a delicious debate, and quite clearly the boundaries of the free market did not extend to moral issues. It is often said that debate was stifled at meetings presided over by the Prime Minister, but this was a very good example of everybody being allowed full rein to argue forcefully for their own corners.

In our Manifesto in 1983 we pledged ourselves to sanction the launch of cable networks to bring choice to consumers not just for entertainment but for the whole new world of TV shopping and other interactive services. Just before the election I got agreement to pay-per-view, and for twelve experimental franchises to be issued. A Cable Authority was established and was soon in the process of evaluating bids for franchises. This came to a shuddering halt as a result of Nigel Lawson's first Budget in 1984 when he proposed a major reduction in corporate taxation, accompanied by the removal of capital allowances. This meant that cable operators – who were new investors and therefore not profitable – would not get any benefit from the lower rates of Corporation Tax but would lose the benefit of the capital allowances which could be set against their income from other sources. At a stroke, the cabling of Britain came to an end. Significant new investment only resumed in 1991, when cable companies were allowed to offer telephony services competing with BT and Mercury.

The Film Industry

After the 1983 Election responsibility for the film industry was added to my portfolio. In the DTI this had been something of an also-ran because it did not sit at all easily in the Department. I came to realize that it should really be with the Arts Ministry, which itself should have been expanded into a major Department responsible for our national culture and language.

The film industry had led a chequered life since the War. There were quite short but golden periods of success – Ealing Studios, the long and profitable series of 'Carry-On' films, and the James Bond films. I found that Britain's most famous and successful international Director, David Lean, was rather looked down upon by the British film establishment. There appeared to be a great breakthrough when Hugh Hudson and David Puttnam won a Hollywood Oscar for *Chariots of Fire* and everyone hoped that a sea change had occurred. Colin Welland even said, when receiving the Oscar, 'The British are coming.'

We had helped the film industry by ensuring when Channel Four was set up that a large part of its output would be provided by independent film producers. In addition to this, London had become a centre for sophisticated cinematic techniques and special effects, as in the *Star Wars* films. There was also a system called the Eady Levy which recycled money from cinemas to the producers in the hope that this would stimulate the creation of successful international films. But only rarely did we break into the really big international market which America and Hollywood continued to dominate. I remember Richard Attenborough telling me that the Eady Levy was so small that *all* its money was not enough to finance even half a Hollywood film. It tended to go towards low-budget UK films – sometimes even soft porn.

I wanted to help the film industry and one side-effect of that concern that I met Harold Wilson and Marcia Williams, now Lady Falkender, several times as they were both very interested in the subject and glad to be involved. Marcia Falkender has sometimes been presented as a hard behind-the-scenes manipulator but, quite to the contrary, I found her frank and pleasant to do business with. Harold Wilson had dealt with the film industry when he had been President of the Board of Trade in the late 1940s. He had kept an interest in it since then largely, I suspect, through the influence of Arnold Goodman. We had lunch together a few times and, apart from his string of amusing reminiscences, I recall Harold's capacity to down gin and tonics, claret and brandy, with no ill effect. In the top echelons of the Labour Party it must have been nature's way of balancing George Brown. The point of these meetings was to secure Wilson's support and approval for the policy that I was preparing, as I did not want it mauled when it went to the Lords. Wilson had introduced the Eady Levy, but its main beneficiary, the National Film Corporation, although it made some good films and one or two very fine ones, had not established itself as a major force in the world of film production. The NFC had become a subordinate source of finance, rather than an important means of initiative and support.

We agreed that the NFC should be replaced by a voluntary agreement whereby the cinemas would support the outstanding British Film School, which was a real centre of excellence, and provide money to stimulate production. This was the basis of the film policy which I announced in June 1984. However, investment in British films, like investment in the fledgeling cable industry, was dealt a near-mortal blow by Nigel Lawson's 1984 Budget when he removed capital allowances. From that time, the terms offered by other countries were simply more attractive to those who backed films. On Budget Day I remember Lew Grade telephoning me at about six o'clock and predicting that investment in films would stop. Producers had just six hours to try to finalize any deals that were in the pipeline before the axe fell at midnight that day. I had not been consulted about the consequences of this Budget proposal. The preparation of the Budget is shrouded with so much secrecy that Ministers are not told of the Chancellor's proposals unless it directly affects their Department. Norman Tebbit may have been told of these tax changes, but certainly this information was not passed on to me. I was furious with Nigel's action as I had been preparing a policy for the cable and film industry which was based upon the continuity of capital allowances. Suddenly the incentive to invest was removed – the dead hand of the Treasury had struck again.

I enjoyed dealing with the film industry as I like going to the cinema. My Special Adviser was later to be Tony Kerpel, who had spent fourteen years on the British Board of Film Censors, so his knowledge of films was encyclopedic. He would tell me which ones I 'had to see'. But the film world is slightly unreal. The main players in it move from triumph to disaster with an amazing facility. A film was either 'a fantastic success' or 'a complete failure'. Or, as Sam Goldwyn once said, 'If they are determined not to come then nothing will stop them.'

Everyone in the film industry had a wonderful capacity to bounce back from financial disaster. They all seemed to live on the basis of Scarlett O'Hara's famous last line in *Gone with the Wind* – 'Tomorrow's another day.' There was always the next picture to be planned and the finance for it had to be found. This buoyant optimism made the film industry appear as if it was full of bankrupts driving around in Rolls-Royces.

Space

I was also responsible for Britain's space programme. We had joined the European Space Agency during Ted's Government to ensure that Europe did not leave this important industry just to America and Russia. We spent about £80 million a year in addition to about £30 million on research into astronomy. This research put us among the world leaders in astronomy. It was a British research vessel, stationed in Antarctica, which first identified and measured the hole in the ozone layer in the mid-1980s. This research was of the purest form and its object was to extend the frontiers of knowledge about the universe. It had no commercial pay-off and it was not intended or expected to, but it had a profound effect on our understanding of how man was damaging the environment.

I tried to ensure that the money which we spent on space, most of which went to the European Space Agency, produced some commercial gain to Britain. France's contribution was the launching capability situated in Kourou in French Guyana. Germany excelled in very sophisticated equipment carried on satellites. We perceived that the manufacturing of the actual satellites – the bus that carried all the equipment – was the best commercial opportunity for Britain. These were built by British Aerospace and Marconi. We were 'in space' for solid business reasons and not for glory.

I had to ensure that we kept on this course and were not seduced into more 'glamorous' projects. On 22 May 1984, following a request from Mr Beggs, the head of NASA, for our cooperation, I gave a presentation at Number 10 on manned space travel. Beggs had been sent by President Reagan to win financial backing from the European space programmes, and especially from Margaret Thatcher. The project, which involved platforms in space from which manoeuvrable space vehicles could be launched, was estimated to cost at least $8 billion in upfront capital with running costs of $1–2 billion a year. When I asked Beggs why Reagan was so keen on this he said that people in America preferred watching manned rather than unmanned space travel on television! The net scientific gain was marginal. However, the arguments of national pride and of keeping up with the Russians, who had been able to match America's space achievements, appealed to Margaret. But as the cost was enormous I persuaded her that we should take this very slowly indeed and work through the European Space Agency.

The use of space for satellite communication and television was due to a discovery by an Englishman, Arthur C. Clarke, who later became celebrated as a science fiction writer. Serving as a young scientist in the RAF during the War, Clarke had identified in an article published in 1945 the geo-stationary orbit. This discovery allowed an object – say a relay device capable of transmitting signals delivered from the earth – to remain stationary by orbiting the earth in the plane of the Equator at a speed that held it steady over some particular location. Clarke deserves recognition for this discovery, because without it we would never have experienced the boom in international communications and satellite television.

America had dominated, and continues to dominate, space from the man-on-the-moon programme to manned space stations. But it is important that Europe does maintain its own capacity to make, equip and launch satellites. I visited the European launcher site in French Guyana – a country of dense equatorial jungle. This was where France had established the infamous Devil's Island penal settlement, also appropriately known as the Green Guillotine. Dreyfus was imprisoned there for seven years, and for a time in a cell which was about twelve feet by eight feet with an open roof. It is a miracle that he survived the fevers and bugs. Right in the middle of this dense jungle, with thick turgid rivers, housing pythons thirty feet long, there is a sophisticated centre of high technology. It is situated there because it is just on the Equator.

The launch that I witnessed was a disaster. The rocket took off with its two satellites worth about £70 million, and after a few minutes an anxious silence descended upon the control room. Something was going seriously wrong. About ten minutes later it was announced that the booster to launch the satellite into its second, higher, orbit had failed. The whole thing was plunging to earth somewhere in the Atlantic off the coast of Africa. The reason was a small mechanical failure in the pump designed to mix the oxygen and hydrogen – worth perhaps £2,000. It was alleged that the French engineers responsible knew it was faulty, but were not prepared to admit it. The engine malfunctioned – for want of a nail the shoe was lost, for want of the shoe the horse was lost, and so on.

It was interesting to see how the French reacted to this crisis. If the British had been responsible then we would have stiffened the upper lip, held a press conference, and explained our failure. Not so with the French. The head of the French team, Professor Curien, disappeared as soon as the failure became clear – apparently to return immediately to Paris and explain this malfunction to the President. He left his juniors to face the music. His career went on unruffled, and he was until the last French election the Minister for Technology. These sorts of mistakes can happen in high technology, as America was tragically to find out with the launch of the Challenger Space Shuttle in January 1986.

CHAPTER 5

Reforming Local Government

Moving on – Red Ken v. Blue Ken – Liverpool and
Rate-Capping

By the summer of 1984, I had been the Minister for Information Technology for three and a half years – a long stint by the standard of ministerial office. It had been for me a very happy time, as I felt that I had been able to contribute something to the success of our country. It had been work largely with specialists at the coalface, and I had not become a well-known political figure, although I had begun to speak at Party Conferences. I gave the CPC Lecture at the main Conference in 1982, using all the new technology – teletext and viewdata – to get my message across, and in 1983 I addressed the Central Council meeting in Harrogate.

These had also been important and full years in our family life. My mother had died in 1981, and I remember being told this news while I was on an official visit to Oman from which I returned immediately. My mother had one of the most generous spirits I have ever known. She thought ill of no one and was a genuinely good person. She had led a happy and blameless life, proud of her children, and she died in the arms of my sister.

Our children were moving through the various stages of education. Both girls changed school at sixteen to do their A-levels in a boys' school, which worked very well: one had gone to Westminster, and one to King's College, Canterbury, where she flourished under the outstanding headship of Canon Peter Pilkington. Our eldest started at St Andrew's University, which was a particularly happy event because that was the university where Mary had studied.

Mary was as always incredibly busy. She had to cope with changing constituencies and moving house in 1983, a time when she was assuming a much more active role in business. In 1975 she had been appointed the first woman director of Thames Television, and in 1982 had joined the UK Board of Barclays. But the job which took up most of her time, and which brought her to national prominence, was the chairmanship of the London Tourist Board from 1980 to 1983.

Mary realized that the full potential of London was not being fulfilled. She gave tourism a much higher profile, notably by establishing a new information centre at the entrance to Victoria Station. This provides advice for all tourists and particularly those who are looking for value for money in London. She was a wonderful breath of fresh air, bringing liveliness and style to the presentation of London. The *Evening Standard*, London's paper, was glad to have an eloquent and attractive advocate of the capital. Mary saw it as one of her prime roles to enlist local councils' support for tourism as a major industry and employer in the capital. With Shirley Porter she got the 'clean and friendly London' campaign off the ground. Mary appeared much more frequently in the press and on London television than I did, and I was very proud of her work there.

Mary went on to become a Director of the London Docklands Development Corporation. However, she had to resign when I became the Minister for Local Government because appointments to this body lay with the Secretary of State for the Environment. It was London's loss, since Mary was keen to develop the tourist potential of Docklands – something which has been sadly lost sight of. Later in 1990, on the day when I became Home Secretary, Mary decided to resign as a Director of Thames Television, which she had served for sixteen years, because there was a possible conflict of interest. In fact this was very slender, as the Broadcasting Act of that year virtually transferred all responsibilities for Independent Television from the Home Secretary to the ITC. Nevertheless, Mary felt she ought to go, and it was Thames's loss. By that time other companies were approaching her and she had joined the Board of the Prudential and later of MFI.

In all of these posts, Mary was always determined to ensure that women were given an equal opportunity to progress in the management of a business. This was recognized when she was asked to become the President of Women in Management in 1989.

In 1983, as a result of Boundary Commission changes, my constituency of St Marylebone was to disappear, with half of it going to North Westminster and half to the South. I certainly had no claim on either of these seats, which were represented by John Wheeler and Peter Brooke. Mary and I had made many friends in the constituency over the past thirteen years, and it was a wrench to leave and to set about finding a new seat for the third time.

I decided that I would apply for only one seat, as I had seen too many colleagues humiliated by applying for several and being repeatedly turned down. Moreover I had set my heart on Dorking, where Keith Wickenden, the talented entrepreneur, was resigning because he preferred business to Westminster. I had known the hills around Dorking during my school days, when we went blackberrying on Fetcham Downs and Headley Common. I was fortunate to be selected in the spring of 1983, and I have counted myself lucky to be able to represent that beautiful area since then.

Red Ken v. Blue Ken

By the summer of 1984, the Government had lost a lot of its shine. It had been humiliated in the Lords over the Paving Bill to abolish the GLC and the Metropolitan Counties, and was beset by serious Shire Tory revolts over rates in the Commons. On 3 August 1984 Margaret Thatcher came down to Surrey to open the new East Surrey Hospital at Redhill, which had just been completed at a cost of £20 million. Even when the Government was spending large sums to improve the Health Service, Margaret's path was still lined with crowds of demonstrators shouting abuse and waving placards. Eight years later in 1992 when Virginia Bottomley, as Health Secretary, came and opened the extension to this hospital there wasn't a demonstrator in sight.

After the opening, Margaret came back to our cottage near Dorking. She looked tired, sank into an easy chair, kicked off her shoes and looked out on our garden bathed in glorious summer evening sunshine. I offered her some of the large, fresh, dark-red gooseberries covered with sugar which Mary had picked earlier that day. She finished off the entire bowl. She was glad that the Parliamentary session was over and she relived some of her triumphant moments in the House of Commons, where just three days earlier she had trounced Neil Kinnock in a censure debate.

However, she went on to say, 'I am very worried about local government and getting all that legislation from the Department of Environment through the House of Lords. But anyway let us all have a break for the moment.' Perhaps she already had in mind that I would strengthen the team if I moved to that Department in the next reshuffle. At any rate, Mary and I took the children off for a family holiday in Italy. For holiday reading I took some of the internal papers which Patrick Jenkin had been publishing, dealing with the abolition of the GLC and the Metropolitan Counties – just in case.

A reshuffle was clearly needed, for Jim Prior had indicated that he wanted to leave the Government. On 7 September he did so, together with Arthur Cockfield, who went to Brussels as a Commissioner and subsequently, in Margaret's words, 'went native'. In this September reshuffle, one of the most significant and bold appointments was David Young to be the Employment Secretary, in the House of Lords. The most important issue according to the opinion polls was the rising level of unemployment. David's imaginative approach did much over the next three years to deal with this problem and to defuse it as a major issue for the 1987 election.

I thought I had been overlooked, for it was only on 10 September, three days later, that Neil McMillan, an outstandingly able civil servant and my Private Secretary, was told to expect a telephone call between 11 a.m. and 1 p.m. from Number 10. I told Neil that if I were to be offered another post I would want to see the Prime Minister personally and not just be told over the telephone. The actual conversation that takes place on these occasions is important because it is one of the few opportunities when a Minister can be quite frank with the Prime Minister.

I saw Margaret in her study and she offered me the post of Minister for Local Government, which was currently held by Irwin Bellwin, a peer who had led the Tories on Leeds City Council. Although he knew the local government world well, it was in the Commons that we needed reinforcement. I told Margaret that after nearly four years of steady achievement in Information Technology I was disappointed not to be going into the Cabinet. It is no good being shy on these occasions. Margaret said that there were two Ministers of State on the brink of the Cabinet and that promotion would come in time. I also asked to be fully involved in all the policy formation concerning local government – rates and the abolition issue – since Irwin, good as he was, had not been. Margaret agreed. When I telephoned Mary to tell her the news she said she was very glad as I deserved a change.

I saw Patrick Jenkin at the Department of the Environment in the late afternoon. He showed a great sense of relief that here was someone who could share the load. I had enjoyed working with Patrick at the DTI. He had hoped that he would be Chancellor after the election, but he was given the short straw of Environment Secretary and he'd had a punishing twelve months. He told me, 'This is my last job. I must move on and earn some money. I missed having a strong Minister of State in the Commons. I would like you to take over the whole of the Abolition Bill and I don't mind at all if you get all the publicity.' As ever, he was generous and kind, and over the next twelve months he gave me his strong personal support. You cannot ask more than that from your Secretary of State. Patrick was full of good intentions, determined to be scrupulously fair, with an absence of ruthlessness which left him open to his enemies but endeared him to his friends. I think I was able to bring to the Department a sharper political cutting edge.

I found the Department in a very demoralized state after being so severely buffeted by the Tory revolts over rates, by Labour local government leaders Ken Livingstone in London, Derek Hatton in Liverpool and David Blunkett in Sheffield, and by a steady stream of cases in the Courts which they lost. The Department didn't believe they could actually win anything.

The handling of the Paving Bill had been a most damaging episode. Francis Pym and Ian Gilmour, both members of Margaret's original 1979 Cabinet but dropped by 1983, opposed the GLC Paving Bill which abolished the 1985 GLC elections and substituted for the GLC a new authority drawn from the London Boroughs to cover the final year up to the GLC's formal abolition in 1986. The Government wanted to avoid holding a deathbed election in 1985 which would only have given renewed electoral authority to a body which would then do everything it could to frustrate its own abolition. The Paving Bill was one way to resolve this problem. Ted Heath was vitriolically opposed to it, and he led eighteen Tory MPs to vote against its Second Reading.

In the Lords what became known as the Pym Amendment was tabled. This proposed that the GLC elections would not be cancelled until the main Abolition Bill had become law, and it was carried in the House of Lords by the large majority of forty. The Government decided that it could not risk a Lords/Commons clash by reversing it in the Commons, and so Patrick Jenkin had to agree that the life of the GLC and the Metropolitan County Councils be extended for another year from 1985 until 1986. Ironically this was the option which Margaret Thatcher had favoured at the beginning. It was a major climbdown for the Government and Ken Livingstone was able to erect a banner on County Hall which read: 'Peers – Thank you for saving London's democracy.'

We would have to win a few battles quickly, and that meant taking on Ken Livingstone. He was doing so well that hardly any Ministers were prepared to debate with him on television. I decided that there should be television debates between us as soon as possible. There was a good case for the abolition of the metropolitan counties and the GLC, but we had failed to put it. The battle lines had been drawn for the 'Red Ken versus Blue Ken' contest, a phrase which first saw the light of day in the *Dorking Advertiser*.

Ken Livingstone had become a nationally known politician when, in a brilliantly planned coup d'état, he seized the leadership of the GLC from the affable but ineffectual Labour leader, Andrew MacIntosh, the day after Labour's GLC victory in 1981. Livingstone used his new position to govern and to dazzle. In June he said:

No one will be left in any doubt that the GLC is now a campaigning organ and a bastion of power for the Labour movement. Part of our task is to sustain a holding operation until such time as the Tory Government can be brought down and replaced by a left-wing Labour Government.

The GLC did not have many responsibilities but it had a lot of money, and Ken Livingstone set about spending it cleverly. His campaign for Fair Fares, which reduced all fares on London Transport by 25 per cent, made him very popular and the Transport Secretary, Nicholas Ridley, very unpopular when he opposed it. Then there was the Ethnic Minorities Committee, the Police Committee, the Women's Committee, the Nuclear Policy Unit, the Greater London Training Board, the Greater London Enterprise Board (funded with over £100 million), the Forum for the Elderly, the London Consortium for the Disabled, and the Stress Borough Programme where GLC money amounting to £30 million was provided to poorer Boroughs.

Livingstone's campaign against the Paving Bill was that Londoners should have a democratically elected assembly. His inspired slogan was, 'Say No to No Say.' He was a gifted publicist who was more popular in the opinion polls than the official Leader of the Opposition, Neil Kinnock. He was London's 'Cheeky Chappy', but behind the bonhomie lay an absolutely committed Socialist. He used his patronage to support those across London who were his political supporters; he gave grants to activist bodies predominantly in the Labour areas; he became the patron of vocal minorities, gays, lesbians and feminists. He was forging a rainbow coalition. As the leader of the GLC, Livingstone also ran the best political poster and advertising campaign since the War, albeit at a cost of £10 million of public money. It employed the classic technique – when you tell a lie, tell a whopper, and then put it on a hoarding. In 1985 Livingstone said, 'The GLC has got more billboards than any other advertiser in London and it has the best sites. The Labour Party can never have access to the funds that the GLC has got.' Against this, the Government seemed heavy-handed, autocratic, old-fashioned and vindictive.

I completely reshaped our counter-campaign both in the Department and the Party. As Local Government Minister I was allowed to appoint a political adviser, and I was very lucky to find Peter Davies, who had been the Conservative Opposition Leader on Lambeth Council. He knew the key players in London local government and his advice and help was invaluable.

The GLC was not the senior partner in local government in London. It accounted for only 11 per cent of local government expenditure, and the only cross-London services for which it remained responsible were the Fire Brigade, refuse disposal and strategic planning. Livingstone, by the clever use of money, had given the impression that the GLC was the fount of all goodness in London. The GLC also dabbled in national politics: it had a foreign policy, an anti-nuclear policy, and a policy for a united Ireland. This led to Ken Livingstone giving unpopular platforms to PLO and IRA supporters.

My first skirmish with Livingstone came on 20 September, which was the date of four test by-elections which Livingstone had arranged. Livingstone himself stood in the by-elections, hoping that the results would give a ringing endorsement to his campaign. George Tremlett, a former Tory Chairman of the GLC Housing Committee and still a sitting GLC councillor, urged Tories to vote for Livingstone as the only way to preserve a directly elected Council. The GLC Tories were well and truly split, unhappy at what the Government was proposing. Although Labour held its seats, the turnout was very low indeed: 8,000 fewer Labour votes were recorded than previously, which showed a remarkable lack of enthusiasm for the GLC by Londoners. What had started as a stunt ended as a fiasco, and Livingstone was off to a very poor start that autumn.

The first opportunity I had to put our case was at the Tory Conference on 11 October. I told the Party that I was not going to attack Livingstone for being a nut and for keeping newts and for supporting gay and lesbian activities. In my view he was a serious politician who was turning County Hall into Tammany Hall. For a body that had few tasks, he had increased the payroll by 1,200 in twelve months, and increased the expenditure from £570 million to £950 million in three years. I published a Cost of Livingstone Index and challenged him to debate on TV.

I started to analyse where he spent his money. I had this to say about the way he directed £5 million of GLC money to feminist activists, for women's groups in Labour Boroughs got five times as much as in Conservative Boroughs:

Islington will get £1.2 million and it is clearly awash with sexual discrimination. Hackney gets £314,000. There the tide is rising dangerously. In Kensington, which gets only £29,000, it is under control. As for Harrow, that is the haven of fairness and equality. Harrow gets nothing. O happy Harrow!

The other important thing that I had to get over to the Tory Conference was that the Abolition Bill was going to get through in spite of opposition from people like Alan Greengross, Leader of the Tories at the GLC, and in spite of a vigorously hostile campaign by Ted Heath. I pledged that the GLC would cease at midnight on 31 March 1986. This meant there were 537 spending days left. The countdown had begun:

There are exactly 537 days left. Only 537 spending days left, Mr Livingstone. The message that I give to you and to your own local councillors, the ratepayers you represent, and the country as a whole is – the clock is ticking, time is running out, the countdown has begun.

I was concerned that there was a group of Tory GLC councillors and some London MPs who hankered after an elected substitute for the GLC. This was supported by people such as Desmond Plummer, a former Tory Leader of the GLC, GLC Councillors George Tremlett and Bernard Brooke-Partridge, and MPs Ian Gilmour, Bill Benyon, Hugh Dykes and John Wilkinson. They were led by Ted Heath, who was in the early stages of his 'she can do nothing right' phase. When it came to the Second Reading of the Abolition Bill, Ted personally attacked the three Ministers at the Department of the Environment for standing on their heads – first Patrick Jenkin, one of his most loyal former Ministers, then William Waldegrave, his former Political Secretary and speechwriter, and lastly myself, his former PPS. He did this in the most virulent terms, but was so rude and spiteful that I simply sat on the Frontbench and laughed. This rather disconcerted him, and he must have felt some disappointment that the Government's majority later that day was 132.

My first debate with Livingstone took place on a programme called 'London Plus' on 17 October. This had been pre-recorded the previous Friday in London, the last day of the Tory Party Conference in Brighton. It was for this reason that Mary and I had to leave Brighton in the early morning of Friday 12 October. As we left the Grand Hotel at 2 a.m. the last person we spoke to was Tony Berry, who was bringing in his little dog after a walk along the promenade. A few hours later he and John Wakeham's wife were among those murdered by the IRA in the bomb explosion that devastated the Grand Hotel.

I missed Tony very much, because we had been close friends for a long time; we had been bridge partners in the House of Commons team, and at Central Office I think he had been one of those who had persuaded Margaret to appoint me to take on Livingstone. He had sat alongside me on the conference platform for my speech on the Wednesday, and had been one of the first to congratulate me on the standing ovation.

In that first television debate with Livingstone the first question put to me was: 'Why do you want to get rid of the GLC?' My immediate answer was: 'It is not to get rid of Mr Livingstone.'

Thames Television also allowed us each to make a ten-minute film putting our respective cases, which was then followed by a debate. The case I was pressing all the time was that the GLC had lost most of its functions and was no longer really responsible for very much. The most difficult argument I had to deal with was that 'London needed a voice', since every other capital city had an elected authority to run it. I accepted that there was clearly a need for a body with overall responsibility for strategic planning, though curiously enough Livingstone had not done much of this, since he was against roads, airports and the private car. The GLC had even notably failed to revitalize Docklands. I argued that London did not need an elected authority since an elected authority was bound to find ways of increasing its powers and its expenditure. London, moreover, did not have one voice but a hundred different voices. The real nub of the Government's case was that the activities of the GLC could be carried out even better by the thirty-two London Boroughs, which had 1,900 councillors compared to the GLC's ninety-two. I also managed to unearth a quote from a talk in 1979 where Livingstone had said, 'I do not believe you need two tiers of local government.'

The Labour Party had one hand tied behind its back since, when it came to the six Metropolitan Counties which were also up for abolition, Labour were not proposing to reinstate them as they believed that the metropolitan districts could do the job better. So Labour accepted the argument for decentralization and delegation outside London, but not inside London. This was a fatal flaw in their campaign against the Abolition Bill.

I piloted the Bill through the Commons, and not surprisingly the greatest difficulty was with those Tories who wanted 'a voice for London'. Just before Christmas, there was a full debate on the floor of the House about an elected assembly for London. The Opposition moved an amendment to prevent abolition until after a Royal Commission had reported, but this was defeated by a majority of over fifty. The critical vote came on an amendment tabled by Patrick Cormack, the Tory backbencher, which said that the GLC should be replaced by a directly elected authority whose functions and powers were to be determined by Parliament after a Select Committee had reported. The Government's majority on this fell to twenty-three, its lowest level since 1979. On this issue the Government had lost more than 100 of its own backbenchers.

On 21 March 1985, Margaret saw one of the more intelligent of the backbench critics, Philip Goodhart, the long-serving Conservative MP for Beckenham, who for a short time had been a junior Minister. He had broken his ankle and limped in on crutches to the Prime Minister's room in the House, where Margaret was sitting at the end of a sofa near the fire with her handbag at her foot. Philip put forward his case for a 'voice'. 'My dear Philip, there is no such thing as a voice for London. Why should Londoners be especially represented when people from Birmingham, Liverpool and Manchester manage without it? Lorries come from the South-West and the North and they have just as much of an interest in road planning in London as Londoners.' Philip's idea of a Select Committee for London was no better – 'Select Committees are unhelpful and all we'll have is another body attacking the Government.'

Philip, who is a dear person, was taken aback by the onslaught. But the Prime Minister realized that the Lords could insist upon some sort of voice for London. Would that be the price to pay for the Bill – would it take the trick? She ended by saying that if we had to have some sort of body it should only meet twice a year and 'no junkets'. It was a remarkable performance which was repeated later that day when she met Alan Greengross, the Tory Opposition Leader of the GLC. It was a lively discussion and it was fascinating to see a Prime Minister with so many other preoccupations prepared to argue at such length with a backbencher and a Tory local government leader.

Later that month there was a meeting at Number 10 to discuss the handling of the Bill in the House of Lords, where Willie Whitelaw was in charge. I started by congratulating Margaret on her speech at the meeting of the Central Council of the Conservative Party at Newcastle which had taken place the previous weekend, and where I had also spoken. She gave me a wintry smile – 'I heard you were brilliant too.' Then to work.

I recommended that there should be no compromise, no Select Committee, and that we should press ahead as we had a Manifesto commitment which the Lords would be reluctant to challenge. Margaret agreed: 'If you have a fall-back position, you don't fight so hard. If you have a fall-back position you fall back into it.' She was getting very fed up with the Lords, who were upsetting quite a lot of our legislation – 'I really won't have the Lords saying that London is so significant that only Londoners should have a voice for London.' It was just as well that Willie was handling this in the Lords, because I knew he would achieve our objective but in a very different manner.

On 15 April, our wedding anniversary, Mary and I had a family dinner party in Soho and then went back to the House of Lords to hear the closing stages of the Second Reading of the Bill. As it was being televised there were very bright lights. After hearing some dull speeches for fifteen minutes my son made one of the most apposite comments about the Upper Chamber: 'They should turn off those lights. They're so bright and hot, they'll dry up some of the Peers who would then snap.' I stayed on to hear Willie wind up and to see us get a good majority.

Liverpool and Rate-Capping

The Government was engaged in a head-on conflict with up to twenty left-wing Labour inner-city councils, and the one which mattered the most was Liverpool. Labour had gained control of Liverpool City Council in 1983, and by 1985 the Militant Tendency had twelve city councillors. The Conservative Party had lost its last Westminster seat in Liverpool in 1983, and the number of Conservative councillors had dropped from twenty four to thirteen by 1984, eventually falling to six and then to just three. The Conservatives were no longer an effective political force in that city. The main Opposition Party were the Liberals who, under Trevor Jones, had been in power for six years in the previous decade. It was part of Labour's case that the Liberals had not faced up to the consequences of their own spending.

In effect, just four people ran Liverpool City. John Hamilton was the Leader of the Council, a tall, trilby-hatted and bespectacled Quaker. He was a decent old-style Labour politician, but actually served as the front man for the Jesuit-educated Tony Byrne, who as Finance Chairman really determined the strategy of the Liverpool City Council. The third person was the thickset Tony Mulhearne, who rarely spoke but was always to be seen in the role of minder to Derek Hatton, the Deputy Leader. It was Hatton who became the public face of the Liverpool Militants – loud, brash, glib and gold-braceleted.

The Council's strategy was to increase spending, particularly on housing, then set an inadequate rate and then blackmail the Government into meeting the deficit. The other parts of this strategy were to set the rate as late as possible, even waiting until after the local elections in May, and at the same time draw the Government into resolving Liverpool's problems. Accordingly, the Council agreed a budget with a deficit of £55 million for 1984–85.

On 9 July 1984 Patrick Jenkin met John Hamilton and tried to be helpful by agreeing to a modest increase of about £20 million for Liverpool's housing. Tony Byrne distorted this and made it appear as a major concession by the Government amounting to £90 million. The Militant councillors held up their left fists in triumph when a rate increase which had threatened to be as high as 170 per cent suddenly dropped to 17 per cent. Hatton said that Jenkin and Thatcher had 'bottled out'. He continued, 'There is no way even Thatcher can take on the might of the working class in this city. This is just the start. Next year we will see not only the defeat of rate-capping and the plans to cut the Metropolitan councils, but we will start to see the kicking out of Thatcher herself.' Hatton was the darling of the 1984 Labour Party Conference. But he had misjudged the Prime Minister, for the one thing she could not stomach was being accused of making a U-turn.

The political significance of this episode was immense. Patrick Jenkin, who had been severely wounded by Militant's twisting of the figures, accused them of 'dancing on his grave'. The Labour Party reluctantly, and with no personal enthusiasm from Jack Cunningham, their Shadow Environment Secretary, now had to be seen to follow Liverpool's lead and be even more determined to defeat rate-capping in

1985. But the reality was that Liverpool's finances were still in chaos. Byrne's destructive strategy was to press on and increase the housing budget to £130 million, claiming that Patrick had promised to support this in July.

In December 1984, following the annual public expenditure settlement, we had to announce cuts in housing capital and Liverpool's allocation was reduced to £37 million. There was now a huge gap, and Liverpool tried to bridge part of it by doing a deal with Banque Paribas, which bought for £30 million the mortgages of the 7,000 houses and flats sold by the Council. This seemed again to be a great triumph for Militant, as the capitalist world had bailed them out. Emboldened by this, the Council now proposed a budget of £374 million, requiring a rate increase of 220 per cent. As a result of creative accounting this was revised down to £285 million and a rate increase of 85 per cent. But it was still far higher than the Government's target for the city of £223 million, so the scene was set for a major confrontation.

When I became the Minister for Local Government in September 1984, I visited Liverpool and was constantly asked whether I would become the Minister for Liverpool. This was a tradition which Michael Heseltine had started in 1981, but I refused to don the mantle, for Liverpool did not deserve such special treatment. Liverpool was heartily disliked by most councils in the North of England because of its constant special pleading, whingeing and militancy. Early in 1985 I met Keva Coombes, then the Labour Leader of the Merseyside County Council, which was to be abolished. He said to me, 'In this part of the world you are abolishing the wrong tier of government. It's Liverpool City Council that ought to go.'

I also met the two Liverpool Bishops, the Roman Catholic Derek Worlock and the Anglican David Sheppard, who were to prove very helpful in trying to find a way through the dramas of the next twelve months. They had their own network of information derived from their parishes, and the message coming back was that the ordinary people of Liverpool were becoming increasingly alarmed at the reckless policies being implemented by the Council. I also spoke to local businessmen led by Desmond Pitcher, the Managing Director of Littlewoods – the only large company whose headquarters were still in Liverpool – and Philip Carter, the Chairman of Everton Football Club. They were very concerned about the bad press that Liverpool was bringing upon itself and the damaging effects upon investment in the city.

I experienced Hatton's loud-mouthed hectoring on my very first visit. He tracked me to a school I was visiting and bellowed down the telephone his demands for more money for a youth service project. I quietly told him to find it himself by putting his own house in order and hung up.

There was a concerted campaign with other left-wing councils to fight rate-capping. But, for a change, a leak actually helped us when early in January the minutes of a meeting of Labour councillors in Brent Town Hall setting out the Labour councils' national tactics were found by Bob Lacey, our Conservative Leader in Brent. Every Labour Council was asked to challenge the rate limit set by the Government and to postpone setting a rate for as long as possible. However, most of the campaigns to resist rate capping turned out to be paper tigers. Merseyside, South Yorkshire, ILEA and GLC all set legal rates after some cliff-hanging meetings. A group of London councils held out, but Hackney fell on 21 May, Southwark on 30 May, and Islington on 31 May. Liverpool held out the longest, but Patrick and I were determined to give them no help.

In the spring of 1985 the District Auditor, who operates quite independently of the Department of the Environment, decided to intervene. The Auditor reminded Liverpool councillors that they had to agree a legal budget and set a legal rate by 1 June, otherwise they faced individual disqualification and bankruptcy. This did not seem to deter many of them. Byrne nonetheless demanded that an incoming Labour Government should indemnify Labour councillors who refused to set a rate. In June, Hatton demanded that the blue-collar workers in Liverpool should 'lock up the city'. One television programme showed film of a priest having to use a hacksaw to cut through the padlocked chain on a school gate, which had been closed by a Militant school caretaker, so that children could actually get into their school. The Council also faced the possibility of giving notice to its 30,000 employees, hoping this would force the Government to give Liverpool yet more money.

On many occasions I had already condemned Liverpool City Council by saying their budget belonged 'in cloud-cuckoo-land. No responsible council could possibly base its plans on such a wild assumption.' This was still my position when I became Environment Secretary in September 1985. On 25 September Hatton called a one-day strike in Liverpool which turned out tens of thousands of people. On the next day I met all the Liverpool MPs led by Eric Heffer, and told them bluntly that we would not be putting an extra penny on the table. The Government was not prepared to increase the Council's borrowing limits to allow them to borrow themselves out of their problems. In addition, I told the MPs that in the following year Liverpool would be rate-capped at a level of £245 million, which was £40 million less than their draft budget. The following day the City Council agreed to issue redundancy notices to its staff, a move which was savagely attacked by Neil Kinnock at the Labour Party Conference in early October.

During the summer months I had kept in contact with Jack Cunningham and Jack Straw, the Shadow Environment Ministers. Jack Cunningham told me that the Shadow Cabinet would not support Hatton, who was loathed in the Labour movement, but they would have to be seen helping the people of Liverpool. That was why David Blunkett, the Labour leader of Sheffield City Council, intervened later. As regards London, Cunningham held Ken Livingstone and the other Loony Left leaders in utter contempt, saying, 'Let them twist in the wind.' Labour's leaders knew only too well the damage the Militants were doing to the Labour Party's electoral chances. In my speech to the Tory Party Conference in October 1985 I attacked Hatton's wreckers:

If any of these councillors are surcharged and disqualified from office for wilful misconduct, they hope that a future Labour Government will indemnify them. Conference, I tell you that you can indemnify local councils for breaking the law but who will indemnify the businesses driven out by Militant folly? Who will indemnify the workers who lose their jobs? Who will indemnify the old people who lose their services? Who will indemnify the children who cannot get into their schools because of the caretakers? Note well that in the Utopia of Militancy it is the caretaker who rules, it is the caretaker who decides who should be taught and where and when they should be taught. Above all, who will indemnify the people of Liverpool who witness daily the dragging down of their great city in the eyes of the world by this Militant mafia?

I also attacked Neil Kinnock, because while Hatton was an easy target for him, Kinnock had done little to confront Militant supporters who were still influential in other councils around the country like Manchester, Southwark and Hackney. Kinnock's anti-Hatton rhetoric was not enough, for in these areas his writ did not run. As I told the Conference, 'The trouble is that Kinnock cannot deliver. Neil Kinnock is walking proof that the biggest drums make the loudest noise because they have the emptiest insides.' There was a temporary respite when David Blunkett, the Leader of Sheffield City Council, agreed to set up an inquiry on behalf of Labour's NEC into Liverpool's financial problems. Thus Liverpool Council had succeeded in sucking in the Labour Party as they had sucked in Patrick Jenkin.

As early as the autumn of 1984 I had advised colleagues that defiance of rate-capping could lead to the Government having to appoint Commissioners to take over the duties of Labour councils. In 1984, and for much of 1985, my fellow Ministers were not very keen to address this contingency. At a meeting on 26 March 1985 Margaret said, 'We don't need Commissioners. No point in discussing them.' At that time she was more concerned about the way the Militants seemed to be getting away with their tricks and putting the Government on the defensive. 'We are not doing enough to expose the Left in the town halls,' she said.

Throughout 1985 the confrontation with Liverpool became more intense. The news which I received from Derek Worlock was very bleak indeed, for Liverpool had become a proving ground for the power of the Militant Tendency. The Council was not prepared to give in, since they saw their defiance as a way to bring down Thatcher.

During the winter of 1985 and early 1986 we had to consider what we would do if local government services collapsed in Liverpool. This Doomsday scenario would mean new legislation to appoint Commissioners who would run all the city's services including education, old people's homes and refuse collection. We set about trying to find people who could do this, but it was clear that Commissioners would need the protection of the police and armed forces, since Militant supporters would not shrink from physically threatening them and their families. The Commissioners would become very unpopular as they implemented policies to restore Liverpool's financial balance. It was a miserable job, and as we considered the various candidates the shortlist became shorter and shorter and actually narrowed down to just one person. It was clear to me that these reserve powers would be very difficult to operate, and certainly we could never hope to do it in more than one or two local authorities.

A special committee under the chairmanship of Margaret Thatcher met that winter to prepare our contingency plans. I found Willie Whitelaw's shrewd and realistic observations particularly helpful. We decided that the Government should offer no special financial assistance to Liverpool, since every other authority in Britain would have exploded with anger. If Byrne and Hatton were prepared to go to the brink then we must be prepared to let them fall over it. We decided to take no steps until services in Liverpool had actually broken down as a result of Militant action, for local people would then appreciate the appalling chaos and demand that the Government act. This policy was known as 'Five Minutes Past Midnight'. It carried huge risks, and required strong nerves, for as D-Day approached it became clear that many people – schoolchildren, the elderly, the sick and the mentally handicapped – would suddenly find themselves without proper services.

On 30 January 1986 I agreed to see a delegation including Hamilton, Hatton, Mulhearne and Byrne, but they were not prepared to budge and neither was I. All too well aware of the way they had misrepresented Patrick, I denied them the opportunity to do the same to me.

We had passed legislation to require all councils to fix their rates by the end of March. This requirement came into force over the last weekend in March, one of the most tense weekends that I have experienced as a Minister. It was expected that as the money had run out, the following Monday would see the start of the breakdown of Liverpool's local services, leading to considerable violence. However, it was not the will of the Government that broke, it was the nerve of Militant. That weekend, on the brink of the abyss, the Council agreed to set a legal budget and to fix a legal rate.

One explanation for this was that the Militants realized that the Government was not going to step in and that they themselves would be blamed for the ensuing chaos. The wrath of Liverpool's people would then be directed against them rather than at the Government. Militant councillors would be disqualified from office, which would leave the Liberals and soft Left to set a rate and run the Council. In the face of this humiliating prospect the rebellion collapsed.

CHAPTER 6

The Community Charge

*The Need for Reform – The Review Group's Work – The
Community Charge 1986 – Cabinet Agreement – The
Fatal Mistakes of 1987 and 1988 – The Underfunding of
1989 – The Community Charge at Central Office –
Epilogue*

Back in the October 1974 General Election, Margaret Thatcher, then
Opposition Environment Spokesman, had pledged to abolish domestic
rates. This had been pressed on her, rather like the policy of fixed
mortgage interest, which she had first argued against but then brilliantly
advocated. The rates were certainly unpopular, and during Ted's premiership and for the short time that he led the Opposition, there had been
strong protests from the Tory rank and file. In 1975 Chris Tugendhat, the
neighbouring MP for Westminster South, and I presented a petition to
Tony Crosland, Labour's Environment Secretary, protesting at Westminster Council's 53 per cent rate increase. We called for total reform of
the rating system.

In addition, successive Conservative Governments could not agree
what the role of local government should really be. Margaret did not have
much time for local councils, which she expected to be the agents of
central government. She said to me once with a resigned sigh, 'I suppose
we need them.' However, many local activists in the constituencies were
councillors, and some MPs had also served as councillors, as I had done,
before entering the House. In addition the Party made great efforts in all
the local government elections to win control of councils. So there was
something schizophrenic in our attitude to local government.

The root of the trouble was the tension between local and central
government. Local authorities were high spenders, led by the Labour
cities but with the Tory Shires not far behind them. When in 1976 the
IMF imposed controls upon British economic policy Tony Crosland, the
Environment Secretary, told local authorities, the chosen instruments for
a more Socialist Britain, 'The Party is over'. But it wasn't. As soon as the

IMF went home, local government expenditure resumed its upward spiral. It is often forgotten that the origin of the recent battles between central and local government began with Labour local authorities in conflict with the Labour Government of 1974–79.

When, in 1979, the first Thatcher Government came to power, a clash with local government became inevitable. Margaret's first priority was to restore sound money by curbing inflation, and this meant reducing public expenditure. Local authorities, particularly Labour-controlled ones, were high-spending engines of inflation, pulling the Treasury along with them. Margaret decided to apply the brakes. In addition, there had been a dramatic change in the kind of people entering local government on the Labour side. A new generation of hard-left activists replaced old-style Labour moderates and deliberately decided to use town halls as a weapon against the Conservative Government. Local government was to become 'a state within the state', the vehicle for delivering Socialism locally in the face of electoral rejection nationally. For all these reasons, the Thatcher Government had no real love of local government.

One of our biggest mistakes was to give local authorities more duties which could only be financed properly by central government grants rather than by locally raised revenue. Councils would carry out their duties conscientiously, some would do it extravagantly, but all would blame the Government for any shortfall in their revenue. It was a relationship which inevitably created continual conflict, mutual recrimination and buckpassing. Councils needed a viable tax base to finance their own services, for which they could then be held properly accountable – accountable both for the level of service and for raising the money to provide that service.

In 1980 the Government started on the right track with its Local Government Planning and Land Act, which abolished many detailed controls. But local authorities accounted for over a quarter of all public expenditure and 11 per cent of GDP. In 1984–85 the services they provided amounted to £45 billion. Owing to the sheer size of such a sum, the Treasury felt that it had to restrict the capacity of councils to spend.

The only effective sanction the Government had was to reduce the central government grant to local authorities in the hope that this would lead to lower rates. It had the reverse effect. Moreover the distribution of grants was quixotic, and particularly irksome when for some convoluted and inexplicable reason the grant to a low-spending Tory authority was cut. The system which allocated the grant on grounds of need was being constantly revised. Graham Page, who had sat as the Tory MP for Crosby and had served Ted as the Minister for Local Government, was the acknowledged expert in the Conservative Party on the system. He once told me, 'Any grant system is flawed. You might just as well take all the money in £10 notes up in an aeroplane and scatter them as you fly over the country.'

In 1982 the Government introduced a new block grant system which was meant to reflect more accurately the real needs of local authorities. At the same time it also introduced controls on capital spending and not just on capital borrowing. In the hope of imposing some discipline on council spending, central Government grants had been cut from 60 per cent of planned expenditure in 1980–81 to 49 per cent in 1985–86. As these measures did not significantly reduce council spending, Leon Brittan, the Chief Secretary, introduced a system of expenditure targets which if exceeded led to the council being penalized by a grant cut. This produced anguish for many Tory authorities, but even this was not sufficient to deal with the small group of high-spending Labour authorities. By 1985–86 council-budgeted expenditure exceeded targets by £850 million, and three-quarters of this was accounted for by just twelve authorities. So in 1984 we passed the Rate Act to give the Government power to cap the rates set by councils.

So a hands-off approach had been transformed into regular and persistent intervention and control. In the space of five years there were five Local Government Finance Bills. The layers of supervision and interference were so Byzantine in their complexity that only a few officials really understood them, just three Ministers were capable of explaining them, and no MP was convinced of their logic. In 1985 Patrick Jenkin persuaded the Treasury, against Nigel Lawson's own wishes, to abandon expenditure targets which had become literally inexplicable. Yet rates were still the system which the Treasury wanted us to retain.

One of the features of 1983 and 1984 were the Tory backbench revolts in the debates at the end of the year after the Rate Support Grant had been announced. Patrick Jenkin had by then become the Environment Secretary and his Minister of State, Irwin Bellwin, an expert in local government, unfortunately sat in the House of Lords, leaving only a junior Minister, William Waldegrave, in the Commons. I remember two debates when William had to wind up after a savage battering from the

Knights of the Shires, led by Geoffrey Rippon, a former Environment Secretary, and Francis Pym, a former Foreign Secretary. William at that time was one of the most junior members of the Government, and he found it very difficult to cope with this heavy barrage from such senior backbenchers.

By the time that I became Minister for Local Government in September 1984 it was clear that something had to be done. There were motions hostile to the rating system tabled for the Party Conference that year, and the one which had been selected was to be proposed by a leading figure in Tory local government, county councillor Emily Blatch from Cambridgeshire.

I noted in my diary, 'I am quite convinced that the present system cannot last more than two or three years. We need a better and more robust tax base for local authorities.' One of the first issues I had to deal with was whether councils which had their expenditure limited and which were refusing to set a rate could in fact be compelled to make a rate. When I warned colleagues at a meeting at Number 10 on 27 September 1984 that we would have to bring in further legislation to compel councils to fix a rate by a certain date, or even give the Environment Secretary powers to determine the rate himself if a council refused to fix one, John Biffen and Willie Whitelaw both groaned at the prospect of even more difficult and contentious Department of Environment legislation. For the first time I said that we might have to consider early the following year the appointment of Commissioners to run those authorities which were determined to resist the Government and flout the legislation. I was anxious to ensure that the Cabinet realized the state of institutional conflict which the present arrangements had created.

It was at this meeting that Patrick Jenkin presented his case for a review of local government finance. In 1980 Margaret Thatcher had asked Michael Heseltine, her new Environment Secretary, to review the rating system in the search for an alternative, but he had concluded that the existing system was the lesser of several evils. In spite of the changes introduced since 1980, this adherence to the rates had become unsustainable by 1984. Patrick now said, 'Our efforts to bring local government spending into line with the Government's public expenditure plans are causing bitter resentment in local government across the board. This is now spilling over into both sides of the House.'

Nigel Lawson objected to a review – the first of his many objections to a fundamental change in local government finance. Keith Joseph and

Nicholas Ridley supported Patrick. I said that I had been appointed to defend the indefensible but had found that it was truly indefensible. The meeting agreed that Patrick, when replying to the debate at the Tory Party Conference, would be allowed to say that there would be a review of local government finance. I noted in my diary, 'I don't relish the prospect at all. This is essential for us but it will be a terrible task for me. The ground has been worked over so many times but we must try and find a way through. The only thing on which virtually everyone is agreed is that no one likes the present system.' In my 1984 Party Conference speech I described the existing rating system as 'a maze surrounded by a marsh and shrouded in a fog'.

The Review Group's Work

The Review Group set up in November 1984 was chaired by me but the work was coordinated by William Waldegrave. It began by seeing whether the rating system, based upon notional rental values which were supposed to be related to the market, could be retained. There were fundamental weaknesses in the rating system. First, rates did not take into account a ratepayer's ability to pay. An elderly widow on a limited income could find herself paying the same high rates as a similar house next door where there were three wage-earners who could easily share the cost between them. People with lower wages spent a higher proportion of their income on rates than the better-off. For people earning £100 a week, rates before any rebate amounted to 6 per cent of their incomes and, after rebates, to 4 per cent. The level for people earning over £400 a week was about 2 per cent.

Second, rates were based upon property values which should have been reassessed at regular intervals to allow for market changes. But because of the reluctance of both Harold Wilson and Margaret Thatcher to bear the electoral flak, the last revaluation in England had been in 1973 – eleven years earlier. Valuers said they would need at least three years to revalue all domestic properties. This meant that the revaluation gap would then be fourteen years, leading to painful and costly realignments. Scotland had just gone through this very process, and the explosion of protest north of the border had reverberated throughout the entire country. Nigel Lawson blamed George Younger, the Scottish Secretary, for not appreciating that the impact of revaluation had to be softened, and eventually and reluctantly an extra £100 million had to be found to do that. Scottish Ministers led by George Younger were by now adamant that the rating system had to go, and they demanded that Scotland should lead the way with a new system. This was reinforced when the Conservatives lost a safe seat in a regional council by-election in George's own highly marginal constituency of Ayr in March 1985.

The unpopularity of the rates was reinforced when Willie Whitelaw returned to London, after a weekend in Scotland, shaken and angry by the blasts of outrage to which he had been subjected when he attended a dinner in Strathkelvin and Bearsden – a constituency he had himself fought in 1950 and 1951. From that moment he was converted to the need for a new system as he realized that rates, especially after revaluation, were no longer acceptable. Margaret was also clear about the dangers of revaluation, and at one early meeting she said, 'We can't have a revaluation in England, it would wipe us out.'

Third, there was a weak and decreasing link between those who voted for local government services and those who paid for them. There were over 35 million electors in Britain of whom only about half, 18 million, were liable to pay rates. But of that number 3 million received partial assistance and another 3 million received full relief through rate rebate. This left just 12 million people paying full rates. In some inner-city areas, which were the biggest spenders and had a higher proportion of low-income earners, domestic ratepayers provided only 20 per cent of the rates bill from their own pockets. In these authorities there was a majority of electors who could vote for more services whilst only a minority had to pick up the actual bill. The rating system encouraged local electors to vote for services for which other people paid. The tax base was too narrow and the burden of rates fell on too few shoulders.

Fourth, the business rate provided over 50 per cent of the rate income for local authorities but local businesses had no effective say on the level of this rate or in how their money was spent. This again encouraged local authorities to be extravagant, since it was voteless businesses, not the electorate, which met half the bill. Some councils were so irresponsible about passing on their high spending through huge business rates that they drove many businesses to close, as happened in Sheffield.

The review group identified three main possibilities for reform: to change the structure of local government; to increase central control by the Treasury; or to design a system that could improve local accountability. They opted for the last proposal, and from this the community charge developed. All the possible ways of raising money locally were looked at.

The review group first examined a sales tax, which would have had to be levied at 6.5 per cent if it were to raise the same amount as the rates. If that tax were determined nationally then there was no local accountability – it would simply be set by central government and collected locally. There would be little discretion left to local councillors, and one could just as well have officials deciding how the money should be spent – as happened in the Health Service. If a sales tax were set locally, either at county level or even at district level, there would be a bewildering variety of prices in what were very small geographical areas. If London had one level and Surrey had another then you could envisage butter being smuggled over Epsom Downs. It was also very difficult to decide how the high yield of a sales tax in major shopping centres, such as Oxford Street, should be redirected to areas that had little retail activity. So a sales tax was dismissed as impractical at an early stage.

The group then looked at a local income tax – the preferred option of the Liberal Party. This seemed to be fair at first glance, since it took into account a person's ability to pay. But a nationally determined local income tax would not enhance local accountability. A local income tax which raised the same revenue as rates would have added 4.5p to the standard rate, but with this figure agreed nationally and collected through PAYE, there would of course be no local accountability. It would be simply another way of funding local authorities with a centrally determined tax.

If the local income tax was set locally, one first had to decide whether it should be set by counties, or by metropolitan borough councils and the district councils. This would have involved over 500 tax-setting authorities. If electors were to be asked to make a judgement on the effectiveness of their local council then that council should have the freedom to set its own level of local income tax. But the complexity of collection would be immense. An office block in central London could have had employees from up to thirty different local authorities on their payroll, and each one would be subject to a different rate of local income tax to be deducted from their wages by their employer. This highlighted the central difficulty – namely that income tax is collected at the place of work, not where the payers live. There were political as well as administrative objections to a local income tax. I was not in favour of giving to

Labour city councils the immense power of a redistributive tax. That would be one way of establishing a Labour Chancellor of the Exchequer in town halls.

The review group also examined property taxes and how to deal with the problem of market values. Any valuation of houses would have to be carried out regularly and be capable of being challenged. I was amused to see that the Labour Party also thought from time to time of retaining a property tax. They came forward with proposals for a floor space tax and later a roof tax. A serious disadvantage of any property tax is that once all the properties in the country are valued, they would appear on a list which could become the database for a capital levy – a great temptation to a left-wing Government.

The Community Charge 1986

Rates were based historically on property because most of the services which they financed originally related to property. Rate revenue in the past used to cover the water, sewerage and gas services, as well as roads and pavements that ran past the property, the street lighting outside and such other services as planning controls and refuse collection. Before the First World War, the rates for these services exceeded the annual yield of income tax, but over the years most of these functions had been transferred to other bodies and local government had concentrated on providing to people, rather than properties, services such as education, social services, housing, libraries and old people's homes. These benefited the local community but were paid for by only a proportion of the beneficiaries. We felt it was only fair that the people and families who benefited from these local services should also pay a charge for them. This would be fairer, since it reflected the number of people in a household using and benefiting from local services rather than simply reflecting the value of the property occupied.

We therefore worked on a scheme for a flat-rate charge payable by all adults over eighteen. This enshrined the principle that everyone should contribute to the cost of their local services. A flat-rate charge was not particularly novel, as other similar charges were already widely used and accepted, such as the road fund and TV licences. However, I made it clear to the review group that such a charge should only be introduced slowly, and initially at a low level. We recommended therefore that the 'community charge' should be introduced at a level of £50 per adult and run alongside the rates until these were phased out. The critical paragraph in the Green Paper of 1986 said:

The Government considers that the change should be made gradually by introducing the Community Charge initially at a low level . . . People will need time to adjust.

The transitional period phasing in the new community charge would last for up to ten years, with the higher-spending inner-city councils being the last ones to retain the rates. This arrangement became known as dual-running, and in my view it was the only feasible way to introduce the community charge. As the Green Paper stated:

Inevitably moves to a community charge in place of domestic rates would involve a degree of disruption and the change could not sensibly take place in a single year.

We also assessed the effect upon various households and published, for the first time, tables of gainers and losers. At that time there were marginally more gainers than losers. Our recommendations showed that these were evenly balanced, with 82 per cent of households either gaining or losing less than £1 a week.

One of the difficulties that I had, as did all those later concerned with the subject, was that we were never able to get from the Department of the Environment exemplifications of the precise impact which the community charge would have upon real voters in real houses. What we wanted was a house-by-house comparison with the rates paid by householders in several streets in a sample area. I believed this to be possible, but the Department resisted it on the grounds that it would only provide a partial snapshot. Instead, the Department gave us theoretical average community charge figures for a local authority. The absence of precise comparisons meant that it was impossible to predict the electoral consequences of the amount people would have to pay for the new community charge compared with their rates. This precise exercise was subsequently conducted by our local government leaders when I moved to Central Office in 1989. We were also hamstrung by the Department's inability to assess what the level of domestic rates would have been for specific households if there had been a revaluation.

We proposed two other important changes, relating to the non-domestic rate and the grants made by central Government. The level of non-domestic or business rates varied widely across the country, from 291p in the £ in Newcastle to 137p in Croydon. Businesses making or selling the same merchandise, or providing the same service, could find that their rate bills could differ by as much as 113 per cent because they were located in different authorities. But councils liked the business rate because it was a milch cow providing over 50 per cent of their total rating income, and in some Labour areas 75 per cent, with no awkward voting objectors. Thus there was no curb at all upon councils' propensity to spend.

We decided that to protect businesses from continual political exploitation there should be a business rate, uniform across the country with its level determined centrally by Government. The annual increase would be limited to the rate of inflation – a proposal widely welcomed by businesses up and down Britain.

But the uniform business rate necessitated a revaluation of all non-domestic properties to reflect how property in London, the South-East and the West Midlands had proportionately increased in value compared to the North-West and the North-East. This exercise was to last three years, and so the non-domestic rate could not possibly be introduced until 1990. It meant that businesses in predominantly Conservative areas such as the South would have to pay more, whereas businesses in the predominantly Labour areas of the North would pay less. That was why it was essential to cushion the impact with a transitional period.

The second change related to the basis of allocating grants. About £1 billion of grant was transferred by an obscure and hidden process from the wealthier London, South-East, and West Midlands to other 'poorer' parts of the country, principally Lancashire, Yorkshire and the North. This equalization of resources, to compensate for low rateable values, had developed over decades and meant that rates were much lower in the North than in the South. There was precious little justification for that, since it was not related to the ability of the householder to pay. A civil servant living in the North, for example, and receiving the same salary as a colleague living in the South, made a windfall gain through this system. Less well-off people in the South were helping to keep down the rates of richer people living in the North. We recommended the introduction of a standard grant to underpin a similar level of service across the country, together with a needs grant to recognize special factors such as the number of elderly people and children in an area, the age of the housing stock and the special needs of inner cities.

The consequences of these changes were that the revenue of local authorities would come from four sources – the non-domestic rate from business; the standard grant and the needs grant from Government; and the community charge from local residents. It was a much simpler and fairer system, but the uniform business rate and the changes of grant would result in a shift of the resources between authorities. We therefore recommended a safety net which would protect the Northern community chargepayer from loss of grant income, but this was at the expense of the gains that the Southern chargepayer was expecting.

The object of the reforms was to devise a system where the charge to each payer for a standard level of service would be the same in different parts of the country. If authorities wanted, for whatever reason, to spend more and to provide a higher level of service, then the income for that would have to be found solely through the local community charge. Hence, every extra pound increase in a council's spending would be met by the community chargepayers in that area, while every pound saved would reduce their charge by the same amount. This created the local accountability which we were searching for.

We also recognized that social security payments to some households would have to be increased, and we estimated an increase to the social security budget of about 4 per cent. However, Norman Fowler had already decided that his Housing Benefit changes would require every ratepayer to contribute at least 20 per cent towards local rates, thus scrapping the 100 per cent rate rebate. This was to lead to a considerable increase in individual bills for some ratepayers and was quite separate from our recommendations for the new community charge.

The review group working on this involved, of course, other Government Departments – the Treasury and Social Security, the Scottish and Welsh Offices, with inputs from Education and Transport. We also benefited from the comments of a group of advisers whom William had asked to assist us. They were headed by his old friend and former boss at the Think Tank, Victor Rothschild, and included the Senior QC Leonard Hoffman, Christopher Foster from Coopers Lybrand, and Tom Wilson, an economics Professor from Glasgow University. Victor analysed our proposals and made a clear recommendation for a flat-rate charge which was supported by Christopher Foster. Tom Wilson did not agree and Lenny Hoffman had reservations. But we believed we had built in sufficient safeguards to meet their concerns and make the community charge acceptable.

Cabinet Agreement

Margaret had set up in October 1984 a separate Cabinet Committee, under her chairmanship, called E(LF) – the Local Finance Sub-Committee of the Economic Affairs Committee. This Committee was to consider 'future policy relating to local government finance' and most senior Cabinet Ministers were members.

One evening early in March, at the Department of the Environment, William and I held a large meeting of advisers and politicians. I went around the table and asked each person to say quite frankly which system of domestic taxation they preferred. No one wanted the rates in their present form, and only one civil servant spoke up for local income tax. The rest thought we were on the right lines. As this meeting was drawing to a close late in the evening there was a tremendous clap of thunder. We went over to the window and watched as great flashes of lightning lit up the whole of Westminster while the thunder continued to rumble. I turned to William and said, 'I hope the community charge won't produce such a storm.' This hope was to be spectacularly dashed.

On 31 March 1985, Patrick Jenkin, William Waldegrave and I presented our preliminary thoughts to a Sunday meeting of Ministers at Chequers. The meeting had as its basis that 'doing nothing is no longer an option'. I had made no attempt to 'soften up' the Prime Minister before the meeting. William ended his presentation with the vigorous and seductive words, 'And so Prime Minister, you will have fulfilled your promise to abolish rates.' Nigel Lawson, who did not like his weekends interrupted though he was later to regret his absence, was represented by Peter Rees, the Chief Secretary to the Treasury. Peter expressed Nigel's opposition to the whole idea of the community charge. He argued that we should retain property as the basis for local taxation. Nick Edwards on behalf of the Welsh Office supported our proposals, as did Michael Ancram, a junior Minister at the Scottish Office, and his Secretary of State, George Younger, who said, 'All my political life I have been waiting for this.'

Margaret was particularly concerned about the number of gainers and losers and the impact upon different households. She wanted more work done on this. She did, however, like the discipline which would be imposed upon local authorities by the new system, which required those who voted for expensive policies to pay for them. Margaret had little fondness for local authorities and was appalled by their overspending.

Above all she wanted a system that would reward the thrifty and punish the extravagant. She also hankered after more explicit controls on local authority spending through extending rate-capping. We explained that our system, if it was allowed to work through gradually, would impose a vigorous discipline on local authorities since it provided them with a wide tax base yet made them, and not the government, directly responsible for the consequent level of the charge. In future, a low level of community charge would depend not upon the quirkiness of the central grant system but upon the efficiency with which a local council provided value for money for its services. The discipline exercised by chargepayers at the ballot box was infinitely preferable to the imperfect discipline of Whitehall.

This Chequers meeting was important in approving the general thrust of our review. In the paper we submitted we had included the ideas of annual elections for councils, and single-tier authorities. The latter was rejected outright at this meeting, and annual elections were put on the back-burner. The minutes – felt to be so sensitive that only five copies were made – acknowledge that 'controversy was inevitable' and that a community charge would be costly and difficult to collect. But the Ministers agreed that the charge was the best way forward provided there was a rebate for low-income families and special aid for the inner cities where the charges were likely to be the highest. We had indicated at the meeting that the average level of community charge to match the yield of domestic rates would be £140. If we had known that in 1990, the first year, the average level of community charge was to be £363 then I am sure we would have suspended work immediately.

On 20 May, William and I presented our proposals for a community charge to the E(LF) Committee, consisting of ten Cabinet Ministers. The key proposal was for a flat-rate residents charge which 'would have to operate with a rebate' for the less well-off. William and I, using slides and visuals, presented the findings of the review. Outside on Horseguards Parade, military bands were rehearsing for the Trooping of the Colour. The Prime Minister wondered whether everyone could hear, and one of her obliging private secretaries suggested that someone could ask the bands to play more softly. As I enjoy brass bands I was only too happy to present our proposals to this musical accompaniment, and was pleased that the Prime Minister declined to interfere with it.

The reaction of colleagues to our proposals was overwhelmingly favourable. Keith Joseph supported the whole concept, saying, 'Accountability means paying and we need a system that relies less on heavy-handed intervention.' Nick Ridley questioned whether the uniform business rate was the best tax for the commercial sector. George Younger asserted yet again that we must do something because of the political pressure in Scotland and was adamant that, 'We must abandon the present rating system.' David Young, too, was in favour but warned against the tax being too regressive. Norman Fowler said that if we delayed, 'We will be criticized for inaction. Press ahead.' Nick Edwards made the useful point that, 'We must cushion the North/South divide and must not overdo the transfer of resources.' Grey Gowrie said it was a 'great plunge to move away from taxing property and should be done with very great care indeed'. Willie Whitelaw said that as the charge would carry all the weight of increased expenditure locally, 'It must be capable of fine-tuning and rebates will be necessary.' As a former Home Secretary he also saw no difficulty in having two registers – one for electors and one for chargepayers.

There were, however, some who were less keen on the community charge. Leon Brittan was very cool and tried to defend the 1982 changes which he had introduced as Chief Secretary. This was quite sharply dismissed by the Prime Minister. Peter Rees, as Chief Secretary, questioned the methods of registration and felt that the forecasts of gainers and losers spelt trouble.

The main opponent was Nigel Lawson, who had submitted a paper from the Treasury which recommended that the Government should 'take over complete responsibility for the financing and some aspects of the management of education'. Keith Joseph opposed this and defended local government's role in education. The Treasury maintained that if education came off the rates then councils could raise the revenue for all the rest of their services from a property tax. This would be kept up to date with an annual programme of rolling revaluation. The Treasury did recognize that 'better accountability requires a highly perceptible and therefore unpopular tax.' So the choice was between a high and painful property tax and the community charge.

The Treasury went on to condemn the idea of a flat-rate charge as 'unworkable and politically catastrophic. A radical reform of the rating system seems more attractive.' However, the Committee dismissed this proposal. I believe that one of the main Treasury concerns was that our proposals would give local government a tax which made it answerable to its electors and, as a consequence, Treasury control over public expenditure would be weakened.

The Treasury cannot bear a rival. It had always been against such proposals. The Prime Minister finally said to Nigel, 'I can see you are against the proposals. Is that right?' He nodded. Then she said, 'I can't have the Treasury being so negative'. But Nigel just ploughed on with his objections. Finally Margaret said, 'Very well. I will do one study and the Treasury can do its own. Then we can compare them and discuss it again'. However, the result of that meeting was to give William and me the task of working up a more detailed proposal for the community charge. It had to be less regressive and had to be introduced in a way that took into account the political difficulties.

During the summer and autumn we undertook further work on the proposals. On 23 September, at a meeting of E(LF), it was confirmed that the local domestic tax should be a combination of a residents charge and a property charge. We provided the first estimates of what this should be – the average charge would be £151, with lower bills in 70 per cent of authorities and higher bills in 30 per cent. In October we agreed that there should be a safety net limiting the effect of the transfer between areas – a subject which Leon Brittan, who represented a Yorkshire seat, was particularly keen on. Nick Edwards supported the proposal that the community charge should start at £50 per person in the first year and increase slowly. When E(LF) approved the Green Paper on 12 December 1985 it was on the basis of a charge consisting of a personal element, together with a property element to be phased out over ten years. George Younger, scorched by Scottish rates revaluation, was so keen on this change that he wanted to do away with the property element for Scotland immediately, saying, 'I wish to proceed separately in Scotland.'

We circulated figures as to what the community charge would be, on the basis of what we had agreed so far. The average would have been £150, and in only thirty-six authorities would it exceed £200, and in six authorities £300. I noted that Mole Valley's charge was likely to be £189 per head. In the event, in the first year it turned out to be £352.

I was summoned to Chequers on New Year's Eve to run through the Green Paper, *Paying for Local Government*, with the Prime Minister. I left her late in the day still, I suspect, regretting that the customary annual festivities were about to disrupt her workflow. One concession I had to make to Margaret was a statement which appeared in paragraph

5.28 of the Green Paper saying that we would retain selective rate-capping, at least until the rates were phased out. I stressed to her again that it was essential for the community charge to be introduced gradually. The new charge and the old rates had to run alongside each other for a time, as without this we would run the risk of asking too much too quickly and it could bring the whole system down.

I was due to present the Green Paper to the whole Cabinet on 9 January 1986, but by then the political world was convulsed by the Westland Affair. It was at that very meeting that Michael Heseltine resigned and walked out. I had previously been to see him to explain our proposals, because although his Department, the Ministry of Defence, had not really been involved Michael had been the Environment Secretary who addressed the rates problem earlier on. He was not at all enthusiastic about the Green Paper proposals, and if he had stayed for the discussion on 9 January I have no doubt that he would have expressed his objections. But as he had left before the discussion, he was fortuitously not bound by the doctrine of collective Cabinet responsibility. He was to make much of this in future years. Nigel Lawson had reluctantly come to agree with our proposals because of the retention of a rates element in the charge. From then on he should have supported the community charge, but I can't say he ever did with much enthusiasm.

On 28 January I finally published the Green Paper, *Paying for Local Government*, and made a statement to the House. Nigel was sitting next to me, and just before I stood up he said, 'This was Ted Heath's commitment. It will be her King Charles' head. You are the only Minister who can sell it.' The proposals were well received by the Tory backbenchers and I sat down to cheers. For some months William and I had been meeting Tory MPs and explaining to them the progress of our review. We had explained our proposals to the Backbench Environment Committee and to the Party's Local Government Committee, because we wanted as many people in the Party as possible to understand exactly what was being proposed.

The press reaction, too, was favourable. The *Daily Telegraph* said, 'Mr Baker's solution is quite the cleverest way yet devised of resolving this problem'. The *Financial Times* recorded that the Tories 'roared approval', and the *Daily Express* supported 'a bold and fair reform'.

The Fatal Mistakes of 1987 and 1988

In May 1986 I was moved from Environment to Education, and although I continued to be a member of E(LF) I was no longer the leading Minister. That fell to Nick Ridley, the new Environment Secretary. During 1986 and 1987 E(LF) had to decide upon the detailed implementation of the community charge. Much of the detail came from the initiative of Malcolm Rifkind, the new Scottish Secretary, because as the charge had to be levied first in Scotland in 1989 there had to be separate Scottish legislation. Important details such as the method of registration, the obligations of the head of household, the joint and several liability of couples who were living together but not married, and the sanctions for non-compliance, were all fashioned from Malcolm's sensible suggestions.

The Committee also agreed that certain groups, such as the mentally handicapped and elderly people living in homes and hospitals, should be exempt from the community charge. In addition, Norman Fowler did not want the charge to have a separate rebate scheme, but the Committee believed this was necessary. As Norman insisted that every charge-payer should pay at least 20 per cent, as they were to do in the case of rates, the basic level of income support had to be increased by £1.30 a week.

One mistake related to second homes, which it was proposed should bear two community charges. I argued that many people had bought such properties as pre-retirement homes and would resent the additional penalty. Willie Whitelaw, who was now presiding over E(LF), was worried about the position of richer people with two homes, since any concession would be seen as giving them a bonus. The compromise was to allow councils to charge less than two full community charges if they wished. None did so, and it was decided to include a 50 per cent discount for second homes as one of the features of the council tax in 1993.

A more serious mistake was made in October 1986 over students' liability to the charge. Malcolm Rifkind recommended that students should be liable for the full charge. As Education Secretary I argued that since students were largely dependent upon other people for their incomes and had two places of residence, at home and at college, they should be exempt. Moreover I foresaw that it was going to be exceptionally difficult to collect the community charge from resentful students who would become very vocal in any protests that would occur. But I got nowhere. Norman Tebbit, the Party Chairman, argued that it would be unfair to exempt students but to expect other young people in work to foot the bill. There were also problems about the definition of students.

So I then began to develop the idea of exempting everybody under the age of twenty-one. If we had done this then I believe we would have neutralized a great deal of the commotion involving younger people and the charge. The refusal to do this was the first of the three major mistakes in the implementation of the community charge.

By the time of the 1987 election the Government had been able to make many decisions about the details of the community charge. In the Manifesto we committed ourselves to saying:

We will legislate in the first Session of the new Parliament to abolish the unfair domestic rating system and replace rates with a fairer Community Charge. This will be a fixed rate charge for local services paid by those over the age of 18, except the mentally ill and elderly people living in homes and hospitals. The less well-off and students will not have to pay the full charge – but everyone will be aware of the costs as well as the benefits of the local services. This should encourage people to take a greater interest in the policies of their local council and getting value for money.

One of the intriguing aspects of the 1987 election was that the Labour Party never really focused upon the community charge as an issue. I understand Jack Cunningham, their Environment spokesman, wanted to do this but Neil Kinnock was persuaded against it by Peter Mandelson. The community charge was considered to be too difficult to understand, and the Labour Party moreover had no clear alternative policy. This was a major omission in the Labour Party's conference campaign.

Our second major, and crucial, mistake involved the removal of the transitional period and the end of dual-running. In September 1986 Nick Ridley, the Environment Secretary, raised for the first time the length of the transitional period and said he wanted to shorten it. The Green Paper had envisaged a transitional period of up to ten years – certainly for the inner-city councils and shorter for other councils – with the community charge being introduced slowly and the rates retained but withering on the vine. To me, this vision of 'dual-running' was an essential part of the introduction of the community charge. In the consultative document issued in July, after the 1987 election, the principle was confirmed. However, Nick recommended that the transitional period should come down from ten to three years and that the initial community charge should be set at £100 a year. John Major, then Chief Secretary, did not agree. At a meeting on 30 July 1987 he argued that the transitional period should be five years and the community charge should be introduced initially at £50 per person. I supported him very strongly indeed, but the Committee agreed to a transitional period of four years and an initial charge of £100.

By now, both the Scottish and Welsh Secretaries wanted to do away with the transitional period. This was not surprising, as the level of rates was much lower in Wales and Scotland, cushioned by the high amount of grant they received. Some English MPs had also come to believe that dual-running was a bad thing, for it meant two local taxes instead of one. Some local authorities, prompted by their officers, argued against the cost and complexity involved. None understood the acute political consequences of abandoning it.

At the 1987 Party Conference, in the debate on the community charge, several speakers argued for its immediate introduction and the abandonment of dual-running. In particular Gerry Malone, who had just lost his seat in Aberdeen South and knew little about the English rating system, said to loud cheers, 'Scrap dual-running.' He now says he was encouraged to do this not by Ministers in the Department of the Environment but by Leon Brittan. Nick Ridley, shortly before his death, strenuously denied that he had arranged this intervention. However, Nigel Lawson was in no doubt whatsoever, and he believes that the Conference debate was rigged.

After the debate, as Margaret left the platform she said to Nick, 'We'll have to look at this again.' It was a fatal mistake, because introducing the community charge in one swoop meant that chargepayers, many of whom had never paid any rates, would now have to bear the full weight of local authority excess spending in the first year. My heart sank, and in E(LF) I did what I could to reverse the decision, but the Conference debate was always quoted back at me. The Conference had not the slightest idea of the consequences of what they had done. They had the illusion that the community charge was so perfect that the nation was just thirsting to take it down in one gulp.

This misjudgement was reminiscent of the only other time in the Party's history when the Tory Party Conference actually made policy.

That was in the 1950s when a vote was carried against the platform committing the Tory Government to build 300,000 houses a year. It led to the building of the great social disasters of high-rise tower blocks and low-cost estates.

Subsequently, on 27 October, Nick submitted a proposal to E(LF) saying that as he had come under substantial pressure from local authorities and MPs to dispense with dual-running, and as this move had attracted great support from the Conservative Party Conference, he was now convinced that dual-running should come to an end. He recommended that councils should be given the right to opt out of dual-running, and it was thought that only about fourteen councils would want to retain it.

During 1987 and 1988 a group of Tory MPs opposed the community charge. In the second reading debate on the Community Charge Bill, on 16 December 1987, seventeen voted against and twelve abstained. The rebels looked to Michael Heseltine, but he left it to his friend, Michael Mates, to take up the running by proposing that the community charge should be banded. This would meet the troublesome and nagging argument about the fairness of the dustman having to pay the same as the Duke. The fact that they paid the same flat rate for TV licences and car tax seemed to be quite irrelevant. Banding, however, would have been very difficult to administer, and on closer inspection looked very much like the local income tax.

On 18 April 1988, the Mates amendment on banding was rejected by just twenty-five votes. Michael Mates was joined by the much subtler and more experienced backbench MP, George Young. He had been a Minister at the DoE when we were fashioning the community charge. When Margaret Thatcher unwisely dropped him from the Government I remember arguing with her to keep him. In November 1988, George was nominated at the *Spectator* Lunch as the Backbencher of the Year. In a witty speech he described one former Minister who had pledged to vote against the community charge and then reneged as 'someone who indulged in a great deal of self-abuse'.

During 1988, as Education Secretary, I persuaded E(LF) to provide an additional £100 million to help the London Boroughs for their takeover of educational responsibilities from ILEA in 1990. This would reduce the demand on the community chargepayers in London, but it was just a drop in the ocean.

During these months the Department of the Environment produced endless revised exemplifications of how all the changes were going to affect individual authorities. I charted the community charge forecasts for Mole Valley. In 1985 it was estimated at £143, in 1986 it was £189, and by the end of 1987, with the effect of withholding the full benefit of the safety net from which Mole Valley would eventually gain, it had reached £252.

The Treasury, whose spokesman was mainly John Major, was clear that we were heading into very serious difficulties. In July 1987, as Chief Secretary, John minuted the Committee saying that, 'We need a safety net (to help the North) and a transitional period (to help households) and a lower initial community charge (to help everyone).' How right he was.

The Underfunding of 1989

On 22 June 1989 there was a crucial meeting at Number 10 under the chairmanship of the Prime Minister when we discussed the level of the local government settlement for the year 1990–91 – the first year of the community charge. Our decision would have a material effect upon the level of the charge. The local authorities had made a bid for £35 billion, and I knew that this was over the top. Nick Ridley, the Environment Secretary, had proposed giving them £32.8 billion and I argued for £34.4 billion.

I had been encouraged to do this privately by Nick, who had rung me at the Department of Education after emerging from a meeting with Nigel at which Nick had been forced to agree to the lower figure. Over at the Department of the Environment Patrick Rock, who was Nick's Special Adviser, was in despair. He knew that Nick had pitched his demand too low, and that really he needed at least a further billion but had been talked out of it by the Prime Minister and the Chancellor. Nick had asked me if I could open up a second front by arguing for more money to underwrite teachers' pay, as this would have the effect of increasing the level of expenditure and the consequential grant to authorities.

At the Number 10 meeting I predicted that the amount proposed by the DoE would be totally inadequate and unrealistic. Local authorities were going to spend close to the figure that I proposed, and a lower figure would in no way influence their spending decisions. It would be sensible therefore to base their grants on the higher figure, or else the Government would be blamed for the ensuing high community charge. Unfortunately the Prime Minister supported Nick's official line. I began to sense a stitch-up by the Treasury when John Moore and Norman Fowler moved to his support, as did Ken Clarke, who vented his usual spleen on local authorities because he knew that if they got an increase in the summer then there would be less for his Health budget in the autumn. At this meeting the only support I had was from Peter Walker.

I thought the meeting was one of the most unrealistic and damaging I had ever attended. Preoccupied with public expenditure control, my colleagues simply could not see the political consequences of the decisions they were taking. The Prime Minister was convinced that unless we had a tough settlement, local government expenditure would go through the roof. Nigel Lawson so loathed the community charge that he was not going to spend a penny on it if he could help it. This was the third major strategic mistake in the introduction of the community charge. I warned my colleagues and commented in my diary, 'This was a bad political decision and it will blow up in our faces next year.'

On 12 July, at the Cabinet meeting to discuss public expenditure, I argued for more money to cushion the effect of the first year of the community charge, but again I lost.

The Community Charge at Central Office

Later in July 1989 I became Party Chairman, and the political impact of the community charge was soon borne in on me at Central Office. Barry Legg, the Chairman of Westminster Council's Finance Committee and later to be the MP for Milton Keynes, brought me the bad news in August that a house-to-house survey in Maida Vale showed that there were seven losers for every three gainers. This spelt electoral disaster. We asked Eric Pickles, the leader of Bradford Council who later became the MP for Brentwood and Ongar, to conduct a survey in Bradford to assess the effect of the community charge in certain wards. This also confirmed that we were on to a loser. I told the Prime Minister that we simply had to have some measures of relief.

I went over to see Chris Patten at the Department of the Environment with the bleak news of our surveys. He had been appointed Secretary of State for the Environment in July, in succession to Nick Ridley, and was straightaway plunged into handling the community charge. Chris, as Overseas Development Minister, had not been involved in any of the previous stages of the charge, for as he said, 'I had been travelling around Africa for three years.' He knew, however, that we had a major political problem on our hands and minuted the Prime Minister asking for £2.5 billion of extra assistance to reduce the burden of the community charge for many households in 1991. When Nigel Lawson read this he exploded and sent for Chris. At their meeting in Number 11 Chris was given a dressing-down by Nigel in front of a rather embarrassed Norman Lamont, who had by then become the Chief Secretary. Chris was told that asking for such a huge increase in money was not the way Cabinet Ministers, particularly new ones, behaved. All proposals involving such large sums had to be cleared with the Chancellor before being circulated to colleagues. So Chris was put in the corner and treated like a dunce.

To resolve this conflict a small committee consisting of Chris Patten, Nigel Lawson and Norman Lamont was set up under Geoffrey Howe's chairmanship. Geoffrey was no real help to Chris, who saw the amount he wanted for a transitional relief scheme whittled down from £2.5 billion to £2 billion, and finally to £1.3 billion to be spread over two years. Chris told both Margaret and Geoffrey that in his view this was totally inadequate.

Nigel Lawson has expressed astonishment that when Chris Patten took office he did not decide to abandon the community charge. Such a view carries naïvety to the point of complete absurdity, for the only person who can stop a new tax is the Chancellor of the Exchequer, if necessary by threatening his resignation. Moreover, the community charge had been worked on for three years; it had been a Manifesto commitment in 1987; it had been introduced in Scotland; and councils in England and Wales were producing registers of chargepayers. The whole local government settlement was based upon the new charge. Chris decided, quite rightly, that he had to continue with the community charge but make it as acceptable as possible. On the very day after his appointment in July, Chris defended the policy in the House of Commons. Indeed, during that autumn and winter the Labour Opposition never tabled a motion of censure on the community charge in the House of Commons, all debates being held on the Government's own proposals or orders. Chris and David Hunt had won the arguments in the House of Commons, but the country was a different manner.

David Hunt, the Minister for Local Government, announced the new transitional relief scheme at the Party Conference in October 1989. The intention was that no one in a two-person household would pay £3 a week more than they did for rates. However, this relief was based on the assumption that councils would increase their spending by only 3.8 per cent, a notional figure that was the basis for the fateful mistake of the July settlement for local government. Since councils were actually going to spend much more than this, many chargepayers who were hoping to pay only £3 extra would instead find themselves paying £7 a week extra. This meant £350 a year more for an individual, and £700 more for a couple. When David Hunt announced the relief scheme he was cheered to the rafters, but his audience had not appreciated that this scheme was related to notional rather than actual expenditure. By the spring of 1990 they knew the real position. Once again we had been scuppered by the Treasury, which had insisted on the use of unrealistic notional figures rather than likely actual figures.

Chris announced that if councils spent at their targeted level of expenditure the average community charge would be £278. But at Central Office we were receiving news from the constituencies that in many cases this figure was wildly optimistic. A steady stream of MPs came in to see me with tales of impending disaster. Douglas Hogg, then a Minister at the Home Office, and Ken Carlisle, the MP for Lincoln, told me in December 1989 that the charge in Lincolnshire would be 46 per cent higher than the average rates bill, and in Lincoln City 60 per cent higher. Douglas said that the settlement had been too tight and what was needed was an injection of £2 billion by way of extra grant, which should be paid for by not indexing income tax thresholds. I sent his advice on to Margaret.

On 10 January 1990 I minuted the Prime Minister privately with my assessment of how the charge was going to affect us in the May council elections. We controlled ninety-six councils and we faced losing at least twenty-two of them. I set out a strategy for fighting the campaign on the basis of some modest further relief. This strategy was to throw the blame for high community charges on high-spending Labour local authorities. I went on to advocate the abolition of the safety net contributions in the first year, as this would certainly help many Conservative areas. Croydon was contributing £59 per head to the safety net and John Moore, the former Cabinet Minister and one of the local MPs, told me that on this basis Croydon's community charge would be £330 and we would lose Croydon Council, as well as two Parliamentary seats at the next general election.

I also proposed that we channel more help to the chargepayer through improving the household relief scheme. We could also increase the grants paid to councils. If that were done towards the end of March, after councils had actually set their community charge, the relief would reduce the level of the charge and not simply go on higher spending. The problem was that every £1 billion of extra grant would only reduce individual community charge bills by about £30. We had created a monster whose appetite was insatiable.

Cranley Onslow, the Chairman of the 1922 Committee, was also under enormous pressure from colleagues. He pressed the Treasury to transfer funds from the income tax payer to the community charge payer. He wanted both the safety net to be withdrawn so that the benefits would flow through immediately, and extra grants which he did not believe would trigger extra spending. But not even the Chairman of the 1922 Committee was listened to.

On the Saturday in March after the loss of the Mid-Staffs by-election, I went to Chequers to have dinner with the Prime Minister, Tim Bell and Gordon Reece. No punches were pulled at this dinner about the unpopularity of the community charge, which by now was universally called the poll tax. Gordon Reece called it Margaret's 'ship money', and Tim Bell said that it needed about £3 billion to make it acceptable to the country.

But Margaret simply wasn't willing to concede this. She did agree, however, that I could say there would be a fundamental review of the community charge involving the crucial element of the Standard Spending Assessments for the following year. I felt that announcing a fundamental review in advance of the local elections was crucial if we were going to defuse public anger over the issue. It was far better to pre-empt the local election results rather than being seen to offer a grudging concession in the wake of a political setback.

On the Monday of the following week, Willie Whitelaw came to see me at Central Office. He said that the most dangerous time for Margaret would be following the May local government elections, and that in May, June and July he expected there would be calls for her to stand down. He also said that when he had left office Margaret had asked him to go and see her at any time when he felt she should stand down. In his judgement that time had not yet been reached, but Willie was clear that something had to be done about the community charge.

On the following day Peter Thorneycroft, another former Chairman, also came to see me and said that Margaret should stay but that the community charge was 'an unmitigated disaster, and something has to be done immediately to reduce its impact'. But the only concession that Chris Patten and I could wring out of our colleagues was that in the community charge rebate scheme the level of disregard of capital for rebate claimants would be increased from £8,000 to £16,000. This helped about 200,000 people.

On 5 April, I presented to the Cabinet our local government campaign with the theme, 'Conservative Councils Cost You Less'. Afterwards I stayed behind for a talk with Margaret, John Major, Norman Lamont, David Hunt and Chris Patten. At this meeting I again recommended the abolition of the safety net in the first year to allow northern areas to benefit from the changes in grants and to remove the contribution which southern areas would have to make. This meant that the community charge would be reduced in much of the South of England. That found no favour because it cost money, but Margaret did say, 'The community charge must come down.' She wanted universal capping for all authorities. At that stage both Chris and John opposed this, as they were appalled at the practical difficulties involved.

On 19 April the Cabinet discussed public expenditure and was told by John Major that the reserves for the current financial year 1990–91 had already been committed, with substantial provisions being made against the two following years. I said that even given these restraints, reducing the community charge had to be our first priority, ahead of income tax cuts or anything else.

There was a further meeting on 26 April when the Treasury moved a little closer to widespread capping, but Chris advocated the selective capping of up to fifty authorities. Malcolm Rifkind, who was now in the second year of the community charge in Scotland, urged us to change as little as possible, saying, 'Stick it out, the second year will be much easier.' Following this meeting Margaret's PPS, Mark Lennox-Boyd, went into the tea room at the House of Commons and gave the impression that we were going to introduce emergency legislation that summer to soften the community charge. Nothing like this had been agreed, and it was a naïve effort to help which just added to the general confusion in the Party.

I was spending a lot of time talking to backbenchers, and there were only a handful who wanted the community charge scrapped. Most wanted it softened, but they approved the general principle behind it, as did the public in opinion polls. I deal with the May local government elections in chapter 14, but their political effect was to show that the community charge was not a universal albatross and that with some sensible changes it could stay, and so, if she displayed flexibility, could Margaret.

There was a further meeting on 17 May, but again there was very little progress, though Margaret had added the idea that councils could be excused from capping if they held a local referendum to approve additional spending. She was really running a one-person campaign on all of this. In June I had several meetings with Chris Patten, since I thought his approach of a more generous settlement and some selective help was much better. Widespread capping, moreover, would need major legislation in the autumn and I feared this could bring back all the debates on banding as well as weaken the support for the charge. At one of the Monday lunches at Number 10, Michael Portillo reported the good news that the latest advice he had received was that the capping powers under existing legislation could be used more widely.

In June the Conservative leaders from the main Conservative councils came into Central Office and told me that they expected expenditure to increase the following year by 14.6 per cent. Clearly the message had just not got through to local government, and I told them their request was totally unreal and unacceptable. I read them the riot act and said that if this was to continue there would have to be capping of all authorities.

On 20 July Chris Patten's proposals for the community charge were agreed. It meant that the charge for 1991 would on average be £379, which was only a little more than 1990. Chris had achieved this by gaining a better level of government grant for the councils together with some selective capping. Relief was at last extended to second homes, bearing in mind the interests of clergymen, people in the armed services and retired people. The safety net protection to the North was extended for another year and transitional relief was increased so that no one should pay more than £2 extra a week in 1991. This was a much better package than Nick Ridley had negotiated a year earlier.

For over twelve months Chris Patten and I, as Environment Secretary and Party Chairman, had borne most of the burden of dealing with the financial and political consequences of the community charge. In the dramatic politics of 1989 and 1990 we had seen it through its first year, had shown that some councils could turn it to their political advantage, and proposed adjustments to set the charge at a more acceptable level. Reflecting on this period long after the 1992 Election, Chris Patten said

137

to me, 'The best political job I've ever done was to introduce the community charge and get it through that year.'

Epilogue

The political consequences of the community charge have been laid at my door, but the painful and voracious creature which emerged as the poll tax was not the proposal put forward in my original 1986 Green Paper. The community charge has been described as 'Thatcher's greatest blunder', and some attribute her downfall to it. I do not agree. The community charge certainly contributed to Margaret Thatcher's unpopularity in 1990, as it was seen as 'her tax'. But it was not the decisive and crucial factor that led to her downfall.

During the leadership election in November 1990, Michael Heseltine, followed by John Major and Douglas Hurd, pledged to undertake a fundamental review of the community charge. In March 1991 it fell to Michael Heseltine, as the new Environment Secretary, to deal the final death blow and to replace the community charge with a council tax based upon the capital value of property. Ironically, by then the community charge had ceased to be a major irritant because Norman Lamont had announced in his Budget what Nigel Lawson had adamantly refused to do since 1986 – funding the charge by providing £3 billion to reduce each chargepayer's bill by £140. As usual, if the Treasury had properly funded the introduction of the charge a year earlier, it would have cost less. VAT was increased to meet the cost, but there was no increase in local government expenditure – the great bogey of the Treasury. So in its second and final year the community charge had at last fallen to an acceptable level. In Mole Valley I had no letters of complaint at all about the charge in 1991. Chris Patten, then Party Chairman, privately believed that the community charge had become acceptable, but in public Ministers had to acknowledge that it was a Thatcherite totem pole which had to come down.

The Conservative Government's attempt to reform local government finance during 1986–90 will be analysed again and again to examine how the search for a better and more accountable local tax became so distorted as to end up a political nightmare.

Certain lessons can be drawn from this episode. First, if the Treasury is not prepared to support a new tax then that tax is doomed. Nigel Lawson as Chancellor of the Exchequer so disliked the whole concept of the community charge that the Treasury refused to provide the sums necessary to ease its introduction. Indeed by 1990, the year that the community charge was introduced, the Treasury had cut central Government grant as a percentage of local government income from 60 per cent in 1980 to only 44 per cent, the lowest proportion it was to reach. The following year, central Government grant leapt to 70 per cent. By contrast, when the Treasury introduced the independent tax-ation of wives, it provided over £2 billion to cushion the transfer, and the reform of the interaction of National Insurance contributions and tax thresholds cost several billion pounds more.

Second, a flat-rate charge is only acceptable if it is set at a reasonable amount. Ministers started with the belief that the average community charge would be around £150, but the actual figure turned out to be more than double this. Serious mistakes were made in 1987, 1988 and 1989, and Ministers were beguiled with the all too optimistic projections which emerged from the Department of the Environment.

Third, a fundamental or indeed revolutionary change to the basis of local taxation needs to be introduced slowly. The abandonment of dual-running in 1987 was the first and most serious mistake. The Tories would have been wiser to have adopted the Fabian concept of 'the inevitability of gradualness'.

The introduction of the community charge was a bold attempt to undertake the reform of local government finance. However, we botched its introduction and have now retreated to an outdated system of property values which bears little relation to the nature of modern local government. Over the years I believe the council tax will bring back many of the problems of the old rating system. There will have to be the regular revaluations which governments came to shirk. There will be demands for higher government grants to reduce the level of the tax as local government expenditure grows. A future government will again have to address the problems of finding a tax that makes local authorities truly accountable by apportioning spending fairly among local electors.

In the great debate about the community charge it is interesting to recall the enthusiastic support for it expressed by so many Ministers. Michael Howard – who, as a distinguished barrister, is used to marshal-ling powerful arguments for his case – said, 'It is only the community charge which measures up to the criteria of fairness and accountability.' In 1988 he assured the Young Conservatives that, 'Our Bill to reform the financing of local government is as important in its own way as the great reform bills of the nineteenth century. The community charge is desperately needed.'

David Hunt told the Conservative Party Conference in 1989, 'Under our new system Conservative councillors and council candidates will have the instrument they need and deserve – a cast-iron link between the bills their voters pay and the amount their council spends ... We all know that the community charge will represent a much fairer and better way of paying for local government.' In 1990, he triumphantly predicted, 'The local community charge is a winner.'

Michael Portillo, who will be in the forefront of politics and will play a major part in any future debate on local government finance, said as Local Government Minister, 'The community charge is an election winner ... The community charge is the most potent weapon ever put into the hands of ordinary voters to defeat incompetent and malign Labour councils.'

All these arguments are as valid today as they were at the time we introduced the idea of the community charge.

CHAPTER 7

Environment Secretary 1985–86

*The Public Expenditure Round of 1985 – Housing, the
Inner Cities and the Environment – Chernobyl – Water
Privatization – Handing over to Nick Ridley*

While I was dealing with the crises over Liverpool, the GLC and local government finance, I had been promoted from being Minister of State to Secretary of State at the Department. On 2 September 1985, Mary and I were in Perthshire at Loch Rannoch when my Private Secretary rang to say that Patrick Jenkin had been asked to go to Number 10 at ten o'clock. Robin Butler, Margaret's Private Secretary, then telephoned through at 10.20 a.m. and said that Patrick was leaving the Government and I was to be offered his post as Secretary of State. The Prime Minister wanted to know my views on her suggestions for my ministerial team: William Waldegrave was to be promoted to do my former job at Local Government; John Patten, who was holidaying in Villefranche, to replace Ian Gow at Housing; and Angela Rumbold and Dick Tracey to join me as Parliamentary Under-Secretaries. I was happy to have such a strong team.

I was dressed for climbing Schiehallion, but was told to come to Number 10 at once. This meant driving immediately to Edinburgh for the shuttle, so when I arrived at Downing Street I was still in my tweeds and Barbour. Margaret said, 'I want you to take over from Patrick, no one is better suited. Patrick has taken it so well.' We had a short discussion about policy and I told her that my initial reaction was to make William Waldegrave responsible also for 'green' matters, as we needed a 'green' Minister to deal with the growing complexity and higher profile of environmental issues. I returned that night to Scotland and on the following day I did indeed climb Schiehallion, my first Munro, over 3,000 feet and Scotland's most beautiful mountain.

Being promoted within the same Department makes life much easier since one is familiar with the issues and the team of officials, but the workload of a Secretary of State is much greater. I was now a member of the Cabinet, and therefore involved in wider policy discussions that went beyond my own Department. At my first Cabinet meeting I was given a seating plan by Sir Robert Armstrong and took my place at the end of the Cabinet table. With each reshuffle I moved closer to the middle.

Patrick had appointed Terry Heiser as the new Permanent Secretary. Terry was something of a maverick among the mandarins. He had left school at sixteen but had climbed his way up through the Department, serving Tony Crosland, Peter Shore, Michael Heseltine and later Nick Ridley. He was wily and very adept at getting the Department's views through to the rest of Whitehall. The Department was a conglomerate based on the former Ministry of Housing and Local Government, and the Ministry of Public Buildings and Works. Its mixed bag of high-profile issues ranged from local taxation and local government to planning, rivers, wildlife protection, environmental and atmospheric pollution, the water industry, the nation's architectural heritage, sport, mineral extraction, and the building industry. It was far too large, and I later recommended that two of these responsibilities – sport and heritage – should be transferred to a new Department of National Heritage.

As Environment Secretary I had four main issues on my agenda. First, the reform of local government finance. Second, to formulate a coherent environmental policy. Third, to sustain the regeneration of urban areas. Fourth, the privatization of water.

The Public Expenditure Round of 1985

One of the first things I had to settle as Environment Secretary in 1985 was the Department's Public Expenditure bid for the coming year. This had of course been submitted by Patrick Jenkin after discussion with his Ministers. We had all agreed to ask for an increase of £600 million for public sector housing. Overall, this programme had been reduced by 49 per cent since 1979. The Department gave to each local authority annually a capital allocation to cover the cost of new building, maintenance and repairs. In 1984–85 this amounted to £1,850 million. For 1986–87 the Treasury wanted me to accept £1,200 million. They were oblivious to the fact that I would soon have to publish a report on public sector housing which revealed that the backlog of repairs amounted to £20 billion. The extra sums that I was arguing for would eliminate the backlog within ten years. The report was political dynamite, as homelessness was increasing by 20,000 a year and about 3,000 people were going into bed-and-breakfast accommodation.

I tried to reach a settlement with the Chief Secretary, John Mac-Gregor, but we were miles apart. So I had to appear before the Star Chamber set up by the Prime Minister to resolve disputes between spending Ministers and the Treasury. This august body, drawn from the Cabinet, was presided over by Willie Whitelaw and had as its members Norman Tebbit, Leon Brittan, John Biffen and Nicholas Edwards. On the afternoon of 24 October I went to my third meeting in Willie Whitelaw's room in the House of Lords. I sat at the end of a long table facing Willie with the rest of the Court seated on either side. Willie straightaway offered an increase of £100 million for 1986–87 and £200 million in each succeeding year. That was quite impossible, for it meant I would have had to acknowledge publicly that the housing programme would be cut by about £400 million. Then the others piled in. Leon acted as the prosecuting barrister – sharp, sarcastic, critical, forensic stuff which only demonstrated that he had a capacity unrivalled in British politics to master the facts and ignore the politics. Norman Tebbit exhibited his least attractive characteristics – bullying and abrasive, openly critical of public sector housing. At one stage I lost my temper with him, which was unusual in Star Chamber, and I said, 'I will not accept your argument nor will any of my Ministers'. There was a deathly pause and Nick Edwards tried to smooth things over. John Biffen was the most sympathetic and tried to explore ways of bridging the gap. Willie Whitelaw tried to browbeat me by saying that the Cabinet 'could cut their generous offer or even withdraw it altogether'.

Norman Tebbit sent me a note saying, 'Do remember for your own sake that it is dangerous to arrive in Cabinet as a residual whose programme must be squeezed to meet the overall target. I can assure you that your 21 colleagues will be unlikely to cut their programmes to bail you out.' I was subjected to these arguments from colleagues for about an hour and a half. Enormous moral pressure was brought to bear upon me, particularly as I was the newest member of the Cabinet and there was some element of 'teaching Baker a lesson' from the start. I refused to accept their proposals.

Following this meeting I flew to the United States in order to open the 'Treasure Houses of Britain' Exhibition in Washington, as the Environment Secretary was also responsible for the historic heritage of our country. While I was there William Waldegrave rang me to report that he had been seen by John Wakeham, the Chief Whip, who had sounded him out as to how strongly he supported me. William had fully backed me, and I told him to tell John that I was quite determined to carry on with my case.

I returned from America on 4 November, and went to see Willie in his room in the Privy Council office, where John Wakeham was sitting with him. Willie said, 'You must settle outside Cabinet'. This was his principal objective, and he increased his previous offer by £100 million. But as I pointed out this was still only an increase of £16 million on the existing level. My colleagues had only shifted the furniture around the house, without increasing either the furniture or the size of the house by very much. After about an hour's discussion Willie accepted this argument and sought to offer me £170 million. It was a very complicated set of figures, because it involved not just an agreement on the capital sum but also the amount of borrowing which we could allocate to local authorities, and this again was a different figure. Throughout all these discussions I felt that Willie was not wholly familiar with the details, but he knew enough about them to know where the bottom line was, and that was what the Treasury expected him to deliver.

At 3.15 p.m. on 5 November I was again summoned to the Star Chamber. I had seen John Wakeham, the Chief Whip, half an hour earlier to confirm my determination. I also asked to see the Prime Minister, who refused as she was not prepared to act as an appeal court while Star Chamber was sitting. This time my colleagues offered an increase of £200 million gross for capital but nothing for borrowing allocations, and this after an hour and a half of discussion. Again I could not accept. I had to be very careful not to lose my temper afresh when Norman Tebbit and Leon Brittan were offensive once again. I was asked for my bottom line, and I replied it was £200 million for capital and £400 million for allocations. I was made to feel isolated and utterly irresponsible for taking this position.

That night we all went to dinner at Number 10 for the Eve of Session Dinner before the Queen's speech. I was now the only Minister who had not settled. Several friends, like David Young, said I should settle. Douglas Hurd asked for a brief so that he could support me if it came to a Cabinet dispute. Peter Walker resolutely supported the line I was taking. Margaret was distinctly cool towards me, and after dinner as I passed a group with her, the Chancellor and Willie Whitelaw, I heard Margaret saying, 'So I must see him.' By this time the press were aware of the dispute, and there had been a very strong leader in the *Daily Mail* fully supporting the line that I was taking. But this was just brushed aside by Willie. Whilst at Number 10 I spoke to John MacGregor in the little room on the ground floor next to the Cabinet Room. I told him my final position. We agreed to meet at 9.30 a.m. the next day at the Treasury.

At that meeting John said he was prepared to move the Treasury's position and I said I was prepared to accept £200 million for capital and £300 million for borrowing allocations. We agreed on these figures. I saw the Prime Minister later that day, after she had responded to the Queen's speech. It had not been one of her best speeches. She was very cool, and rebuked me by saying, 'We are a team, Kenneth.' She then said she was going to criticize the report on council house renovations I was about to publish. I asked her not to do this because it would be politically foolish. Although we were successfully selling council houses there was a large number still left in the public sector and whose condition was deteriorating. I wasn't prepared to give an inch on the need for these repairs. My job was to make sure that colleagues understood the housing crisis facing the country, and I was not going to run away from it.

I don't believe that if I had seen Margaret separately I would have got a penny more. She was as unsympathetic to the cause as was Norman Tebbit. I was amazed by the whole episode, which illustrated the crude system of picking off one Minister after another. Ministers collectively were simply not allowed to discuss an overall strategy or to determine priorities as between one area of expenditure and another. All that mattered was that the expenditure level pushed through Cabinet the previous July was met at all costs. There was no real balancing of political priorities. The issue became not the priorities of spending but the importance of protecting the Chancellor's position. I was surprised at the sheer clumsiness of it all. The whole system seemed based upon public school bullying and parading the awkward soldier in front of the regimental colonel.

Two days later, Peter Davies, my Political Adviser, bumped into Bernard Ingham, the Prime Minister's Press Secretary, at a dinner in Brooks's Club, where Peter was asked, 'Why is Ken feeding black propaganda to the press?' Peter replied he thought that was more in Bernard's department, but Bernard had the last word when he said darkly, 'Ken has bridges to build with the Prime Minister and Willie Whitelaw'.

Other friends congratulated me afterwards. Apparently John

Wakeham told Gordon Reece that I had played it brilliantly, as I had got more than anyone expected by going to Star Chamber. Well, that might have been one assessment but it seemed a hollow victory to me. I am quite sure the whole episode confirmed in my colleagues' minds that I was a natural big spender. Indeed the Treasury coined a phrase about my stance based upon the slogan of the John Lewis stores – 'Kenneth was never knowingly underbid.' This gave a false impression, but I did not lose any sleep over it.

Housing, the Inner Cities and the Environment

One of the consequences of this settlement was that the Urban Programme directed at the inner cities had to be cut back from £338 million to £317 million for 1986–87. I was very disappointed with this, because as Local Government Minister since 1984 I had devoted a lot of energy and commitment to help regenerate the run-down parts of our cities. As I had fought a London East End seat and represented two inner London Parliamentary seats I had, perhaps more than most of my colleagues, seen at first hand the economic and social problems of urban decay.

In 1985 I therefore decided to transfer £400 million of grant from the Shires to the inner cities. There was a protest vote in the House of Commons in February 1986 and fifty Tory MPs voted against my announcement, led by Jim Prior, Francis Pym and Ian Gilmour. I thought it was extraordinary that these three former Cabinet Ministers who had been foremost in criticism of the Thatcher Government's 'heartlessness' should behave in this way. When it came to it they voted for their own Shires rather than for the wider interest they espoused.

David Young and I were very concerned about the employment consequences of inner-city decline, and during the winter of 1985–86 we worked on several measures to mitigate this. Central Government could only give urban grants to local authorities, some of which used them sensibly to create a better environment or more attractive areas for local businesses, but others spent the grants on their latest fads. So we introduced legislation to pay grants direct to private developers of any future city projects and committed £20 million for this. At the same time we increased to 70 per cent the discount for people buying their council homes, since home ownership was one of the best ways to improve a housing estate.

We also wanted to make market forces work more effectively, and

1 My grandparents, Margaret Desmond and Ted Baker, on their
wedding day

2 My parents, Amanda Harries and Wilfred Baker, on their wedding day,
1926

3 Riding my first hobby-horse

4 A brisk walk to the beach at Bournemouth in 1937 – my father, mother,
sister Dodie and me

5 Celebrating Victory 1945 – Holy Trinity School, Southport. I am third from the left
6 National Service – The Mortar Instructor silent upon a peak in Libya, 1954

7 Secretary of the Oxford Union – with future Tory MPs Alan Haselhurst,
Andrew Rowe, Tony Newton and Labour's Tony Crosland

8 Campaigning with Mary and our two daughters, 1970

9 The Lord Chancellor, Quintin Hailsham, enjoying a joke made by his successor during the St Marylebone by-election, 1970

10 Margaret Thatcher's first official engagement as leader of the Conservative Party in March 1975 was to plant a lime tree in my constituency. Some unkindly said that she was burying Ted.   11 But Ted wouldn't lie down – 1977

12 Exploring the world of Information Technology with my son, and our cat

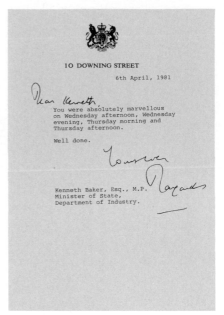

13 Launching 'Micros in Schools', 1981
14 The thanks of a demanding mistress for the long Parliamentary session
on the 1981 British Telecom Bill which paved the way for BT's privatization

15 The Wizard of Information Technology, 1983

16 Blue Ken versus Red Ken – debating the abolition of the GLC,
October 1984, as Minister for Local Government

17 Laying the foundation of the Salford Quays Development in Manchester,
April 1986, as Secretary of State for the Environment

"It's madness! It looks like this Government is prepared to sell off everything but the kitchen sink!"

18 Announcing the privatization of the Water Industry, February 1986

"It's galling having to admit it, but a little wetness has its uses!"

19 This cartoon was presented to me by Sir George Young and the other
Ministers at the Department of the Environment when I moved to
Education in May 1986

therefore introduced a simplified planning zone for the inner cities. The idea was to cut out the red tape and speed up the actual process of development. This idea had emerged from a group of major developers including John Sainsbury, Clifford Chetwood of Wimpeys, and Idris Pearce of Richard Ellis, who had been called together by the Prime Minister and met every six months at Number 10 under her chairmanship. They reviewed the whole planning system to find ways of reducing the bureaucracy and the time taken in approving major developments. This group was a goad to the Department of Environment, and it was a very clever way for the Prime Minister to keep her eye on an area where she suspected things were not going well. She wanted to spur her Ministers to be more vigorous in their pursuit of the Thatcherite revolution.

In 1985 the Government had been taken to task by a Commission appointed by the Archbishop of Canterbury to look into inner-city issues. Its Report, called *Faith in the City*, was dismissed by one Minister, who was never identified, as 'Marxist theology', for it was certainly more secular than spiritual and advocated a substantial increase in financial support for local authorities. But I knew it was not just a question of more money for the inner cities. It was important that resources were properly targeted, because more money for the inner cities in the 1960s and 1970s had simply produced the vast impersonal council estates which caused so many of our present problems. I met Robert Runcie, the Archbishop of Canterbury, and David Sheppard, the Bishop of Liverpool, to defuse the resulting brouhaha. I encouraged the Church of England to involve itself in small-scale community developments like housing cooperatives within deprived city areas. The vicar with an inner-city parish, in my view, needed to be much more than just another social worker in clerical garb. The problem with this Report was that the whole philosophy behind it seemed too collectivist and failed to recognize the valuable role of individuals in improving their own communities.

It was while at the Department of Environment that I became personally involved in working against drug abuse. On behalf of the Department I presented a grant to the YMCA in South Shields to set up a unit helping glue sniffers overcome their addiction. I decided to raise money personally to help in the fight against this appalling problem and in 1986 organized a sponsored walk in the Peak District which raised £5,000 to help young people in the North East. On a later visit to

Liverpool I met SHADO (Self Help Against Drugs Organization), an advisory service run by the determined Ann Milling, and based in Croxteth where the problem was not glue sniffing but heroin addiction. Since that time Mary and I have organized an annual sponsored walk which now raises £50,000 for SHADO. Until this year the walks were run by Father Paul Thompson, who had a genius for friendship, but alas he died all too young in March 1993.

We take on our walks some of the young recovering addicts and I have learnt a great deal from them about the dangers and temptations of addiction and how difficult it is to kick the habit. Mary and I have enjoyed getting involved with all the helpers, supporters and young recovering addicts and have been very glad to make some personal contribution to helping deal with this serious problem.

It was essential that we should do everything possible to use the large amount of derelict land in our cities for housing, since this would have the additional benefit of taking pressure for new building off some of the undeveloped country areas. The Department was always pressing me to increase the amount of housing built in the South-East, but all the delegations I received from MPs in Berkshire, Hampshire and Kent strongly opposed any further urban sprawl. I told the House Builders Federation in 1986 to 'think small', as we were ruling out the sort of large new settlements which Michael Heseltine had floated in the early 1980s. He had favoured the building of a new town, nicknamed 'Heseltown', somewhere in North Hampshire. I urged the builders to make the most of in-filling both in cities and country towns and also to seek out development land in urban areas.

The Green Belt has been one of the most successful developments in English planning this century, but it has not prevented urban sprawl stretching out virtually all the way from London to Brighton or from London to Reading. However, it did manage to check the further development of Oxford, which I visited with the two local Members of Parliament, John Patten and Steve Norris. I stood on Magdalen Bridge and announced strict limits on any further developments in the city of Oxford. I thought it was important to retain Oxford's unique character, and this meant stopping the ever-growing urban development to the north and south.

Despite the fact that environmental issues were now coming to the forefront in every political debate, Margaret was at that time very cool about 'green' policies, which she considered to be expensive and not absolutely necessary. Two years earlier, in May 1984, when I was still an Industry Minister, I had attended a Sunday seminar at Chequers about acid rain. The advice given by the scientists, including Herman Bondi, was very clear: acid rain was caused by emissions of carbon dioxide and nitric oxide from power stations and vehicles, and we should do something about it. The Prime Minister was very concerned about the cost of adding desulphurization plants to power stations, saying, 'We cannot afford them.' Walter Marshall, head of the Central Electricity Generating Board and then very much in favour with Margaret, since he had helped her defeat the miners' strike, used the scientists' analysis to argue for greater investment in nuclear power stations which, he claimed, were more environmentally acceptable.

I had been invited to this seminar, no doubt in the hope that I would say that industry could not bear the costs, but if that was the case Margaret must have been disappointed. It was clear to me that we would soon have to put policies in place to deal with the problems of acid rain and atmospheric pollution. Margaret was anxious to explore if there were other reasons to explain why trees were dying in Scandinavia, but no convincing reasons could be found.

I now asked William Waldegrave, who I knew shared my attitudes, to take responsibility for the development of environmental policies. Environmental issues had become more dominant, particularly among young voters, and in the 1986 European elections the Green Party made their most significant breakthrough. Margaret was a late convert to the importance of these environmental issues, but once she had been persuaded she put her stamp of authority on them. In September 1988 I was present at the dinner of the Royal Society held in the Fishmongers' Hall when Margaret delivered her first major speech on the environment and committed the Government to a conservation policy. William Waldegrave was sitting just one seat away from me, and after Margaret sat down he whispered to me, 'I never thought I'd live to hear it.'

At the beginning of 1986, Peter Davies, my Political Adviser, decided to leave the Environment Department to join the Conservative Research Department and thereafter fight a Parliamentary seat. He was a considerable loss, both as a friend and as a reliable source of astute advice. I chose as his replacement Tony Kerpel, who had been Leader of the Conservatives on Camden Council. He proved to be an outstanding Political Adviser.

In America, a Senator has a staff of twenty, and in Europe a

Commissioner can appoint his own personal Cabinet to expand his political presence. But in Britain the great tradition of the talented amateur prevails. Each Cabinet Minister is allowed one Special Adviser, whose appointment has to be confirmed by the Prime Minister. It is a unique and special relationship, requiring mutual respect, discretion and loyalty. Although they rank as temporary civil servants, Special Advisers alone in a Department handle Party political issues and their job disappears with their Minister.

In addition to being a councillor, Tony had been National Chairman of the Young Conservatives, and a Parliamentary candidate, and therefore brought a great deal of political experience to his new post. He was the shrewdest of all the Whitehall Political Advisers and we became close friends. This, together with the fact that we saw eye to eye on nearly all issues, enabled him to speak for my views when journalists could not speak with me directly.

Tony was at my side for six years from 1986 to 1992, winning the respect of civil servants and Party officials as he followed me from Department to Department, and fighting two General Election campaigns with me as I criss-crossed the country. He has given me a lot of sound advice. The only advice I gave him in return was initially to suggest that his writing read too much like a leader for the *Times*. In political speeches to Conferences, one rarely wants sentences to extend over one line, occasionally over two, but never over three.

In 1989, Tony learnt that he had cancer, and underwent surgery followed by a year of chemotherapy. I gave him all my support during this time, and with his great and determined spirit he pulled through, and we were able to resume our active political partnership again.

Chernobyl

In April and May of 1986 it fell to me as Environment Secretary to cope with the political as well as the radioactive fallout from the worst environmental disaster to affect Europe – the meltdown of a Soviet nuclear reactor at Chernobyl, in the Ukraine. Unlike most disasters, which become apparent as soon as they occur, this one crept more slowly into European consciousness because of the Soviet Government's obsessive secrecy, which prevented official news of the accident being released. The first evidence of something having gone wrong came from Finland and Sweden, where monitoring revealed abnormal amounts of radioactive fallout in the atmosphere. The news gradually emerged from a reluctant Soviet Government that on 26 April there had been a terrible accident at the Chernobyl nuclear power station. A fire had destroyed buildings and released large amounts of radioactivity over the surrounding area and into the atmosphere. Wind patterns were now carrying this over western and northern Europe.

Although immediate concern in Britain had been for the people of the Ukraine and Byelorussia, and the safety of some 100 British students and teachers in the Kiev and Minsk areas, alarm soon focused on how we in Britain would be affected. For understandable reasons the public began to get very worried, for there are few things more emotionally charged than anxieties about radioactive fallout, a threat which one cannot see, hear or feel, yet one that is all-pervasive and potentially fatal. Two months earlier, I had to deal with a small leak of radioactive material from Sellafield, which was not serious, though that did not prevent the European Parliament voting to close down the plant. But Chernobyl was on a quite different scale, and something like panic began to spread over the country.

The first instinct of a Government on such occasions is to want more information. The National Radiological Protection Board in Oxford and Glasgow, and the Central Electricity Generating Board power stations, which all had their own monitoring equipment, began extensive monitoring of the United Kingdom. This indicated no immediate increase in radioactivity. There was further monitoring by the United Kingdom Atomic Energy Authority, and the Ministry of Agriculture, Fisheries and Food, which had collecting posts on the east coast and also on high-rainfall areas in North Wales. Milk samples and water samples were taken, and we monitored certain foodstuffs, and in particular sheep in North Wales and Cumbria which had been grazing on high hills affected by rain contaminated with radioactivity. It was obviously important that we knew as soon as possible which foods might be safe or unsafe for human consumption, in order to take the necessary precautions or give reassurances to a worried population.

However, the other information we required was not readily forthcoming. This was information from the Soviet Government itself about the extent of the disaster at Chernobyl and also whether the radioactivity had been contained or was continuing to pose a threat to Europe. American satellite reconnaissance photographs had seemed to indicate that a second reactor was on fire. If so, this was disastrous news. I would have expected that since the Government, through the Ministry of Defence and the Foreign Office, had access to intelligence information gained from satellite surveillance this question could have been clarified. To my irritation it was not. Instead we relied, like everyone else, on news reports and copy filed from journalists in the Soviet Union. I remember one morning, shortly after the crisis broke, the spectacle of each of my Ministers standing at my table reading a different newspaper in order to ascertain from journalists' reports the sort of information we should have been getting through the Government's own sources.

The second instinct of a Government on such occasions is to rush to its own defences. Since we too had a nuclear power programme it was inevitable that one of the first questions asked was 'Could it happen here?' The answer we were able to give was that the Chernobyl reactors were graphite-moderated, natural water-cooled reactors of a hybrid type for which there was no equivalent in the West. Furthermore, we built nuclear power stations to much higher construction and safety standards than did the Soviets. The British nuclear energy industry had had a good safety record over the previous twenty-five years, and so the awkward question of whether a similar disaster could happen in Britain never really became a major issue of public debate.

What soon became clear in the handling of the Chernobyl emergency was the complete lack of coordination between Government Departments. Several Departments and their Ministers had interests in the various aspects of the crisis, including Michael Jopling and John Gummer at Agriculture, Peter Walker the Energy Secretary, Nick Edwards the Welsh Secretary, George Younger the Scottish Secretary, and myself as Environment Secretary. The Ministry of Agriculture, the Home Office and the Department of the Environment all had monitoring capabilities. The problem was that the scientists engaged in each of these monitoring exercises tended to produce contradictory readings. This presented considerable difficulties, because it meant individual Ministers giving different assessments to the House of Commons.

I remember on one occasion listening to the phone call as William Waldegrave argued with John Gummer over different figures for radiation levels which our respective Departments were going to put out. Ministers quickly had to become acquainted with the minutiae of radiation measurement. The unit of radioactive decay was called a becquerel, and when these went above a certain level in foodstuffs, it meant that action had to be taken. The *Guardian*, in what I assume was an intentionally funny misprint, referred to 'becquerels' as 'buggeralls'. It was good to know that for some, even a radioactive cloud had a humorous lining.

I had expected that Willie Whitelaw, the Deputy Prime Minister, would coordinate all Ministers' actions, and I was therefore surprised that not only did he not do this but also that there was no calling together of the specially formed crisis committee in the Cabinet Office.

On Thursday 1 May, two days after I had made my first short statement to the House on the dangers of the fallout from Chernobyl, I was due to speak to an evening meeting at the Ryedale by-election in Yorkshire. I had intended to speak about our plans to reform local government finance, but Tony Kerpel urged me instead to pick up the leading role in handling the Chernobyl crisis by calling for the International Atomic Energy Agency to hold a full international investigation into the design, operating conditions and circumstances of the Chernobyl accident. My Private Secretary, Robin Young, was horrified by this idea. He felt that since responsibility for nuclear matters was shared between several Departments, there were risks in me as Environment Secretary being seen as the leading minister. However, I agreed with Tony that it would look rather strange if at a time when only one story was dominating the news, a story in which I had Departmental responsibilities, I did not make any reference to the issue. We swiftly drafted my speech, and the draft immediately fell foul of both Peter Walker and Geoffrey Howe.

It is a Whitehall convention that when a Minister speaks on an issue which impinges on another Minister's responsibilities then that speech or statement has to be cleared by the other Department. Peter, as Energy Secretary and therefore responsible for nuclear power, objected to a reference which said, 'We know that accidents can happen – it would be dishonest to pretend otherwise – but we do everything we can to ensure that what happened at Chernobyl cannot happen here.' Deleting this was in the honourable tradition of saying the *Titanic* was unsinkable.

Geoffrey Howe, on behalf of the Foreign Office, insisted on the deletion of: 'This paranoid obsession with secrecy has become a pattern of Soviet Government conduct so deeply ingrained that even a change of leadership has failed to alter this attitude . . . Offers of missile cuts and on-site inspections in the arms controls field contrast starkly with the failure of the Soviet Government to alert their international neighbours to the radioactive clouds heading their way.' Removing these justified rebukes for fear of offending Soviet sensibilities about 'glasnost' was Geoffrey Howe in Noël Coward mode playing 'Don't let's be beastly to the Soviets'.

My speech, now somewhat shorter, received front-page coverage in the *Times*, and Margaret immediately summoned me to Number 10, where she asked me to take charge of coordinating Government responses to the crisis. On 6 May I made a statement to the House setting out the latest information the Government had through its monitoring channels, so that we could help calm mounting fears. Michael Jopling believed that the levels of radiation in milk were 'miles below the safe limit' even for children, so I decided to ask three rhetorical questions at the dispatch box. These were: 'Is it safe to drink milk? Yes. Is it safe to drink water? Yes. Is it necessary for children to take iodine tablets? No.'

However, this situation was obviously subject to change, and indeed bad weather and storms over Scotland brought levels of radiation to the point where people were advised not to drink fresh water. Further precipitation in Wales meant that many sheep grazing there had absorbed significant levels of radioactivity – indeed the shadow of Chernobyl still hangs over those areas worst affected at the time. In the short term my statement to the House served to calm things down and the crisis passed. It was very clear, however, that the Government machinery to cope with such a crisis was woefully inadequate. Had a similar disaster occurred at a nuclear reactor in northern France, giving us far less warning time and with a radioactive plume affecting the heavily populated South and South-East of England, the effects could have been incalculable. William Waldegrave sent an excellent confidential memorandum to the Prime Minister about the future handling of any similar crisis. Appropriate machinery for handling such an eventuality has, I believe, been set up by the Cabinet Office.

One of the major consequences of Chernobyl was to place a question mark over the case for nuclear power stations. The Government had stoutly defended the economic and environmental case for nuclear power over some years. In particular we had pointed to France, which had a major programme of building and operating nuclear power stations without any incident because these had been properly managed. The failure of Chernobyl was as much a failure of Soviet management as of Soviet technology. When the Cabinet discussed Chernobyl that week,

Norman Tebbit sent me a note after I had reported. He wrote, 'Then we must blame Communism, not nuclear energy for the disaster.' This rather overlooked the lesson of the Three Mile Island incident, when an American nuclear power station had narrowly escaped disaster.

Water Privatization

Following the successful sale of British Telecom, and Cable and Wireless, in which I had been involved as Industry Minister, the Government had also decided to privatize British Airways, British Gas and British Leyland. Now at Environment I found myself responsible for yet another nationalized industry – state-owned water, which was composed of large regional water boards and a clutch of smaller privately owned water companies.

As the Minister for Local Government in 1985 I had explored ways in which this industry could be privatized because I wanted it to benefit from being run by commercial managers rather than public servants. Some of the water companies themselves wanted the freedom to expand their service activities overseas, which was denied to them as a state-owned industry. Privatization would also allow the new water companies to go to the private market, rather than the taxpayer, to seek finance for their capital demands, which were immense. Recent history had shown that in every round of public expenditure cuts the first thing offered up to the Treasury was the capital programme of the water industry. In 1985 this had led the Government to intervene and insist that Thames Water should increase its charges above that which the Authority thought necessary to maintain its investment programme. It was a very unhappy relationship.

However, the Water Authorities were 'large natural monopolies', and we could not encourage alternative competitive supplies of water to individual households. Authorities would, however, through their performance, be able to compete with each other in attracting funds from the capital markets of the world. The privatization of water was therefore different from the privatization of other utilities, in that it would require strict regulation, particularly on quality and health grounds, but we had the precedent of Oftel, the regulator for the telecommunications industry.

As Secretary of State I went round in November 1985 to see John MacGregor, the Chief Secretary, in that rather gloomy room at the

Treasury which is the graveyard of so many Departmental hopes. I told him that having taken through the privatization of BT I was working on the privatization of the Water Authorities. John was amazed and delighted, pledging his strong support with colleagues, some of whom we guessed would be apprehensive. One of his officials present at the meeting, who later left the Treasury, told me that they could hardly believe such a proposal would ever emanate from the Department of the Environment.

On 2 February 1986 I announced to the House that the Government intended to privatize the water industry. Although the *Daily Telegraph* welcomed my announcement by saying, 'The arguments for a sale are compelling,' for some Tories this was a privatization too far – it was selling the family silver. It took three years to take the necessary legislation through the House and to prepare the prospectus. In the spring of 1989 one of the factors in the Government's unpopularity was our determination to go ahead with this privatization. Margaret Thatcher became very fed up with the criticism over this, and at our Local Government Conference in Spring she said publicly that water privatization 'had not been handled well or accurately'. She later said this was meant to be a criticism of the way the media had covered the issue, but inevitably it was seen as a swipe at Michael Howard, the Minister of State who was handling this measure.

The privatization of water was absolutely essential if we were to replace the network of Victorian sewers, improve the quality of our sewage disposal and therefore the cleanliness of our rivers and beaches, and maintain the quality of our drinking water. All water companies are now free to go to the capital market for the huge sums of money they require for these modernization programmes. It is only through higher investment that water quality can be improved, and £5,000 is being spent on this by the water companies each minute each day for the rest of this century.

Just as I had been encouraged in their privatizations by George Jefferson at British Telecom and Eric Sharp at Cable and Wireless, so I was encouraged by the Chairman of Thames Water, Roy Watts. He was a stout-hearted advocate of privatization, as were most of the chairmen of the other local regional boards, who were tired of the long-drawn-out process of trying and failing to get adequate funds from governments of whatever complexion. The Labour Party committed itself immediately to renationalization, a policy it was not to abandon until after the 1992 Election.

Handing over to Nick Ridley

In the wake of the Westland Crisis in the spring of 1986 there was speculation about Margaret's position. During a regional political tour, I used the opportunity of a visit to Chester, where I was speaking for Peter Morrison, to urge the Party to put all this behind us and think of the future. I said, 'The itchy search for new leaders must cease. There is so much chatter about the leadership that no ring is large enough to accommodate all the hats being thrown into it.' The bookies at that time were quoting the following odds on various contenders: Peter Walker 9–4; Geoffrey Howe 5–2; Norman Tebbit 7–2; Douglas Hurd 4–1; Ken Clarke and Kenneth Baker 14–1; and Michael Heseltine 20–1. There was no mention of John Major, who at that time was a junior Minister in the Department of Health and Social Security.

As Party Chairman, Norman Tebbit was now openly favouring a ministerial reshuffle so that the team for the next election could be put into place. Norman Fowler and even Rhodes Boyson were being considered as possible successors to Keith Joseph at Education. The front runner was actually Nick Ridley, then Transport Secretary, but in the event Nick succeeded me as Environment Secretary, and his main responsibility for the next three years was the introduction of the community charge.

I first worked with Nick in the late 1960s. At that time, he was as keen on Europe as Peter Walker was cool. Both of their positions were to change over the years. Nick used to host lunches in a small terrace house near Lambeth Palace, where Enoch Powell, whom he had supported in the 1965 leadership election, was a frequent guest. Even in those early days Nick was opposed to unnecessary and extravagant public expenditure. I remember in May 1969, after a lunch at the Savoy which the 1922 Committee had given Ted Heath, walking back with Nick through the Embankment Gardens. I remarked with pleasure on the large beds of beautiful tulips. 'Kenneth,' said Nick gloomily, 'don't forget that beautiful as they are it's all public expenditure.' Nick's natural insouciance was enhanced by the wreaths of cigarette smoke and scattered ash which always surrounded him. He was a heavy smoker – the only one, apart from Tony Newton, in Margaret's Cabinet.

Ted Heath appointed Nick as an Industry Minister in 1970, but he got into hot water following the collapse of the Vehicle and General Insurance Company. Without really reading it through, Nick had signed a letter to the Labour MP for Northfield, Ray Carter, which admitted that a leak from the Department had precipitated the crisis. This was to plague Nick and eventually lead to a full Tribunal of Inquiry under the 1922 Act. Thereafter, Nick moved imperceptibly into that area where there was speculation about his dismissal. In 1972, when Ted decided to move him and offered him instead the Arts portfolio, he rejected it and happily returned to the Backbenches.

In Ted's great economic volte-face of 1972 Nick was strongly opposed to the new interventionist policy, preferring Enoch Powell's mesmeric castigation of all prices and incomes policies. Throughout his life, Nick espoused liberal economics – minimum state involvement, privatization and low taxes.

Under Margaret, as Transport Secretary, he acquired the soubriquet 'Von Ridley' through his passionate determination to privatize the bus services, which he successfully carried through. He was ultra-Thatcherite, and Margaret came to look upon him as the closest of all her colleagues, one on whom she could rely in any circumstances. She always made a point of attending his Conference speeches which, while not spellbinding, not even after he had managed to use the new-fangled autocue, were clear and intellectually distinguished expositions of Thatcherite economics. He was a strong supporter of the community charge, but as Environment Secretary he took one decision – to end dual-running – and acquiesced in another – to fund it inadequately – which turned it into a political disaster.

Nick was coolly contemptuous of television, newspapers, political journalists, most backbench MPs, and quite a few of his Cabinet colleagues. He was not burdened by concern for political niceties, and on one occasion as Environment Secretary, when dealing with the continuing financial follies of Liverpool Council, proposed in a confidential minute that his Department should appoint people with the title of 'Overseers' to supervise Liverpool's finances. Tony Kerpel raised this with me and then tactfully pointed out to Nick's Special Adviser that since 'Overseers' were the men who thrashed hapless black slaves in *Uncle Tom's Cabin*, or administered the Poor Laws in Dickensian England, this title would not go down particularly well in Liverpool. The idea was dropped.

Nick loved to get away to fish, to garden and to paint. One of the secret pleasures of a Cabinet Committee would be to sit next to Nick and watch his doodling. As a grandson of Lutyens he drew with great delicacy and precision. While the rest of the meeting debated the burning issue of the moment, he would create the most wonderful vistas of urns, porticos, festoons, trees and the occasional naked lady. He was a most gifted watercolourist, and I have had a lot of pleasure from the two paintings of London churches which Mary bought from him when she was Chairman of the London Tourist Board.

Nick was a throwback to another age. The caricaturists loved him because compared to the suburban flowering of most of the Cabinet here was an exotic and rare hybrid – a thing most wonderful to behold and quite definitely unique. He was a warm and kind person whose appearance and style made him appear aloof and disdainful, but this was a false impression. After his death, the fishmonger who runs the excellent fresh fish stall in Tachbrook Street market which Nick frequented said to me, 'It's very sad about Mr Ridley. He was a wonderful person.' He continued with real pride, 'I've got some of his paintings of the river – they're very beautiful. He is a great loss.'

CHAPTER 8

Education Secretary

The Need for Education Reform – My Approach –
Dealing with the Bushfires – Resolving the Teachers' Pay
Dispute – City Technology Colleges

The early months of 1986 had been very bad for the Government. The Prime Minister had survived the Westland Crisis but only just. Two senior Cabinet Ministers – Michael Heseltine and Leon Brittan – had resigned largely as a result of the way the Government was being run. Opinion polls put Labour ahead, and in the local government elections the Party Chairman, Norman Tebbit, was held responsible for the loss of over 700 local government seats. In education there was widespread dissatisfaction with the state system, exacerbated by a lengthy series of teacher classroom strikes some of which were deliberately targeted to hit the constituencies of Cabinet Ministers. Keith Joseph, the Education Secretary, had let it be known that he wanted to step down.

Speculation built up that in the next reshuffle I would move to the Department of Education and Science. I did nothing to discourage such talk because I wanted to do the job, and about three weeks before the shuffle I told this to David Young knowing that he would pass it on to the Prime Minister. I believed that the biggest challenge facing our nation, and which seven years of Conservative Government had not really addressed, was the quality of state education experienced by 93 per cent of the country's children. Both as a Member of Parliament and as a Minister I had seen the deterioration of the education system and had clear ideas about what should be done.

On 21 May 1986, the day of the reshuffle, I was asked by Nigel Wicks, Margaret's Private Secretary, to go to Number 10 at 9.30 a.m. When I saw the Prime Minister in her first-floor study she told me that Keith, who was 'a wonderful man', had wanted to leave the Government for some time but because of the troubles during the winter had felt he had to stay on. Margaret offered me the post of Education Secretary, saying, 'We are not getting credit for what we have achieved in education, and there are lots of problems which I want you to sort out.'

She made no request for a fundamental overhaul but I told her that I had three priorities. First, to deal with the group of immediate problems, and for this I would need more money. Margaret smiled but did not nod. Second, I had to resolve the very damaging teachers' strike. Third, I told her that within six months I would bring forward proposals for a fundamental reform of the education system. Her reply was simply, 'Get on with it.' Margaret did not mention vouchers, selection, the curriculum or any of the other matters on which I knew she held strong views, and I did not press her to express them. She did, however, warn me about the Department. She had clearly had a searing time dealing with the officials there when she herself had been the Education Secretary from 1970 to 1974 and she believed that these officials had thwarted Keith too. I remembered her saying to Keith at a meeting in 1983, 'You have an awful Department.'

There had also been rumours that the University Grants Committee was about to recommend the closure of a university due to a shortage of funds. I had seen a minute by Keith Joseph warning the Prime Minister of this in January 1986. I thought it prudent to make clear from the beginning that I was simply not prepared to consider closing a university. Indeed, I believed that there was an urgent need to expand higher education. Margaret nodded.

When I met Keith later that afternoon in his room at the House of Commons, he started by saying, 'I have no bitterness. I have been wanting to go since before Christmas.' He then gave me a list of some thirty issues which I would find in my in-tray. Many of these were small, detailed points. I remember in particular his interest in music teaching, and some aspects of the GCSE which he had introduced to replace the 'O' and 'CSE' level examinations. Keith gave me the good advice, 'Don't make the same mistake I did of attacking the teachers.'

Keith's attitude confirmed my belief that it is better for politicians to decide themselves when they want to leave the centre stage rather than wait to be pushed off it. It allows them time to make the necessary changes in their own minds and attitudes in a measured and considered way rather than having to react to a painful crisis. Talking to Keith it was clear that here was a man who had decided for a variety of personal reasons to leave the glare of public life. He was a kind, generous and courtly person. Not a worldly man, Keith was never involved in intrigues or secret meetings. He found much of the small change of politics tedious and uncongenial. His intellect made him one of the mainsprings of Thatcherism and her leading guru, although opponents less charitably dubbed him 'the mad monk'.

Having served as a Cabinet Minister under Ted Heath, Keith had come to realize that the interventionist policies of 1972–74 were not only disastrous but fundamentally wrong. Keith made bold speeches after our February 1974 defeat that were embarrassingly frank. I remember attending an election planning meeting in Ted Heath's London house one Sunday evening during the October 1974 election. The other members of the Shadow Cabinet discussed ways to sharpen their attack upon Harold Wilson, but Keith wanted them to discuss unemployment and how it was only the market that would produce more jobs. 'Dear Keith is at it again,' was the general feeling. In fact 'Dear Keith' was to have a great impact upon the policies of state disengagement, the introduction of market forces, and the progress of privatization that marked the Thatcher years.

He and Margaret founded the Centre for Policy Studies which, together with the Adam Smith Institute and the Institute of Economic Affairs, was to become such an influential powerhouse of ideas and policies for 1980s Conservatism. It acted as a focus for talented intellectuals of the Right, many of whom were to make a significant impact both as policy initiators and as elected politicians.

As Education Secretary, Keith had put the issue of quality back on to the agenda. He had dared to raise the question of what should be taught in our schools and how this could be improved. To this end Keith had formulated a number of proposals which had been put to the Cabinet's H Committee for consideration. As Environment Secretary I was a member of that Committee, and therefore involved in discussing these embryonic ideas. In July 1985, Keith had proposed a scheme for a dozen or so Government-maintained primary schools to be set up by charitable trusts or sponsored by entrepreneurs, and which would be able to charge modest fees.

In March 1986, H Committee gave approval for a feasibility study, but by that time the scheme had become subsumed within a much wider discussion of radical options. Keith wanted 'to launch a sweeping reform package in a statement before the Party Conference'. This would include a scheme to allow businessmen and groups of parents to take over county schools, though the idea of fees had been dropped. There was no mention of a parental ballot, which I was to introduce in my reforms. The package also envisaged a greatly expanded Assisted Places Scheme, which had been introduced in 1980 and which subsidized places at independent schools for children from less well-off families. There was to be a statutory review body for the pay and conditions of service of teachers. There was also to be a separate education grant regime, with grants paid to local authorities and schools according to monitored performance and on the basis of cost-effectiveness, value for money, and quality.

However, Keith rejected a proposal for parental credits which would have given autonomy to schools by giving them per capita funding. This was a variation of the controversial education vouchers scheme which had for a long time been floated by the Conservative right wing as a way of increasing parental choice. The scheme was seen at that time as so radical as to be unacceptable. There were, however, other ways of delivering those objectives dear to the heart of the voucher enthusiasts.

At the end of March, Norman Tebbit minuted the Prime Minister setting out a scheme for a customer/contractor relationship by which the Government would make payments to LEAs to educate children to a specified curriculum and to specified standards. If the LEA failed to fulfil the contract, then the Government, with power transferred from producer to contractor, could insist on changes. This scheme would provide an opportunity to move at a later date to a more fully market-based system including, conceivably, credits.

Nigel Lawson had his own views, which went much further. He favoured removing from local authorities any responsibility for education expenditure. He proposed that the grants which went to local government to cover their education expenditure should instead be treated as central government expenditure to be funded from the centre. Without any further need to finance education, local authorities would then only have to raise the revenue for their other services. This was known as 'taking education off the rates'. A variation of this was to take away from local authorities the amount spent on teachers' salaries, as these were centrally negotiated. This would have created a national education service. Fortunately the Cabinet was not persuaded to go down that route.

When I took over as Education Secretary it was with the full knowledge of these education ideas which had been under confidential discussion. I have thought it worthwhile to explain what ideas were circulating among colleagues because it is a common misconception both among the public and commentators that Ministers arrive in a Department and immediately begin fashioning their own policies. In fact incoming Ministers are usually faced with the task of implementing what their predecessors have set in motion. But even when there are no major ready-made programmes to pick up, newcomers can draw on a fund of knowledge regarding their new brief from their membership of relevant Cabinet Committees. So it was with my transfer from Environment to Education. Although I have been criticized for making policy on the hoof, and writing the education reforms on the back of a cigarette packet, I had actually for some time been a member of the sub-committee considering education, and since teachers' salaries formed such a large part of local government spending I had had, as Environment Secretary, a very direct interest in education policy.

My Approach

Until now, the genesis of my Education Reform Bill has not been made public, and this accounts for several critics believing that the reforms were rabbits pulled from a hat, or the product of little thought. This was most certainly not the case. Jim Callaghan had highlighted the problem, and over the years many piecemeal proposals had been floated, but no one had yet grasped the nettle of a major legislative overhaul. While Keith Joseph had planted many of the seeds for what would become elements of the Education Reform Bill, I realized that the scale of the problem could only be tackled by a coherent national programme, and time was not on our side. I knew what I wanted in the package, and knew I would have to drive it through my Department, persuade the Prime Minister and colleagues that it should be adopted in the form I wanted, and then steer a major piece of legislation through Parliament and around all the obstacles which the vested education interests would throw in its way.

To be successful, a politician has to have both a clear vision and the determination to pursue it. By the 1980s I believed that there was an overpowering need for educational reform. The English education system had lost its way in the 1960s. The Butler Act of 1944 had been based upon three types of school – Grammar, Secondary Modern and Technical – with selection at the age of eleven as an essential part of this. Within twenty years this tripartite system had been abandoned, and replaced with the new concept of comprehensive schools, pioneered by the Labour Party and accepted by Conservative Ministers, notably Edward Boyle. The old system was viewed as socially divisive, relegating far too many children to a 'second-class' education, and the development of the technical schools had also been abandoned for the same reason.

Comprehensive schools were sold to the British public on the basis that they would become as good as grammar schools. Moreover, in this New Jerusalem bigger schools would be more effective at delivering a truly comprehensive education, and this led to schools with 1,500–2,000 children in some of our cities.

I had been amazed that Britain had decided to abandon the structure of its education system in this way, and as each year passed it became clearer that the high hopes of the comprehensive movement had not been fulfilled. We began to make comparisons with other countries, particularly Germany and France. In West Germany, nine out of ten sixteen-year-olds got a Hauptschule certificate covering Maths, German, a foreign language and two other subjects. The equivalent in England was the Certificate of Secondary Education Grade 4, and only four out of ten English school leavers achieved this standard. The staying-on rate of our sixteen-year-olds was one of the lowest in the developed world, and employers complained continually about the low levels of basic literacy and numeracy of job applicants. Although our universities had a high international reputation, the proportion of working-class students at Oxford and Cambridge was lower than it had been in the late 1940s. What is more, only 12 per cent of our eighteen-year-olds went on to higher education. Children deserved better.

As the incoming Education Secretary I had two watchwords: standards and choice. Those twin themes, exemplified by the introduction of a national curriculum with testing, and city technology schools and grant-maintained schools, were the ways I intended to achieve my overriding aim. This was to improve the quality of education for *all* our children in whatever part of the country they lived. If one concentrates upon the cleverest children it is not too difficult to create some outstandingly good schools. But the real test of an education system is how it deals with the children of average and below-average ability and how it can open for them the doors of opportunity. All children, even those who seem the least able, have within them something that can be brought out. One of my favourite quotations comes from *Timon of Athens*, 'the fire i'the flint shows not till it be struck'. The task of the good school and the good teacher is to find that flint and to strike from it a spark.

Moving from the Department of the Environment to the Department of Education and Science at that time was like moving from the manager's job at Arsenal to Charlton. You crossed the River Thames and dropped down two divisions. The DES was based in Elizabeth House, a drab sixties tower block perched above Waterloo Station. It had been designed by John Poulson, the architect later jailed on corruption charges, and the unkind joke went that Poulson deserved ten years just for building Elizabeth House. The Secretary of State's office on the east side of the building overlooked the Charing Cross line, and as trains rumbled over the Thames the din as they crossed Hungerford Bridge would drown out conversation in my office. Double-glazing had recently been installed to cater for this problem, but it meant that in the summer, with the sun streaming directly into my room, one faced the choice between frying at meetings or opening the windows to be deafened by trains.

The Ministerial team awaiting me consisted of Chris Patten, George Walden and Bob Dunn. Relations between Chris and Bob were poor because they came from opposite wings of the Party, an antipathy reinforced by what Bob saw as Chris's inclination to side with leftish civil servants, and what Chris saw as Bob's reliance on Stuart Sexton, Keith Joseph's right-wing Political Adviser. Chris had the office next to me, but instead of a party wall between us the rooms were divided by sliding doors. My first sight of Chris as a ministerial colleague was when his leg appeared as he drew apart this boudoir apparatus, followed by the rest of him. As the Ministers all sat in my office for our first chat about the situation in the Department, with the thundering of trains outside, I had to ask Chris to speak up. Bob Dunn beamed and said, 'That's the best idea I've heard in this Department for years.'

The nominal Head of the Department as its Permanent Secretary was Sir David Hancock, who had come from the Treasury and took very seriously his role as Accounting Officer for the universities, and the world of higher education. I came to count on David to ensure that the Department delivered what Ministers wanted. But schools policy remained the fiefdom of those officials brought up and bred in the DES tradition. They had seen to it that key policy battles with Ministers had been won by civil servants. Keith's idea of education vouchers had been scuppered by them first delaying, and then proposing a 'super voucher' scheme which was so radical it frightened the Cabinet and was rejected as unacceptable.

There were four Deputy Secretaries, the most powerful of whom was Walter Ulrich, in charge of the Schools Branch. A prodigious worker and talented draftsman, Walter was no particular fan of Government policies. As Secretary of State my working method in every Department I headed was to hold round-table meetings. I would sit on one side of the table, flanked by the appropriate Minister and my PPS, and my minute-taking Private Secretary. Around the side of the table would be my Political Adviser and the Chief Information Officer. On the side facing me would be the civil servants. When the Permanent Secretary attended these meetings he would sit immediately opposite me, even if he was not the policy expert on the subject under discussion. This seating arrangement deferred to his status as Head of the Department, and he would be flanked by other officials in descending order of seniority. But at the DES, it was always Walter Ulrich who sat himself in the seat opposite me, so that he would be my main interlocutor when we discussed schools policy. Nor did he allow his subordinates too many contributions. David Hancock would be relegated to sitting at the end of the table, and on one occasion the unofficial relationship became crystal-clear. Walter was holding forth on some policy or other when I put forward an alternative view about which David had sent me a minute. 'Who came up with that?' demanded Walter contemptuously, not knowing it was his senior. 'I did,' said David plaintively, and everyone burst into laughter at this vivid illustration of their relationship.

Even Secretaries of State were not immune from Walter's formidable intellectual bullying. It was one of Bob Dunn's complaints that when Ministers in Keith's time eventually reached a political decision about a policy matter, Walter, if he didn't like it, would unpick it by sending a dissenting minute and then re-argue the issue face to face with Keith. Bob felt that too often both Keith and Chris Patten would end up admiring Walter's fine Wykehamist mind and concede the intellectual point rather than persist with the political argument. Early on, Walter tried the same tactic with me, but I made it clear that I had an agenda which I expected officials to deliver. There was only room for one boss in my Departments. Walter and his colleagues came to understand that, and once we had established what our relationship was to be I found Walter and the DES civil servants as capable of producing good-quality policy papers as any of their colleagues in other Departments. I was also very lucky to have Rob Smith and Tom Jeffery as my Private Secretaries for most of my time at Education. They were outstandingly able and acted as a buffer between me and the Department.

It soon became clear that not only was Departmental morale poor – the teachers' walkouts, Keith's unhappiness, and shortfalls in funding had all contributed to that – but ministerial morale was also low, due in no small part to an inability to push distinctively Conservative policies past powerful civil servants' opposition. Of all Whitehall Departments, the DES was among those with the strongest in-house ideology. There was a clear 1960s ethos and a very clear agenda which permeated virtually all the civil servants. It was rooted in 'progressive' orthodoxies, in egalitarianism and in the comprehensive school system. It was devoutly anti-excellence, anti-selection, and anti-market. The DES represented perfectly the theory of 'producer capture', whereby the interests of the producer prevail over the interests of the consumer. Not only was the Department in league with the teacher unions, University Departments of Education, teacher-training theories, and local authorities, it also acted as their protector against any threats which Ministers might pose. If the civil servants were the guardians of this culture, then Her Majesty's Inspectors of Education were its priesthood. Reports on schools were written with an opaque quality which defied any reader to judge whether the school being inspected was any good or not.

Lest this analysis be dismissed as typical Tory prejudice I would refer to Bernard Donoughue's book on his experiences as the head of James Callaghan's Policy Unit in the Labour Government. One of Callaghan's first speeches as Prime Minister in 1976 was on education. He delivered it at Ruskin College, Oxford, where he called for more vigorous educational standards, greater monitoring and accountability of teachers, and greater concentration on the basic skills of literacy and numeracy. But, as Donoughue writes, 'The education profession reacted, predictably, with less generosity than the public. The NUT was furious. The Department of Education was shocked.' The Green Paper which followed the Callaghan speech was 'sparse in content and complacent in tone'. The officials at the DES and the education establishment had seen to that. This was 'Whitehall at its self-satisfied, condescending and unimaginative worst'. Labour too had been thwarted by 'the resistance of professional vested interests to radical change'.

This whole episode illustrates the cross-party view on the hidebound nature of the education establishment and the consensus which existed between politicians on the problems which had to be tackled. Of course there were disagreements on how to tackle them, but I was determined not to be baulked as had my predecessors. For a variety of reasons the education system needed radical change if it was to match the needs of twenty-first-century Britain. If this meant foregoing the usual snail's pace at which reform in education was conducted, then so be it.

Dealing with the Bushfires

I soon discovered at the Department of Education and Science that there were a number of issues, relatively small in themselves, which were causing an inordinate amount of trouble. These I dubbed 'the bushfires'.

The first was a rumpus over the introduction of the new GCSE exam which, it was claimed, was under-resourced, with certain books and equipment unavailable. Clearly, we had to give more help to schools, and I minuted the Prime Minister on 1 June asking for £75 million more for books, and also building repairs which were urgently needed. I reminded her that I had specifically said I would do this when she appointed me. I heard on the grapevine that the Prime Minister was very annoyed by this request and disinclined to allow it. She felt that I was placing a gun to her head, but I was in the strong position of just having been appointed to 'sort out the mess in education'. I was summoned to appear before her and Willie at Number 10.

Brian Griffiths, the Head of the Number 10 Policy Unit, came to see me late one night in the House of Commons to suggest that I should present a more subtle case. This was the first time I had met Brian who, as a distinguished academic himself, had a particular interest in education. We were to work very closely together over the coming years, during which Brian helped me in brokering various settlements with Number 10. Benefiting from his advice, I was able to persuade the Prime Minister and Willie that something had to be done about school books and buildings. I was told that my request for school repairs would have to wait until later in the year, when it would be favourably looked upon in the Public Expenditure round. However, I did obtain an immediate injection of £20 million for the GCSE which was spent in secondary schools on books and equipment. This certainly eased the introduction of the new exam and led to the NUT abandoning its boycott.

The second bushfire was the nature and content of sex education in schools. Some on the Tory Right did not want any such education, while others on the Labour Left wanted it to be more explicit. I wanted to ensure that schoolchildren did not learn just about the mechanics of sex – whether in the playground or in the classroom – but also learnt to appreciate the importance of love, the long-term nature of relationships, and the acceptance of marriage as the stablest of all relationships. I secured this aim by tabling amendments to the Education Bill currently going through the House. These ensured that family values formed the basis of sex education and gave the governing body and parents the right to review the material to be used in individual schools.

The third bushfire was the issue of corporal punishment in schools. I dealt with this by announcing that there would be a free vote in the House of Commons on allowing parents, governors and school heads to decide whether to retain corporal punishment. In effect, the vote ensured that corporal punishment in state schools was ended, but it could still be administered in independent schools.

The fourth issue was the composition of school governing bodies, which I believed were not truly representative of the community and were too dominated by teacher interests. We amended the Bill to ensure that each governing body had some local business people on it. They, after all, were likely to employ local school-leavers and I wanted to involve them in improving the educational process.

The fifth bushfire was an impending crisis in the polytechnics. These had been one of the great successes of the last seven years, but I was told they were going to have to cut back and recruit fewer students that autumn. This was clearly ridiculous, and I found from within my budget some more money to allow them to continue to expand.

The sixth important issue was the way in which freedom of speech had been curtailed on some university campuses where left-wing student unions had banned certain right-wing speakers. However objectionable any view may be, a university should be the very last place in which the expression of opinion is restricted. I decided that we would include in the Education Bill amendments to ensure that free speech was preserved on the campuses. It was a great disappointment to find Vice-Chancellors only lukewarm in support of a measure they should have been in the forefront of proposing. It contrasted oddly with the line they were to take on academic freedom when we proposed the ending of tenure for academic staff.

We were able to put out all these bushfires through announcing a package of measures to the House on 11 June – just five weeks after I had been appointed Secretary of State. Getting these issues resolved so quickly was important because it showed everyone that we were determined to achieve our objectives.

While dealing with these day-to-day problems I set in hand plans for longer term extensive reform. The Department was willing to discuss these as concepts, but when it came down to practical implementation they were far less keen. Some of the ideas we discussed were very controversial. The best way of dealing with them was to thrash them out at our large round-table discussions, during which I encouraged officials to speak up, particularly the junior ones. This was not entirely welcome in a Department that was very conscious of its internal hierarchy.

Resolving the Teachers' Pay Dispute

On becoming Education Secretary I inherited a long-running pay dispute with the teaching profession. Keith Joseph wanted to introduce a new structure for rewarding teachers and had brought forward his first proposals in the spring of 1985. The negotiating procedure of the teaching profession was conducted through the Burnham Committee, which involved the six teacher unions, the local authorities who were the employers, and two civil servants from the Department of Education and Science, who had no vote but represented the Government, as it provided over 50 per cent of the funds through the local authority grant. Burnham, created after the First World War, had been reorganized by Edward Boyle following a protracted dispute in the 1960s. It was dominated by the left-wing NUT and by left-wing Labour councils. As I told the Cabinet Committee, it was a case of 'the NUT negotiating with the NUT'. The six unions could agree on almost nothing, not least because of the rivalry between them for members. The local authorities, mainly Labour-led, tried to manoeuvre the Government into coughing up large public-sector pay claims, while Ministers declined to approve such costly settlements. It was a recipe for deadlock.

As Environment Secretary I had attended the Cabinet Committee, MISC 122, which had been specially formed to deal with teachers' pay. I had seen Keith Joseph and his Minister of State, Chris Patten, put forward costly proposals, all of which came to grief. I decided as Education Secretary that it was essential to resolve this dispute as soon as possible. The first minute which I sent to the Prime Minister on 2 June started with the sentence, 'I find that large parts of the education system are demoralized.' The main reason for this was that teachers were taking industrial action because of low pay and children were being sent home as their teachers walked out of the classrooms. This, in my view, was utterly unacceptable and a betrayal of the teachers' professional position. I was shocked that people who claimed to be professionals were prepared to throw the education system into chaos. I decided to appeal to those teachers who did not agree with the call to strike action and to all parents who were appalled by it.

One of the things I soon discovered was how close, and indeed cosy, was the relationship between the teacher unions and the Education Department. The unions seemed to come in almost daily, and even had rooms at the Department designated for their use. This was all part and parcel of the culture of the education establishment which had reigned since the 1960s. It was very different from the relationships I had seen as a Minister in the Department of Trade and Industry, and the Department of the Environment. As Environment Minister during the rate-capping disputes, I had marginalized the local government unions and their leadership by reducing the frequency of the meetings they had come to expect. It had been a successful strategy, and I therefore decided to adopt it at Education. While I would, of course, meet with the unions, these meetings would not be as frequent as in the past and none of the unions should feel they could just drop into the Department and see me at any time.

In Keith's time as Education Secretary, the Treasury had frequently intervened in pay negotiations since they were alarmed at the cost of his proposals. It was the Treasury's idea to involve the Advisory Conciliation and Arbitration Service, ACAS, in the teachers' pay dispute, which I thought was unnecessary. The Treasury also proposed the setting up of the Main Committee to report on the pay of teachers solely in Scotland, as they thought it would set a helpful precedent by recommending a low figure. I remember Nigel Lawson saying that Peter Main was an old friend of his. This friendship did not extend to him producing a report helpful to the Government. Quite the reverse. Main recommended a pay increase for teachers of 16.4 per cent in Scotland, and this became the bottom line for a settlement in England. The recommendation cost £2.9 billion over four years, and was higher than the offer of £2.1 billion I had tabled for the next meeting of Burnham in Coventry. It was twice as high as Keith Joseph's offer of £1.25 billion a year earlier. Once again the Treasury's short-term meanness had led to longer-term higher costs.

A MISC meeting in October 1986 agreed that it would be impossible to settle for anything less than the Main recommendations. I told this meeting that Burnham would not produce a settlement even on this basis, because the teacher unions were now arguing among themselves about how the money should be distributed. The large unions wanted to use most of the pay award in a flat-rate increase across the board for all their members. I was totally opposed to this union approach, which was dignified with the term 'Collegiate rewards'. Teachers were to be treated like college dons who were all paid the same, apart from increments recognizing long service and a handful of senior posts.

I was not prepared to accept this system and proposed an alternative which introduced five additional allowances to reward the quality of teaching in the classroom as well as extra responsibilities. Salaries of head teachers and their deputies would also increase substantially, so that for the first time a head teacher in a large secondary school could earn over £30,000 per year, which was more than the basic pay of a professor at most universities. I set down three conditions for this offer: the extra pay costs should not exceed £600 million a year; the acceptance of the five incentive allowances; the job of teachers should be specified in a contract, including five days for training. These were later to become known as 'Baker Days'. To keep the initiative I set out the terms of my offer in a letter to all head teachers. This was the first time that a Secretary of State for Education had attempted to communicate directly with the profession. I also wanted to ensure that every teacher knew the details of this very generous pay offer, and the only way to communicate this to them was to take full-page press advertisements consisting of a 'Dear Teacher' letter.

As I had forecast, the unions could not agree to the three conditions, and predictably they demanded more money – a further £80 million. They also wanted a lower number of incentive allowances because of their opposition to differentials within the procession. Rambling negotiations continued under the Burnham Committee, and I remember receiving calls from my officials at midnight reporting yet more impasses. It was my custom each Christmas to take the staff of my Private Office out to a cinema and then to supper. In December 1986 I had to take a call about the latest state of play in the teachers' pay talks while standing in the foyer of a cinema in Tottenham Court Road. This was typical of the frenetic and crisis-laden atmosphere which resulted from the endless union disagreements.

These negotiations on pay had now dragged on for over two years, and I could not allow them to continue to disrupt the schooling of millions of children. I won the approval of my colleagues to abandon the whole Burnham system and then examined the possibility of a pay review body, which a large part of the teaching profession wanted. But I was only prepared to introduce this if there was a no-strike clause, and teacher unions wouldn't wear this. I therefore proposed to set up an Interim Advisory Committee on pay to determine the pay and conditions of teachers each year. The difference between this and a Review Body was that the IAC had to operate within a ceiling of overall expenditure set by the Government. This in effect removed all negotiating rights for pay and conditions from the teacher unions. I was surprised at how supine the Labour Opposition was when faced with such a radical proposal. As I said to the House on 27 November, 'Our children are entitled to better schooling and this has often been denied to them over the last two years. The House, the public and all parents will understand that the Government must put our children first.'

On 8 December I introduced the Bill on Teachers' Pay and Conditions. I wanted to resolve this matter quickly and so I persuaded Willie Whitelaw and John Wakeham to ensure that the Bill went through all its stages in the Commons before Christmas. The Committee and Report stages were taken on 9 and 10 December right through the night, as a result of which we lost the following day's business in the House.

I asked Henry Chilver, the Vice-Chancellor of Cranfield, to chair the IAC and I also appointed to it Ray Carter, a former Labour Minister and a fellow collector of first editions. He proved to be an inspired choice, for being close to the Labour unions he persuaded them to accept much of what the Committee recommended. Over the next four years I was happy to see the IAC improve the remuneration, standing and morale of the teaching profession more significantly than had the previous forty years of Burnham.

I could not resolve the pay dispute until March 1987 when the Teachers' Pay and Conditions Bill had passed through the House of Lords. I had modified my October proposals slightly so that the basic pay of teachers would increase by £600 a year, and there would be five levels of incentive allowances for able teachers ranging from £500 to £4,200. This meant that within three years over half of all teachers would have an incentive post carrying one of the allowances. I was in fact 'imposing' a 25 per cent salary increase on teachers over an eighteen-month period.

The two main teacher unions, the NUT led by Fred Jarvis and Doug McAvoy, and the NASUWT led by Fred Smithies and Nigel de Gruchy, opposed both the principle of the Bill and the details of the offer. In the spring term of 1987 they balloted their members to get approval for strike action, which consisted of half-day national stoppages when children were sent home, and then local stoppages affecting ten or twelve areas at a time. In April 1987 this highly damaging action was endorsed by the teacher unions at their Easter conferences, and they committed themselves to even more strikes.

I felt that I was helped by the Easter teacher union conferences, which always receive a lot of news coverage as they are the only political events taking place over Easter. TV and radio networks are only too happy to include speeches from the most militant and rampant teachers whom parents would not want to see anywhere near their children. Once again the unions overplayed their hand. After my offer a MORI poll revealed that 54 per cent of parents agreed that teachers were not underpaid.

On 14 May the NUT and NASUWT, having lost public sympathy, had to recognize the strikes were a flop and called them off. This heralded a period of six years where there was no disruption in our schools. It was a period of calm, commitment and progress. I said at the time, 'Teachers are being given a substantial pay increase combined with a clear definition of their responsibilities. I believe that parents will expect teachers to respond by giving their commitment to uninterrupted and effective education.'

When I became Education Secretary I was determined to bring the teachers' pay dispute to an end. It had been a running sore for too long and it had been inflamed and sustained by small groups of militant teachers in the NUT and NASUWT. There was one union, the Professional Association of Teachers, led courageously by Peter Dawson, which boldly stated that on no occasion would its members ever take industrial action. PAT's membership numbers rose to 40,000 while those of other unions were falling. I believed it was utterly wrong for teachers to take any form of industrial action, for it damaged their reputation in the eyes of the country, and in the eyes of parents and children. By walking out on classrooms, teachers were setting an appalling example to the very children who should be looking up to them. I do not believe that people who consider themselves professionals, as many teachers rightly do, should ever engage in industrial action. In return society should treat them with respect.

During the June 1987 Election I was followed around by militant teachers, and there were some very lively and packed meetings which I enjoyed immensely. Fighting broke out at a meeting in Oxford East where I was speaking for Steve Norris, and in Leicester where I was supporting Peter Bruinvels a large police presence was needed to control a big contingent from the Socialist Workers' Party and Militant, who turned on members of the audience when they could not get at me. At these election meetings I needed more police protection as Education Secretary than I later did as Home Secretary! I also became a major target for the teacher unions because the system I had set up was delivering a better deal on pay than they had ever been able to negotiate.

City Technology Colleges

My first policy initiative was the creation of the City Technology Colleges (CTCs). As the Minister for Information Technology I had seen how quickly children and young people responded to technological education. My early Micros in Schools scheme and the establishment of a network of Information Technology Centres were proven successes. Seeing that the Department of Education was cool towards technological education and reluctant to impose a curricular commitment to it, David Young had provided £100 million from his own budget at the Department of Employment to provide technological and vocational education for fourteen- to sixteen-year-olds. This was the Technical and Vocational Initiative (TVEI).

Initially, the local education authorities who actually ran schools had been suspicious of TVEI, since it came from non-education sources. But seeing the opportunity of more money for classroom use, even the Labour-controlled LEAs overcame their prejudices and TVEI was being adopted throughout the system. Good as this scheme was, and I visited several schools where it worked well, it was still limited.

As Environment Secretary I had seen how the housing sector had been improved by the increase in choice of tenure. The monolith of public-sector council housing had given way to new decentralized and small-scale initiatives such as housing associations and housing cooperatives. These engaged the energies and commitment of local people and had given them more power over their lives in a key area directly affecting their well-being.

I felt that education was in a similar position to that of housing twenty years earlier. Ninety-three per cent of children attended state schools while 7 per cent were in the independent sector. There was a small island of private education alongside a great continent of state education, and I wanted to provide between them new areas of wider choice. While limited choices existed in the form of Church schools, a few grammar schools and the Assisted Places Scheme, I believed we needed a greater diversity of schooling provision. We had to shift power towards the parents and children who were the consumers of education, and away from the education administrators and vested interests who were the producers of education.

I also wanted to pick up Keith Joseph's banner and to raise the standard of education for that large number of children attending state schools but who, for whatever reasons, were not getting the best possible education. I saw technology as their route to better education, but was reluctant to entrust any new initiative to the reactionary local education authorities. Moreover, the rest of my thinking behind the introduction of City Technology Colleges would be anathema to them.

First, the curriculum had to be made more relevant to Britain's national needs and the future employment opportunities for young people. We had to educate the young of today for the jobs of tomorrow. The curriculum would therefore need to be technologically orientated and involve employers and industrialists. Changing the culture of education in this way meant giving employers and industrialists the opportunity to enter 'the secret garden' of education.

I was also keen to involve employers and industry in both the funding and the running of a new type of school. The CBI and individual employers were always complaining about the declining standards of school-leavers applying for jobs and coming forward for training. Well here was a chance for them to put up or shut up – not that those who declined to put up did shut up. Continuing employer/industry involvement in this new breed of schools would cement the permanence of the link between education and the world of employment. We had to overcome the idea that industry was simply being tapped for money and could then be told, 'Thank you, now go away.' The private-sector sponsors of the CTCs would be actively involved on the CTC governing body and the progress of 'their' school. This continuing relationship would be a crucial part of the CTC. In some respects we were recreating the great civic endowments of the last century, where wealthy benefactors had achieved immortality through the generous endowment of great public projects in their home cities.

My second aim was to use the CTCs as beacons of excellence and exemplar models for what could be done in other state schools. I wanted a new ethos which entailed giving more powers to head teachers to set the tone of their school, to spend their budget as they wished and to hire the staff they wanted. There had to be the possibility of a longer school day, and a four- or five-term year which made better use of the capital investment which a school represented. We wanted CTCs to be testbeds for new teaching methods and new school management methods which could then be emulated by other state schools. This belief in levelling up rather than levelling down was to be the antithesis of the Labour Party's policy, which had been to destroy good schools in the cause of egalitarian mediocrity.

For the CTC experiment to work it was vital that CTCs should not be accorded such favourable treatment that success could easily be dismissed by opponents with, 'Oh, we could have achieved the same results if only we had the same amount of money or were able to select pupils.' From the very start of the CTC initiative I fully understood that CTCs' running costs could not be funded at a level greater than that of comparable LEA schools. The importance of the CTC pilots was what they *did* with the money received for their running costs, which would be at broadly the same level as that for other LEA schools. Furthermore, pupil admission had to be on an all-ability basis and not simply cream off the most academically gifted children. After all, I was trying to show what could be done to raise standards for children of average ability.

My third aim was a social one. In the United States, the Magnet Schools programme was revitalizing education in rundown inner city areas. Such areas manifesting large-scale social problems had led to 'white flight' to the suburbs and a residue of poor, badly educated people whose children went to sink-schools where truancy and drug-taking was rife. This cycle of poverty and despair was being broken by the setting up of special magnet schools where an ethos of pride and discipline had done much to restore confidence among children and parents. Although British cities did not display the same extremes of the problems one could see in American cities, I was nevertheless concerned about the phenomenon of the middle-class drift to suburban schools which left inner-city schools with an increasingly problematic pupil population. That was why the primary locations for CTCs were to be in selected disadvantaged inner-city areas.

We also wanted CTCs to be involved in the wider community through the provision of adult education, skills training, recreation and sports facilities after school hours. CTCs should be seen as a resource for all the people living in an area. In this way they would give a positive incentive to people to continue living in the urban locale of a CTC rather than moving away.

At this time these areas were mainly Labour-controlled, and we knew that the Labour LEAs would be hostile to a Government initiative designed to help the very people whom the Labour Party claimed to care about. However, what we had not anticipated was the total obduracy of Labour councils towards this initiative. While they looked upon CTCs as cuckoos in the nest, that had also been their attitude to TVEI. Even the DES officials thought that the LEAs had learned from their experience with TVEI money that not everything on offer from the Government was tainted. However, we were to be greatly disappointed by continuous Labour obstruction to the siting of CTCs in those areas they controlled.

The first stage in working up these ideas into policy proposals was to hold round-table meetings with my senior officials. These began on 16 June, and when on 23 June I met Margaret to discuss a number of education initiatives, I told her that by the time of the Party Conference in October I wanted to announce some twelve to twenty technical schools directly funded by the DES on a per capita basis. She gave me a green light to develop the idea, and during July I began an intensive series of meetings in the Department.

The first paper on 4 July was titled *Trust-Sponsored Secondary Schools in Inner Cities*. It proposed the establishment of between twelve and twenty 'trust schools' for pupils from eleven to eighteen years old, which would be free, offer a technical curriculum, attract inner-city pupils, and be owned and controlled by trusts. Pupils would be selected on the basis of parental commitment; there would be a cross-section of ability; and the governing body would be free to negotiate the pay of teachers. Eight of the schools would be located in areas chosen from the Inner Cities Initiative, while others would be based in areas ranking high in the Environment Department's index of deprivation.

When we met to discuss this paper one week later I said that I wanted to minute the Prime Minister about CTCs before the recess. We felt that the schools should be called city colleges, and our discussions focused on how these schools could be prevented from becoming institutions catering mainly for middle-class pupils. There could not be selection if these schools were to become beacons for other inner city schools. The Department therefore stressed that the attitude of parents should be crucial in pupil selection.

Shortly after this meeting I received a minute from Tony Kerpel, who objected that these key meetings setting the CTC agenda were being conducted solely between myself and senior officials without significant input from ministerial colleagues. He was concerned that DES officials were hijacking the CTC initiative and imposing their version, which simply represented a rehash of the very comprehensive schools we felt had failed. Tony argued that if the new schools were to promote excellence then selection on merit should not be ruled out. He felt that children, and not only parents, should be assessed regarding suitability for the education offered by city colleges.

On 15 July, therefore, I cancelled the next meeting which was due with officials and instead had a meeting only with my Ministers – Chris Patten, Bob Dunn and George Walden, together with our PPSs, Alistair Burt and Virginia Bottomley, and Tony. We agreed that the objectives of the scheme were to set up schools outside LEA control; to establish the principle of contracts and per capita funding; and to deal with the problems of inner-city youth. The scheme should not reopen the grammar school debate.

This was a clear indication that we were not loading the dice in favour of such schools succeeding by simply creaming off the academically brightest pupils. We also decided that heads and governing bodies should be responsible for admissions. Pupil selection should reflect a child's primary school record and aptitude as well as the attitude of parents, and a long-term commitment by the family to education. I remember George Walden arguing passionately that these new schools had to help able children from working-class backgrounds to ascend the ladder of social mobility. This had been his own background, which had led him to the Foreign Office and then the House of Commons. George was, and continues to be, an eloquent critic of poor education standards and an exponent of the priority which Government needs to attach to education and training.

The success of each school should be monitored through output measures such as exam results, low truancy rates and high staying-on rates. We also agreed that sponsors for the new schools would want statutory protection through a seven-year contract to ensure that their financial investment in the new schools could not simply be expropriated by any incoming Labour Government. We knew that the Labour Party would threaten to abolish CTCs once they were announced, and did not want prospective sponsors scared off by this threat.

On 28 July I minuted Margaret with these proposals, setting out the political as well as the educational objectives, and pressing for an early announcement. She commented back that these schools should be called City Technological Colleges and might be based in the suburbs as well as in inner cities.

In September the full CTC proposal was circulated to other Cabinet colleagues and on 25 September the Prime Minister chaired a meeting at which the initiative received collective agreement. I said that CTCs would establish a way forward beyond the next election, since they embodied three new principles: a direct link between these schools and the DES; per capita funding; and a centrally determined curriculum. Together with the fact that these schools were to be independent of the LEAs it is clear that the thinking and discussions about CTCs broke crucial ground for some of the main changes eventually included in the Education Reform Act which we developed some months later for the 1987 Election Manifesto. City Technology Colleges were the first challengers to the LEAs' monopoly of free education. As prototypes, they laid the ground for the emergence of the grant-maintained schools which in many respects are the direct descendants of the CTCs.

There were still a couple of political wrinkles to be overcome however. Tony Kerpel felt very strongly that I should announce the CTCs' launch in my speech to the Party Conference. Not only should I, as the new Education Secretary, have something positive to tell the Conference, but Conservative Central Office under Norman Tebbit was also asking each Cabinet Minister to announce a policy initiative. October 1986 was the famous 'Next Move Forward' Conference, orchestrated by Saatchi and Saatchi, which was intended as a shop window for a possible 1987 Election. We needed to demonstrate as a Government that far from running out of ideas we still had plenty of radical new policies.

The Department was adamantly opposed to my announcing the CTC network at the Party Conference and predicted that to do this would so politicize the policy as to guarantee future opposition from the Labour and Liberal Parties. Tony argued that even if I announced the CTC initiative at a meeting of the Church of England Synod it would still get the thumbs-down from Labour. I ought to make the announcement to cheers and not to groans. I agreed with this, and included the announcement in my Party Conference speech. Everybody's predictions were fulfilled, as I received huge cheers from the Conference and huge opposition from the Labour Party and the education establishment.

The other wrinkle was thrown up by the Prime Minister's meeting of 25 September when it was argued that in making my announcement the introduction of parental fees at a later stage 'should not be precluded'. I was not at all happy with this, and minuted Margaret appealing to her political judgement, saying that there were 'overwhelming disadvantages in acknowledging the possibility of charging fees for CTCs. One of the strengths of the scheme is that it will provide a ladder of opportunity to families unable to afford private education. At this stage any mention of fees would reduce its political appeal, particularly among our own supporters.' Although the question of fees subsided at this point, it was later to resurface with damaging consequences during the 1987 election campaign.

One week later the DES published its brochure on the City Technology College initiative detailing the objectives of these new schools and the preferred locations. To get the scheme off the ground we needed sponsors. Our initial thinking in the Department had been that CTCs would incur a capital cost of around £2 million to set up. £1 million would be the cost of acquiring existing redundant schools which local authorities had closed or were intending to close because of falling pupil numbers. We were told that as the buildings were going to be retained for educational purposes we would not have to pay the market value for sites or premises.

The other £1 million was needed for the refurbishment and equipping of the new schools. So when I announced at the outset of the scheme that private sponsors would make 'a substantial contribution towards the costs' it was envisaged that the private sector would be contributing at least £1 million per school. Indeed, that was the amount which all of the principal sponsors put up for each CTC. But what pushed up the price of the CTC initiative was the dogmatic refusal by Labour LEAs to part with their redundant schools. I remember during one visit to Leeds driving past a school which was completely boarded up but in perfectly good structural condition. It was in precisely the sort of area which would have benefited from a CTC. However, Leeds LEA refused to part with the premises, and for all I know it remains a disused education building to this day.

The LEA boycott did not simply push up the cost of CTCs by forcing the Government to build most of them as brand-new schools. The LEAs also denied their own areas this new initiative by compelling us to look, in some cases, to areas outside the inner cities. The key to success was not simply which Party controlled the local education authority but which Party controlled planning for the relevant area.

In the case of Nottingham, the Conservatives narrowly won control of the City Council, and the City planning committee rushed through permission for a CTC against the wishes of the Labour-controlled Nottinghamshire Education Authority. Bradford Council did the same when Eric Pickles was its Tory leader. However, even the fact of a local education authority being Conservative-controlled was no guarantee that we could get what we wanted. There were bitter arguments in Conservative-controlled Trafford Council when provisional agreement to site a CTC in the area was vetoed by the Council on the grounds that they feared the CTC would cream off the most able pupils from their one remaining grammar school, whose continued survival had been a local election pledge.

Where it was not possible to overcome LEA or planning objections we approached the nearest sympathetic Conservative authority to the one where we wanted to site our CTC. I was grateful to Peter Bowness, Leader of Croydon Council, and Bob Meachum, the Leader of Solihull Council, both of whom agreed to make available to us schools in their area which were suitable for conversion into CTCs. We were able to draw the catchment areas to include working-class neighbourhoods in the adjoining Labour-controlled councils of Lambeth and Birmingham so that we could fulfil the original social remit of CTCs.

The first sponsor I approached was James Hanson, the Chairman of Hanson plc, one of the most successful and fastest-growing industrial holding companies in the UK. Over lunch I described the CTC idea and told James that we needed an initial commitment of £1 million per school. He was attracted by the idea of changing the nature of education to make it more practical and useful for many of our young people, and simply said, 'Yes.' We started to plan for what would become the first of the CTCs at Kingshurst, Solihull, on the outskirts of Birmingham.

Although Solihull was not an inner-city area, the CTC was to take over the closed Kingshurst Comprehensive School, which was itself located in a problem overspill estate. The Conservative-controlled Local Education Authority was willing to sell the school and we jumped at the opportunity. I went up to Kingshurst with Gordon White, the joint Managing Director of Hansons, and it did indeed become our first CTC. Tony Gill of Lucas Industries, an important Midlands company, became a joint sponsor and this CTC has now been supported by forty-five businesses including GKN and IMI. Kingshurst's first head teacher was Valerie Bragg, who came to the school from the maintained sector and gave the new CTC the drive and leadership needed for it to open on time.

I then approached Harry Djanogly, whose family had built up the textile company, Nottingham Manufacturing. Harry was an old friend, and many times I had heard him complain of the poor quality of education of the sixteen-year-olds who applied for jobs in his factories and businesses. Harry also agreed to help, and a further £1 million from his own Trust was committed for a CTC in Nottingham. This was built from scratch on a derelict site, on the other side of the road from a small mosque, in a rundown residential area of the city. Ken Clarke and I, together with the development team, met on a damp grey day and, wearing hard hats, we went through the motions of groundbreaking with a mechanical digger. The low-key event was recorded for posterity by a camera crew making a Conservative Party Political Broadcast. Today this school is flourishing and enjoys support from several local companies including Boots, Marks and Spencer, and W. H. Smith.

Next, Stanley Kalms of Dixons, who had also criticized the quality of technical education, agreed to support a college because it was 'an opportunity that can't be passed over'. But it proved difficult to find a location in the North of England, which was where Stanley wanted his school. Eventually a site was found in Bradford, and again the school was built from scratch. It is now the most popular school in the city, and among its sponsors are Kodak and Hoover. Sir Geoffrey Leigh, the Chairman of Allied London Properties, said he would sponsor a CTC in Dartford, Kent. That school, which was a refurbishment, is now up and running and is also sponsored by the Wellcome Foundation.

Several other leading industrialists and business leaders also agreed to sponsor CTCs. Pat Sheehy of BAT, and John Hall, sponsored the Middlesbrough CTC; Peter Vardy, and Laings, the Gateshead CTC.

Hugh de Capell Brooke donated a fifteen-acre site, and was generously supported by Garfield Weston for the Corby CTC. Michael Ashcroft of ADT sponsored the Wandsworth CTC, with support from UNISYS. Martin Landau and Forte plc sponsored the Derby CTC. Eric Sharp at Cable and Wireless, and Lord Wolfson, jointly sponsored the CTC opening in autumn 1993 in Bristol.

Philip Harris, who had run Harris Queensway, was so committed that he sponsored two CTCs in South London. I was particularly glad that Mercers, the City Livery Company which had funded my own school during the sixteenth century, and Eric Pountain of Tarmac, decided jointly to sponsor the Telford CTC. The Haberdashers Company donated their two New Cross schools for incorporation into the CTC network. Britain's major record companies, under the umbrella of the British Record Industry Trust, with enthusiastic support from George Martin and Richard Branson, sponsored the Croydon CTC specializing in performing arts, which the press dubbed our 'Fame' school. We even persuaded the Church of England to rebuild the Bacon's School in Bermondsey as a CTC, with substantial help from the Docklands Development Corporation.

Acquiring each site was a drama. Although the Roman Catholic Church frowned upon CTCs we found that they were quite willing to realize the capital values of closed schools by considering their sale to the CTC Trust. This dose of Catholic pragmatism was matched by an even heftier dose of Jewish philanthropy. Of such unlikely bedfellows is social progress made. It was interesting that many of the larger, more traditional companies did not support CTCs. Our most enthusiastic supporters were the entrepreneurs, those who had built their own businesses or broken through the crust of the Establishment. Altogether we raised over £36 million from private sources for the capital costs of the CTCs, and funds for curriculum development are still increasing. It was the largest sum of money ever raised from the private sector for an education project.

Although we had set up a small team at the Department to launch and develop the CTC programme, we still needed someone who was totally committed, professional, and could actually deliver it. We therefore set up the CTC Trust as an external agency supported by DES money, to pursue this initiative. The person I appointed to head the Trust was Cyril Taylor. We had first met when he was a Conservative councillor on the GLC and a strong supporter of its abolition. Cyril had given me a great deal of help in 1985 and 1986 when I was Environment Secretary. He also brought with him considerable experience as an entrepreneur and educationist, thanks to his professional experience in running the American College in London. Cyril made the CTCs his first priority and handled brilliantly the unwieldly and complicated mechanics of raising money, interesting sponsors and keeping them enthused, finding sites, negotiating the terms with local authorities and local politicians, and helping to find key personnel such as project managers for each CTC and the head teachers to develop their academic side. Without Cyril's enthusiasm, drive and cheerful determination we would never have got CTCs off the ground.

The creation of the CTC initiative was an interesting case study in the development of a new policy. When one wishes to innovate, there is usually a choice between using existing institutions with their established practices and reforming them from within, or starting completely anew. The advantage of reform from within would have been that it would have cost much less since we could have used existing schools owned by the local education authorities. The disadvantage, however, was that we would have had to start a reform programme with the existing staffs of schools, and we could have been sure that some would have tried to slow down or wreck the reform process. I found that there were many good teachers who felt they were being held back by the heavy hand of local education authorities and the reluctance of the teacher unions to envisage new patterns of education and management.

I felt that there was an urgent need to inject all those new features embodied in the CTCs into the education system. However, the education monolith is resistant to any quick change. Initiatives become bogged down in a welter of consultation, with the result that analysis leads to paralysis. One must remember too that in 1986, the very same teachers who had been unable to agree about even their own pay deal would hardly have been likely to agree about a package of radical education reforms. A pilot network of CTCs, however, would show what could be done, and it could also be put in place relatively quickly. The pilot network of CTCs was designed to have an influence on the rest of the education system, not to replace it. In this they certainly succeeded.

Labour's Education spokesman, Jack Straw, was critical that the initial money earmarked for the CTC programme – £86 million over three years – would be going to a group of some twenty schools. He wanted the money to be parcelled out among all maintained secondary schools. However, since there were around 4,000 secondary schools this would have meant an annual benefit of only £7,000 per school. Given that the average annual school budget was already £1 million it was hardly likely that such a small extra sum would make any significant improvement to an individual school, compared with the exemplar effect of CTCs.

I was amused by Labour's accusation that the CTCs were 'a gimmick which would benefit only a small proportion of all pupils'. With the same breath Labour would then argue that CTCs would 'wreck the education system', despite the fact that only a handful of LEAs out of the ninety-six in England were likely to have a single CTC in the pilot network. I had to point out that either CTCs were a drop in the ocean or they were a major threat to the LEAs, but they couldn't be both at the same time.

There is now a network of fifteen CTCs. They have yet to reach their full intake, but to date there are nearly 8,000 pupils and 700 teachers. CTCs are immensely popular, and each is oversubscribed many times, with parents and children eager for the education on offer. In the visits I have made to them I have been impressed by the dedication of the staff and their wholehearted commitment to a very different teaching regime. One of the attractions to teachers of working in CTCs is that they can work as a team and be innovative, free from the distractions of teacher union disputes, or the hindrances of local bureaucracies.

I am very proud of the CTCs because they will provide first-class education for tens of thousands of children over the decades to come. Already, two of our goals are being achieved. Truancy rates are consistently less than normal, and staying-on rates are as high as 90 per cent. I wanted City Technology Colleges to become beacons of excellence, setting standards that others would want to follow, and that too is happening. The Technology Schools Initiative launched in December 1991 is aimed at spreading a CTC-style curriculum throughout the maintained sector. Currently some 200 secondary schools are participating. The 1993 Education Bill allows for a new programme of technology colleges with CTC curriculum characteristics and sponsor governors. This is a direct response to schools which want to be modelled on CTCs.

The CTCs were key in the process of education reform because they were the first element to be announced, and incorporated many of the changes that I wanted to introduce into the whole system – parental choice, per capita funding, local managerial control, and independence from the LEA. If I had started out by focusing just on per capita funding and tried to get the support of my ministerial colleagues and their Departments, then the whole process would have become bogged down in the Whitehall system. That is what happened to Keith Joseph's ideas. The Department of the Environment would have been suspicious of per capita funding as it would have had a major impact upon their grant-making powers; the Treasury would have been deeply suspicious because of its potential to increase expenditure; and the Health Department would have been suspicious and seen the CTC initiative as a forerunner for changes to the Health Service. No, the only way was to get something up and running which incorporated the essence of much-needed reforms. That way everyone could see the reforms in operation, understand their significance and realize that we meant business.

CHAPTER 9

The National Curriculum

*Shaping the Curriculum 1986–87 – Creating the
Curriculum – Tests – English – Maths – Science and
Other Subjects – Religious Education*

In 1976 James Callaghan, as Prime Minister, had made the speech in which he questioned the quality of state education. Over the next ten years under both Labour and Conservative Governments the Department of Education started to bring the nature of the school curriculum into public debate. Keith Joseph made several speeches about the quality of education, and his White Paper, *Better Schools*, tried to focus upon this. He was also concerned about the various extraneous subjects that schools were now teaching, calling it 'the clutter in the curriculum'. But when he took proposals to colleagues, and to the Cabinet Committee of which I was a member, the discussions were rambling and inconclusive. Most Ministers around the table could not distinguish between the curriculum, covering the full range of knowledge that a child has to absorb, and the syllabus, covering the detailed programme of study leading to an exam. Their views were drawn mainly from their own experience of education or occasionally based on that of their children.

I was convinced that the key to raising education standards across the country was a national curriculum, and when I told Margaret this soon after my appointment I also said I wanted some time to work on it before involving colleagues. I found that the Department had spent a lot of time on this subject, but the work lacked coherence. Keith Joseph had argued for a national curriculum to be introduced by agreement and consent; other Departments had wanted subject syllabuses; and the Treasury sounded a warning bell that this would all mean more teachers. I inherited a decision taken just before my appointment that an agreement on a national curriculum 'should not be thrown away by imposition'.

It took me, however, no time at all to discover that there was no chance of getting a voluntary agreement. The education establishment in university Departments of Education were deeply suspicious, some teachers were determined to fight to the death for their own subject specialisms, while others objected to the whole principle of an imposed national curriculum. It was also clear that there would be great difficulty getting agreement on the content of each subject – even unemotional ones like maths.

At a meeting with the Prime Minister on 23 June which was principally about my early thoughts on City Technology Colleges, the independence of polytechnics and the training of head teachers, I also raised with Margaret my preliminary ideas about the curriculum. We would have to be quite specific about the range and content of subjects so that pupils, teachers and parents would know the progress which could be expected in schools from the ages of five to sixteen. There would have to be targets of attainment at various ages to check a child's progress, which for English would mean specifying the range of books children were expected to read and understand. This range should be wide, and draw upon the great literary inheritance of our country. At the end of our meeting Margaret generously said, 'I am most encouraged by the range and interest of the ideas under discussion.'

After the summer recess I saw the Prime Minister on 18 September with Brian Griffiths to secure her support for delegating budgets to schools, and to discuss my thoughts on higher education and student finance. I took the opportunity to raise further thoughts about the curriculum. I was particularly concerned about the teaching of English, for if a child could not decipher a page of writing by the age of seven, then he or she would suffer a handicap during their school-days and probably for the rest of their lives. Employers were complaining constantly about the level of literacy and numeracy of sixteen-year-olds. We had also just registered the fact that there were about 6 million adults in the country who, after eleven years of compulsory state education, still had difficulty in reading and writing. I suggested that we begin our review of the curriculum by establishing an inquiry into the nature of English with the objective of establishing what should be taught in our schools about our language. Such a question could not arise in France, where schoolchildren receive as a matter of course a uniform grounding in their language, its development, structure and grammar.

This had virtually ceased in British schools, where teaching had fallen victim to the ludicrous political fashion which argued that language was an instrument of class. As a way of breaking down class and ethnic barriers there was therefore to be no 'correct' form of language. Any-thing was acceptable, and indeed reflected or added to the 'rich variety' of our culture. Formal grammar and correct spelling and punctuation were dismissed by some teachers as irrelevant or at best secondary to the need for 'children's rich imagination, and creative expression'. That this meant a generation of children for whom the construction of a written letter, or completed application form, was beyond them mattered not one jot to the ideologues who had captured much of the education world. So it was the teaching of English that was to become one of the major battlefields in our campaign for education reform.

To chair the Committee reviewing the teaching of English, I appointed Sir John Kingman, the Vice-Chancellor of Bristol University and a distinguished scientist. It was better to appoint a scientist rather than an English specialist in order to avoid the doctrinal debates which racked university English faculties in the 1970s and 1980s. However, the Kingman Report proved a disappointment, because one of its con-clusions was that standard English should be regarded as merely one of several dialects. Standard English may be only one version of English among many, but it is the one that is used in the world of work, politics and the media. It appeared that even the guardians of standards had become infected with fashionable nonsense.

The Department was glad to be given the green light to develop proposals for a National Curriculum, a policy for which they had a considerable degree of sympathy. I was given much help in developing this by Eric Bolton, the Senior Chief Inspector of Schools. However, the public had as yet no idea that this was on the education agenda. So I decided to tell them, but without first referring back to colleagues, which would have been usual before making such a major policy announcement. I did not want my curriculum proposals sunk in a mire of other people's individual memory and prejudice.

To pre-empt this, I decided to reveal the curriculum proposals on the Sunday television programme, 'Weekend World', which had scheduled an interview with me for 7 December 1986. 'Weekend World' was the lunchtime current affairs programme which Matthew Parris, a former Member of Parliament and now a *Times* columnist, had taken over from Brian Walden. Matthew was finding the interview pretty routine until, without much prompting, I announced that I intended to establish a National Curriculum for all schools. The programme was very pleased that it got the headlines the following day. It was a gamble, but when I saw Margaret shortly afterwards she rather approved of this calculated bounce, a leaf out of her own book. 'Kenneth,' she said, 'never underestimate the effectiveness of simply just announcing something.'

I took my announcement a stage further in January 1987 at the North of England Conference – the traditional start of the education conference year – and again at the Society of Education Officers Conference. I now wanted to prepare the education system for radical change. I believed that the National Curriculum had five objectives. It should: first, set a standard of knowledge which would give a clear incentive for all our schools to catch up with the best and challenge the best to do even better; second, provide teachers with detailed and precise objectives to support their work; third, provide parents with clear, accurate information about their child and their school; fourth, ensure continuity and avoid the duplication which many children suffered when moving from one school to another; and fifth, help teachers concentrate on the task of getting the best possible results from each individual child.

Traditionally, in Britain it was the head teacher who decided the curriculum. But after the demise of the 11-plus, the only external standard was the GCSE exam at sixteen. This had left some schools and some LEAs adrift in a sea of fashionable opinions about what students should not, rather than should, be taught and at what age. Children of similar ability were achieving widely different standards depending on what part of the country they lived in. Whether children received good or poor education in the State sector had become a lottery,

I knew our children deserved better, and I believed that not only parents but teachers too would welcome the national framework I was proposing. As I said in April 1987, 'We can no longer leave individual teachers, schools or local education authorities to devise the curriculum children should follow.' The debates with the Prime Minister about the proposed National Curriculum took place in the spring of 1987. Added urgency was given to our discussions by the likelihood of a summer General Election and the need therefore to tie up details by April for inclusion in our Party Manifesto. I was planning for a balanced curriculum of ten subjects covering the school years of five to sixteen, with achievement targets for each subject.

However, a National Curriculum was not sufficient by itself to improve education standards unless, during the children's time at school, their progress was measured at regular intervals. This meant introducing the sort of regular testing which was a feature of other countries like France and Germany, both of which had a long-established National Curriculum. The purpose of these tests was not to pass or to fail, like the old 11-plus. It was to identify what extra help a child might need in a particular subject and at a particular age. Testing would also provide objective information for teachers, pupils and parents as to how a pupil was doing. At the Young Conservative Conference in February 1987 I announced that there would be tests at seven, eleven and fourteen, leading to the GCSE at sixteen. This was welcomed by the *Times* as 'a logical extension of the National Curriculum'. At their Easter Conference that year, the NUT rejected both the National Curriculum and testing.

At our meeting on 3 March the Prime Minister warned against over-elaboration of the Curriculum and said that she wanted to concentrate on the core subjects of English, maths and science. In the debates that took place between us both before and after the Election this proved to be the central issue. I believed that if we were to concentrate just upon the core subjects then schools would teach only to them and give much less prominence to the broader range which I felt was necessary. Some of the other subjects would be relegated or even ignored. I wanted to ensure that every boy and girl took not just science but also technology up to the age of sixteen. Furthermore, our national record in foreign languages was abysmal, since many children started to study them at eleven years old but gave them up at fourteen. I wanted to ensure that not only was the teaching of languages more relevant and more practical but that all children had to continue with them up to the age of sixteen.

I also wanted to ensure that as regards history our children would leave school with real knowledge of what has happened in our country over the last 1,000 years. In many school visits I found children being taught about dinosaurs for the second or third time. It would have been a rather more helpful preparation for life if they could have distinguished between Charles I and Cromwell, and known something about the Victorian Age and the Second World War, rather than being able to identify the differences between a brontosaurus and a tyrannosaurus. Geography too was important, but it was in danger of disappearing into the less rigorous form of environmental studies, rather than retaining its value as a more structured body of geographical knowledge starting with where Birmingham was in relation to London or Edinburgh. I also wanted to include art, music and sport in the National Curriculum.

In April 1987 I secured the Prime Minister's approval to set up two working groups on maths and science to develop a curriculum for these two subjects. I wanted to get the groups going before the Election, and so on 7 April I announced this to the Education Select Committee chaired by Bill van Straubenzee, himself a former Education Minister who had worked under Margaret in the 1970s. The MPs were rather surprised to hear this statement of new policy made to a Select Committee.

This intense round of meetings with Number 10, and the preparation of policy papers by DES officials, allowed us to set out a full programme of major education reform in the Conservative Manifesto for the 1987 General Election. In our 1979 Manifesto there had been just three inches of text on education, and in 1983 just one page. But in 1987 our proposals extended over eight pages of the Manifesto. When it was launched at Central Office on 19 May, at a large and crowded meeting of Ministers, our education plans were hailed as the flagship of the Manifesto. However, three days later on 22 May the Prime Minister plunged the policy into confusion.

Asked about education and the funding of the proposed grant-maintained schools at the morning press conference, when Defence was meant to be the subject, Margaret said, 'We are not excluding the possibility that they may raise additional sums.' This was a not unreasonable thing to say, because parents at many state schools already organized fundraising campaigns for things like school trips and extra school equipment. However, the press interpreted Margaret's comments as the Prime Minister being willing to contemplate fees. She was also asked about the admissions policy for grant-maintained schools, and said, 'If schools go independent, it will be up to them to pursue their own admissions policy.' This reply was simply wrong, and may have been a case of Margaret speaking from the heart rather than from her brief.

It had been clearly agreed in the discussions between us that grant-maintained schools could not change their character and become selective schools. As regards fees, it had also been agreed that despite some yearning to reintroduce the old direct grant schools there was no intention of reintroducing financial contributions from parents. Since I had taken Margaret and senior colleagues through the details of these policies on several occasions I was intensely annoyed that our flagship was now receiving inaccurate directions from the bridge.

I was told of Margaret's gaffe while I was broadcasting in a three-way debate with the Labour and Liberal Education spokesmen, Giles Radice and Paddy Ashdown, on BBC Radio's Jimmy Young Show. One book about the 1987 election wrongly suggested that I could not be found at this crucial moment, but in fact Norman Tebbit, the Party Chairman, sent an aide to the studio while the programme was on the air to alert me to the problem. I rang Norman at the end of my debate and he said that we had to kill the story straightaway and I must get out a 'no fees' statement. A further problem arose when I tried to get hold of a transcript of what Margaret had actually said, rather than be drawn into commenting on press reports of what she had said and thereby open up an unnecessary rift. It took Central Office ten hours to produce the transcript. I spoke to the Prime Minister later in the day, and although she was worried about this story which was now dominating the headlines, there was as usual no apology.

During the formulation of education policies Margaret was always returning to refight battles she had lost and I suspect that on this occasion she was trying to keep open the option of fees and selection. In the event, any possibility of these, which I certainly never wanted, was utterly destroyed by her gaffe. This whole episode also meant that as regards the education issue, where we had clearly had a lead over the other Parties, we were now thrown on to the defensive. The press also had an opportunity for running stories claiming that Margaret and I were divided on education – hardly the most helpful start to an election campaign. I had to work into the early hours of Saturday morning with Tony Kerpel, and Rob Smith my Private Secretary, in order to prepare a definitive speech for Saturday lunchtime. The speech was effective in setting out the authoritative version of our education policies, and Norman Tebbit also issued a release which clearly set out the Party's position.

At the election press conference on education, brought forward to Wednesday 27 May, I restated our policy very clearly by saying, 'The Government is wholly committed to the principle of free education within the state sector. Grant-maintained schools will not be allowed to charge fees.' I also said, 'Grant-maintained schools will retain their character and range of ability intake. When a school becomes grant-maintained it will retain the same character as when it was an LEA school. The grammar school will remain a grammar school, a comprehensive school will remain a comprehensive school, and a secondary modern school will remain a secondary modern school. If a school at a later stage wishes to change its character then it can apply to the

Secretary of State under procedures akin to those of Section Twelve of the 1980 Education Act.' This took the heat out of the issue, and the election news agenda moved on. However, this episode was an unwanted distraction from the positive campaign I had been intending to fight, and proved to be something of a curtain-raiser to the long-running saga of 'Who's in charge of education?'

After the Election, I secured the approval of Number 10 and my colleagues to a consultation paper on the Curriculum which was published on 24 July. But that was not the end of the matter. The Prime Minister, although she spoke up at meetings for art and music – 'I so enjoyed them myself at school' – believed that they should not be part of the prescribed curriculum. She also thought that history, geography and technology should not have attainment targets like the three core subjects. If this had been agreed I would have had to concede the disintegration of a genuine curriculum and the reappearance of three core subjects – English, maths and science – as the sole curriculum requirement. This, to my mind, would have been a curriculum more suited to the nineteenth century than the twenty-first. I argued at length with Margaret and colleagues so that they would understand that if we did not have a full prescribed curriculum we would achieve very little improvement in the overall standards of education. Those schools that were not up to scratch would simply carry on as they had been for a large part of the day.

Our debates in the summer and autumn of 1987 focused on the amount of time that a ten-subject curriculum would take up in the forty-period week. The lobbies for the minority subjects became really busy – classics and home economics were particularly vocal. I believed that the prescribed curriculum should take up to 80 or 85 per cent of the teaching time, but of course for brighter children it would be less. But Margaret wanted the time for the National curriculum to be reduced to 70 per cent; she felt that what schools did with the rest of the time was up to them. This issue came to a head at a meeting of E(EP) on 28 October, when the minutes recorded that art and music should not be compulsory subjects and that the main curriculum should only take up 70 per cent of the time. Furthermore, attainment targets for all subjects other than the core should be dropped. I took the most unusual step of challenging these minutes in a personal minute to the Prime Minister. This is almost unknown in Whitehall, and it goes to the very heart of the Cabinet Committee system, because I was challenging the accuracy of what was recorded as having been agreed. I was implying that the minutes reflected Margaret's personal views rather than the sense of the meeting.

Much of Government depends upon the way in which the minutes of Cabinet and Cabinet Committees are actually expressed, and their distribution across Whitehall is eagerly awaited. It is not unknown for Ministers to leave a meeting with no precise idea as to what has been decided, but the minutes will tell them. The British Civil Service at its best will draft according to that splendid piece of doggerel:

And so when the great ones depart to their dinner,
The Secretary stays, growing thinner and thinner,
Racking his brains to record and report
What he thinks that they think that they ought to have thought.

I was asked by the Prime Minister to withdraw my minute, but I refused to do so and saw her privately. I said, 'If you want me to continue as Education Secretary then we will have to stick to the curriculum that I have set out in the White Paper. I and my ministerial colleagues have advocated and stoutly defended the broad curriculum. We have listed the ten subjects and I set them out before the Select Committee in April. You will recall, Prime Minister, that I had specifically cleared my statement with you.' Moreover, the Education Reform Bill was going to be introduced in three weeks' time, and this part of it had already been drafted. The Parliamentary draftsmen were working flat out drawing up the rest. I simply couldn't change the clauses dealing with the curriculum even if I had wanted to, and I didn't. This was a tough meeting but I was simply not prepared to give in to a last-minute rearguard action, even when waged by the Prime Minister herself. The broad-based curriculum was saved – for the time being.

Creating the Curriculum

It was much easier to introduce the principle of a National Curriculum than to get it up and running in the schools. In former days, the Department would have set up a Working Group to proceed at the leisurely tempo of a Royal Commission, consulting widely and reporting in three years. But the decline of education standards in Britain demanded swift action that would begin to have a real impact on schools. This was never going to be easy, but I was determined to drive it through and I wanted the curriculum for each subject to be published for consultation within a year. I wanted to introduce the maths and science curriculum for five- to eleven-year-olds in September 1989, and the English curriculum in September 1990. It was in any event going to take up to seven years to introduce all the subjects at all levels and to introduce the testing and assessment arrangements.

Because of the enormous task of creating a National Curriculum for the first time in our history, and the need to take along with it all the vested-interest groups including teachers, the Education Act had established two independent bodies to be the twin guardians of the curriculum – the National Curriculum Council (NCC) and the Schools Examination and Assessment Council (SEAC). Both would have to work very hard to meet my timetable. I always envisaged that these two Councils would be combined after their initial pioneering work had been completed, as has now happened under Sir Ron Dearing.

I appointed Duncan Graham to be the Chairman and Chief Executive of the NCC. He had been the Chief Education Officer of Suffolk and had uniquely been appointed from that post to be the Chief Executive of Humberside County Council, so he was both an educationist and an administrator. I liked his down-to-earth, very Scottish approach. He was not in thrall to the prejudices of academics, and the fact that we have a National Curriculum at all owes much to his dogged determination and commitment.

Duncan fell foul of officials in the Department of Education who spent a lot of their time trying to second-guess the work of the NCC. He also fell out with Ken Clarke, a successor Secretary of State for Education, who sacked him, I thought unfairly, because Ken and his Ministers had become impatient with the complex detail and prescriptive nature of the curriculum. But the whole purpose of a curriculum is that it sets out in detail the progressive growth in knowledge which a child has to experience. Vagueness and lack of detail will allow an inadequate and lazy teacher to skip important parts.

Tests

I also appointed Philip Halsey, a former head teacher who was about to retire from the DES as a Deputy Secretary, to the extremely difficult post of Chairman of the Schools Examination and Assessment Council. This Council had to create a system of testing and assessment. Many teachers, various experts in the assessment of children and virtually everyone in University Education Departments were passionately opposed to the whole idea of testing and assessment. There was, and still is, a large body of teachers opposed to any sort of testing because they see tests as a pass/fail system. They believe there must be prizes for everyone. The result was that the only compulsory test that children had in their years of education from five to sixteen years of age was the one at the end of compulsory schooling – the GCSE. For that exam there had to be syllabuses, set subjects, and books. The absence in Britain of any regular standard assessment of children's school performance was unique for a developed country. But trying to introduce such a system became one of the most emotive aspects of my reforms.

The purpose of introducing regular testing to underpin the National Curriculum was not to try to fail children but to determine what they had actually been able to absorb and assimilate at a particular time in their education. Only in this way would teachers be able to determine whether their pupils needed special assistance or help, or if there were concepts which the pupil had difficulty in understanding, and what additional teaching or help could be provided. Far too many teachers were suspicious of testing because it might also reflect badly upon their own teaching ability, and would highlight one school's performance relative to another with a similar pupil intake.

I also wanted the results of the tests to be published, so that parents and the local community would be able to see how well a school was doing. These were the famous 'league tables'. Again that was anathema to most of the profession, but it was something which parents wanted to know. I ensured that the requirement for publication was embedded in the legislation, otherwise successor Secretaries of State might well have been persuaded to go soft on this. The argument against the publication of results was that they would not adequately reflect the social background of a school. This argument raged, and continues to rage, for all too often educationists wanted to explain away the poor performance of, say, an inner-city school by reference to the socio-economic circumstances of the area in which the school was located. Certainly one should not discount such factors entirely, and the social problems of some inner cities make such things as truancy and discipline much more difficult to cope with. On the other hand, even in these areas there can be very good schools with a high level of achievement. It depends essentially upon the leadership of the Head and the quality of the teaching. I believed that teachers should not be looking for excuses to explain away poor performance but looking for ways to improve that performance.

I insisted that the tests be written – pencil and paper – and not just teacher assessments at the key stages of seven, eleven and fourteen. SEAC started to establish a most complicated and elaborate system of Standardised Assessment Tasks for each subject which were supposed to lead to these tests. Little was actually agreed before I left the Department, but I had a feeling that this elaboration would cause trouble in the schools and fail to accomplish its objectives. Testing needed to be much simpler.

English

The Kingman Committee reported in April 1988 and it was, for me, a disappointing report. I had hoped that they would recommend a model of the English language which would serve as a basis for teachers to be trained to teach it and for pupils to learn how to use language fluently and correctly. In the 1960s and 1970s the teaching of English had fallen victim to left-wing dogma. This meant that little was taught about formal grammar and punctuation, legibility was not important, spelling mistakes were frequently not corrected and, for some teachers, it was no longer crucial for children to read and study some of the great writers of the past because their texts were 'too difficult'. The prevailing philosophy in many schools was that children learnt English through their everyday use of the language, and their creative writing should not be hampered by the fussy use of capitals, commas, full stops, adverbs, adjectives or participles. This might have been acceptable if it had produced a more literate generation of children with a thorough grasp of the language, but it hadn't. Moreover those who dared to question the prevailing philosophy were looked upon as old-fashioned throwbacks to an age of elitism.

It was because I love the English language and literature so much, and had drawn so much pleasure from it in my own life, that I wanted everyone else to have the chance of enjoying it. I did not expect every child to read the more obscure plays of Shakespeare, or the longer novels of Hardy, or immediately understand Gerard Manley Hopkins or T. S. Eliot, but children had to start down the road which would lead to an appreciation of our literary heritage. Teaching had to convey the magic and the power of the English language.

Following the Kingman Report I appointed a Working Group to draw up the curriculum on English, under the chairmanship of Professor Brian Cox from Manchester University, who had been one of the co-authors of the right-wing 'Black Papers' in the 1970s. The Group was given the task of drawing up a teaching programme to ensure that all school-leavers would be competent in the use of written and spoken English by the time they left school. I also asked the Group to include recommendations on what books children should have been expected to read by certain ages. This was not meant to produce a narrow exclusive list. However, the Group's report was not as helpful as I had hoped over the question of teaching grammar, and the attainment targets set for the ages of seven and eleven were too vague. But I did welcome their commitment to standard English and to correcting such colloquial inaccuracies as 'we was', 'he ain't done it', and 'he writes real quick'.

The Education Reform Act established a procedure for drawing up the Curriculum which did not allow Ministers simply to write the Curriculum as my French counterpart, M. Chevènement, had done. Under the Act, responsibility for this lay with the National Curriculum Council, whose task was to produce a curriculum for each subject. I asked the NCC to use the Cox Report as a basis for their wider consultations and their final recommendations to me about the nature of the English curriculum. Duncan Graham, the NCC Chairman, shared my view that the teaching of English had become too casual and relaxed. He made the attainment targets much more precise, and has subsequently admitted that he would have preferred to go much further and be more specific than the NCC wanted. In particular, he believed that the NCC should have published clear guidance on the teaching of reading, as this would have avoided a great deal of dispute about the place of literature in English teaching.

The English curriculum for primary schools which I presented to Parliament in March 1989 laid down that children should be taught grammatical terms such as sentence, noun and pronoun, verb, adjective and tense, and to use standard English. Children should also be encouraged to memorize the spelling of words and to learn poetry by heart. This was the only direct recommendation that I had asked the National Curriculum Council to incorporate, for I was convinced that it would be beneficial for children. I was very encouraged, therefore, to receive a letter from the Poet Laureate, Ted Hughes, in which he repeated some of the observations he'd made when presenting prizes in the *Observer*'s children's poetry competition. He wrote:

In English students are at sea, awash in the rubbish and incoherence of the jabber in the soundwaves – unless they have some internal sort of anchor/ template of standards. Classroom grammar kits and teachers' prayers can't contain the guardian angel/demon of English for kids who have no other access to it but TV, their pals and their parents who had only TV and their pals, and some mysterious gulf where the natural eloquence of the illiterate are also lost. What kids need, say I, is a handful of songs that are not songs but blocks of achieved and exemplary language. When they know by heart 15 pages of Robert Frost, a page of Swift's 'Modest Proposal', and Animula etc., etc., they have the guardian angel installed behind the tongue. They have reefs of language for life to build and read around, a globe of 'precepts' and a great sheet anchor in the maelstrom of linguistic turbulence (now we are really at sea).

I went on in my little chat to point out that a very ordinary actor would learn by heart, say, half of *The Rattlebag* for a single week of performances. He would think nothing of it, so I urged them to learn the whole book – a page a day, or a page per week, or even a page each month. I said a few more things about language, that it is an artificial human invention and doesn't simply grow like hair or nails but it has to be learned like skill at tennis. I told some various tales from research into this sort of thing. How language is always trying to leave us and how we keep it only by constant practice and improve it only by deliberate training – exactly like playing an instrument, running or any sport.

I was not so ambitious as the Poet Laureate, but I was glad to have his endorsement for my own feelings about learning poetry by heart.

Maths

I had hoped that, in contrast to English, the drawing up of the maths curriculum was going to be fairly straightforward. I had told the Education Select Committee that 'the Government wants the National Curriculum to be as good as the best minds in this country can make it.' I therefore took a good deal of trouble in appointing the members of each Group in order to balance the various strands of thinking in each subject, as I wanted to gain as great a degree of consensus as possible. I appointed as Chairman of the Maths Working Group, Professor Blin-Stoyle, a scientist, with as other members of the Group a so-called 'progressive' – Hugh Berkhart – and a so-called traditionalist – Sig Prais.

Sig Prais had produced research which was highly critical of British pupil performance in this area. If I had asked him and his colleagues simply to draft the maths curriculum then the education establishment would have rejected it outright. The Group's interim report was, however, disappointing and I was astonished to find it reflecting the deep doctrinal divisions that exist in maths on such issues as the learning of multiplication tables, the use of calculators, whether long division should be taught, and whether children should learn calculus before the age of sixteen. The Group had not begun to address the task of setting out a progressive programme of study with clear attainment targets at each level, for to some this was anathema.

This made me very exasperated. I had a frank and angry meeting with the Maths Group in September 1987, when I made it clear that their work had turned out to be an academic exercise with no practical outcome. I decided to replace Blin-Stoyle with Duncan Graham, who had served as a member of the Group, because I wanted someone who would deliver quickly. In my letter to the Committee I said:

I have to say that I regard it as essential to establish a clear structure of age-related targets in order to give teachers, parents and pupils a clear frame of reference against which to measure progress within common targets accessible to all pupils. It should be possible to specify the normal range of attainment and the key age points . . . I want the Group to tackle this as a matter of urgency.

I also made clear in the letter that traditional teaching methods should be taken fully into account:

Your final report will need to recognize the risk as well as the opportunities which calculators in the classroom offer . . . In particular I want the group to consider the balance between open-ended practical problem-solving approaches and the more traditional pencil and paper practice of important skills and techniques.

In maths I was clear that children should continue to learn their tables. Although they should also be taught how to use calculators, the discipline of learning tables should come first. By then, I had become suspicious of certain phrases widely used in education which had a meretricious ring about them. One was 'problem solving' and the other was 'child-centred'. These were euphemisms for a much softer and less demanding approach to teaching.

I was disappointed when Sig Prais resigned from the Group, for I had hoped that he would argue his point of view with the others. Nevertheless, within six months Duncan Graham produced a maths curriculum which was well received by both myself and the world of maths teaching. At last we had the first subject in place.

Science and Other Subjects

The Science Working Group under Professor Jeff Thompson was rather more plain sailing. They drew up a curriculum that covered the three sciences of chemistry, physics and biology and also poached a good deal of earth sciences from geography. They recommended that there should be a balanced science curriculum leading to a dual science award at GCSE level which would take up about 25 per cent of teaching time in schools. I thought this was too demanding for some children and that the enthusiastic specialists on the Group were pre-empting too much of the forty-period week. The NCC came to a similar conclusion and recommended that there should be two science options in the curriculum – a dual science taking up 20 per cent of the week or, for some pupils, a single science taking up 12.5 per cent of the week. The Science Group reported on the same day as the Maths Group, 16 August 1988, and this meant that we could start teaching the curriculum for those two subjects in schools from September 1989.

Quite apart from science, I had always believed that there was an overwhelming need for all children – the academic as well as the less academic, girls as well as boys – to be trained in the practical skills of computing, design, engineering, and business studies. Some schools were already teaching craft design technology, which had developed partly from woodwork, metalwork and art. Often alongside this was home economics. Many of these subjects were popular, since they seemed to have for many children a greater relevance to their lives after school than the more academic subjects they were studying. The task of pulling all this together was difficult, but to bring it under the umbrella of the National Curriculum we appointed a Technology Working Group under the chairmanship of Lady Parkes. She was a Governor of the BBC, had a strong technological background and proved to be an excellent Chairman. She had the task of creating an entirely new curriculum subject and stood up well to the various pressure groups of teachers who were all demanding more time for their own subject specialisms. Technology had been one of the most neglected backwaters of English education, but Lady Parkes and her Group produced a challenging new curriculum.

The least controversial of the Working Groups was the one on languages chaired by Martin Harris, the Vice-Chancellor of Essex University. There were two key issues. First, too many children gave up a foreign language at the age of fourteen because it was just too difficult. Second, the teaching had to be more practical, with more conversational French and less Racine. The Group also had to decide what range of foreign languages should actually be taught. This was particularly important, as many children of Asian origin in Britain could already speak fluent Punjabi, Urdu or Hindi. We therefore decided to divide languages into two groups, the first consisting of the main European Community languages, and the second consisting of commercially important languages such as Russian, Japanese, and those of the Indian subcontinent. Every child had to choose a first compulsory language from the first group, while second languages could be selected from either the first or second group.

In 1989 the French Government, for purely nationalistic reasons, asked the European Commission to agree an obligation for schools throughout the European Community to teach two foreign languages. The French felt that if only one foreign language was specified, then right across Europe children would opt to study English as their foreign language in preference to French. I successfully resisted the Commission's proposal. When I had announced that children should study at least one foreign language, some criticized me for being unambitious. But in my view it was totally unrealistic to expect all children to learn two foreign languages, as the French Government wanted. While some children can cope with two languages and it comes easily to them, others find it very difficult to manage even one. Indeed, at that time only 40 per cent of children studied a foreign language beyond the age of fourteen.

The Chairman of the Geography Working Group was the former diplomat, Sir Leslie Fielding, then the Vice-Chancellor of Sussex University, and again this proved to be a successful appointment. Within the year he produced an excellent curriculum with a good emphasis on geographical knowledge. He had clearly taken to heart that piece of doggerel:

Geography is about maps
And History is about chaps.

But the history curriculum was much more contentious. The Chairman of the Group was Michael Saunders Watson, whom I had first met when, as Chairman of the Historic Houses Association, he mounted a quite superb exhibition in Washington of artistic treasures still owned by historic houses in Britain. He was the spokesman of the Association, and I was impressed with his speeches and his love of history and tradition. At Rockingham Castle, which he owned, Michael had converted a stable wing into a centre for local children who could study the history of Rockingham and the surrounding area.

The history curriculum was as difficult to fashion as was the English curriculum, because each Minister involved had his own views about the subject. The teaching of history was seen as doubly important because it conditions children's attitudes to their own country and often to politics. Margaret Thatcher saw history as a pageant of glorious events and significant developments, with our small country having given the world parliamentary democracy, an independent judiciary and a tradition of incorrupt administration. The British Empire had been a civilizing influence on mankind.

History had been the subject of my degree, and I had produced an anthology of poetry which told the history of England from Boadicea to Elizabeth II. I was keenly interested in the work of this group. When I visited history classes in schools around the country I saw a variety of teaching practices, some of which involved children being asked to imagine that they lived, say, in the Middle Ages, or in London during the Great Plague. Historical imagination is the ability to transpose oneself into another age or another personality. It is an important part of historical understanding, and certainly the greatest historians are able to do it. But the young children who were being asked to transpose themselves into the Middle Ages simply had not been given enough basic factual knowledge to enable them to perform this complex task. These children probably drew most of their information from films about Robin Hood. I stood in the ranks of those who saw the systematic and disciplined acquisition of historical knowledge as the essential basis of this curriculum.

The early drafts of the history curriculum arrived before I moved to Conservative Central Office, and I was disappointed with the lack of emphasis on the teaching of hard facts and their chronology. The drafts clearly needed strengthening from the point of view of knowledge. Both of my successors were to make major changes to the history curriculum. Ken Clarke decided that the history curriculum had to end twenty years before the present day. Presumably he felt that anything more contemporary would become highly politicized, which was not desirable in classrooms. While there had certainly been too much emphasis upon current affairs in history teaching, this step seemed too rigid a demarcation. Children today are much more familiar with recent events through their reporting on television, and are often well informed about them. That is why I believe that children would benefit from a historical understanding of how we have arrived at present-day positions.

Religious Education

The Butler Education Act of 1944 had been essentially a religious settlement, as indeed had most of the earlier Education Acts this century. In 1987, therefore, I did not have to frame my Education Bill with the powers and responsibilities of the Churches and other faiths in Britain at the forefront. I was concerned, however, that certain aspects of the Butler settlement, such as daily worship and the teaching of Religious Education, had in many schools fallen by the wayside or been transformed into other studies. So the first clause of the 1987 Bill stated clearly that one of the purposes of education was the spiritual education of the child, which went together with their mental and physical development. I also strengthened the 1944 Act by making it a duty for Heads, governors and LEAs to provide religious education. In the Commons there was little debate on these aspects of the Bill, as the Opposition Parties were largely secular and the Tories were concerned specifically about the position of the Church of England. The Lords, however, had markedly different attitudes.

The Churches wanted religious education to stand alongside the other ten subjects of the curriculum, though they did not want it to become a formal part of the curriculum since the details of the syllabuses would then have to be determined by a secular body, the National Curriculum Council. I was able to satisfy the Churches by making religious education part of the 'basic curriculum' of the school. In fact it was given special status, definitely *primus inter pares*.

In the House of Lords there was considerable unease about the way in which the religious provisions of the 1944 Act had fallen into disuse. A group of peers saw this as an opportunity to win back lost ground. They were led by Caroline Cox and David Renton, who recruited the support of Alec Douglas-Home, Peter Thorneycroft and John Boyd-Carpenter, and got the nodding approval of the Duke of Norfolk for the Catholics and the Chief Rabbi for the Jews.

At that stage the word 'Christian' did not appear on the face of the Bill, but the Anglican members of this group wanted three things: first, religious education to be a compulsory subject; second, a daily act of collective worship to take place; and third, that both of these should be predominantly Christian with due allowance for the other faiths. The Bishops, whose spokesman was Graham Leonard, the Bishop of London, were initially very cool. Graham had the unenviable task of bringing together the other Christian denominations – the Methodists, the Free Churches and the Catholics – and also dealing with the other faiths such as the Muslims and the Sikhs. But he was under pressure from the Anglican group of fellow peers, whom he dubbed 'the Tribe'. I visited him at his lodgings in Westminster and sat with him in his dining-room under the portrait of Bishop Juxton, who he reminded me had assisted Charles I to the last. As the portraits of Charles I and Archbishop Laud looked down upon us I thought this was an auspicious beginning.

On 12 May 1988 in the Lords 'the Tribe' insisted that collective worship should be preceded by the word 'Christian' – they wanted to start the day with a hymn and a prayer. They wanted to divide the House for a vote, and this was only averted by the Chief Whip, Bertie Denham, deciding not to put any Government peers through the Lobby when the Division was called. This meant the question was held over. Graham Leonard was opposed to the word 'Christian' being on the face of the Bill because the other faiths would certainly object and the various groups of Christian denominations had widely differing understandings as to what Christian collective worship was. Graham told me that he had agreed with the Archbishop of Canterbury that if this amendment was pressed then the Bishops would vote against it, even though this would take quite a lot of explaining to the public by producing headlines such as 'Bishops Vote Against Christian Worship'. This was averted by Graham promising to bring forward his own amendments to strengthen the Christian element in the Bill at a later stage.

To break the impasse I became a broker between 'the Tribe' and the Churches. I was very conscious that the key figure to win over was Alec Douglas-Home. Graham got the agreement of the other interested religious parties to an amendment which would re-establish the local Standing Advisory Council for Religious Education (SACREs). In each local authority these would all be asked to determine a new school syllabus for religious education, and the members of these committees would consist of the various Christian denominations with the other faiths, but no humanists. Graham had therefore been persuaded by the pressure in the Lords to strengthen the Christian element in all of this whilst respecting the other faiths. The phraseology that found its way onto the Statute Book owed a good deal to Nick Stuart, now the Schools Deputy Secretary at the Department of Education. He had suggested to me earlier that the SACREs should 'reflect the worship, thought and action of the principal religious traditions represented in Britain recognizing that those traditions are mainly, though not exclusively, Christian'. This approach could also be applied to the daily act of collective worship.

I then had to persuade 'the Tribe' that this was a victory for them. They, however, decided to regroup on higher ground. They now wanted not so much collective worship but separate worship, provided that teachers were qualified to give it. This would have allowed all the other faiths the right to their own religious education and worship within school hours. I took the precaution on 9 June of explaining all this to the Prime Minister, since she had a high regard for Caroline Cox and had been briefed to support her by Brian Griffiths. But Margaret agreed that these latest demands were going too far. She was very firm and decisive in rejecting them and gave her support to Graham Leonard's proposals. I contacted Alec and he too was satisfied and pleased that the Church had at last moved towards them. It was, however, touch and go right up to the Third Reading in the House of Lords on 7 July. But by that time a backlash was emerging from the teachers and teacher unions.

This had been a very tricky issue to handle, but one in which I was personally very interested. I think Graham Leonard struck the right balance. The religious aspects of education had certainly been strengthened, and I do not think that would have happened if we had attempted to do this initially in the Commons. But then reform comes in many shapes and sizes.

*

CHAPTER 10

Increasing Parental Choice

*Delegated Budgets – Per Capita Funding – Open
Enrolment – Grant-Maintained Schools – Parental
Ballots – The Abolition of the ILEA – Getting the Bill
Through*

In addition to raising standards through a National Curriculum I also
wanted to increase the range of choice for parents in the state system. I
wanted to give real meaning to one of the most famous statements of
intent in the 1944 Education Act. Section 76 of that Act, which was
more honoured in the breach than the observance, boldly stated:
'Pupils should be educated in accordance with the wishes of their
parents.' Parents who could afford private education had choice. The
private sector in education was important, for it had some of the best
schools in the country, but it catered for only 7 per cent of all children
at school. Keith Joseph had helped independent schools in 1980 by
introducing the Assisted Places Scheme which provided financial
assistance for about 30,000 children from low-income families whose
parents could not afford the full fees. Proposals to extend this were
expensive, and would have been seen as benefiting a small minority
without addressing the problems of the overwhelming majority. I
agreed to a limited extension of the scheme, but that did not bridge the
huge gap between the small island of independent education and the
vast continent of state education.

I wanted to create a variety of halfway houses between the two
systems. In the 1960s and 1970s I had been impressed by the way in
which the division of housing between council estates and private
estates had been slowly eroded through the sale of council houses. The
social division of the housing market had begun to disappear. I wanted
the social separation of a divided educational market also to disappear.
The best way to achieve this was to extend the choice available to
parents by creating new opportunities. I wanted parents to be able to
choose between comprehensive and grammar schools, between single

sex and co-educational, between Church and non-denominational schools, and I added to that variety City Technology Colleges and grant-maintained schools.

Hitherto most thought on education reform had centred upon increasing the powers of the Department and reducing the powers of the local education authorities. I was deeply suspicious of such a change, which merely reflected competition between bureaucracies. I wanted to empower local schools and colleges, and thereby give real influence to parents and children – the consumers of education. I was quite confident that this would energize the whole system. It was a latter-day version of 'trust the people'.

I started first with the management of schools. The principle which we argued over was decentralization, and the metaphor which I coined and used again and again was the hub and the rim of the wheel. I wanted to disperse responsibility away from the hub and down the spokes to the rim. The argument ranged over what was the rim. The Deputy Secretaries in the Department, Walter Ulrich, Philip Halsey and the Senior Chief Inspector of Schools, Eric Bolton, were all involved in this discussion, as was Nick Stuart, the Principal Finance Officer and an experienced DES hand. Some favoured the LEAs being the rim, but for me the rim consisted of the individual schools and colleges. Slowly the Department was won round. It meant that schools would become self-managed, independent of the LEAs, and be given control over their own budgets.

I was impressed with the success of pioneer schemes of delegated budgets in schools which I had visited in Cambridgeshire and my own county of Surrey. These experiments had been running for two or three years. They were welcomed by the teachers, the governors and the parents, all of whom liked the extra responsibility and greater freedom that a delegated budget gave them Expenditure on such items as repairs to school buildings, and the purchase of equipment and books, was the first to be delegated. This was slowly extended to cover the full range of a school's budget but did not, at that stage, include teachers' salaries, which still amounted to about 75 per cent of a school's expenditure. The Department was reluctant to delegate responsibility for collective provision such as school meals, because LEAs usually organized these for a number of schools. But I wanted to improve the quality of school meals, and the quickest way to do this was to make each school responsible. Following successful pilot schemes this too was delegated to the schools. The delegation of budgets could not simply come about by good practice, since some LEAs and their directors were hostile to any reduction of the control that they had over their schools. So the local management of schools became one of the pillars of our reforms.

The consequence of this was that school governors would have to assume greater responsibility for the running of their school. Various schemes that Keith had brought forward had been rejected by colleagues on the grounds that people would not volunteer to serve as governors if they had too much to do. This was rubbish, and defied my experience, which was that if you gave people significant responsibility then they would come forward to exercise it. In 1986 I had amended the Education Bill to involve local business people and more parents in the running of schools. Too often governing bodies were dominated by teachers, associates of teachers or the unions. I now wanted to involve further and engage the commitment of the consumers of the services – the parents and the employers. This has worked well. Many people have put themselves forward as school governors, and this has not just been in the middle-class suburban areas. School governors have found that under the new arrangements, they have been involved not just in deciding details for speech day or the school sports day but in the whole running of a school – the maintenance of the building, the appointment of staff, and the reputation of the school in the local community.

Per Capita Funding

Alongside delegated budgets we developed a scheme of per capita funding. This had come to nothing in the past, since it had been perceived as a method of paving the way for a system of parental vouchers with which parents could select the school their children would go to. Under the existing system, parental choice was limited and it was the local authority which really determined the school a child would attend. The idea of vouchers was to make parents customers by enabling them to shop around between different state schools, and this meant a radical change in the provision of a public service where local authorities rationed school places. The Party was split about vouchers, and Keith had discovered the practical difficulties. I wanted to achieve the results of a voucher system, namely real choice for parents and schools which responded to that choice by improving themselves.

An essential second step was to establish per capita funding for each pupil so that if a school attracted more pupils it would receive more money, while a less popular school would lose money. The actual per capita amount to cover the cost of education for each child was roughly £900 a head for primary schools, and £1,500 for secondary schools. But we soon discovered that there were wide variations between education authorities and that similar schools in the same authority received very different amounts of money. We had to establish a formula that would eventually iron out all these differences and treat schools on an equal basis. It would, of course, have to take into account the extra costs of small schools and rural schools. We received a lot of complaints, which in effect amounted to special pleading for past spending inconsistencies, but over the following three years the system of per capita funding became established. Having established this principle in schools we were able to extend the same principle of money following the student to Further and Higher Education. It also became the principle behind the Government's health reforms, in which money followed the patient.

Open Enrolment

The third step was to move to a system of open enrolment which would allow parents to choose a school for their children as long as that school had the capacity to take them. Far too many schools were half empty, kept empty by local education authorities who did not want to close down other schools in a particular area. Children were often allocated by their local authority to a less popular school, in order to justify keeping it open, when the popular school these children would have preferred to attend actually had spare places available. This policy was known as 'artificial ceilings', and had the absurd consequence of leaving empty desks in popular schools. In such a system the poor school had no incentive to improve itself, since it always received from the LEA its annual allocation of children. The idea of 'open enrolment', including as it did the principle behind the vouchers policy, encountered considerable opposition within the Department because of the belief that education was like a see-saw – if one end rose because of improvement the other end would sink under the weight of failure. This analogy failed to take into account the motivation of those in less popular schools to improve their performance or even change their staff.

Grant-Maintained Schools

Delegated budgets, per capita funding and open enrolment led to the possibility of schools becoming independent of the local education authority. This was the genesis of Opting Out. As Education Secretary, I had been faced from day one by pressure from the Treasury to close schools because there was a substantial number of surplus places in both primary and secondary schools. This had arisen out of the expansion of schools in the 1960s and 1970s to meet the 'baby-boom', but the birthrate had now declined and the number of school places had to contract to match the reduced demand. Indeed a committee was set up under the former head of the Scottish Education Department to find ways of speeding up the closure process for individual schools. This meant attaching even less weight to the view of parents and local MPs about the emotive issue of local school closures.

As proposals from the LEAs to close schools thudded onto my desk, I became increasingly uneasy. Too many LEAs wanted to close good small schools, often those in villages. The argument advanced was that of saving money, but what was seldom taken into account was the quality of education and the good start in life that these schools gave to children. Within days of becoming Education Secretary, and following pressure from the Treasury, I was persuaded to issue a draft circular recommending that small schools with fewer than three teachers and fifty pupils should be closed. There were 2,000 such schools in England and Wales, and as the proposals came in to me over the following months, I realized that I was being asked to close some very good schools. Many of them contributed significantly to the social cohesion of a village. This circular was a mistake, and a year later in May 1987 I withdrew it. It was a U-turn I was happy to make.

Some LEAs were still being vindictive towards former grammar schools which had by then become comprehensives but which still tried to maintain something of their old ethos. These schools were frequently discriminated against by an LEA through its power to affect pupil admissions and reduce capital spending. In such cases those parents who had positively wanted such schools for their children were being denied choice, and the schools themselves were frequently put forward by hostile LEAs as candidates for closure.

Here again I wanted to give parents more power. One night after a vote in the House of Commons in December 1986, I went to see

Margaret and talked her through the idea of schools opting out of LEA control and then being financed from grants paid directly by the Department. This would only be possible after a regime of delegated budgets and per capita funding had been put in place. Standards in schools which opted out would continue to be monitored by school inspectors, but local bureaucratic control by the LEA would disappear. I told Margaret that this proposal would appeal particularly to schools under threat from hostile LEAs, and this included the remaining grammar schools. It would also give parents in those LEAs with poor reputations, particularly some in the inner-city areas, an escape route by making their schools self-governing. Margaret was very attracted to this idea, but I explained that we would also have to decide the mechanism for triggering the opting-out process. I was attracted to the idea of a parental ballot, since the success of our trade union reforms had rested on the idea of giving a voice to the silent majority.

Parental Ballots

Devising a democratic process to allow schools to opt out proved to be a contentious business. We decided that the first stage had to be a majority decision by the governing body. Later, as a result of pressure from faint-hearted Tory MPs, we had to introduce a second stage where governors had to confirm their own decision a month later. If they decided to go ahead, then a ballot had to be held among all parents of the children attending the school. Once again we had to resist pressure from some Conservative MPs and the Labour Party who, this time, wanted to include in the ballot the parents of those children who were about to enter the school. Opponents even tried to create difficulties about defining who were parents by raising the qualification of divorced, separated or step-parents to vote in an opt-out ballot.

As some school governors were nominated by the LEA, which itself could be opposed to opting out, it was essential that the trigger for a parental ballot did not lie exclusively with the governors. So we provided for a situation where 20 per cent of the parents could trigger a ballot and thereby begin the opting-out process. We next faced the problem of defining how many parents needed to vote in favour of opting out in order to carry the day. We proposed that a simple majority of those voting should suffice. But Labour and the Liberals, supported by some Tory MPs led by Keith Hampson, wanted the minimum number of parents required to vote for opting out to be raised to 50 per cent of those entitled to vote, a level of approval which had not been achieved by any postwar Government. Indeed, after studying his own election results, I pointed out to Keith Hampson that he himself had never achieved such a high approval rating from voters in his Leeds constituency. On the criterion of 'needing to obtain 50 per cent of those eligible to vote' he would never have been elected to the House of Commons where he was now suggesting that this be applied to parents who wanted to see their schools opt out.

Even with the legislation in place, the conduct of the ballots rapidly became an issue. Local education authorities fought hard not to lose any of their schools. They campaigned vigorously, in some cases unscrupulously, using groups of teachers and parents, and in some cases issuing thoroughly misleading leaflets to children to take home to their parents. In some instances this was done with the full approval of Chief Education Officers who, as public servants, should have been neutral. I had no powers to stop this but I made it clear to the LEAs that if they continued to misrepresent the effects of opting out, and continued to fund such campaigns from public money, then I would amend the law further to reduce their powers. It is a sorry reflection on some LEAs that they continued their trickery, and it was necessary for John Patten's 1993 Education Act to ensure a level playing field.

Some LEAs also became very spiteful towards those schools trying to opt out. Heads and teachers were told in confidence that they would have no future with the LEA if they pursued this course of action; surplus land attaching to the school was suddenly transferred from it; books were clawed back from school libraries, and LEAs threatened to withdraw the use of shared educational facilities such as swimming pools and sports grounds. They even refused to allow sports teams from LEA schools to compete with those from schools which had opted out. When one considers all the obstacles that were put in the way of a school wanting independence from the LEA, it is remarkable that so many still persevered to gain their freedom.

During 1987 and the passage of the Bill I gave assurances that GM schools would retain their character and reflect this in their admission policy. This would not preclude them from applying, like any other school, at some later date for a change in status. I also had to make it clear that if a grant-maintained school failed, it would not automatically revert to the LEA. In order to help opted-out schools determine their own staffing we agreed that they would not be obliged to take on all the existing staff, and the Government would pay compensation to any former teachers who were not taken on by the new grant-maintained school. It was also agreed that the two criteria which would guide the Secretary of State in giving his approval to schools wanting to opt out were the viability of the school and the capacity of the governors to run it. It was important that the new grant-maintained status did not simply become an escape route for those schools where closure was justified.

Further attempts to shackle the process and make it ineffective were made when the Bill was in the House of Lords. The Bishops were no help and it was the Catholic Church which led the opposition. I had three meetings with Cardinal Hume, the Archbishop of Westminster, in the Cardinal's Palace alongside Westminster Cathedral. On entering the building, one ascends a wide oak staircase and proceeds along spacious corridors, passing nuns silently gliding by, to arrive in the Cardinal's room. Ensconced in large comfortable chairs, surrounded by scholarly ambitious young priests, and flanked by Bishop Konstant of Leeds, the Catholic spokesman on education, the dialogue with the Cardinal began. I was conscious that I was not dealing merely with a local education authority, or merely a trade union, or even the British Cabinet, but with one of the great and enduring institutions of Western civilization. The tall stooping figure of its representative, Basil Hume, is well known. He conveys a sense of holiness, kindness and courtesy, and it is not easy to argue with such a saintly man. But within that scarlet and purple apparition was the sinewy force of a prelate concerned with temporal as well as spiritual power.

The Cardinal argued that there was a fundamental doctrinal objection to grant-maintained schools which made them unacceptable to the Catholic Church. It centred upon the position of the Bishop, who derived authority over his flock directly from the Pope, who had received his from St Peter and thence from God. The Bishop was the father of his followers and nothing should come between them and him. So our opting-out proposals by which Catholic parents could choose to make their school independent of the LEA, even though it would remain Catholic, destroyed that relationship. It removed from the Bishops their final say. The Cardinal also said that he had received a letter from the Pope confirming this. I was amazed that the Holy Father had taken such a close interest in my Education Bill. The Cardinal in effect was arguing that all Catholic schools should be excluded from the provisions of the Government's legislation. The Church should prevail over the State.

These discussions were held with great courtesy and solemnity. I could not help but recall my studies at Oxford of the English Reformation, and I was reminded of the same arguments which Henry VIII used to challenge the powers of the Papacy. The great question then was 'Cuius regio, eius religio' – 'Whose region, his religion.' Henry VIII also challenged the imperium of the Pope in England – 'Imperium in imperio', 'the state within the state'. This was now being re-argued in the last decade of the twentieth century. In the Anglican tradition I argued for the supremacy of Parliament, for at the end of the day the issue was who should determine the law relating to the education of English children in England.

The Cardinal was appalled that Catholic parents and teachers would actually campaign against the educational advice of their Bishops. He was personally in a difficult position because as Archbishop of Westminster he was responsible for the Catholic schools in his diocese. One excellent school, Cardinal Vaughan, wanted to opt out after the Archbishop had proposed to remove its sixth form in order to create a Sixth Form College. The parents persevered, and a lively debate surfaced in the Catholic newspapers – 'Archbishop against the parents'. Even when the vote of the parents went in favour of opting out, the Archbishop was still reluctant to accept it. As the Secretary of State had the discretionary power to approve or reject an opt-out proposal after the ballot, the Archbishop actually asked me to set aside the wishes of his own flock. I much enjoyed our long deliberate talks, and found the Cardinal the most formidable of my opponents, since he reflected the settled authority of centuries. But parental choice was one of the pillars of our reforms and I was not willing to concede a step. Indeed I gently chided him for some inconsistency, since as a former teacher at Ampleforth he had taught in a school that only existed because of parental choice – the choice of parents to pay fees. Moreover, Ampleforth had a sixth form.

When it came to the Church of England the person I dealt with was Graham Leonard, the Bishop of London. I enjoyed our relationship since we are both High Anglicans, though at times the advice Graham received was, I thought, neither High nor particularly Anglican. The Church of England, like the Catholic Church, was opposed to grant-maintained schools though its arguments were not quite so classy. It did not like parental choice. The argument which I heard time and time again was that if one let good schools opt out, the less good schools would suffer. That was rubbish. A local school that is seen to be good sets standards for others to emulate or even surpass. I wanted to break away from the even monotony of mediocrity. But if the poor school could not be improved then it would be better to close it down. I had been impressed with some of the schools that Bill Bennett, Reagan's Education Secretary, had taken me to see in the worst inner-city areas when I visited America. There I saw schools held together and inspired by charismatic heads – real leaders who were very often black. I also visited one school in Spanish Harlem which had been so bad that it was closed down and then reopened with a whole new team of staff, and as the director cheerfully said, 'We did a paint job on it as well.'

We needed an agency to promote grant-maintained schools and I asked Steve Norris, then the former MP for Oxford East, whether he could find money from the private sector to start one. He set about this with his usual determination and efficiency and we were soon able to employ Andrew Turner, from the Conservative Research Department, to counter the black propaganda of the LEAs. In May 1989, after Steve was re-elected to Parliament, I invited Bob Balchin to take over the chairmanship. Bob, who had built his own business in the private education sector, was a keen enthusiast for GM schools and also brought to the Grant-Maintained Schools Trust his administrative experience as a former director of the St John's Ambulance Brigade.

The Trust has now developed into the Grant-Maintained Schools Foundation, providing information about the status and procedures for becoming grant-maintained, and advice during the transitional period. Initially I had been told by the DES that it would not be a correct use of public money to fund such a body. Too many officials had views on GM schools which varied from scepticism to hostility. However, I discovered that the Department had formed its own unit in the 1960s and 1970s to promote comprehensive schools and this had been headed by Nick Stuart. The Department then agreed that it would be appropriate to provide a grant to the Foundation – grant-maintained schools had become officially respectable.

The Education Reform Act went onto the Statute Book in July 1988, and the first schools began the lengthy process that was to lead to their freedom. Within a year I was able to approve and visit the first one, Skegness Grammar School, followed shortly by St James's in Bolton. I was very glad to see that the hopes which I had had for liberating the energy and commitment of teachers and parents were being fulfilled. Many more schools followed, and by April 1993 over 500 grant-maintained schools had been approved. The target for 1994 is 1,500.

The pace of opting out became another area of difference between Margaret and myself. In an interview she gave to Peter Jenkins in September 1987, after the Election but before the Bill was even published, Margaret said, 'I think most schools will opt out.' This contrasted with my refusal to predict the number of schools which would opt out. The press jumped on this as further evidence of a Thatcher-Baker rift over education, but my clear view was that since the whole thrust of our policy was to extend parental choice, it would be parents, not the Government, who decided the pace of change. My objective was to ensure that the first wave of opted-out schools should consist of good large schools which would succeed in their new independent role and be a successful example to others. Since the whole process was quite clearly going to be an evolutionary one, my own position was to state that there was not going to be an immediate mass movement into the grant-maintained sector. Yet again, as regards education policy, Margaret had rather strayed from the script.

A late and reluctant convert to the growing popularity and success of opting out was the Labour Party. It was only in June 1992, after Labour's fourth successive election defeat, that their Education spokesman, Jack Straw, at last came round to accepting grant-maintained schools. On behalf of the Labour Party, he recommended that local authorities should no longer oppose applications for GM status.

The creation of grant-maintained schools, and the prospect of eventual large-scale opting out, did raise the whole question of whether the local education authorities should continue to exist. In discussions during 1986 and 1987, the Department of the Environment, led by Nick Ridley, wanted schools to be funded solely by a per capita grant to be topped up with fees. The Treasury was quite prepared to take on the funding of schools centrally. This would have been the nationalization of the education service. But the Department of Education and Science consisted of just 1,500 civil servants, 500 of whom were in Darlington administering the complicated Teachers' Pension Scheme. The rest were responsible for administering funding for the universities, the polytechnics and the science programme, running the school inspectorate and generally supervising the education system. They could not possibly take over the day to day administration of 30,000 schools, 400,000 teachers and 7.5 million children. I wanted radical changes, but only to be introduced at a pace which the system could absorb. Most of my colleagues lived in the world of theory, whereas I had the responsibility for making the changes work. This meant retaining the role of the LEA for at least the time being, and I secured the Prime Minister's approval for this.

It was clear that I had to pull all the elements of reform together, since Ministers in other Departments had quite unrealistic views of what could be achieved. I was not prepared to go slithering down the path which Keith had been obliged to tread. Therefore over the Christmas break in 1986 I had drawn up my own blueprint for change and presented it to the Prime Minister (see Appendix 2). I formally minuted her in February with these plans, emphasizing that the major objective over the next five years was 'to put in hand a series of reforms which taken together are more fundamental than the 1944 Act'.

However, getting colleagues to agree the details of this huge programme of reform proved very difficult because of other Departments' interests, the memory and prejudices of Ministers, and the deep suspicion of the Prime Minister about any proposal emanating from her old Department. The Ministers who attended these meetings in 1986 and 1987 will remember them as being among the most lively and forceful debates on any issue of policy.

I recall one important meeting on 25 February 1987 when we spent two hours trying to agree the details of delegated budgets, grant-maintained schools and the role of the LEA. Margaret wanted to quicken the pace on devolution, which would have spelt the end of LEAs in a matter of months. I had to explain that MPs and Tory educationists, quite apart from the teaching profession, would not take change at this pace. There was a series of quite furious exchanges about this. I stuck to my position, which meant that there were a number of draws, and I was asked to bring back the policy again in a slightly different form. I would often respond with such lengthy and detailed papers that the close attention of colleagues could not always be guaranteed.

On one occasion during these heated discussions I said to Margaret how little she had done as Secretary of State for Education. This produced a lull in the exchanges, as she was rather ashamed of her own record at the Department, where she thought she had been bamboozled by officials. The statistics showed that she had closed more grammar schools in her time than had any Labour Secretary of State.

The meeting resumed in the afternoon to deal with the future of polytechnics. The session was less heated and I won agreement to remove polytechnics from the LEAs and to issue very soon a consultative paper on the Curriculum. After these two lively meetings I went back in the early evening to Downing Street to meet two directors of polytechnics, Ray Ricketts of Middlesex and Ken Durrands of Huddersfield, whom Margaret had invited to see her. They were strong allies in the move for the independence of polytechnics, and by seeing people like these Margaret was able to keep in touch with grassroots professionals. She was reinvigorated by their robust attitude. At some stage Ken Durrands said that when it came to education policy he was Genghis Khan. Up shot Margaret's arm from where she sat on the sofa – 'Please, me Mrs Genghis Khan.'

That evening, Mary and I went to see a wonderful production of *Les Liaisons Dangereuses*, an appropriate entertainment in view of the day's proceedings.

These meetings were heavy battering, and I didn't have many friends who spoke up for me. When the Prime Minister was in full flight others tended to duck for cover. Nigel Lawson, commenting on these meetings, wrote, 'Kenneth remained in unruffled good humour throughout this process.' At the end of one such meeting, Margaret said to me, 'You take it so well.' On another occasion, after a long heated meeting, she leant over the table and said, 'Kenneth, in five minutes I am due to see the King of Jordan about peace in the Middle East. You are going to make me late. Why can't you agree?' I replied that since I did not want my proposals to disrupt the Middle East peace process we would have to resume on another day.

I believed that this was the only way to deal with the Prime Minister. It was no good being a wimp: if people stood their ground and argued their case well, then she respected them for it. I enjoyed arguing with Margaret – it was important not to be cowed, and I tried to encourage some support for my position from the others around the table. I usually got some help from the other Ministers with responsibility for Education – Malcolm Rifkind for Scotland and Peter Walker for Wales. But colleagues would cheerfully let the stormwaves wash over me first.

The Abolition of the ILEA

As the MP for St Marylebone, I saw the Labour-run Inner London Education Authority operating at close quarters. I was very unimpressed.

I did not believe that the children of my constituents were getting the quality of education they deserved. Yet ILEA remained above criticism.

ILEA boasted that it was the largest education authority in the world, with a budget of over £1 billion; that its architectural department had won prizes for design (actually it had built some of the most hideous schools); that it had the huge problem of dealing with children speaking over a hundred different languages; and that its further and adult education was the envy of the world. But it also had some of the worst exam results in the country, so the input of resources bore little relation to the educational output. It had sink schools where the passing fads of inadequate and politically motivated teachers had been given full rein. The left-wing politicized bureaucracy which ran ILEA was arrogant. It never listened to my constituents, to the local London Borough councillors, or to me or any other London MP.

I was soon plunged into a conflict with ILEA over its plans to turn St Marylebone Grammar School into a comprehensive. This school was one of the best in my constituency, if not in central London. It had been founded in the 1790s, and for two centuries had provided excellent education for London boys. It was situated at a cramped site on the Marylebone Road – not that poor premises have much to do with the quality of education that goes on inside a school. It had an excellent Head in Patrick Hutton, who was later to become the Head of Wolverhampton Grammar School. Yet ILEA was determined to destroy St Marylebone Grammar.

In the 1960s, the concept of the comprehensive school had been established. It had been sold to the British public on the basis that selection was divisive, that some children would be permanently excluded from the best, and that every comprehensive school would be as good as the grammar schools. The campaign for universal comprehensive education was racing ahead when Margaret Thatcher became Education Secretary in 1970. Given her hostility to 'progressive' education policies it is a surprising fact that she approved more schools converting from grammar to comprehensive than any of her predecessors – something for which she never forgave herself or the Department of Education and Science. But that did not stop me from leading a campaign in the early 1970s to save St Marylebone Grammar School. I took a delegation to see Margaret, and we won – but not for long.

In the late 1970s, I wrote several articles for the *Evening Standard* advocating the abolition of ILEA – 'the last of the big spenders'. ILEA educated 4 per cent of the country's children but spent 8 per cent of the country's budget for schools. With Labour in power and Shirley Williams as Education Secretary, ILEA, led by Ashley Bramall, who was also Chairman of Governors of Marylebone Grammar School, decided to strike the school down. It was to close and the boys were to go to another secondary school half a mile away, a school known in the neighbourhood for its violence, vandalism and poor standards. We fought hard, but ILEA manipulated its majority on the governing body to close down St Marylebone Grammar. It was an act of educational vandalism based on bigotry. I vowed that I would do everything I could to bring an end to an Education Authority where dogma took precedence over good education.

The political indoctrination which typified ILEA went very deep. I recall attending an open day at the ILEA Theatre just off the Edgware Road. A group of teachers, all under thirty, had prepared a programme of social history for primary schools. It was the story of the great class struggle. All the pictures were about the Dockers' Strike of 1889, the Match girls and the early trade unions, with the bosses portrayed in top hats, with cigars and Rolls-Royces. The teachers had even devised a board game to be laid out on the floor of a gym where lines of blue and red squares representing the two interests intertwined. Where the two lines crossed, the square was called 'conflict'. When I remonstrated and argued for impartiality, I was bluntly told that there was no other version of history which was true. No, ILEA was incapable of reform. It had to go.

In 1980 I was asked by Mark Carlisle, the new Conservative Education Secretary, to draw up for him a report on ILEA. I set up a Committee with his Special Adviser, Stuart Sexton, as its secretary. The Committee met privately, but when its existence became known it was dubbed 'The Sherlock Committee', possibly a pun on Sexton Blake. We recommended that ILEA should be abolished and its education responsibilities transferred to each of the inner London Boroughs.

This decision drew down upon us the organized wrath of ILEA. We were dismissed as ignoramuses, wanting to create the smallest and therefore the most inefficient education authorities in England; writing off the educational hopes of millions of children; sacrificing a great tradition and an Authority that was the envy of professional educationists around the world, especially in Africa and India. This sandbagging from ILEA, led by its Chief Education Officer, Peter Newsam, was so intense that the Government lost its nerve and distanced itself from our report. ILEA and particularly Mr Newsam enjoyed attacking our proposals, especially as I had called in 1980 for his resignation. This had followed a devastating report by 200 school inspectors on ILEA's inadequacies and failures. There was a crisis in the classroom and nothing was being done about it.

Mark Carlisle and Rhodes Boyson, his junior Education Minister, had hoped that we would come up with a scheme to create four separate ILEAs or elected school boards. But we did not shrink from saying what had to be done. The education establishment knew that ILEA was one of the gems of Labour Party social engineering. The fact that its education standards were appalling was apparently nothing to do with ILEA. It was supposedly all down to the socio-economic background of the inner city. The Churches supported ILEA because their education advisers too succumbed to the same flawed thinking. So had a handful of local Tory councillors who liked the size and dignity of a large body that gave them status and spent large sums of money. It provided them with something to do, and flattering occasions to speechify, but thankfully there were not many Tory ILEA enthusiasts.

On 5 December 1980 I received a very anodyne letter from the Prime Minister thanking me for our report and saying that it would be taken into account in the Government's review. Clearly, it was going to be shelved. The letter had been drafted in the DES, and shirking the ILEA issue was clearly the order of the day. So at that stage we could not expect any great change. It was a remarkably unradical Government.

When the decision was taken to include the abolition of the GLC in the 1983 Manifesto, I urged that we should go a step further and abolish ILEA as well. But the Government's view was still uncertain. A meeting was summoned on 14 April in the Prime Minister's Room in the House of Commons to hear the views of London Conservative Members. Rhodes Boyson wanted to dismantle ILEA, but still hankered for school boards; David Mellor, Geoffrey Finsberg, Bill Shelton and Peter Brooke advised a more cautious approach, since they were concerned about ILEA stirring up parents with alarmist stories during the forthcoming General Election campaign. Keith Joseph was worried too about the role of the Parent Teacher Associations as campaigning bodies. Only Margaret and I continued to favour abolition. She was particularly pleased about my support and said, 'I'm glad that you still support abolition. I'd been told that you had weakened.'

However, it was clear that the abolition of ILEA was not going to be included in the Manifesto. So I recommended that ILEA's constituent London Boroughs should be given an opportunity to opt out of ILEA and become their own education authorities if they wished. But in the event, our policy in the Manifesto was limited simply to reviewing the position of ILEA.

The review proposed that following the GLC's abolition, ILEA should be established as a directly elected authority consisting of two or three members from each London Borough. This formed part of the GLC Abolition Bill, and the first elections were held in March 1986. Far from abolishing ILEA it consolidated its authority and gave it the power to precept on the individual London Boroughs. It also gave ILEA a new, unwarranted, legitimacy by introducing directly elected membership of the Authority.

However, the new directly elected ILEA was no better, indeed it provided a political platform for the same sort of left-wing politics we were seeing in the town halls. Furthermore, ILEA showed itself totally incapable of dealing with militant left-wing teachers who, among other things, absented themselves from their schools to take part in political demonstrations. Together with ILEA's promotion of homosexual literature, and the anti-police attitude fostered by teachers in some schools, the Authority became a byword for swollen bureaucracy, high costs, low academic standards and political extremism.

In April 1987 I minuted the Prime Minister about the future of ILEA and came down in favour of allowing individual Boroughs to secede from ILEA and assume responsibility for their own education services. This was agreed in May and included in our 1987 Election Manifesto. The dismemberment of ILEA had to be done slowly, and it was important to achieve it through the democratic process. In this way, ILEA would shrink and eventually cease to be viable, thus justifying its winding up. However, I had always envisaged that once the Bill was published and going through the House it would be possible to modify these proposals to accelerate the process.

The Education Reform Bill also removed ILEA's responsibility for further and higher education. This meant moving the arts colleges away from ILEA's control and into the free-standing and newly created London Institute. I also promoted the idea of splitting up ILEA's network of adult education institutes and associating them more closely with the areas in which they were based. I wanted ILEA to revert to its basic function, which was the schooling of children from the ages of five to eighteen. The new power to opt out of ILEA was quickly seized upon by Conservative Boroughs like Wandsworth, Westminster, and Kensington and Chelsea. These were Conservative-run Boroughs, dedicated to reducing local taxes, and they resented a Labour-run Authority being able to levy a precept on them, thus forcing up local taxes. It looked as if a rump of Labour Boroughs would remain and form themselves into a little ILEA. However, it wasn't long before territorial ambition overcame Socialist fraternity. It began to dawn on the individual Labour Borough leaders that there was no geographical or educational sense in continuing membership of a shrinking rump. Moreover, many Labour London Boroughs came to see the virtue of controlling their own education, for they actually had very little love for ILEA itself. So ILEA's Labour allies began drifting away.

In September 1987 I suggested that the Secretary of State for Education should have a reserve power to dissolve ILEA if eight Boroughs out of the thirteen opted out leaving a non-viable rump. In October, ILEA's Chief Education Officer, Bill Stubbs, suggested it would be better to abolish the Authority outright, and this line was echoed by editorials in all the heavyweight newspapers. Their argument was that ILEA's abolition and an orderly transfer of education to the Boroughs was preferable to death by a thousand cuts. At that stage, one of the Boroughs deciding to opt out was Wandsworth. In November there was a crucial by-election in the Borough on which hung control of the council. Labour called for this by-election to be treated as a referendum on whether Wandsworth should opt out of ILEA, and had high hopes of winning. But David Fanthorpe, the Conservative candidate, who was also the education desk officer at Conservative Research Department, won decisively, confirming popular support for Wandsworth's decision. This was another nail in ILEA's coffin.

As the Bill progressed through the House an amendment was moved reducing to five the number of Boroughs whose secession would trigger the abolition of ILEA. At that time three Boroughs – Wandsworth, Westminster, Kensington and Chelsea – had decided to opt out, and the City of London and Tower Hamlets were considering doing so. It was clearly unsatisfactory to allow the future of ILEA to become paralysed by continuing uncertainty about its future, and 109 Tory MPs signed an Early Day Motion to abolish ILEA altogether. Early in 1988 I minuted colleagues seeking their approval to do this. It was readily given, but

Margaret was very worried about the capacity of Boroughs like Lambeth to provide a good education service. One of her cleaners lived in Lambeth and had told her the horrors of living under that left-wing council.

At this stage Michael Heseltine and Norman Tebbit, an unholy alliance, joined the bandwagon and added their considerable weight to the demand for ILEA to go, and on 4 February I announced the abolition of ILEA to the House. I knew that Michael would not be able to resist the temptation to claim credit for this and to preen himself a little. Just as I predicted, he did. But I was ready for him, and after thanking him for his support I added, 'Nobody should underestimate my Rt Hon. Friend's ability to hurl himself through a half open door.' The gale of laughter was as gratifying to me as it was discomfiting for Michael.

In order to shore up its prospects of survival, ILEA organized a parents' referendum designed to influence the House of Lords to vote against our ILEA abolition proposals. The Authority spent public money campaigning against the Bill and showed itself in its true colours – a platform for Labour politicians first and a concern for education second. ILEA could not even resist rigging their referendum by allocating to every parent one ballot paper for each child they had at ILEA schools. So some parents had five or even six votes each! Just over half the ballot papers were returned, and not surprisingly the majority of these favoured keeping ILEA. But there was no way of knowing the number of individual parents actually involved in this phoney voting exercise, and inner London ratepayers, who had to foot ILEA's bills, were not allowed a say.

Since the Lords' vote in the summer of 1988 was crucial, and we were by no means certain of a majority, I asked the Party Chairman, Peter Brooke, for a small amount of money to allow us to commission a public opinion poll which might give a more helpful indication on attitudes to ILEA. The Centre for Policy Studies agreed to be the sponsoring organization and Tony Kerpel, Sheila Lawlor of the CPS, and Gordon Heald of Gallup had regular meetings to devise the questionnaire. The results, released on the eve of the Lords' vote on 17 May, were helpful to us and undermined ILEA's referendum. Among parents in London 52 per cent were not worried about the abolition of ILEA compared with 43 per cent who were. Of Londoners as a whole, 63 per cent were not worried about the abolition of ILEA and 32 per cent said they were. We won the Lords' vote by 236 to 183, a healthy majority of fifty-three.

This whole process is an interesting example of how a policy which was politically unacceptable in 1980 had, by 1987, become inevitable. ILEA would not have fallen to a frontal assault at the beginning because it had too many friends among the vested interests – Labour politicians, teachers, politically organized Parent–Teacher Associations, the education establishment of London, the colleges and universities, and the Churches. ILEA had to be given a chance to assist in its own destruction, and this it managed to do under the leadership of Frances Morrell and Neil Fletcher, both of whom were influential figures in London Labour politics. It is a measure of how little ILEA is missed that today no one proposes it should be recreated.

Getting the Bill Through

In getting the Education Reform Bill ready for presentation I had a lot of help from Bob Dunn and Angela Rumbold. Angela had replaced Chris Patten as the Minister of State, and brought to us her experience as a former Chairman of a London Borough education committee. On 18 November we were able to publish the Bill as the first major legislation of the new Parliament. The officials at the DES worked extraordinarily hard during the passage of the Bill, and throughout this period the Department proved it had climbed back to First Division status.

In contrast to the community charge, which had become popularly known as the poll tax and 'a bad thing', with education reform we succeeded in capturing the high ground. The Bill started life rather uninspiringly called the Education Bill, but then became the Education Reform Bill because education reform was regarded by the public as 'a good thing'. Education commentators went a step further and on account of the scale of legislation called it the Great Education Reform Bill, whereupon the education world dubbed it the GERBIL. Since gerbils are cuddly and friendly creatures, this delighted us. Even Labour spokesmen fell into the habit of referring to the Gerbil, and so on this occasion the name of Government legislation never became a focus for protest or unpopularity.

There was nearly a last-minute hiccup when I received a call on my car telephone from the Attorney-General, Paddy Mayhew. He was very worried about the Bill being drafted too quickly. It was a complicated

Bill which, in his words, was 'looking for judicial review'. He was very reluctant to give his approval and would have preferred me to delay it. But I couldn't delay; indeed procrastination would have been fatal. Paddy's anxieties have proved to be unfounded. There has been virtually no challenge under judicial review to the main provisions of the Act.

There were some Tories who, for various reasons, opposed parts of my education reforms. When I announced the City Technology Colleges, Demitri Coryton, Chairman of the Conservative Education Association, condemned them on TV. Some Tory Education Chairmen, conscious that the effect of the reforms would reduce the role of LEAs, strongly opposed opting out. David Muffet, the robust Education chairman of Hereford and Worcester, who looked and spoke like the former colonial administrator he had been, said at the 1987 Party Conference, 'Do not demolish the house just to get even with the Philistines. It didn't do Samson any good.'

In November 1987 our opponents received succour from a most unlikely source when Willie Whitelaw said in a radio interview with Peter Hennessy that the House of Lords would probably reject opting out. This was said even before the Education Bill had been published. Both Number 10 and I were very fed up, and messages were passed to Willie. He then sent me a letter of apology saying that he would do everything to get the Bill through. But, alas, the spectre of eventual castration had been raised and it cheered the sceptics.

In the debate on the Second Reading, Ted Heath, to Labour cheers, opposed every main proposal arguing, 'This Bill is divisive and it will be fatal to the education of large numbers of children.' He questioned parental choice, doubted whether school governors wanted more power, attacked the prescriptive curriculum, supported the retention of ILEA and demanded that opting out should be 'dropped completely'. Until that moment I had not been aware that Ted had very much interest in education, indeed as far as I could recall this was his maiden speech on education policy. It was all part and parcel of his opposition to absolutely anything the Government was doing. It was therefore not surprising that he didn't vote for Second Reading.

However, Tory backbenchers overwhelmingly supported what we were doing, none more so than James Pawsey, the Member for Rugby, and Chairman of the Conservative Education Backbench Committee. Jim was always a great help in organizing Conservative backbench questions and interventions during education debates, and robustly defended our policies on television. If a Minister is not able to depend on such colleagues for support then life can be difficult, but in Jim I had an ally who was always supportive and reliable.

It was because there were so many possible pitfalls in the passage of the Bill that I decided to take it through Committee myself. I believe this is something which Secretaries of State should do with major legislation, but quite apart from that I enjoyed debating in Committee. Jack Straw was Labour's new Education spokesman, and although we did not spare each other in the debates there was a mutual respect. He was much more effective than his predecessor Giles Radice had been, and he kept us on our toes. That is more than can be said about the Liberals' Education spokesman, Paddy Ashdown, who approached these debates with an open, if not empty, mind. He had few ideas about education and took his briefing from one of the teacher unions. He would sit in the Committee staring up at the ceiling and listening to the debate whose arguments he was clearly hearing for the first time. Then he would speak on the spur of the moment, neither praising nor damning our proposals but preferring to be querulous.

This was the first time I had seen Ashdown operating at close quarters, and he was mightily unimpressive. He was the coming man, rugged and with a romantic military past, and clearly had his mind on the Liberal Democrats' leadership, for which he was campaigning during this period. But as I said of him in the House:

He likes parent power but not too much; he likes choice but not too much; he likes delegated budgets but not too much; he likes excellence but not too much; he has conducted a sustained exercise in restrained enthusiasm. As he flits from one half-belief to another thinly held conviction he has become the snapper-up of unconsidered half thoughts.

I have had little reason to change that impression over the intervening years.

CHAPTER II

The Expansion of Higher and Further Education

Higher Education – Student Loans – Academic Tenure and Pay – Further Education – Teacher Training – Science – Epilogue

By the time I became Education Secretary the Tories were at loggerheads with the world of higher education. There were many reasons. Mark Carlisle, the Education Secretary from 1979 to 1981, in the wake of the tough Budget of 1981 had imposed significant cuts in university funding. Oxford and Cambridge were to some extent cushioned by the historic wealth of their colleges, but other universities were severely affected – Salford University had its grant income cut by 40 per cent.

Keith Joseph, Mark's successor, bore the brunt of the student protests which were actively inflamed over these issues. He encountered huge crowds of protesting students wherever he went. After his car had been surrounded and almost overturned he received extra police protection when visiting the campuses. Travelling once with him in his car, I found that his driver kept a large wooden truncheon under the front seat.

When I became Education Secretary, I too experienced some of these violent demonstrations. During a visit to a further education college in Buckinghamshire, militant students sat down in front of me wherever I went and then tried to throw themselves in front of my car while hurling abuse at me all the time. I discovered early on that the young female students were the more vicious, with a range of vituperation that was probably the most imaginative thing of which they were capable. I also discovered that in virtually every college and university there was a small, active and militant group, usually from the Socialist Workers' Party and often closely associated with a similar group in the town. Their purpose was to gain as much publicity as possible from disruption.

There were large demonstrations at Cambridge, Sussex and Sunderland Polytechnic, and these became very intimidating, as the students were quite prepared to promote violence against the police or visiting politicians. During one visit to Leicester University in October 1988 militant students formed up outside the building I had entered and laid siege to it. My party, including two security men and the local MP David Tredinnick, who had been an officer in the Guards, decided to push our way through this crowd. We were hit with sticks and I was knocked to the ground. The demonstrators drew some blood and my spectacles were broken. However, I continued my visit because I was simply not prepared to let these thugs get away with this sort of bullying behaviour. It amounted to a complete denial of what a university stood for – free speech and the tolerance of dissenting views.

The cuts of 1981 were the first time following the Robbins Report and the great expansion of universities that any Government had dared to question the funding of higher education. The university world was convinced that the philistine Thatcher Government was determined not only to stop the expansion of higher education but actually to reduce it. They had come to expect governments to meet their demands for more expenditure in a totally uncritical way, and were not prepared to face up to any changes which would allow expansion to take place at a realistic unit cost. The academic establishment at the universities was the first professional middle class group whose practices and interests were challenged by the Thatcher Government.

Change was necessary because Britain was running a high cost education system with a relatively low level of output. Only one in eight of our eighteen-year-olds went on to higher education, yet we were spending a higher proportion of our GDP on higher education than any other Western European country apart from the Netherlands. Expenditure per student was higher even than in California, whose per capita GDP was double that of the UK.

The reason for the higher relative costs in Britain was that the University Grants Committee, which was the body funding the universities, had developed an ingenious system where a unit of resource was established which represented the amount needed to teach one student. This formula became sacrosanct and meant that if student numbers were to be increased then the amount paid through the unit of resource had to be increased pro rata. Since the student/lecturer ratio was never questioned, this meant that the cost of expanding university education was very high. Lecturers were unlikely to challenge a system which guaranteed them some of the smallest classes in any developed country.

Growth in student numbers was limited, since a university was not encouraged to increase the number of its students by accepting some at a lower marginal cost, which was just what the polytechnics were doing. It meant that in effect the number of students at our universities was determined by how much money could be squeezed out of the Treasury each year.

I wanted to see a system where expansion would be determined by student demand. So the first action we took was to abolish the 'unit of resource', which had become a rationing system. We replaced it with a system of per capita funding with different rates for arts, science and medical students. This would encourage universities to increase their income by attracting more students and providing them with an incentive to expand at a lower cost.

I also wanted to see universities become more independent and draw their income from a range of sources, particularly private ones. That was the sure guarantee of academic freedom. Universities and polytechnics had to be autonomous to maintain their vitality, to manage themselves effectively and to be accountable to the individual student, the economy and the society that sustained them. In a speech at Lancaster University in 1989 I said:

The necessary autonomy of higher education does not derive just from grants or endowments from the State, but by diversification. For the foreseeable future, the scene will be dominated by the role of the State in funding higher education. But provided access is preserved – particularly for the less well-off – I see funding and accountability being increasingly diversified as higher education institutions interact with a whole range of the vital forces in society.

In that speech I also encouraged universities to be more flexible and imaginative in the sort of courses they should offer to students in this more market-oriented atmosphere. For example, the traditional three-year degree course of study of one subject would be supplemented by a wide range of combined courses running for two or four years, part of which could be taken outside the institution. This was the pattern of American higher education, responsive to the market and to young people's demands, and growing from the bottom up rather than being imposed from the top down as are most of the university systems on the continent of Europe. Diversification and differentiation were the ways forward.

British universities had become over-reliant on the taxpayer compared with universities in Japan and America. American universities had much closer links with industrial companies and private foundations. These provided over £4.5 billion a year, which was three times the total expenditure on higher education in Britain. There was only one significant example of this sort of relationship in Britain – at Salford University, where straitened finances had led the Vice-Chancellor, John Ashworth, to develop successfully the industrial links which produced a significant proportion of his university budget. In order to encourage this sort of partnership we changed university funding rules to allow research laboratories to keep the money which they earned from industrial contracts and to benefit from the patents of any inventions arising from their work.

The number of students receiving higher education had increased by 200,000 since 1979, with most of that increase in the polytechnics. I planned that the total number of students should go up from 906,000 in 1986 to 952,000 in 1990 – an increase of 50,000. This figure was in fact surpassed in the autumn of 1987, and by 1990 there were over 1,100,000 students in our polytechnics and universities. At the start of the 1980s one in eight eighteen-year-olds went into higher education; by 1990 it was one in five. I was not satisfied with that, and before I left Education, in my January 1989 Lancaster speech, I set a target of one in three by the year 2000.

In contrast to the universities, the polytechnics had decided to expand by reducing the unit cost of their students. They had also been very imaginative in creating new courses and combinations of courses, and had involved business companies as much as possible. Tony Crosland had established polytechnics as an additional tier of higher education in the mid-1960s, largely from a sense of frustration over the attitudes of the universities. The county councils were the parents of the polytechnics but their children had now outgrown them. Polytechnic capital expenditure was caught up in the general controls of local authority expenditure operated by Government. Moreover, some councils interfered in the affairs of polytechnics in a petty and sometimes political way. Some were now much larger than most universities, such as Manchester Polytechnic with over 20,000 students, and ILEA had under its control a whole clutch of polytechnics in London.

In 1980 Mark Carlisle, then the Education Secretary, had met a wall of opposition when he tried to make the polytechnics independent of local government. By 1986 this opposition had virtually evaporated.

Indeed two polytechnic directors who were former Labour Members of Parliament – Gerry Fowler and Chris Price – were two of my strongest supporters for the independence of their institutions. I announced this policy in time for the 1987 Manifesto. It has proved to be hugely successful and popular. The polytechnics have used their freedom to expand and improve.

In February 1988, at a meeting of E(EP), there was a long and heated exchange about the funding of polytechnics and universities. I wanted to secure more independence for the University Funding Council and the Polytechnics Funding Council, but Margaret was deeply suspicious. I wanted the PFC to have a 'duty to advise me' but she believed this would turn them into a strident lobby for more money. One of her greatest anxieties was the creation of bodies she believed would then become demanders for more state funding. We argued at length and the exchange between us became heated. At one time she spat out at me, 'You'll be wanting £50 million next. You usually do.' Most of my colleagues were silenced by such comments. But I just ploughed on because I believed I was right and anyway most of the people around the table agreed with me. Eventually I persuaded Margaret to agree that the UFC and the PFC would have a 'power' to advise, which was virtually the same thing.

Another battle I had to win was to resist Treasury demands that the UFC and the PFC in making their grants would take into account any money raised by polytechnics and universities through their own initiatives. This would have penalized their success, and it ran counter to all that I was doing to encourage colleges to go out and raise money in the way that American universities did. This episode demonstrated to me how important it was to free higher education from the top-down planned control of the Treasury.

Student Loans

The second reason why British university education was so costly in relation to other countries was the high cost of student maintenance. Keith Joseph had decided in 1981 to require students from overseas at British universities and polytechnics to pay their full tuition fees. Largely as a hangover from our imperial past, overseas students had been able to study in Britain for their degrees without having to pay for their tuition. This had become a sacred cow which supported students from the Far East, India and Africa, as well as Europe and America. We were the only country in the developed world that was so generous.

The new requirement for overseas students to find their tuition fees unleashed a furious barrage against the Government, who were accused of being mean, short-sighted, market-dominated bigots who put money before learning. The impact was mitigated by an increase in the number of scholarships for poorer overseas students which was provided from the education and overseas budgets. But despite the protests, the Government held fast to its policy that students from wealthier families in Hong Kong, Malaysia, India, America and Europe should pay their way. In 1980, before the change, there were 75,000 overseas students in the UK. By 1990, despite having to pay fees, the number had risen to 88,000. Indeed British higher education institutions went out to sell their courses right across the world, since the money they got for tuition was a valuable source of extra income. In 1987 I attended a great market in Hong Kong where in a matter of two days, one hundred British institutions attracted thousands of potential new students.

In 1981, 1982 and 1983 Keith Joseph had increased the student maintenance grant by less than the rate of inflation. He had decided to divert funds from student support to university support. Most of the taxpayers who provided the money for these grants did not themselves benefit, and nor did their children, whereas those students who did go to college were all given the great personal and financial advantage of a university education. In these grant changes the poorest families were protected but middle-income families had to pay more. In 1984 Keith went further by abolishing the minimum maintenance grant paid to all students and he also planned to require better-off parents to make a contribution towards the tuition fees of their children. The back-benchers of the Tory Party rose in wrath at these proposals directed at the very heartland of their middle-class supporters who had become very vocal in their protests.

Keith's announcement coincided with the Enfield by-election, caused by the death of Anthony Berry in the IRA bombing of the Grand Hotel, Brighton. With student fees now an election issue, Keith had to climb down and he withdrew his proposed parental contribution for tuition. He returned to this particular fray in 1985 when he tried to persuade colleagues to accept the idea of giving students loans instead of grants. He was supported by Nigel Lawson but rather surprisingly he was vehemently opposed by Margaret Thatcher and by Cecil Parkinson, who argued that he would never have gone to university if there had been a loan scheme.

When I became Education Secretary in 1986 I inherited a further cut in the amount for student maintenance grants, and in the amount of social security payments for which students were eligible. This caused a great furore. Student maintenance grants had fallen in value by 20 per cent since 1979, and as a result social security payments to students had risen by £120 million. Norman Fowler, the Social Security Secretary, wanted to reduce this cost by excluding students from Housing Benefit. I persuaded colleagues to rescind some of these cuts, which would have caused real hardship, and as part of the deal I offered to set up a review committee under George Walden, then the Minister for Higher Education, to examine the whole question of student finance, including the possibility of introducing 'top-up' loans. I persuaded Margaret to be more receptive to the whole concept of student loans, and in our 1987 Manifesto we specifically said that we would consider top-up loans to supplement grants as one way of bringing additional new finance to the funding of higher education.

We were the only developed country in the world that did not have some form of student loans, but it had been a taboo subject for too long. In 1988, the 390,000 students receiving awards cost the taxpayer about £500 million in maintenance grants alone. We had developed a system of funding higher education to suit a small and exclusive minority. I wanted to expand the numbers without reducing standards, so that far more young people would benefit and Britain would have a better-educated workforce. Moreover, it was estimated that higher education provided a direct financial return to students, who were able to command starting salaries 25 per cent above the average after graduating. So it was only fair that the cost of higher education should be shared not just between the state and students' parents, but also with the students themselves.

After the Election, with the enthusiastic support of Robert Jackson, the new Minister for Higher Education, I held a series of meetings with John Major, who had just been appointed Chief Secretary at the Treasury. I was delighted to find that he did not accept the traditional Treasury hostility to student loans. The Treasury had always opposed loans because any system would inevitably increase public expenditure during the first few years before graduates started earning and could begin to make repayments. Indeed, the scheme that I was to agree with

John Major had an initial cost to the taxpayer in the first twelve years of about £700 million. But John saw the advantages of increasing the finance available to students, and I thought this was particularly far-sighted because he himself had not been privileged to study at college or university.

Together we prepared a scheme to allow students to obtain a Government loan of up to £420 a year, beginning in autumn 1990. These loans were to have a real interest rate of zero, in other words they were interest-free, but the principal sum to be repaid would be uprated each year in line with inflation. Students would not have to begin repayment until nine months after they had finished their course, and even then payment could be deferred if a graduate's income was low and fell below a certain threshold. These conditions made the top-up loans available to students the cheapest money in town, and far cheaper than the over-drafts which many of them were running up with their banks.

These generous terms had been agreed by John Major on the under-standing that at the same time social security benefits for students would be ended. We had been committed to that as early as 1985, and I certainly felt that there was no worse way for students to start out in life than learning to navigate the complex social security benefit system. The level of the loan ensured that most students were compensated for any loss of benefit. However, as there were some who could be worse off we provided three access funds each of £5 million, available to the universities, the polytechnics and the colleges of further education, to be spent at their discretion to support their students. This was an addi-tional and important source of income to these institutions and was under their complete control.

Another important part of our package of changes was to freeze the existing student maintenance grant. As this fell in real terms so students would be encouraged to take up larger loans to compensate for this. Over the years there would be a gradual reduction in the burden of student support falling on the taxpayer, and a greater assumption of responsibility by students for their own finances through the interest-free loans.

These proposals were approved by colleagues in November 1988, and I published a White Paper, saying on its introduction in the House:

These proposals represent an important step away from the dependency cul-ture. Students will have a financial stake in their own future and this will encourage greater economic awareness and self-reliance. The burden of student support on taxpayers and parents will be reduced. For the first time there will be a guaranteed extra source of income for students over and above their grants and parental contributions.

This last point was very important, because in the surveys we had undertaken we discovered that despite protests that the Government was planning to cut student support, the fact was that 35 per cent of students did not receive the full contribution from their parents which it was assumed they were getting. Many families who could afford it were failing to fulfil their obligations to their student children. We were now going to make money available direct to the student to cover that shortfall. When I was a student myself, I had had a means-tested award which I supplemented from my own savings made during my period of National Service. I also worked during vacations. I would certainly have liked to benefit from a top-up loan available on the terms that I announced.

Our proposals were attacked by all the reactionary forces in education – the National Union of Students, the Labour Party, the Liberal Party, and the Tory Reform Group. The main arguments against loans were that they would deter students from entering higher education – 'a mortgage on knowledge' said Jack Straw – and that they would plunge students into debt. We countered by pointing out that in the rest of the world, where loans were the norm, the number and proportion of young people entering higher education was much higher than in Britain. As for debt, most students already left university with debts, only these were called 'bank overdrafts' and incurred interest payments, which would not be the case with loans.

But our proposals were widely welcomed outside the education world – indeed the major criticism was that the actual level of the maximum loan was too low and should be higher at around £1,000. Even the ranks of Tuscany could scarce forbear to cheer – the *Times Higher Education Supplement*, no friend of the Government, said, 'The case for loans now has an unstoppable momentum.'

One of the trickiest aspects of the top-up loan scheme was how it should be administered and how the loan element should be repaid. At the Department we examined the arguments for whether repayment should be made through the income tax and national insurance systems, or through the banks. Robert Jackson favoured the banks as he considered it vital to break the nexus between the state and the funding of higher education. He had been impressed on his visits to America by US participation rates and how students paid their way through college. He was a strong believer in 'private money being engaged in the higher education process'.

On the other hand, Tony Kerpel believed that loans should be repaid through additional income tax once a graduate had started to earn salary. This would appeal to a sense of social equity – like higher-rate income tax – would be easy to collect, and would create a virtuous circle by which graduate repayments would be seen to fund new generations of students. It was also a painless way in to the eventual charging of repayable tuition fees if the Government later wanted to move that way. Angela Rumbold also had doubts about relying on the banks, and argued that since the banks were being asked to lend money at a zero rate of interest, then what was in it for them?

However, John Major was strongly opposed to introducing a graduate tax, as he and the Treasury thought this would undermine the pristine purity of the tax system. They wanted the banks to be the agents to provide and secure the repayment of loans. As usual, the Treasury prevailed, and it fell to me to try and negotiate this with the banks. David Hancock and I met Tom Boardman, the Chairman of the Clearing Banks, and Robin Leigh-Pemberton, the Governor of the Bank of England, and for a time we thought we had won them over. However, some of the banks' feet became colder and colder when, instead of seeing student loans as a means of introducing students to their other services, they came to believe that loans would have exactly the reverse effect as students protesting against the scheme switched their accounts away from participating banks. Concerned that our principal agents were about to quit the field, John Major too spoke to the banks, but to no effect. Eventually in 1989 we had to set up a separate loans agency based in Glasgow to handle the whole scheme. I was disappointed with that, and quite frankly if I had known this was going to be the outcome I would have persevered with proposals for repayment through the tax system.

The first loans were made available in the academic year 1990–91. Loans worth around £17 million were made to over 180,000 students, about 28 per cent of the total eligible in the UK. In the second year this had risen to £139 million covering 261,000 students, 37 per cent of those eligible. The latest published figures show that at the end of 1992 there were some 403,000 borrowers with loans outstanding of £322 million. So a radical change in the way we financed student support, which had been greeted with protests, is now widely accepted as the way forward and has been accompanied by an unprecedented expansion in actual student numbers. Higher education is no longer the preserve of an elite, and the old system which rationed entry has been replaced by one which is consumer- and demand-led.

Academic Tenure and Pay

In our attempt to change attitudes in the universities Robert Jackson and I had to tackle the problem of academic tenure. Robert was himself a fellow of All Souls, and he vigorously challenged the universities' slovenly attitudes to tenure, pay, and the split between teaching and research. He didn't win their gratitude for that. In fact Robert was refreshingly robust and took the argument to them on their own grounds. I believe he was the most effective Minister of Higher Education during the 1980s.

There were two basic principles: first, academics had lifelong tenure of their posts in universities; second, they were paid on the basis of collegiate rewards whereby everyone received approximately the same pay – there was no real distinction for merit. This ancient principle was not appropriate for an age where academics in certain disciplines could earn higher salaries outside the university world. The idea of jobs for life was also fundamentally wrong, as it meant that a lecturer in his late twenties could get an appointment for the rest of his or her life irrespective of how good their research or teaching was.

These changes were hard fought by the universities. I encountered heated debates in common rooms up and down the land, being told that the whole fabric of university life would collapse because lecturers and professors would be exposed to anxiety and competition. A more subtle argument, which developed as the Education Reform Bill went to the House of Lords in 1988, was that the withdrawal of academic tenure would reduce the freedom for academics to speak their mind. It was therefore a direct threat to academic freedom. This debate, supported by people like Roy Jenkins, was at first conducted on an elevated plane where it was argued that the freedom of academics to dissent from the prevailing views of the day, and particularly the views of the Government, had to be protected. The claim that the withdrawal of academic tenure would prevent dons from attacking Thatcher and all her works was simply ludicrous. Many academics seemed to me to spend most of their time doing exactly that.

The debate soon narrowed down, as it so often does in the universities, to the nervous and personal worries of some academics. They wanted protection for academics from an efficient manager responsible for college finances who simply wanted to ensure that every lecturer was pulling their weight either in teaching or research. Mark Richmond, the urbane Vice-Chancellor of Manchester University and Chairman of the Vice-Chancellors' Committee, sent me a letter in which he pointedly referred to 'malign administrators'.

I became so tired of such niggling special pleading that we arranged a meeting with some of the Vice-Chancellors led by Mark Richmond and Sir Patrick Neill, the Warden of All Souls who was himself a distinguished academic lawyer. The Government's side was represented by James Mackay the Lord Chancellor, Robert Jackson, and myself. The Vice-Chancellors started by arguing that they wanted an explicit undertaking on the face of the Bill to protect academic freedom. As Mark Richmond said, 'This flag is flying high on the flagpole and you'd better do something about it.'

James Mackay, who has the sharpest mind in the Government and the softest way of showing it, slowly dissected the Vice-Chancellors' arguments and mercilessly shredded them with his silky charm. He argued that if the principle of academic freedom was enshrined in statute then it would be impossible to dismiss any lecturer, because such a dismissal would threaten their academic freedom of expression, and this would fly in the face of the Bill's purpose. We wanted to meet their concerns by providing a proper appeals procedure for academic staff. James intended to introduce late in the Report Stage in the Lords a minor amendment to establish a complaints procedure, but he did not mention this at the meeting because an inch offered in March could become a yard by the end of July. As a result of the Bill, academics have since 1986 been appointed on short contracts which can of course be extended by universities if lecturers are seen to be making a positive contribution to the purpose of that university.

I was also unhappy about the standard level of collegiate salaries, and managed to introduce differentials and significantly higher salaries for professors. Oxford, for example, had the tradition of paying all its professors the same salary, about £30,000 a year, whether they taught law or Sanskrit. This was utterly unrealistic and also served to artificially depress rewards for top academic staff. As a result of a belated recognition of market forces and some pressure from us, Oxford began to pay more for some professors in certain posts than others.

At about this time, considerable publicity was being given to an alleged brain drain of top British academics who were being lured to lucrative appointments at American universities. Yet when we argued for the introduction of that same system of differential pay, in order to retain our top academics in Britain or even attract American academics here, we were attacked for introducing Mammon into the temple. It seemed to me extraordinary that while the Government was criticized for creating a brain drain by not allowing enough money for higher academic salaries, it was also criticized for wanting to make more money available to those who were motivated to leave Britain in search of higher rewards abroad.

Further Education

The major problem, and indeed the greatest area of opportunity, in post-sixteen education in Britain was not in higher education but further education. This whole sector had come to be regarded as the 'Cinderella service' of the education system. Yet the more further education colleges I visited the more I became impressed with their work. They provided practical training in a wide range of subjects from computing and engineering to design and business studies, foreign languages, car maintenance, plumbing, hairdressing, building, photography and tourism. There were over 1,750,000 students both full-time and part-time, and 63,000 full-time lecturers in over 400 local education authority colleges. The students were willing to work hard to get qualifications and most of the teachers and lecturers were down-to-earth people who were very concerned about getting jobs or improving careers for their students. They worked closely with local businesses and had tremendous enthusiasm. I thought the ability of all those in further education was underrated.

Further education colleges were being held back by their local authority controllers, yet they were clearly capable of operating independently. As a start in July 1987 I persuaded my colleagues on E(EP) to extend the scheme of delegated budgets for schools to cover also FE colleges and to reconstitute their governing bodies so that at least half the membership came from local businesses and the local community.

FE students studied for a very wide range of qualifications. Forty-one per cent of all A-level students were in these colleges, but most of the courses were provided by bodies like BTeC, City and Guilds, and the Royal Society of Arts, which had their own qualifications. There were also the various diplomas and certificates of the different trades and professions. It was such a bewildering variety that David Young, the Secretary of State for Employment, and I set up a Committee to coordinate all of these into the National Vocational Qualification. We wanted to establish clear stages of progress which provided a ladder beyond the GCSE and allowed non-university students to work towards the equivalent of a degree at any stage in their life. The fruits of this policy are now coming through.

I was so attracted by this whole sector of education that in a speech to the Association of Colleges of Further and Higher Education in February 1989 I set out a new ambitious programme of expansion. Post-sixteen education and training had been one of the failures of English education. In 1979, only 41 per cent of sixteen-year-olds continued in full-time education, with a further 14 per cent in part-time education, making 55 per cent in all. This compared to 80 per cent in America, Japan and the Netherlands. The National Curriculum was intended to encourage higher staying-on rates, but I wanted quicker progress.

First, we did all that we could do to ensure that this sector of education was well funded. Second, Robert Jackson and I went out of our way to publicize the activities of further education and enhance its status. Third, financial delegation was only a first step, and before I left the Department in July 1989 I had begun work to allow these colleges to become as independent as the polytechnics. My successors passed the necessary legislation, and from 1 April 1993, 480 further education and sixth form colleges became independent.

I happened to be attending a meeting with some academics on 31 March 1993 when I was approached by the Principal of an FE college who had actually been present at my speech in 1989. He thanked me warmly and was thrilled and excited that at midnight that evening he would become the head of an independent college. All our efforts have been rewarded, for in 1992 the participation rate at sixteen reached the record level of 77 per cent – 67 per cent in full-time and 10 per cent in part-time education. The changes of 1993 will lead to even higher levels of participation, and this means that more of our young people will acquire skills and qualifications to match or even surpass our competitors, and more older people can decide to enhance or upgrade their skills by working for a further qualification.

Another major innovation was to apply the principle of money following the student. In 1983 Henry Chilver, the remarkably innovative Vice-Chancellor of Cranfield University, and I as Minister of Information Technology, had put a proposal to Keith Joseph to establish a new IT university on a campus near Milton Keynes. We recommended that students should be funded for this with a per capita grant from the Department of Education and Science. It was the first time that this concept had been put to the DES. Unfortunately, this idea had not been fulfilled before I left the Department of Trade to become Minister of Local Government. It survived only in a rather watered-down form relating to postgraduates, but I had learnt a lot from preparing this scheme with Henry – indeed it was the basis for many of the education reforms relating to schools.

Robert Jackson took up this ball for further education and proposed that the per capita grant should not just be provided to colleges but actually given to students as a training or education credit. Students would be entitled to a credit if they enrolled on a course of further education, study or training at an FE college. They could therefore take this funding with them and 'buy' the course that suited them most and which would then be provided by any FE college or a private training operation. The consequence of this would be that the provision of training would be market-led by the student's own wish for a particular course. It meant also that colleges would have to compete for their students. This was indeed a revolutionary step and has been developed by succeeding Ministers. It is now incorporated into the system, and no doubt will one day apply to universities and polytechnics as well.

Teacher Training

There are just over 400,000 teachers in our schools, and each year it is essential to recruit at least another 20–30,000. There are also over 400,000 ex-teachers, many of whom are women bringing up a family. The first priority therefore was to encourage married returners. The second was to recruit teachers for the shortage subjects – in 1986 we were short of 400 maths teachers and 150 physics teachers.

A teacher had to qualify either by studying a four-year degree course leading to a BEd degree or by taking, as a postgraduate, a one-year course leading to the Postgraduate Certificate of Education. The courses for these two qualifications were provided by the teacher training colleges and the university departments of education. I visited several of these and found they varied in quality, for some were very theoretical and in all there was insufficient practical training for actual teaching in the classroom. Many people who were thinking of entering the teaching profession, when it had not been their first job, were discouraged by the requirement to go back to college on a student grant. This chilled the enthusiasm of many people in their late twenties or thirties who had a lot to contribute to teaching if only a better way could be found into the profession.

I started therefore to develop new ideas for the training of teachers on the job – learning under careful supervision in the classroom with a minimum of time spent in college learning the theory. Candidates had to be at least twenty-six years old, with a minimum two years' experience of higher education, and hold a GCSE or its equivalent in maths and English. This led to the innovation of a teacher 'licensed to teach' after one year's practice in the classroom under the supervision of an experienced teacher. The 'licensed teacher' was an important step in breaking down the whole mythology of teacher training. Some Authorities, for example Surrey, found difficulty in recruiting teachers in maths, physics, science and technology. Yet there were many people who had studied these subjects at college or who had practised them in the armed services and now wanted a career change. The licensed teacher route appealed particularly to them. There have been few dropouts from this scheme, and the first licensed teachers entered schools in September 1989. So far over 1,500 licensees have started work.

In June 1989 we estimated there was going to be a shortfall of 20,000 teachers by 1995 and that already there were shortages in key subjects such as maths and sciences. Having already introduced the system of Licensed Teacher Training, I now proposed the introduction of Articled Teacher Training designed to attract graduates who possessed a degree in one subject but did not want to go back to college for another year. They could work in a school for two years as paid trainees, and I recommended that initially there should be up to 500 of these places.

We then started to look at the full-time BEd undergraduate courses in universities and polytechnics. I found in some that the student in the first year had barely any experience of actually being in the classroom. This seemed to me totally absurd. I believe that a high proportion of teacher training time should actually be spent in schools learning to teach children. The unions were deeply suspicious of these proposals, since teachers had won their particular status of being highly qualified after years of struggle. But the whole system had become far too obscurely theoretical and elaborate. I therefore put in hand the reforms which my successors were to implement to change the nature of teacher training.

Science

One of the undoubted successes of British education has been its scientific achievements. Since 1970 British scientists have won fifteen Nobel Prizes, which per capita puts us ahead of any country. British scientists have discovered, invented, or pioneered work on penicillin, monoclonal antibodies, DNA, nuclear magnetic resonance, synthetic pyrethroid insecticides, liquid crystals, fibre optics, the ozone layer, and many other areas of knowledge. Government spending on science since 1979 had increased in real terms by 26 per cent and the science budget for 1988–89 was £1.4 billion. However, it was simply impossible to satisfy the science lobby, which demanded even more, arguing that the Government's duty was to meet those demands. It was one of the ironies of the 1980s that Margaret Thatcher, herself a chemistry graduate, should be disliked by the scientific world after having increased expenditure by 25 per cent in real terms. Even this wasn't enough for them. The British Government was spending £2.6 billion a year on all civil research and development, with science accounting for £1.4 billion. The purpose of this expenditure was threefold: to advance knowledge, to improve technological capability, and to produce qualified manpower. Science needed more scientists, and therefore the National Curriculum reforms ensured that all children studied science up to the age of sixteen – a necessary first step.

The Government's spending on science was not out of line with other countries at about 0.6 per cent of our GDP, which was more than the USA, about the same as Japan, but less than France and Germany. British industry's spending on Research and Development – about 1 per cent of GDP – did not compare well. Industry in the USA, Japan and Germany all spent significantly more than British companies. Industry had to do more, and I made it clear that we would not support 'near market' research whose purpose was to develop a specific product or process for commercial sale.

We wanted the fruits of Government-funded research to be used by industry but Britain's record in technology transfer has been poor. We therefore decided to allow Government laboratories, university laboratories and the National Research and Development Council to keep the royalties and profits which they could earn from the exploitation of their work. This was intended to stimulate them to establish more cooperative arrangements with companies big and small.

In 1987, David Young, now the Secretary of State for Trade and Industry, and I set up the LINK programme which brought together government and university research with companies in five key areas including molecular electronics, advanced semiconductors and industrial measurement systems, and for which we provided £83 million. The whole thrust of these proposals was to open up the doors of science's ivory towers so that business people would be welcome and academics would serve as consultants or directors of private sector companies. I had seen this relationship working effectively on visits I had made in 1981 and 1983 to Silicon Valley, on the west coast of America.

Scientific research was funded principally from two sources, the research councils and the universities – the two sides of the dual support system. The work supported by the research councils was of excellent quality, but they had been subjected to public spending restraints in the early 1980s. Like Keith Joseph I was alarmed at the number of research projects graded as Alpha which emanated from laboratories around the country but which could not be funded. Setting out to increase the research council funds, I found a rather unexpected ally in the Prime Minister.

In 1987 Margaret decided to chair a Committee to coordinate government research spending. She was targeting the substantial research budgets which each Department had and which received relatively little scrutiny from their Ministers. The deal that I did with her was that any savings we managed to make in these individual Departments' budgets would be transferred to the central science budget which I controlled. There was a series of bloody clashes, particularly with George Younger at Defence, which had by far the biggest budget. As a result of this I was able to secure a 12 per cent increase in research council funding in the year 1988–89. As this was principally a rechannelling of existing funds it was supported by John Major, the Chief Secretary.

It was also necessary to change significantly the funding of research in universities. Under the existing system, an allowance for research amounting to a premium of about 40 per cent was attached to each undergraduate science student, and this was one of the factors that drove up the high unit cost of education in Britain. It also meant that universities were being supported for research without any regard to their performance or capability. So we decided to separate the money that went to universities between teaching and research. Moreover, the research funding was to be allocated to universities on the basis of a periodic peer-group assessment of their performance. The great centres of scientific excellence like Oxford, Cambridge, Imperial College and University College, London, and Manchester University welcomed this decision, as did certain other centres of excellence, but some university departments objected to their poor performances being shown up so clearly in the league tables. We also transferred £300 million from university spending to the research councils so they could fund more appropriately the overhead costs of research projects and not simply their running costs. All this amounted to significant changes which had at their heart the concentration of spending on performance, and value for money.

Margaret was suspicious of large, grandiose projects, and particularly of large international ones like CERN in Geneva, whose purpose was to produce energy through nuclear fusion. In the 1970s Margaret had come to learn that grand European science was very expensive, poorly managed and not particularly successful in making breakthroughs. Britain's continuing membership of CERN was brought into question, and Robert Jackson was dispatched to Geneva to ask awkward questions about the value for money of this substantial project. When this became known, the wrath of the physicists fell upon the Government. We learnt that particle and nuclear physics were the root of all progress, the path to all goodness, and essential for humanity and the universe. Today, other countries, realizing the vast sums of money that have been spent on international science to little effect, are also asking the sorts of questions we were asking in the 1980s.

There were new areas of research for which new money had to be found and the most notable of these was AIDS. From 1986 I had served on the Cabinet's AIDS Committee under the chairmanship of Willie Whitelaw and later of Norman Fowler and John Moore. The advice of the Chief Medical Officer was very bleak. The disease was spreading rapidly and there was neither a cure nor a preventive vaccine. The first thing the Committee did was to sponsor some awareness advertising on

TV, since in those days there was much less discussion of AIDS, which was still seen as a problem confined to the homosexual community in America and the heterosexual community in East Africa.

We decided to be frank about the consequences of this new disease and explain how it could infect heterosexuals as well as homosexuals, although this view was itself a matter of controversy. A video was prepared for schools setting out the problem and dealing frankly and visually with the use of condoms.

In the end Willie Whitelaw found all this rather distasteful, and some of the material that we had to view set his eyebrows quivering and his jowls shaking. I was a little surprised that someone who had been in the Army could be so sensitive about sexual matters. But Willie's political antennae told him that AIDS was a huge problem which had to be addressed and that it was right that he, as Deputy Prime Minister, should give it his support and authority. I submitted proposals to increase the amount of research on AIDS and in November 1986 the Committee agreed to an extra £17.5 million over three years. There were good laboratories at St Mary's Hospital and at Cambridge University which were well experienced in dealing with gene disorder and virus infection. Ultimately, this whole area is one where a lot of money has to be spent in the hope that there will be a breakthrough.

Because AIDS was an unknown quantity we were inundated with requests for epidemiological surveys to chart the existing rates of infection, the speed of its transmission and those groups most likely to be at risk. Early in 1989, the two Health Ministers, David Mellor and Ken Clarke, proposed that there should be a Government-sponsored survey of the sexual behaviour of 20,000 British people in the year 1990. This was to determine whether we had got the balance right in our advertising campaign, and whether we should still be so concerned about AIDS affecting the heterosexual community. George Younger, Douglas Hurd and I opposed this survey and stopped it. We believed that such a survey would become just another Kinsey Report, revealing that Britain had become a more promiscuous society – which we knew – and more experimental in the realm of bisexual relationships – which we also knew. A new survey therefore would neither increase the sum of human knowledge nor do anything actually to help AIDS sufferers.

Epilogue

By the summer of 1989, the Education Reform Act was being implemented throughout the country. But the dynamic of change needed more focus and on 14 July I took DES Ministers and senior officials down to Chevening for a seminar on the next phase. I wanted to see a transformation in the system of teacher training by building upon the changes we had already introduced, and increasing the amount of training in the classroom. We also discussed the future role of the local education authorities, which would be diminished following the impact of delegated budgets and grant-maintained schools. The whole movement of reform was rolling forward. However, it was going to be several years before all the changes in the Act could be fully incorporated into the education system. A period of consolidation was now required or, as one commentator put it, 'A really boring Minister, devoid of charisma, short on vision, is just what education needs.'

So what had been achieved over the past three years? I believed that a complete reform of the English education system was vitally necessary and the best way to achieve this was to follow Milton's advice, 'To strike high and adventure dangerously.' The improvement that I wanted could not be secured just by tinkering or slapping another coat of paint on the rusty and crumbling framework.

I knew that to secure change one must have a clear objective, one must work at the details carefully, planning forward all the various Parliamentary stages in both Houses, and one must not waver. The greatest and most important of these is not to waver. There were many who wanted to derail the engine of education reform – the teacher unions, the education establishment, some teachers, and both the Liberal and Labour Parties. I was amazed that the Labour Party, which had always attached such importance to the role of education throughout its history, seemed oblivious to the fact that fundamental change was necessary. But they couldn't shake off their historic link to the entrenched 1960s attitudes of some teacher unions. As I said in one of my Party Conference speeches:

We will not heed any longer the views of the frayed Fabians and champagne Socialists who told us that we were not fit to run an Empire but who denied our children the competitive skills they need for this new world.

There were also Tories who were opposed to the reforms. Some on the left did not like the City Technology Colleges and grant-maintained schools, while some on the right did not like the National Curriculum. There were also faint-hearts in the House of Commons, but I was not prepared to concede an inch to them because Tory backbenchers soon know when they have a Tory Government on the run.

The only way to secure these reforms was to ensure that the pace and momentum did not slacken. I was fortunate to remain as Secretary of State for Education for three years, which meant that I could pilot the whole process of reform from the first discussions through to implement-ation. As I said to the Party Conference in 1987, 'I have put my hand to the plough of education reform and I will carry through to the end of the furrow.'

By the time I had left the Department we had made considerable progress establishing the City Technology Colleges network, the first grant-maintained schools were about to opt out, the formula for delegated budgets had been agreed, per capita funding was being introduced, the necessary arrangements for open enrolment were under way, elections for more broadly based school governing bodies had been held, the GCSE was bedded down, A-levels had been preserved, many more children were staying on at sixteen, record numbers were going on to universities and polytechnics, teachers' pay had been increased substantially, teacher recruitment was going well, the National Curriculum for three subjects had been agreed, and work was in hand for the other seven subjects. A lot had been achieved, but I was under no illusion that it would take many years for the full effect and benefit of the reforms to work through.

One regret I have is that I did not ease the introduction of the National Curriculum by increasing the number of periods taught each day by just one, thereby adding five extra forty-minute periods to the teaching week. If we had done this then there would have been all the flexibility needed to accommodate the existing curriculum alongside other subjects like classics, a second foreign language, and home economics. I had con-sidered doing this in 1989, but it would have involved renegotiation with the unions about teachers' contracts which stipulated the number of hours a teacher had to work each year. The teacher unions would have certainly opposed such a change, and it would have thrown the whole system into turmoil again just at the time when I was wanting a period of stability to implement the rest of the reforms. However, the whole issue should now be raised again because the City Technology Colleges have shown how imaginative a curriculum can be when the length of the teaching day is increased.

I was fully conscious that the success of all these reforms would depend upon the teachers, and that we were asking a great deal of them. But I had little regard for the leadership of the large teacher unions which was narrow, selfish and bigoted. During the many meetings I held with the teacher union leaders never once did they raise the central issue of improving the standard of education – it was always more pay for less work. Children came a long way down their list of considerations. However, I followed Keith Joseph's first wise advice to me and never attacked rank-and-file teachers themselves. I have always been keenly aware of the crucial importance of teachers in our society, for the last three generations of my own family had all seized opportunities which only education had opened up for them. Moreover, my grandmother had been a teacher, one of my great aunts had run Catholic Education in south Wales in the early part of this century, several other relations were teachers, and my wife had been a teacher for over seven years. I was determined that teachers' status should be enhanced in the eyes of the public, and this meant putting behind them – I hoped forever – any thought of industrial action. They could look forward instead to an era when they were better paid, better trained, and working in better schools.

CHAPTER 12

Living with Margaret

Arguing the Toss – Controlling the Purse Strings –
Leading from the Front – Getting the Message Across

When I first joined the Cabinet in 1985 its meetings tended to be formal, with routine reports from the Leader of the House about the next week's business, followed by the Chief Whip on voting arrangements, and the Foreign Secretary on world affairs. Occasionally there would be quite short discussions about the matter of the moment and future legislation. After the Westland Crisis in 1986 there was a definite shift to longer and fuller discussions. When I became Chairman of the Conservative Party I introduced political discussions after the formal Cabinet meeting.

Much of the debate on major governmental issues was held in Cabinet committees, and for particularly critical issues Margaret took the chair herself. The EA Committee dealt primarily with economic affairs but could handle almost anything else. Margaret also set up a variety of miscellaneous committees to deal with specific matters such as the education reforms, teachers' pay, the health reforms, science expenditure and broadcasting policy. As she chaired all of these, her influence was pervasive.

Margaret's conduct of these meetings was unique. She usually had three sets of briefings for the issues being discussed. One came from the Cabinet Secretary, carefully crafted and recommending the official line to take; one from Brian Griffiths' Policy Unit, and a third sometimes appeared from her handbag – although few would know who had written it. All her briefing papers were heavily underlined and sometimes highlighted in yellow. There is no doubt she did her homework.

Sometimes Margaret would start a meeting by summing up, 'Well I don't know why we are meeting. It is quite clear this matter must be settled and in fact I thought it was. So shall we just check some of the details?' From that moment everyone knew, if there had been any doubt, exactly what her views were. On other occasions, knowing that there was a major dispute between two Government Departments, say on defence expenditure or the future of the motor industry, she would let Ministers present their case. But whatever the discussion one of the first people to be brought in would be the Chief Secretary, the titular controller of the public purse though Margaret's fingers were always tightly around its strings.

Margaret categorized her Ministers into those she could put down, those she could break down, and those she could wear down. She never respected wimps or those who were meekly compliant, but she did respect those who stood their corner. Being a strong and determined character herself, she recognized those qualities in others. But there were always some whom she knew she had to deal with much more carefully.

I never heard Margaret tangle with Peter Walker, who was given complete licence to attack Nigel Lawson's economic policy. She was always aware that he could return to the Backbenches and become the focus of centre-left discontent. But she got pretty impatient with Geoffrey Howe's scrupulous expositions on foreign affairs. This reflected her deep suspicion of the Foreign Office, which she thought was spineless, wet, feeble, and one of the institutions most responsible for Britain's decline over the decades. However, this did not prevent her from holding some individual diplomats, like Crispin Tickell, in high regard and appointing others, like Antony Acland and Robin Renwick, rather than politicians, to key ambassadorships like that in Washington.

The first Cabinet meeting after her great election victory in 1987 was held on 18 June. It was a very hot and stuffy day, but Margaret chose the middle of Geoffrey Howe's report on foreign affairs to say, 'Please open the windows. We can't have people falling asleep.' It was not entirely clear whether the soporific effect she had in mind was induced by Geoffrey or the heat. She didn't mind vigorous debate but Ministers had to give as good as they got. The only way was not to treat her as the all-powerful Prime Minister but as someone whose arguments had to be met and, if necessary, rebutted. There were very few open disagreements between Margaret and Nigel Lawson. Most of their disputes took place in smaller gatherings or tête-à-tête. Indeed Margaret went out of her way at all her meetings to buttress the authority of the Treasury and the Chancellor. The only sharp exchange I ever heard between her and Nigel was over the community charge at our meeting in May 1985.

The Cabinet Committee debates on the education reforms during 1986 and 1987 were forceful and robust. The Richter scale, which her Private Office kept unofficially to record the liveliness of meetings, hit record levels. Verbal blows were traded as I fought off some extraordinary notions, not only from Margaret but also from other colleagues, about how the education system should be reformed.

Another Minister who stood his corner was Ken Clarke, particularly during the period when he was fashioning the health reforms. Margaret had her own briefings on this issue from various informants working in the Health Service. This would enable her to suddenly come out with a piece of detailed information which was probably only half true but had the effect of undermining Ken's arguments. Ken would never use one sentence when three could do the job, and after one of their meetings Margaret said to him, 'The trouble with you is that you talk too much. You remind me of Robert Carr.' That certainly rang a bell with me. I remembered in 1973 Robert taking over from Reggie Maudling as Home Secretary and presiding as Chairman of the Home Affairs Committee. Reggie would shamble in to the Committee, which met on a Friday morning at ten o'clock, and dispose of the business within an hour. By contrast, Robert would open up a debate on each subject and treat the proceedings as a seminar, forcing colleagues to cancel their lunch dates. Margaret did not like seminars. Crispness was all.

On some occasions the Prime Minister was quite willing to argue with literally everybody around the table about one issue. These were remarkable tours de force in which conflicting ideas flashed about and there was no attempt to reach a consensus. After one particularly gruelling meeting I remember Chris Patten saying to me, with reference to the temporary contraction of the fingers on Margaret's right hand, known as Dupuytren's Contracture, 'The thing she suffers from is also known as Coachman's Grip.' This was an eighteenth-century ailment acquired by coachmen who clutched reins too tightly and for too long.

On 20 April 1989, after the Hillsborough Disaster in which ninety-five people were crushed to death during a massive crowd build-up inside one end of the Sheffield Wednesday football ground, there was a discussion about the Football Spectators Bill. This Bill, which was currently before Parliament, set up a compulsory system of identity cards for members of football clubs and was being driven hard by Margaret, who saw it as a way of combating football hooliganism. There had, however, been a great campaign in the football world, supported by many Tory Members of Parliament, to abandon the Bill. The Chief Whip and the Leader of the House both advised that there was not a majority to carry the measure. Douglas Hurd, the Home

Secretary, also wanted postponement, but Margaret was totally opposed to this. She began by reminding us of 300 deaths in other football stadium disasters, and 6,000 violent incidents all connected with football, arguing 'Three hundred dead is no cause for delay.' Nigel Lawson still supported postponement, to which the Prime Minister replied, 'Do you want a problem or an agreement?' Geoffrey Howe, and Ken Clarke, who as a soccer fan knew a lot about the game and about football grounds, both argued for delay. Margaret crisply asked them, 'Well, what would you do?' Norman Fowler, sensing the flow of the tide, supported the Prime Minister, as did Nick Ridley.

During this debate, Margaret used a technique which I had seen her deploy on other occasions with devastating effect. She called for the Popplewell Report on football ground safety to be brought in, and then read aloud sections from it which supported her case before telling us all about the horrors of inaction. A sort of truce was agreed whereby Douglas Hurd promised an interim report from Lord Taylor, the Judge appointed to conduct an inquiry into the Hillsborough Disaster. We agreed to re-examine the Bill in the light of that report. But Margaret remained in quite a huff, and continued to read the Popplewell Report all through other Ministers' reports. This was another interesting example of her doggedness, her resistance to advice when she had made up her own mind, and the very spirited way in which she argued. In the event the matter was delayed, which was a sensible response.

While Margaret could argue her case in the Cabinet and in the House of Commons, when it came to the House of Lords others had to do it for her. Margaret was very happy that Willie Whitelaw was around to handle the Lords for her from 1983. There was a large crossbench element in the Lords which was broadly opposed to virtually everything that Thatcherism stood for. If these peers allied with Labour the Government could not muster an effective majority. Willie Whitelaw and Bertie Denham, who was an outstanding Chief Whip, time and time again had to conjure up majorities on very controversial issues. Willie's successor, John Belstead, had a much more difficult time and had to report fairly regularly to Cabinet that yet another amendment had been lost in the Lords.

In February 1988, at a meeting on the Education Reform Bill, I told Margaret that we would probably have some real trouble in the Lords about the definition of academic freedom. John Belstead chose that moment to intervene and confirm my advice. Margaret turned and said to him, which I could never imagine her saying to Willie, 'Be robust, we can't be defeated on this in the Lords. They have no business to change this. Be robust.' In fact, it wasn't so much robustness as patient persuasion that was needed. But the flow of defeats continued.

A year later in February 1989 the Lords were mauling the Bill to establish identity cards for football supporters, and limbering up to maul Douglas Hurd's Broadcasting Bill and his Security Services Bill. Margaret was appalled that so many Tory peers did not turn up to vote for Tory measures. She asked John Belstead indignantly, 'What are all the Tory peers whom I have created doing?'

However, on some matters Margaret certainly did want to take the views of her colleagues, and particularly on important political decisions. One of these was the timing of the 1987 General Election. Not only did Margaret want to hear colleagues' views but she genuinely wanted to be in a position to say that she had considered these carefully. In March 1987 there was a very long discussion after Cabinet on the timing of the forthcoming election. The press had virtually decided that it was to be in June, which was Margaret's 'lucky' month. As the power to decide the General Election date is one of the few party political advantages of incumbency which a Prime Minister has, she was struggling to keep open other options. Despite a Conservative lead of around 11 points in the opinion polls, some Conservatives did not believe we could win a summer election and we would do much better in the autumn, after the summer recess.

The civil servants left the Cabinet Room and Margaret asked each Minister to give their view. Norman Tebbit, as Chairman of the Party, was circumspect and did not advocate a particular date. He urged us to go at the Labour Party and not build up the Alliance by attacking them too much. John Biffen made some very sensible comments about how to tackle the Alliance and then came out for an autumn election, as did George Younger, Geoffrey Howe and John Moore. Tom King said that unless the May local election results were decisively in our favour we should go for the autumn. Ken Clarke suggested that the Prime Minister should declare now that she was going to go for an autumn election. 'No, no,' she said. 'The only weapon I have is surprise.' Peter Walker and Paul Channon plumped for June, together with Michael Jopling who, concerned that delay might mean a deterioration in the Party's position, said, 'Too many things come out of the blue.' David Young also preferred June, advising her to 'take the tide', while Nick Ridley said just one word, 'June'.

Quintin Hailsham said that we should not just rely on negative campaigning by knocking the Opposition so much. Disgruntled Conservatives had to be persuaded to vote for us for positive reasons. He recommended that the Prime Minister should not make up her mind just yet. Willie Whitelaw, winding up the discussion, said, 'If the window is wide open, go through it in June. But it is highly unlikely that it will be wide enough to know clearly enough.'

This was a most interesting discussion, and the Prime Minister intervened at various times in favour of both June and September. She knew there were likely to be leaks from this meeting simply as a result of Ministers speculating with their journalist friends about the date of the next Election, and was being careful not to reveal her own preference. My own view, which I expressed at the meeting, was that it had become almost impossible to avoid going to the country in June, particularly with the unemployment figures beginning to look a little better. Later that evening, Margaret said on television that she wanted to serve two more terms – that is until 1997.

Controlling the Purse Strings

Margaret had a determination bordering upon obsession about public expenditure. She had seen a succession of weak Governments surrendering to the emotive pleas of lobbies pressing for higher expenditure. For her, controlling Government spending was the number one priority, and it required all her willpower to get her colleagues to accept this. Each July the Cabinet agreed the spending totals for the following year. Margaret began these meetings with dire warnings about the pressures that had been building up: they were even greater than ever before, and colleagues had to back the Chancellor. Every Minister then commented, and anyone who even hinted at some relaxation of the limits got a frosty and dismissive stare. The only Minister to whose disagreement Margaret listened, with her head bowed, was Peter Walker, who invariably spoke up for the other point of view. At the end of the meeting the heavies like Cecil Parkinson and Norman Tebbit would come in. Then came a summary by Willie Whitelaw which would fully endorse the Prime Minister and the Chancellor.

These meetings intimidated Ministers into collective responsibility for public expenditure. The spending target then became inviolable, and in the autumn Margaret would report regularly as to how the Chief

Secretary was getting on in his bilateral negotiations with individual Ministers and how everybody was expected to help him. Indeed, she looked upon the Chief Secretary almost as her own deputy rather than the Chancellor's.

I recall several incidents going back to the early 1980s when Margaret intervened to control expenditure. The Cabinet wanted to hold back the Boyle recommendations on MPs' pay and allowances. This was the Cabinet's reaction to virtually every report that came from the Top Salaries Review Body, and throughout the 1980s Ministers were regularly asked to agree to less than had been recommended. As a member of the 1922 Executive I attended a meeting in February 1980 about the Boyle Report when it was clear that the backbenchers wanted all of their recommended pay increase. Margaret had reluctantly accepted the Report but objected to the proposal that MPs should have free rail travel for journeys anywhere in the country. It was certainly a good populist line to be against that.

This was very much Margaret's pattern of behaviour. When she was forced to accept something she didn't basically like, her technique was to focus on one small element, blow it up out of all proportion, and make people feel guilty about contradicting her on that one point. It somehow sweetened the bitterness of the bigger pill she was being asked to swallow. However, in July the backbench MPs resisted the pressure from the Prime Minister, Willie Whitelaw and a three-line whip, and insisted upon the full 9.6 per cent of the Boyle recommendation. But Margaret had the last word, and shamed Tory MPs into voting against unlimited free rail travel.

On 18 June 1982 I was present at a meeting to discuss whether we should sell two frigates to Pakistan. Margaret liked Pakistan, which was a good friend of Britain, but the Treasury in the shape of Leon Brittan, and the Department of Trade in the shape of Arthur Cockfield, were not in favour of finding the money to subsidize the cost of building the ships. Margaret was supported by John Nott, the Defence Secretary, and myself from Industry. She summed up by saying, 'You must find a way. You are accountants and accounting is all about taking a sum of money from one person and giving it to someone else. Sort it out.' She wasn't just interested in selling frigates to Pakistan, but wanted the business because it meant jobs back home for our shipyards. Time and time again she said, 'I want to spend money on real jobs', even though this might mean, on occasions, very un-Thatcherite economics.

Although Margaret had given defence expenditure priority even she was aware this could not go on forever. In September 1983, after a meeting about the cost of British troops in Germany, she said, 'We can't go on indefinitely with a three per cent real terms increase in defence expenditure.'

Margaret's opposition to increasing public expenditure was so profound that she would not even agree to proposals from her greatest supporter, Keith Joseph. On 20 October 1983, as Education Secretary, he had proposed an increase in expenditure by the research councils of a further £50 million per year for the next three years. Keith argued that the councils were turning down first-class research projects because of earlier cuts in funding. He was nevertheless strongly opposed by the Prime Minister who said, 'You just can't have any more money. We don't need more pure scientific research. What we need is to apply more effectively what we have done already.' As usual, she was more than half right. The fact that she was arguing with her strongest supporter and closest friend in the Cabinet was even more piquant. She eventually half-pleaded with Keith, 'You are making me say "No". It is not fair. You are making me appear a battleaxe.' Keith got something, but not his £150 million.

In 1984 the annual battle on the public expenditure round created a crisis for the Cabinet. The Treasury wanted to cut capital expenditure on the building and maintenance of council housing by £600 million. Patrick Jenkin, the Environment Secretary, was totally opposed to this cut, as was Ian Gow, the Housing Minister, who told Margaret he would resign if it went through. Ian wryly told me that despite her evident fondness for him she had accused him of being a 'wet'. When Ian was moved later to the most junior post in the Treasury he thought it was because of the stand he had taken over this issue. Patrick Jenkin decided to take it to Cabinet, refusing to settle through the normal channels. Most unusually the full Cabinet was adjourned for half an hour while this matter was settled. Patrick won, but I do not think Margaret ever really forgave him for it.

In the July 1986 Cabinet on the public expenditure proposals – the first such debate I had attended – Nigel announced there was little scope for any increase in expenditure. I entered the round-table discussion rather late and argued for greater flexibility to allow some increases for education and housing. The Prime Minister suddenly turned to me and asked the direct question, 'Do you agree with the planning totals?' I said that I did but requested flexibility interpreting them. But having asked me, Margaret then had to go around the rest of the table, which was her way of getting collective approval for Nigel's package. Peter Walker was the only Cabinet Minister who bluntly said that he didn't agree and argued for a higher spend.

Another example of Margaret's determination to hold down expenditure was the discussion about the increase in charges for eye and dental tests in November 1988. John Major, as Chief Secretary, had just agreed to increase NHS expenditure by £2,000 million. To offset some of this, charges for eye and dental tests were to be increased to raise £140 million. At the Cabinet on 1 November the Chief Whip and the Leader of the House reported that we would lose the vote later that day unless we changed our policy. The Prime Minister insisted that we must win with no change of policy.

Ken Clarke, as Health Secretary, raised the question of where his extra money would come from in the event of us losing the vote. The Prime Minister rounded on him, telling him to stand firm and to hold to the Autumn Statement which John was announcing that afternoon. 'The Party must know that if we don't get these increases in the charges, then there's going to be less extra money for the NHS,' she said. She then deployed one of her most effective weapons – the power of the Prime Minister at the dispatch box – by saying, 'I will say all this when I answer questions this afternoon. You Ken must say the same in your opening speech.' Ken was rash enough to try again on two separate occasions to get Margaret to change her mind, but she was very sharp and squashed him.

The Prime Minister was adamant on this issue. Both David Waddington and John Wakeham had suggested that one way to avert the crisis was to exempt old age pensioners from the charges. This would cost some £27 million. John later told me that if Willie Whitelaw had still been around he would almost certainly have persuaded Margaret to accept this. But there was no Willie and she would have none of it. Margaret was flying solo and demanding that the Party should follow her lead. During the day the Whips worked away at the rebels and even asked me to speak to Simon Coombs, a potential rebel who had been my Parliamentary Private Secretary back in 1981.

The debate was raucous and lively. David Mellor, Ken Clarke's deputy at Health, was so astonishingly rude in his winding-up speech that we all thought he would drive any doubters into the Opposition lobby. He was gratuitously rude to Jerry Hayes, the Conservative MP for Harlow, who had written an article on oral cancer for the London *Evening Standard*. David said that Jerry had been 'remunerated well enough to enable him to pay for his next check-up'. However, we won the vote for increased dental charges by sixteen votes, and eye charges by eight. After the first vote I was sitting alongside the Prime Minister and she said that it looked as if we were going to lose the second vote. She was due to leave London early the next day for an official visit to Poland and said rather tartly to me, 'It is intolerable that I have to face the Party and Jaruzelski in the same week.'

This crisis was of Margaret's own making. Any other member of the Cabinet would have climbed down, but her mission was to keep the finances of the country in proper shape. The Party was taken right to the brink and Margaret was quite prepared to risk humiliation. None of that changed her determination. No Chancellor of the Exchequer or Chief Secretary could have had better support from their Prime Minister than that. Margaret took her responsibilities as First Lord of the Treasury very seriously indeed, and she did not mind how unpopular she became. She knew that if she gave in to one case there would be another twenty waiting to march forward. I recalled her comment at a meeting two years earlier, 'The bigger the handout, the bigger the queue.'

The Prime Minister stood out against increases of expenditure in even the most humane cases like war widows and haemophiliacs. She did so not because she didn't see the strength of their case but because it would set a precedent for many other claims. Towards the end of 1989, as Party Chairman, I pressed her to concede on both of these issues, since Ministers were being carved up on television when defending what seemed to be indefensible policies. Margaret withstood my pleas but I pressed again and eventually concessions were made.

In the autumn of 1989 I strongly supported Chris Patten in his attempt to soften the first-year impact of the community charge. This of course involved more money. Margaret bluntly turned down our appeal saying, 'The reserves have virtually gone, there is nothing left.' However, she was not unaware of the political importance of public expenditure and at one of our early meetings raised the question of the poor quality of the fabric of our museums. Five of the museum directors, encouraged I believe by Grey Gowrie, had written to her and convinced her of the strength of their cause. 'They have a good case,' she said. 'We are going to spend quite a lot of money between now and the next election and we must target it.'

By April 1990, the finances of the country had deteriorated and we had to consider postponing either the National Health Service reforms or the introduction of Community Care, which was being transferred to local authorities. Margaret's view was, 'I am now inclined to say this can't be done by local authorities because they already have too much on their plate. The Treasury simply does not have any more money. Our backbenchers have spent it.'

Margaret was prepared to court considerable personal and political odium in these fights over public expenditure, and she didn't let down her Ministers who were taking the same line. I think she realized that when she departed from office whoever followed would slacken the rein, but she could never have thought it would be slackened so much. At a dinner hosted by Conrad Black, before Christmas 1992, Margaret was incandescent about the looseness of Treasury control and the prospect of a huge deficit. 'It is madness,' she said. 'We can't go on like this.'

Leading from the Front

The British people always respond to strong leadership. Margaret knew that and gave it to them. She led from the front even though some following her often fretted about her pace and direction. Just a fortnight before she lost the leadership of the Conservative Party she said in an interview, 'Had I faltered we would have neither the success nor the international reputation we have.' She added one of her rare comments upon her position as a woman: 'When a woman is strong she is strident. If a man is strong he is a good guy.'

As a woman, Margaret had come under critical fire from feminist writers and intellectuals. The irony was that their objections to her were usually based upon the special pleading argument, 'What has she done for women?' It completely eluded her critics that Margaret had triumphed in the predominantly male world of politics without anyone having 'done' anything for her, and that as a product of the meritocracy she believed others too could achieve what she had done. In fact the feminists totally overlooked Margaret's actual achievement in winning and keeping the premiership, thereby creating a fantastic role model for women. They simply wished that she were a different type of woman, preferably hand-wringing rather than handbagging, and moist-eyed for others of her sex. They could not forgive Margaret for playing the matter of gender straight down the line, ignoring the 'issue' as they saw it of sex, and simply getting on with the job. During the drafting of the 1987 Manifesto I suggested to Margaret that we should include, as part of our record, the fact that nearly 50 per cent of students at our universities and polytechnics were now female. She dismissed this as being irrelevant.

The quality that marked Margaret out from all of the other possible leadership contenders was her strength of purpose and character. She had a clear vision for Britain – property-owning, low-taxed, free from trade union domination, less state ownership, and proud and strong in the councils of the world. Like her or loathe her, people knew what she stood for and where she was going.

Margaret was vilified by her opponents, looked down upon by the chattering classes, and viciously caricatured, but she didn't give a damn. She was not called the Iron Lady for nothing. During the hard months of 1989 and 1990 I knew that we had a leader who would not buckle under pressure and whine to journalists about the way she was being treated. Her armour made her impervious to the sort of criticism which withered gentler souls.

One of the few times I heard her react to press coverage was during a Saturday morning visit to Downing Street in the summer of 1990 when, over a whisky, we were discussing how to put across the Government's record more effectively. She said, 'I don't expect gratitude, no politician should do that, but I would hope to be treated fairly and at the moment the press are not giving us any credit for our successes.' If this was a complaint, then it was by the Captain on behalf of her team, rather than for herself.

Margaret did not pore over newspapers, contenting herself instead with seeing the early editions of the *Financial Times* at midnight. She once said to me, 'I don't spend much time on the newspapers.' However, she was kept abreast of the main stories, and particularly of the performance of her Government and Ministers, through selected cuttings and briefings from Bernard Ingham. Some looked upon Bernard Ingham as the Rasputin at her Court, more powerful than Ministers, and prepared verbally to execute anyone who dared challenge his Tsarina. Although there was some basis for this belief it exaggerates his influence. Bernard was no Rasputin, but his relationship with Margaret could be described, to borrow the words of W. E. Henley, as 'She's the tenant of the room, he's the ruffian on the stairs'.

Bernard was one of the most loyal supporters Margaret had, defending her when few could think of a good word to say in her favour. He represented her views, not only when she had expressed them, but when he had 'divined' them. His power of divination was acute and his mode of expression blunt. Over the years, Ministers who had been bruised by Bernard came to resent his influence, and many Tory backbenchers felt he had become one of the Downing Street Praetorian guard, shielding Margaret from even her friends in the Parliamentary Party. This contributed to the feeling that what Number 10 needed was a changing of the guard.

Margaret had certain deep-seated instincts which coloured the decisions she took. These decisions were not taken quickly or lightly, and she would subject each issue to a good deal of collective thought, analysis and discussion, but having decided upon a course of action with her colleagues, she would pursue it with vigour, determination and resolution. Her instincts were drawn principally from her family and childhood. They were reinforced by her experience as a junior Minister in the Ministry of Pensions, where she had worked with John Boyd-Carpenter – a period to which she referred quite frequently – as well as by her time as the Cabinet Minister responsible for Education – a period to which she referred very little.

Her experiences as a junior and senior Minister made very lasting impressions upon her. I remember a discussion in November 1982 when Patrick Jenkin was defending his Department's advice over one aspect of privatization. Margaret rounded on him and said, 'Since Keith left your Department the advice you get has been more interventionist. When I was Parliamentary Secretary in the Ministry of Pensions I saw how civil servants changed their advice as the Ministers changed. I served under three Ministers and I remember well how the advice to them changed.'

In 1981 Margaret had been persuaded by Alan Walters that, in spite of the fact that Britain was going through the worst recession since the war, a tough Budget was needed. That Budget was essentially hers, and I doubt very much whether it would have emerged from the Treasury without her prompting. It was a very risky course of action and I remember going into the House on Budget Day at about 2 p.m. having been a Minister of State for just three months. I saw Jim Prior sitting alone, not on the Frontbench, but at the back of the Chamber. He looked very flushed and angry, saying, 'I can't tell you any details but this is an appalling Budget. We have gone mad and I don't know whether I shall stay on board.' He did stay, but this episode indicated that Margaret was prepared to risk ministerial resignations if that was the price for imposing such tough economic medicine. She gave an equally clear and determined lead during the Falklands War in 1982 and the miners' strike in 1984.

I have no doubt that this determination to stick with her policies and avoid U-turns stemmed from her experiences in Ted Heath's Government. In March 1979 I was not yet a Minister, but as a member of the Executive of the 1922 Committee, I went with colleagues to see her at Downing Street. She turned to me at one stage and said, 'You remember, Kenneth, when we were in Ted's Government, that there were U-turns and they didn't work.' I said, 'Margaret, you'll remember that you were a member of the Government that made the U-turns. I joined in 1972, after they'd been made!' Michael Jopling, the Chief Whip, nearly choked on his whisky.

In the early 1980s Margaret knew that she had to be resolute about the deployment of NATO Cruise missiles. The West, primarily America and Britain, had to demonstrate to Brezhnev and his successors that we had not lost or weakened our resolve to resist Soviet threats. When the Soviet Union deployed its SS20 missiles it was essential that the West countered this immediately. Our demonstration of firmness showed to the Soviets that they and the Warsaw Pact could not pressure the West into accepting one-sided disarmament. In fact the United States, by planning to outspend the Soviets on defence, forced the Soviet Union to recognize its own need for reform and change.

Subsequent to these events and a new basis for understanding between East and West, Margaret formed a special relationship with Mikhail Gorbachev, telling the Cabinet on her return from her first meeting with him in Russia, that he was 'someone we can do business with'. In 1989 Gorbachev received the freedom of the City of London, and as I left the Guildhall where the ceremony had taken place I met Cecil Parkinson. We both marvelled at this extraordinary turn of events. 'Gorbachev,' said Cecil, 'spends so much time with Margaret because he knows that she is the toughest of the West's leaders.'

In April 1986 President Reagan asked for British assistance in the bombing raids he intended to launch against Colonel Gaddafi in Libya. The Prime Minister was asked to give approval for American bombers to fly from British airbases. Her answer was 'Yes.' In her report to Cabinet on 15 April she said that we had been asked to give immediate help to America and that, 'This is the right decision in the long-term interests of Britain. The US keeps hundreds of thousands of troops in Europe to defend Europe. She is entitled to ask to use our bases.' This decision had been approved by a small group of Ministers including Geoffrey Howe and George Younger. Willie Whitelaw said, 'When I was told, I fully supported this decision.' Some other Ministers including Norman Tebbit, Nigel Lawson and John Biffen expressed misgivings, and I too was doubtful whether such a raid would achieve any objective. But Margaret countered this by saying, 'We would have been in a much worse position if we had withheld our support.' Nigel Lawson ruefully and pointedly said, 'The Americans owe you a lot for this,' rather ignoring that the Americans had jeopardized their own Latin American policy by helping us during the Falklands War. The fact was that Ronald Reagan had done Margaret a favour and she was now repaying him.

Later that year Margaret stood out against the moves to impose economic sanctions against South Africa. She was virtually the only major world figure to resist sanctions from the beginning. She believed they were completely misconceived because they would drive De Klerk and South Africa's whites into isolation which would only serve to entrench apartheid. She was also concerned that sanctions would hit South Africa's economy and actually bring suffering upon the black workers whom sanctions were supposed to help, although this was not the view of the ANC. The Commonwealth heads of Government attacked Margaret for not supporting sanctions, but she said to the Cabinet on 27 November 1986, 'We are the one country in the world which must stand strong on everything.'

Margaret was always looking for new policies to maintain the thrust of Thatcherism. In the spring of 1989 interest rates were high, the balance of trade was moving into the red, and the Government was unpopular. Margaret decided to take the initiative by abolishing the Dock Labour Scheme, whose effect had been to protect for life the work of dockers. This had made many British ports uncompetitive, and it was amazing that it had survived for ten years. Any move to change or scrap the scheme had been rejected because of the possibility of a national dock strike. Now, despite the Government's economic troubles, Margaret was quite prepared to risk taking on the dockers. When Nigel Lawson said that the £ would withstand the strain of any strike, Douglas Hurd said the police were prepared to deal with one, and Norman Fowler said a Bill could be drafted and on the Statute Book by the summer, Margaret decided to go ahead.

This was a good example of Margaret deciding to move quickly into a rather unexpected area to sort out a mess, to right a wrong, and also to revive the flagging fortunes of her Government. There was no doubt this legislation would be popular with our Party and our backbenchers, even though it ran the risk of provoking a strike. But Margaret felt she had to keep the Thatcherite revolution going forward, if only in the belief that if she stopped pedalling then everybody would fall off the bicycle.

Margaret rather liked the soubriquet of 'The Iron Lady', and she did nothing to discourage comparisons with Joan of Arc. Like St Joan she too had her voices, and a woman with 'voices' can change history.

Getting the Message Across

Margaret looked upon her annual speech to the Tory Party Conference as one of the major events of the political year. She spent days working on her speech with a team of people who would gather in a room adjacent to her suite in the Conference Hotel. Led by her Political Secretaries, first Stephen Sherbourne and latterly John Whittingdale, they produced endless drafts which would be embellished by Ronnie Millar and John O'Sullivan. From time to time Chris Patten or John Selwyn Gummer were summoned to provide some telling phrases. These great set pieces had two purposes. First, to commune with the Party faithful and to consolidate Margaret's grip over the Party. Second, to ensure that the success and the agenda of her Government led that day's television news programmes and the Saturday morning papers, and carried through to Sunday's papers. Margaret also used her speeches to give very clear signals about her personality, perhaps the most striking example being her 'the Lady's not for turning' speech.

The second means of communication which Margaret came to master was the television interview. Adroit and experienced as her interviewers – Robin Day, Brian Walden, David Dimbleby and Alastair Burnet – were, Margaret developed a technique to dominate her interviews. This was developed carefully, usually with Bernard Ingham and her Political Advisers. Its aim was to get across to viewers the simple message she wanted, regardless of what she was asked. Although Margaret did not watch much television, apart from the news, she realized that the impression she gave on screen was just as important as what she actually said in the interview. In both Party Conference and television appearances she used her clothes, style and manner to convey the strength and vitality of her character, employing with devastating effect the fact that she was a woman.

Margaret's third means of communication was through the House of Commons, especially when Prime Minister's Questions became televised twice each week. She turned Prime Minister's Questions into a major news story that would lead the evening television news on Tuesdays and Thursdays. The two fifteen-minute slots were an ordeal for which she prepared very carefully. Over a sandwich lunch at Number 10 she would spend at least two hours with her Private Secretaries and Political Advisers trying to guess which issues would come up and polishing sharp responses, particularly to the questions that Neil Kinnock was likely to raise.

Margaret would enter the Chamber of the House of Commons at about ten minutes past three, carrying a sheaf of notes. These were not contained in a folder but were separate sheets for each subject. Comments and phrases in her own hand would be scribbled on each sheet. John Major prefers a loose-leaf folder in which each subject page is divided vertically, with typed comments and replies heavily underlined. Margaret was always nervous before being called to answer Prime Minister's Questions at the Dispatch Box. When she took her place on the Frontbench she preferred not to speak to those sitting beside her. She would flip through her notes trying to memorize the most salient points and devastating ripostes, humming quietly to herself under her breath. When Prime Minister's Questions were over at 3.30 p.m. Margaret's team would meet again in her office in the House of Commons to hold a post-mortem. Bernard Ingham would come down from the Press Gallery, and if Margaret had made an inadvertent comment or a factual slip he would return to give journalists the correct message.

No picture of the Thatcher years would be complete without a reference to Denis Thatcher. He was at Margaret's side, or one pace behind her, on foreign visits, at official dinners, and at Party Conferences. He was a familiar figure at the various Conference receptions with his cigarette and gin and tonic, making refreshingly blunt comments about 'pinkoes', 'commies', 'whingers', and the Church of England. He had a very expressive way of shaking his head and turning up his eyes when someone he disapproved of was mentioned, and would say, 'Well what can you expect?' Some of Margaret's comments about the performance of industry, and the sloppiness of accounting of some great company that had got into trouble, I knew would have come from

Denis's own experience in the world of business. The best of the 'Dear Bill' letters in *Private Eye* were like listening to Denis speak.

Denis was utterly loyal to Margaret, whom he worshipped. The press came to like him because he was utterly genuine and unpretentious. Journalists were full of admiration and some amazement that he had survived so well being married to such a strong and vibrant personality. At all the critical moments in Margaret's political life one must never forget that it was Denis who was at her side and who was her closest confidant, the last person to say good-night to her and the first person to talk over the morning news with her. In my experience he never intervened directly in any current political issues, but his influence remained profound.

CHAPTER 13

The Party Chairmanship

*The Tenth Anniversary – The Absence of Willie – The
Currie Crisis – The Political Position in 1989, and the
Party Chairmanship – The Dismissal of Geoffrey Howe –
Reform at Central Office – The Party Conference 1989*

As the tenth anniversary of Margaret's 1979 election victory
approached, the Party prepared to celebrate. On 3 May, the 1922
Committee entertained her to lunch at the Savoy and presented her with
a silver rose bowl. In her speech she reminisced about her long period in
office, reminding us about the great events of her premiership – the
tough Budget of 1981, the Falklands, and the miners' strike. Much had
been achieved but there was much more to do. Socialism had to be
defeated, and her message was 'keep at it'. There was no element here of
valediction.

Shortly before the anniversary day, 4 May, Margaret had appeared on
the steps of Number 10 holding her recently born grandchild in her
arms. This was seen as a dynastic gesture and was accompanied by
Margaret's appropriation of royal syntax when she declared, 'We have
become a grandmother of a grandson.' This use of 'We' instead of 'I'
became the subject of much public fun. At Number 10 on the anniversary evening there was a happy celebratory dinner with the Cabinet
Ministers and their wives. There were six tables set out in the drawing-
rooms on the first floor and the Prime Minister was seated between
George Younger and John Wakeham. Geoffrey Howe sat at another
table next to Denis Thatcher. It was a truly Thatcherite function, as
each of us had paid for ourselves and our wives to enjoy the very English
dinner of salmon, lamb and raspberries. Such self-financing economics
did not, however, blunt the jollity of the occasion.

Geoffrey Howe, who together with Peter Walker and George Younger
was the only surviving member of Margaret's first Cabinet, made a very
warm congratulatory speech. He declared that Margaret was the greatest
peacetime Prime Minister of the century and that her place in the

history of our country was secure. It was a charming and amusing speech, and I thought that after this performance he really ought to be appointed her official biographer.

Many people felt at the time that it would have been better if Margaret had decided to retire on this her tenth anniversary. She had by then secured her place in the history books as an outstanding leader who had arrested the decline of Britain. She could bow out in glory. This was certainly the view of Denis and her close confidants and advisers – Tim Bell and Gordon Reece. At one of their meetings Tim had said to Gordon, 'It is up to you, you must tell her very firmly that she should stand down'. 'I can't,' said Gordon, 'I love her.' 'Steady on,' said Denis. 'She's my wife.'

I don't believe that Margaret for one moment contemplated retirement. She was not in the mould of Keats' 'St Agnes' – 'purposing each minute to retire, she linger'd still.' Margaret wanted to stay for two reasons. First, she liked being Prime Minister, the power, the influence, her personal position in the world, and she still had abundant energy. Second, if she stood down at that time the succession contest would have been between Geoffrey Howe and Michael Heseltine, and she didn't think that Geoffrey would win. She was not prepared to hand over the Party to Michael, who in her view represented all the things from which she had saved her country and her Party.

The Absence of Willie

There is no doubt that from 1988 the Government was weakened by not having Willie Whitelaw in it. Attending a carol concert in Westminster Abbey just before Christmas in 1987, he had collapsed with a mild stroke. His absence from the centre of the Conservative Party was a severe loss. He had been around the heart of politics for a long time. During Ted's premiership he and Peter Carrington were the two heavyweights who in difficult times would call upon Ted and then something would happen or would stop happening.

As a former Chief Whip, Willie had a deep understanding of the nature of the Parliamentary Party, and that made him earthily realistic about what could be achieved in politics. Ted's Government missed him when he was moved away from the centre in 1972 to run Northern Ireland, which then totally preoccupied him. He was brought back as Employment Secretary late in 1973 to try and stop the rot, but by then the waves that were to sweep Ted out of office were too strong for him to contain.

Having lost the subsequent leadership election against Margaret, he decided that his role was to help her as much as he could – Melbourne to Margaret's Victoria. In Government his was the shoulder to cry on. He was the father confessor to whom Ministers could confide their anxieties and the wily old politician whose counsel was always worth hearing. Hundreds of Ministers felt that in Willie they had a friend at Court. Not that he always helped them, because his agenda was to deliver what Margaret wanted. She once described his role, using the inadvertent *double-entendre* 'Every Government should have a Willie.' At Cabinet he would say little, listening to what was said by others, though in fact he knew the views of everyone around the table on every major topic. What he was wanting to hear was whether individual Ministers would actually articulate their views, and how that articulation would be met by colleagues. Then, in a few words, he would sum up in a way that guided the decision in the direction the Prime Minister wanted. It was brilliant man-management.

Willie has a wonderfully open and genial character that evoked an affectionate response. I never saw anyone who could move so rapidly from torpor to anger within a few seconds – jowls shaking, shoulders heaving and those great oyster eyes turned up. Then, just as quickly, peace would descend. Shakespeare said 'sudden storms are short', but these storms were wonderful to behold and usually left the landscape a little altered. Willie also had a habit, when concentrating hard, of looking down and pulling his eyebrows with his right hand as if he was encouraging the grey cells into action. The more he twisted his eyebrows, the more you knew how tricky the problem was.

Willie developed political astuteness to a high art. He understood basic human nature. He wasn't much good with figures but he had a shrewd idea of the political impact that any financial decision would make, and for Margaret this common-sense, down-to-earth advice was essential. Willie was no intellectual and had no pretension to be. He was disarmingly diffident about his own powers, and once said to an aide as he walked down the Committee Room Corridor of the House of Commons, 'The Tory Party doesn't like brains. Thank God I don't have any.'

The Currie Crisis

On 3 December 1988, on a Saturday morning, the junior Health Minister Edwina Currie, had made a statement on television saying that most egg production in the UK was contaminated by salmonella. I mention this episode because it became a sort of turning-point for the Government where everything that happened subsequently seemed to go wrong. Edwina's statement was not rebutted quickly on Sunday because John MacGregor, then Agriculture Secretary, was in Montreal attending GATT talks and unable to appreciate the row that was building up back home. This proved to be a fatal absence. The fallout became very serious indeed. Scared shoppers stopped buying eggs, egg production dropped by between 50 and 70 per cent, producers were closing units and issuing writs against the Government, and hundreds of thousands of birds were being killed. Edwina had precipitated 'the slaughter of the innocents'. Her position became untenable when one major egg producer began legal proceedings against her for damages.

Ken Clarke, Edwina's boss as Health Secretary, could have resolved the matter by either forcing Edwina to retract or modify her statement, or saying something himself. But, for whatever reason, the smack of firm government failed to descend. The Cabinet discussed the eggs crisis twice at length on 8 and 15 December. Everything that MAFF and the Health Department did to try to clarify the position dug them deeper and deeper into the hole. Backbenchers, under pressure from the egg-producer lobby, were demanding Edwina's resignation, and on the 15th the Prime Minister said, 'This situation is now a crisis.' It was partly resolved by Edwina resigning the next day, but this was a crisis of her own contrivance, with the other Ministers involved making a real mess of the crisis management.

Despite the furore, Edwina could have survived if she had simply apologized for saying that 'most' egg production was infected and then set the record straight. But she was unable to adopt this politically prudent approach. Colleagues, who had never borne much love for Edwina and her flair for self-publicity, were loath to rally round. Two years later Edwina was to demonstrate her mercurial temperament again when, in the leadership election, she became one of the first to announce the view that Margaret should go. Coming from someone who had always proclaimed herself a Thatcher-clone and built a career in praise of the Prime Minister – she even said to Margaret during an intervention in the House in July 1990, 'May I say that my Rt Hon. Friend the Prime Minister is looking jolly nice today' – this seemed a mite opportunistic.

The Political Position in 1989, and the Party Chairmanship

In the summer of 1989 the economy was heading into a recession, the balance of payments was moving into the red, unemployment was beginning to rise, high interest and mortgage rates were driving our supporters away in droves. The Party in the country was beginning to question our capacity to win, and there were grassroots rumblings about water privatization, the health reforms and the community charge. In the House of Commons there was a significant group of MPs who were convinced that we could not win another election with Margaret as leader, and Michael Heseltine was campaigning vigorously around the country for himself.

By the end of the Parliamentary session in July, the Government was looking tired. Its main Bills establishing the community charge and the education reforms were on the Statute Book. Already, politicians were beginning to think about the next Election. Fresh blood was needed in the Cabinet and at the junior levels. The main difficulty was the log-jam in the three top posts. Geoffrey Howe had been the Foreign Secretary, and Nigel Lawson the Chancellor, since 1983. Douglas Hurd had been the Home Secretary since 1986. Few thought that this team, which had been the winning team of 1987, was likely to be the one which would lead us at the next Election. Margaret pre-empted a long summer of gossip and speculation by bringing forward Government changes to July rather than wait until the more usual time of September. This was very sensible timing and allowed new Ministers to use the summer to settle into their new Departments.

It was widely expected that the Prime Minister would appoint a new Party Chairman. Since becoming leader, Margaret had had five different Chairmen – Peter Thorneycroft, Cecil Parkinson, John Selwyn Gummer, Norman Tebbit, and Peter Brooke. After the 1987 Election, Norman Tebbit had made it clear that he wished to leave the Government. That raised the question of who would succeed him as Party Chairman. Having served as Norman's deputy during the Election campaign, David Young would have been a logical candidate, and indeed at the time of the Party Conference his name began to feature in speculation about who Margaret would appoint as her new Chairman. It did not take long for the counter-briefing to begin.

Norman and David had not enjoyed the most comradely partnership during the Election campaign, and Norman was now making things as difficult as only Norman can. But he also appeared to have powerful allies in Willie Whitelaw and John Wakeham. One argument against David was that he had never fought a Parliamentary election and so did not have sufficient understanding of the Party in the House of Commons. But the main argument used against David's appointment to head Central Office was his understandable wish to remain Secretary of State for Trade and Industry, a job he relished. It was argued that combining the two posts could lead to a conflict of interest in cases where David had to make rulings involving companies which were also contributors to Party funds. There were precedents for Chairmen of the Party also holding senior ministerial rank, but in David's case the argument seemed to cut some ice.

As the speculation grew, one solution put forward was that David should give up any responsibility for company mergers in order to resolve possible conflicts of interest arising. However, he was not prepared to be hobbled in this way and decided that in these circumstances he would rather not be considered for the Party chairmanship.

It was a sad episode, because David is a talented manager and Central Office would have benefited from his critical eye. But his mind was made up and Margaret turned instead to Peter Brooke, Paymaster General at the Treasury, to take on the job. Peter was the son of former Home Secretary Henry Brooke, well liked, and generally regarded as a safe pair of hands. He is a Tory of the old school, with a dry rather Edwardian wit, a charming and civilized man, who is courteous and painstaking in his dealings with colleagues and officials. This made him popular with the staff at Central Office, where Peter, himself a management recruiter, undertook a reconstruction of Departments. But the European Election campaign of June 1989 was not regarded as a success, with criticism directed against the Party for negative advertising, and the Labour Party scoring its first national campaign success since 1974.

It is traditional for Conservative Prime Ministers to appoint 'peacetime' and 'wartime' Chairmen. Peter had fulfilled the 'peacetime' role, which is to manage and reshape Central Office in the post-Election years. Now the Prime Minister was looking for a 'wartime' Chairman to get the Party headquarters into shape for the General Election campaign. Because our Euro-election defeat was blamed largely on presentation, the general consensus was that the Party needed 'a communicator'. This term is the TV-age equivalent of the Blarney stone, and some politicians are deemed to be communicators and others not. I was generally regarded as one of the Tory Party's communicators. The problem for those deemed to be communicators is that they are also deemed to be nothing more. A communicator is not readily regarded as also being capable of thought, new ideas or administrative ability. So to bear the label 'communicator' is a not unalloyed blessing.

Most of the press speculation centred on Norman Fowler and Tom King, though my name was occasionally mentioned. Some political colleagues had approached me and said they would like me to take on the Chairmanship. They wanted me to make it clear that I was seeking this position, but I was not willing to do that. I had no great desire to take on the role, for I was very happy at the Department of Education, and getting the Education Bill on to the Statute Book was only the first step along the road to education reform. I would have been happy to continue to implement the Act because I was passionately committed to improving the quality of education in our country.

Moreover I knew perfectly well that the job of being Chairman had always been a bed of nails. The only Chairman who had enhanced his reputation in recent years was Cecil Parkinson, who masterminded the 1983 Election victory. Cecil had been very popular with Central Office staff, and the campaign – in particular the service to candidates – had been a great success. But even Cecil would acknowledge that with Margaret enjoying her Falklands War prestige, and with Michael Foot leading a totally discredited Labour Party, the Conservatives were odds-on favourites to win. Norman Tebbit had run the 1987 Election campaign, but had not emerged with the same acclaim. In part this was unfair, because Norman delivered an enormous 102-seat majority and was the architect of a remarkable victory for which he has not had the credit he is due.

There were lessons to be learnt from all this. The Election campaign in 1991, or 1992 if Margaret broke with precedent and went for a full five-year Parliament, was going to be much more difficult. The Chairman would have to fashion victory against the background of a declining economy, a new and unpopular local tax system, and increasing Party divisions on Europe. During an Election the relationship between the Leader and the Chairman has to be very personal and close. If I became Party Chairman I would have to stand four-square with the Prime

Minister on all these issues. There could not be a cigarette paper's width of difference between us. If there was, Bernard Ingham would see to it that Prime Ministerial displeasure seeped into lobby briefings, and the rifts experienced by Norman would open up again.

I asked Tony Kerpel what he thought of my taking on the Party chairmanship in the run-up to a General Election. He thought for a moment and then replied, 'Victory is hers, defeat is yours.' He had reservations. First, he thought there were good reasons for me to stay at Education for a full five-year term. That would kill the mischievous comment that I moved on before having to face the consequences of my own legislation. It would also enable me to bed down in my own way the education reforms which I had introduced. Second, he felt that I was a good manager of a Department and could get officials to give their best. Certainly the DES had been transformed into a frontline Department. By comparison Central Office, which he knew, was not amenable to the same skills and could be a nest of intrigue with its factionalized departments.

These arguments chimed well with my own thoughts, so I did nothing to encourage the idea that I wanted the post. I knew of course that if Margaret did offer it to me I would have to accept, but I was also confident that I could do it well. Occasionally my name was mentioned as a possible Leader of the Party, but I knew that no Party Chairman since the War had gone on to become Leader of the Party. This view was confirmed when on one evening in July 1989, Mary and I went to have a drink with Willie and Celia Whitelaw at their mews house. Willie, returning slowly to public life, was very concerned about the growing unpopularity of the Government. He believed the Prime Minister did not really understand how serious this was. He thought that I would be an ideal Chairman for the Party but said, 'It's tricky and I doubt whether it will really progress your career.'

In fact, I was rather surprised that Margaret would even consider me, for I was not a member of her inner circle as Cecil had been, nor one of her speech writers like John Selwyn Gummer, and not particularly a soul-mate such as Norman Tebbit had been for a time. However, the longer I served Margaret the more I came to respect and like her. I think that she respected me, though not just as a Minister who could handle difficult problems and take through reforms which although not hers were definitely in the Thatcher-mould, but also because I was not to be browbeaten. On the whole Margaret preferred people to agree with her, but she never had any real respect for the craven.

On Monday 25 July, I was asked to go to Number 10, arriving just before 10 a.m. As soon as I arrived I was shown up to the small study on the first floor. Margaret said that she wanted me to go to Central Office as Party Chairman, and serve in the Cabinet as Chancellor of the Duchy of Lancaster. Margaret hoped that I would improve the presentation of the Government's record, but I knew that poor communication of Government policy was only part of the trouble. The Government seemed to have lost its way and lost some of its magic touch. I was clear that if we were to win the next election there would have to be some changes in economic policy and in the introduction of the community charge. It was not just a matter of better presentation. Margaret told me that she was very worried about the economy but 'our first priority must be to get inflation down. Mortgage and interest rates will follow, and then we'll be all right.' That was to be our central problem for the next three years.

I told Margaret that as Party Chairman I would give her my total personal loyalty. That must be the essential bedrock of the relationship between the Chairman and the Leader of the Party. In any Conservative Government there are two crucial relationships: the Prime Minister with the Chancellor of the Exchequer, and the Prime Minister with the Chairman of the Party. If the first is not right, then the Government will soon fall apart. If the second is not right, then the Party in the country and in the Commons will be riven by internal feuds.

I was determined that this should not happen. I did not want a repeat of the tensions between Central Office and Number 10 which occurred during Norman Tebbit's time. That became the guiding principle of my chairmanship. It has been said that Margaret wanted a Central Office machine that was good enough to win elections for her but not good enough to challenge Number 10. Under my chairmanship, Central Office was not going to become an alternative power base for a challenge superficially supporting the Prime Minister but surreptitiously undermining her position. Indeed, if I had not taken this line from the beginning then I believe the Tory Party, in the dramatic events which were later to unfold, would have broken into two camps. That division would have continued long after the change of the Party leadership.

The Dismissal of Geoffrey Howe

The Prime Minister also told me of the immediate consequences of my move – John MacGregor, at Agriculture, was to take my place at Education, and Peter Brooke, the current Party Chairman, was to go to Northern Ireland. I was not told of any other moves and I did not ask about them, for on these occasions Prime Ministers are particularly reticent. They know that as the day unfolds there will be some Ministers who object to what is going to happen to them, some who can't be contacted, and some who – as I would in the future – decline the offer of an alternative position. The lunchtime news, and the *Evening Standard*, led with my becoming Party Chairman. There was no inkling of other changes. The headlines were to be very different by tea-time.

Before I left Number 10, I bumped into Peter Brooke and we spent about half an hour together in the little antechamber on the ground floor of Number 10, where he fully and frankly debriefed me about Central Office. He gave me a rundown on the staff, the position in the constituencies, and the large financial deficit that I was about to inherit.

I had lunch at the *Daily Express* with the Editor, Nick Lloyd, but I was unable to give him any tasty morsels if only for the very good reason that I did not know any. It was only towards the end of the afternoon that it became clear the Prime Minister had decided to remove her Foreign Secretary. The dismissal of Geoffrey Howe as Foreign Secretary was to prove an unhappy episode for both him and Margaret. Geoffrey was surprised and hurt. He did not expect that this would be his reward for long years of loyal and important service. It lit the fuse which was to explode in his speech in November 1990, triggering the leadership contest which ended in Margaret's own resignation.

Geoffrey had been one of the principal architects of Thatcherism. His control of economic policy as Chancellor of the Exchequer from 1979 to 1983, and particularly his Budget in 1981, had established the essential framework for the Government's success. In pursuing his policies, Geoffrey had withstood a massive amount of condescending and coruscating attacks. Denis Healey, in a much-quoted phrase, said that being attacked by Geoffrey Howe was like being 'savaged by a dead sheep'. But Healey was always better at being a bar-room bully than a Chancellor of the Exchequer, where his own record was one of humiliating failure. As Chancellor, Geoffrey had also received a letter signed by 364 economists condemning his policies and predicting that these would lead to ruin and decline. Mary and I were dining at Number 11 on the night the letter was delivered, and as we left I saw Geoffrey glancing through the early editions of the morning papers. He said laconically, with a sigh, 'I'm surprised that they only found 364.'

Geoffrey bore all these attacks with a patient air that never ruffled his innate amiability. He knew that his policies were right and that they would produce, as they did, lower inflation, high growth, and the possibility for the first time since the war of repaying some of our National Debt. He was secure in his reputation and he will be seen as a great Chancellor.

He went on to be Foreign Secretary – a post he enjoyed – although his tenure will be seen as good rather than great. For, after four years as Prime Minister, Margaret had become not only familiar with world issues but intrigued, involved, and with a firm set of views of her own. Moreover, she was a world figure who immediately commanded attention at every international gathering that she attended. She was 'the cynosure of neighbouring eyes'. It was what *she* said that counted. Each of Geoffrey's moves had to be made in the knowledge that the Prime Minister was not only interested but might have a different stance, and perhaps express this in a blunt, more vivid and perhaps not entirely helpful way. The breaking-point was Europe, in particular the Single European Act of 1986 which Margaret felt coerced into agreeing, and the terms for joining the Exchange Rate Mechanism of the European Monetary System, which the Prime Minister had reluctantly agreed to at Madrid in June 1989 under pressure from her Chancellor and Foreign Secretary. This tension led to Margaret's decision to move her Foreign Secretary and free up one of the 'big three' jobs for a protégé.

Geoffrey's dismissal from the Foreign Office was a profound shock to him and Elspeth. He was offered instead the post of Leader of the House and Lord President of the Privy Council. During the following day, Geoffrey's friends gave their version of events and allowed it to be known that he had been offered, as an alternative, Douglas Hurd's job as Home Secretary. This in turn gave offence to Douglas' friends who believed the Prime Minister considered him expendable – hardly fair reward for Douglas' long stint in the salt mines of the Home Office.

Geoffrey had turned down the Home Office, but had asked in addition to being the Leader of the House to be made Deputy Prime Minister and to have the chairmanship of the Star Chamber Committee that dealt with public expenditure. All this was readily granted by the Prime Minister.

On the Wednesday, there was a further embarrassment when Bernard Ingham was asked by journalists what the post of Deputy Prime Minister entailed. In typically brusque fashion, Ingham was utterly dismissive, implying that the title meant nothing. But he was taking his cue from Margaret who, eighteen months earlier, had said that the post of Deputy Prime Minister was no longer needed.

The fact that Geoffrey had to ask for this additional title made his consolation prize even more hollow. When confidence has been lost between a Prime Minister and another Minister then neither titles nor seats on Cabinet Committees make much difference. When Jim Prior ceased to be Employment Secretary he asked to be a member of the important economic sub-committee of the Cabinet. It really made no difference. He found very soon that Northern Ireland occupied virtually all his time. He may have saved face but he lost the game. In this case, the chairmanship of Star Chamber meant absolutely nothing since the committee was never convened that autumn.

Margaret had really decided that she did not want Geoffrey any longer to be her Foreign Secretary. In such circumstances it would have been better for them both if the breach had been complete and if Geoffrey had left the Government altogether. But politicians nearly always find it difficult to go. The glare of the footlights holds them to the stage.

For Geoffrey, the next eighteen months were to be lonely, frustrating and humiliating. I did what I could to work for a better personal relationship between him and Margaret, but too much had happened, too much had been said. Churchill said of Curzon, 'The morning was golden, the noontide was silver, and the evening was bronze.' It would have been better for Geoffrey to have avoided the evening, for he is one of the nicest and most decent people in British politics. He was always ready to pause in the Lobby to have a word with the most junior Member; always willing to speak at a constituency dinner; always keen to help the young and aspiring candidate. Geoffrey was reflective and thoughtful, rightly proud of the policy initiatives he had put in hand and particularly of the work he had done in founding the Bow Group. He engendered great loyalty from his friends, including Ian Gow, who was also deeply attached to Margaret and had been her best Parliamentary Private Secretary.

The dismissal from the Foreign Secretaryship was not made any the easier by the fact that Geoffrey and Elspeth were also made homeless through it. They had two official residences – one at Carlton Gardens in London, and the other at Chevening, in Kent.

This issue of the houses, or 'Sir Geoffrey Houses' as some wits dubbed it, became something more than a storm in a teacup. Chevening, more beautiful than Chequers, is a splendid Georgian mansion, stuffed full of mementoes of William Pitt the Younger, which was given to the nation by the last of the Stanhope family. It is a gracious house with a large park and lake, a great library formed over 300 years, and fine furniture. Over the years Geoffrey and Elspeth had come to look upon Chevening as their home. Lying alongside Stanhope's books, visitors would find gifts that had been given to Geoffrey as Chancellor and Foreign Secretary.

Margaret harboured the suspicion that Geoffrey and Elspeth were using Chevening as a sort of alternative power-base to Chequers, for they were generous hosts. Such suspicions were totally without foundation. The guest book at Chevening shows that Geoffrey and Elspeth invited a wide range of friends to their weekend parties, mixing together politicians of all sorts, business people, diplomats, writers, constituents, and their own family. After dinner, most of their guests were encouraged to play a simplified form of snooker called 'Slosh', which allowed even the most inexpert to score occasionally. Weekends at Chevening were convivial, not conspiratorial. Guests took away happy memories of Geoffrey's chuckling and courtly kindness, and Elspeth's intense and infectious gaiety. Chevening was part of their lives, but they made the mistake of falling in love with it. Ministers should never forget that they are merely tenants who have a leasehold, not a freehold.

The only way that Geoffrey could be found a home quickly was for Margaret to ask Nigel Lawson to give up the use of Dorneywood, the other official residence, in Buckinghamshire. This was not welcome news to Nigel and his wife, Therese, since they enjoyed living in that comfortable house. By mid-week, all of this estate agent aspect of the reshuffle had become public. When Geoffrey rose in the House at 3.30 p.m. on Thursday he was greeted with long and warm cheers. But when he uttered the customary words of the Leader of the House, 'The Business of the House next week will be . . .' a Labour wit shouted out, 'House hunting.'

The shuffle was much wider than expected. George Younger and David Young stood down. Paul Channon at Transport and John Moore at Social Security, both of whom were having a bad patch and exceptionally bad luck, were asked to leave. The new Cabinet was meant to be the team for the Election. Cecil Parkinson moved from Energy to

Transport, though he would have preferred the Foreign Office. Chris Patten joined the Cabinet as the Environment Secretary, and Norman Lamont as the Chief Secretary, something which he much desired and had deserved for a long time. John Selwyn Gummer also entered the Cabinet as Agriculture Secretary, and Virginia Bottomley joined the Government as a junior Health Minister. The *Economist* called the reshuffle 'Mrs Thatcher's bid for posterity'. The future, it said, lay with Major, Patten and Baker, and 'if she triumphs then one of them is almost certain to succeed her', a perceptive analysis, albeit one fulfilled in totally unforeseen circumstances.

The reports of my own move from Education Secretary to Party Chairman were predictable. They uniformly stressed my 'presentational skills' and how these would help the Party better to communicate its policies. Some raised questions about my legacy in previous Departments. The newspapers also pointed out for their readers what I already knew for myself – that the new job represented opportunities for the succession to Margaret but also pitfalls in the event of an unsuccessful Election campaign. The *Times* and the *Daily Express* reported, 'Ladbrokes, the bookmakers, last night made Mr Baker favourite to succeed Mrs Thatcher at 2–1, Mr John Major was quoted at 7–2, Sir Geoffrey Howe and Mr Michael Heseltine 4–1, and Mr Cecil Parkinson 5–1.' I was not tempted to place any bets.

By the weekend, a shuffle that had been intended to rejuvenate the Government had rather added to its troubles. On Wednesday, Margaret told me, 'The gloss has been taken off.' By the weekend, Labour had a lead of 9 per cent in the opinion polls. On the Saturday night, I was rung up by Brendan Bruce, Director of Communications at Conservative Central Office, with the news that the *Observer* was going to run a story that Willie Whitelaw thought the shuffle 'a ghastly mistake'. They claimed that he had been telling his friends that while he liked Chris Patten's appointment to Environment, and mine to Central Office, he thought Geoffrey and Douglas had been treated badly.

This was the first of the many minor and major crises that I had to deal with as Party Chairman. Margaret and I were annoyed that the episode had been kept alive by this further twist. So, on Sunday, I tracked Willie down to where he was staying with Peter Carrington and spoke to him on the telephone. Willie said, 'I am very, very sorry and the story is completely untrue.' He issued an appropriate statement but the damage had been done.

That weekend, Margaret was disappointed even though she had got into place the people she wanted. She was saddened by what she thought were confidential discussions being leaked to the press – and here Geoffrey's friends did not help him – and remarked, 'I don't think that the Privy Councillor's Oath means anything to some people.' This got the relationship with her ex-Foreign Secretary and now her new Deputy off to a very poor start.

But things had not been handled well. Three of the most senior members of the Government had been hurt, surprised and embarrassed. On the following Monday, Geoffrey and Elspeth went off to France in high dudgeon, with Geoffrey denying that he would be standing against the Prime Minister in any leadership contest that autumn. Much of the week's troubles could have been avoided if Margaret had softened the blow by allowing Geoffrey to keep Chevening. These little things matter. But she was determined to deprive him and Elspeth of the use of this house. It was an unnecessarily spiteful act which Margaret was to regret.

There was, however, one clear beneficiary from the week's events. John Major, then Chief Secretary to the Treasury, was totally surprised and taken aback at becoming Foreign Secretary. He had not had the slightest inkling of what was in store for him. Indeed, at lunch on the Monday, after seeing me on television go into Number 10, he had rung up to find out what was happening since he hadn't heard a thing.

It was typical of John and Norma that despite all the excitement of that day, with the new phenomenon for them of personal protection officers and security, and the massive briefing which the Foreign Office was preparing for him, they kept a longstanding invitation to dine with us at our Pimlico house that night. Mary Soames, Winston Churchill's daughter, joined us and couldn't conceal her sheer delight at so unexpectedly returning to the centre of political events by dining with the new Foreign Secretary and the new Chairman of the Party on the very day they were appointed. It must have seemed just like the old days.

Alastair Burnet, who was not that evening appearing on 'News at Ten', also came to dinner. He believed that the shuffle was a stroke of genius since it had rejuvenated the Government. John was a good deal more modest. After dinner he told me that he was amazed that Margaret had offered him the Foreign Secretaryship. He said that he really wanted to be Chancellor of the Exchequer, and he did not want the leadership. He was not to wait long to get his first choice.

Reform at Central Office

When I took over as Party Chairman I did not have to make many changes to the Central Office organisation that I inherited from Peter Brooke. Brendan Bruce had been recently recruited from the advertising world to be Director of Communications. Although he had not had much experience of politics he brought to Central Office a good understanding of marketing and the importance of strategic thinking. He was not a politician's Director of Communications, for he was far too intelligent and shrewd simply to agree with the last person who had talked to him. He was well supported by the head of the Press Office, Christine Wall, who having worked with Margaret at Number 10 had wide and useful connections across the media and was respected for her sound political judgement. John Lacy was the Director of Organization and Head of the Agents, and together with Tony Garrett had already started to analyse the key marginal seats, assessing our strengths and weaknesses, and allocating new support where necessary.

Robin Harris was Head of the Research Department, but he soon decided that he wanted to go and work for Margaret in the Policy Unit at Number 10, and since then he has become the principal writer of her memoirs. To replace him I appointed Andrew Lansley from the British Chamber of Commerce, who had previously been a civil servant working as Norman Tebbit's Private Secretary. Andrew built up a strong team of young men and women who were to serve the Party well in the coming years. During the 1992 General Election some of them became known as the Brat Pack, and several have since become Political Advisers to Ministers. I was impressed with the calibre of the young people attracted to working in the Research Department. It continued to live up to its reputation of being a very good recruiting ground for future Conservative politicians. Margaret shared this view. After a meeting in August she said, 'You have some marvellous people in Research – unrivalled.'

I was also determined to reinforce the professional expertise of the Party, because that's where we have a clear lead over Labour and the Liberals. In his political novel, *Beauchamp's Career*, Meredith commented upon the Tories' legendary efficiency, 'Tories dread the restlessness of radicals and the radicals are in awe of the organization of Tories.' I decided to increase significantly the number of new agents in training. It costs about £10,000 to train an agent, and I set a target to increase the number by eighty, which meant an investment of at least £800,000. This was money really well spent. We took in some very able people, many of whom I hope will be serving the Party for several decades to come.

I also wanted the constituencies to have the latest computer technology to allow them to target individual electors and interest groups by direct mail. This was another excellent investment. Increased subscriptions soon pay off the initial cost of a computer, which can then be used as an electioneering tool. I decided to provide computers and staff in the key marginal seats which could not afford them, and this proved to be of critical importance in the 1992 Election.

I had asked Margaret, at one of my first meetings as Party Chairman, to allow the Cabinet after their Thursday morning meeting to remain in session for a political discussion without, of course, the civil servants remaining. There are few opportunities for a broad collective political discussion between Ministers where the overall effects of Government policy, rather than narrower Departmental interests and the issues of the moment, are discussed. Margaret really agreed to this innovation, and we started to have a political discussion after most Cabinets. I found this essential in focusing the attention of colleagues on promoting the record of the Government as a whole and concentrating upon how they could contribute to winning the next Election. These meetings became a regular feature for the next two years, and Chris Patten continued them when he became Party Chairman.

I was strongly supported by my team at Central Office. Tom Arnold, MP for the highly marginal seat of Hazel Grove, was the Vice-Chairman of the Party who dealt with the selection of candidates. This is a critical task, since Central Office compiles and keeps a list of approved candidates who have passed through a selection process, and from this the local Associations can shortlist applicants for interview. The fact that the 1992 intake of MPs is one of the ablest for some time is due to Tom's work over seven years. David Young was the Deputy Chairman, and some commentators said that he had been appointed to keep an eye on me on behalf of Margaret. They didn't understand the relationship between us. We had been close friends since those early days in Trade and Industry, and we had kept very much in touch with each other over the years.

One of my first decisions was to ask David to review the substantial refurbishment programme of Central Office which Peter Brooke had announced in October 1988. By the time I had taken over, it was costing some £4 million and no separate funds had been raised to finance it.

Modernization was needed to allow for new technology, and to create out of the existing warren of little offices and inadequate press facilities the sort of flexible building suitable for a modern election campaign. Central Office was also to have its own television studio where candidates and MPs could be trained, and from where Party spokesmen could do down-the-line interviews. I wanted to know whether it was possible to delay, alter or even halt this programme, which was bearing heavily upon the Party's finances. But David's report showed that it would in fact cost as much to cancel or delay as it would to go ahead. It was, however, a mistake that the project had been set in hand without the money first being raised by the Treasurers.

In August, Thames Water, which occupied the next-door building, decided to move and the opportunity arose to acquire their office. Both David Young and Idris Pearce, the Party's property adviser, strongly advised that we should buy it in order to concentrate on to one site the various outlying posts for which we were paying rent, and in order to provide the possibility of comprehensive redevelopment of the site one day. The net result was that the first year of my chairmanship was conducted against the background of whining drills and heavy hammers as modernization proceeded floor by floor.

The cash position of the Party was not good. In addition to the £4 million needed to refurbish Central Office, there was still the £1 million for the advertising of the ill-fated European Election campaign. Faced with this, I decided that there should be no increase in the overheads and running costs of the Party unless specific funds had been raised to meet them. The responsibility for raising money for the Party rests with the Treasurers who are appointed by the leader of the Party. It is absolutely right that the Chairman should have no direct role in raising money. He should never put himself or the Party in the position of being beholden to anyone. I never asked anyone for a penny, and that's how it should be.

The Party had been very lucky in having as its Treasurer for over ten years Alistair McAlpine. Alistair had a legendary reputation for raising money. He has a huge range of interests and friends, and is a successful businessman in the family's property and building companies. He was born shrewd. Alistair is a patron of the Arts, putting together collections as varied as eighteenth-century garden implements, modern statues, fossils, books on parrots, and early primitive art from the Pacific Islands. He is also a dealer in antiques, one of the world's natural traders but with a fine eye for the beautiful and exotic. He is by nature gregarious, and a lover of fine wines and the very best champagne which he used to cheer up anyone whose spirits were flagging.

Alistair presided over the most popular parties at the annual Party Conference. Late on Wednesday and Thursday nights his chubby crew-cut figure, wearing his inevitable Garrick Club tie, could be seen chuckling, gossiping and thrusting champagne upon the eager and indiscreet collection of Ministers, journalists and hangers-on, only some of whom had received formal invitations to his party. But Alistair's affability concealed a sharp and occasionally ruthless judgement. This he elegantly displayed in his Machiavellian study into the motivation of courtiers called *The Servant*. He did not suffer fools gladly, and would not hesitate to make scathing comments about those whose performance fell short of his own standards.

Alistair was the staunchest advocate of the independence of the Treasurers, and he instructed each of the Chairmen whom he served that they should have nothing to do with the raising of money for the Party. For ten years he had enjoyed the confidence and friendship of Margaret Thatcher. I was very sorry therefore to know that he wanted for personal reasons – he had had a triple heart bypass operation – to stand down. It took two people to replace him, Max Beaverbrook and Hector Laing. I also appointed a senior expert to develop direct mail as a means of raising cash for the Party. This had been tried by both Cecil Parkinson and Norman Tebbit, but it had come to grief over the opposition of some constituencies. This time more care was taken, and it became a useful additional source of revenue.

The Party has to raise over £10 million a year from the constituency associations around the country and from individual donations large and small. The raising of cash by the Associations gives them a real sense of purpose alongside their campaigning and electioneering. I would not want to see that replaced by state funding. The need to raise money to maintain the activity of a political party necessarily involves the commitment, and the voluntary work, of many millions of people. If all of a Party's finances came from the state, based upon the number of votes cast at a General Election, then would there be any real need for local organizations? Everything could be done from the national headquarters with local and national advertising campaigns. The local Associations would wither. If people believe strongly enough in a political party, whether they be Socialists, Liberals or Conservatives, then they should commit their own time and money to furthering their cause.

The current financial difficulties of Central office have sometimes, and unfairly I must say, been laid at my door. The facts are that when I became Party Chairman in July 1989 the decision to modernize Smith Square had already been taken by my predecessor Peter Brooke, and work was already well advanced. However, the initial costs of this work only showed up in the April 1989–90 balance sheets during my Chairmanship, as did the costs of the June 1989 European Election campaign which were also incurred under Peter's Chairmanship.

The expanded Press Office was fully staffed when I took over, and the only senior manager I appointed was one to organize direct mail as a fundraising operation. I did increase the training of agents but these extra costs were met from funds raised separately by John Lacy. The major item of expenditure authorized during my time was the cost of advertising for the local government elections in May 1990, and this came to about £600,000.

Subsequent to my leaving Central Office in November 1990, my successor as Chairman, Chris Patten, appointed his own Director of Communications and engaged Saatchi & Saatchi on a full service contract for what proved to be a long run up to the 1992 General Election. Part of the costs of these decisions fell in the April 1990–91 financial year during which I was Chairman for the first eight months. The fact remains that the period of appointment of Party Chairmen bears no relation to the period of the Party's annual accounts. It is therefore quite easy to draw erroneous conclusions about who was responsible for what expenditure unless individual Chairmen's tenure of office, coupled with their spending decisions, are identified separately in the Party's annual financial year accounts.

The Party Conference 1989

The first meeting that I had at Central Office on Tuesday 30 July was with Sir Peter Lane, then Chairman of the National Union Executive Committee. He was the elected head of the organization which represents the voice of the voluntary workers of the Party. It is the National Union which is responsible for organizing the autumn Party Conference and the spring Central Council. It runs the two conferences each year, selects the motions to be debated, and chooses the speakers. So it is essential that there is a good working relationship between the National Union and the Chairman. I wanted to ensure that a new fresh message of confidence emerged from the Party Conference in October, and so planning the Conference was the first task. We had to focus upon the future and the next Election.

As part of the planning, I decided that the Party needed a new logo. The one that we'd had for the last ten years looked like a small squashed ice-cream cone. The Labour Party had ditched the red flag for the red rose. We had no need to do anything as symbolical as that, but we did need a symbol that was new and inspiring while preserving a degree of continuity. Brendan commissioned Michael Peters, the design firm, and Fiona Gilmore came up with several alternatives. Much research was done on Olympic torches, Roman torches, torches with hands and without hands, and eventually we settled on the present logo, a flaming torch. It is much more lively and meaningful than the old one and was rapidly accepted as the Party's symbol. Margaret agreed it at a meeting on 5 September, saying, 'It's much better – it's active. Labour's rose is passive.'

When we formally launched the new logo for the press and television, cartoonists and commentators had a field day. They saw in the new logo significances which had entirely escaped us. The flames of the torch were said to represent Margaret's hairstyle, and the hand holding the torch was symbolic of her passing the Party on to me! From some Associations came the predictable grumbles about anything that was new. Their overriding concern was what to do with stocks of the old letterheads.

The Conservative Party paper, *Newsline*, was also revamped. The Research Department then set about analysing and destroying Labour's policy document, *Meet the Challenge, Make the Change*, a quarry of uncosted and extravagant pledges which we ensured the Labour Party was never able to shake off. The Labour Party could not resist the temptation to have a policy on everything, which was a sure way of alarming the maximum number of people. They had their agenda and we had to pin them down to it. We did.

I also wanted the Party to look to the future and face up to winning the next election. As we had a Cabinet with many new faces, we decided after considering many alternatives that the best theme for our Party Conference was 'The Right Team for Britain's Future'. This would promote the strength of the new talents which had been brought in at the reshuffle. The Labour Party was to have some fun with this in the following months when three Cabinet Ministers resigned for a variety of personal and political reasons.

I wanted the Party Conference in Blackpool to be the opening salvo of what was likely to be a long Election campaign. We were trailing Labour in the opinion polls. The morale of the Party had to be lifted, and Ministers had to think first and foremost of what they could individually do to win that Election. This was overshadowed by our growing economic difficulties. The boom of the last two years was over. Inflation had risen to 7 per cent and the balance of payments deficit was £20 billion. There was no question of the next Election being held in the boom conditions of 1987.

By the beginning of October 1989 a good old-fashioned run on the pound was under way. We were proposing to stem it with the equally old-fashioned remedy of raising interest rates. Some Ministers had been hoping for a cut in interest rates before the Conference. I was concerned about the economic effect and the political damage that higher interest rates would have, and I said this to Margaret several times. On 4 October I took the unusual step of writing to her personally from Central Office:

If interest rates are raised, the British economy will go into recession in 1990. I do not think it will be possible to pull it back by 1991. Instead of raising interest rates I hope it will be possible to allow sterling to fall somewhat. Existing interest rates which are high by international standards show our commitment to fighting inflation.

That view was not to prevail. Some £2 billion had been spent from the reserves to support sterling but it was not enough, and on Thursday 5 October Nigel Lawson increased interest rates by 1 per cent to 15 per cent. This took us back to the levels that we had had to introduce in the 1979–81 recession. Politically the timing was difficult. It was the last day of the Labour Party Conference, and Neil Kinnock jubilantly hit out at the failure of our economic policy. Nigel Lawson in an interview said that the increase, while necessary, was 'awkward', 'uncomfortable' and 'embarrassing'. Nigel Lawson's luck had run out. This was not a happy curtain-raiser for our Party Conference the following week.

The Monday of a Tory Conference is normally a quiet day, when the Party faithful gather from across the country. I was already there to check the arrangements with Harvey Thomas, the Director of Presentation and designer of the platform layout for the Conference. While I was with him in the Winter Gardens, I was pinned down by a television crew and Peter Allen, the ITN reporter, who told me that the pound had sunk through the 3-Deutschmark level to a two-year low. That was the level which Nigel Lawson said had to be maintained at any cost.

I could not side-step or avoid the TV crews in Blackpool, since I was the only Minister available to them on camera during the day. I spoke to Nigel who was at home in Leicestershire. He was very worried and gave me the rather unhelpful advice that there must be no comment about the pound! Nigel was due to come up to Blackpool that afternoon because, although his speech to Conference was not until Thursday, he had to attend the Agents' Dinner on Monday night at which the Prime Minister would speak, since his Agent was the Secretary of the Agents' Association. The dinner meant that Nigel, who had managed to keep a low profile during the day, would have to appear at the Imperial Hotel with all the world's press in attendance.

Only those who have been to a Tory Party Conference, and stayed at the Conference Headquarters hotel, know the intensity of the occasion. The lobby is stuffed with journalists; in the bars constituency representatives and Party officials mingle with Cabinet Ministers; radio mikes are pushed up in front of you; television crews record you entering, being searched, checking in, and chatting to friends. If you have to wait for the lift then you are trapped, and comment can only be refused by being churlish.

Gossip and rumour thrive under the intensity of the television lights and the liberality of the hospitality. 'Who's she talking to?' 'Is it true he's not coming?' 'His wife usually comes, where is she this year?' 'You know he's not staying for the final speech.' 'They're not on speaking terms.' 'Denis isn't coming till Friday.' 'The Chief Secretary is in his room and he's getting nowhere, there'll be a Star Chamber this year.' 'Just look at him, flushed already.' All such observations flourish in this atmosphere of convivial intrigue. They are nourished by the heat, the crush and the alcohol and are turned into exotic stories, romantic, fantastic, spiteful and malicious. Nigel was about to step into this raging hothouse.

Judith Chaplin, Nigel's special adviser, who was later to become the MP for Newbury, and also to die tragically early, rang us from Nigel's car as it approached the Imperial Hotel in Blackpool. 'Should we come in through the back door?' she asked. 'No,' I said. 'Nigel must not sneak in through the kitchens. It has to be the front door.' By now, however, the world's press was waiting for him. I told Nigel that I would meet him at the entrance and physically get him through the press and up to his room. However, before meeting him I had to hold the opening press conference where, for forty-five minutes, I had to field probing questions on the sterling crisis from the entire political press corps. So much for Nigel's advice to keep off the subject. The first question, from Robin Day, was, 'Do any of you remember a more difficult situation at the beginning of a Party Conference?' I agreed it would be interesting.

When I met Nigel on his arrival he looked harassed and annoyed. There was a shrugging impatience about him. I am sure that he was fed up with having to face all the carping hacks who only two years earlier had praised him as the greatest Chancellor since the War. Here was a man close to the end of his tether.

Getting Nigel up to his room was a problem. Getting him down was another. I collected Margaret, and together with Nigel the three of us in evening dress walked down the staircase of the Imperial Hotel shoulder to shoulder, serenely and calmly breasting the shouting ranks of assembled hacks, impervious to their impertinent jibes. At the dinner, Margaret in a corner was a sight to behold. She really came out fighting. She loyally defended Nigel and our record.

Next day, the *Daily Mail* led with a front-page editorial demanding Nigel's resignation. Nigel had decided, however, to get out of the hot-house world of Blackpool and had returned late on Monday night to his Leicestershire home. This became the mysterious 'flight of the Chancellor' and the papers were soon full of pictures, taken through his study window, of him working on his Conference speech – another annoying intrusion for a man who felt he was being unfairly hounded. I spoke to Margaret at the Church Service which starts our Conference. She said, 'I am very worried about the *Daily Mail* leader and I have spoken to Nigel to reassure him of my support.'

So the Party's spirits needed rallying and its nerves steadying. The keynote speech on the first day is the Chairman's. I really cut loose and made as strong and as fighting a speech as I had ever made. I defended Nigel for his courage – rather than his judgement – saying, 'He didn't shrink from doing what was right.' But I then went on to the attack. The Liberals and the Social Democrats were going through a great name crisis trying to decide what to call their joint Party. I jibed that, 'They have had more names than Imelda Marcos has shoes.' I also attacked the Greens, who were still showing up reasonably well in the polls – 'Green politicians are like tomatoes, they start green and end up red.'

I took head-on the Party's anxieties about water privatization, the Health Service reforms and the community charge, arguing that it was right not to falter but to press ahead. I told the Conference, 'We have not been re-elected at two successive General Elections in order to manage this nation's decline in a more genteel fashion than the Labour Party. We have been re-elected to shake off the shackles of the past, and to release the energies of the British people. It isn't our radicalism which should make people uncomfortable. It is Labour's nostalgia for the failures of the past.'

I ended with Henry V's clarion call to duty – 'He which hath no stomach to this fight, let him depart.' Little did I anticipate that the first person to follow that stirring call was going to be the Chancellor of the Exchequer himself!

The speech went down well, and I received a two-minute standing ovation, which is the way the press measures political popularity. Willie Whitelaw thought it was 'the best speech I have ever heard at a Party Conference'. Robin Day was kind enough to say, 'It reminds me of Iain Macleod.' It got the Conference off to a good start, and that's what the Chairman has to do on the first day.

Some important policies were announced at the Conference. Chris Patten made a good speech on 'green' issues. David Hunt announced a package of relief amounting to over £1 billion for the community charge. Nigel's speech had been the occasion for a great show of solidarity – the Conservative Party knew its duty. Although Geoffrey Howe was Deputy Leader he did not have a Department to answer for and therefore no slot to speak at the Conference. Though I had been anxious to fit him in, the National Union declined to make a special slot for him, and this led to inaccurate comment that he was being sidelined. He spoke to a fringe meeting of the Bow Group and called for 'a listening Party', by which he meant it ought to listen to him.

There was one curious incident at the Conference. It occurred at 2 a.m. on Wednesday morning while I was working on my second speech in my room with Tony Kerpel and Brendan Bruce. I received a visit from Tom Arnold, who had with him the Chief Constable of Lancashire, the Deputy Chief Constable, and an Army Colonel. Tom was in charge of the day-to-day security at the Conference.

At the weekend some vapours thought to be of EGDN had been discovered on the fourth floor of the hotel. Ethylene Glycol Di-Nitrate is a substance given off from nitro-glycerine and from objects which have come into contact with nitro-glycerine. The Army had picked up traces of this and had sent it to be analysed. They said that their equipment was very new and not entirely reliable. They told me that they had just received the news that the sample showed traces of EGDN vapours. This could be anywhere in the hotel, and to find the source the hotel would have to be evacuated and virtually gutted. The sources could be Semtex explosive which had been stored alongside nitro-glycerine, or clothing that had come into contact with nitro-glycerine.

The Colonel advised me that the hotel should be evacuated at once, as Semtex or nitro-glycerine might be anywhere. The Chief Constable was less clear. No previous example of Semtex and nitro-glycerine being stored together had been found on the mainland, and he was very doubtful of the risk that was involved.

In the light of the appalling IRA Brighton bombing of 1984 this was clearly a very important matter and a very difficult decision. The Prime Minister and several Cabinet colleagues were asleep in their rooms that night. I had no intention of waking them up. We discussed the threat for some time and I decided, and the decision had to be mine alone, that the hotel should not be evacuated until I had spoken to the scientists after further tests in the morning. I was simply not prepared to turn out everybody in their pyjamas and nightdresses in the middle of the night and cause a major disruption. The world headlines would have been of another assassination attempt on Margaret Thatcher, and that would have been a considerable publicity coup for the IRA. I would not give them that prize. We continued work on my speech and then I went to sleep, although Mary was rather more worried than I. At eight o'clock that morning the boffins arrived and said the vapours were not EGDN.

It had certainly been difficult to weigh up the balance of probabilities in the early hours of the morning and to make the decision I did. Brendan thought the decision was a brave one. Tony thought it was risky.

The Chairman has to speak again on the last day. I decided to go for a rather jolly, cheer-up rouser and have a dig at the BBC by holding an audience poll. I said:

There are many more of you here than take part in most opinion polls. You come from all over the country. You represent a balance between men and women. You represent all backgrounds and all ages. And when it comes to political affiliations, I consider that you are as representative of a balanced cross-section as a typical BBC 'Question Time' audience. I'm going to ask you three questions and you either have to answer yes or no. My first question is: Has this been a successful Conference?

The audience shouted back 'Yes.' But I wasn't satisfied. 'Not every newsroom in the country heard that. I will ask you again. Has this been a successful Conference?' This time the Conference understood what was wanted and roared back, 'Yes.'

I continued: 'Now my second question is, and I want you to take the roof off – I want the decibels to break the microphones of the BBC – my next question is, will we win the next General Election?' Another great roar came back.

Finally I said, 'My third question in this opinion poll is the most difficult of all. Think about it carefully. Do we have the right team for Britain's future?' There was a huge roar of 'Yes', at which point I sat down.

One commentator called my speech brazen, but I wanted to send our troops back happy. Tony Kerpel called it 'the Uncle Ken at the end of the pier show'. But one person decidedly unhappy, indeed angry, was Barbara Maxwell, the editor of BBC TV's 'Question Time', who wrote to me saying:

I am a grown up and regard your reference to 'Question Time' as highly damaging and I think it disgraceful that a national Party Chairman, for the sake of an easy, rabble-rousing 'joke' to his own supporters should defame my professional integrity and competence and the reputation of a highly respected programme . . .

I declined to apologize and pointed out that since the BBC dished out criticism of politicians, it should not be so sensitive about getting some back.

Margaret's final speech was as usual rapturously received, and this time at my suggestion it contained more spiky attacks on Labour and Neil Kinnock. It had been a tricky week. The Labour lead, due to the inevitable increase in mortgage rates, went from 6 to 10 points. Nonetheless I had fired the first opening shots in the 1991 or 1992 Election campaign. It was not going to be a short dash. It was a long race. On Saturday Peter Jenkins, the political columnist of the *Independent*, gave his view that the co-favourites in the succession stakes were Michael Heseltine and Kenneth Baker. But then, as any bookmaker knows, favourites don't always win.

CHAPTER 14

Gathering Clouds

The Position of Michael Heseltine – The Resignation of
Nigel Lawson – The First Leadership Election – The
Stalking-Horse Candidate

The Party Conference had not been made any easier by the high profile and ambitious presence of Michael Heseltine in Blackpool. On the eve of the conference on Monday, BBC TV showed a 'Panorama' programme which portrayed him in a very attractive light with growing support among backbenchers. On the Tuesday, Michael spoke to a packed meeting in the Grand Theatre, making a root-and-branch challenge to the whole of the Government's economic policy. He dismissed Nigel Lawson's approach to the trade deficit as 'naïve', and urged intervention to stimulate manufacturing industry. He was making it clear for all to see that 'there was an alternative'.

So throughout 1989 and 1990 there was a shadow candidate for the leadership who was articulate in the media, active in the constituencies, and popular in the country. The threat that he posed was a very real one, and to most of the Cabinet it was not just a case of keeping Margaret but also stopping Michael. Those who had known him well, like Norman Tebbit, Cecil Parkinson, Willie Whitelaw and Douglas Hurd, were utterly convinced that a Heseltine takeover of the Party would be disastrous. In the actual leadership election of November 1990 only one Cabinet Minister, David Hunt, declared for him. In those frantic days the overwhelming motive which explains how various colleagues acted was the desire to 'stop Heseltine'. It is interesting to analyse why he excited such antipathy in the upper echelons of the Party.

I first met Michael Heseltine during my first term at Oxford in 1955, when he returned as an ex-President to speak at the Union. Handsome, tall, elegant and witty, wearing a white tie and cut-away evening coat, he seemed the very essence of young England. Admired by his friends, feared by his enemies, he appeared the personification of the successful Oxford life – a man destined to lead his country. In that Union debate I remember a series of exchanges between Michael and another former President. It was a few minutes of glittering and breathtaking spontaneous repartee which I was only to find out later had been carefully rehearsed by both of them.

Michael and I crossed paths when we were both junior Ministers in Ted Heath's Government. He was one of Peter Walker's team of Ministers, and Michael had attached himself to Peter's star which was in the ascendant. I remember Michael saying to me at one of the Christmas parties which Michael and Rosemary Wolff held, 'My object in politics is to help Peter to get to the top.' This was not just naked ambition. Michael, like Peter, had a disposition towards the 'Grand Plan' in which the government set targets and provided funds for continuous involvement in economic and industrial affairs. That was the spirit of the times and of the Heath government. Industries had to be saved in spite of their inadequate management, crippling industrial relations, and inferior products. This generation of politicians were the children of Macmillan, and the disciple of the market and the opponent of corporatism – Enoch Powell – had been banished.

Michael really came to national prominence in the late 1970s as the darling of the Tory Party Conferences. His speeches were not to be missed, and were received with such rapture that Margaret preferred to watch bits of them on television. A good natural speaker, Michael nevertheless worked hard preparing his speeches and rehearsing their effective delivery. He was at his best when attacking the Labour Party with anger, scorn and humour. He was by far the best stump-orator in the Party – the occasion was all. In retrospect his speeches don't read that well and few memorable phrases were coined. But these speeches were tailored to the occasion and usually moved the Party workers to a frenzy. As one wag remarked, 'Michael has the knack of finding the clitoris of the Conservative Party.'

Margaret appointed Michael Secretary of State for the Environment in 1979. He set about selling council houses, reforming the administration of his Department and changing the rating system. His most notable achievement was the work he did in Liverpool following the riots of 1981. Then he played the role of the energetic executive, the busy and successful managing director, bringing together public and private sector leaders and businessmen, galvanizing the whole system and inspiring others. This is what Michael did best and the people of Liverpool to this day have a warm affection for him.

In 1982, Margaret moved Michael to Defence to deal with the vociferous minority of nuclear disarmers protesting about the deployment of Cruise missiles. Michael argued the Government's case with flair and swagger, although eyebrows were raised when he donned a camouflage jacket to visit a new base where confrontations with a few frumpy woollen-hatted protesters were expected. Nevertheless there was now the perceptible sense of a man walking on water. Popular and successful, he was used to getting his way, and that led to his fatal clash with Margaret over the Westland Affair in 1985.

Michael wanted a European consortium to save Westland, an ailing British helicopter company. Margaret felt that if a deal with the American Sikorsky company could be done then so be it. The issue also involved Leon Brittan, the Trade and Industry Secretary, who sided with the Prime Minister. The matter was particularly sensitive because Michael and the Prime Minister had differed a year earlier over the placing of an order for two frigates. The initial proposal was to place them both with Swan Hunter, but Michael wanted one frigate to go to Cammell Laird to help ease unemployment on Merseyside, and because the yard had resisted a strike. Michael won against the Prime Minister's wishes, and he felt this precedent coloured the subsequent events.

But now the formidable power of Number 10 was being wielded with all its overarching and personal authority to ensure that on this occasion the Prime Minister's will prevailed. It was not so much the future of the Westland Company that was at stake, it was the nature of Prime Ministerial government.

On 12 December 1985 at the full Cabinet, Michael decided to raise the question of Westland because a meeting of the Cabinet Committee, EA, which had been dealing with this matter had been cancelled by its Chairman, the Prime Minister. It is customary for Cabinet Ministers to advise the Cabinet Secretary if they wish to raise any issues or, alternatively, to submit a paper. On this occasion Michael had done neither. The Prime Minister was annoyed with him for raising the Westland issue, saying, 'No notice has been given to Leon Brittan or to me.' Michael pressed on, insisting that this was a matter for the Cabinet. When Margaret interrupted him he said, 'Don't interrupt me.' Margaret then said that her decision as to what could be raised in Cabinet accorded with tradition – 'That's the position. I'm sorry.' Michael replied, 'You're not in the least sorry.' There was cold anger on both sides, and I had never seen such a bitter exchange between colleagues, certainly not in front of a full Cabinet. I thought to myself that this issue would run, and that Michael was taking on the Prime Minister in a very personal way.

Michael felt that he had been denied proper access to the Cabinet system of government and that Departments and Ministers, guided by Number 10, were determined to defeat him in this battle of wills. I believe that he conducted himself bravely, if not wisely, during this whole episode. He fell because he did not secure the tacit support of any of the older and more senior members of the Cabinet. Michael was a loner, and at that famous Cabinet meeting on 9 January 1986 he experienced the loneliness of the isolated politician.

The first thirty minutes of the discussion had gone reasonably well, with the views of both sides being put. Leon Brittan, who had responsibility for the aircraft industry, had firmly got back into the act, which I had believed was the purpose of this meeting. But new life was breathed into the whole issue by Nick Ridley intervening about the ministerial statements that Michael had issued off his own bat. Nick asked, 'What was their status?' and, 'What about future ones?' Margaret said that in view of other Departments being involved, Michael's statements now had to have prior clearance by Number 10. That was too much for a proud man, a man with a good record of achievement whose judgement had not been challenged before now by colleagues on an issue where he had ministerial responsibility.

Michael realized that he was no longer his own master in an unprecedented ministerial turf war. Whether that was fortuitous or whether it had been planned in order to provoke his resignation I cannot say. Others may know. But whether by chance or design the result was inevitable. Margaret said, 'You will make no further statements or answer questions. This is the decision of the Cabinet and I must ask you to accept it.' Michael replied, 'I cannot hesitate in supporting what I have said.' Then with dignity he closed his red ministerial folder, rose from his chair which was next but one to mine, and said, 'There has been a breakdown of collective responsibility and I must therefore leave the Cabinet.'

I was at that time the most junior member of the Cabinet, and I was amazed that not one of the experienced older Ministers such as Willie Whitelaw, Quintin Hogg or Geoffrey Howe, who had heard these exchanges, said or did anything to avert Michael's walkout. Everyone was stunned by this dramatic resignation. Margaret suggested we should have a coffee break, and as we trooped out of the Cabinet Room Willie

Whitelaw, John Wakeham and George Younger stayed behind. After fifteen minutes the rest of us were summoned back and told that George Younger was the new Defence Secretary and Malcolm Rifkind the new Scottish Secretary. I had the distinct feeling that the Defence Secretary's vacancy had not caught them unawares.

For the next four years Michael was Margaret's successor-in-waiting, the alternative leader-in-exile. He was able to use his personal wealth to maintain a ministerial schedule and office, touring the constituencies, and winning friends among Conservative backbenchers and grassroots supporters. It was taken for granted that, despite his disavowals, Michael was building a base of support for the day when he would stand for the Party leadership. But Michael also stood for something different – an interventionist policy in industry, closer union with Europe and, above all, a different style of leadership. He became better known and more popular than any member of the Cabinet. Michael was persistent in promoting his own campaign, though it always fell short of a direct challenge to Margaret. He openly challenged the effectiveness of Thatcherite policies and implicitly challenged Margaret's leadership. But he never explicitly challenged her position. Even after 1987, he kept on saying he was sure she was going to lead us to victory in the following Election, and repeatedly gave assurances that he would not stand against Margaret before that Election.

I believe there were three reasons for Michael's failure to become Party leader and his gaining so little support from senior members of the Party. First, the policies he advocated amounted to an abandonment of part of Thatcherism. While this appealed to the Heathite wing of the Conservative Party, it was anathema to all those Members who had been swept in on Margaret's coat-tails in 1983 and 1987. They did not share Michael's enthusiasm for 'big Government' and high-spending intervention which, they feared, would jeopardize the anti-inflation and tax-reduction achievements of Thatcherism. Moreover, their heroine was Margaret Thatcher, and anyone who dared to challenge her was guilty of the ultimate Tory heresy, disloyalty.

Second, although Michael had admirers of his visionary leadership there were many others who were suspicious of where his judgement might lead us all. The Tory Party likes its leaders to have a lot of bottom, and the ship to have a good cargo of ballast. The difficulty with Michael was that his sails were always unfurled, billowing out with the following wind and taking the ship to God knows where. Liverpool, Westland, and the 1992 pit closures had three things in common – Michael knew what he wanted, he believed he was in the right, and he was impatient to get on with it. He became frustrated if others tried to apply the handbrake.

Third, there was a question mark over his sometimes volatile temperament. I was in the House for that famous event in 1976 when Labour's Bill to nationalize the shipbuilding and aviation industries was passed by one vote after a Labour Whip had broken a prearranged pair. Incensed by this breach of Parliamentary practice on such a controversial Bill, Michael seized the Mace and waved it in the face of the Labour Members who were singing 'The Red Flag'. It was a dramatically defiant gesture but Willie Whitelaw, with jowls quivering, shook his head and said, 'That won't do. That won't do. You can do anything in this House except touch the Mace. Oh, no, no, no.' Afterwards I went to the Smoking Room, where several of the older Tories were saying that Michael would have to resign from the Shadow Cabinet. When I told Michael this he laughed, saying, 'The House may not like it but the public will love it.' As usual Michael had an eye for the audience.

Michael and I have always got on rather well. He wore his ambitions quite openly, and even though we were on different sides in the 1990 leadership election there is no rancour. I remember, shortly after becoming Party Chairman, going out with Mary to have dinner in his Northamptonshire home. Both Michael and Anne are rightly proud of their beautiful house with its landscaped grounds which they have created. Michael spoke with enthusiasm and real feeling about a painting which they had recently bought. As to politics, he knew that the community charge, high interest rates and Margaret's standing were going to provide him with tremendous opportunities to promote himself as an alternative. Some time later, after the battle for the leadership had been resolved, we met late in the House one evening. In reflective mood he asked me what I would like to be remembered for and I replied, 'My education reforms.' I then asked him the same question. He paused and said, quite truthfully I believe, 'My arboretum.'

The Resignation of Nigel Lawson

After the Conference, I went to America to see whether the Republican Party had anything from which we could learn. I met the late Lee Atwater. He was the Chairman of the Republican Party who had run George Bush's 1988 campaign, having previously run Ronald Reagan's

1980 campaign, when he'd helped to rubbish Bush in the primaries. Bush's election to the US Presidency was largely credited to Lee Atwater because he'd been the one who realized the importance of the Willie Horton parole case which allowed Bush to brand his Democrat opponent Michael Dukakis as weak on law and order. Atwater made Norman Tebbit look like a blushing violet. His short sentences were punctuated with blunt expletives describing various people. He was always searching for the weak points of his opponents – usually below the belt – and unashamedly played the racial card.

I found the Republican Party puzzled. They were pleased that Bush was enjoying a honeymoon, with a 75 per cent popularity rating, but locally Republicans were losing seats. Bush was doing well overseas and badly at home. They were confident of winning in 1992 but the Party was working itself up to ensure that someone other than Jim Baker would stand in 1996.

The Republicans had mastered the arts of direct mail and telephone canvassing. We had much to learn from them on that, but little to learn from their TV campaigning. Fortunately, one cannot buy time on British television for political advertising. If one could then the Tory Party would have needed at least another £20 million. But the real objection to paid political advertising on TV is that it promotes the most negative campaigning. TV political advertisements in the States have become an art form – no longer than twenty seconds, for that is the timespan of viewers' attention, and into that has to be packed innuendo, scorn, venom, a smear, and an unanswerable lie. The object is to create suspicion, fear and positive dislike of one's opponent.

America has got to disentangle money from politics. Candidates spend years paying off their campaign bills, which means that those who control the money bags have too great an influence upon candidate selection and candidate attitudes. Robert Walpole and the Duke of Newcastle would certainly feel at home in the politics of America today.

I returned from America on Thursday 26 October in time for Cabinet, not expecting anything untoward. The only trouble had been the publication over the weekend of an article written by Professor Alan Walters. He had previously been the Economic Adviser to Margaret during Geoffrey's Chancellorship but had then resumed his academic career in America. He had been re-employed by Margaret as a part-time adviser at £31,000 a year. In his article, which had been written some eighteen months earlier for an American magazine, Walters said that the European

Monetary System was 'half-baked' and claimed that 'since I soon earned Mrs Thatcher's trust I acquired a considerable influence on economic policy'. The *Daily Telegraph* had a leader in black capitals headed 'Quiet Walters'. On Wednesday, during a censure debate in the House of Commons, Nigel Lawson condemned advisers going into print. Later that day Margaret, who had just returned from the Commonwealth Conference in Kuala Lumpar, agreed that Walters should not say anything in public about Government policy. At Question Time on the Thursday, she dismissed Kinnock's attack with a phrase that was to be much quoted – 'advisers advise, and Ministers decide.'

I had been invited to meet the Executive of the 1922 Committee privately at 5.30 p.m. to explain to them my proposals for improving the publicity of the Party. At about two minutes to six, when the main meeting was due to start, Terence Higgins, a member of the Executive, came in and asked me to have a word with Mark Lennox-Boyd, Margaret's PPS, who was waiting outside. When I left Committee Room 14, I had to push my way through not only the mass of MPs wanting to get in but a large number of journalists shouting questions about Nigel. As we hurried along the corridor Mark whispered in my ear that Nigel had resigned and would I go at once to Number 10.

When I got to Margaret's study I found John Major sitting in the chair next to the fireplace looking rather stunned. 'Nigel has resigned and I have asked John to take over as Chancellor,' Margaret said. Bernard Ingham was there working out answers to all the inevitable questions. He and John left together.

Alone with the Prime Minister, Andrew Turnbull and Charles Powell, I told her of my complete amazement at the turn of events. Margaret was very calm, sitting in her usual chair by the fireplace. But I sensed anxiety under the surface. I said, 'You are now in danger. This is not a little local difficulty, it's a crisis. Nigel has a real standing in the Party and you have rejected his advice, preferring to listen to Alan Walters. However wrong Nigel is, and however right Alan may be, is not the question. The Party in the House won't like this at all and there'll be calls for Alan's resignation.'

Another Private Secretary came in with the news that the House of Commons had been suspended, with Labour MPs singing 'The Red Flag', and it had been told there would be a government statement later that night. 'There you are,' I said. 'The position will be unsustainable if Alan has not resigned by the time the House resumes. MPs will demand his scalp or yours.' Margaret replied, 'Alan has done no wrong and it would be unfair to sack him.' This was typical of her loyalty to her staff.

I suggested that Brian Griffiths, a close friend of Alan's, should speak to him in America immediately. Before he did I said to Brian privately that Alan must understand that it was a question of him or the Prime Minister, and she was in a tight corner. Brian brought back the news ten minutes later that Alan had said he would go. Margaret spoke to Alan on the telephone and I drafted the statement to be issued by Number 10:

Sir Alan Walters has contacted the Prime Minister from America. He is deeply shocked at the news that the Chancellor has resigned. Sir Alan is convinced that he has acted totally correctly but his sole concern is that confidence should continue in the government and its policies. He therefore thinks that at this juncture it would be advisable for him to step aside as an adviser to the Prime Minister and this he is doing.

'Step aside' was a delicate euphemism for the inevitable.

This matter was resolved by 6.35 p.m. and I then urged Margaret to announce her new appointments by 8.00 p.m. so that they would be on the 9 p.m. television news. It was absolutely essential that John Major's appointment as Chancellor should be announced quickly in order to steady the markets. Unfortunately, neither the Chief Whip, David Waddington, nor the Deputy Leader, Geoffrey Howe, could join us, as they were both coping with the crisis in the House, which had been suspended under a barrage of Points of Order and demands for a statement. I suggested that Margaret should send a note to Geoffrey, which she wrote immediately at her desk, setting out what had happened over the Lawson/Walters saga.

She then turned to me and asked about the Foreign Secretaryship. There were three candidates: Cecil Parkinson, Tom King and Douglas Hurd. Cecil was getting to grips with the difficult portfolio of Transport, which had ended the careers of at least two Secretaries of State, and as he was one of the 'great communicators' of the Party he was needed in that important domestic area. Tom King had only recently settled into Defence. So I recommended Douglas. Charles Powell nodded vigorously, on behalf of the Foreign Office, and Margaret did not demur.

This move meant that Margaret could appoint David Waddington, the Chief Whip, to be Home Secretary. She was delighted, saying, 'At last a right-winger at the Home Office.' But filling the Chief Whip's post proved more difficult. The Deputy Chief Whip was Tristan Garel-Jones, who was burdened with the reputation of being devious and a master of backstairs intrigue. Moreover he was not trusted by the right wing of the Parliamentary Party, who believed that he spent his time promoting Chris Patten. Since no one else in the Whips Office could be promoted over him, former Whips came into the reckoning, and Alastair Goodlad's name was briefly considered. Then we looked down the list of Ministers of State and Tim Renton's name was suggested. Tim was currently serving as Minister of State at the Home Office. He had been close to Geoffrey Howe, which Charles Powell thought was a positive advantage.

Tim came from the centre of the Party, though having served as a junior Minister in the Foreign Office he strongly supported their pro-European line. He was highly principled, having resigned in 1981 as the Chancellor of the Exchequer's PPS over the introduction of a retrospective tax on banks. Tim was the essence of decency but lacked the guile and willingness to bully and threaten, which are the characteristics all Chief Whips must have. I suggested to Margaret that she sleep on the decision and consult John Wakeham, but the urgent desire to complete a full list of Government changes that night prevailed. Tim's appointment had the effect that, at a later critical time, Margaret was to have as her Chief Whip, a crucial position, someone who was neither an ardent admirer nor particularly sympathetic to her ideological views.

The consequence of this change was that there was a slot in the Home Office, and I suggested that David Mellor be moved from Health, where his abrasiveness was proving to be no emollient counterpart to Ken Clarke. This meant that Virginia Bottomley could be promoted – a move which was described as, 'A wholesome English Rose at Health.'

It was ironic that this political crisis produced such a political improvement in the strength of the Government. John Major was in the post he most wanted; Douglas Hurd had the job for which his career had prepared him; David Waddington would be a tough Home Secretary; and the Health team had a more acceptable face.

The House was to resume by 7.50 p.m., and so I took all this information over to Geoffrey, and particularly the news of the Walters resignation. Elspeth was with him, very angry that Geoffrey had not been told of Nigel's resignation and not been offered a bigger role in the Government. Geoffrey's absorbent bulk fielded the flak in the

House, which he did very well despite cries of 'Where is she, where is she?' Someone shouted from the Labour Benches, 'In the bunker.' The Labour MPs sensed blood, which was not surprising for there was a lot of it about.

After this I went to Douglas' room in the Commons, where I found him surprised but delighted. I had decided that it made sense for me to appear live on the television news programmes to stabilize the position, and Douglas thought that would be helpful. His parting advice to me, delivered with a grin, was 'Kenneth, don't smile too much.' That evening I praised Nigel's record and regretted his departure, which had the desired effect of smoothing his ruffled feathers. At any rate, Nigel kept his own counsel and at this stage also kept his version of events to himself.

Nigel was, after Keith Joseph, the most intellectual member of any of Margaret's Cabinets. He coined the phrase 'Thatcherism' and provided much of the economic thinking which transformed the economy in the early and mid-1980s. He was Chancellor for longer than anyone since Lloyd George, and he abolished several taxes, substantially reduced Income Tax, reformed Corporation Tax and secured a repayment of some of our National Debt. He had a roguish charm and was a good companion at dinner, a civilized raconteur and a stimulating conversationalist. But he was not someone to listen to when it came to investing the family legacy. He didn't care much about his appearance: his vanity was reserved for his reputation. I remember him getting very cross during an economic debate in 1980 when he was Financial Secretary to the Treasury. In a slip of the tongue I did not refer to the 'medium-term financial strategy' but to the 'medium-term financial secretary'. This was not an inadvertent witticism, just a silly mistake, but a prickly Nigel reproached me later for what he took to be an insult.

Nigel tended to be a loner. He shunned the conviviality of the Smoking Room, and did not try to attract any group of followers. Impatient of criticism, and so convinced of the rightness of his own case, he often thought that a contemptuous dismissal of a patently weak case was enough. If he didn't get his way, which was not often, he would retire hurt from the field but would still conduct the game from the boundary.

Nigel has written a formidable defence of his own economic policies. He abandoned monetary targets as a means of controlling inflation in November 1985, preferring to rely upon the exchange rate of sterling. In his resignation speech he said that the exchange rate was 'a central part of the essential market discipline'. He wanted to buttress this by joining the ERM (although he was never in favour of EMU and a single currency). But Margaret would not agree and so Nigel, in a prolonged and disdainful sulk, decided that sterling would shadow the Deutschmark as an alternative.

Shadowing the Deutschmark meant that the UK had to reduce its interest rates just as it was experiencing a boom which required interest rates to rise. This was aggravated by the reaction of the Western world to the dramatic fall of 20 per cent on the world Stock Exchanges on Black Monday, 19 October 1987. Britain, together with the other major Western economies, decided to prevent a recession like that of the 1920s and 1930s by introducing measures to stimulate their economies. In Britain the tap marked 'money' was turned on, but it was left running for far too long.

One year after Nigel Lawson left the Treasury, John Major decided to take sterling into the ERM in October 1990. At that time Germany was having to find vast sums of money, over 120 billion Deutschmarks a year, for the reunification of East and West Germany. Chancellor Kohl had taken the decision that this had to come principally from borrowing rather than an increase in German taxes. This inevitably meant that German interest rates had to be high just at the time Britain needed hers to be low, since we were sinking deep into a recession. During this whole period the German and British economies were not in the same cycle. The experiment from 1987 to 1992 of shadowing the Deutschmark and joining the ERM proved to be economically and politically disastrous.

Easy credit and deregulation had led to a house price explosion, and distortion of the housing market. Nigel had tried to check this by restricting mortgage relief to only one person where a couple were living together but not married. But this was done in such a leisurely and careless way – announced in March but not implemented until August – that it actually stimulated the boom as couples rushed to buy before the deadline. The inevitable property crash began in 1989, and we are still seeing the effects today. The economy was plunged into recession. 1990 and 1991 were Nigel's legacy.

The plain fact was that the Chancellor and the Prime Minister were not in agreement over the basic economic policy of the Government. Nigel wanted to join the ERM, he wanted a consumer credit tax, and he wanted an independent Bank of England. Margaret would have none of these. She had remained a monetarist and was opposed to going into a fixed exchange rate system, particularly one that was tied to the Deutschmark. On 25 October 1989 she had said, 'You simply cannot have a system with a currency like sterling playing under that higgledy-piggledy set of rules.' However, if the Chancellor and the Prime Minister do not agree, it is very difficult for the Prime Minister to overrule her Chancellor in the day-to-day management of the economy. This was why Margaret reappointed Alan Walters. She wanted an intellectual economist to provide her with the ammunition and the arguments against her intellectual and stubborn Chancellor.

I remember attending the *Spectator* annual lunch on 25 November 1987 when Nigel was awarded the prize for being 'Parliamentarian of the Year'. I noted in my diary, 'probably Nigel's peak'. Margaret should have moved Nigel to another job in the autumn of 1988. After the Madrid Summit in June 1989, when Nigel and Geoffrey Howe pinned Margaret down to agreeing that sterling should enter the ERM on certain conditions, there were even stronger grounds for her to move or sack him. But Margaret was in a corner, and she was forced to accept these conditions, although when she spoke of them she emphasized the ones closest to the brake and furthest from the accelerator.

By then Margaret had lost all confidence in Nigel's judgement. I remember Brian Griffiths telling me that after one clash between them Margaret had said, 'The trouble with Nigel is that he's a gambler.' I once asked Margaret, after she had lost the leadership, why she had not sacked Nigel following the Madrid Summit. After a long pause she said, 'In 1989 I couldn't. I might well have had to go as well.' If one looks at economic policy from 1987 to 1989 I have little doubt that Margaret's views were instinctively right and that Nigel's were wrong.

Nevertheless, Alan Walters was the occasion rather than the reason for Nigel's resignation. Not surprisingly Nigel was hurt and angry because his judgement was always being questioned, which is difficult for a proud man. In his letter of resignation, he said that the essential requirement for full agreement by the Prime Minister and the Chancellor of the Exchequer 'cannot be satisfied so long as Alan Walters remains your personal economic adviser.' In his speech he referred to the Walters article as 'the tip of a significantly ill-concealed iceberg'.

Margaret did not want Nigel to leave, but he did. He had come to the end of his tether since his luck had run out, and now Walters' indiscretion offered him the perfect opportunity to quit. In July, writing to Tory backbenchers, Nigel had said, 'It now looks very much as if inflation may already have peaked.' It was then at 8.3 per cent. It was to rise by October 1990 to 10.9 per cent. Nigel had seen the Treasury forecasts and he knew that what lay ahead was two years of acute economic difficulty, and thus two years of apology.

Following Nigel's resignation, the Party in the country and the House remained remarkably calm. Keith Joseph rushed to the defence of Margaret, saying, 'There is no one to match her.' He was also one of the first to condemn Nigel's policy, arguing, 'Nigel Lawson made a misjudgement.' On Friday, and at the weekend, I set about putting out more stabilizers. John Major issued a strong statement about sterling; I persuaded Geoffrey Howe, after a pro-Europe speech, to go on the radio on Sunday to emphasize the unity of the Party, and Douglas Hurd went on 'Panorama' on Monday. The message from the constituencies was clear: 'We will be all right at the grassroots but get your act together at the centre. We can't have any more of this.' It was much the view taken by the 1922 Committee when they had lunch at Number 10 with Margaret on the following Monday.

Some commentators said that this whole episode went to the very heart of Margaret's style of Government. But the fact was that she disagreed with her Chancellor on a central issue of economic policy. She was quite entitled to seek advice from whomsoever she wished, and it was unacceptable for a colleague, however senior, to put a pistol to her head in the way that Nigel had done. How would Churchill have reacted if one of his generals had told him to sack Lindemann?

Margaret's authority had been challenged quite openly by Nigel, and she defended her position robustly. In an interview with Brian Walden on the following Sunday, she repeated that Nigel's position had been 'unassailable', but added that 'somehow Nigel made up his mind that he was going'. As to her bullying her colleagues, she said, 'I like strong men and strong women about me – that's the way we have strong Government.' One could not but admire her resilience. Her popularity rating the following week fell to 24 per cent – the lowest since polling started. Labour had a lead of 15 points. But even Nigel in his resignation speech said that he was confident that we were going to win the next Election under her leadership.

The First Leadership Election

In the autumn of 1989, Parliament was sitting to finish off the legislative programme and there was no let-up in the Government following its Thatcherite agenda. Ken Clarke, the Health Secretary, was standing up to the ambulancemen in a pay dispute which was growing bitter and emotional; Michael Howard was pushing ahead with water privatization; Chris Patten was preparing for the introduction of the community charge; John Wakeham was busy with electricity privatization; Nicholas Ridley was refusing to help the Barlow Clowes investors; Tom King was refusing to improve the pensions of war widows; and the new Chancellor, John Major, in his Autumn Statement, warned of a sharp economic downturn. He emphatically, and indeed prophetically, said that the object of his policy was 'to bring inflation down and decisively down'. The Government was certainly not going out of its way to make itself popular.

The Government had been shaken by Nigel Lawson's resignation and there was a feverish atmosphere in the House. Strange rumours began to circulate about another Cabinet Minister having to resign on the grounds that he had engaged in insider dealing. There was no foundation whatsoever in these rumours, but Cecil Parkinson's solicitors had to condemn them as 'baseless'.

Europe was still the key issue. On 2 November, John Major explained to the Cabinet his proposal on Economic and Monetary Union. He intended to publish a White Paper containing the Treasury proposal which had been prepared by Nigel Lawson. This advocated the emergence of a hard ECU which could be traded alongside the individual currencies of each country and could come slowly and eventually to replace them, as and when each country wished to do so. This was a good positive proposal, but alas it found few friends.

On that same day I went to Worcester to speak for Peter Walker, and during the drive back to London he strongly attacked Nigel's policy and said Margaret's approach had been right. This was indeed a welcome change of tune, for Peter was perceived as a critic of the Prime Minister's economic policies.

Himself associated with the Heath/Barber boom of the 1970s, Peter was aware that the Treasury was creating too much credit and that this was going to lead to disaster. Having been tarred with responsibility for the house price explosion of 1972, Peter had developed strong views on the dangers of stoking up consumer credit. Now he thought that Nigel had become a disastrous Chancellor, saying, 'He's done more than we ever did.' One has to remember that Margaret and he had served for four years in Ted Heath's Cabinet, where Peter was the more senior, the rising star and even the heir apparent. Margaret always treated Peter with great care and respect, and I never heard her criticize him in private though there were some ironic and amusing exchanges in Cabinet from time to time. When Norman Fowler was clearing his White Paper on training on 1 December 1988, the Prime Minister turned to Peter seeking his approval and said, 'Wales is all right?' I intervened and asked, 'Is that a statement or a question?' The Prime Minister quickly replied, 'It is a rebuttable presumption.'

The Party and the Government badly needed a period of calm consolidation. It was not to get it. The first bombshell came from Margaret herself. On 5 November, in an interview with the *Sunday Correspondent* – a newspaper which has since disappeared from the scene – Margaret indicated that she intended to step down from the premiership after the next Election. 'People would think it was time for someone else to carry the torch,' she said. This interview was given off her own bat and none of her close advisers was told. When I spoke to Margaret about the effect of her remark she said, 'I had to say it, Kenneth. When I said before the last Election that I would "go on and on and on", I was accused of being arrogant. If I went on to the following Election in 1996–97 I would be approaching seventy. There must come a time when I should stand down, and I have cleared the air. After the next Election, other people will emerge as possible leaders, including your own good self, Kenneth.' This only half cleared the air and did not clear the way for anyone.

Many people simply did not believe that Margaret would leave office voluntarily. But one group thoroughly dismayed by the prospect of her departure was the loyalist Right of the Parliamentary Party. A deputation went to see her to dissuade her from such a notion. They felt that by saying what she had, Margaret had not only fired the starting gun in the leadership succession stakes but had also imperilled the Party's electoral prospects. After all, if she was to step down after a General Election victory who would the voters who had supported her be getting as a successor? Neil Kinnock, the Labour leader, was quick to jump on this point, arguing that at the next Election Margaret would be a lame duck and the electorate would not know for whom they were actually voting.

Thatcher one day, who the next? This position was inherently unstable and electorally damaging.

I persuaded Margaret to soften her line and to give an interview to Robin Oakley, the political editor of the *Times*. This appeared on 24 November. Far from clarifying the situation it actually worsened it. Asked about her interview in the *Sunday Correspondent* and her hint of resignation, Margaret told the *Times*, 'I have had so many protests about my answer that by popular acclaim I am quite prepared to carry on.' Apart from the note of hubris, to hold out the prospect of a premiership without end was bound to be a provocation to those in the Party who wanted to see a challenge to Margaret. Their silence had been assured by the prospect of voluntary departure indicated to the *Sunday Correspondent*. Now the *Times* was telling them that she might fight two more Elections, implying another six or seven years in Downing Street.

Margaret was due to be interviewed on BBC TV's 'Panorama' on 27 November. That morning, my team from Central Office met Margaret and her Downing Street team for one of the regular weekly sessions to coordinate Government and Party presentation. Tony Kerpel predicted that David Dimbleby, the 'Panorama' interviewer, would question Margaret about her conflicting answers on how long she intended to remain Prime Minister. Tony suggested that the answer to Dimbleby should be, 'I would like to go on as Prime Minister for as long as the electorate and the Party want me to.' This would combine humility with realism, and steady the Party's nerves. Margaret carefully noted this down. During the 'Panorama' interview this question was indeed put to her. She stuck to the formula answer and it had the desired effect.

Margaret was also questioned about a Downing Street lunch with backbenchers following Nigel's resignation. The backbenchers let it be known afterwards that they had told Margaret to get her act together, and I had confirmed this in a news interview with Michael Brunson, the political editor of ITN. However, Margaret, sensitive to having received any such rebuke from her MPs, denied that any such words had been used, a denial which the *Daily Mirror* made its front page story next morning – 'Whoops! Now Thatcher Drops Herself In It With Baker'.

The second bombshell was the growing certainty of a leadership contest before Christmas. Under the rules for the election of the Leader of the Conservative Party, nominations from candidates have to be put in at the beginning of each session of Parliament. This means that each year there is the possibility of an election. However, every year since

1975 there had only been one nomination, and that was for Margaret Thatcher.

This year, the only realistic prospective challenger was Michael Heseltine. The radio wavelengths and television spectrum were full of his denials, but on 20 November Michael was photographed with Anne at their house near Banbury. In my experience, when the press were summoned to Banbury, Michael meant business. In an interview on television he said, 'I think ambition is a very laudable human quality and if, in the service of the Party, I had to play the ultimate role it would be a great honour.' Ian Gilmour had tilled the ground earlier in the month in a speech to the Tory Reform Group in Cambridge. He called for 'a change in content and style. The British people like strong government at home and abroad but centuries ago they rejected divine right.'

The Stalking-Horse Candidate

The idea of a 'stalking-horse' candidate began to emerge. The full range of those who were disenchanted with Margaret, or had been dismissed by her, were considered as possibilities. Ian Gilmour, David Howell and Barney Hayhoe were frequently mentioned as possible challengers.

During this period, I spent a lot of time touring the country speaking to Party meetings. On 10 November I spoke in four different constituencies and addressed over 1,000 supporters. There was no doubt that they were solidly behind Margaret. That night I stayed in Cheltenham, watching television late into the evening. One channel had Charles Laughton in the magnificent black and white film of *Jamaica Inn*. But there was something much more dramatic happening on the other channels. This was the night when the citizens of Berlin scaled their wall, danced on it, and ended thirty years of division and dictatorship. It was wonderful to see the Iron Curtain swept aside and thousands of people crossing into the West.

There was a race crowd at the hotel in Cheltenham at which I was staying. At midnight there was a bomb scare and we all had to turn out in our pyjamas, dressing-gowns and coats and stand shivering in the car-park. As I was the cause of this discomfiture, I felt the only answer was to buy drinks all round when we got back into the warmth of the hotel and continued to watch history being made in Berlin. The race crowd, some of whom had already had a good day at the races, were full of advice as to how to win the next Election and we remained doggedly cheerful.

I spoke to Margaret over the weekend. She was thrilled by the events in

Berlin: 'All part of my vision of a wider Europe.' She was buoyed up again. Losing her Chancellor was in a different league to the new pattern of world politics that was emerging, and for which she could take considerable credit.

The opening of Parliament on 23 November was the first time that a debate had been televised. Margaret, in a suit of cobalt blue and a dagger brooch, made a spirited defence of her beleaguered Government, but the press said that honours were divided between her and Neil Kinnock. The sixty-nine-year-old Baronet and MP for Clwyd North West, Sir Anthony Meyer, also spoke on the first day, attacking the Prime Minister's attitude towards Europe. On the following day, he announced that if no one else would challenge the Prime Minister, he would.

In the light of events exactly one year later, it is interesting to recall that in response to the Meyer challenge, Geoffrey Howe had said, 'I urge any Parliamentary colleagues who might be thinking of forcing the Party into a leadership election not to do so. A contest would only damage the Party.' Michael Heseltine followed up with his own statement, saying, 'I have made it clear that I will not challenge Mrs Thatcher. That remains my position.'

Meyer had joined the House of Commons from the Foreign Office and for him the issue of Europe was the heart of politics. Meyer called himself an 'extreme moderate' – the only Tory MP to vote against the Falklands expedition. Not surprisingly, at the same time as he announced his candidacy for the Tory leadership he was fighting off a lengthy campaign of de-selection in his own constituency. He saw himself as a Trojan horse, but he was soon dubbed 'the stalking donkey' or the 'pantomime horse'. He frankly, and rather engagingly, admitted, 'I am so dim and obscure that no one has paid any attention to what I have said up till now.' He was accompanied everywhere by his loyal and devoted wife, whose shoulder-length grey hair, cheerful demeanour and spriteliness became familiar on television. The tabloids made much of this aristocrat who dared to challenge the grocer's daughter. They dug and dug until they found a black actress, called Simone Washington, with whom it was alleged Sir Anthony had conducted an affair. He ignored this and declined to sue for libel. Meyer conducted his daring but hopeless campaign in a dignified way, never descending to personal abuse. That was left to others. Ted Heath, smelling blood, called Margaret 'a narrow little nationalist'. Michael Heseltine issued a statement dissociating himself from Meyer, who no doubt felt that there was a certain nobility in laying down one's life for a friend who disowned him.

Willie Whitelaw condemned Meyer's action, as did Cranley Onslow on behalf of the 1922 Committee, dismissing it as irrelevant, and Geoffrey Howe, who urged everyone to support Margaret because she would 'lead us to victory in the next election'. In the House of Commons, Jonathan Aitken called the challenge 'the charge of the light-in-head brigade'. On Tuesday 28 November, the Prime Minister received a huge ovation from her backbenchers in the House of Commons, and in the election for the Executive of the 1922 on the following Thursday, there was a sharp shift to the right.

The procedure for electing the Leader of the Conservative Party involves a wide process of consultation. Over the weekend of 2 and 3 December, the fourteen Area Chairmen of the National Union consulted the Chairmen of each Association and reported the result to Sir Peter Lane. Candidates' and peers' views were also solicited, and these groups reported to the Executive of the 1922 Committee. There was overwhelming support for the Prime Minister, and the only group which supported Meyer were the Conservative MEPs in the European Parliament.

Over that weekend I met with my constituency Party officers in the Mole Valley, who were unanimous in their support for Margaret. On the Saturday, I went with Mary to Chequers for the lunch the Prime Minister was giving for Lech Walesa. He was not yet the President of Poland, but without him the Polish people would never have been the first to break from the Soviet hegemony. For that his place in history was secure. I was immensely impressed by the calm determination of this famous leader. His stocky figure with his straggly moustache embodied the spirit of the people whom he had so inspired. He was strongest on politics. On economics, I don't think that he fully appreciated the changes that would have to be made in Poland if it was to become a capitalist market economy. His views on the consequences of the breakdown of the Soviet Empire were very perceptive. He forecast that there would be many local national wars, masses of refugees swirling around in Central Europe, and a mass migration of people. Western Europe should be prepared and willing to act to mitigate the political turmoil which would ensue.

I stayed on to have a talk with Margaret, who had a very heavy cold. Although she was under the weather she was quite relaxed about the leadership election but regretted that we all had to be going through it.

She had decided not to campaign herself, not to canvass MPs, and not to ring up colleagues.

However, the challenge was taken seriously by others. George Younger, who had left the Cabinet in July in order to become Chairman of the Royal Bank of Scotland, was appointed Margaret's campaign manager. He and Ian Gow, who was in hourly charge of the command post, organized a strong team of supportive MPs to canvass the electoral college, which was of course their 374 fellow MPs. In this election, Tristan Garel-Jones was instrumental in organizing a wide canvass of Members. He appointed a team, known as 'The Twelve Apostles', who supported Margaret but who were not particularly obvious supporters. None of the twelve knew who the others were but each was given a list of people to sound out. It was done in a very clever way and produced a very accurate sample of opinion.

Margaret was abroad for the first days of the campaign, but on American breakfast television she was robust, saying, 'I am combative. In what I am doing I believe we will win the battle of ideas. I believe that if we did not fight we would not be where we are.' That was a good statement of Margaret's basic attitude to politics.

At the weekend, I had told her that we must expect a vote of between forty to fifty against her. That was also George Younger's assessment. My other advice was that we should put the whole episode behind us as quickly as possible. As Party Chairman I wanted to ensure that there was going to be no residue of bitterness. There must be no witchhunts of MPs who were opposed to Margaret. We should do everything we could to ensure that there was no rerun of the leadership election in a year's time.

The ballot took place on Tuesday 5 December in a Committee Room in the House. The ballot closed at 6 p.m. and Cranley Onslow announced the result twenty-five minutes later: Thatcher 314, Meyer 33, abstentions 24, 3 non-voting. In effect, fifty-seven MPs wanted the PM to go. The *Daily Telegraph* said in a banner headline, 'Thatcher secures 85% support'. George Younger, however, told Margaret that the figure of discontent was greater than fifty-seven and closer to 100. Loyalty had secured the lower figure. George also told her that she should move Bernard Ingham and Charles Powell out of Number 10, as their combined influence was resented by many Tory MPs.

Margaret heard the news during her weekly audience with the Queen at Buckingham Palace. She returned to Number 10 through the back door and I met her with George Younger and Bernard Ingham. We had prepared a statement and, as she still had her heavy cold, we armed her with cough sweets and pills and went out on to the steps of Number 10. Margaret made her very matter-of-fact victory statement: 'I am very pleased with the result. We can now get on with the real issue of tackling inflation. Prime Ministers have a lot of work to do. There is a great pile of it inside and it would be better now if I left you to get on with it.' Then we all went back indoors for some champagne. Denis had been celebrating in his own way, and Margaret rather sweetly said that he too had got a lot of catarrh that night.

One of the lighter episodes during this leadership contest was a competition among advertising agencies to devise the best slogan for each of the four other possible leadership contenders. Michael Heseltine's was, 'The best man to fill her boots is the man who never licked them'. The one picked for me was a picture of Michael waving the Mace, subtitled 'Look back in Anger', side-by-side with a picture of a serene Kenneth Baker subtitled 'Look forward with calm.' Geoffrey Howe's slogan was 'After Iron, Velvet.' Chris Patten's, negative and obscure, was 'The Conservatives could lose the next election. Here's Howe.' In the event none of these slogans was ever needed.

Some commentators claimed that Margaret's position was strengthened by this election. I never saw it that way, and she acknowledged this when she said to me, 'It is not good for the Party' – a view echoed by Chris Patten. What the election revealed was that a group in the Party was deeply dissatisfied with Margaret and her style of leadership. Certainly, the Labour Party loved every minute of it. Since it was all happening against the background of totalitarian regimes being overthrown in East Germany, Poland and Romania, Jack Cunningham asked Geoffrey Howe at Business Questions, 'Will he confirm that totalitarianism is finally crumbling and will we soon see free elections for the leadership of the Conservative Party?'

The 1989 leadership contest was a serious challenge by a frivolous candidate standing as the representative of those who had been dismissed, disappointed or disenchanted by Thatcher. Yet if Anthony Meyer and his supporters had been in power in the 1980s, there would have been no restraint upon public expenditure, no tax cuts, no curbing of trade union bosses, no unleashing of that spirit of enterprise, no re-establishment of our position abroad. The great achievements of the Thatcher years would never have happened, because these were due entirely to Margaret's individual character and her boldness. She said to me at the first meeting I had with her as Party Chairman on 31 July, 'We have done things people had not dared to do.' There would have been no daring or doing if the old guard had been in charge.

The issue of Europe had dominated the politics of 1989. It had played a significant part in the demotion of Geoffrey Howe, the resignation of Nigel Lawson, and the leadership challenge of Anthony Meyer. The year went out with a bang at the Strasbourg Summit. Britain's solo opposition voted against the Social Charter made the vote 11–1 and Margaret Thatcher tried to prevent the beginning of the process of renegotiation which came to a head at Maastricht two years later. With the Eastern European bloc falling apart, the European Community seemed to be the stable and prosperous ideal which every country wanted to join. The federalists were in the ascendant. Chancellor Kohl's great year lay ahead of him and the Kohl–Mitterrand axis bolstered by the EC Commission President, Jacques Delors dominated Europe. Margaret Thatcher's view seemed to some to be petty, limited and pedestrian. The others seemed to have a bright confident future all mapped out. How different things turned out to be by 1992. At the press conference at the end of the Strasbourg Summit, Mitterrand said at one stage, 'Shall we have a break?' Margaret's rejoinder was, 'No, let's go on,' whereupon all the lights fused and Margaret's voice rang out through the darkness, 'Why can't we discuss the Social Charter now?'

CHAPTER 15

A Choppy Spring 1990

Developing a Conservative Strategy – The Political
Troubles of the Poll Tax – The Central Council and
Norman Tebbit's Re-Emergence – Local Government
Elections: the Westminster and Wandsworth Effect

As we entered 1990 I had four things on my agenda as Party Chairman – to avoid another bruising leadership election; to mitigate the effects of the poll tax in the spring and move to a fundamental revision; to bridge the gap in the Party between Euro-fanatics and Euro-sceptics; and above all, to develop a strategy for winning the next Election.

It was simply not possible to go on reacting tactically to the various crises, putting out the blaze here or there like some political fire brigade. In September 1989 the Prime Minister had seen a presentation of the research work we were doing and had asked, where do we go from here? I decided to hold a weekend seminar in January at Hever Castle, where we could hammer out an election-winning strategy. I took with me the top management at Central Office – David Young, the Deputy Chairman; Tom Arnold, the Vice-Chairman; the inner team of Tony Kerpel, Brendan Bruce and Andrew Lansley; those experienced election campaigners John Lacy, Tony Garrett and Shirley Stotter; John Hanvey, our pollster; Christine Wall, head of our Press Office; Professor Brian Griffiths, the head of the Prime Minister's Policy Unit; Tim Bell, who saw Margaret regularly to advise her on the Government's PR; Stephen Sherbourne, her former Political Secretary; and David Willetts, the astute Director of the Centre for Policy Studies, the think-tank which Margaret and Keith Joseph had set up to propagate free-market policies.

I began by saying that we could not win the next Election if we adopted an attitude of 'business as usual', the trap into which most governing Parties fall. We needed a plan, an assessment of Conservative and Opposition strengths and weaknesses, the maximization of our assets and a flexible strategy which while giving us direction could also accommodate new factors.

The Labour Party was benefitting from a reduction in support for the Liberal and Social Democrats and that meant that we needed to get more votes than in 1987 in order to win. From where would we get those votes? We needed to analyse where the Green vote, which had increased significantly in the 1989 European Parliament elections, had come from. Although Labour was in better shape than before, the lesson of 1987 was that presentation alone didn't win elections. Finally what approach should we adopt to the argument that the Labour Party had changed? It was vital for us not be diverted by the crisis of the hour. Our job was to determine the ground on which we chose to fight the next General Election.

I had also invited to our meeting Dick Wirthlin, the American pollster who had been a key adviser to President Reagan. He had developed a method of polling which identified emotions and values as the key element in determining how people were going to vote. This differed from most polling, which identified key issues and then asked how people were going to vote on the basis of these issues. Dick's method had been the bedrock of the successful Republican campaigns in 1980, 1984 and 1988.

Dick's particular contribution was to point out that while incumbent leaders always wanted to fight the next Election on their past record, what voters actually voted for was prospects for the future. It was 'Hope for the future' for themselves and their families which was the key to voter behaviour. This was a lesson President Bush would have done well to heed in 1992, when his doomed re-election campaign rested heavily on his record in office. Dick's analysis of British voters showed that the major driving factor was 'hope' followed by a 'sense of security'– including 'opportunity' and 'peace of mind'. This led us to concentrate on the positive elements of the Conservative appeal. A Conservative Government would have to convince people that they would have a better future for themselves and their families under us, rather than under any other Party. So we had to present a future of increasing opportunities and wider choice for everyone. The underlying message had to be one of hope, but without using the word itself in slogans.

But since we had been in office for eleven years there also had to be continuity with the recent past. The vision for the 1990s had to be based upon the enterprise culture which Thatcherism had developed in the 1980s. We had to continue to extend opportunities for people to own their own homes, to choose schools for their children, and to keep a higher proportion of what they earned. These policies had transformed society in the 1980s and should be continued into the 1990s.

It was clear from John Hanvey's polling analysis that we had lost support among the critical C2 voters who had given us victory since 1979. These voters, often described as 'the Basildon Factor', or 'Essex Man', were upwardly mobile and aspiring working-class with an attachment to what modern Conservatism could deliver. They had been particularly hard hit by high mortgage interest rates and the poll tax. Indeed when one examined the proportion of income taken up by high mortgage rates this factor had much more impact upon disposable incomes than the poll tax. But it was the new poll tax which had become the lightning conductor for discontent with the mortgage rates. However, Labour still held no emotional attractions for the C2 voters and it was up to us to win them back.

We also recognized that the most powerful argument we would have to counter was the 'Time for a Change' factor. But this was balanced by poll findings showing that when it came to voters' perceptions of which Party offered the best leadership, Margaret remained far ahead of Neil Kinnock. In fact the credibility, or incredibility, of Kinnock as an alternative Prime Minister was itself a powerful factor in voter opinion, something we were to turn to time and again in our attacks on Labour.

Tim Bell reported on the mood of the media which, he said, were looking to criticize us. Not only were newspapers becoming increasingly competitive and therefore seeking out crisis and controversy, but editors and journalists too were voters and did not like high mortgages. Despite their view that the Government was doing badly, there was still a general belief that the Conservatives would win the next Election. Televising the House of Commons had boosted Margaret's stature and not done Neil Kinnock any favours.

We had a report from John Lacy about the help needed in marginal seats. He had identified ninety marginal seats divided into four groups depending upon their marginality, and of these which could be won from Labour or Liberal Democrats. We wanted to direct financial help to these seats to employ Agents or secretaries, and to provide them with computers. This was the first time that such a thorough programme of support had been put in place to help save or win marginal seats. Tom Arnold subsequently interviewed each of our marginal seat MPs, or the candidates where we were hoping to win the seat, to see how Central Office could help them.

We also discussed how to tackle the Opposition Parties. We

specifically agreed not to attempt to appeal to the Liberal Democrat vote – the supposed middle ground of British politics. I was clear that if we did, then we would sink into the unidentifiable and unrecognizable marsh of mushy policies that would appeal only to those who were unlikely to vote for us in any event. The problem about seeking the middle ground of British politics is that it turns all too quickly into no-man's-land.

But the critical part of this discussion was how we would tackle Labour. My feeling was that we had to show that at the next Election voters faced a real choice between a Conservative Britain and a Socialist Britain. My clear view, agreed to by the strategy group, was that we should not accept Labour's propaganda that their Party had changed significantly. The change from the Red Flag to the Red Rose in 1986 was merely symbolic. Peter Mandelson, Labour's Communications Director, had been brought in to create an image of modernity and moderation. He had been rewarded with opinion polls showing 60 per cent of people believing Labour had changed, albeit for largely electoral reasons. But I believed that Labour remained Socialist and that it was our task to persuade voters back to that point of view.

Neil Kinnock, when pressed, still described himself as a Socialist, although the word had totally disappeared from Labour's lexicon. It didn't fit the music of the Mandelson Sonata. So we had to bring out how Labour were still the Party of high spending, high taxes, state interference and state ownership. Their 1989 policy document, *Meet the Challenge, Make the Change*, was stuffed full of commitments which proved this. During the coming year, the careful tracking and analysis of the flood of Labour policy documents by the Conservative Research Department was to give us invaluable ammunition in supporting this approach.

The Hever strategy meeting concluded with the adoption of seven strategic imperatives. These were:

- Reinforce the perception of 'Hope' tied to 'the Future', upheld by 'Peace of Mind' and 'Opportunity'.
- Further reinforce the strong leadership image of the Prime Minister.
- Use fully the advantage of incumbency, particularly in the timing of the campaign.
- Maximize the political advantage of our superior organization and financial resources.

- Neutralize voters' negative attitude to our handling of the NHS and community charge.
- Develop the offset issues of the Environment and Education/Training and blunt Labour's attack that we are 'unfair, do not care, and are building a selfish society'.
- Highlight Labour's vulnerabilities.

The conclusions of Hever were presented to the Prime Minister on 20 January and she accepted my underlying strategy. She was keen to do so because the research finding that worried her most was that far too many people believed that the Labour Party had changed. 'Kenneth, we must stop that impression. It's totally false', she said. So there was unanimity at the top of the Party leadership about the way Labour had to be attacked, and this tactical approach was enshrined in the campaign which I was to launch in May, entitled 'Summer Heat on Labour'.

Following this endorsement, I saw separately each of the leading Cabinet Ministers in charge of the main domestic Departments to take them through our analysis and our conclusions. I wanted to persuade them to direct their own policy thinking along these lines. But some Conservatives rejected this approach and argued that we should accept the perception that Labour had indeed changed. We should attack them instead for their cynicism in abandoning their principles, which meant that their word could not be trusted in the future. This argument seemed to me to be fatally flawed. I was not prepared to abandon the high ground that Labour were still essentially a Socialist Party. Once that ground was conceded it would become very difficult to persuade voters of the risks they were taking by voting Labour. Our strategy depended on presenting a stark choice to voters. I argued that as the next Election came closer we would have to remind the British public again of the past horrors of Socialism and the real dangers of a future Socialist government. If we had, in the meantime, accepted that Labour had shed most of its old commitments then our attack would be totally blunted, since where was the threat?

I also thought that to ask voters to reject Labour for abandoning their principles was a pretty damp squib. Most voters are cynical enough to believe that politicians and Parties regularly abandon their principles so why should the Conservatives be making such a big fuss over it.

However, when John Major became Leader, and Chris Patten his Chairman, they took this unconvincing line for several months,

presumably in an attempt to win back votes from the Liberal Democrats. It didn't work. As the Election neared, inevitably they swung
back to the Hever approach of presenting the electorate with a stark
choice. The whole thrust of our campaign was an attack on a Labour
Party which remained socialist. In our Manifesto the two banner words
in the shortened version were 'choice' and 'opportunity'. The best
ammunition that we fired against Labour was directed against their
high-tax policy. The 1992 Conservative Manifesto was the last great
promotion of Thatcherism and its success over the previous twelve
years. There could be no other message, even though the carrier of that
message had changed.

The development of the Hever strategy proved its use during the rest
of the year by giving us a definite sense of direction. It enabled us to
seize the initiative and to try setting the news agenda by attacking
Labour, something quite unusual for a Conservative Party in government. It also gave a theme to my speeches as Party Chairman, so that in
addition to the issue of the day I also set out arguments which helped to
position the Labour Party in relation to ourselves.

In a key article for the *Times* on 14 March I wrote:

Practical politicians should not ignore the Zeitgeist, but neither should they
forget what it was that won voters' support for one Party at the ballot box and
condemned other Parties to opposition.

It is important to appreciate that the Conservative policies of the last 10 years
were not devised in a vacuum. They were a crucial element of the philosophy
which has inspired the Government throughout its three terms in office.

Unlike the Labour Party, we Conservatives have no intention of trimming
simply in order to reverse temporary unpopularity at the polls. I cannot believe
that people are now asking the Government to turn around in its tracks and
depart from the philosophy and principles that have put our nation on the road
to economic and social recovery.

Are our critics really saying that just as the nations of Eastern Europe are
throwing off the stifling effects of socialism and turning to us for advice on how
to create free markets and consumerism, we should retreat into that same failed
economic system?

If I thought the British wanted those things, I would know we had failed. But
I don't believe they want to repeat past failures. They want to see Britain
building on the achievements of the past decade, and that will be the agenda on
which we fight the next Election.

We returned to the Hever Strategy at a meeting in London on 7 June
at the St Ermin's Hotel. There we reviewed the extent to which we had

made progress with our objectives, and further specific tasks were allocated to individuals, and new publications agreed which supported the strategy.

At working meetings in October 1990 we decided to increase our attacks upon the Liberal Party, particularly in the South-West, and to focus even more sharply upon Labour's tax plans and the damage inherent in their economic policies. We also focused on the absence of any effective Labour alternative to the community charge. Never before had such detailed planning been undertaken so far in advance of a General Election, and when I left the chairmanship in November a clear basis had been established for a winning Election strategy.

I have dwelt on the Hever meeting in some detail not only because it was significant historically but also because some in my successor's circle tried to put it about that on entering Central Office the strategy cupboard was bare. That was a malicious untruth. The new team may not have liked what was there, but they were to adopt much of our thinking as the basis of their General Election campaign in 1992.

The Political Troubles of the Poll Tax

The first three months of 1990 were an almost unmitigated disaster for the Government. Just about anything that could go wrong did go wrong. On 2 January Norman Fowler resigned from the Cabinet as Employment Secretary on the grounds that he wanted to spend more time with his family. I was saddened to hear this, as he had been a successful Social Security Secretary in charge of a Department which is traditionally difficult for the Government. There, he presided over a huge increase in expenditure and had gained credit for this. He was a safe pair of hands, and his successors were to have a much rougher time.

Norman had told me that he had intended to resign the previous October and had informed Margaret of this, but following Nigel's resignation he had decided to stay on. He must have been disappointed not to have been offered either the posts of Party Chairman or Home Secretary in the reshuffles of 1989. He had started his journalistic career as the Home Affairs correspondent of the *Times*, and I believe he cherished an ambition to be Home Secretary. Following the 1992 Election he accepted the Party Chairmanship offered to him by John Major, so clearly the demands of his family had waned.

Just two months after Norman's resignation, on 5 March Peter

Walker announced after a press leak in the *Sunday Times* that he too intended to step down from the Cabinet and to leave the House at the next Election. He also wanted to spend more time with his family and to resume his business life.

There was some sympathy with Nick Ridley when, in a debate in the House of Commons rejecting the Opposition's call for him to resign, he acidly said that the last people he wanted to spend more time with were his family. As a result of these changes Margaret was able to bring some good new blood into her Cabinet: Michael Howard at Employment, and David Hunt at Wales. But the overall impression was that seasoned and experienced Ministers had seen the storm cones hoisted and had decided to abandon ship.

There were also a number of revolts by Tory MPs in the Commons. One should not think this was a characteristic acquired under John Major's subsequent premiership. The revolts started on 3 January. A group of MPs demanded that the Uniform Business Rate had to be softened because it was going to drive many firms out of business in the South-East. On 11 January, twelve Tory MPs abstained in a vote on ambulancemen's pay. On 19 January, thirty-one Tory MPs voted against the Government and eight abstained on the poll tax, reducing the Government's majority to thirty-six. In February, Norman Tebbit had marshalled eighty Tory MPs against the Government's Bill to extend British citizenship to 50,000 heads of household in Hong Kong. On 14 March, the Government was actually defeated by a further backbench revolt on the issue of income support for elderly people in council homes. Tim Renton, the Chief Whip, said that he had a list of about seventy Tory MPs who had stopped supporting the Government on certain matters.

Norman Tebbit had put himself at the head of a campaign to stop the Hong Kong Bill. He urged Associations to write to me as Party Chairman; he pressed for the issue to be on the agenda for every Party conference – Central Council, Young Conservatives, and the Women's Conference; he planned to hold up the Bill in the House of Commons and to deny it a guillotine, which meant the final stages would be taken in the spillover period in the late autumn of 1990. This would have had the effect of wrecking the Party Conference, since there would have been a demand for this most emotive issue to be debated at the Conference itself. I did not welcome such subversive tactics from the former Chairman. Margaret told me that in her view it was treacherous and said of Norman's motives, 'I think basically it is spite.'

It was not surprising to see the popularity of the Government slump. In January, Labour's lead was 10.5 points; in February 15.5 points; at the beginning of March 18.5; and by mid-March 21 points – the largest lead since 1974. Margaret Thatcher had become the most unpopular Prime Minister since records were started, and for the first time since he had become Leader of the Labour Party, Neil Kinnock surpassed the Prime Minister in the polls.

The magnificent John Stokes – upright, Christian, patriot – who sat for Halesowen, spoke up for the conventional decency of middle-class middle England. He said in the House that he went into pubs a lot, where they didn't normally talk about politics, but now they were and that was very worrying. The economic news was also terrible. On 15 February, mortgage rates went up to 15.5 per cent – the highest ever level. John Major was savagely attacked in the Commons, but he insisted that the reduction of inflation was the Government's key target and forecast there would be an economic recovery in 1991.

But the issue which dominated the whole of the political debate at the beginning of 1990 was the new Community Charge, dubbed by Labour the Poll Tax. Chris Patten had wanted to mitigate its effect, but his pleas for more money to do this had been brusquely rejected. In a debate in January he was roughed up by Tory backbenchers – many of whom were now running scared, afraid of losing their seats.

Early in January I sent a minute to the Prime Minister saying that we could lose control of twenty-two Councils in the May local government elections and hundreds of council seats around the country. I set out all the various ways by which we could mitigate the poll tax. But ultimately it came down to more money from the Treasury to ease the pain which they themselves had caused by insisting upon a tight settlement for local government expenditure. In a meeting with Margaret on 11 January, when this was discussed, I had to accept the fact that the Treasury was not going to provide significant extra funds. In the light of all the public opinion signals and the misgivings I was hearing from our local authority leaders, this was a major mistake.

Chris and I decided that we should develop two lines of defence which could also be turned into attacks upon Labour. First, however unpopular the poll tax, Labour had no alternative. So we goaded Bryan Gould, Labour's Environment Spokesman, until on 10 February he produced one – a combination of a capital value tax and an income tax. This ludicrous dual tax was a godsend and we dubbed it 'The Roof

Tax'. Second, we had to show that it was the high-spending, wasteful Labour councils which were setting the highest poll taxes. Although there were some high Tory poll taxes too (I remember Windsor in particular), the highest were to be found in the Labour bastions in the inner cities. Indeed we unearthed a document containing advice from the Labour Party to Labour councils encouraging them to spend up, set a high poll tax and then blame the Government for it.

On 1 March, Chris had to publish figures which revealed that the average poll tax would be £370 a head instead of the earlier estimate, which we had been rash enough to publish, of £278. The headlines screamed '£100 more per head'. On that day we lost control of West Oxfordshire District Council, in Douglas Hurd's constituency, when some Conservative councillors resigned from the Party because of their opposition to the poll tax, and declared themselves as Independents.

Seventy Tory MPs demanded that education be taken out of local government finance in order to reduce the poll tax. But Margaret dismissed this as 'retrograde and leading to a colossal increase in income tax'. The Government moved a little way early in March when it increased the Transitional Relief Scheme by £50 million. This gave a further 1.5 million people about £30 relief. It was too little and was far too difficult to explain.

Our campaign to show that well run Conservative councils could produce a low poll tax was given a great boost on 3 March when Wandsworth declared a poll tax of £148 – the lowest in the country, alongside Westminster, which set a poll tax of £195. Alas, there weren't many like that. When Labour-controlled Haringey Council declared a poll tax of £572, fighting broke out in the Town Hall. All over the country town halls were besieged, council chambers were invaded in Thamesdown, Southampton and Norwich, and councillors were physically attacked in Bristol and Nottingham. In Hackney a large protest meeting turned into looting of local shops. Public order was at risk.

I wrote to Neil Kinnock demanding that he condemn the Anti-Poll Tax Federation as a front for the Militant tendency, and disown the twenty-eight Labour MPs who had pledged not to pay the poll tax and were thus breaking the law. 'What have you done to stop the Militants?' I asked. He scornfully dismissed this, but on 9 March our case was strengthened when Tony Wedgwood Benn defended and advocated 'conscientious law-breaking'. At this late stage the Government could do little to reduce the damaging impact of the poll tax. Chris and I pressed

John Major, the Chancellor of the Exchequer, to do something in response to all the pressure that we had had over the last few months and to use his Budget to mitigate some of the effect of the poll tax.

On 20 March, John got the loudest cheer in his Budget when he announced that the amount of capital which would be disregarded in calculating poll tax rebates would be increased from £8,000 to £16,000. This was a particular help to elderly people who had quite modest savings but who had been debarred from benefiting from the rebate scheme. Our backbenchers and councillors liked this. But the gloss was soon taken off the announcement when it emerged that John had forgotten to say how Scotland was to be treated, where they had been paying the poll tax for a year. Malcolm Rifkind was reported to be considering resignation. For two days the Government dithered, and then it gave in and extended the benefit retrospectively to Scotland. This measure of relief, though welcome, was really marginal in its effect. It certainly had no beneficial effect in the by-election at Mid Staffordshire which was held two days after the Budget and which we lost with a 21 per cent swing against the Conservatives.

This was the first by-election for which I had been responsible as Party Chairman. John Heddle, the popular local MP, had committed suicide in December when it became impossible for him to meet the financial obligations of various property deals he had embarked upon at the peak of the property market. I remember when the news of his death was brought into me at Cabinet on 19 December and I passed the note over to Margaret. I could see from her eyes that she was hurt and saddened by it.

It meant of course that we would have a by-election at an acutely difficult time. The candidate was Charles Prior, a nephew of our former Cabinet colleague Jim Prior, and in almost any other circumstances he would have been a very good candidate. But there was only really one issue in the entire campaign, and that was the poll tax. The Conservative candidate could only be a target for protest votes.

Mid Staffordshire was normally considered to be a safe Conservative seat, with a majority of 14,654 at the 1987 General Election. At the by-election this was transformed into a Labour majority of 9,449. The Labour candidate, Sylvia Heal, presented an untypically moderate and sensible face for Labour, although her winning strategy was to say absolutely nothing during the entire campaign. Even the press became utterly frustrated by her convent-like refusal to utter a word. I accused Labour of adopting 'The Sound of Silence' as its new theme song. Neil

Kinnock flew in by helicopter provided by a local millionaire Socialist – all part of the new image – but even he maintained silence about policy. Labour felt they had only to say nothing in order to achieve victory, because the Government was twisting in the wind. My comment on the result was, 'Labour was the passive beneficiary of the protest vote.' Sylvia Heal was a well-liked Member of the House of Commons, but in the Election of 1992 she lost the seat as Mid Staffordshire, in post-poll tax mood, returned to the Tory fold.

This by-election was a severe blow to the morale of the Party, but was not unexpected. Margaret took the unusual step of writing to me as Party Chairman and publishing the letter. In it she said, 'All those who took part in the Mid-Staffordshire campaign can take pride in fighting so hard and in showing so clearly the mettle of the Conservative Party. We are not a "fair-weather" Party. We are not for trimming and turning. We believe in long-term policies of the kind we have implemented so successfully over the last eleven years.'

The Central Council and Norman Tebbit's Re-emergence

At this time Margaret Thatcher's position came under withering fire, often from her own Party. Michael Heseltine and Geoffrey Howe rivalled each other in their protestations of support for the Prime Minister. Then at the beginning of March a rumour, starting in the Far East, swept across the markets that Margaret Thatcher had actually resigned. This was accompanied by stories that some Cabinet Ministers had discussed whether she should stand down, which led Margaret to say that she had 'the most united and cooperative Cabinet I have ever had during my whole term'. As a member of that Cabinet I can certainly confirm that this was the position in Cabinet meeting after Cabinet meeting. However, speculation was rife and most commentators believed that there was inevitably going to be a leadership election again later that year. Michael Heseltine was clearly the front runner, and to such an extent that on 30 March front page stories were running that if Margaret stood down then Norman Tebbit would throw his hat into the ring against him.

Norman Tebbit had lunched with Gordon Greig of the *Daily Mail* and Trevor Kavanagh of the *Sun*, two of the most experienced and war-worn political journalists. They hunted together with a good nose for the scent of a scoop. They reported that Norman was prepared to stand for the leadership, should there be a vacancy, because above all he wanted to stop Heseltine. Norman did nothing by accident, and this was a hand-grenade lobbed into the Party's Central Council Meeting, which was to start the following day at Cheltenham. As a former Party Chairman, Norman knew that by tossing his hat into the ring at this precise time he would cast his shadow over the conference, and put the leadership issue right back onto the front pages.

From time to time politics throws up a real one-off, and Norman Tebbit was one of these. He had cultivated a brutal and confrontational style which stood out in a Party that preferred the dagger to the cudgel. His blunt way of expressing himself won him devoted friends and implacable enemies. He had a unique capacity to polarize opinion. The right-wing Federation of Conservative Students loved him for his 'get on your bike' attitude and unfurled banners at the 1985 Conference saying, 'Tebbit is pure Gold.' It was one of the strange ironies that as Party Chairman he had to disband this strident body as it had become an extreme and disruptive force within the Party.

Norman and I had worked as fellow Ministers of State under Keith Joseph in the Department of Industry. I had all the new industries and he had all the old ones – we were known as Mr Sunrise and Mr Sunset. Later, as Secretary of State for Employment, Norman's greatest contributions to Thatcherite policy, and the ones in which he took the greatest pride, were his measures to reform trade union law and to reduce the power of the trade union bosses. He did this with relish. He was not as radical when he became Secretary of State for Trade and Industry. It was known that he was working on a plan to reduce regional aid, which he didn't much favour, but his eventual proposals were rather mild, with lower grants but spread over a wider number of eligible areas. This was a clever scheme, but it was a case of the film not living up to the trailer.

John Selwyn Gummer passed me a poem which he had written during the meeting which discussed Norman's proposals:

Lines on the softening of an image

When will Tebbit take again
His leathers and his cycle chain
And bring his knuckle-duster back
And give the clout that now we lack?
Soon – oh soon – lest we forget
And count him as a closet wet.

Norman had a well deserved reputation for stubbornness. In July 1984 Ken Warren MP, the Chairman of the Select Committee on Trade and Industry, had asked to see the corporate plans of British Shipbuilders. Norman, as the Secretary of State, instructed Graham Day, the Managing Director of British Shipbuilders, not to send the plans to the Select Committee. He had no confidence in the Committee, thought their prying would be unhelpful, and referred to them as 'children'. Norman's non-compliance with the wishes of the Select Committee became an awkward Parliamentary issue for the Government, and a meeting was held in the Prime Minister's room in the House to resolve it. It was a very acrimonious discussion, since Norman was isolated yet expected his colleagues to rally to his support. He even demanded that John Wakeham, the Chief Whip, should whip the Party to support him, which John flatly refused to do. Even Willie Whitelaw said in exasperation, 'If you can't do a deal with Ken Warren then you're not fit to be a Minister.' I believe that Willie later apologized to Norman for saying this.

Norman had been a popular Chairman of the Conservative Party, running the very successful pre-Election Conference of 1986 and the Election campaign itself in 1987. Before the bomb outrage at Brighton, which left him injured, he was often seen as Margaret's natural heir. But he realized that this could not be, especially when he decided to devote a large part of the rest of his life to caring for his wife, Margaret, who had been even more seriously injured in the Brighton bombing. Nevertheless Norman never totally rejected the possibility of standing, especially if it was to beat Michael Heseltine.

Mary and I were woken up at 6.30 a.m. on the Friday morning to be told the news that Norman's interest in the Party leadership was all over the front pages. By the time we got to Cheltenham I had decided how this would have to be handled to prevent it dominating the whole weekend. In my opening speech I gave a very clear message to the Party:

Loyalty and unity have always been the great strengths of our Party. Disloyalty and disunity have always been the great burdens of the Labour Party. Any house divided against itself will fall. So the lesson is clear.

Talk of a leadership election, the canvassing of candidates openly or surreptitiously, when there is no vacancy, and there will be no vacancy, is welcomed only by our opponents. I say to you – let this idle chatter cease. We have serious work to do.

I warn our opponents and our critics, never write off the Conservative Party. Our record is the record of fighters not quitters.

Margaret arrived on Saturday the following morning, and told me she had been up until three o'clock working on her speech, which also took up the theme that there was no vacancy and that she hadn't come like a Colonel to Cheltenham to retire. She tried to turn the tables by putting herself at the head of those protesting about high poll taxes, which was a clever anti-ministerial change of role. 'Some poll taxes are a scandal,' she thundered. She pledged herself to protect the community charge payer from 'overpowering taxation', and received a rapturous reception. But I had a great sense that we were having to run very hard just to stand still.

There was a huge police presence in Cheltenham which diverted a column of poll tax protesters away from the Conference Centre. Mary and I set off with Brendan Bruce to return via Gloucester, where we stopped to see that magnificent Cathedral. It was another gloriously warm, sunny day. As we passed through Devizes, Brendan picked up a newsflash on his portable television, 'Poll Tax Riots in Central London'. This was the most violent demonstration in our capital for many, many years. The police had been openly attacked. About 3,000 politically motivated protesters, including anarchist groups like Class War, had taken over what was intended to be a peaceful rally in order to turn up the political temperature. Television film, seen widely around the world, showed young men and women, some masked, attacking police, looting shops and setting fire to cars. These scenes, so untypical of Britain, made a considerable impact. We appeared to be trembling on the edge of anarchy, and the very authority of Government was being challenged – all because of the reform of local taxation.

Local Government Elections: the Westminster and Wandsworth Effect

Following on from the Mid Staffs by-election, the local government elections on 2 May were going to be a major test of the Government's popularity. If the polls were to be believed we were facing obliteration at local council level. Labour's lead had increased to an all-time record of 24 points, and during the campaign an ICM poll showed that their lead among skilled manual workers, Thatcher's greatest supporters since 1979, was as high as 42 per cent. Leaders of Tory councils brought dismal reports to Central Office. Of the 4,500 seats being contested we were defending 1,400 and we could lose 400 of these. I had to stop this apparently terminal decline in the Party's support. The only way was to run a campaign that was both positive and attacking. One never wins elections by being defensive and apologetic, so I launched our campaign on 4 April, a fortnight before Labour.

Back in January, Tony Kerpel had stressed the importance of not treating the local elections as a secondary matter. He urged me to fight a high-profile campaign in order to create the perception that once again Central Office had an election-winning machine. He argued that it was particularly important to focus on London because of the media attention concentrated there. This made sense because in 1990, while there were elections for every London Borough and the metropolitan districts, there were no local elections in large parts of the country. So the national debate could be focused on London, where we could establish a stark contrast between high and low levels of poll tax in neighbouring Labour- and Conservative-controlled councils.

The poll tax was the only real issue. Despite being a high-risk strategy I decided that we would take it head-on and go out to sell its advantages. Our private polls showed that 71 per cent of the public accepted the basic principle of the poll tax, namely that all adults should pay something towards the cost of local government. We had to emphasize, therefore, the importance and value of local accountability. The thrust of our campaign, developed with Brendan Bruce and Tim Bell in March and later approved by the Cabinet, was 'Conservative Councils Cost You Less'. The converse of that was that Labour councils cost you more. We hammered home this message for four weeks. In London we were able to show that a community chargepayer could save £3 a week by voting Tory. We focused especially on the high-profile councils of Westminster and Wandsworth, where the Tories were led with verve by Shirley Porter and Paul Beresford. With spirit and imagination both had cut back expenditure but improved services. They were the flagships of efficiency in local government, together with Bradford, where the Tories were led by Eric Pickles and the poll tax was £276. I published a 'Chargeometer', designed like a large thermometer, which showed the ten highest poll tax Labour councils in red at the top and the lower poll tax Tory councils in blue at the bottom.

Labour's campaign was muffled and muddled. They tried to repeat their Mid Staffs by-election strategy of relying entirely upon the protest vote and mounting a general attack upon the Government. They only mentioned the poll tax once in their last Party Political Broadcast, an astonishing error. Under pressure to come clean with a more credible

20 Introducing change and taking the brickbats as Education Secretary

If you see Ken...

tell him you want your rights back!

16 October 1987   Volume 179 Number 16   £1

Education

Mutual admiration society. The Prime Minister Mrs. Margaret Thatcher earned a pat on the back from her education secretary Mr. Kenneth Baker, as she rose to applaud his speech winding up the education debate at the Conservative Party conference in Blackpool last week. Mrs. Thatcher herself put education top of her priorities two days later, when she announced her undiminished commitment to establishing 'independent state schools' free from local authority control. (PA Photos).

21 Sorting out the teachers' pay dispute, 1986

22 A touching scene at the end of my Party Conference speech, October 1987

23 Visiting my old school in Southport

24 Showing Raisa Gorbachev a primary school in Oxfordshire, 1987

25 Trying to persuade Vice President Bush to focus on education in the US
Election, with Bill Bennett, President Reagan's Education Secretary, 1987

26 Meeting Mikhail Gorbachev with the Prime Minister at Brize Norton,
and Alan Clark preparing a diary entry, 1987

27 General Election 1987 – on the campaign trail with Tony Kerpel, my
Political Adviser

28 As Party Chairman with the Cabinet, September 1989 – a new style of
photograph for the new Government

"CARRY YOUR BAG MISSIS."

29 Warding off the first challenge to Margaret's leadership, 1989

30 The Party Chairman and the Chancellor of the Exchequer turning up the
Summer Heat on Labour, 1990

31 A jaundiced view of my handling of the Local Government Election
results, May 1990

32 The Party Conference 1990 – one month to go before Geoffrey's
resignation speech and Margaret's fall

I can't understand it, Kenneth Baker is usually so gentle. He's never done anything like this before

33 A canine view of my Dangerous Dogs Bill, 1991
34 As Home Secretary, launching plans for Britain's first National Lottery, 1992

35 Relaxing with Mary in our garden

Labour alternative, Bryan Gould had transformed the 'roof tax' into a 'floor tax' based upon the space occupied by a household. This simply added to the general confusion about Labour's plans. Labour was also unable to shake off the high-spending reputation of its inner-city councils, all of which had high poll tax levels.

I finished the campaign by visiting Hazelbourne Road – the boundary between Tory Wandsworth with a poll tax of £148 and Labour Lambeth with a poll tax of £496. This was one of the few election campaigns where the theme remained constant throughout and where the message on the final day was the same as the message on the first.

It was also a very enjoyable campaign – supported by Chris Patten and by David Hunt, the Local Government Minister, whose enthusiasm for the poll tax had led him to declare, 'The community charge is a winner.' The fact that we had our backs to the wall added to the vigour of it all. We also had effective newspaper advertisements setting out simple facts about the poll tax – '10 things you should know about the Community Charge'. Many people said that in all the hullabaloo surrounding the poll tax they hadn't taken these facts on board until they read our advertisements.

The final weekend polls made grim reading. The *Sunday Times* predicted a 600-seat loss, and this was echoed by the *Independent* and others. Nationally, NOP and MORI had put Labour ahead of us by between 23 and 28 per cent. In London, Labour was 20 per cent ahead. Special NOP polls put Labour 4 per cent ahead in Wandsworth and 5 per cent ahead in Westminster. On Wednesday 2 May we held our final press conference of the campaign and, despite the polls, predicted that we would hold the councils we controlled, win back Hillingdon and make gains in Ealing. On election day, I told Margaret to prepare for bad news but to leave some room for optimism.

That evening I watched the results coming in with my Local Government team in Central Office. The first results had pointed to a Labour landslide and the early edition of the *Sun* announced, 'It's Blue Murder for Maggie'. However, just before midnight we began to get reports that we were actually making significant gains and winning seats from Labour in Wandsworth, Westminster, Southend and Hillingdon. By about one o'clock in the morning it became clear that there was no Labour landslide and that our strategy of concentrating upon certain councils had paid off. Our message about the poll tax had got through.

Far from losing our London flagships, our majority on Wandsworth

Council had increased dramatically from one to thirty-five, and on Westminster Council from four to twenty-nine. Conservatives became the controlling Party in Hillingdon, we won Southend and Hastings, and held on to Trafford. Perhaps sweetest of all, we gained control of the Labour Borough of Ealing where Neil Kinnock lived. The only disappointment was at Bradford, where the loss of five seats meant that we also lost control of the council. But overall, it had been a better night than even the optimists had predicted.

The later edition of the *Sun* said 'Kinnock Poll Axed'. I had had a £5 bet with Kelvin Mackenzie, the paper's editor, that we would hold Westminster and Wandsworth. It showed how desperate things were when the editor of Margaret's greatest fan club thought we'd had it. Kelvin later generously sent me a letter with his fiver saying he would stick to editing rather than forecasting.

Early the following morning, and after only a few hours' sleep, Brendan Bruce and I began to visit every radio and television programme asking for us. The raw figures showed that the Conservatives had a net loss of 172 seats nationwide, compared with an anticipated loss of 600, while Labour had a net gain of 277, and the SDP/SLD a net loss of 88. In London we actually achieved a net gain of 35 seats, and Labour a net loss of 23.

These results were far less bad for us than all the predictions and polls had forecast. They were also demoralizing for Labour, who had done far less well than they needed to if they were to win a General Election. So these results, relative to expectations, created the clear impression that we had won. The fact that I rammed home this message throughout Friday morning caused the Labour Party to protest that we were stealing the election, but there was no way I was going to miss the opportunity of capitalizing on the better than expected results of a good campaign. Victories in two of our flagship councils proved that where a reasonable poll tax was set due to good housekeeping, then people would vote for Conservative government.

Returning to Central Office after doing the rounds of studio interviews, Brendan arranged for me to be filmed emerging beaming from my car holding up the *Sun* front page. I was then filmed in the office congratulating staff. At lunchtime I took the winning team from Central Office to lunch on the Terrace of the House of Commons. As we entered, Nicholas Soames bellowed out, 'Victory from the jaws of defeat. Well done!' I appreciated rather more Willie Whitelaw's sober assessment when he came into Central Office a few days later – 'It was a superb campaign, a real coup, and you've certainly saved Margaret. After this, I don't think there will be a leadership election later this year.' But we agreed that in order to defuse the issue, other councils' poll taxes would have to come down to the Wandsworth/Westminster levels the following year.

In the afternoon I invited the Sunday lobby journalists to my room to ensure that the week's events were reflected helpfully in Sunday's newspapers. I reminded the journalists of their predictions only a week earlier that we would be routed, and how we had succeeded against all expectations. For once the journalists had the grace to look sheepish.

I should add here that despite the results which we were publicly claiming as a victory I was very well aware of the negative results as well, particularly those outside London falling in constituencies which were marginal seats. I knew that for those Conservative MPs, the thought of colleagues hanging on in London while they lost their own seats was not a prospect which would diminish their opposition to the poll tax and Margaret's stubborn adherence to its unamended form. What the local election results had done was to buy time for the Government to have another look at the poll tax to see how it could be made more acceptable. That was the real achievement of our campaign.

Some commentators said the local government elections had been a great presentational success, but it was much more than that. We had decided to take head-on the issue which was making the Government massively unpopular and to go out and confront our critics. We showed in those areas where the discipline of the poll tax was working through that we could win seats. We had managed to arrest the decline of the Government's fortunes, and Labour's national lead after the local elections came down to 15 per cent. James Baker, the American Secretary of State on a visit to Britain, told Douglas Hurd that weekend, 'Political success depends upon perception, and you won because people perceived that you'd won.'

The 1990 local elections were also the first real indicator that even consistent opinion poll results could be an unreliable guide to how voters would actually behave on the day. This was not a case of one or two rogue polls. Every poll had predicted a bad result which simply did not materialize. However, it was not until the 1992 General Election, when again the polls consistently indicated a Labour win, that even commentators and pollsters seriously acknowledged the limitations of modern polling as a guide to voter behaviour.

Following the local elections, Geoffrey Howe loyally reaffirmed his support for Margaret in an interview in which he asked the rhetorical question, 'Whose spirits failed – hers or theirs?' Michael Heseltine's friends were nonplussed. The better-than-expected results for the Government immediately chilled any hopes Michael may have had for continued pressure on Margaret, and an opening for a leadership challenge by him. His camp responded by saying that 'the brilliant political achievement' of winning seventeen seats in Wandsworth and thirteen in Westminster was only made possible by the Department of Environment switching grants to those Boroughs. That was absolutely untrue.

Michael had expected the leadership issue to come to a head in July through the culmination of a disastrous six months which would have included a terrible drubbing in the local elections. This would have led to such a volume of protest that Margaret would have had to stand down. Certainly Michael and his friends were taking soundings with Party Officers to gauge their reaction to a change of leadership, and I was told that Michael had discussed the constitutional implications with Michael Havers. All this had to be put into reverse after 5 May.

Shortly afterwards, Mary and I went to see *Coriolanus* at the Barbican. We found ourselves sitting directly behind Anne and Michael Heseltine. Coriolanus was played by Charles Dance, a tall, handsome actor with long, flowing blond hair. Coriolanus, proud and defiant, is rejected by the people and in turn he rejects them, striding off the stage with the superbly dismissive exit line, 'There is a world elsewhere'. The gossip columnists had great fun in reporting that Michael had gone to see this play and that I was sitting directly behind him for this dramatic portrayal of thwarted ambition and hubris.

In the market of political reputations the word went round to 'buy Bakers and sell Heseltines'. Even the *Observer* said, 'The local elections ruin Heseltine's hopes.' The Scottish Party Conference was held at Aberdeen just a few days later, and once again I hammered home the message about the leadership:

We have moved through difficult waters, but we are heading for the clearer open sea where the wind of public opinion can fill our sails. But as we make our way through I know one thing for certain – we should not, we must not, and we will not drop the pilot.

Five days later Michael set out in an article in the *Times* some rather modest proposals for reforming the poll tax, and on BBC TV's 'Question Time' that night he said quite specifically, 'Margaret Thatcher will lead us into the next Election and we will win under her leadership.' For a time I thought he actually meant it.

CHAPTER 16

Summer Heat on Labour

*Improving Relations with Germany and the CDU – The
Party's Help to East European Countries – Armenia – The
Resignation of Nick Ridley – Preparing for the Next
Election: Summer 1990*

The better than expected local election results transformed morale at
Central Office. At last we had a victory of sorts, and it was the Labour
Party which was looking down in the mouth. The leadership issue was
off the boil and the question was how to take advantage of this new
political climate. I decided that we had to capitalize on the relative
success of our local government campaign and keep up the momentum
during the normally flat summer months as Parliament hastens towards
the end of its session, with MPs looking forward to their summer break.
Our bright team in the Research Department had relished their
attacking role and wanted to continue being let off the leash to engage in
more of the same.

We put our heads together and came up with the 'Summer Heat on
Labour' campaign, whose symbol was a wilting version of Labour's red
rose. The themes, in accordance with our Hever strategy, were that
deep down Labour hadn't really changed, and behind their mask they
remained Socialist. Labour's policies were not credible and didn't add
up without extra taxation to finance them. Neil Kinnock was not a
credible alternative Prime Minister. In addition to turning the heat on
Labour and melting their policies we also wanted to use the campaign to
rehearse lines of attack which if successful could be used subsequently
in a General Election.

The campaign was launched on 22 May at a press conference at the
Charing Cross Hotel and was deliberately timed to pre-empt Labour's
latest rehash of policies entitled *Looking to the Future*, which was
scheduled for publication the next day. This document was meant to be
a preliminary manifesto on which Labour would fight the General
Election. I persuaded John Major, as Chancellor of the Exchequer, to

join me in launching our campaign. Initially his staff were reluctant to have him descend to this 'political' exercise, since Chancellors are supposed to be above this sort of coarse Party knockabout. However, I felt that having a Departmental heavyweight at the press conference would not only attract journalists but indicate to them the seriousness with which we took our attack on Labour. There was also discussion about putting a price tag on Labour's policies just as we had done in 1987, when John MacGregor had conducted a highly successful exercise as Chief Secretary. But the Treasury team were reluctant to get down to costings at this stage, partly because they thought the time was too far in advance of an Election and therefore premature, and also because the Labour Party kept retreating from spending commitments and fudging its promises with each new policy document.

However, John Major finally agreed to join me for the Summer Heat on Labour launch, which turned out to be the first Party political news conference he had attended. He was surprised at the hostility of the questions we faced, although by this time in my chairmanship it had become second nature to me and I wasn't exactly short of practice. John was pressed hard about the state of the economy and the political consequences of high interest rates and inflation. He dealt with the questions well, and launched a pertinent assault on Labour's plans for the economy, asking what was Labour's strategy for controlling inflation since they were against raising interest rates, and by how much would they raise taxes to meet their spending plans? 'Millions of people will pay more tax and finance Labour's plans,' he said. 'No one should believe the Labour Party have changed. They haven't. They have no policy on inflation, they have no will to control expenditure, they have no idea how to run the economy. All they have to offer is debt, devaluation and decline.' Little did one know it at the time, but this script was an uncanny forerunner of the themes John was to use in his own 1992 Election campaign to such good effect.

For my part I attacked Labour's policies as meaning higher national and local taxes, the confiscation of shares, no nuclear defence policy, easier industrial strike action, and lower education standards. We had two particularly effective posters. One stated 'Labour's Tax Plans Won't Hurt Everybody. Only Those With Jobs, Homes and Savings'. The other said, 'What's Yours Will Be Ours – Labour's Plans For Shareholders'. When, next day, Labour published *Looking to the Future* we analysed and challenged them on all those policies they had conveniently omitted but which had been in their previous policy bible, *Meet the Challenge, Make the Change*.

Labour was clearly trying to scuttle away from close examination of its policies and trying to make it impossible even for journalists to keep track of what was still official policy, what was no longer official policy and what remained official policy by default. During this and later periods I was quite dismayed by the readiness with which journalists accepted Labour spokesmen's interpretations of their own policies rather than the meaning, or lack of meaning, of Labour's own words in cold print. During this time the media uncritically swallowed Labour claims without recourse to either the proverbial pinch of salt or the sugar coating.

Our response was *Labour – Behind the Mask*, a snappy thirty-page booklet which nailed the Labour Party on, among other things, economic policy and tax, renationalization, undermining the nuclear deterrent, Labour's indebtedness to the trade unions, Labour and the hard Left, and Neil Kinnock's convolutions on policy. This was followed over the next few months by further documents on Labour and the economy – the *Essential Guide for Business*, the *Red Tape Review* – Labour's plans for more bureaucracy – *Labour and the Unions*, and *What They Claim and How They Voted* – the contradiction between policies Labour said they wanted to see and the way they had voted against these policies in the House of Commons.

Our rolling barrage of attacks on Labour was aided by the confusion exhibited right at the top of their Party. On BBC TV's 'Panorama' in June, Neil Kinnock said that 'Fourteen out of fifteen working taxpayers' would be no worse off under Labour. The next day his Shadow Chancellor, John Smith, had to correct him by saying that Mr Kinnock had meant 'fourteen out of fifteen basic rate taxpayers' would be no worse off. In fact he too underestimated the impact on basic rate taxpayers of scrapping the National Insurance upper earnings limit, which Labour was pledged to do. Neil Kinnock later compounded this technical error with a basic arithmetical gaffe. Arguing that only the rich would have to pay more tax under Labour he was at a loss to explain how the £2 billion this would raise was sufficient to fund the extra £3.3 billion Labour planned to spend. We had much fun with this, and these episodes did register in journalists' minds as further question marks over Neil Kinnock's competence.

Kinnock's big problem was that he was not numerate. That had been Alec Douglas-Home's weakness too as Harold Wilson had been able to demonstrate. Today a political leader has to be able to master statistics and figures with as much ease as the politicians of the nineteenth century used Latin and Greek epigrams. Kinnock had been elected Labour Party Leader in 1983 following Michael Foot's disastrous General Election campaign, in which support for Labour had dropped to its lowest ever. However, Kinnock too came from the left of his Party, and clung tenaciously to political views which the broad mass of voters utterly rejected. The Labour Party had chosen two losers in a row.

Denis Healey had tried to school Kinnock in economics and world affairs, playing the role of Melbourne to Kinnock's Victoria. Just before the 1987 Election I found myself sitting next to Denis at an all-Party lunch at the Savoy, and he spoke of Kinnock in glowing terms as 'the Younger Pitt'. Such fantasies, particularly coming from someone so worldly-wise, deluded the Labour Party into believing they were going to oust Margaret's Government. However, Neil Kinnock will go down in history as a good manager of his Party because, despite two General Election defeats under him, he held Labour together and bequeathed as a legacy a Party which seemed to the electorate much less divided than the one he inherited.

As Chairman of the Conservative Party I decided that there were three lines of attack on Kinnock: first, his innumeracy; second, his total lack of government experience; third, his convinced Socialism. Some MPs told me that we should also attack his wife, Glenys, who exercised a formidable political influence over him. The gibes directed against her were cheap and tacky. I laid it down that while I remained Chairman there was to be no attack from Central Office on Glenys Kinnock, nor would I condone one by any Minister or MP. The country was going to choose between Margaret and Neil, not Denis and Glenys.

Our constant monitoring of Labour, and our challenges to the Shadow Cabinet, went on right through the summer. There was now no such thing as an August holiday or a recess for the Party machine, as Andrew Lansley and his team in the Research Department ensured a rolling programme of high-quality attacking material. My only disappointment was that the media accorded these critiques less credit and coverage than they deserved. But given the media's general propensity to write off most of what the Government did at this time, we could have brought down the tablets of stone from Mount Sinai and still only received minor coverage on page 5 of most newspapers.

However, it is of some satisfaction to know that much of the work done analysing Labour's policies during this period was to be recycled later and used to greater effect when the political climate had changed and the media began to look at Labour and its leadership with a more critical eye. Shouting 'Where's the beef and what's the cost?' only has resonance when journalists realize that they too will have to share the same menu and the same bill. Harris polls showed that the Summer Heat on Labour campaign did have some impact on voter perceptions. Aside from Labour's lead being cut significantly from 18 points in May to 8 points in September, more respondents now said that Labour was poorly led, subject to left-wing influence, and that a Labour government would lead to higher taxes.

Improving Relations with Germany and the CDU

In the spring and summer of 1990 I visited our MEPs in Strasbourg on three occasions as I wanted to improve their relationship with the rest of the Party. They had had a meeting with Margaret, shifting rather uneasily on the small gilt and red velvet chairs which are provided at Number 10 for these occasions. The more federalist MEPs had been kept well in check by Sir Christopher Prout, the Conservative Group's leader, but Margaret did not disguise her coolness towards greater European unity. I also attended several sessions of the Parliament in Strasbourg, but its practices and procedures are so very different from our own that I came back with no desire to increase its powers at the expense of Westminster.

I also visited Bonn and Berlin, as I was keen to forge a closer link between the Conservative Party and our German counterparts, the Christian Democratic Union. Germany was in the process of reunification negotiations and the CDU were to fight the first pan-German elections in December. It was critical that they should win, not least because their Socialist opponents had pledged to withdraw a united Germany from NATO.

Volker Ruhe had been appointed as the new young Secretary General of the CDU. He was well known in English Conservative circles, and of all German politicians he has a greater understanding and sympathy than most for British attitudes and concerns. So his appointment made it a propitious time to establish stronger ties at senior level between our two Parties.

Anglo-German relations had been dented in recent months by a widespread misconception in the FRG that the British, and Mrs Thatcher in particular, were opposed to reunification. This was because there had been a spat over Chancellor Kohl's apparent reluctance to accept the postwar border with Poland, which gave rise to the fear that Germany was looking to reincorporate its former Prussian territory into the new Germany. Margaret had said that the existing Polish border must remain, and this had been interpreted as an objection to the whole reunification process. One of my tasks was to make clear to our hosts our exact position on this issue.

My visit was welcomed by the CDU, as it was the first occasion on which serving CDU and Conservative Party Chairmen had met. The fact that the Heads of Government relations were not particularly good – Margaret and Helmut Kohl were never close – gave an added impetus to the Party Chairmen being able to communicate by establishing an alternative channel. Two months later one of the first fruits of this relationship would be trying to explain away Nick Ridley's criticism of the Germans!

My visits to Berlin and Bonn were arranged by the Konrad Adenauer Foundation, the 'Embassy' of the CDU around the world. The London office was run with distinction by Ludger Eling, whose influence in developing good relations between British Conservative and German Christian Democrat politicians has been considerable. My programme, in addition to meeting politicians and Government Ministers, included an address to the Konrad Adenauer Foundation in Bonn on the theme of 'Conservatism in the 1990s'. I was accompanied by Tony Kerpel and Edward Llewellyn, the bright young international affairs desk officer from Research Department. Edward has since become Chris Patten's political adviser in the Hong Kong Governor's office.

We began with a visit to Berlin, which still had the air of a newly liberated city. It was an enormously exciting time politically, and one had a constant sense of history in the making. The Berlin Wall had begun to come down six months earlier and it was now quite hard to find sections of the wall remaining. One long piece still standing by the Potsdamer Platz was being chipped at by a small army of souvenir hunters and had as many holes as a Swiss cheese. Streets and vistas previously brutally divided by the wall were now open again. For the first time in thirty years, one could walk from the Reichstag Building, under the Brandenburg Gate, to Unter den Linden and the great Imperial government buildings which lead to Alexanderplatz. We stopped at the makeshift stalls selling Soviet and East German uniforms and cap badges, the detritus of military occupation and dictatorship providing the raw materials for capitalist commercialism and Western souvenir collectors.

In the late afternoon sunshine we drove out towards Wannsee for a walk along part of the cleared area fringed by woods, circling West Berlin like some medieval moat, which had once contained the wall, its mined strip and military road. We came upon a junkyard full of dismantled watchtowers lying on their side, entire sections of the wall, and the electrodes with now severed wire which had once topped it. It was like an unofficial museum which represented the recent dark past yet made one hopeful about a new and better future. Tony and Edward collected several chunks of whitewashed concrete wall, which they later had to lug through airport security to the amusement of the Germans happy to see foreigners carting their debris away.

That evening we drove to the Glienicke Bridge, scene of dramatic spy exchanges during the years of the Cold War. East Berliners were queuing outside West Berlin telephone boxes at the western end of the bridge because the reliability of the phone service enabled them to contact relatives and friends with a speed unknown to their own telephone service. Such were the daily realities of life under the two neighbouring political and economic systems.

In my address to the Konrad Adenauer Foundation in Bonn, I spoke of the success of Conservative policies in Britain during the 1980s. I also went out of my way to bridge the apparent difference of views between Helmut Kohl, who wanted to press on with faster integration between EC partners, and Margaret Thatcher, who wanted the new democracies of Eastern Europe to join the European Community. I told my German audience:

Together, we can look forward to building a new Europe in which democracy and the social market economy stretch from the Atlantic to the Urals. As partners in the European Community, we are already actively discussing ways to deepen our cooperation, and we are proceeding rapidly with the completion of the Single Market, itself a powerful force for European unity.

I do not share the view of some who see the development of Europe as a choice between either widening the association of nations or deepening the areas of formal cooperation. I believe that in the last decade of this century we have the opportunity to both widen and to deepen our association throughout the whole continent. We have a unique chance to instigate a political and economic renaissance which builds upon the rich tradition of European nationhoods and civilizations.

Ten months later John Major, as the new Prime Minister, was also to address the Konrad Adenauer Foundation in Bonn, where he included his now famous quotation: 'I want us to be where we belong – at the very heart of Europe, working with our partners in building the future.' I suppose the difference between Margaret and John might be summed up as John wanting to be at the heart of Europe while Margaret appeared to prefer being at its throat.

I had two lengthy meetings with Volker Ruhe during which we discussed ways of increasing Party cooperation, and I sought his help in securing for British MEPs their membership of the European People's Party group in the European Parliament. We also discussed our assistance programmes to the new democratic Parties in Eastern Europe. Since Volker spoke fluent English I invited him to give the prestigious CPC lecture at our Party Conference in October 1990. Volker has since become Defence Minister and is regarded by some as a possible successor to Chancellor Kohl.

Kohl undoubtedly wanted to secure his place in the history books as the man who reunited Germany. Generally rated as a rather dull provincial figure, he was in fact a tenacious Party leader, brutal with rivals, and he possessed a shrewd appreciation of the historic moment, which if political leaders are lucky, might occur once in their lifetime. Kohl had seen that moment and intended to grasp it.

Several months later I attended the great CDU rally which formally united the Parties of East and West Germany in a great burst of patriotic pan-German fervour. With tears running down their cheeks, the delegates fervently sang 'Deutschland, Deutschland, über alles'. I saw Kohl at the reception afterwards, sitting at the centre of a great oak table in the old medieval High Hall, eating a vast plateful of frankfurters and sauerkraut. His Party workers stood around in respectful silence watching their leader eat, as courtiers must have watched their medieval kings in the past.

To Kohl must go the credit for seeing Gorbachev's last uncertain year in power as the window of opportunity to do a deal which would restore Germany to a geopolitical whole. Who was then to know that in reaching for his star Kohl was also to precipitate an economic recession and social unrest in Germany, and economic instability throughout Western

Europe? The root cause of this was Kohl's bribe to the East German electors of one Deutschmark for each worthless Ostmark, and his underestimate of the huge costs of East Germany's reconstruction.

On my first visit to Germany I had been told that the cost of reunification would be DM 60 billion; on my second visit it was DM 80 billion; and on my third, DM 120 billion. But whatever it cost there was the overriding and historic mission to reunite the Fatherland. All this had the consequence that German interest rates had to remain high, and other European countries had to follow suit just at the time when their interest rates should have been coming down. In September 1992 the markets called the bluff and sterling crashed out of the ERM, allowing the British Government to break free from the German domestic ball and chain.

Whether Chancellor Kohl was right to pay this price for the reunification of his country, and his victory in the subsequent federal elections, only time will tell. It may be a case of short-term pain for long-term gain. But in May 1990, before this chain of consequences became apparent, one could not fail to be excited by the sense of historic developments in Germany. Without a war, which so many had feared for decades, the Iron Curtain was falling. The postwar division of Europe which had formed the backdrop to all our lives was ending, and for a brief period the future appeared to be one of optimism and fresh opportunity for the continent of Europe.

The Party's Help to East European Countries

In 1989 the events unfolding in Eastern Europe were truly historic. The Soviet Empire was breaking up. When Gorbachev refused to send Russian troops to help East Germany's Communist Party boss Erich Honecker, then for all the Soviet satellite regimes the game was up.

I met Gorbachev and his wife, Raisa, three times, and in somewhat unusual circumstances. In December 1987 Gorbachev, then on his way to America, decided to stop over to see Margaret Thatcher, who had been playing an important intermediary role between him and President Reagan. The meeting took place at the Brize Norton Royal Air Force base, where the two leaders talked for about two hours. Mrs Gorbachev was in the party and as she had expressed an interest in education I arranged for her to visit the nearest local primary school in Oxfordshire. I accompanied her and together we watched the Nativity play, which must have been a new experience for her. I had taken one of my officials who spoke Russian and he told me that the KGB were telling Mrs Gorbachev that this was a special school just for the children of officers – like the ones they had back home for the children of the political elite. I was glad that one of our normal primary schools was so highly rated by the KGB.

That was the first time I had met Raisa Gorbachev, and I was struck at how 'Western' she appeared. The wives of previous Soviet leaders looked as though they would have been happier staying in the kitchen and chopping up cabbage. Not so Raisa. She was very well turned out and clearly had a political presence. On arriving at the school, as soon as she got out of the car she went straight over to the group of parents being held back by the police and where the cameramen were located. Through an interpreter she talked to the parents in a friendly and open way. Raisa seemed to embody the openness and freshness of all that was happening in the Soviet Union.

She could understand a little English, but we really chatted mostly through the interpreter. I found she wanted to talk about Dickens. I was delighted to oblige, and later I presented her with a first edition of *Little Dorrit*. She was also very interested in British painting and knew the work of Reynolds, Lawrence and Gainsborough. On one occasion I took along with me large colour books from the National Gallery and National Portrait Gallery. She was able to identify and discuss many of the paintings.

On another visit to the UK in April 1989, I again escorted Mrs Gorbachev to various events in London. On these occasions she quite liked to discuss politics as well as the latest news about what was happening in Western Europe – who was up and who was down. She was particularly interested in Margaret's popularity. I asked about the political developments in Russia, and she was proud that there had been elections for the Supreme Soviet in which 90 per cent of the people had voted. But she added, 'My husband does not think that you need have more than one Party. Countries with many Parties are often poor and some fight for the fun of it. Eighty-two per cent of our candidates are Party people.' Clearly, she saw no need for opposition candidates.

She was very aware that her husband was a man of destiny. I also noticed how close they were. There was a political as well as a personal intimacy. During the Brize Norton visit we returned from the school rather late, and Margaret and Gorbachev were having to wait for us. As soon as she arrived Raisa went straight up to her husband, who asked her what she had been doing and whether it was interesting. She wanted to know what he had been doing and then straightened his tie. It was clearly a working partnership.

When I met Gorbachev he recognized me as the escort to his wife but he was also aware that I was Education Secretary. We talked about education reform in the Soviet Union and he invited me to come and see what was happening there, which I subsequently did. In the week I spent visiting schools and universities in Russia, I found that the selective schools where the children of the political elite were sent were very good and similar to our grammar schools. There was a heavy concentration on learning a foreign language and being able to speak it fluently. I met several fifteen- and sixteen-year-olds who had a good command of English but who had never left Russia. We therefore started an exchange programme for British and Soviet children, and several hundred have since benefited from visiting the others' country.

Apart from languages, Soviet education appeared to me to be very rigid and limited. It didn't have the resources for proper technological education. At one school, I was shown with pride their sole computer – a Sinclair mini, which was then being sold in America at $99. They were very lucky to have just one computer. However, the standards in mathematics and physics were very high.

In higher education too, the university system had been stifling variety and independence for eighty years. In Moscow and Leningrad I spoke to large student gatherings of over 1,000 young people. They were fascinated by and interested in Western politicians and democracy, and clearly resented the ever-present prying of the KGB. In all universities the KGB controlled the photocopiers and the loudest cheer I got was when I said, 'There should be a Xerox copier in every Department.'

I suggested to Gorbachev when I met him later that he should find ways to release all that hidden talent in Soviet schools, colleges and the teaching profession. He agreed that the key to education reform was decentralization, as in everything else. But the difficulty with education, as with the Soviet economy, was that a fundamental change was needed in those attitudes ingrained into three generations since 1918. People were afraid to make their own decision, relying instead on direction from Moscow.

The pace of change in Eastern Europe was dramatically accelerated by the fall of the Berlin Wall in November 1989. Poland had for some time seen a struggle between the ruling Communist Party and workers led by Lech Walesa. Hungary had been liberalizing its economy quietly over several years. Czechoslovakia was experiencing the velvet revolution. At Conservative Central Office in London we had received requests from new political Parties in those three countries for help in establishing the democratic processes. Much of the help we gave in those early days was in the form of truckloads of paper, ink and stickers. We also sent training teams from Central Office to teach campaigning skills and to help the development of local branch structures for new centre-right Parties.

I told Margaret Thatcher in January 1990 that CCO had been approached by the Democratic Forum Party of Hungary and really we ought to do something to help them. I therefore made two visits, one to Austria and one to Hungary. In Vienna I met Andreas Kohl, the Secretary General of the European Democratic Union, the grouping of centre-right Parties to which we belonged, and he told us as early as the autumn of 1989 that Yugoslavia was going to blow apart. His analysis was news to me because the West was showing little interest in Yugo-slavia, and yet clearly the racial and religious tensions were set to explode.

I then went on to Hungary, where we met all nascent political parties. We identified Jozsef Antall and his Democratic Forum as our counter-part most likely to win the forthcoming Election. He was by no means the favourite at that time but I arranged for him to come to Britain to meet Margaret at Number 10 in advance of the Hungarian elections. He was very grateful for this opportunity, as he wanted a photograph to be seen back home of him talking with Margaret Thatcher – the symbol of freedom. One should never underestimate the value which visiting politicians – particularly those seeking office – place on meeting sitting leaders. Much good will can be accrued by backing future winners. The converse is also true, as we saw in 1992 when Central Office officials went over to the United States to help George Bush.

I also visited East Germany, Poland and Czechoslovakia, where I again tried to identify those Parties which the Conservative Party should associate with and assist. Czechoslovakia was easier to gauge than Poland, since it was clear that Vaclav Klaus, who was then only just beginning to emerge, was the politician and economist closest to the Conservative belief in free markets. The Slovak Prime Minister Meciar made it clear to me that the Slovaks wanted their independence from the

Czech lands and were already planning how to manage their own economy. He wanted to send 500 young men and women to Britain to work in the private sector to see how things were done. I told Margaret that on her visit in the autumn she would be asked by the Foreign Office to make speeches advocating the unity of Czechoslovakia, but in my view the split-up of the country was inevitable.

Margaret was also very keen for us to develop contacts in Eastern Europe, saying, 'We must support parties of our own beliefs against Communists and Socialists.' I therefore appointed Sir Geoffrey Pattie MP, who had been a former Defence Minister, as Vice-Chairman of the Party responsible for Eastern Europe. British Conservative MPs and MEPs visited conferences of the new Parties, and also played a supporting role in their elections, particularly those in East Germany. Although my ministerial jobs had all been concerned with domestic issues I was very keen that the Conservative Party should play an active role in international affairs, especially at such a critical time for the development of democracy in Eastern Europe.

Margaret was very proud of her own contribution to the freedom movements in Eastern Europe. She remembered vividly her first visit to Russia. In Poland, the people almost worshipped the ground she walked upon. In February 1990, when discussing a speech she was preparing, she said that 'neither Gorbachev nor De Klerk would have begun their reforms if it had not been for Reagan and me. In both countries it will take time to build up the new world. Now that some have smashed the system and the central control, others have seen how it can be done.'

Armenia

In July I accompanied Margaret to the Soviet Union in order to open the school in Armenia which I had arranged to finance as Education Secretary following the earthquake in 1988. I met up with Margaret first in Kiev, where she spoke on a Saturday afternoon to the Ukrainian Parliament. The representatives waved their pale blue and yellow national flags, and cheered her as the Messiah of Freedom and Liberty leading to independence for their country. We flew to Armenia on a plane provided by Mr Gorbachev, but he chose not to accompany us, as just one visit to the earthquake-stricken town of Leninakhan was enough for him.

Armenia was at that time still part of the Soviet Union, but just about the only presence from Moscow that was evident were the KGB bodyguards who surrounded us. The streets from the airport to the town were filled by thousands of people who overflowed from the pavements and made the passage of our cars almost impossible. When we were about 300 yards from the school, Denis Thatcher and I struggled out of our cars and then forced our way through the crowd to get to the Prime Minister. To see such enthusiasm and warmth was very moving, although the KGB were deeply contemptuous of the way in which the Armenians had allowed the security of this visit to collapse. The KGB decided that Margaret should not walk through the town centre as they couldn't be sure of protecting her, although everybody was cheering her. So we all set off in a large coach with Margaret standing at the front beside the driver, clearly visible through the large window and waving to the crowds outside – a sort of Maggiemobile. The crowds, recognizing Margaret from photographs and television, threw flowers in the path of the bus. To them she was the symbol of freedom and independence, whereas the absent Gorbachev represented oppression.

The people were very friendly but the town still looked as if it had been blitzed. Damaged buildings had not been pulled down, roads had not been repaved or repaired and vast numbers of people were still living in tents. The vaunted Socialist economy had not even provided bricks, cement, electric wire, slates or good workers. We had to send virtually all the building materials for the school out from the UK, together with brickies, plasterers, electricians and plumbers to ensure that the school was actually built. The school was named after Lord Byron, whom the Armenians saw as a freedom fighter, and it has three shifts of children using it every day.

The Resignation of Nick Ridley

Our attitude to the European Community continued to trouble the Party. Margaret could see the push towards greater political and monetary union that President Mitterrand and Chancellor Kohl were now mounting, and she was determined to resist it. She did not want a United States of Europe. For her, the future of Europe depended upon the vitality and energy of its individual nation states, rather than a supranational state. This was a Gaullist view and, I believe, a realistic one. But the European political mood in 1990, following the reunification of Germany, favoured greater economic and political union. Margaret was not alone in her scepticism about the pace of European union. At the Welsh Conference in the summer John Major warned that the Twelve were 'nowhere near ready for the imposition of a single currency, a central bank or a single interest rate'.

In July the issue of our relations with the Germans came unexpectedly to a head when a lunch discussion between Nick Ridley and Dominic Lawson of the *Spectator* was reported verbatim. Nick had reluctantly agreed to be interviewed at his home and appears to have been lulled into relaxing his ministerial vigilance by Lawson's assurances that he only wanted to be helpful. Nick had agreed to the conversation being tape-recorded but assumed that since the occasion was private the verbatim conversation would not be reported. How wrong he was.

Nick had been very frank and had expressed his anxiety about the growing power of Germany and the threat he believed this posed to Europe. He was also disparaging about Chancellor Kohl. The *Spectator* compounded this report by putting on its front cover a devastating cartoon by Garland. This depicted Nick with a paintpot in his hand running away from a large poster of Kohl onto which had been daubed Hitler's moustache and hairstyle. I thought this cartoon did more damage than the article itself by suggesting that Nick had compared Kohl with Hitler, which he simply had not. Nick was deeply hurt that confidences expressed in his own house had been given such wide coverage.

This episode was bad news for the Government. Paradoxically it was Nick's closeness to Margaret which undid him rather than protected him. Because Nick was always assumed to be in tune with Margaret's views – as indeed he was – for her to have kept him in the Cabinet would have appeared as though she accepted his publicly aired views as a surrogate for her private ones. Every time Douglas Hurd trotted off to see the Germans there would have been the unspoken question in the air, 'Who really speaks for Mrs Thatcher – you or Mr Ridley?' Nick was facing the fallout from his interview while away on a ministerial visit to Hungary, and so was less able to marshal his defence than if he had been in London.

I persuaded Margaret to say at Question Time that Nick's views, 'which had been withdrawn, did not represent the Government's view or indeed my views'. During that Thursday the overwhelming view of the Party in the House of Commons was that Nick would have to go – an opinion that was certainly shared by John Wakeham and Tim Renton, the Chief Whip. Margaret, however, was fiercely loyal to the one member of the Cabinet who was closest to her. She believed that he had been betrayed by Dominic Lawson.

The press was virtually unanimous in condemning Nick's comments, although his constituents in Cirencester rode in behind 'old Nick'. Enoch Powell also rallied to him, saying, 'It shows how the wind blows – the comment will be understood by those in the know.' Chancellor Kohl was dismissive about the article, and the German press put Nick's comments down to the recent defeat of England's soccer team by Germany in the World Cup. Michael Forsyth, the Scottish Chairman, issued a statement supporting Nick Ridley. Steve Norris, the Member for Epping Forest and Nick's PPS, loyally talked up Nick's position to the press. When Nick returned to London he was met at the aeroplane steps by Steve, who protected him from the press pack by driving him away from Heathrow at top speed in a BMW. There was much speculation on the news about whether Nick would or wouldn't resign.

On the Saturday I spoke to Margaret at Chequers and she told me that Nick had decided to go, and that Peter Lilley would replace him. Peter would be the tenth Secretary of State for Trade and Industry in her eleven years – this post had become a veritable graveyard. I was very sorry that Nick's ministerial career should end in this shabby way. Charles Powell told me that early on Thursday, Margaret had realized that Nick's position was likely to become untenable but she was not going to sack him. She would let events take their course, even though it was an uncomfortable two days for her. Downing Street was due to announce the shuffle on Saturday lunchtime, but as the hours dragged by announcement came there none. Steve Norris was undertaking energetic briefing on Nick's behalf which threw his resignation into question. Such tenacity was to be admired, although not by the Whips, who like life to be orderly.

This episode, however, did not die a quiet death. On Sunday the press reported a leaked Foreign Office document about a seminar on Germany which Margaret had presided over at Chequers in March. Among those attending was Norman Stone, the Professor of Modern History at Oxford. This leaked report underlined the fact that Margaret was suspicious of the character and power of Germany. Douglas Hurd tried in a series of deeply uncomfortable interviews to dispel this impression.

These two episodes reveal how the carefully constructed Cabinet consensus on Europe had collapsed. However, the British people out in the country had other things to think about. The summer of 1990 was one of the hottest on record. There were long, baking, sunny days with hosepipe bans over virtually the whole of Britain. Most people were worried about a prolonged drought. In May I had attended a meeting at Number 10 where a group of meteorologists, set up by one of the Heads of Government summit meetings, reported on the 'Greenhouse Effect'. Their news was very gloomy. The hole in the ozone layer was going to get larger and, as a result, over the next century the average temperature could increase by 4°C. This would lead to major climatic changes in the world and a rise in sea levels over the century of as much as 60 cm as the polar ice-caps melted. As we trooped out of Downing Street and sweltered in tropical temperatures it seemed as if the summer of 1990 was going to be the harbinger of ecological disaster. But as with all predictions one should take them with a grain of salt. The summer just two years later was one of the wettest on record.

Preparing for the Next Election: Summer 1990

In June I had meetings with Brian Griffiths, John Wakeham and John Whittingdale to start the planning of policies for the next Election. I proposed to the Prime Minister that she should set up Departmental policy groups in the autumn, each headed by a Cabinet Minister, to produce further new ideas by the early spring of 1991. The composition of the groups would be determined by each Cabinet Minister but I was anxious to ensure that the officers of the Backbench Committees should be involved, together with outside experts. There was to be a Steering Committee chaired by the Prime Minister and consisting of Geoffrey Howe, Douglas Hurd, David Waddington, John Major, John Wakeham and myself. I was particularly keen to ensure that Geoffrey Howe was fully involved in this process and fully committed to its outcome. We put this to Margaret on 28 June and she approved it and agreed to announce it to the 1922 Committee when she made her end-of-session speech to them in July. She also made clear that she would take personal control of the Manifesto – 'I shall do the Manifesto myself.' This is the prerogative and indeed the practice of Prime Ministers which John Major was also to follow.

Policy was developing throughout the summer. At the Women's Conference, Margaret committed us to extending nationwide the successful scheme of converting rents to mortgages which had been pioneered in Scotland. To me this was an essential part of our future housing policy, and a natural extension of our very successful campaign of selling council housing. We also announced an important new policy to make runaway fathers more responsible by making them pay contributions for their children to the mother. This was a scheme developed by Tony Newton and became an important part of our social policy. Chris Patten was also preparing a White Paper on the environment, which was published in September. This committed the UK to dealing with CO_2 emissions and other pollution problems on a much faster timescale, as well as encouraging energy conservation. There was no question of the Government running out of ideas.

At the end of the Parliamentary session, we were beginning to see some bright spots. Margaret was in good form, and in the newly televised Prime Minister's Question Time regularly demolished Neil Kinnock at the dispatch box. She had developed a more freewheeling style and was much better when she departed from her written brief. I remember one exchange with Michael Foot, who had condemned her for causing the fiasco over football identity cards. He suggested that she ought to do what she'd always done in the past and pass the blame onto someone else by finding a scapegoat. Margaret's tart response was, 'I do not need his assistance now just as I didn't need it when he was Leader of the Opposition and got the chop.' The opinion polls showed that Margaret had regained her lead over Kinnock, and that on the crucial issue of handling the economy the electorate trusted the Tories more than Labour.

At the end of July we won a council by-election at Hillingdon with a swing of 9 per cent. The polls showed that Labour's lead had now been reduced to 8 per cent. Clearly I had to start planning for an early General Election, and I identified all the possible dates in 1991 on which we could hold it. The local government elections in May 1991 were going to be difficult, as there were no flagships and we would be fighting in over 12,000 seats. In early August I discussed possible election dates with Margaret. I said that any decision to hold a June 1991 General Election would have to be taken a month earlier on Sunday 5 May when we had analysed the local government election results. But these were likely to produce at best a confusing picture and at worst a pessimistic one. Margaret agreed and said, 'June is most unlikely. There is no point in going a year early unless you can win.'

Because of this uncertainty about the precise timing of the next General Election I decided that the autumn 1990 Party Conference would not be a 'shop window' Manifesto conference like 1986, but one of consolidation. The slogan that we chose to capture this theme was 'The Strength to Succeed'. This particularly emphasized the quality of leadership for which, our research showed, Margaret was most admired.

Because I did not believe that we should be stampeded into a 1991 Election I did not want to see an inevitable momentum building up for any particular date in 1991. If 1992 suited us better then that date too had to be kept open. I thought at that stage that a late autumn Election after the 1991 Conference was the most likely, but it was far too early to say whether we were going to be sufficiently ahead in the polls to go at that time, and so to chill speculation I spoke to the press in terms of 1992. This was the theme that Margaret also took up when she spoke to the Tory peers in her end-of-session speech in July. We should plan for 1992 but be prepared to hold an Election in 1991 if the circumstances looked favourable.

The most significant event which came to dominate politics over the next six months was the invasion of Kuwait on 2 August by the Iraqi dictator Saddam Hussein. Margaret was actually in America and staying with President Bush at the time. There is no doubt that her tough attitude and experience of the Falklands War stiffened the resolve of the President to resist this act of unprovoked aggression. The chance of the two leaders being together as the news came in made the Anglo-American 'Special Relationship' central in leading world opinion. It was the bedrock of the allied campaign. Europe failed to speak with a united voice and only France was really prepared to stand alongside us, though President Mitterrand wavered at various critical moments. The Prime Minister condemned Europe's reaction as 'slow and patchy'.

This international crisis allowed Margaret to appear on the world stage in the role that she liked best – The Iron Lady. She remained in London for most of August. In the middle of the month she held a press conference to condemn Saddam Hussein's ruthless use of the British residents he had taken hostage, particularly a young British boy. The Prime Minister made clear that we were not prepared to negotiate over these hostages, and when Parliament was recalled on 6 September she committed British troops to a ground war if necessary. The build-up to this conflict dominated all the news. In September the polls recorded that Margaret's popularity had risen sharply. In May it had been

Thatcher 28: Kinnock 30. By September it was Thatcher 41: Kinnock 35. The public was also showing 85 per cent approval for the determined and strong line the Conservatives were taking.

The full Cabinet received reports of the position in the Gulf on 6 August. This time there was to be no inner War Cabinet. There was unanimous support for the line that the Prime Minister was taking. Two squadrons of Tornados had been dispatched. We were going to stand shoulder to shoulder with America and do everything we could in the United Nations to gather collective world opinion behind us. Margaret said, 'Iraq must withdraw unconditionally from Kuwait.'

In September, after taking a very short holiday in Switzerland, Margaret set off on her travels again. This time she visited Czechoslovakia, Hungary and Poland. It was her first visit to Czechoslovakia, and once more she was welcomed as a conquering heroine and the symbol of freedom. Later that month she went to the United Nations for a meeting on World Children's Year. There was no doubt that there was far too much international travelling in Margaret's schedule, but she liked it because she was a world figure and wherever she went she commanded absolute attention. But she should have spent more time back in the UK for, as I frequently told her, 'The plaudits are abroad but the votes are back home.'

CHAPTER 17

The Ides of Margaret

The Fall of Margaret Thatcher – The Murder of Ian Gow –
Joining the ERM – The Party Conference October 1990 –
The Eastbourne By-Election – Geoffrey Howe's
Resignation – Towards the Kill

Many people like to believe that great events have great causes. This belief is reassuring because it can provide a simple explanation for complex and perplexing situations. People are happier when they can recognize patterns that derive from logic or their own experience of human behaviour. History, however, allows us to make a more careful analysis at a distance both personal and temporal which usually shows that the earlier assumptions were too simplistic. Historians, who seek to explain great events as the result of a cumulative movement of powerful forces built up over the years and incapable of being arrested by human action, deceive themselves and their readers. All too often great events come about as the result of unpredicted, unrelated and often bizarre little events occurring in a haphazard and unexpected way.

One of my history tutors at Oxford was A. J. P. Taylor, who liked to shock his young students by saying that the Great War had no great cause, it just happened. He wanted to challenge the certainty of the young who had carefully learnt for their A-levels the causes of the First World War starting with Germany's ambition, passing on to the collapse of the Austro-Hungarian Empire, and through to the unpreparedness of France and Britain. Taylor wanted to overturn this neat and simple interpretation of history.

In charting the decline and fall of Margaret Thatcher, I have come to the conclusion that there is no simple explanation that predetermined its inevitability. With the gift of hindsight, the 1980s look like a decade with an integrity and completeness of its own. Three leaders dominated its politics – President Reagan, President Gorbachev and Prime Minister Thatcher. Britain was there among the top three countries, punching in a class well above its weight simply because of Margaret's unique character. Britain's policy of less state intervention, lower taxes, the control of public expenditure, the reduction of the power of organized labour, the stimulation of the enterprise economy, the spread of wealth through home ownership and wider share ownership, and a rugged, simple patriotism was given a name – Thatcherism. Because the 1980s was her decade, one should not assume that Margaret Thatcher had to end with it. Her fall was not inevitable.

It is not sufficient to say that Margaret Thatcher fell because of the deep unpopularity of the poll tax, or because of her policy towards Europe, or because of the economic mess of 1990. All were contributory factors but were not the sole determinants. Other matters such as the presence of an ambitious alternative leader, and the disgruntled attitudes of Ministers sacked, Ministers slighted or Members of Parliament overlooked, all made their contribution, as did the conduct of her campaign and her personal reluctance to canvass support. Some of the events that led to the dramatic crisis of 20 November were quite trivial but, happening as they did in the circumstances that emerged, they led to an outcome which would have been very different if they had happened at a slightly different time or in slightly different circumstances.

The flickering lamps of history will show many ruts in the road, many stones, winding diversions, cunning traps and treacherous slopes. They will not reveal a highway leading directly to a given destination. There was in my view nothing inevitable about the events of autumn 1990 which led to Margaret's fall. That came about through an amazing mixture of accident, mistake, ambition, intrigue, slighted pride, misplaced optimism and faulty judgement.

The Murder of Ian Gow

I was sitting in Central Office at nine o'clock in the morning on 30 July when John Whittingdale, the Prime Minister's Political Secretary, rang from Number 10 to say that they had received a report of an explosion at Ian Gow's home in Eastbourne. I sat there in a state of chilled shock, hoping anxiously not to hear the worst, but within an hour it was confirmed that Ian had been killed by a bomb planted under his car outside his house. My first reaction was of sheer overwhelming anger that an old friend, a wonderful husband and father, a courageous and warm-hearted person had been murdered by the IRA.

Ian's fearless criticism of the IRA had made his face well known in

Republican circles. He never shrank from telling the truth about terrorist attacks, about the IRA, and about the evil and wicked acts which they perpetrated. He was Mr Valiant-for-Truth.

Anyone in public life who condemns terrorists makes himself and his family potential targets. He can take more precautions, fit more alarms and have more police protection, but he knows that by speaking out he is putting his life at risk. Ministers who have responsibilities in these matters have to face these risks, but for backbenchers it requires a fearless courage to do so. Ian had that courage.

Ian and I had been friends for many years. In the 1970s Mary and I lived for a time at The Old Rectory in Selmeston, a village about eight miles from Ian's house. He and Jane came over to have tea in our garden and we often dropped in to see them at their home, quaintly called 'The Doghouse'. It was a very happy family home where Jane played the piano and Ian played cricket with his sons in the garden.

In the leadership election of 1975, Ian helped to run Geoffrey Howe's campaign, but he had subsequently become very attached to Margaret. There was no MP closer to her. He worshipped her and Margaret gave him the total and complete trust she usually reserved for members of her family, but that is what Ian had virtually become. He was the best Parliamentary Private Secretary she ever had. In those difficult and dark days of 1979–82, Ian was ever present in the House of Commons, in the Tea Room, the Dining Room, the Chamber, the Lobby, the Library, listening with sympathy and talking with frankness. Members from all wings of the Party felt they had a friend at Court.

I wasn't asked to join the Government for two years, and in that time Ian and I often lunched and dined together, sometimes at the Cavalry Club, where Ian invariably started by offering his guests a White Lady. We later served as Ministers of State together at the Department of the Environment, where Ian was responsible for Housing. He was not very happy there. He wanted to reform the Property Services Agency and to make fundamental changes in housing legislation, but in both of these aims he was thwarted. He went on to the Treasury as Financial Secretary, but never really cared for ministerial life.

When the Anglo-Irish Agreement was signed in November 1985 Ian decided that he had to resign, despite the fact that it had been negoti-ated by the two politicians he had served most loyally – Geoffrey and

Margaret. As a staunch Protestant and Unionist Ian felt that Ulster had been betrayed. As a man of stern and unyielding honour he put principle before office.

It is often difficult for people outside politics, and sometimes inside, to appreciate that very capable Members of Parliament do not always wish to be Ministers or even want to go on being Ministers for long. Ministerial life is not the be-all and end-all of political involvement. Ian was always happy on the backbenches looking after the interests of his Eastbourne constituents. He really did love being the Member of Parliament for that town, and they loved him. His personal popularity helped him to hold that seat against the local Liberals who had captured control of the council. But the seat was secure as long as Ian remained the Member.

Many of Ian's contemporaries have happy and fond memories of him. One of mine was that when engaged in economic discussion he would slowly take out his wallet and extract from it a piece of well-folded paper which he then proceeded to read. It was the letter written in 1976 to Denis Healey by Mr Witteween, the Managing Director of the IMF, in which the IMF imposed conditions upon the British Government for the loans it made to bail Britain out of its economic crisis. Ian read this catalogue of shame lugubriously, and with a sense of shocked outrage that Socialist mismanagement had reduced Britain to such a humiliating position. Ian's manner of speaking was polished and rotund, which could make him appear pompous, but there was not a less pompous Member of Parliament in the House. The smile and the chuckle were never distant.

Ian's funeral and requiem mass took place on a blindingly sunny day at the High Anglican Gothic Church of St Alban's in Eastbourne. Peter Ball, the monk who was the Bishop of Lewes, gave a moving address full of love and reassurance. A bugler from Ian's regiment sounded the last post and his coffin left the church to the great hymn 'I vow to thee my country'. This always brings a lump to my throat, and on this occasion it also brought tears to my eyes.

After the funeral Ian's closest friends went back to 'The Doghouse', where we all joined in what could only be described as a wake held in the garden. It was almost as if Ian's spirit was there. Jane, with that serenity and assurance that comes from deep and abiding faith, was determined not to be sad. Over the last week many friends had rallied to help, and we had been asked with others to send down some food so that Jane would not have to worry about feeding the large number of people who had descended upon her home. I was amazed that she had noticed our contribution and even thanked us for it. It was her way of saying that life had to go on. Out of this dreadful tragedy came the inspiration of hope and the realization that death would have no dominion.

Ian's murder was a great blow to Margaret. Two of her closest friends, Airey Neave and Ian, had been killed because of their brave defence of the Unionist cause in Northern Ireland. They had also been targeted because of their close association with her. The IRA could not get at the Prime Minister, but they could get at her closest friends. On hearing of Ian's murder Margaret was overwhelmed by grief and immediately went down to Eastbourne to console Jane. Margaret had not only lost a close confidant, but a very astute politician who knew how the winds blew at Westminster. Ian was someone who in the months ahead could have been a bridge between her and Geoffrey Howe, and would have been a key figure in preventing any leadership election taking place. In the event that it did take place, Ian would have worked as subtly and, I consider, as successfully for Margaret as he had done in 1989. Margaret was eventually to lose by only four votes. Ian, quite apart from his own vote, would have made up that vital difference.

Joining the ERM

As summer moved into autumn the economic position did not improve. Inflation hit an eight-year peak in September at 10.6 per cent; the trade gap in the same month was £1.1 billion and John Major admitted that the economy was slowing down. The Liberal Democrats had just shed the SDP and were trying to get recognition for the new name of their Party – but they were not relevant. The Labour Party was trying to keep as quiet as possible, still hoping that circumstances and the unpopularity of the Government would deliver them victory in the Election whenever it came. At the Labour Party Conference, Neil Kinnock just managed to stop a resolution reducing defence expenditure by £7 billion, but he did commit his Party to increasing pensions and social spending by £4 billion.

The last day of Labour's Conference was overshadowed by John Major's statement on 5 October that sterling would enter the Exchange Rate Mechanism at a middle rate of DM 2.95 to the pound. The Cabinet had not been told about this on the Thursday, but I had got wind of it. A fortnight earlier, as Party Chairman, I had visited John in his room at the Treasury to discuss his speech to the Party Conference. He was gloomy, as he saw no opportunity of reducing interest rates in the near future. He said to me, 'Inflation is the number one enemy and joining the ERM would help. Douglas thinks so too.' This was the Auld Alliance of the Treasury and the Foreign Office revisiting the Madrid Accord. John wasn't quite telling me that he intended to join the ERM, since the timing of this was one of the Treasury's inner secrets, but he was hinting that he was going to do it. I warned him against joining, but in any event I didn't think he would actually be able to persuade Margaret to do it.

I went to see Margaret at Number 10 on the evening of 4 October and urged her not to join the ERM and certainly not at the rate of DM 2.95 to the pound. I considered that as Party Chairman I had a duty to ask the Prime Minister at the very least to think again about this dramatic change which had been agreed, apparently bilaterally, between her and her Chancellor, because I feared for the economic and political consequences. It was unusual, if not unacceptable, for any other Minister to enter the secret and closed area of exchange rate policy. The forbidding threat of 'market considerations' apparently ruled out collective discussion, and the group that made the decisions was as small as possible – Number 10, the Treasury and the Bank of England. Now that sterling is out of the ERM, I am certain that any decision about its future relationship or status could not be taken by such a small group. One of the consequences of this episode is that in future the full Cabinet would have to consider such a significant and central matter and the House of Commons would have to debate it.

I have never been in favour of a system of fixed parities which included sterling. In 1925 Churchill put Britain back on the Gold Standard, and later he recognized this was his major mistake which made the slump much worse. We did not really begin to recover until 1931, when we left the Gold Standard. Churchill's comment on his unhappy tenure as Chancellor was that he wished 'that finance had not been so proud'. I was a junior Minister in 1972 when the Bretton Woods System finally collapsed. We had done all that we could to maintain it but it, too, was doomed. I welcomed the fact that we would be returning to floating exchange rates.

I had seen the damage that Nigel Lawson's policy of shadowing the Deutschmark since 1987 had done. It had increased the money supply and intensified inflationary pressures just at the time when we should have been increasing interest rates to dampen down the boom. The undoubted collective view of most economists was that by joining the ERM Britain would be able to contain inflationary pressures better. In the *Daily Telegraph* Sarah Hogg, later to become head of John Major's Number 10 Policy Unit, regularly argued that 'the ERM is the best solution for all our woes'.

I warned Margaret that by joining we would be tying ourselves to the German economy just at the time when it was going to have to face the massive cost of reunification. I could not see any prospect of interest rates falling, and as we would no longer be in control of our own interest rates we would be boxed in during the run-up to an Election. Margaret was not enthusiastic about the ERM but she had been persuaded, it was the only way to get a cut in interest rates, and that was her prevailing passion. John Major had proposed a 1 per cent cut, and this Margaret seized upon. She said, 'Kenneth, I have secured a one per cent cut and when we join we will be able to adjust the value of sterling. I have been assured that we will have that flexibility.' The decision had been made and I could not dissuade her. I then argued against DM 2.95 and said that if we were to go into the ERM it should be at DM 2.70 or lower. Again, I had no success.

The decision was a major disaster and committed us to enduring a deeper and longer recession than we need have suffered. However, the press was unanimous in praising the Government. The *Financial Times* stated authoritatively that 'the time was ripe'. The *Guardian* heralded it as 'a long-term move of enormous economic importance which would lead to a further reduction in interest rates'. The *Independent* crowed that, 'Joining the ERM will have much more far-reaching economic consequences in speeding the pace of integration in Europe'. Alan Budd in the *Times* rejoiced, 'At last! ERM is the end of an experiment.' Sarah Hogg in the *Daily Telegraph* was triumphant. A profile in the *Sunday Times* said of John Major that he was 'a new model for the Tories as they look to the post-Thatcherite years'. The only sceptical voice raised was from that fine and far-sighted journalist Peter Jenkins, who wrote, 'It could prove that Mrs Thatcher has joined when the time was wrong.'

The Party Conference October 1990

The Party Conference took place in Bournemouth, which had only quite recently joined Blackpool and Brighton as a venue for our annual jamborees. Most politicians prefer Blackpool because the Winter Gardens, with its upper balconies which crowd the audience in, is a large theatre whose style and character create a political atmosphere. By contrast, the sterile modern auditoriums of Brighton and Bournemouth, which seat their audiences far from the platform, leave the politicians addressing a void. The conference hotels are different too. The Imperial at Blackpool and the Grand at Brighton, now rebuilt after the bombing, evoke memories of Victorian naughtiness and opulent Edwardian weekends. But the Bournemouth conference hotel, perched on a cliff, is straight out of an Agatha Christie novel.

The Party faithful assembled on the Monday of Party Conference week to comments that John Major, by taking sterling into the ERM, had paved the way for a 1991 Election. My strategy was to leave that question open. The divisions in Europe within the Party were being loudly probed. Michael Heseltine, in a prophecy that sounded good at the time but which was to be overturned within two years, said that joining the ERM was 'the first heroic step,' but Nick Ridley warned that the pound was overvalued at DM 2.95. In her speech to the Party Agents on Monday night Margaret brushed all this internal debate aside and set the ship to 'full steam ahead for the fourth term – whenever that may be'.

Labour's lead in the opinion polls had dropped from 17 to 12 points, which was some small comfort. The theme of the Conference was 'strong leadership', which played to our strength just when the invasion of Iraq seemed imminent. There were four sub-themes developed by Ministers – 'opportunities for all'; 'choice and higher standards'; 'a cleaner, greener, safer Britain'; and 'leadership in an uncertain world'.

In my opening speech I concentrated on attacking Labour, which had been the theme of our summer campaign, focusing upon their plans for a massive increase in state planning – Labour's proposed 2,012 new bodies would create a mountain of bureaucracy. The Party faithful always warmed to that message. I descended to doggerel – Neil Kinnock had said at Labour's Party Conference that the Conservatives would 'cut and run in '91'. I replied that, 'In '91 or '92, the Government will still be Blue.' Only at Party Conferences can one be forgiven for such things. I also reminded the audience of our council election successes and our victory in capturing Ealing, where Neil Kinnock lived – 'We have saved Mr Kinnock from the cost of living under a Labour council. We must now save him from the cost of living under a Labour Government.'

371

The Conference got off to a fairly slow start but gathered speed as the week wore on. My final speech contained a lot of knockabout and audience participation, and during it we showed our latest Party Political Broadcast. I was amazed at how few Party workers had seen it. We had tried very hard to improve the quality of our PPBs, and on Brendan Bruce's advice we had asked John Salmon to make the last three. They were outstandingly good. His latest depicted Socialism with some very striking visual effects – one of a red rose in a lapel held in place at the back by a Campaign for Nuclear Disarmament badge; and a doom-laden clanging door as Socialism shut on Britain.

Jeffrey Archer, who had spent many days going around the constituencies where he was a popular draw, spoke in the Friday debate about Party organisation and presentation. He was fed up with the many MPs who were whingeing at Westminster and his attack upon them was loudly applauded. Jeffrey declared his strong support for Margaret by saying, 'We've got the leader we want, and Labour has got the leader we want!' This was a warm-up for the grand finale of the Leader's speech.

Margaret had been up till 3 a.m. polishing and gilding her speech. The amount of work which both she and Ted Heath put into their Conference speeches was never, in my view, repaid by subsequent quotation from them. They fitted the hour. Each year the press claim that the speech to be made by the Leader is the most important one that has ever been made – needed to hold the Party together, to restore morale and to inspire the Party workers in the country. The pre-billing is quite absurd and the effect is usually transient. Margaret spoke of the future and saw 'an open, classless Britain' which she certainly saw herself as leading. She perceptively described herself as 'the pushy woman who always gets to the head of the queue'.

The Party certainly ended the week in better shape than it started. Ted Heath, who still saw himself as a world statesman with a major role to play on the international scene, tried to steal the limelight from the Prime Minister. On the last day he held a press conference in Bournemouth where he announced that he was going to visit Saddam Hussein to negotiate the release of the British hostages. This was just at the time when Saddam Hussein had realized that holding hostages was damaging his standing in the world and was looking for ways of releasing each national group. Ted's press conference was designed to dominate the news programmes, and so it did. I could just imagine how Ted would have felt if Alec Douglas-Home, after he had ceased to be the Leader of the

Party, had ever tried to upstage him in this sort of way.

I tried to send the Party workers away happy and confident. One of the weekend journalists said the Party was lucky to have as Chairman a man 'with such enviable bounce', but another said, 'A Chairman has to do, what a Chairman has to do.' However, those who attended this Conference, or watched it on television, will remember the uniquely moving scenes on the Thursday afternoon when the Party invited on to the platform the emerging Party leaders from Eastern Europe: Jan Carnogursky from Czechoslovakia; Jozsef Antall, recently elected Prime Minister of Hungary; the Speaker of the East German Parliament, Sabine Bergmann Pohl; and most memorably a Pole and a great advocate of privatization, Andrzej Zacwislak, who brought a great roar from the Conference when he said, 'In my country we have a saying: Socialism cannot be improved – it must be removed.'

Some of these people had been imprisoned and tortured, but all had fought to see the end of the stifling, harsh rule of state Communism. The Conservatives had always predicted the death of Socialism, but no one really expected East Europe to disintegrate so quickly. At the Conference we, too, experienced that feeling of joyous hope that was expressed at the beginning of the French Revolution by Wordsworth – 'Bliss was it in that dawn to be alive'.

The Friday of the Party Conference was Margaret's sixty-fifth birthday, but we had deliberately played this down and avoided a sing-song of 'many happy returns'. On the Saturday evening Margaret hosted a birthday party dinner at Chequers for her closest friends – Jeffrey and Mary Archer, John and Alison Wakeham, Tim and Virginia Bell, Gordon Reece, and Mary and me. I gave her a large coloured Victorian print of Lord Salisbury rolling up his sleeves and saying, 'What a good team we've got, there's a lot of work to do.'

Margaret was very tired and almost dropped off to sleep during the dinner. Jeffrey Archer, at our end of the table, decided to liven things up, by joking, 'Hello, hello, hello, why doesn't a Sloane Ranger like a gang bang?' I responded, 'Jeffrey, tell us why doesn't a Sloane Ranger like a gang bang?' Jeffrey replied, 'Because afterwards there are too many thank you letters.' This produced a burst of laughter, and Margaret sprang into action again. She leaned forward saying, 'Kenneth, Kenneth, what's happening at your end of the table?' I thought it better not to tell her.

I did, however, make a speech at the end of the dinner saying that we were with her completely, she had our support, we wanted her to lead us to victory in the next Election, and we would fight for her to the end. As we were leaving Chequers I said cheerfully to John Wakeham, 'I hope this isn't the last time that we will all be here.'

The Eastbourne By-Election

Ian Gow had been murdered on 30 July, and there is a convention that a by-election has to be held within three months of a vacancy occurring. There is no law on this, but the convention had developed because in the 1960s Harold Wilson had tried to avoid difficult by-elections by postponing them. The by-election which I won at Acton in 1968 was held almost six months after the suicide of the sitting Labour Member. In this case the end of October was the outer limit, and we chose 18 October, in the week after the Party Conference. We were defending Ian's majority of 16,900, but from the start, and bearing in mind the Mid Staffordshire result, I knew things were going to be very difficult.

Ian had a strong personal following, and the canvassing revealed that many people felt there should be no by-election at all and that a Tory Member of Parliament should simply be appointed. Not only was this unrealistic but it would have played very much into the hands of the IRA, part of whose strategy is to disrupt the democratic process in Britain. Our campaign was not helped by Eastbourne having a poll tax of £395, one of the highest in the country. This was no Tory flagship. In addition, the Liberals had a strong position on the local council.

I would have preferred to have a local candidate, as I think this tends to work better in by-elections, but the Party Chairman has no influence at all in such matters. In the Conservative Party, the choice of candidate is up to the local Association. This is unlike the Labour Party, which simply dumped its sitting candidate about six weeks before the election, replacing a hardline non-poll taxpayer with a soft centrist.

Our candidate was Richard Hickmet, who had previously sat as the Member for Glanford and Scunthorpe. From the beginning of the campaign he was subjected to a series of personal attacks because of his Turkish ancestry and his support for Turkish Cypriots. Abusive pamphlets about him circulated in the constituency, and one can never quite gauge just how influential is such a whispering campaign. But undoubtedly it did not help our cause or promote the peace of mind of our candidate.

We tried to focus upon the full range of national issues, but each press conference came back to the circumstances which caused the by-election. Richard Hickmet in his speech to the Party Conference had dwelt far too much upon Ian and terrorism, but as he pointed out, 'It was impossible to ignore the circumstances which brought the by-election about.' Neil Kinnock could not avoid speaking of Ian's murder when he visited the constituency. I went down to support Hickmet twice, and on the eve of the poll our senior Agent John Lacy, who is a betting man, said the bookies in Eastbourne had stopped taking bets on a Conservative victory and he thought we would win by 2–3,000 votes. I was much less optimistic and told Margaret to expect a very bad result as we could even lose.

On polling day I was guest speaker at the Royal Institute of Chartered Surveyors Conference in Birmingham. Travelling back to London by train that afternoon I kept in touch with our Agents to see how the vote was shaping up. They were cautiously optimistic. But I was less confident. The sniff that I had got on my visits was that many Tories would be staying at home, and in the event that is what happened. Tony Kerpel was travelling with me, and aware of my misgivings he suggested that commentators would throw at me the jibe which Margaret had made at the expense of the Liberals during her Party Conference speech. She had likened the Liberals' new logo of a soaring bird to a dead parrot, a reference to one of John Cleese's famous Monty Python sketches, the humour of which had to be explained to Margaret. Critics were now bound to say that the parrot was very much alive. We agreed to shrug off a good result for the Liberals by saying, 'The parrot has twitched.' I used this line in the following morning's interviews, and it caused much laughter even among the normally blasé studio technicians. When the Liberal victor, Mr Bellotti, was introduced into the House of Commons he was greeted with cries of 'Pretty Polly', and Denis Skinner shouted out, 'Go on. Give 'em a peck.'

The poll was 10,000 fewer than it had been at the General Election, and the Liberals won a spectacular victory with a 4,500 majority. At the BBC TV by-election programme that evening Charles Kennedy the young Scottish MP who is now President of the Liberal Democrat Party had told me before we went on air that the Liberals did not expect to win, although they did expect to reduce significantly the Conservative majority. He was genuinely surprised at the actual result. That, however, did not prevent his leader Paddy Ashdown proclaiming that the Liberal Democrats 'are now establishing themselves as a decisive force in the defeat of

Thatcherism in Britain'. Not for the first time his claims were extravagant and absurd. But one could not disguise that this was a disappointing and poor result and was another bloody nose for the Government.

I reminded the country and the Party that the Eastbourne result was almost identical to the by-election at Ryedale just before the 1987 General Election. Then, a Conservative majority of a similar size had been overturned by the Liberals, but the seat was won back by the Conservatives in the ensuing 1987 General Election. Indeed the same turnaround happened at Eastbourne in the 1992 General Election.

By-elections are very uncertain guides to what will happen in the long term. They are snapshots depicting the fortunes of the Parties at a fleeting moment of time. I speak as the victor of two by-elections in Acton and Marylebone. I won Acton in 1968 with a swing of 16 per cent, but in spite of assiduous constituency work the seat went back to Labour in 1970.

For the incumbent Government, by-elections are nightmares to be endured. I recall Chris Patten, who as Chairman in 1991 and 1992 was to experience his own nasty and difficult by-elections which we also lost, plaintively asking me, 'How on earth can you win a by-election?' Margaret never attempted to answer that question. She simply avoided creating unnecessary by-elections. But the lot of the Party Chairman is to carry the can. Iain Macleod was blamed for the loss of Orpington to the Liberals, and I was for Eastbourne. Even Cecil Parkinson and Norman Tebbit had their share of lost by-elections. But then Party Chairmen have to have broad shoulders.

The effect of the Eastbourne by-election defeat was to strengthen further the belief among doubting Tory MPs that Margaret could not win the next Election. It undid much of the good work created by our local election and 'Summer Heat on Labour' campaigns. While it did not directly cause the challenge to Margaret's leadership, it certainly contributed to the climate which made a leadership challenge thinkable again.

Geoffrey Howe's Resignation

When Parliament resumed, Europe continued to trouble us. Tony Favell, the Member of Parliament for Stockport, resigned as John Major's Parliamentary Private Secretary because of the ERM, and on 23 October eleven Tory MPs voted against the ERM. I toured seats in the North of England and found morale just about holding. In the polls we were 10 points behind, but it was encouraging to see a recovery in the Liberal vote which was going to be essential for our victory.

Over the weekend on 28 October the Italians, who held the European Community Presidency, called a special summit in Rome to deal with the impasse on agricultural reform and international trade. However, Andreotti, the Italian Prime Minister, had other fish to fry. He had seen Chancellor Kohl earlier in the month and they had agreed to push ahead more quickly with economic and monetary union. This meant accepting a single currency by the end of the century and establishing a central bank by January 1994. The proposal was carried by eleven votes to one. Britain was isolated, and the *Independent* crowed, 'Mrs Thatcher stands alone.'

This move had not taken Margaret and Douglas Hurd completely by surprise, for private warnings had been passed to Andrew Turnbull, the Prime Minister's Private Secretary, but this did not prevent Britain being isolated. Giulio Andreotti, supported by his large, ebullient, jazz-loving Foreign Minister, Gianni de Michaelis, had in effect hijacked the Summit. Robert Jackson told me that by bringing this to a head and exposing the isolation of Britain, an Italian Prime Minister had for the first time set the stage to bring down a British Prime Minister. It is even more ironic that this pair of scene setters are now themselves the subject of inquiries into alleged corruption linked to the Mafia.

Douglas later told me that Margaret had handled the discussions well, but freed from her script in the televized press conferences afterwards she went over the top. She said that our European partners were living in cloud-cuckoo-land. When I saw her on the Monday I suggested that, while she was quite right to resist this federalist push, her rhetoric should be more about fighting *for* British interests rather than fighting *against* the other eleven countries.

Margaret made a statement in the House of Commons on the Tuesday, when she dismissed a below-par Kinnock as 'Little Sir Echo'. However, the importance of her statement rested in something she said towards the end of her questions. Jacques Delors had said that he wanted 'the European Parliament to be the democratic body of the Community; the Commission to be the Executive; and the Council of Ministers to be the Senate'. When pressed on this Margaret defiantly cried out, 'No. No. No.' Geoffrey Howe was sitting on one side of Margaret and just about managed to smile – that is while he was on camera.

The Prime Minister at bay was a wondrous sight. She didn't like being cornered and she fought back like a tigress. Margaret was not prepared to surrender any more sovereignty, and she included future generations who she claimed would be betrayed. This was real conviction politics, boldly enunciated with little thought of the immediate consequences. Margaret's report on the Rome Summit to the Cabinet that Thursday was followed by a great tirade against Europe. No one intervened.

By then, the press were beginning to speculate about Geoffrey's position. The *Daily Mail* reported that some MPs were urging Margaret to sack him, and the *Daily Express* said that he intended to stand down at the next Election. During the Party Conference, at a fringe meeting, Geoffrey had said that 'the European train is about to leave for a still unidentified destination but certainly in the direction of some sort of EMU. Shall Britain be in the driver's cab or in the rear carriage?' I always felt that train metaphors in relation to Europe were misleading. In a well run railway you only get on if you know where the train is going, and if you miss that train then there is usually another one later. That is exactly how we came to join the European Community.

While Margaret was in Rome, Geoffrey took the opportunity to promote his views by accepting an invitation to appear on Brian Walden's Sunday television programme. This was clearly deliberate, for Geoffrey did not want to be excluded from the European debate. However, this interview only confirmed my view that doing political television on a Sunday is on the whole not good for politicians. It is designed principally for a small audience, of whom a large proportion consists of journalists looking for stories for Monday's papers. They certainly got one from Geoffrey. He dismissed opposition to a single currency by saying, 'I don't think that can be the right view to take.'

At the Cabinet on 1 November it was clear the Prime Minister and her Deputy were worlds apart. One of the jobs that the Leader of the House has to do each year is to marshal the Queen's Speech. This involves protracted debates with Ministers to agree the number of Bills that can be presented, and ensuring that Parliamentary Counsel are well advanced in the drafting of the Bills that have to be taken early in the session. Geoffrey had been patiently working on this from the early summer. During the Cabinet meeting the week before, Margaret had addressed some sharp questions to Geoffrey about how prepared the legislation was.

A week later she now returned to this theme with vigour. She was unnecessarily rude to Geoffrey over the details of the legislative programme, and for about ten minutes she asked a series of niggling questions about which Bills were and were not ready for introduction.

The clear implication was that Geoffrey had fallen down on his job and that the new session would get off to a slow start. This was quite untrue, and Geoffrey replied patiently, but he was clearly uneasy and embarrassed at suddenly becoming the victim of Margaret's wrath. The rest of the Cabinet were also embarrassed, and tried not to catch each other's eyes by finding a great interest in their papers.

In these exchanges a particular aspect of Margaret's femininity emerged. When men fall out and argue they can be very coarse, angry and blunt. Margaret was never coarse and I never heard her use swearwords. But sometimes her emotions got the better of her and she felt compelled to speak her mind and say what she really thought. I do not believe a man would ever speak in this way to another man in front of others. Part of Margaret's vivid character came from this spontaneity, but what her exchange with Geoffrey showed was that whilst she could be kind and generous she could also say very personally hurtful things and wound to the quick.

That evening Mary and I were going to see Derek Jacobi as Kean at the Old Vic. On the way to the theatre I received a telephone call from Number 10 saying that Geoffrey Howe had resigned and would I go to Number 10 immediately. I left Mary at the theatre and returned to Downing Street, where I found the Prime Minister sitting in the Private Secretary's room adjacent to the Cabinet Room peering rather myopically at Geoffrey's letter of resignation. I thought that she suddenly looked a lot older.

In his letter of resignation Geoffrey said that now Britain was in the Exchange Rate Mechanism we should play a more positive role in developing economic and monetary union. 'I am deeply anxious that the mood you have struck, most notably in Rome last weekend and in the House of Commons this Tuesday, will make it more difficult for Britain to hold and retain a position of influence in this vital debate.'

I was then asked to do what I could on the two television news bulletins to explain what had happened – just as it had fallen to me to do this when Nigel had resigned a year earlier. There wasn't very much I could say but I emphasized the phrase in Geoffrey's letter about 'mood' – he didn't like the Prime Minister's style.

Once again it was Europe which had provided the breaking-point between the Prime Minister and a senior Minister. Peter Jenkins strikingly described Europe as 'the Bermuda Triangle for those who sail with Mrs Thatcher' – Heseltine, Ridley, Lawson and now Howe were its victims and soon it was to claim the skipper herself. Back in July I had told the Cabinet that in my view, 'The Delors package would be highly divisive. It has the potential to destroy our Party.' At the time it seemed that virtue and common sense were on the side of Geoffrey nobly fighting against a bigoted, narrow-minded little Englander – the Prime Minister.

It was apparently obvious to all that the great prize was EMU and that the ERM was the golden path that led to it. How could anyone who was serious about the real interests of Britain as a partner in Europe not realize this? Yet within two years the ERM was collapsing and Britain had been forced to withdraw. The train which was leaving the station and didn't know its destination had been derailed. The track which was to lead us to the heart of Europe had led us instead to the humiliation of Black Wednesday. In 1992 the federalist push in Europe was checked. There can be little doubt that history, or 'events, dear boy' as Macmillan used to say, has vindicated Margaret Thatcher's doubts rather than Geoffrey Howe's hopes.

But Geoffrey's resignation wasn't just about Europe. He had been humiliated by his abrupt dismissal as Foreign Secretary a year earlier. Without a major Department behind him he seemed remarkably lifeless. The withdrawal of his official residence at Chevening, and his exclusion from the policy formation of the Government: all these things had contributed to bringing him to the point when he decided to soldier on no more. It had been rather expected that Geoffrey would fill Willie Whitelaw's role – a senior elder statesman at the right hand of the Leader and securing collective support for her. But that was never the relationship. Nor was Geoffrey an alter ego for the Prime Minister, a substitute or an alternative, nor a spokesman for her in her absence. That, too, was not his role. Having been at the centre of policy-making since 1975, Geoffrey felt frustrated and marginalized. His speeches and interviews were the shadowy ways in which he tried to continue to influence the course of events. He had become like the Vice-President of the United States – loaded with titles and prestige but having little real power.

It was the personal relationship that had become too difficult. I had seen Geoffrey on several occasions over the years take a great battering from the Prime Minister. He had a wonderful capacity to absorb the punches. He would quietly rearrange his papers and come back plodding persistently, patiently and reasonably to regain the lost ground. This endeared him to his colleagues and won their respect, but by now the Tory tortoise had run out of patience. For Geoffrey the events of that week, Margaret's statement in the House of Commons and their exchange in Cabinet were an outburst too far and an insult too many. The cause of Geoffrey's resignation was ultimately personal, and basically it all came down to the incompatibility of their two characters.

I spent the following day visiting constituencies. The Party workers were rattled, and some were openly hostile to the Prime Minister – 'You can't win with her.' But others were more robust – 'She's our only trump.' There was a mini reshuffle, and I was called to the telephone during a visit to an aerospace factory to discuss some of the changes. Margaret wanted to bring Norman Tebbit back by making him Education Secretary. I talked with Norman about this, but he wanted to stay outside Government to concentrate on his business interests. Ken Clarke went to Education, John MacGregor to be Leader of the House and, ironically, William Waldegrave, a strong pro-European, joined the Cabinet as Health Secretary. By the weekend we were 14 points behind Labour in the polls. I was very worried that Geoffrey's resignation would precipitate a leadership election, something which I had hoped our successes in the spring and our campaigns in the summer had prevented. Several Members of Parliament from marginal seats telephoned me over the weekend to convey their anxieties.

Michael Heseltine fired off a six-page open letter to his Constituency Chairman and then left for a visit to Jordan. Michael was openly critical of Margaret Thatcher's style but he said that he would not stand against the Prime Minister and that she would lead us into the next Election and win it. His supporters, however, were very active, for they sniffed blood. In a poll at the weekend, 71 per cent of MPs who were asked said that Margaret should stay, 14 per cent that she should go, and 13 per cent didn't know.

Towards the Kill

Michael Heseltine's open letter addressed to his constituents, but really meant for the country, focused upon the disunity of the Government which was revealed by Geoffrey's resignation. It also echoed the reasons for his own resignation in 1986. 'If decisions continue to be taken and imposed that do not carry the collective endorsement, the stresses will continue to show and be our undoing,' he wrote. This was directed at the Prime Minister's style of Government. Michael Portillo, Francis Maude and Archie Hamilton, all Ministers of State, issued a statement supporting the Prime Minister, and Tom King, an old friend of Heseltine's, said that the letter was 'extraordinarily ill-advised'. Douglas Hurd, at the weekend, insisted that there was no split on policy – that is to say he supported my interpretation that Geoffrey's resignation was not about substance but about style.

There was the usual lunch at Number 10 on Monday and Margaret was very relaxed. The general feeling was that Michael had overplayed his hand. Bernard Ingham had already talked of Michael having to 'put up or shut up', and this was the line taken by the *Daily Mail*. Later this was said to be a crucial factor for Michael in deciding whether he should stand. I don't think so at all. Michael was waiting to see what was going to happen, how events would turn out, and whether they were going to provide him with an opportunity. Indeed, two days later on 7 November, the day when Parliament opened, he said in the *Daily Telegraph*, and I believe this reflected his real state of mind before Geoffrey's speech, 'I have made my position clear. I am not going to take part in that process. I think Mrs Thatcher will lead the Conservative Party into the next Election, and the Conservative Party will win it.'

In the evening Ken Clarke and I dined together to talk about education, but we of course discussed Geoffrey's resignation. Ken had no time for Michael and thought he 'should stop messing around', which he publicly said a few days later. On the Monday evening, Michael's constituency officers met in Henley to consider his letter to them. Quite unbeknown to me, the Area Agent of the Conservative Party, Donald Stringer, had been invited by the President of the Henley Association to attend this meeting. In the heady atmosphere that was building up this was seen as 'the hidden hand' of Central Office. That simply wasn't true. I only learnt of Donald's presence from the newspapers the following day. The Henley officers went on to publish a letter supporting Margaret Thatcher's leadership. This was interpreted as a rebuke to Michael but, in fact, the letter was more ambiguous. Michael clearly had the support of some of his activists.

I was receiving a very mixed bag of comments about the Prime Minister, and at Central Office the new Deputy Chairman, David Trippier, told me that Margaret was 'past her sell-by date'. All this was taking place against the background of two difficult by-elections in Bootle and Bradford, which were both Labour seats. I told Margaret that we were going to do very badly in both, with the possibility of a lost deposit in Bradford. John Lacy this time accurately forecast the result, and at Bradford the Conservative candidate came a poor third. I don't think that these results were particularly significant but they were one of the factors that Michael Heseltine was to cite as illustrating our poor performance in the inner cities – an area where he believed he could re-establish the Party's position.

The Prime Minister made a strong and confident speech when the new session of Parliament opened on 7 November. Cranley Onslow, the Chairman of the 1922 Committee, after securing Margaret's agreement, announced the timetable for the annual leadership election which was usually a formality. The nomination list was to close at midday on Thursday 15 November, just a week away. Margaret's nomination, in the names of Douglas Hurd and John Major, was promptly submitted. Geoffrey Howe let it be known that he intended to make a statement in the House early the following week just before the nomination list closed.

On Thursday 8 November, John Major published the Autumn Statement of Expenditure for the following year 1990–91. He forecast a smaller balance of payments deficit and he still intended to make a debt repayment – those were the days! John performed well in the House, where he had become much more confident at the dispatch box. He squashed Dennis Skinner, who called his statement 'a cock-and-bull story', by saying a public sector debt repayment of 'only £3 billion was not a beast I recall during the period of the last Labour Government. He mentions a cock-and-bull story and we all know which of these he talks.'

I told Margaret of the two by-election results early on Friday morning. The poll tax had been the real killer but, as she said the results were 'better than we feared'. After the Remembrance ceremony at the Cenotaph on Sunday Margaret told me that she thought it likely that Michael would stand. Tom King was very angry at the very idea of a leadership election even being discussed when British troops were committed on the ground in the Gulf. Douglas Hurd told me after the parade that it looked like war before Christmas. He meant war in the Gulf.

Sir Peter Lane, the President of the National Union, rang me on Sunday evening to say he had been receiving calls from all over the country from leading Party workers. There were some criticisms, but the overwhelming view was strong support for the Prime Minister and considerable annoyance that the Party was wounding itself in this way. On Monday 12 November I saw Willie Whitelaw, who did not think this was the right moment for Margaret to go, but he did say that if a third of the Parliamentary Party voted against her then she would have to go.

Willie was determined to do everything that he could to stop Michael Heseltine, and he thought that Douglas Hurd was the best hope to do this. At lunch that day, Margaret was in very good form and looking forward to her speech that evening at the Guildhall.

The Guildhall speech is the annual dinner for the new Lord Mayor, with the City at its most glittering in all its medieval and seventeenth-century trappings. When I talked to Denis before the dinner he was very fed up, saying, 'We are destroying ourselves.' Margaret wore a great black velvet cloak with a high wide collar which made her appear even more regal. Her tone was defiant as she said, 'I am still at the crease though the bowling has been pretty hostile of late. No ducking, no stonewalling, the bowling is going to be hit all over the ground. That's my style.' Margaret's supporters loved this sort of bravura performance where the melodrama was enhanced by her extraordinary get-up. But it reinforced the antipathy of all those who couldn't stand her or her style. Even so, no movement from Michael. He returned hurriedly from Europe, where he had been making a speech.

On Tuesday 13 November, the House was packed for Geoffrey's resignation statement. It had to wait while Peter Lilley, the Trade and Industry Secretary, made an important announcement extending competition in the telecommunications industry. This was really the fulfilment of the policies I had put in hand seven years earlier. However, that Tuesday will not be remembered for Peter's statement. Ted Heath was present wearing his usual expression of grumpy impassivity. He must have sensed that one of his long-cherished ambitions, to see his successor fall, was close to realization. Michael Heseltine was also there on the front bench below the gangway, smiling and cheerfully confident. The Prime Minister was flanked by John Major and myself.

Geoffrey's speech was heard in silence apart from sharp intakes of breath and gusts of laughter. It was a devastating direct attack upon the policy and style of Margaret's leadership. I couldn't help recalling the speech that I had heard him make in Number 10 Downing Street at the dinner in 1989 to celebrate Margaret's tenth year in office. His speech on that occasion was a paean of praise and seen as a preliminary to sanctification. On this occasion his speech was coolly dismissive and seen as the preliminary to assassination. He wielded the dagger of Brutus. Geoffrey had decided that Margaret should go and that this was the last opportunity before an Election to bring her down. He set about his mission with relish.

He began by saying:

It has been suggested – even, indeed, by some of my Rt Hon. and Honourable Friends – that I decided to resign solely because of questions of style and not on matters of substance at all. Indeed, if some of my former colleagues are to be believed, I must be the first Minister in history who has resigned because he was in full agreement with Government policy. The truth is that, in many aspects of politics, style and substance complement each other. Very often, they are two sides of the same coin.

Geoffrey went on to condemn Margaret's approach to Europe, referring to:

The nightmare image, sometimes conjured up by my Rt Hon. Friend, who seems sometimes to look out upon a continent that is positively teeming with ill-intentioned people, scheming, in her words, to 'extinguish democracy', to 'disown our national identities' and dissolve to lead us 'through the back door into a federal Europe'. What kind of vision is that . . .?'

Europe was the issue and Margaret was prepared to use all her power and office against greater European union. Geoffrey made it clear that he had extracted from her the Madrid commitment to enter the ERM under certain conditions. Then he attacked her dismissal of the hard ECU proposal, which John Major had put forward, in these terms:

How on earth are the Chancellor and the Governor of the Bank of England commending the hard ECU as they strive to be taken as serious participants in the debate against that kind of background noise? I believe that both the Chancellor and the Governor are cricketing enthusiasts, so I hope that there is no monopoly of cricketing metaphors. It is rather like sending your opening batsmen to the crease only for them to find, the moment the first balls are bowled, that their bats have been broken before the game by the team captain.

Geoffrey ended with an open call for others to stand against Margaret:

The time has come for others to consider their own response to the tragic conflict of loyalties with which I have myself wrestled for perhaps too long.

The reaction in the House of Commons was profound. Just a few could remember Nigel Birch's devastating attack upon Harold Macmillan during the Profumo Affair, when he quoted from Robert Browning's poem 'The Lost Leader' – 'never glad confident morning again'. Geoffrey's speech was in that class. Margaret, unlike Macmillan, did not slouch from the chamber. She kept her composure, and her face remained tight as she muttered to me on the bench, 'I didn't think he would do something like that.'

Geoffrey will be remembered for this speech more than anything else he has said. He discovered rather late in his life the gift of invective. Denis Healey had once cruelly said that to be attacked by Geoffrey Howe was like being savaged by a dead sheep. It was a pity that Geoffrey's invective had never been used so sharply upon the Opposition. Quite apart from its effect upon the Prime Minister, Geoffrey's speech was reckless and irresponsible because it sought to impale the Party on the single issue of Europe. He had become so preoccupied with this that he overlooked the fact that there were deep divisions within the Party on that subject. He was being just as divisive as Margaret in the line that he was taking. The Conservative Party has to be kept together on Europe by a judicious balance.

Charles Irving, the now retired waspish and witty MP for Cheltenham, said to me as we passed in the Lobby, 'It took Elspeth ten minutes to write that speech and Geoffrey ten years to make it.' After Geoffrey had sat down, I went round to John Major's office in the House of Commons where I found him pacing nervously up and down and quite devastated. We discussed the consequences of the speech and the possibility of a leadership challenge. John said, 'She must go on.' He knew that Margaret would have been very hurt, and he went round to her office to offer his support and comfort. I joined them later. Margaret now knew that a leadership election was inevitable – the speech had been the setting event for Michael Heseltine.

Norman Tebbit and I dined together that evening. He thought that Margaret would win a leadership contest but that above all Michael Heseltine had to be stopped. If there was a second round he didn't favour Douglas Hurd, and he wasn't at all clear who would be able to stop Heseltine or whom he would support. He was not tempted to enter the contest himself, but he never completely ruled out that possibility.

The following morning, Michael Heseltine declared his candidacy at a press conference on the steps of his house in Belgravia. 'I am persuaded,' he said, 'that I would now have a better prospect than Mrs Thatcher of leading the Conservatives to a fourth electoral victory.' He also promised a fundamental review of the poll tax. Michael was impatient to seize the leadership and he knew that this was his best chance. The Prime Minister was winged, probably fatally, and destiny was beckoning him to take over. Despite months of protestation that he would not stand against Margaret, Geoffrey's speech provided the let-out for Michael to realize his long-cherished ambition.

The campaign teams of the two candidates quickly got into position. Michael's campaign was led by Michael Mates, the burly former Army officer and backbench MP who had run Willie Whitelaw's campaign back in 1975. He was joined by Keith Hampson, Michael's former PPS. Margaret's campaign was nominally under the leadership of George Younger, but as the Chairman of the Royal Bank of Scotland, business engagements meant that George was not able to spend much time in the House talking to MPs. Norman Tebbit, in effect, became the unofficial leader of Margaret's campaign, with Norman Fowler as a spokesman for Margaret. Peter Morrison, Margaret's PPS, ran a team of MPs headed by Michael Neubert and Gerry Neale to canvass the Parliamentary Party. There was no doubt that they missed Ian Gow.

The Party Chairman has a difficult role in a leadership election. I made my personal position clear in a statement on 14 November when I said:

I believe this challenge to Mrs Thatcher's leadership is unnecessary and unwanted. We must concentrate on the task of fighting the Labour Party and ensure that the achievements of Mrs Thatcher's Premiership and the Government are not put at risk.

My own position is clear. I am one hundred per cent behind Mrs Thatcher. It is to her political skills and unprecedented electoral successes that Conservative MPs owe their position. She is entitled to expect our loyalty in return. Mrs Thatcher's leadership qualities are the greatest political assets which the Conservative Party and our nation have.

The Leader of the Conservative Party is elected solely by the electoral college of MPs, and Central Office has no constitutional role in this. I was determined therefore that the position of Central Office should not be used to influence MPs as to how they should vote. I issued written instructions to the staff of Central Office, which became known as the Baker Rules, to guide conduct over the following days. (They are printed as Appendix 3.) Alistair Burt gave a copy to Michael Heseltine's campaign to reassure them of Central Office's position. There were good reasons for issuing these rules.

First, there was a significant minority in the Parliamentary Party who were opposed to Margaret but who, nonetheless, remained members of the Party in receipt of the Conservative whip. They would certainly object most strongly if Central Office was seen to be stridently campaigning for the Leader. Moreover, after the ballot they would still be in the Party, and I wanted to ensure that whatever happened the Conservative Party was not going to be divided. If the Party machine had been used to try to influence Members of Parliament then I think that a much more fundamental split in the Party would have emerged. I was determined to avoid this.

Second, if Central Office had intervened in the constituencies by trying to bring pressure on MPs to support Margaret then, I believe, many MPs would have resented this very strongly. Indeed, such activity would have been counterproductive. Michael Heseltine's camp were just waiting for this, and if they had been given any grounds to protest at interference by the Party machine then I am quite sure it would have told against Margaret.

The Whips' Office is in a similar position. The Chief Whip, Tim Renton, knew that the Parliamentary Party was divided and that he could not use the usual processes of persuasion. This had led Ted Heath in 1975 similarly to suspect that Humphrey Atkins, then his Chief Whip, had not done enough to support him. I believe that Margaret also had this suspicion of Tim Renton, but the fact is that in a situation like this the Chief Whip is in a very difficult position. Tim summoned a meeting of the Whips and told them that they had to remain neutral and not favour either of the candidates. 'Does that mean that we can do nothing to help the Prime Minister?' one of them asked. Tim's reply was, 'You do nothing.' However, Tim could, like me, have disclosed his personal position by issuing a statement of support for Margaret, but he chose not to do so.

'Treasons, Stratagems and Spoils'

Margaret's Poor Campaign – Monday 19 November:
Eve of Poll – Tuesday 20 November: Election Day –
Wednesday 21 November: Return to London and the
Cabinet – Thursday 22 November: The Curtain Falls –
Tidying up – Epilogue

Margaret had decided that she would run her campaign as a national and world leader. Yet that was how Ted Heath had run his unsuccessful campaign in 1975 while Margaret, the challenger, had spent her entire time talking to and meeting with the Conservative Members of Parliament who are the sole electorate.

It is an occupational hazard of Prime Ministers that in their translation from politician to statesman they forget the base arts which won them office in the first place. The Civil Service machine at Number 10, with Rolls-Royce precision, takes over the lives of Prime Ministers from their Party, their friends, and their family. Prime Ministers have to be very determined to find time to drop into the Tea Room of the House, to walk over to Party headquarters or to invite a few colleagues and their wives to dinner or the theatre. And so it was with Ted and Margaret.

Cranley Onslow, the Chairman of the 1922 Committee, had been completely flabbergasted when Margaret decided to hold the leadership election on Tuesday 20 November. He had been to see her to discuss various dates, yet she had specifically chosen the time when she was going to be abroad. He sought to dissuade her but she had made up her mind very clearly about this. Cranley got the impression that it was her decision and not Charles Powell's or Bernard Ingham's. Margaret knew that on the Friday before polling day, the second day of the campaign, she would be visiting Ulster. On the Sunday she was scheduled to be in Paris for two days in order to sign the treaties which symbolized the end of the Cold War. These dates occupied the fourth, fifth, and sixth days of the campaign.

This decision to absent herself from the fray was a major mistake by

Margaret. On several occasions I urged her to postpone the Ulster visit and let Douglas Hurd, as her Foreign Secretary, sign the Paris treaties in her stead. Who now remembers which political leaders attended that Paris meeting?

Moreover, Margaret was going to be escorted around Ulster by Richard Needham, one of the Northern Ireland Ministers, who only a few days earlier had referred to her on a car phone as 'that cow'. This conversation had been intercepted by one of the terrorist organizations and released to cause embarrassment to him and to her. Margaret's absence from her own campaign was doubly damaging because her proposer, Douglas, in any event a fairly diffident campaigner, was going to be in Paris with her. John Major, her seconder, was not in London at all, as he entered hospital on the Saturday for a wisdom tooth operation and was literally silent on Margaret's behalf.

Michael Heseltine, in the meantime, was campaigning vigorously for himself. He had never really cared for the social life of the House of Commons, but from Thursday morning he haunted the place. I had never before seen him in the Tea Room, and he only went into the Smoking Room after he had made a successful speech. He was rarely to be seen in the Dining Room. But now he was everywhere, striding down the Library corridor, and standing in the Members' Lobby with a list in his hand containing the names of MPs his team had told him to speak to. Over the weekend, Michael gave television interviews and was much photographed with his family at their country house. These were the obligatory obeisances to the outer world which any candidate has to make. More important work was done on the telephone talking to the doubters among Tory MPs.

Even as late as Friday and Saturday, I urged Margaret to stay in London on the following Monday, but she was determined to go to Paris. Margaret had decided that the best way for the Party to see her was as a world leader. On Thursday, five days later, after she had resigned, we were sitting around the Cabinet table in a prolonged wake. The conversation turned to her campaign and she leant over the table and said to me, 'You told me that I would have had to do something about the community charge. I would have found that difficult. You also told me that I would have had to ring up MPs and spend my time in the Tea Room. That's not for me after eleven years.'

The rules for the election of a Conservative Party Leader require certain things to happen. Each MP has to sound out the views of his or her Conservative Constituency Association, which they should take into account but are not bound to follow. I met the officers of the Mole Valley Association and they were unanimous in their support of Margaret, but they made it clear that they wanted certain changes, particularly to the community charge.

Many MPs rang me up over the weekend and my estimate was that they broadly supported Margaret. Sir Peter Lane, the President of the National Union, also had to collect the views of the Area Chairmen who in turn had spoken to the Chairman of each Association. Only one Area Chairman supported Michael Heseltine. Peter was frequently told that if Heseltine were to win then the Party would split, because his campaign to bring down Margaret was seen as disloyal. If Michael had won it would have been very difficult indeed for him to have kept the Party together and I suspect he would have had to call a General Election very quickly. On his side there would have been the many Conservatives whose instinctive attitude is to support the Leader of the day whosoever it may be. But, certainly, some Ministers would not have served under Michael, and the Thatcherite MPs would have tried to destroy his authority.

Margaret decided to communicate her views to the public and the Party, who she hoped would influence their MPs, by giving newspaper interviews to Charles Moore of the *Sunday Telegraph* and Michael Jones of the *Sunday Times*. She had rejected the idea of television interviews, despite the fact that Michael was ever-present on the screen. She robustly defended her record and her style while dismissing the idea that she couldn't unite the Party. 'So who are these unifying figures?' she asked. 'I have had to fight so many things through. I still have much to do. The younger generation are very much for the things I stand for.' Margaret had been nettled by Geoffrey's reference to a 'ghetto of sentimentality'. 'Absurd,' she said. 'I don't live in one. Nothing wrong with being proud of our own traditions. Everything that is regarded as civilized came from different parts of Europe and not from one central domination.'

On Saturday evening I went down to Chequers with Mary for dinner. We arrived just as Margaret had finished giving an interview to Simon Jenkins for Monday's edition of the *Times*. This turned out to be a good deal more abrasive than her previous interviews, and the *Times* headline on the Monday was to read, 'Thatcher accuses Heseltine of Labour policies'. This attack was misjudged, and more damaging to Margaret

391

than to Michael, but I had arrived too late to do anything about it. When Richard Ryder, the Financial Secretary to the Treasury, whose wife Caroline had been Margaret's diary secretary, and who therefore knew Margaret well, learnt over the weekend from Simon Jenkins about the interview, his heart sank as he felt it would seriously damage Margaret's chances. This proved to be the case, for on Monday the interview was not well received by Tory MPs.

At dinner that night the other guests and their wives were Tim Bell, Gordon Reece, Alistair McAlpine and John Whittingdale, together with Margaret's campaign team of Peter Morrison, Michael Neubert, Gerry Neale, and Mark and Carol Thatcher. Over dinner I told Margaret again that after it was all over we would have to do something fundamental about the community charge, for this was the clear message coming back from MPs. I didn't get the customary blunt dismissal.

After the dinner I gave a short toast to longevity, and while the less active members of the party retired to the drawing-room the rest of us got down to the practicalities of the campaign. The Sunday papers were all going to carry polls saying that the Tories would have a much better chance under Michael Heseltine. I wanted Margaret to appear on television late on Sunday and again on Monday, but she was leaving for Paris the next afternoon. Peter Morrison reported that as a result of the team's canvassing she would get between 230 and 240 votes and Michael would get below 100. I considered this was far too optimistic, as from my own soundings the Heseltine vote was already in excess of 120 and could reach 150. Earlier in the week Tim Bell, Brendan Bruce and Tony Kerpel had estimated a ballpark figure which gave Margaret 200 votes, Michael 140, with forty abstentions. This made the result too close to call, given the extra margin required for victory. The atmosphere at Chequers was far too complacent, and much of the discussion centred upon what we would have to do in order to unite the Party after Margaret won. Gordon Reece stayed behind after the dinner and made a last attempt to persuade Margaret not to go to Paris. 'Gordon,' she said, 'if I pull out now, MPs will say that I am running scared and think I am going to lose. That would be even worse. No, the decision is made.'

The Sunday press was very hostile to Margaret. Andrew Neil at the *Sunday Times*, the Murdoch press flagship, came out against her. But then he had always favoured a Heseltine/Walker alliance, indeed he had worked with Peter Walker earlier in his career. Stewart Steven at the *Mail on Sunday*, an important newspaper for Conservatives, also came out against Margaret. So predictably did the *Observer*, the *Independent* and the *Sunday Correspondent*. Only the *Sunday Telegraph*, the *Sunday Express* and the *News of the World* remained loyal to her. Ladbrokes made Margaret favourite at 1–3, with Heseltine quoted at 7–2.

I spent much of the day on the telephone checking, reassuring, persuading and assessing. Both Chris Patten and Richard Needham told me that some Ministers would vote against Margaret. Richard said, 'She is in for a real shock,' but Chris believed, 'She'll win on the first ballot, probably quite easily, but it will be pretty bloody.' John Lee, my former PPS and a close friend, who represented the marginal seat of Pendle which had been particularly hard hit by the poll tax, was actively campaigning for Michael Heseltine. He predicted that Michael would do very well, and that there would be a second ballot which Michael would win. Douglas Hurd, on the other hand, said he had a hunch that Margaret would win. This was after a good deal of telephoning, which led him to say: 'There's a pricking in my thumbs.'

Monday 19 November – Eve of Poll

On Monday, the day before the election, I spoke to John Wakeham – an experienced hand who had been Chief Whip, Leader of the House, and was now Energy Secretary – and told him early in the morning that in my view it was going to be very close and we should prepare for a second ballot. We agreed to meet later that morning to discuss this in the Prime Minister's room at the House of Commons. At this meeting George Younger, John Moore, John Wakeham, Norman Tebbit, Cranley Onslow, Tim Renton, Peter Morrison and Gerry Neale were present. We assessed the possible results. The voting system was complicated. To win on the first ballot a candidate was required to have an overall majority of those entitled to vote plus a 15 per cent margin over the next candidate. Since the electoral college numbered 372 votes, then in order to win the Prime Minister needed a minimum of 187 votes and to be fifty-six votes ahead of Heseltine. The difficult area lay where the Prime Minister got between 187 and 210 votes, while Heseltine got between 132 and 155 votes. This would mean a second ballot. This would be conducted along simpler lines, with an overall majority being sufficient without the requirement of an extra margin. If a third ballot was required because of other candidates entering the race then the system used would be the single transferable vote.

This exceptional and extraordinary electoral system had been devised by Humphrey Berkeley in 1964, and it has been much criticized. However, many people around the world marvelled at a procedure that allowed a Party with a large overall majority to change its popular and successful leader – a world figure – within the short space of two weeks and without rancour and mayhem, while remaining a united Party still in office. Although the 1922 Executive decided in 1990 to change the rules slightly by requiring more Tory MPs to sign any proposal for a leadership candidate to stand, the rules have remained essentially the same.

Tim Renton felt that if Margaret won only 187 votes then she couldn't go on as Leader to the second ballot with only half the Parliamentary Party supporting her. Peter Morrison maintained that she would want to fight a second round because even with those figures she would have won the majority of the votes cast. If Margaret continued to stand, then no member of the Cabinet would be willing to stand against her. The only possible new entrant of any significance would be Geoffrey Howe. The discussion then turned to what Margaret should say if there was no decisive result. Norman Tebbit was certain, saying, 'If she does not immediately make a clear statement of her intent to carry on, then it is a lost cause and she has to withdraw. So to keep her options open she must make a clear statement.' George Younger said that if the result was inconclusive then, 'Several people have told me that she must think very carefully, as several members of the Cabinet will advise her not to go on.'

I put forward the view which I had earlier expressed to John Wakeham, that Margaret should not be so definite. I suggested three alternative statements for her to make – 'I intend to let my name go forward to the second ballot'; 'I wish to consult my colleagues'; and, 'It would not be appropriate for me to say any more until I return to London.' I suggested the latter two, because much of the criticism directed against Margaret was that she did not consult her colleagues, and it would be better if she said she intended to return to London to consult them. This would have two advantages. First the Heseltine camp would be thrown into confusion, and secondly by the Wednesday morning there would be a whole army of people – Ministers, Party officers, and MPs – marching to Downing Street insisting that Margaret had to continue.

However, other views prevailed. I think that those colleagues thought my views were too defeatist. Peter Morrison was clearly impatient at even having to discuss all this, since he believed that such an outcome was beyond the bounds of possibility. It was then agreed that the form of words to be used by Margaret would be: 'I am pleased that more than half the Parliamentary Party voted for me and I would like to thank all my supporters. Nevertheless, I am disappointed that it is necessary to have a second ballot. According to the rules laid down by the 1922 Committee nominations are now open for the next round. I can confirm that it is my intention to let my name go forward to the second ballot.' All that I had secured in the way of time to consult was the insertion of Margaret's 'intention' to stand.

We then briefly discussed what would happen in the event of a defeat, but one which still required a further round of voting without the Prime Minister. This was uncharted ground, and a brief on the constitutional consequences had been prepared. The Palace was keen that the Prime Minister should continue until a successor had been elected.

During the course of Monday I spoke to John Wakeham, Tim Renton and briefly to Norman Tebbit about the need to find a 'stop Heseltine' candidate in the event of Margaret being fatally wounded. Towards the end of the previous week it looked as if Douglas Hurd was the front runner for this position, although he had told his PPS, Tim Yeo, the MP for Suffolk South, 'Don't go scurrying around the House on my behalf.' But Douglas had said over the weekend that in certain circumstances he would be prepared to stand for the leadership, but 'not against her'. However, the weekend press had questioned Douglas's capacity to campaign effectively against Neil Kinnock in a General Election. Norman Tebbit did not want 'Hong Kong Hurd' and preferred John Major, but the difficulty was that John was too young, untried and not very well known. Norman thought that if he stood himself he would only get between twenty and forty votes. For myself I thought that Michael Heseltine, after a leadership election which divided the Party, would not beat Kinnock in a General Election and that the only one who could be counted upon to do that was Margaret.

In the afternoon I went to see Willie Whitelaw in his small, narrow office in the House of Lords. He was still of the view that if a third of the Party voted against Margaret, that is to say 124 MPs, then she would have to go. Willie was very concerned about Michael Heseltine. He wanted Douglas as an alternative leader, but 'he is happy as Foreign Secretary and he is not really suited for a ruthless campaign against Kinnock. The trouble with Douglas was the same with me in 1975. He doesn't really want the job.' Willie then also said, 'I expect John Major will stand. Many will vote for him thinking that he is on the right wing. They'll be disappointed and soon find out that he isn't.'

I spoke on the telephone to John Major, who was recuperating at his Huntingdon home after the operation on his wisdom teeth, and said, 'We really miss you from the campaign. It's touch and go.' I had also heard that Norman Lamont and Robert Atkins, over the weekend, had been promoting John as a candidate in the event of Margaret's defeat. 'So many people are talking up your chances that I assume there is some campaign running on your behalf,' I said. John vehemently denied this, and said he had been discouraging his friends from promoting his name as a candidate.

Later that night I went to see Peter Morrison, who said that his latest canvassing returns showed that the Prime Minister could get as many as 245 votes but probably would receive 230 after allowing for the 'fib factor'. Michael Heseltine would get 100 if he was lucky. I took a £10 bet with Peter that Michael Heseltine would be nearer to 150 than 100, in the hope that Peter would see that there was still work to be done.

Tuesday 20 November: Election Day

Margaret's campaign team reconvened on the Tuesday morning at 11.15 a.m. and confirmed the line which the Prime Minister had by then agreed. I again urged more flexibility, as I had learnt that some Ministers who would vote for her in the first ballot might not vote for her in the second. My view was still that she should come back to the UK and consult her colleagues about going on, as a decision made in Paris would be seen as high-handed. Norman Tebbit was very opposed to this, saying that if she didn't straightaway declare she was going on 'then support would immediately haemorrhage'. I said, 'What can we do about Ken Clarke, Chris Patten and Douglas Hurd?', as I anticipated their hostile reaction to this line. John Wakeham optimistically said, 'If she makes that statement they will have to back it.'

The atmosphere in the House prior to the voting was quite calm. Packs of journalists stood outside Committee Room 12, as did some members of the Labour Party, like Dennis Skinner, sneering and sniping. At 6 p.m. John Wakeham, Norman Tebbit, Gerry Neale, Michael Neubert, Tim Bell, Gordon Reece, John Whittingdale, David Waddington, John Moore, Mark Lennox Boyd, Tony Newton, Alistair McAlpine, Brendan Bruce, Tony Kerpel and I gathered in the Prime

Minister's room in the House of Commons. The general air was still a confident one. At 6.30 p.m. Ian Twinn, the MP for Edmonton, came down and gave us the figures. It was bad news: 204 for Margaret, 152 for Michael Heseltine, and sixteen abstentions. The Prime Minister had a majority of fifty-two, just four votes short of the fifty-six majority that she needed. If two Conservative MPs had voted the other way she would have been safe. Tim Renton telephoned the news to Peter Morrison in Paris. After briefly digesting the figures Margaret came straight out on to the steps of the British Embassy and rapidly descending them asked where the 'pool' microphone was. The BBC's intrepid political reporter, John Sargeant, who had been addressing the camera and had his back to Margaret, was alerted to her arrival and achieved his place in history by spinning round, defying Bernard Ingham and thrusting the BBC's microphone into her face, crying out, 'Here's the microphone Prime Minister.' Margaret then made her prepared statement, saying, 'I am naturally very pleased that I got more than half the Parliamentary Party, and disappointed that's not quite enough to win on the first ballot. So I confirm it is my intention to let my name go forward for the second ballot.'

As I had predicted, this was a mistake. The comments back at Westminster that evening were that the Prime Minister had reached this decision all alone; it was typical of her style, and far too gung-ho. The speed and brusqueness of the announcement represented all that her critics found wrong with her style. I left the House to appear on the TV news programmes where I stressed that Margaret had got 55 per cent of the vote and that under any other system this would have led to a clear victory. With a majority of fifty-two, winners do not throw in the towel. I also said that the Cabinet was united behind Margaret. This proved to be a rather rash statement. Margaret phoned me from Paris to thank me for my efforts and I said to her, 'You must get back to London. Can you be here tonight?' But she said she had to attend an official dinner and a musical entertainment.

I was later told that Douglas Hurd, who was with Margaret in Paris, became annoyed when Charles Powell, Margaret's civil service Private Secretary, urged him to sign Margaret's second ballot nomination form. As Foreign Secretary, Douglas rightly felt that it was improper for a civil servant to act in this way, but he was also angry at being bounced into immediate support for Margaret.

On returning to the House of Commons I was passing through the small antechamber behind the Speaker's Chair when I met a group of five Cabinet Ministers. They were Chris Patten, William Waldegrave, Malcolm Rifkind and Tony Newton, and the group was led by Norman Lamont. They told me that they had met earlier in the evening, with several other Ministers and MPs, at the home of Tristan Garel-Jones in Catherine Place. They had gone on to see the Chief Whip, Tim Renton. They were looking worried, and a bit flushed and flustered. Norman Lamont acted as spokesman and said that it was their unanimous view that 'Margaret should withdraw, as she will lose the second ballot, although we will all vote for her.' The clear impression I got was this group were searching for an executioner. They had tried the Chief Whip and now they were trying to recruit the Party Chairman. The fact that I was not prepared to play this role dismayed them all and angered some.

Later that night the news leaked out that this group of five Cabinet Ministers, together with another five or six Ministers and Whips, had been invited by Tristan Garel-Jones, the Deputy Chief Whip, to a meeting at his house. The participants had been selected carefully and their anxieties, apprehensions and ambitions must have been fully known. Norman Lamont thought that he was being invited to a small dinner party, although in the event only drinks were served. Chris Patten believed the invitation was an impromptu one. Search parties were sent to look for Ken Clarke, but he was actually appearing on TV that night extolling the leadership qualities of the Prime Minister. Others had known of the meeting before noon, that is to say six hours before the close of poll.

Some at the Catherine Place meeting genuinely believed that Margaret could not win on the second ballot. Others saw this as an opportunity to get rid of a Leader they did not like and who they thought was an electoral liability. The only factor uniting these two groups was a determination to stop Michael Heseltine. This meant persuading Margaret to stand down to allow other candidates to enter the lists. But there was no agreement as to who those candidates should be, or whether there should just be one candidate to oppose Heseltine. The majority of those present supported Douglas Hurd, which surprised Norman Lamont. He was fully committed to John Major as an alternative candidate and resented some disparaging remarks made about John.

There was some surprise that Alan Clark was at this meeting. He was the amusing and eccentric Defence Minister, who one felt was never really busy, at least in his own Department's work. He was an ardent admirer of Margaret, and clearly on the right of the Party. Tristan had been astute in inviting him, since it gave the impression to the rest that the Right was deserting Margaret, which it was not. Alan had been at loggerheads with his boss, Tom King, the Defence Secretary, over the need for a new defence strategy, and he'd used his back channels to Number 10 to get his views across. He was contemptuous of Tom, whose stolid approach had served him well in several Departments and made him well liked in the Party, but to everyone's surprise Alan suggested that Tom should stand as a candidate for the leadership. This was met with incredulity.

The Catherine Place meeting was important because it cemented together a disparate group of individuals who then became committed to a common purpose. Over the previous days there had been many discussions and conversations which revealed a considerable degree of disgruntlement with Margaret. But the Catherine Place meeting became a setting event because individual disgruntlement was turned into collective action. If any were inclined to waver in their support of Margaret they now knew that they could count upon a degree of collective support for this position. I am sure that every person who attended this meeting would deny that he was a plotter, and some would never have seen themselves in that light. But in effect when a collective course of action has been agreed upon to achieve a common goal then there is that sense of purpose which every plot has to have. While daggers were not issued, guns not loaded, gunpowder barrels not installed, instead regulation grey suits were issued for the solemn procession of those who were to see the Leader the following day with their avowals of total loyalty accompanied by frank assessments of her inevitable defeat. Of such stuff is modern political assassination made.

Following this encounter I continued my rounds and met several other MPs who were still in the House. But I only found one, Dudley Fishburn, who was thinking of switching to Michael Heseltine in the second vote, though the Whips in their trawl had identified twelve switchers. The very thing that the proponents of a clear statement had sought to avoid – the ebbing away of support for Margaret – was happening. But those who wanted Margaret to remain as Leader and contest the second ballot were at that time silent, unaware of the campaign to get her to stand down.

Back at Number 10 that evening Brian Griffiths, faithful and industrious to the last, was preparing yet another paper on the reform of the poll tax. Over at Tim Bell's office, Nick True, later himself to be a member of

John Major's Policy Unit at Number 10, was working with others on a strategy to save the Prime Minister when the fax machine began to churn out Brian Griffiths' latest proposals. It was rather like issuing new hymn sheets to the band on the *Titanic*.

Wednesday 21 November: Return to London and the Cabinet

Early the following morning I had a meeting at Central Office with my inner team, plus Tim Bell and Gordon Reece, all of whom wanted Margaret to go on. We hammered out a campaign for the second round, the key to which was that Margaret was the only candidate who could stop Heseltine. Certainly, the Frightened Five of the night before were not agreed on any alternative candidate who would be able to win against the strong Heseltine campaign machine, which now had considerable momentum. Our strategy consisted of Margaret making no more attacks upon Michael, getting her to campaign personally among MPs, and involving actively in her campaign Douglas Hurd, John Major, Norman Fowler and Chris Patten. The strategy also depended upon a united Cabinet backing her.

At midday I went to see John MacGregor in the Lord President's office in Whitehall. We sat in the two red leather easy chairs facing the large bow window of that rather empty room looking out on to Horseguards Parade. At John Wakeham's suggestion, John MacGregor had been sounding out the Cabinet and had discovered that ten of them thought Margaret would be defeated if she went on. They felt it would be better if either Douglas or John Major were to stand, or even both of them. John MacGregor had also contacted middle-ranking Ministers, not asking them this same question, but he found that there was virtually no change in the way they intended to vote. Those who had supported Margaret intended to continue doing so.

Tim Renton joined us and said that in addition to the twelve MPs whom he'd identified as going over to Heseltine the night before, the Whips had found an additional thirteen, bringing the total to twenty-five. But he thought that was the full extent of any defection. This could only be a vague estimate, and should have been presented as such, since several of the Whips had not been able to contact the MPs with whom they usually dealt. Overall, the Whips' Office view was that it was still Margaret who had the best chance against Heseltine, but Tim told me privately that it was too close to call and he thought Michael could win.

During the morning Margaret had returned from Paris. She met John Wakeham and Norman Tebbit in her sitting-room on the first floor of Number 10. John had just arrived after having launched at the Cumberland Hotel the prospectus for the sale of the twelve regional electricity companies. His advice to Margaret was clear: first, there was no dishonour in standing and being defeated. Second, if she was not going to stand, then the question everybody had to ask was who else could lead a united Party? As Margaret appeared to be the only person to fit the bill he considered this to be her key card.

I went over to Number 10 and joined Margaret and the others just after 1 p.m. in the Cabinet Room, where we had sandwiches and some white wine. The sandwiches were rather better than usual and they passed up and down the table, but the Prime Minister only nibbled at one. She asked me to report first. I said that the reaction from the Party workers that morning via messages sent to Central Office had been 90 per cent in her favour. There was great apprehension about a Heseltine takeover of the Party. Margaret was seen as the only one who could win against Michael. I then set out my strategy for handling the second round.

Margaret next turned to John MacGregor, but he did not tell her the views of the ten Cabinet Ministers opposed to her standing, since Cranley Onslow and Norman Tebbit, who were sitting at the table, were not themselves Ministers. But John did tell Margaret about the views of the Ministers of State, and Tim Renton told her about the Whips' soundings. Cranley Onslow reported that he had summoned that morning a meeting of the 1922 Executive and they did not want Michael Heseltine to become Leader. There was no strong feeling that Margaret should stand down from the second ballot, but some wanted a wider choice of candidates. Norman Tebbit said little at this meeting but he emphasized the point that if Margaret was not the candidate then who would be the Cabinet's choice to stop Heseltine?

Margaret listened very carefully to all of this and was very calm throughout. She had become convinced that she had a mission to save the Party from Michael Heseltine because he believed in everything that she had opposed for the last eleven years. I reminded her that this time she would have to campaign personally.

I learnt later that while we were lunching at Number 10, three of Margaret's closest friends, who were also lunching together, rang John Major at his home in Huntingdon. They urged him to return to London immediately and to go on television to express his strongest support for the Prime Minister. His surprising reply to these entreaties was, 'I'll have to think about it.'

After our meeting in the Cabinet Room broke up, Margaret went to prepare her statement to the House of Commons on the outcome of her Paris meeting. In the hall outside the Cabinet Room John MacGregor said to John Wakeham, 'I didn't have a chance to tell her that the Cabinet is not unanimous.' I went with John Wakeham to the Political Secretary's office, just outside the Cabinet Room, to discuss who should be Margaret's campaign manager for the second ballot, because George Younger clearly could not spare the time. John suggested Ken Clarke, which I thought was utterly unrealistic as I had been told that his views were exactly the same as those who met at Garel-Jones' house. John was then amazed to find that he could not persuade three of his ex-Whips, Alastair Goodlad, Tristan Garel-Jones and Richard Ryder, or his own Parliamentary Private Secretary, Andrew Mitchell, to join him in running Margaret's campaign. They all thought she would lose. So by four o'clock Norman Tebbit, who had already taken over much of the direction of Margaret's inner office, put out a statement that John Wakeham was to be her campaign manager – an announcement which considerably annoyed John.

When Margaret left for the Commons at 3.15 p.m. to make her statement on the Paris CSCE meeting she said to shouted questions from reporters as she was getting into her car, 'I fight on. I fight to win.' Her Paris statement was a strong performance in which she dominated the House. After she sat down in the Chamber, she was taken to the Tea Room by Norman Tebbit – a long overdue appearance among the electorate.

At four o'clock Michael Heseltine came to see me in my room at the House. I had wanted to discuss with him details of how the next round would be conducted as far as the Party was concerned. The room happened to be his old one when he was Secretary of State for Defence, and he went straight to the most comfortable sofa. He knew that Margaret intended to stand and was quite relaxed and confident, indeed he was happy about it. He believed he was going to win, and he was on a high. His adrenalin was pumping and, full of confidence, he said to me, 'This is a wonderful ego trip.' He also added, 'Don't worry Kenneth. There'll be a big job for you.' I forebore to ask him what that was going to be.

I passed Margaret as she was returning to her own room at 5 p.m., and at that time she was still determined to fight on. In Paris the previous evening, Peter Morrison had advised Margaret to see the Cabinet individually on her return. He had given this advice because he wanted to avoid a row, as he had heard that two Cabinet Ministers – Ken Clarke and Malcolm Rifkind – could possibly resign if Margaret continued in office. He believed this would have been exceptionally damaging if these resignations had taken place after a collective Cabinet discussion. But on her return Margaret had not definitely accepted Peter's advice because she then asked John Wakeham for his view. He said quite decisively that she should see her Ministers individually. Margaret's first reaction was to say, 'I can't. I've got to make a statement to the House and then see the Queen.' John said, 'You will just have to make the time.' I think the advice from Peter and John to see the Cabinet individually was a major mistake, particularly as the first question put to each Minister by Margaret was, 'Do you think I should go on?'

Prior to this fatal exercise Peter Morrison told the Prime Minister of the soundings which John MacGregor had taken that morning. Margaret then went to the Palace for her regular audience with the Queen. Afterwards she would have preferred to return to Number 10 to work on her speech for the censure motion tabled by Labour who were hoping to exploit Tory divisions, but instead returned to the House to see the Cabinet one by one. Margaret briefly saw two trusted friends who were not in the Cabinet, Francis Maude and Michael Forsyth. Francis followed his Treasury colleagues' line that she couldn't win and that above all they must stop Heseltine. But Michael told her she would win and she must go on.

John Whittingdale, Margaret's Political Secretary, had realized that Margaret needed formal renomination and this required John Major's signature, alongside that of Douglas Hurd. Alistair McAlpine later told me that Margaret telephoned John at Huntingdon and asked, 'Will you please second my nomination?' There was a long pause, and she repeated the question. He replied, 'If that's what you want me to do, I'll do it.' John Whittingdale was told that no civil servant could handle the nomination paper and it had to be done through someone on the Party side. So Jeffrey Archer was asked to arrange for the nomination paper to be delivered to John Major at Huntingdon. The paper read, 'The undersigned is willing to stand as leader of the Conservative Party.' Margaret had signed it and had been proposed by Douglas Hurd. John Major's signature was needed to second it. As Jeffrey was leaving at 5.30 p.m., Bernard Ingham rushed past him saying, 'Jeffrey, you couldn't write it. Jeffrey, you couldn't write it.' Bernard rather over-looked the fact that he was addressing this comment to one of the world's bestselling authors of political fiction novels.

The Prime Minister began seeing the Cabinet one by one at about 6 p.m., and the next two hours proved decisive. Margaret sat on the end of the sofa next to the fireplace and her Ministers sat on the sofa facing her. Only Peter Morrison was present for all the interviews. The first person to be consulted was Douglas Hurd, to whom I spoke afterwards in the Speakers' Corridor. He said he had agreed to nominate her again – 'Well I'll do it because she wants me to do it and that's that.' He did not tell Margaret that in his opinion she shouldn't stand but did tell her that she must stop attacking Michael Heseltine. Cecil Parkinson was an early visitor and told Margaret that she must carry on and would win with a better campaign.

The Cabinet Ministers were now all coming to the House of Commons in order to see the Prime Minister. The exception was David Hunt who, being abroad, telephoned his support. The Prime Minister's room is on the same level as the Chamber of the House of Commons. It is reached by a narrow corridor that passes the Chancellor of the Exchequer's Room and crosses a landing on the backstairs that lead up to the first floor where the Cabinet Ministers' rooms are located. There was much toing and froing on that staircase for the next three hours. Suddenly I met Alan Clark on the backstairs. Like the Ancient Mariner he was stopping one in three. He urged me to get Margaret to fight on, for 'she may lose but she might win but if she is going to go down, she must go down fighting'.

I went up to Chris Patten's office, right at the end of the Ministers' corridor, where I also found Ken Clarke, Tristan Garel-Jones, Richard Ryder and Alistair Goodlad. Chris said with some heat as soon as I stepped into the room, 'Her decision to go ahead is disastrous.' I replied that in a head-to-head single contest with Michael Heseltine, Margaret was the only one who could beat him. 'If she stands she will win,' I said. Chris replied, 'All right, if she wins she wins by a few votes, but what has she won? What sort of victory is that – a broken Party? She should stand down and let other people come forward. Anyway, the evidence I'm getting is that she won't win.'

I was not convinced of that at all. In a Heseltine-Thatcher run-off it was clear there was not going to be an overwhelming majority for either candidate. But what was clear was that this group of Ministers really did want a change of leader. Ken Clarke was even angrier, saying, 'If she decides to stand then I want a full meeting of the Cabinet tonight.' I was to hear that request several times over the next two hours. I replied, 'Your demand is unnecessary because the Cabinet is meeting tomorrow at 9 a.m. and anyone can say what they want around the table. However, I do agree it would have been better to have thrashed it out with all the voices around the table rather than Margaret seeing each of us individually.'

This group was very angry that I had advised Margaret to stand again. But they failed to appreciate that this was not simply my personal view. As Chairman of the Party I was faithfully and accurately reflecting the overwhelming view of the Party activists, including these Ministers' own constituency officers. They wanted a grey-suited executioner from Central Office but were disappointed that I refused to sign up to their cause.

John Wakeham had urged each member of the Cabinet as they went in to see Margaret to be absolutely frank. In the event that was unnecessary advice. By 6.30 p.m. he had compiled a list of those Ministers who had told her she could not win. He had recently added to this list the names of Peter Lilley and Michael Howard, two of Margaret's soulmates.

Peter Lilley had decided after the first vote that Margaret would not win the second ballot. He seems to have been particularly influenced by certain Members of Parliament, such as Andrew Mitchell and James Arbuthnot, saying that they could no longer vote for her. Peter had written a letter to Margaret setting out his views but which he never actually sent, since Cabinet Ministers had by then been asked to go and see her personally. Peter still has this letter. In his interview with Margaret he said that he had come regretfully to the view that she could not win. This had a profound effect upon her. Those who positively wanted her to go could not have expected to have had such an ally from her wing of the Party.

While I was with John Wakeham, John Gummer arrived. He was also one of Margaret's greatest supporters and had contributed to some of her best speeches. But he too was convinced that she could not win and sadly told her so. Shortly afterwards I went to one of the Ministers' rooms in the Upper Corridor where I found Tom King, Malcolm Rifkind and Peter Brooke, who was wearing a white tie as he was off to some City function. Peter said that as Ulster Secretary he was out of touch with backbench opinion but would support Margaret in the second ballot. Tom, instinctively loyal and representing the Shire element of the Tory Party, said that he too would support her but that she should make clear she would stand down at some time in the future. I, of course, knew Malcolm's position from the night before. He calmly restated it, and added that if Margaret only won the second ballot narrowly then her authority would be fatally undermined. He intended to tell her that.

I went in to see Margaret at about 7.30 p.m. By this time she had also seen David Waddington, Ken Clarke and Chris Patten. She had received so much bad news that she was now adding to her comments the droll observation, 'It's a funny old world.' David, the Home Secretary, Margaret's former Chief Whip and one of the most loyal members of her Cabinet, pledged his support for her whatever she was going to do but said that in his view she would lose. Ken Clarke, on the other hand, had been her bluntest visitor. Although he had great respect for Margaret he had come to the conclusion that she was now an electoral liability to the Party. He had told me that, 'She couldn't count on my vote next time.' He told her that going on was like the Charge of the Light Brigade. He said, 'The fight is over. The battle is lost. You should withdraw from the field'. He made clear that he could not go on defending her as he had done on television the previous night. Margaret tried to rally him to her support but failed. Ken spent the rest of the evening in the House, busily contacting other Tory MPs and telling them that if Margaret stood again, 'I will resign as we are crashing on to great folly'. When he left the House late that night he was convinced that she was going to go on.

Margaret's talk with Chris Patten had been courteous and dignified. His advice was that she would not win, but if she decided to stand he would not resign. William Waldegrave was one of the last Ministers to see Margaret and he found her rather flat. He told her, 'I will vote for you on the second ballot.' 'William,' she said, 'that's not enough. Will you campaign for me?' 'Yes, but I don't think you can win,' he replied.

Norman Tebbit then joined us, taking a very confident line that everything would be all right. However, Peter Morrison had been present at all the interviews and by eight o'clock he was of the view that Margaret would decide she really could not go on. At about this time, the '92 Group, led by Edward Leigh and Gerald Howarth, demanded to see her; about ten Members, some of whom earlier in the morning were doubtful that she could win, were now quite convinced that she could because wavering votes were coming back to her. These loyalist MPs had obviously been prompted by the rumours beginning to circulate that the Cabinet had gone soft.

I went back to Chris Patten's room and found much the same group as before gathered together. They were angry because they thought that even after meeting them Margaret had decided to carry on. 'Intolerable, she's bounced John and Douglas,' they said, and again I had the demand for a meeting of the Cabinet at 11 p.m. that night. They were angry that the Catherine Place scenario of a contest involving new candidates looked like being frustrated. However, John Wakeham, who had also seen several of the Cabinet Ministers after their meeting with Margaret, was now clear that she could not go on.

One of the problems of the last days was that John Wakeham had been preoccupied with the privatization of the electricity industry. He was not completely up to date with backbench feeling. This meant that one of the most experienced politicians in the black arts of persuasion, cajoling and threatening was reduced to relying on hearsay. John expected Margaret to win, but when the possibility of defeat arose during the course of the afternoon, he was at sea. I remember him sitting in the antechamber outside the Prime Minister's office slightly bewildered and making up lists of those for and against. John has a tidy Whip's mind, which focuses sharply upon immediate events and tries to find a safe course through them. He had decided that the crucial matter was the opinion of the Cabinet. In what had become a very ragged afternoon and evening his approach was, 'This is a Party problem. Well let's see what can be done about it.' My own approach was, 'We must do all that we can to save Margaret.'

Following all her interviews I saw Margaret just before she left her room. She was pale, subdued and shaking her head, saying, 'I am not a quitter, I am not a quitter.' But the tone was one of resignation, not defiance, and as our eyes met we both knew that this was the end. She left to return to Downing Street alone. On that short journey, realizing that she would have to resign, not because of electoral defeat but because her own Cabinet had deserted her in her hour of need, she could have been forgiven for recalling Richard II's comment on his former supporters who had turned upon him, 'Yet I well remember the favours of these men: were they not mine? Did they not sometimes cry "All Hail!" to me?'

At 8.30 p.m., after Margaret had gone back to Number 10, only Peter Morrison, Norman Tebbit, Ian Twinn and I were left drinking in the little antechamber to Margaret's office in the House of Commons. Although she had not told anybody of her intention, for she was going back to talk to Denis, we all knew that she was going to stand down. One straw in the wind was that she had asked Peter Morrison to contact John Major to ensure that he had a proposer and seconder ready in the event of a wider contest. Moreover, Margaret had now to prepare her speech for Labour's censure motion the following day.

It was an extraordinary and fatal procedure to have Cabinet Ministers going in one by one to see their Leader. Almost certainly working on hearsay alone, they could not have talked a great deal to the many Members of Parliament who were about the House. They had no idea either about who they wanted to succeed Margaret. Alan Clark had put the idea that she should allow other Cabinet Ministers to stand in addition to her. For example, if Ken Clarke stood Alan felt he would siphon off some votes from Michael Heseltine – 'about thirty votes, the readers of the *Guardian* Women's page'. As the night wore on, Norman Tebbit became angrier and angrier at what he saw to be the weakness of Margaret's colleagues. He stormed off to do the late-night news bulletins determined to assert that she was going to stand, but as he left he said angrily, 'This is the last time I am going to lie on her behalf.'

The No Turning Back Group had been holding one of its regular dinners at the Institute of Economic Affairs in Lord North Street. News began to filter through to them that the Cabinet was not supporting the Prime Minister and was advising her to resign. Three of the group went back to the Smoking Room in the House of Commons – Michael Forsyth, Michael Portillo and Michael Fallon, who came to be known as 'The Three Michaels'. They sat in such gloomy silence that Michael Forsyth said it was the only time he had actually heard the clock tick in the Smoking Room. They decided that they must go to Number 10 immediately to express their support for the Prime Minister. They went over to Downing Street, where Neil Hamilton joined them, but for a time they were not allowed to see Margaret. They had done their own analysis of support and were convinced that she could win the second ballot and that she had been given incorrect information by her Cabinet. They were allowed to join her in the Cabinet Room where she was working on her speech. Neil Hamilton told her of their analysis and their support, but John Selwyn Gummer, who was also present, repeatedly contradicted their point of view.

In the meantime, Jeffrey Archer's chauffeur had driven to Huntingdon so that John Major could sign Margaret's nomination paper. The chauffeur then returned with it to his flat on the Albert Embankment. But Jeffrey couldn't sleep while he had this vital piece of paper next to him and so he decided to take it round to Number 10, handing it over to John Whittingdale at about 1 a.m. Jeffrey still believed at that time that Margaret was going to stand in the second ballot. Gordon Reece, on the other hand, had divined that she wasn't. He told Tim Bell, who was at a dinner party at the home of Nick Lloyd, the editor of the *Daily Express*. Tim then told Nick that he'd heard Margaret was likely to resign but Nick, believing this was too speculative, declined to lead his paper with that story the following morning.

Later that night I spoke to my friends John Lee and Alistair Burt, who were both Heseltine supporters. They were confident that Michael was going to win. Very much later I went off to a restaurant to join Mary, her brother, and two of our Scottish friends, who had all been to see 'Fidelio' at Covent Garden.

It was the end of a long and historic day in the history of the Conservative Party. The Prime Minister had started the day as the Leader determined to go on. She reaffirmed this when she went to the House in the afternoon, but by 8.30 p.m. that evening her confidence had been shattered by a succession of Cabinet colleagues telling her that she could not win and indeed ought to stand down. That night in Downing Street, as she penned her final speech as Prime Minister, she must have thought there was little truth in David Maxwell-Fyffe's celebrated comment that 'Loyalty is the Tory Party's secret weapon.'

Thursday 22 November: The Curtain Falls

Early on Thursday morning I was telephoned by Andrew Turnbull from Number 10 and told that the Prime Minister had decided to resign. A great leader of our country, a very great Prime Minister, had been struck down by a collective loss of nerve among her colleagues. It was the end of an era and of a very great Prime Minister.

When I arrived at Number 10 I found my fellow cabinet colleagues waiting outside the Cabinet Room in a funereal and uneasy silence, not at all keen to catch each other's eye. The Prime Minister came down the stairs a little after nine o'clock, and with head lowered went alone into the Cabinet Room. After a few minutes we were called in to take our places. Margaret looked very red-eyed and under considerable strain. She began by saying that before the formal business of the Cabinet she wanted to make her position known. She started to read from the paper in front of her, but when she reached the part which said, 'having consulted widely among colleagues', she broke down and could not continue. The words choked in her throat and she wiped away tears from her eyes. She started again falteringly and said, 'I am so sorry.' Cecil Parkinson, sitting next but one to her, suggested that the Lord Chancellor should read the statement. Margaret blew her nose, shook her head and continued, 'I have concluded that the unity of the Party and the prospects of victory in the General Election . . .' here she paused again and choked on the words, but went on, '. . . will be better served if I stood down to enable Cabinet colleagues to enter the ballot for the Leadership. I should like to thank all those in Cabinet and outside who have given me such dedicated support.'

David Waddington was dabbing his eyes at this stage, and others were close to tears. Some, while remaining expressionless, must have been relieved. But nobody around that Cabinet table had ever thought they would witness such a scene. Margaret went on, 'It is vital that we stand together. The unity of the Party is crucial and that's why I am giving up. I couldn't bear all the things I have stood for over the past eleven years being rejected. The Cabinet must unite to stop Michael Heseltine.'

Slowly Margaret recovered her composure. It had been a moving scene. Never before had she broken down in front of her colleagues. But at the end she was a real person of flesh and blood, not the cold, unfeeling automaton she was so often portrayed as. Then the Lord Chancellor, James Mackay, read the passage which Robin Butler the Cabinet Secretary had prepared for him, recording the Cabinet's tribute to Margaret's leadership of the country.

As Party Chairman I said, 'You have and will always continue to have the love and loyalty of the Party. You have a special place in the heart of the Party. You have led us to victory three times and you would have done so again.' Speaking as one of the longest-serving Cabinet Ministers, I added, 'Those who have served you recognize that they have been in touch with greatness.' Then Douglas Hurd said he wanted to place on record the superb way in which Margaret had carried herself at the Paris Conference over the last three days, especially with the pressures of the leadership election upon her.

We then turned to other matters, the business of the House and so on. When it came to Foreign Affairs, Margaret gave a spirited, very detailed and long report on her talks with Gorbachev and Bush. She was clearly getting back into her stride. But towards the end of the meeting I could see she was close to tears again.

We were all asked to stay on for coffee, which we then had sitting around the Cabinet table. We talked about the future. Margaret was very keen and insistent that it should be a member of the Cabinet who was elected to succeed her. 'I think the Cabinet will have to do everything it can to ensure this. You will have to work very hard,' she said.

During this meeting I passed a note to Douglas Hurd asking whether he had come to any agreement with John about the candidacy. I had assumed that some time over the last twenty-four hours they must have talked together about this and come to an arrangement. Douglas sent back a note saying they were going to issue a joint statement declaring that they had worked very closely together and would continue to do so but, in all the circumstances, the best way of uniting the Party would be for both to go forward in the next ballot. It would be a friendly contest. Douglas drafted this statement then and there and passed it to me. It was perfect, a masterly composition. One of Douglas' great gifts is his capacity to draft elegant statements at the drop of a pen. Norman Lamont, who had been promoting John's cause for some time – he had actually canvassed Cecil Parkinson twenty-four hours earlier – could now openly become John's campaign manager. It was clear to me that despite the disavowals of the two protagonists a good deal of preparatory work had already been done by the two camps to marshal their campaign teams.

Cecil was quite scathing about the whole situation. He said both campaigns would be negative if the contestants were going to be friendly. 'If they are going to be friendly, why bother to turn up and vote for them?' As the meeting broke up I told Cecil and Douglas that as Chairman of the Party I would make a statement to the cameras outside Number 10 on behalf of the Cabinet. I jotted something down outside the Cabinet Room, and then went out to the massed cameras opposite the front door of Number 10 and said,

This is a typically brave and selfless decision by the Prime Minister. Once again Margaret Thatcher has put her country and the Party's interests before personal considerations. This will allow the Party to elect a new leader to unite the Party and build upon her immense successes.

If I could add just a personal note, I am very saddened that our greatest peace-time Prime Minister has left Government. She is an outstanding leader, not only of our country but also of the world. I do not believe we will see her like again.

I was deeply moved by the events which I had just witnessed. I was very close to tears myself in the Cabinet Room. I had started by being cool about Margaret Thatcher, but over the years I had come to admire her. She has traits of character which can make her not particularly endearing. As Prime Minister she was personally dominant, supremely self-confident, infuriatingly stubborn and held a strange mixture of broad views and narrow prejudices. But Margaret also had a strength of character that made her a natural leader. She was a patriot, always putting the interests of Britain first. She also realized that Britain had to be saved from economic and institutional collapse. No Prime Minister I have known since the War would have seen through that tough Budget of 1981 which deepened the recession we were then going through but proved to be the foundation of the prosperity of the middle and late 1980s. No Prime Minister I have known would have had the courage to launch a sea and land offensive 8,000 miles away to secure the independence of a small group of colonial islands. No Prime Minister since the War would have withstood a miners' strike for over a year. And, no Prime Minister since the War would have reduced the power of organized labour in the way that Margaret did.

After the Cabinet was over I returned to Central Office where many people were in tears. Some had worked closely with Margaret since 1975 and seen her win three General Elections. They could not understand the ingratitude of the Parliamentary Party. I called all the staff together and spoke to them for a few minutes, for they were all very saddened and shocked. Then John Lacy and I went off to the memorial service for Lady Douglas-Home. I found myself in the pew next to Denis – his last official appearance. Margaret couldn't attend the service, as she was at Buckingham Palace letting the Queen know of her decision to resign.

It is extraordinary how in great moments of crisis I seem to be attending memorial services. I remembered Rab Butler's service at the time of the outbreak of the Falklands War. As I left Westminster Abbey, Alec Douglas-Home said he was very pleased I had been able to attend on such a historic and critical day. He is such an unassuming, gentle and lovable person.

In the afternoon I went to the House of Commons where the Prime Minister was answering questions. She had put on a bright blue suit, different from the dark one she wore at the Cabinet meeting that morning. She was crisp and witty. Elaine Kellett-Bowman, the Member for Lancaster, who had been at college with Margaret, was almost in tears when she asked her to accept 'the love and affection of millions of people in my part of the world who over the years have looked to her with the greatest admiration and delight'. Sir John Stokes, echoing the famous comment about Marie Antoinette, asked whether the Prime Minister agreed 'that the age of chivalry has gone and been succeeded by economists and calculators. Does not she look back with pride and satisfaction on all those years when she was leader of this country and a world statesman?' Margaret's graceful reply was, 'The age of chivalry will not have gone while my hon. Friend is a Member of this House.'

Opening Labour's censure motion, Neil Kinnock made a good attacking speech, but he was holed below the waterline with a simple question about the single currency. Margaret rose to enormous cheers. She strongly defended her record and it was a vintage performance. As she had said to me on the day before, 'I will defend my Government's record even if I have to resign before doing it,' and she came out fighting with all guns firing. At times she was almost skittish, especially in dealing with an intervention from Dennis Skinner, who suggested that she could become the Governor of the European Bank. 'What a good idea,' she replied. Margaret laid into Labour and it was a bravura performance. Dave Nellist, the left-wing MP for Coventry and no friend of Margaret, shouted out, 'Why did they sack you?', a question which many Tory MPs were also asking themselves. Margaret ended with these words:

Twice in my time as Prime Minister we have had to send our forces across the world to defend a small country against ruthless aggression: first to our own people in the Falklands and now to the borders of Kuwait. To those who have never had to take such decisions, I say that they are taken with a heavy heart and in the knowledge of the manifold dangers, but with tremendous pride in the professionalism and courage of our armed forces.

There is something else which one feels. That is a sense of this country's destiny: the centuries of history and experience which ensure that, when principles have to be defended, when good has to be upheld and when evil has to be overcome, Britain will take up arms. It is because we on this side have never flinched from difficult decisions that this House and this country can have confidence in this Government today.

One could not help but admire the sheer verve, vivacity and bounce that Margaret could demonstrate on the very day that she had resigned. It was a remarkable performance acclaimed by friend and foe alike.

This confirmed my conviction that if Margaret had decided not to resign but instead contest the second ballot then, having made a speech of this calibre in which she totally dominated the House of Commons, she would have won. Her task then would have been to reunite a divided

Parliamentary Party in the teeth of a media barrage directed against the Conservatives. However, with the Gulf War about to erupt into open conflict in early January I believe that the Party issue would have become submerged in the wider national consideration about the fighting itself. Margaret would have been in her element as the Warrior Queen, and following the recapture of Kuwait and the defeat of Saddam Hussein would probably have called a General Election. Although the poll tax would still have been an issue, I believe that the severity of the leadership challenge to Margaret would have persuaded her to make significant adjustments to it. One should also remember that at this time inflation was falling, there was no apparent economic recession, and the issue of Europe had not reached crisis point. In a head-to-head battle with Neil Kinnock, Margaret would have won a fourth successive term, albeit with a reduced majority. All this, however, is one of the great 'ifs' of history, and the muse of history has no compassion for the future.

After the vote that evening, I had a long whisky with Margaret in her room. She was still resilient and looked as if she had freshly stepped off a boat after a great tour. We talked about her campaign, and how John and Douglas' campaigns could be improved if they were handled professionally. John came in for a chat, and I advised him to say something soon about overhauling the community charge. He was very cautious because as Chancellor of the Exchequer he knew what this was likely to cost. But he couldn't afford to remain too cautious, since the community charge was a key issue in the leadership election and Michael Heseltine had won great support by promising to review it.

Tidying up

Now bereft of their leader the Thatcherite MPs were very angry. Chris Chope had broken down when he heard of Margaret's resignation, and Michael Forsyth came over to me in the House canteen to say he probably wouldn't vote for any of the candidates in the second ballot. He also thanked me for standing by Margaret to the end saying, 'The Right didn't think you would!'

The Cabinet agreed to my suggestion that we should buy for Margaret a valuable pair of eighteenth-century silver candlesticks. I thought the very least my fellow Cabinet members could do was to give the leader they had deserted something in silver.

On the following Monday, Margaret and Denis came to say their farewells at Conservative Central Office, the building in which her Election successes of 1979, 1983 and 1987 had been planned. We gave Margaret an engraved tray and Denis a hip-flask. In her short speech Margaret said that she was no longer in the driving seat but that she was still going to be on board in the back. This gave rise to headlines the following day of 'Margaret The Backseat Driver'.

Later the same day Margaret gave a lunch for her oldest political friends in the long panelled room on the first floor of Number 10. It was a sad and nostalgic occasion. Keith Joseph, Nick Ridley, John Wakeham, Cecil Parkinson, John Moore, Peter Lilley, Michael Portillo, Neil Hamilton, Michael Forsyth, Archie Hamilton, Edward Leigh, Peter Morrison and Peter Thorneycroft were among those present. At the end, Keith Joseph said, 'You have done more than any of us ever thought possible and ever hoped to do. You were a great leader, a giant. "A beautiful giant".' And that was our toast. Margaret, speaking for the last time in that dining-room where she had greeted so many Heads of State, said, 'We are the faithful. Never forget that we have given a lead to the world. If Britain does that then other countries will follow.' Her last words were, 'Don't falter now.' The toast which she proposed was, 'To the future.'

As Party Chairman, I still had to see the three candidates to agree arrangements for the large Party meeting to be held in the Queen Elizabeth II Centre on 4 December following the result of the second ballot. This meeting was the official 'laying-on of hands' for the new leader. I met the three candidates on Monday 26 November and quickly got an insight into their campaigning and state of minds. Michael was full of confidence and ebullient. As he left my room in the House of Commons he threw over his shoulder an appetizing morsel: 'The Palace has been in touch.'

When I saw John in his room he was sitting quietly watching the early news on television surrounded by his campaign team. They had just told him that the 1922 Committee had been informed by Sir Peter Lane that the Party in the country was 3:1 for him. John must have had twenty to thirty MPs actually working for him. His was a real campaign, and there was no doubt that his team had hit the ground running.

I met Douglas a little later in the Foreign Secretary's room in the House. He had only one aide with him. When I explained the details for the 4 December meeting he said that he might not be able to attend as there was a NATO ministerial meeting that day. He was already telling himself that he was going to continue in the role of Foreign Secretary rather than Prime Minister.

Douglas came from a political family, though his early career had been spent in the Foreign Office, which was his first and abiding love. That is the clue to his character. Like an Ambassador or a Permanent Secretary, Douglas believes that most problems only need to be subject to rational management in order to be resolved. Douglas is not driven by a clear political ideology. He lacks both ambition and vanity, and he cultivates a passionless, effortless style. He is reactive rather than proactive. As Home Secretary measures were either pressed upon him by the flow of events, like the reform of the firearms laws in the wake of the Hungerford shootings, or by Mrs Thatcher, who bullied him into the Broadcasting Bill.

Douglas had never been one of Margaret's intimates. He was embarrassed in July 1989 to learn from the press that his job as Home Secretary had been offered to Geoffrey Howe, while he was to get the consolation prize of the Leadership of the House. But following Nigel's resignation he got the job that he had always wanted – Foreign Secretary. As Margaret's Foreign Secretary he was, like Geoffrey Howe, doomed never to be master in his own house. He always had to defer to Margaret, and must have looked forward to a change in the Party leadership, as he then would be in undisputed charge of Britain's foreign policy.

Douglas had regularly featured in lists of possible future Conservative Party Leaders, but in 1987, when Home Secretary, he said, 'Tory Home Secretaries do not get standing ovations nor do they become Leader of the Tory Party.' He was actually only right about the latter. At the Tory Party Conference in 1990, when it still looked as though there was going to be no leadership contest, he replied to a question about his own ambitions by saying, 'I have other ideas for the rest of my life.' Within six weeks, however, he had been persuaded to stand as a candidate in the second ballot. Doomed to come third, he ran an elegant campaign supported by Chris Patten and William Waldegrave, who saw him as a caretaker who would shortly make way for a candidate from their wing of the Party – most probably Chris himself. Douglas made the best crack of the campaign. When asked why, like the tortoise, he was limping along behind the hare he replied, 'May I remind you who won that race?'

Douglas has great gravitas but lacks the common touch. He knows this and public opinion polls confirm it. But if the British public do not see him as a leader with whom they can identify they certainly see him as a man who they can respect. Douglas is a gifted writer and has the ability, a real mandarin skill, of being able to draft a summary or communiqué quickly and without need of correction. I have enjoyed his novels and short stories, and when eventually he decides to retire, diplomacy's loss will be literature's gain.

In the late 1970s, after Douglas had been selected for an Oxfordshire seat, we kept bumping into each other in Old Palace Yard since we both employed the same constituency secretary, Judy Smart. She dealt with us both with great patience and firmness, but in due course I noticed that Douglas was getting rather better attention. This was not surprising, since they had fallen in love. It has proved to be a happy marriage.

On Tuesday 27 November 1990, the day of the second leadership ballot, Margaret answered Prime Minister's Questions for the last time. After she had finished I went to her room in the House of Commons where she said to me, 'Kenneth, I am very glad I didn't go on. The last five days would have been awful.' That evening, the result of the second leadership ballot was declared – John Major 185, Michael Heseltine 131, and Douglas Hurd 56. That left John just two votes short of an overall majority, and Michael Heseltine withdrew at once. Three years after joining the Cabinet, John Major had become Leader of the Conservative Party and Prime Minister of the United Kingdom.

Epilogue

Over the previous weekend I spent time reflecting upon the extraordinary events which had led to the downfall of a remarkable woman. While it was a personal tragedy for Margaret, these events did not unfold like a Greek tragedy, for Margaret's decline and fall was not written in the stars. Although the poll tax was unpopular, Margaret and the Government could have survived. Indeed, the poll tax too could have survived if it had earlier been made as palatable as it was to become in 1991. Although the emerging divisions on Europe were more serious, and the Europhiles were determined that Margaret should go, they had always held that view. But if it had not been for the provocation of Geoffrey Howe's resignation speech then there would have been no leadership contest, and I do not believe that these larger issues would have caused Margaret's downfall.

Nor do I subscribe to the view that the Parliamentary Party, believing they could not win with Margaret, decided cynically to ditch her. Some certainly thought she was a loser, but most others believed she was still a winner, as the vote on the first ballot showed. As for that group of

Ministers who helped to bring her down, they did not give me the impression that they had engaged in stealthy plotting or the careful planning and forethought required for such an exercise in political calculation.

Misfortune and misjudgement also played their part. Events occurred which no one could have foreseen and which did not help her position. The tragic murder of Ian Gow deprived her of a close and influential friend during the last few weeks. Margaret had also surrounded herself with a group of senior colleagues who were not as close to her, or as personally devoted, as earlier ones had been. Geoffrey Howe the Deputy Leader, and Tim Renton the Chief Whip, were never real fans of Margaret, nor did they become her confidants in the same way that John Wakeham and Cecil Parkinson had been. This intensified Margaret's sense of isolation.

There were also the sins of commission and omission. Those around Margaret, who were after all her personal appointees, made mistakes. Her rather lackadaisical leadership campaign run by George Younger lacked urgency; the canvassing of MPs was insufficiently shrewd, and the analysis too complacent; the advice of Peter Morrison and John Wakeham to see the Cabinet separately led to the sapping of Margaret's will to fight on; and I reproach myself for not insisting upon a full Cabinet meeting. As to the omissions, things were not done which should have been done. A different Chief Whip could have been more demonstrably energetic on Margaret's behalf. Douglas and John, who were, after all, her proposer and seconder, could have summoned television news cameras on the Wednesday morning in order to express their support for Margaret, and to appeal to the Cabinet to back her. If the central team of advisers and supporters does not generate enthusiasm for the Leader, then no one else will.

Then there were Margaret's own mistakes. It was a mistake to hold the leadership election while she was absent in France; a mistake not to canvass support personally; a mistake to attack Michael Heseltine in the *Times* so strongly; a mistake to react so quickly in Paris; and a mistake to see her Cabinet Ministers individually. To the extent that Margaret made these decisions herself, she was the architect of her own downfall. Even so, her reasons for making these decisions were neither perverse nor irrational.

During Margaret's last months as Prime Minister I was close enough to her to understand her attitudes and feelings. When it came to the leadership contest itself I could appreciate her believing that, as a world figure, she had to attend the Paris conference which was to mark the end of the Cold War, an ending which she herself had done so much to bring about. Her country would expect her to be there. As for canvassing personally, didn't all those Conservative MPs already know her character and ideas? If they didn't now, would they ever? Having achieved what she had, could she not expect that her Party and her colleagues in the House of Commons would acknowledge her record and allow her to decide for herself when she would step down? She was rightly proud of what she had done to reverse the decline of Britain, but all her achievements were now being threatened by her main opponent for the leadership. Margaret was hurt that after eleven years, the Party which she had brought back to power, the Government which she had fashioned, and the Cabinet she had appointed should even think of turning against her. And when all is said and done, if only two MPs had voted differently then all these feelings would have been vindicated. It was, as Wellington said of another occasion, though that occasion was a victory, 'a damn close run thing'.

Underlying the events of Margaret's last year were her relationships with Nigel Lawson and Geoffrey Howe. In my view she should have moved or dismissed Nigel Lawson in 1988 – but she didn't. Margaret feared, as she later admitted to me, that Nigel would not have gone quietly and would have made her own position untenable. She therefore decided to move the apparently less dangerous Geoffrey Howe, who she thought did not have either the capacity or the will to cause her much trouble. Her misjudgement of the character of her two most senior colleagues gave her initially an unnecessary sense of alarm and finally an unjustified sense of confidence.

Even so, Margaret should have been able to expect that her Cabinet would support her. But some of her Cabinet now clearly wanted her to go. As the leadership ballot is secret, one will never know whether some members of the Cabinet voted against her in the first round. But to forestall the haemorrhage of support which occurred after that first ballot Margaret should have called all her Ministers together to see how many around the table in open debate would have told her to go. The Cabinet needed to be pulled together. Willie Whitelaw could have achieved this, but John Wakeham did not have the seniority or authority, and any appeal on Margaret's behalf by me, as Party Chairman, would inevitably have been seen by colleagues as *parti pris*, since my political fortunes were inextricably linked with hers. There was no one to call the players together to give them a team talk.

I reflected also upon the consequences for me of these events. Prior to becoming Party Chairman my name had been mentioned frequently as a possible future Party Leader, but I never laboured under the illusion that becoming Party Chairman would increase my chances, for no Party Chairman has succeeded to the leadership of the Party. This is because when things go wrong the person most criticized after the Leader is the Chairman.

I had told Margaret on my appointment that she would have my total loyalty whatever happened. I stuck to this, but it was not just a question of loyalty, important as this is in politics. I supported Margaret Thatcher because she was a great Prime Minister who had saved Britain from decline. On the big issues of the economy, the trade unions and Europe she had been right. Lower public expenditure, lower taxes and supply-side economics had produced high growth in the 1980s and it was only Nigel Lawson's policies that removed the gloss towards the end. Margaret had taken on the trade unions and reduced their overweening power, thus making British industry manageable and competitive again. She had passionately resisted moves towards a more centralized federal European state. On the smaller issues too she was usually more right than wrong.

Margaret could be exasperating, dogmatic, wilful and a poor judge of people, but I have no doubt that the balance of history will come down firmly in her favour. In my view it was important that the mixture of policies we followed in the 1980s, towards which I had initially been rather cool, but had come to support with enthusiasm, should be retained, developed and built upon in the 1990s. I believed that we should have continued with these policies and with their architect. Others thought differently.

During the course of 1990 my name disappeared from any realistic speculation about who would become the Tory leader after Margaret, but this did not surprise or hurt me, for I had not planned my life to that end. I had never looked upon the Party chairmanship as a stepping stone to Number 10, and that was a realistic assessment. Moreover, accepting Ted Heath's invitation to become his PPS after he had lost the premiership in 1974, and accepting Margaret's invitation to become Party Chairman after her tenth anniversary in 1989, could hardly have been described as acts of calculated political ambition. Opportunists only follow the sunrise. Loyalists stay on for the sunset.

Journalists and commentators have frequently called me ambitious – an impression presumably gained from my character, which is naturally ebullient, cheerful and confident. I have always found politics a stimulating profession and enjoyed the company of those involved in practising or reporting it. But by temperament and analysis I had neither the burning ambition to lead the Party nor the pure calculation which drive those who hunger for the highest office. Unlike Michael Heseltine, I had not written on an envelope forty years earlier a political career path ending in Number 10. As a keen bridge player I know only too well that while you play your hand to the best of your ability you still have to play the hand you are dealt. The essential determinant of political success is being the right person in the right place at the right time.

I find it amusing that journalists, that most sceptical if not cynical profession, should place so much belief in the ability of any politician to plan rationally for an eventuality that may lie decades ahead. Politics is a wholly uncertain occupation. Press cutting files are filled with the political obituaries of potential Party Leaders who fell at the early hurdles of ministerial careers, never mind the later ones. Party Leaders emerge in response to their Party's perception of what is required at that moment in time to lead the Party to electoral victory and what is most required to unite the Party. The ultra-ambitious politician may therefore find himself or herself completely out of tune with these requirements by the time a leadership election comes along.

In the case of Margaret, it was obvious that any successor would necessarily have a different temperament and a different character. It was also likely, since the next leader would in all probability be leading the Party through the last decade of the twentieth century, that it might be better to look at candidates from the younger generation of Cabinet Ministers. The Parliamentary Party chose John Major because it wanted a broad continuation of Thatcherite policies and also a change of style. Only the passage of time will tell whether both of these expectations have been met.

CHAPTER 19

Becoming Home Secretary

*Criminal Justice – Miscarriages of Justice – Dangerous
Dogs – Joy-Riding, Bail Bandits and Squatting –
Frontier Controls and Conflict with Europe – Asylum*

I knew that now John Major was Prime Minister he would want to
make some changes for his first Cabinet. I felt quite certain that I
would not be left as Party Chairman, for I was far too associated with
Margaret, and John would want his own man in that key post. At
lunchtime on Wednesday 28 November I was asked to see John in his
study at Number 10, where he was sitting in Margaret's old chair with
a glass of milk beside him. He said to me, 'You've had to bear the
enormous burden of the Government's unpopularity and Margaret's
unpopularity over the last year. You often had to do this alone. I
would like to lessen that burden slightly and I would like you to be
Home Secretary.'

I was very pleased and honoured to be offered one of the three great
offices of state. John also told me that he was appointing Chris Patten
as Chairman of the Conservative Party, which I thought was sensible
for they got on well together. In the run-up to and during a General
Election the Party Leader and the Chairman must be able to work very
closely. John went on to ask me about Margaret, saying, 'How is she
taking it?' 'Pretty badly,' I replied, 'but she is glad you won.' I went
on, 'Margaret is going to be a difficult act to follow, not least, because
a whole generation of politicians have only known her style as Prime
Minister. You have a different style. That was the main reason why
you won. You should make the most of it.'

It was subsequently reported in the press that John had first offered
the post of Home Secretary to Michael Heseltine, who had been disappointed to get the Department of the Environment. Michael, so it was
said, wanted one of the two economic jobs – the Chancellorship or the
Department of Trade. But John told me on Friday, while we were
waiting in Buckingham Palace before taking our oaths and receiving our

422

seals of office, that he had definitely not offered the post of Home Secretary to Michael or anyone else besides me.

I went back to Central Office to say my farewells. It had been a turbulent time, but for the most part I had enjoyed it. The staff had been very loyal to me, and I had made a point of spending a lot of time in Central Office, where I was particularly well served by my Personal Assistant, John Gardiner. I was then driven by a police driver in my new official car to the Home Office, that fortress-like, top-heavy building in Queen Anne's Gate. I was whisked through the metal gates and the manned barriers, and into the brick courtyard. A small door on the far side led to the Ministers' lift which took me up to the large and splendid office of the Home Secretary. It was an office that I knew well, having visited it several times for meetings with my Tory Home Secretary predecessors, Willie Whitelaw, Leon Brittan, Douglas Hurd and David Waddington.

I was greeted by Sir Clive Whitmore, the Permanent Secretary, who had been the Private Secretary at Number 10 in 1981. It was he who had telephoned me in Sussex asking me to come to London when I was offered my first job in Margaret's Government. I was briefed on security and told that from that moment I would have personal bodyguards and police protection. This was a new experience, and over the months ahead Mary and I were to come to know our personal protection officers very well. Working closely together meant establishing a proximity and trust which created a sort of extended family relationship. I never ceased to admire the way the officers adapted so rapidly to different Ministers and their families who all lived in their own particular ways. I even managed to get some of 'the boys' to try their hand at fly-fishing up in the hills of Wester Ross.

When I became Home Secretary, Alistair Burt, who had been my Parliamentary Private Secretary for six years, felt that he wanted more freedom on the Backbenches and also more time to defend his marginal seat in Bury. He had been my loyal and hard-working link with back-benchers during the exciting years in Education and at Central Office. We had become firm friends and I understood why he wanted a change. I asked Steve Norris, MP for Epping Forest, to take over as my PPS. Steve had virtually single-handedly set up Crime Concern to involve businesses in the fight against crime, and he had helped me with the Grant-Maintained Schools Trust. Steve was articulate and robust, and he too proved a great pillar of support. Alistair and Steve are now Ministers and both will, I believe, go far in the Party.

Before the deluge of formal briefings could begin I took stock in my own mind of the nature of my new job. First, we were not doing very well as a Government on the law and order issue, despite this being perceived as a Conservative strength, and it was clearly going to feature in the forthcoming General Election. There was a lot of ground to make up. Second, the range of responsibilities in the Home Office was so wide that it touched the lives of most people most of the time. Having watched Home Secretaries from Reggie Maudling onwards, I knew that the job was a strange mixture of short-term often difficult crises and longer-term policies which could have a profound impact upon the development of our society. But if a Home Secretary could survive the crises then he did have an opportunity to set in hand changes which could influence the way in which society was developing.

Third, as a job, the Home Secretaryship had proved to be both a poisoned chalice and one of the most difficult for a Tory Minister. The Home Secretary was blamed for rising crime and for not giving in to the public clamour to bring back capital punishment. Willie Whitelaw, Leon Brittan and Douglas Hurd all had harrowing times with the Tory Party Conference, where they had been lambasted for their 'wetness'. David Waddington had been the only Tory Home Secretary since the 1960s who favoured hanging, and he had been loudly applauded for expressing this view at the 1990 Party Conference. There were debates in the House of Commons every two or three years on the question of capital punishment. In the debate which followed Leon's appointment he stumbled over the issue. He argued that although he had been an abolitionist up to that moment, he was now in favour of restoring capital punishment for terrorists. This pleased no one, since it amazed his old abolitionist friends and failed to convince the pro-hanging lobby who recognized that the execution of terrorists would solve little. This was also the view of all Ministers who had ever served in Northern Ireland. Leon's political reputation never really recovered from that speech.

I too have never favoured the restoration of capital punishment because I did not believe it was a deterrent. That view has been borne out by the experience of those states in America which now have executions. The death sentence there has done nothing to abate violent crime and murder. Furthermore, a series of cases which had cast doubt on the reliability of convictions for terrorist offences had resulted in the Court of Appeal freeing the Guildford Four and the Birmingham Six. Had capital punishment been in existence then it is likely that those found guilty would have been wrongly executed. Since there is no appeal from the grave, erroneous convictions cannot be reversed or compensated for. These were the views I expressed in December 1990 when there was another debate and the House had probably its last chance to restore capital punishment. If that Parliament, with its large Conservative majority, did not restore hanging, then I did not think any other future Parliament would. There were large majorities in the lobby that night against the restoration of the death penalty, and I remarked to John, who was sitting beside me on the Bench, 'Well, we are ropeless now as well as classless.'

I do not believe that any Home Secretary enters that great office with a long agenda of things to be done. Much of the responsibility lies in maintaining and sustaining the process that upholds law and order in the country. The Home Secretary is also much more the victim of day-to-day events than any other Minister. He is answerable for many decisions, some of them highly controversial, which are actually taken by other people – Chief Constables, Prison Governors, Probation Officers and the Parole Board. But in the public's eye the Home Secretary is held to be not just answerable but also responsible for these decisions, many of which have to be taken quickly and under considerable personal pressure by the people involved.

In another respect too, the Home Secretary is in a different position from other Ministers, as he has to take many decisions directly affecting the liberty of individuals without any consultation with colleagues. This gives the Home Secretary a rather lonely position in Government. Many of these decisions fall on the fine line between the personal liberty of the individual and the powers which Parliament has given to the various state institutions answerable to the Home Secretary. On many occasions the Home Secretary has to maintain a balance between the power and authority required to maintain an orderly society and the rights of individuals which are embedded not in a written constitution but more in our way of life.

On assuming office I did know that there were two areas that would need a major overhaul. First, having witnessed the twenty-three days of rioting at Manchester's Strangeways Prison during David Waddington's time as Home Secretary, it was clear to me that the whole prison system needed fundamental reform. This was an issue which most Home Secretaries had shied away from. There were literally no votes in prisons.

The second area was the seemingly inexorable rise in the level of crime. All the efforts of Willie Whitelaw and Douglas Hurd had not abated, let alone reduced, this rise. From my time as Education Secretary I knew that a tendency to anti-social and then criminal activity started at a very early age. If we were to create safer and more peaceful communities then the activities, interests and responsibilities of the Home Office and Education Department had to be coordinated. When a young man is sentenced in the dock and the prison door clangs shut behind him, then that is evidence of a failure at a much earlier age. I recognized that there was a lot to be done in the field of crime prevention by checking the slide into crime by boys and young men. I knew as Home Secretary that I would have to carry the Party with me on law and order, but I was never worried that this would be a problem while I was at the Home Office. My colleagues knew that I would have no truck with a soft approach to crime.

Becoming Home Secretary did have one tangible benefit, and that was the use of Dorneywood, the red-brick house in Buckinghamshire which had been given to the nation by Sir Courtauld Thomson for the use of Ministers of the Crown. It is the third of the official residences, and although the smallest I thought it the most comfortable. The special individual character of Dorneywood which marks it out from the other houses used by Ministers is its warmth – not just the physical warmth of the log fire in the drawing-room on a winter day, but the homely atmosphere of welcome and comfort that pervades the whole house.

Thankfully it is built of brick and roofed with clay tiles, rather than the cold formality of stone, stucco and slate which characterizes residences like Chevening. Visitors from all walks of life can relax in Dorneywood's intimate atmosphere, for the rooms are not too grand and are on a human scale. There are spirits in every house, and the guardian that presides over Dorneywood inspires friendship and intimacy.

Mary and I decided that to make the best of Dorneywood we would use it to entertain at the weekends not only our family and friends, MPs and journalists, but also men and women from the remarkably wide range of responsibilities that lay within my remit at the Home Office. We wanted our guests from the world of the police, prisons, race relations, security services, education, racing and broadcasting to meet and mingle with each other.

We had a very happy time at Dorneywood and took away many lasting impressions: the games in the barn which every guest would be encouraged to play; the lovely gardens with their delicious early blackberries; the bagatelle, where players fret to enter the house annals and sometimes question the veracity of their predecessors; and the relaxed happy dinners in front of Rex Whistler's romantic panorama. For Mary and me, although Dorneywood was never to be a substitute for our home in the constituency, which remained a place where we caught up with the backlog of weeding and reading, it was a very useful adjunct to the work of the Home Secretary. The running of Dorneywood costs the taxpayer nothing, since it was very well endowed by Sir Courtauld Thomson, and the Minister living there has to pay for his personal expenses.

I appreciate how unhappy Nigel Lawson must have been to be told that he had to give up this house in order to allow Geoffrey Howe to move in after he lost Chevening in July 1989. Nigel had enjoyed living at Dorneywood with Therese and their two children. One of the testimonies to that enjoyment lies in the book recording the bagatelle scores. Only those who score over a thousand points are entered. This is a very difficult thing to do with just twenty balls, and no one did it in our time. Churchill achieved it once, as did the young William Waldegrave while visiting Dorneywood as a schoolboy when Alec Douglas Home lived there; and so did Celia Whitelaw, clearly a demon player. But the recent star was Nigel Lawson – five entries of one thousand points are recorded against his signature. He must have spent literally hours and hours at the bagatelle board – a happier and more predictable pastime than coping with the economy or Margaret.

On Thursday 29 November John presided over his first Cabinet meeting, and after we had all sat down he looked around the table and smiled saying, 'Well, who'd have thought it?' John's style of chairing the Cabinet was quite different from Margaret's. John encouraged discussion and elicited colleagues' views, something which Michael Heseltine in particular made the most of at this his first Cabinet for six years. One of John's great talents is his skill at handling difficult meetings and teasing out a consensus. It was a much chummier atmosphere, and as we left the Cabinet Room Ken Clarke said to me, 'I wish there had been more discussions like this during the past few months. Perhaps she would have avoided some of the pitfalls.'

For the next eighteen months during John's short honeymoon and the long run-up to the 1992 General Election the Government did indeed manage to avoid major pitfalls. But after the Election it became apparent that not even the friendliest and fullest Cabinet discussions could prevent the Government slipping on a choice selection of banana skins.

Criminal Justice

The Home Secretary is responsible for the maintenance of law and order with specific responsibility for the police, prisons and criminal justice system. The latter is one of the most important, and in my experience most interesting, of the Home Office responsibilities. The decisions in this area are, in the widest sense of the word, 'political', though not Party political. They are political in the sense that Home Secretaries have to respond to the views of the public who 'want something done' about mugging, 'joy-riding', gun crime, or child murderers. The Home Secretary is the buffer between the understandable concerns of the public and the capability of the forces of law and order to respond effectively to these concerns. Home Secretaries have to deal with these specific problems as they arise. Douglas Hurd had responded to the murders at Hungerford by tightening the gun laws, I responded to concern over dangerous dogs and joy-riders, and Ken Clarke responded to the public outcry about the apparent unfairness of unit fines. At times, however, the Home Secretary has to resist the popular clamour if in his judgement there is no effective or practical remedy.

The Home Secretary's duties are quite separate from those of the Lord Chancellor and the Attorney-General. The Lord Chancellor is the head of the judiciary responsible for judges and the administration of the Courts. The independence of the judiciary from political influence is one of the bulwarks of our free and fair system of justice. The judiciary interpret and administer the criminal law, but changes to that law lie with the Home Secretary and Parliament. That division of responsibilities is, in my view, correct and should remain, though there are certain semi-judicial functions of the Home Secretary which could be transferred to other bodies. The Attorney-General is responsible for the Crown Prosecution Service, which is a separate and independent body. So there is a tripartite division of responsibilities, but in the public eye it is the Home Secretary who bears responsibility for the coherence and ultimate effectiveness of the whole criminal justice system.

In November 1990, as the new Home Secretary, I inherited a Criminal Justice Bill which made important changes in sentencing policy. Douglas Hurd at a 1987 Leeds Castle seminar had started the process of examination that led to the proposals in the Bill. These had been confirmed and approved by his successor, David Waddington. The Bill had two purposes. The first was to ensure that violent criminals spent a longer proportion of their sentence in prison, as it had become quite common for such criminals to be released after having served only a third of their sentence. This meant that neither the criterion of punishment, nor that of custody to protect the public, was being sufficiently met. Violent criminals now have to serve at least half their sentence behind bars, and in certain circumstances more than half.

Second, if it could be avoided less serious criminals should not be sent to prison. The reason behind this thinking was that prisons in the UK were seriously overcrowded and full of petty criminals. Far too many young men were being sent to prison, where they learnt very little other than to be better professional criminals. One of the controversial proposals in the Criminal Justice Bill was to forbid Courts to take into account the previous record of the accused. As a non-lawyer I was amazed at this proposal, but I was assured by John Patten, then Minister of State, and by Home Office lawyers who had been preparing the Bill for the previous three years that this corresponded to best judicial practice. Moreover there was not a squeak of objection from the judiciary led by Lord Chief Justice Lane, or from the Magistrates Association, as the Bill went through the House.

The first real complaint I received about the effect of the Bill was, strangely enough, at a meeting with Prison Officers in Winchester Prison. They complained that in future prisons would have a much higher proportion of violent and sexual offenders and would therefore be more difficult to control. The Prison Officers regretted the departure from their care of the rather more gentle prisoners such as cheque-bouncers, fine-dodgers, and driving offenders.

The other controversial element of the Bill was the introduction of unit fines. This proposal responded to frequently heard complaints about the inconsistency of sentencing across the country. Magistrates or Judges could give widely different sentences for seemingly similar offences. Unit fines were designed to improve consistency and also to take into account the financial position of the person to be fined. A fine of £200 for a wealthy man charged with drunk driving was neither a punishment nor a deterrent. Similarly a fine of £200 for someone on Income Support was unlikely to be paid and might probably result in the person going to jail. Here, the Government was meeting the Duke and Dustman 'unfairness' argument which had bedevilled the community charge. We were 'banding' fines according to ability to pay. Much good did that do.

The Bill, which I introduced to Parliament within days of taking over at the Home Office, proceeded through both Houses after exhaustive debate and with general plaudits.

However, in the early months of the new unit fine system coming into effect, some indefensible and risible fines were imposed, resulting in highly publicized cases of well-off people paying ludicrously high sums for offences such as dropping litter. Under pressure, Ken Clarke decided to withdraw the new system. But he made clear that it was important to retain the principle of taking into account a person's ability to pay so that the punishment for a crime was appropriate.

Miscarriages of Justice

I was soon plunged into another controversial aspect of the criminal justice system, that of allegations of miscarriages of justice. Most of these stemmed from trials in the 1970s of people accused of terrorist offences, though other cases were also submitted to me, including that of the three men who had been found guilty of murdering P. C. Keith Blakelock during the Broadwater Farm riot. Although the Home Secretary cannot set aside the verdict of a jury he must examine allegations of miscarriages of justice which may involve tampering with or falsifying evidence, the deliberate omission of evidence, or any other matters which could lead to the verdict being considered unsound. Technological advances, in particular the ESDA test which reveals what police officers have originally written in their contemporaneous notes, were being used to discredit police evidence in certain cases.

Both of my predecessors had referred to the Court of Appeal the alleged miscarriages of justice concerning the so-called Birmingham Six and the Guildford Four. Because there are few things more grave than deliberate miscarriages of justice I believed it was my duty to deal promptly with any case submitted to me. The fact that some cases might cause 'political embarrassment' did not concern me at all. In addition to ending the suffering of innocent people who should not have been in prison, I was anxious about these cases seriously undermining the public's confidence in and respect for the police and the courts.

If a Home Secretary believes there is a possible miscarriage of justice, the only course of action open to him is to refer the case to the Court of Appeal, which then examines the new evidence. I found this system cumbersome and inappropriate. In the spring of 1991 the court of Appeal was reviewing the case of the Birmingham Six. Like David Waddington, I felt that the likely release of people who had served long sentences but who should not have been convicted on the evidence presented revealed some serious weaknesses in the criminal justice system. The best way to address these and to restore the public's confidence was to have a thorough review of the whole system. James Mackay the Lord Chancellor, Paddy Mayhew the Attorney-General, and I agreed upon a range of issues to be examined by an inquiry. I suggested to the Prime Minister that it would be appropriate for a Royal Commission to be appointed to conduct the review of the criminal justice system in order to emphasize the review's independence from the Government. This was the first Royal Commission for over fifteen years and Lord Runciman agreed to be its Chairman.

The Royal Commission's terms of reference allowed it to range very widely over many other matters in the criminal justice system. This, however, was only one part of its work. We also wanted it to look at confessional evidence, the role of the prosecuting magistrate – which I personally did not favour – and the right to silence, which I believed was being widely abused. I was very concerned to hear from police officers how some suspects, particularly those arrested in connection with terrorist offences, would not give any information and even basic facts such as their name and address. They would simply stare at the wall in front of them for weeks or even months until their trial. This determined and total lack of cooperation could not be reported to the Court or the jury, who were simply told that the accused were exercising their right to silence. I believed that at the very least the way in which this right was exercised should be revealed to a jury.

Having dealt with several cases of alleged miscarriages of justice I came to the conclusion that the system needs to be changed. Such allegations should not come to the Home Secretary for him to consider whether they should be referred to the Court of Appeal. They should instead be submitted to a separate Authority which would investigate them and examine any new evidence. That Authority should have extensive powers of investigation and examination. If it found that allegations of a miscarriage of justice were not frivolous but cast serious doubts over the soundness of a verdict, then it would refer the case either to the Court of Appeal or to a separate Court which would reopen the matter in a less formal way than the usual adversarial style of the British Courts.

There was another area where I was glad to change the duty and responsibility of the Home Secretary. In the days of capital punishment it fell to the Home Secretary to exercise the royal prerogative of mercy and to decide whether a condemned person should be executed or reprieved. Largely as a legacy of this the Home Secretary has to decide when those sentenced to mandatory life imprisonment, mainly for murder, should be released. Home Office Ministers, guided by what the trial judge and the Lord Chief Justice say, decide how many years must pass before the possibility of release can be considered. This is known as the tariff. The Home Secretary then has to consider whether a prisoner should be released. Such prisoners are released on licence, which means that for the rest of their life they can still be called back to prison at any time.

When a life sentence prisoner becomes eligible for release on licence the case is submitted to the Home Secretary. This is done in a most scrupulous and fair way. Each file that came to me was three or four inches thick, with reports from all the various people who had been involved with the prisoner during his time in custody. Before reaching the Home Secretary each case is reviewed and commented upon by the Lord Chief Justice. These are very personal decisions for the Home Secretary, and each incumbent of that office owes it to the convicted person, and to the family of the victim, to examine each case most carefully since a person's individual liberty is involved. This, however, must always be weighed in the balance against whether that person would constitute a danger to society if they were released.

There are two types of life sentence. Mandatory sentences, for very serious crimes such as murder, are where the judge has to give a life sentence. Discretionary sentences, for such crimes as manslaughter, are where a judge may give a life sentence or a set term of imprisonment. As a result of recent appeals by life sentence prisoners to the European Court of Human Rights, the Home Secretary's role in determining the date of release for prisoners serving discretionary life sentences was successfully challenged. I therefore agreed to a new system which made two important changes. First, the trial judge, rather than Home Office Ministers, now determines the number of years which a convicted person sentenced to life imprisonment has to serve as a punishment for his crime.

Second, when that sentence has been served the prisoner may petition to be released, because as he was sentenced to life imprisonment his release is not automatic. This appeal is examined by a panel of three people from the Parole Board, headed by a judge. The panel can direct the Home Secretary to release a prisoner on licence if they believe that he is not a danger to society. Such decisions are essentially judicial, and better removed from the Home Secretary. It is only a question of time before this new system is extended to the review of mandatory life sentences for the most serious crimes.

A Home Secretary has to be prepared to deal with changes in the criminal justice system on a much shorter timescale than that of a Royal Commission, particularly when certain new offences arise or existing offences have not been adequately dealt with. It fell to me to deal with four such matters: dangerous dogs, joy-riding, bail bandits and squatting.

Dangerous Dogs

In the spring of 1991, the media reported a series of savage attacks by dogs which Home Office experts told me were seasonal occurrences. The worst of these attacks were by the notorious pit bull terrier, and the menace of these particular dogs was compounded by increasing evidence that they were being bred quite specifically for their power and viciousness. Pit bulls were being used for illegal dog fighting. Pit bull magazines carried coded advertisements in which a dog described as 'heroic' would have fought and won at least one fight, and those described as 'very heroic' had fought more than once and would probably bear the scars to prove it. Pit bulls were also being bought by criminals such as drug dealers who found the dogs a useful legal alternative to carrying a weapon.

On 8 May there was a shocking attack by two pit bulls on Mr Frank Tempest in Lincoln. I was shown the hospital photographs of Mr Tempest's horrific injuries, which had left him with nothing resembling a face, just a raw mass of red flesh. Mr Tempest later courageously called a press conference to support legislation against pit bulls. This serious incident was followed by an attack on a two-year-old girl at home caused by a pit bull owned by her grandparents. I felt that these attacks could no longer be ignored and asked officials to see what could be done about pit bulls and other dangerous dogs. The issue was made more complicated by the fact that the largest number of reported dog bitings was caused by Alsatians and other domestic breeds whose owners would never have regarded their pets as dangerous. But I considered that pit bulls represented a quite different scale of menace and caused far worse injuries than other dogs. Home Office officials put up endless difficulties about devising a law which could define different breeds and deal with a situation where an estimated 10,000 pit bulls were already in Britain. Was I proposing to confiscate all these dogs from their owners? Would the dogs be destroyed? How would the owners react and what would be the Home Office's liability? The problem was that if we did not act quickly, then simply by force of nature the number of pit bulls would increase as breeding went on and the problem would then become even more intractable.

Matters looked even worse when I was told that a well-known breeder had imported a Japanese Tosa dog, a fighting breed which can weigh up to 17 stone, and was planning to commence breeding this monster. So I was already planning to act when, on Saturday 18 May, a six-year-old Bradford girl, Rukhsana Khan, was seriously injured in yet another attack by a pit bull. The television news showed the little girl lying injured in hospital and her parents crying by her bedside. The pit bull issue was now up and running.

On the Sunday, I was being interviewed on television by David Frost, primarily about the state of the Conservative Party in the wake of our defeat at the Monmouth by-election. But discussion turned to the issue of pit bulls and what could be done about them. Instead of promising the slaughter of the ten thousand – which had been my inclination and which would have won public approbation – I produced the rather lame official line that legislation to curb dangerous dogs would be difficult to pass and that the whole issue was very complicated. The next day I was lambasted by some of the tabloid newspapers, and Number 10 sought guidance for Prime Minister's Questions on Tuesday. I told John that we must act but that this required emergency legislation. The Chief Whip, Richard Ryder, was uneasy about Government action and had told me previously that having almost been defeated in 1989 over dog licensing, 'The last thing we want is any more dog legislation.' However, John agreed with me and gave the green light to go ahead.

The question now turned to exactly what could practically be done and who would do it. I soon discovered that while many people loved dogs, others loathed them. There was a danger of over-reaction, with demands to have all dogs muzzled and to put Rottweilers, Dobermans and Alsatians in the same category as pit bulls. This would have infuriated the 'green welly' brigade. However, the 'pit bull lobby' came to my aid by appearing in front of TV cameras with owners usually sporting tattoos and earrings while extolling the allegedly gentle nature of their dogs, whose names were invariably Tyson, Gripper, Killer or Sykes. There was one vivid illustration of this misrepresentation when a Thames TV news cameraman crouched to push his lens too close to a pit bull's face. Viewers saw the dog's gaping jaws as it lunged upwards into the cameraman's groin. There was an audible yell, the camera swung upwards and Thames viewers saw lots of blue sky accompanied by the sound of growling and shrieks.

The animal lobbies were very divided on the issue of controlling dangerous dogs. The Kennel Club supported the idea of pit bulls being put down. They did not register pit bulls as one of their recognized breeds and felt that as fighting dogs they had no place in our society. The RSPCA, while having no love for pit bulls, shrank from the physical elimination of the breed, preferring instead that the dogs should be neutered and then die out over time as the breed became extinct. Furthermore, the RSPCA used the opportunity to raise its cherished aim of the introduction of a dog licensing system – which I opposed. I was not in the business of legislating to control chihuahuas when I wanted to rid the country of pit bulls. The vets were also reluctant to destroy pit bulls en masse, believing that this went against their version of the Hippocratic Oath. But one dog expert assured me that 'All pit bulls go mad.' Unlike other recognized breeds they were unpredictable and could not be reliably trained. Steering a course acceptable to all these differing viewpoints strained patience as well as imagination, and I knew that whatever course of action I took I would be attacked by one group or another.

On 22 May I announced to the House of Commons my intention to introduce legislation to ban the breeding and ownership of pit bull terriers and other dogs bred especially for fighting. I then embarked on further meetings with the animal interest groups which, in addition to the RSPCA and the Kennel Club, included the Joint Advisory Committee on Pets in Society, the Canine Defence League, the Royal College of Veterinary Surgeons, and the British Veterinary Association. The issues we debated included whether to identify dogs by implanting micro-chips under their skin, or by tattooing them. This led to humorous exchanges about exactly who would volunteer to tattoo a pit bull's inside leg, and whether the dog's tattoo should match that of the owner. Would pit bulls have 'love' and 'hate' inscribed on each knuckle?

On 10 June I introduced the Dangerous Dogs Bill in the House of Commons. Owning and breeding these dogs was to be made illegal, which meant they would eventually disappear in Britain. If owners wanted to keep their pit bulls then the dogs would have to be neutered, insured and registered, otherwise they would be destroyed with some compensation being paid to the owner. Although we anticipated difficult court cases over the definition of a pit bull, I thought it better to risk those difficulties, because having realized the danger of these dogs it would have been irresponsible to have done nothing. The Bill was broadly supported by all Parties (although the Labour Party wanted me to go further and compulsorily muzzle Rottweilers and Alsatians), and passed through all its stages on the floor of the House in just one sitting. The only crucial vote came on an amendment to introduce a full dog registration scheme, which we won at one o'clock in the morning by 303 votes to 260, with several Conservative MPs voting against the Government. The Dangerous Dogs Act became law on 24 July 1991, and has saved many children and adults from vicious attacks by pit bulls.

This episode showed that the Government and Parliament could act quickly to deal with an urgent situation. The Home Office was able to devise legislation to deal with a specific problem which they would have preferred to have left alone. Subsequently, I was to find that quite a large number of Home Office officials were crossing their fingers and hoping that similar emergencies would not happen in their own area of responsibility.

Joy-Riding, Bail-Bandits and Squatting

In the early autumn of 1991 there were outbreaks of violence, hooliganism and looting in several council housing estates across the country. These were not on the same scale as the riots of 1981 and 1986 but they did create pockets of lawlessness in the Handsworth area of Birmingham, the Blackbird Leys Estate in Oxford, and the Meadow Well Estate on North Tyneside. The common thread in each of these incidents was the mindless violence of young boys and men who stole cars principally for 'kicks', frequently crashing them and then setting them on fire. This activity was given the misnomer of 'joy-riding'. In several instances innocent bystanders and the joyriders themselves had been injured or killed.

In the case of Oxford, the Chief Constable of Thames Valley, Charles Pollard, had described to me two months earlier the problems on the Blackbird Leys Estate. In the early hours of the morning stolen cars were being driven dangerously and at very fast speeds around the estate by young hooligans who were virtually defying the police to stop them. The Chief Constable decided to arrest some of the gang ringleaders in order to bring an end to the lawlessness. It was this action which precipitated the riots.

The public were outraged by the violent scenes which they saw nightly on their television screens, and also by the light sentences meted out to the young offenders. If the police were lucky enough to arrest any of the car thieves they would usually be released on bail and continue with their criminal activities. We proposed toughening the law by introducing a new offence of Aggravated Vehicle Taking, with a maximum sentence of five years. The chances of securing a conviction were increased by reversing the burden of proof so that the person who had stolen the car had to prove that he was not personally to blame for any subsequent damage. Often it was possible to identify the original thief but the actual car would have been abandoned and only found several days later after much damage had been caused. I was accused of introducing instant legislation, but I make no apology for toughening the law in this area.

John Patten and I also took initiatives with car manufacturers and the insurance industry to try and make cars safer and more burglar-proof. Car crime accounted for nearly 40 per cent of all recorded crime in the UK and was the principle reason for the very sharp increase in reported crime in 1990–91. John Patten had the main responsibility for dealing with the crime figures. We summoned the rather reluctant managing directors of all the main UK car companies to the Home Office and exhorted them to fit burglar alarms and more secure locks to their cars and to consider introducing immobilizers. Initially the car manufacturers were not particularly keen to spend money on these changes, which did not significantly increase car sales. However, after several meetings our message got through to them and car security moved higher up their agenda.

John Patten and I also met the representatives of the insurance industry who had become alarmed when insurance losses for car thefts rose to £600 million a year. The insurance companies increased their premiums for those types of car most likely to be stolen, and gave rebates to clients who had fitted security systems to new cars. These were sensible initiatives to prevent crime and were just as important as measures to detect and punish car thieves.

I also wanted to deal with Chief Constables' frequent complaints that young criminals, particularly car thieves, were being given bail against police recommendation and then went out the very same day to commit more crimes. These were the so-called 'bail bandits'. My proposals to create an additional offence of committing a crime whilst on bail encountered legal objections, and I had to be content with a less draconian measure. British Courts now have to take into account, when deciding the length of a sentence, the fact that further offences may have been committed while the accused was on bail.

Another area of the law which had always seemed unsatisfactory to me was that relating to squatting. The Home Office had previously been most reluctant to consider any changes, since it opened up the much wider question of trespass. Since 1977 the position was that if squatters occupied a property in which the owner was actually residing then the police could be called in to help evict the squatters. But squatters very rarely chose homes of that type, preferring instead to occupy an empty flat or house waiting to be sold or where the owner had died, or a second home, or a shop. In these cases the criminal law did not apply and the owners had to start lengthy eviction procedures in the civil courts, during which time the property might have been vandalized, neighbours intimidated, and the peace of the neighbourhood shattered.

There is no solid argument in defence of squatting, no matter how compelling the squatters' own circumstances are claimed to be by their apologists. It is simply wrong that legitimate owners should be deprived of the use of their property. Squatting was common in many parts of London, some northern cities, and several towns on the south coast. It had also become common for empty shops to be taken over and shoddy goods offered for sale from them. This provided unfair competition for neighbouring shops and the shop squatters usually disappeared before the law caught up with them.

I asked the Home Office lawyers to come up with some positive proposals and they did not disappoint me. On 15 October 1991 I published a White Paper setting out the changes that we believed to be necessary. Essentially we intended to extend the criminal law to cover the activities of squatters. This was a good example of where, with some determination and great encouragement from backbench MPs, it was possible to improve the law. After I had announced these proposals in the House of Commons I sat down to cheers, and several Tory MPs said they would like the same ideas applied to the general law of trespass in order to deal with gypsies and New Age Travellers. We then set in hand an examination of that most complex area.

Frontier Controls and Conflict with Europe

The first international meeting I attended was the 6 December gathering of European Interior Ministers known as the TREVI group. We met as a Council of Ministers because internal affairs and immigration are not within the competence of the Treaty of Rome. This meant the European Commission did not organize, run or dominate these meetings. TREVI is a good example of the effectiveness of intergovernmental cooperation working in practice. The Vice-President of the European Commission, the German Liberal, Martin Bangemann, attended as an observer by invitation only and sat brooding and impatient surrounded by a small group of his officials. He wanted to bring home affairs, immigration and asylum within the competence of the Treaty of Rome. This would make the European Commission the driving force behind immigration policy and convert TREVI meetings to the same status as the Environment and Agriculture Committees which have the power to make Community law, impose penalties and decide policy by majority voting. The Benelux countries and Germany were prepared to pool sovereignty in this way but I was strongly opposed. Subsequent TREVI meetings over the next eighteen months confirmed my belief that the best way forward was through intergovernmental cooperation.

I was briefed for this meeting by Anthony Langdon, the Deputy Secretary in charge of the Immigration and Nationality Division. Unlike most briefings, which are formal affairs to familiarize a new Home Secretary with a particular area of a Department's responsibility, what Anthony told me was to have a profound effect upon my future attitude to a crucial area of Government policy – that regarding Europe.

I was told that Article 8A of the Single European Act was being reinterpreted by our Community partners in such a way as to change completely its original intention. The Single European Act, consolidating the Treaty of Rome, had been agreed by the Government in 1986. Article 8A stated, 'The internal market shall comprise an area without internal frontiers in which the free movement of goods, persons, services and capital is ensured in accordance with the provisions of this Treaty.'

Margaret Thatcher, advised by Geoffrey Howe and Douglas Hurd, had secured a General Declaration appended to the Single European Act which stated:

Nothing in these provisions shall affect the right of Member States to take such measures as they consider necessary for the purpose of controlling immigration from third countries, and to combat terrorism, crime, and traffic in drugs and illicit trading in works of art and antiques.

We had believed that this Declaration allowed Britain to maintain its own immigration controls; indeed if it had not I am sure that Margaret would have refused to approve the Act. The Declaration represented a British opt-out. But we were now being told that the Declaration was worthless.

It had been commonly understood that 'the free movement of persons' in Article 8A meant citizens of European Community countries. I was amazed to learn, therefore, that 'persons' was now being interpreted by European Commission lawyers as meaning *anyone* who lawfully entered the European Community. This meant that an EC Member State's embassy or consulate anywhere in the world could give permission for someone to enter that EC country, and once there, that person would be subject to no further border checks if they decided to travel on to any other EC country. Thus the Portuguese consulate in Mozambique, or the German consulate in Brazil, by issuing a visa, could actually determine who ultimately entered Britain following arrival in the European Community. This was a complete bombshell. At a stroke, the lawyers' new interpretation would blow our immigration controls out of the water. We had never envisaged that freedom of movement within the European Community meant that we would be obliged to admit non-EC citizens without any right to control their numbers.

Immigration is a sensitive matter at the best of times, but I thought that if the vulnerability of our opt-out from Article 8A became widely known and understood it would provoke an explosion of public anger and become a major political issue. I was determined not to be the Home Secretary who dismantled Britain's frontier controls and rolled over at the behest of Brussels. I was soon to find that my opposite numbers, the Interior and Justice Ministers of other EC countries, had virtually given up entirely on their border controls either out of despair or resignation. The Italians felt that their coastline was impossible to patrol, the Germans felt that their land border with Poland could not be guarded, and the Dutch didn't seem too bothered about who came into their country. The Dutch Immigration Minister simply said that her country could not police their borders and, with an air of cheerful indifference, added that liberal Holland didn't really mind who turned up or how long they stayed. I told her that any country doing that was saying to the rest of the world, 'Our doors are open, come in.'

German attitudes were to change considerably when the rapid influx of refugees and migrants from Eastern Europe provided fuel for the extreme Right. The French had already experienced the rise of the National Front under Jean-Marie Le Pen, following North African immigration into cities like Marseilles, Lyons, and even Paris. But unlike my colleagues abroad, I was not going to sit back and let the problem develop before taking action. Britain had a proud record of relatively harmonious race relations, and immigration was not much of an issue. I wanted to keep things that way. I therefore made it clear that whatever the Single European Act said, we were going to keep our frontier controls, our requirement for visas for some nationals, and passport checks for everybody. Since, unlike other EC countries, we have the advantage of being an island, controls at our ports and airports were relatively easy to maintain and I did not see why we should give up that advantage.

When I expressed my views on Article 8A, Bangemann said that he planned to arrive in Britain at one minute past midnight on 1 January 1993 – the date when we were expected to abandon our frontier controls – without his passport and demand entry. I replied that he would not be let in. If he insisted he would be detained and put back on the first plane to Germany. Bangemann muttered threats about retaliatory action against Britain unless we complied. My response was that British citizens would be quite happy to have to show their passports when visiting other EC countries if that meant that we could control who entered Britain.

This episode had a profound effect upon my attitude to the European Community. I had always favoured entry into the European Economic Community and I continue to support our membership of an economic community which serves the interests of its member nation states. But I have never favoured the diminution of sovereignty and absorption into a superstate, which is what the EC institutions in Brussels seem increasingly determined to drag us into. It had certainly never occurred to me, nor I am sure to Margaret, that signing the Single European Act meant signing away control over Britain's immigration policy, and I was shocked that a Declaration which we had solemnly agreed was now considered to be worthless. My concern, however, was not shared by senior Home Office officials, who appeared rather resigned to Britain's eventual compliance. Their view was that if we resisted the new interpretation of Article 8A then we would be in breach of the agreement and be taken to the European Court. But my attitude was to wait and see if any European Court ruling would happen and then be prepared to wave two fingers, rather than abandon border controls in anticipation of a defeat.

The prospect of a conflict with the European Commission over our resistance to open frontiers hung over my period as Home Secretary. Furthermore, it was not just a question of immigration. I was also concerned about the weakening of our capacity to combat terrorism, crime and drug trafficking. In the run-up to the Maastricht Treaty negotiations in December 1991 I minuted the Prime Minister urging him to do two things. First, not to surrender to the Community British rights to control our own borders. This line was held at Maastricht, but it was clear to me that the Commission would return to the issue at an early opportunity. Second, there must be no going back on the undertakings given to the House of Commons by Margaret Thatcher, which meant that we could continue to operate our own immigration and frontier controls. This would require the British Government to secure either the reaffirmation of the 1986 General Declaration or a renegotiation of Article 8A.

I met the Prime Minister and Douglas Hurd separately on two occasions to urge this, and whilst they agreed that an extension of the Community's competence in this area should be resisted, they felt unable to raise the whole interpretation of Article 8A and the Declaration. Perhaps they believed that to do so would throw a spanner in the Maastricht negotiations, and thought it was a matter which would be counterproductive to reopen with EC colleagues. I was very disappointed that this fundamental European challenge to our sovereignty was never raised at the Maastricht meeting. We still remain on a collision course with the European Community over maintaining our frontier controls, and when this collision occurs it will be the ultimate test of 'Who governs?', the national or the supranational state.

Since I left the Government I have been criticized by former Cabinet colleagues for my cool attitude towards European political integration. It was even suggested that after the Maastricht negotiations I had led the chorus of congratulations in Cabinet to the Prime Minister. This is simply not true, as will be revealed when the Cabinet minutes are published.

My cooling towards Europe had in fact been developing for some time. While I was at the Department of Education I had seen how the European Commissioner for Social Affairs, Mrs Papandreou, manipulated the Council of Ministers and sought to extend Community powers into areas for which it had no responsibility. The Commission had become the driving force behind interventionist policies. Britain could only really count on Denmark's vote to support the lines that we took. Later, as Party Chairman, I visited the European Parliament in Strasbourg and tried to understand and appreciate it. But I came back from it only convinced of the advantages of our own Westminster Parliament.

Now, as Home Secretary, I was fighting a rearguard action to prevent the Community taking control of immigration and asylum policy. These were two of the most sensitive political issues for each European Community country, including Britain. I had no confidence that the Commission would be able to act more effectively than each country was already doing itself. The Schengen Accord, whereby certain countries including France were to do away with their frontier controls, was unacceptable as far as the UK was concerned. I also believed that this Accord would wither under the pressure of immigration and asylum in the 1990s, and this in fact is now happening. The new French Government has insisted on new conditions for adopting Schengen and set as its own national target an end to all new immigration.

So my cooling towards the sort of European union which Kohl, Mitterrand, Delors and Bangemann want had been building up for some time. I ensured that those parts of the Maastricht Treaty dealing with frontier control did not extend the Community's competence. But neither did they clarify the confusion which weakens our position. Important as it was, however, frontier control was a secondary issue at Maastricht. The heart of the Treaty was Economic and Monetary Union, which itself rested upon the Exchange Rate Mechanism which we were told was inviolable. When Britain was forced to withdraw from the ERM in September 1992 it seemed to me that the *raison d'être* behind Maastricht had collapsed and that the right thing to do was to renegotiate the Maastricht Treaty. This is the line that I have consistently taken since then.

Asylum

In the late 1980s an increasing number of people claiming to be political refugees arrived in Europe seeking asylum on the grounds that they had 'a well founded fear of persecution'. This was the definition of such refugees enshrined in the 1951 United Nations Declaration. But most of these people were economic migrants rather than political refugees. Whatever their real status, the fact remained that hundreds of thousands of nationals from countries in Africa, Asia and the Middle East were now travelling to European countries and then claiming political asylum.

In the 1970s Britain had received 1,000–2,000 asylum applications each year, rising to 5,000 applications in the mid-1980s. By 1989 this figure had risen to 15,000 applications for asylum and the figure shot up to 45,000 applications in 1991. Each asylum application had to be assessed separately and was subject to an appeal process, which meant that it took up to two or three years to decide whether an application was genuine or bogus. During the time it took to decide this claim an applicant could remain in Britain, eligible for both local authority housing and social security benefits. The British immigration services at Croydon, responsible for deciding these cases, were overwhelmed with a backlog of 60,000 cases to consider. It had become evident that most so-called asylum seekers were immigrants trying to exploit a humanitarian procedure in order to queue-jump and evade normal immigration controls. The Government remained committed to genuine refugee cases, indeed over the period 1979–89 we had granted refugee status to some 34,000 applicants. But what was now happening was a complete abuse of the asylum procedure intended to help genuine refugees.

I reported on the gathering crisis to the Cabinet on 13 December 1990, and was given the go-ahead to produce proposals to stem the flow of bogus asylum seekers into Britain. David Mellor and Michael

Heseltine were particularly helpful – David because his own constituency was being affected by asylum-seekers jumping the council
house waiting list, and Michael because he realized that this was a
politically explosive issue which could blow Europe apart. On 15
January I submitted proposals to increase the number of staff at Croydon by 500 so that the administrative process could be quickened. We
also needed new legislation to speed up the whole process of determining applications and the subsequent appeals. Asylum applications
fell under the Home Secretary's responsibilities, but appeals came under
the Lord Chancellor. The object of the Bill was to complete the process
of determination and appeal within twelve weeks. Those who were
found not to be political refugees would either have to leave the country
or be deported.

We also doubled to £2,000 the penalty paid by airlines which accepted
passengers without proper entry documents. We tightened the social
security arrangements for assessing applicants for benefits, since we had
unearthed many fraudulent multiple applications. To check this more
effectively we proposed to fingerprint applicants in order to prevent
impersonation. These measures were agreed by the Cabinet on 9 May
and I received strong support from David Waddington and Peter Lilley.
The proposals were ultimately incorporated in the Asylum Bill, which
did not have enough Parliamentary time to complete its progress before
the General Election in April 1992.

However, the fact that we were now acting to stamp out abuses of the
asylum procedure began to show results very quickly. By the spring of
1992 4,628 people who were already in Britain and had applied for
asylum by post were offered early interviews by the newly strengthened
immigration staff at Croydon. Only 821 of the asylum applicants bothered to turn up. This figure, together with the fact that three-quarters of
asylum applicants were already in Britain as visitors or students at the
time they made their applications for asylum, seemed to me to speak
volumes about the problem we faced. The issue of bogus asylum-
seeking was entirely separate from legitimate immigration, for which
British Governments of both political parties had created a fair system of
controls, although the Labour Party now favoured relaxing some of
these. However, the number of people entering Britain using the asylum
route was getting out of hand and I told John, 'The build up of
migratory pressure and the way in which we handle it will be one of the
most difficult issues facing us over the next decade'.

This pattern of asylum-seeking was being repeated all across Europe on an even larger scale. The biggest number of asylum seekers applied to Germany, which received around 250,000 applications in 1990, rising dramatically to 400,000 in 1992. Following the reunification of Germany the policing of the German/Polish border became impossible. It also became relatively easy for people from Eastern European or Balkan countries to cross the German frontier. This fact, coupled with Germany's constitutional obligation to accept refugees, created a tinderbox situation which any moderately intelligent politician should have been able to foresee. In the summer of 1990 I visited the German Interior Minister, Wolfgang Schauble, who was confined to a wheelchair after an assassination attempt. I found that although he was concerned about the asylum problem he was quite relaxed that the Germans could handle it. In the following weeks, outbursts of neo-Nazi violence, rioting, arson and murders targeted at asylum-seekers and immigrants took place in many German towns. When I met Herr Schauble again in the autumn he was now alarmed and said, 'Immigration is our biggest problem. We have got to act to check the flow.' It was, however, to take the murder of more innocent people at the hands of neo-Nazis before the Social Democrats and Liberals would join the Christian Democrats to repeal in 1993 the relevant parts of Germany's constitutional obligation to refugees.

France, which received about 70,000 applications for asylum, was particularly worried about the numbers of migrants coming from North Africa. The population growth of the Maghreb was one of the highest in the world and its economy could not sustain this. Illegal immigrants were using small boats to cross the Mediterranean, landing in France or Spain, where they either claimed political asylum or simply disappeared into the immigrant communities already established in particular cities in those countries.

Even Italy, which over the centuries has sent so many of its people across the world, was also a target for asylum-seekers. In the spring of 1991 boatloads of Albanians tried to land at southern Italian ports. After the first boatload of people had scrambled ashore, an arrangement had to be made which in effect set aside the international rights covering asylum-seekers. The Italian Interior Minister, Signor Scotti, later to come under investigation for allegedly receiving Mafia bribes, asked each EC country to accept a quota of Albanians. All refused. It was now becoming clear to EC member countries that this was the thin end of a very large wedge. Mr Scotti was in some despair, because Albania was not the only country from which migrants were arriving in Italy. One third of Genoa's population was now immigrant, while outside Rome there was a camp of 1,000 Bangladeshis. 'What have we done to deserve that?' asked Signor Scotti plaintively.

This shared experience of economic migration reinforced my argument that it would be a dangerous folly to abandon EC internal frontier controls. But only Denmark took the same resolute line as Britain, although the French were becoming increasingly worried, not least because of the rise of the National Front. At least I had the satisfaction of knowing that, unlike some of our EC partners, we in Britain have not suffered the upsurge of racial bigotry and extreme right-wing viciousness which has resulted from the supine and indifferent attitudes shown by those elsewhere who should have known better.

The uncontrolled movement of people who are in fact economic migrants seeking to establish residential rights in more prosperous countries is one of the biggest problems facing Europe. Until EC member countries can both agree on and operate rigorous and effective frontier controls so that each member state can rely on the other to maintain equivalent entry standards, then national controls must remain in place.

It was over an asylum case in November 1991 that I was found to be guilty of contempt of Court, thus making legal and constitutional history. Peter Lloyd, the Minister who dealt with immigration matters, had approved the refusal of an asylum claim from a Zaïrean teacher and approved his deportation. On two separate occasions the High Court and the Appeal Court had upheld this decision. Lawyers acting on behalf of the Zaïrean nonetheless continued trying to prevent the deportation and sought an injunction just at the time the man was being put on a plane at Heathrow. Home Office officials decided at that stage that they could not stop the deportation. The lawyers then found a Judge in Chambers who issued an order requiring me as Home Secretary to return the Zaïrean from Kinshasa, to which he had now been flown. This matter was referred to me on the following day.

The specific issue was whether I, as Home Secretary, was obliged to follow the Judge's order. The advice given to me by the Home Office lawyers and Treasury Counsel was absolutely unequivocal, namely that the Judge was acting beyond his powers in issuing the order, and that a temporary injunction could not be taken out against the Crown. Six months later the Appeal Court by a majority decision of 2:1 decided that, 'Ministers and Civil Servants are accountable to the law and to the Courts for their personal actions.' This was clearly a constitutional novelty, as it sought to draw a distinction between me acting as the Home Secretary and me as an individual. Yet it was only as Home Secretary that I had the power to exercise the decisions I did. However, the Court also held that I had not deliberately defied the Court or held myself above the law. Indeed on the day following the deportation we successfully challenged the Judge's power to issue the order and it was withdrawn. Nonetheless the Appeal Court and the Master of the Rolls decided to use this case to challenge the executive power of Government. The central constitutional issue was whether a Court can have coercive jurisdiction over the Crown. In July 1993 the House of Lords delivered their judgment. They departed from a previous judgment which stated that there was no power in domestic law to grant injunctions against the Crown. The Lords now held that the Crown and its Ministers may be made subject to the coercive jurisdiction of the Court. This will have significant constitutional consequences. I was glad, however, that speaking specifically of my position, Lord Woolf, the Law Lord who actually delivered the judgment said, 'He was acting on advice. His error was understandable and I accept that there is an element of unfairness in the finding against him personally'.

CHAPTER 20

The Home Office and After

Supporting the Police – Preventing Criminality –
Reforming Prisons – Privatization of the
Management of Prisons – The Brixton Escape – The
National Lottery – Racing – Winning a Fourth Term –
Standing Down

All my political life I have had a very simple attitude to the police – they deserve our full support. They have a difficult and at times a dangerous job; they have to deal with some vicious criminals; and, uniquely in the world, they do it mostly unarmed. During my time as Home Secretary, one sergeant was murdered and I visited two officers in hospital who had almost had their throats slit in a knife attack. There were also examples of exceptional courage by police officers in dealing with terrorists. In the urban disturbances of autumn 1991 the police had to tackle violent crowds of hooligans to stop them burning houses, looting shops and stealing cars. As I said on several occasions, the police were 'the thin blue line between order and chaos'.

These views of mine were total anathema to the Left, who generally believed that police were corrupt, violent and indifferent to citizens' rights. Nor did my views appeal to the Liberal Party. However, I did not shrink from expressing them strongly. My purpose was not to get an easy cheer at the Tory Conference, but to use the authority of my Office to support the police and sustain their morale at a time when they were subject to an avalanche of critical attacks in the media. Indeed, my views on law and order reflected the attitudes of the overwhelming majority in the country.

This did not mean I believed the police were beyond criticism, or did not require reform. Some allegations of miscarriages of justice raised serious questions about their investigatory practices. There are some bad police officers, some who are racially biased, and some who are unnecessarily violent when restraining suspects. But the police are trying to put this right. Since 1985 they have operated under the Police and Criminal Evidence Act which requires interviews in police stations to be tape-recorded. This has removed the major complaint arising from the interviewing of suspects and witnesses. In London, Peter Imbert, the Metropolitan Commissioner during my period as Home Secretary, launched major campaigns to recruit more black, Asian and female officers.

I found, however, that while several of my ministerial colleagues and Tory MPs supported the police in public, they were highly critical of them in private. There was impatience, if not anger, that although we had spent 87 per cent more in real terms since 1979, and had increased police numbers by 27,000, there had still been a substantial rise in crime. 'Where is the value for money?' asked my colleagues.

I had even heard Margaret Thatcher criticize the management and leadership of the police. She regretted that they did not have an 'officer class'. Chief Constables and senior police officers all rise through the ranks. That is not usually the case with Generals, Admirals, and Air Marshals, who will have joined the armed services as young men to be trained as officers. Margaret wanted the same for the police, complete with a police version of Sandhurst. But analogies with the armed forces are simply wrong. Not only are police tasks quite different but they have to be carried out in quite different circumstances. The police live within the community they are protecting. They do not live isolated in barracks. In their daily tasks they meet ordinary people all the time, providing a great sense of comfort and reassurance by their manner and their presence. They also have to deal with many truculent youths who resent them, but with whom they have to establish a relationship.

What I think Margaret was getting at was that not enough bright young people, particularly graduates, joined the police. This I found simply not to be true. In a uniformed force of 127,000 police officers there were 7,000 graduates, a higher proportion than in the armed forces. When I visited police training courses I found that there were many recruits entering in their late twenties or early thirties who had been in the armed services, or had a professional training, or a degree. Some were discouraged by the emphasis on patrol work and police station duties, so it seemed to me that the best response was to provide a fast track for the speedy promotion of the ablest, one which would allow a bright young entrant to reach the post of Inspector or Chief Inspector within four to eight years. Although this was not welcomed by some forces, I insisted that it be accepted across the country.

I didn't hear the Sandhurst approach from John Major, but he too was sceptical about the performance of the police and did not seem over-enamoured of the performance of his own county force. This was very much 'The Treasury line', and I believe it was encouraged by his Private Secretary, Andrew Turnbull, who had often nodded agreement whenever I heard Margaret expressing herself strongly on this subject.

At one of our earliest meetings I told John that the police were very stretched and I intended to bid for an extra 1,000 police officers that year. The Chief Constables were asking for 7,000 more. I was surprised to find David Mellor, the Chief Secretary, so unsympathetic. He had of course to resist pressure from every spending Department, but his time as a Minister at the Home Office certainly had not turned him into a friend of the police. He said, 'They are overpaid, we've thrown money at them, and we have the highest level of crime in our history.' Leading figures in the Conservative press were also expressing considerable doubt about the effectiveness of policing. I remember Max Hastings, the editor of the *Daily Telegraph*, saying, 'The only time most middle-class people meet the police is when they are being asked to blow into a bag or when they are being told that their burglary can't be investigated for two days.' Nonetheless, I was glad to secure the extra 1,000 officers.

One of the main problems was that there were too many chiefs, and not enough police officers on the beat. There were too many head-quarters staff, and too many senior ranks which had been created simply for career progression. I believed that the answer was to break down the big units and to increase local autonomy in the way that I had been able to do in my education reforms. This meant splitting police forces into smaller operating units directly responsible for one geographical area. There were already some experiments along these lines called 'geographic policing' or 'community policing' in Surrey and South London. Each area would have its own police force of between thirty to sixty officers. They would stay in that area for several years, and the Inspector in charge would come to be recognized by the community as their own Chief Constable. The local community would also become involved, so that their eyes and ears would be recruited in the fight against crime. I was very impressed by a pilot scheme of community policing which I visited in Wandsworth where the increase in crime had fallen from 15 to 5 per cent.

The Home Secretary has no power to instruct local police forces what to do. Instead, he issues guidance through the Chief Inspector of

Constabulary, who at that time was Sir John Woodcock. John and I agreed that community policing was to be the way forward for policing in Britain, a radical and very important decision. But we found it was difficult to implement because of the rigid shift system which governs policing. A police officer is told as much as a year in advance which shift he or she will be working on, and shift loyalty is almost as strong as force loyalty.

The Police Federation, which represents all ranks up to Inspector, was reluctant to change a system full of special payments for extra time at the beginning and end of shifts. Community policing needs flexibility so that fewer police officers are on duty in the quiet times and more at the busier times. The reluctance to accept part-time or flexible working certainly discouraged many women officers from remaining in the force. I managed to persuade the Federation at least to accept job-sharing, so as to encourage experienced police women to stay on. But this was only a start on the long road leading to the abandonment of the rigid attitudes and practices which characterize large parts of the police.

Community policing will improve the quality of the police service and its effectiveness much more than controversial mergers of police forces, or proposals to exclude local councillors from police authorities. Returning the power of decision-making to local people who understand their own needs has been one of my guiding principles in every Department I have served in.

Preventing Criminality

Through a variety of inner-city projects the Home Office financially supported a wide range of schemes to prevent crime. These ranged from a taxi service run by women for women in Coventry, to inner-city after-school care programmes to keep children off the streets until their parents came home from work; the provision of alarms for elderly people living alone; the organization of voluntary street wardens to keep an eye on elderly people; improving the lighting of some streets and car-parks; and the provision of bars and bolts on some housing estates. This was money well spent. Even so, we were fairly criticized for not spending more. But I had to fight for every penny with the Treasury, who as usual were sceptical.

Valuable as these schemes were, they all dealt with the consequences of crime rather than its causes, but I wanted to try and stop young boys slipping into crime in the first place. Research showed that this slide started with boys playing truant, and then moving on to dabbling in drugs, shop-lifting, stealing bicycles, breaking into cars and houses, and joy-riding. A high proportion of crime was committed by young males below the age of fifteen who had become experienced criminals with the prospect of spending a large part of their lives in jail.

I was quite convinced from my time as Education Secretary that it was better to identify troublemakers at an early age and intervene then rather than later. As Home Secretary I approved the spending of £13 million to provide just sixty places in secure lock-up accommodation for fifteen- to sixteen-year-olds on remand. This brought home to me the cost of mopping up a problem which would have cost much less if preventive action had taken place earlier.

I invited to a series of lunchtime meetings leading people who could have an impact on these matters – the Archbishop of Canterbury, the Chief Rabbi, Catholic Bishops, leaders of the Hindu and Muslim communities, teachers, Chief Constables, social workers, prison governors, housing managers, youth workers and those working for charities and voluntary bodies concerned with children's welfare. The consensus was that the problem was concentrated on some housing estates where family support was inadequate or absent and lawlessness was endemic.

Following these meetings, John Patten and I developed a strategy which we called 'Preventing Criminality' and which involved setting up local task forces that would bring together all the various agencies – public and private – to focus on and coordinate help for the most troublesome children. This meant identifying the 'problem kids'. There were objections made on the grounds that by identifying these children one stereotyped them for life. My answer was that such children usually identified themselves, frequently by regular truancy and petty criminal acts. Such children at an early age, certainly at the primary level, should be sent to special schools. When I was Education Secretary I had been told repeatedly that difficult children should be left in mainstream schools in the hope that they would mend their ways through not being isolated. But all too often this did not work, and classes continued to be disrupted by these problem children.

Virginia Bottomley, then the Health Secretary and with her experience as a children's psychiatric social worker, supported these proposals but I could never persuade Ken Clarke, then Education Secretary, of the importance of this initiative, which he blocked. Later, as Home

Secretary, he may have found for himself how much more costly it was to deal with failed youngsters than it would have been if efforts had been made earlier to prevent these young people going off the rails. We need more special schools at the primary level, and there is one in Oxford – Northern House School run by a firm and enlightened head teacher, Ray Howarth – which I have subsequently visited and which could serve as a model.

Reforming Prisons

I asked my Private Secretary, Colin Walters, to arrange a series of regular visits to prisons, as I wanted to see for myself what they were really like. This was rather unusual, for most Home Secretaries do not spend much time visiting prisons. I came across one official who had been in Reggie Maudling's Private Office and he told me that after being Home Secretary for about eighteen months it was suggested to Reggie that he should visit a prison. 'Do I really have to?' was his reply. Willie Whitelaw had had his fingers burnt over the proposal to subject young offenders to a 'short, sharp shock'. This had been in our 1979 Manifesto, but after a brief experiment it had been abandoned as it had no proven effect upon recidivism.

Most Home Secretaries cross their fingers and hope that things will not go wrong in prisons while they are in office. Unfortunately, things went very wrong for David Waddington in April 1990 when a group of violent prisoners seized control of Strangeways Prison and held it in a defiant siege for twenty-three days. A decision was taken on the second day of the riot, without David's knowledge, that force would not be used to regain control of the prison. This riot was one of the most damaging experiences for the prison service and its reputation. The total bill for rebuilding Strangeways, holding prisoners in police cells, and officers' overtime, came to £120 million. I was utterly determined that while I was Home Secretary there would be no repeat of this sort of episode.

Each day incidents occur in prisons which result in the disciplining of prisoners. Some of these incidents can get out of hand, particularly on a warm summer evening when prisoners are made to return to their cells. I was determined not to be kept in the dark about prison disturbances and insisted on being told immediately there was the possibility of an incipient riot. I was also determined not to allow the control of another prison to be lost. I arranged to be told of each incident, and I would then speak directly to the Governor to find out what his plans were to regain control. In every one of these cases the riot was ended within six hours, but they often involved violent struggles and hand-to-hand fighting.

The riots at Strangeways, and other prisons, were protests against the conditions of prison life. I was well aware that the public have little sympathy with these protests and that as far as they are concerned the best treatment is 'lock 'em up and throw away the key'. But such treatment invariably meant that most prisoners left prison with a more hostile attitude towards society than when they entered.

Within a few days of my appointment I visited Wandsworth, a large Victorian prison which housed a thousand remand prisoners awaiting trial in London courts. I was shocked to find that some prisoners were kept in their cells for twenty-two hours a day. Their main communal activity was slopping out the plastic buckets which served as their lavatories during the night. There was little time or opportunity for education and training. One Prison Officer said to me, with his peaked cap pointing almost vertically down his nose, 'We don't have much trouble in this prison, sir.' Over the next year I visited many different types of prison and came to the conclusion that all prisons are grim but some are grimmer than others. The deprivation of liberty is a major punishment in itself, and anyone who doesn't believe that should actually visit a prison. A prisoner's character and personality become slowly submerged and subdued under the institutional regime.

Prisons are needed for three purposes. First, to punish the offender, and second, to protect society. But the third purpose is to release the prisoner as a better person than when he entered, and if possible with a skill so that he has a chance of going straight. Of course prisons should not be holiday camps. They should be austere, and certainly all the ones I visited were – cells have only a bed, a locker and a chair – although long-term prisoners are allowed to keep a canary or a budgerigar. Most prisoners are locked up at nine o'clock at night and unlocked the following morning at eight. But prisons should also be decent places, and the punishment element should not include daily humiliation. Slopping out was a dirty practice and I decided that it should end.

The building plans I inherited would still have left some prison cells without integral sanitation until well beyond the end of the century. I wanted all cells to have integral sanitation, or alternatively prisoners to have controlled access to shared facilities during the night, by the end of

1994. This cost £30 million, and when I asked the Chief Secretary, David Mellor, for the money I am glad to say that he readily agreed. As a former Minister for Prisons, he too had found slopping out to be unacceptable and so I was able to announce the end of this practice in a package of measures in February 1991.

On my visits to prisons most Governors told me that they had little problem with drugs in their prisons, but in fact I found that soft drugs are endemic and that they, together with hard drugs, were often smuggled in during family visits. I also found, particularly in young offenders institutions, that bullying was rife. This was a particularly bad problem in the young offenders institution at Feltham, but then it had always been a mistake to build a prison as large as this on the outskirts of London, where it had to house some of the capital's most defiant, truculent, rebellious and violent youths.

The Prison Officers' Association told me repeatedly that the answer to all problems in the prisons was more staff. Yet the number of Prison Officers had increased by 4,000 while the number of prisoners had actually dropped by 6,000. At the end of the War there were six prisoners to one Prison Officer, and that ratio had dropped to just two prisoners per officer. One of the major obstacles to reform within the prison system in fact was the Prison Officers' Association itself. They supported practices which led to inflexibility and overmanning.

A particular problem was that in a trade union deal in 1989, Douglas Hurd had conceded that Prison Governors should only be promoted from the ranks of Prison Officers. A Prison Governor would therefore have had to have spent a large part of his career as a warder on prison landings. What was needed was an injection of new ideas and wider management experience, which could only come about through recruitment of people who had not spent their entire career in the enclosed and isolated atmosphere of prison life.

The attitude to the wearing of uniform typified much of what was wrong in the prison service. I was amazed that at my first meeting with the Prison Governors' Association their opening question was not about my penal policy but whether I would allow them to wear uniform instead of civilian suits. The Governors told me that this would enhance their status, reinforce their authority, and mean they would be smartly turned out on official occasions like attending funerals. When I visited prisons in other countries in Europe and America I did not find any Governors wearing uniform. I also noted that Prison Officers did not wear intimidating jackets and peaked caps, but pullovers. This in no way reduced their authority within the prisons, but in Britain caps were seen by many Prison Officers as the ultimate expression of their authority. Some carefully pressed down the peak to run almost vertically down their forehead and over their nose.

All this intensified the atmosphere of potential conflict. One must recognize, however, the very difficult task that Prison Officers face. They have to control a mass of men, most of whom are frustrated, bored and on a short fuse. Most are devious, some corrupt, and there are some to whom violence is a way of life. Since weightlifting and bodybuilding are two of the most popular pastimes in prisons, some prisoners are also very strong and powerful men.

I did not advocate a 'softly, softly' approach, but I did believe that if society treated convicted criminals as animals then they would behave like animals. The authority of a Prison Officer should depend not upon what he wears but upon his strength of character, fairness, firmness, consistency in dealing with prisoners, and the back-up he knows he can count upon. The Report on the Strangeways disturbance produced by Lord Justice Woolf recommended that caps generally should not be worn in prison, that the doctored peaked cap should be banned, and that each Prison Officer should be identified by a name badge. All of this the POA opposed.

Clearly changes were necessary. The prison estate had been neglected for years, but both Willie Whitelaw and Douglas Hurd had secured a significant increase in the building programme. Since 1987, ten new prisons had been opened and eight more were being built. A large proportion of the prison estate had been built in the nineteenth century and was now overcrowded and insanitary. The building programme created 10,000 new places, and unfortunately all of these were needed, as the prison population was rising to 50,000. Early in 1991 I decided to make some changes in prisons. I approved the provision of telephones in more prisons, as most prisoners are worried about what is happening to their families outside and it is sensible to allow them access to a telephone, provided of course that they pay for the calls themselves. Similarly I did not consider the routine censorship of letters, which took up a lot of Prison Officers' time, to be necessary except for dangerous prisoners, those suspected of trying to escape, or those wanting to interfere with witnesses.

While there was hardly likely to be general acclaim for such changes they were warmly welcomed by Judge Stephen Tumim, the Chief Inspector of Prisons, who had started to publish his reports which were highly critical of conditions in individual prisons. Similarly, Lord Justice Woolf, whose Report into the Strangeways riot I published in the spring of 1991, produced a milestone in penal reform. Both Woolf and Tumim wanted the regime in prisons to be more positive and constructive. So did I. Prisoners should be kept busy, either improving their education or acquiring useful skills.

Privatization of the Management of Prisons

I asked Angela Rumbold, the Prisons Minister, to go and see for herself the experiments in the private management of prisons in America. David Waddington had been impressed by what he had seen in Australia, and I too was later to see for myself the success of privately managed prisons in the United States, and the contracting-out of many prison services in France. On Angela's advice we decided to contract out the management of the new remand prison in Yorkshire, The Wolds, even though remand prisons present difficult problems through the constant changeover of prisoners and the more relaxed regime to which prisoners awaiting trial are entitled. I visited The Wolds both before and after it had opened. The senior management had been drawn from the prison service but the Prison Officers had been recruited from other walks of life and were therefore not indoctrinated by POA attitudes. Prisoners were allowed out of their cells for fourteen hours a day and there was generally a more relaxed atmosphere. This was likely to be initially abused by some prisoners who were used to the more restrictive regimes in the old Victorian prisons. We were able to extend privatization to more prisons and this has been warmly supported by my successors.

The Brixton Escape

On Sunday 8 July 1991 Mary and I were at Dorneywood preparing to host a summer party for my Private Office staff and their families. At about eleven o'clock I was telephoned by Heather Wilkinson, my Assistant Private Secretary, who gave me the bad news that two men remanded in custody on terrorist charges had shot their way out of Brixton Prison after attending chapel, and had then shot a passing motorist and escaped. Thus began the single most difficult episode during my period as Home Secretary.

I immediately telephoned John Major to tell him what had happened, and he was sympathetic and supportive. Nevertheless, it quickly crossed my mind that this could be a resignation matter, and I telephoned Tony Kerpel to get his reaction. His view was, 'If the escape is due to a policy failure then you might well have to resign. If it's due to an operational failure then that's down to the prison staff. Nobody expects the Home Secretary to personally lock up every prisoner in every cell in every jail.' Over the next few hours I received updates about the escape, and the media had the first details by lunchtime. The two escapees were last seen at Baker Street tube station, having abandoned their hijacked car and taken a taxi the rest of the way. In fact they did not surface again until April 1993, when they were rearrested in the Irish Republic.

It was clear that I would have to make a statement to the House about the Brixton escape, and on Monday morning I met with officials to establish the facts. To the amazement of everyone, Chris Train, the Director-General of the Prison Service, who had said on Sunday's television news that security at Brixton was 'adequate', told us that there was an unsubstantiated report that a prison officer, said to have been collaborating with the Staffordshire Police, knew that the two IRA prisoners had been interested in getting hold of a gun. Since this was unconfirmed and no one could answer the questions I raised about it, I could not refer to it in the statement I made in the House that afternoon. But I did specifically ask Judge Stephen Tumim, the Chief Inspector of Prisons, who was to carry out a full inquiry into the escape, to look into these new allegations.

At 3.30 p.m. on Monday, I gave the House the fullest account of the escape I could, and promised that subject only to security requirements I intended to publish Stephen Tumim's Report at the end of the month. In the meantime I had ordered Prison Governors to review their procedures for holding all high-risk prisoners when out of their cells. Roy Hattersley, Labour's Shadow Home Secretary, made the most of this chance to attack me, but Merlyn Rees, the former Labour Home Secretary and Northern Ireland Secretary, was both circumspect and constructive in his intervention, having himself faced the sort of problem I now did. It was not a comfortable time, but I was determined to discover what had gone wrong so that we could try and stop it happening again.

Stephen Tumim conducted his inquiry with both speed and thoroughness, and delivered his Report at the beginning of August. It did not make happy reading. Not only were there security weaknesses at Brixton Prison, but there had indeed been prior knowledge of an escape attempt. A Prison Officer had struck up a relationship with the two IRA prisoners and learnt that they were interested in obtaining a gun. This information had been passed to a Staffordshire police officer. He in turn passed it on to the Metropolitan Police, who then informed the Prison Department and the Governor of Brixton. On receiving this information the Governor had the Prison Officer transferred to another jail, but did nothing to separate the two high-risk IRA suspects, who were still kept in the same wing of the prison and allowed to attend Mass together.

There had clearly been a very serious failure of communication between the Home Office Prison Department and the Brixton Governor. Officials neither fully appreciated nor acted with sufficient urgency on very serious warnings. Furthermore, none of this information had been communicated to Ministers prior to the escape. The report concluded that the Brixton escape had been an operational failure of security at the prison.

Stephen Tumim initially recommended that for good security reasons only a small part of his Report should be published. I argued that this was unacceptable, as it would lead to cries of 'cover-up', and that we had to publish as much as possible. Stephen's view was that to publish the whole report would endanger remaining security at Brixton and jeopardize the safety of individual prison officers. I had to accept this advice from the Chief Inspector of Prisons, and so a truncated version of his Report containing that information which we could reveal was published on Monday 5 August.

The fact that a large part of this eagerly awaited report remained unpublished served only to resurrect speculation about the escape. The suspicion arose that there had been a covert operation in the prison, and the most inventive journalists theorized that the security services had set out to help the two IRA men escape so that they would be led to IRA safe houses and other terrorist contacts in the UK. This theory was utter rubbish. If ever there was a case of cock-up rather than conspiracy then Brixton was it. However, as long as parts of the Tumim Report remained unpublished there was nothing I could do to dispel such untruthful speculation.

Since I had returned from a holiday to spend three days in London for the publication of the Tumim Report, I now left London to collect Mary from where we had been staying. But within twenty-four hours a media storm had broken out. My Private Office and the Home Office press office were totally phlegmatic about the calls for my head. They had seen this all before and regarded it as going with the territory of being Home Secretary. But Tony Kerpel phoned me to say that I was getting the worst press he had seen me receive in six years. I decided to come back to deal with it, and Mary and I returned to London that night. On Friday I spent much of the afternoon individually briefing the political correspondents of the Sunday newspapers in order to get over the facts of the Brixton saga and squash the wilder stories. By the weekend, the newspapers carried much more balanced and sober accounts of this inglorious episode.

However, as far as the House of Commons was concerned, the Labour Party still continued to make accusations of a cover-up. Their spokesmen implied that I had foreknowledge of police warnings about the Brixton escape and had not given as full an account to the House as I could have done when making my original statement. This was totally untrue, and a definitive answer from me to a Written Question from Peter Archer, Labour's Shadow Attorney-General, finally killed the issue in December.

In classic Civil Service fashion the Home Office's own disciplinary inquiry found nobody responsible for the extraordinary breach of security at Brixton. As for the question of my own position, most senior Ministers get demands for their resignation at some time during their careers, and this is something to which serious consideration has to be given. Several of my predecessors as Home Secretary had faced similar calls: Roy Jenkins over the escape of George Blake from Wormwood Scrubs; Willie Whitelaw over Michael Fagan's break-in to the Queen's bedroom; Douglas Hurd over the daring helicopter escape from Gartree; and David Waddington over the Strangeways Prison riot. But on none of these occasions did these Home Secretaries feel there were genuine grounds for resignation. In each case the failure was one of operational security on the ground, and not one resulting from policy for which the Home Secretary is directly responsible. I believed that the Brixton escape fell into that category.

The National Lottery

For a long time I had been in favour of a National Lottery. Most other European countries had them, and I did not believe that a British lottery would have harmful social consequences. Because of our membership of the European Community it was likely that German, French and Spanish lottery tickets would soon become available in the UK. It would have been ludicrous for our people to be able to contribute to other countries' lotteries while denying them the right to buy British lottery tickets. Indeed a British National Lottery could raise a great deal of additional money for good causes such as charities, art, sport and the national heritage, which were all areas the Government wanted to support but for which there was never enough money.

Since the Home Secretary is responsible for the control of gambling, it fell to me to take the initiative about getting a National Lottery off the ground. My predecessors had never felt sufficiently interested to do anything about it, and the Home Office had traditionally frowned on any extension of gambling, but I saw this as a chance for the Government to introduce a little gaiety into British life. Prior to the 1991 Budget I met the Chancellor, Norman Lamont, to discuss the possibilities. I told Norman that any proposal would need to be very carefully worked up and developed because there were various vested interests, particularly the Football Pools industry, which would do everything to stop a National Lottery. One could not simply announce that the Government was in favour of a lottery, for it would need careful preparation and collective discussion, but I would be happy to prepare a paper for colleagues to consider at Cabinet.

What Norman did not tell me was that he was working on a scheme to head off a National Lottery. John Major, when he was Chancellor of the Exchequer, had done a deal with the Pools companies whereby Football Pools duty was reduced in exchange for the Pools using that money to help fund the rebuilding and improvement of football grounds. John had wanted to develop this further and passed the ball to David Mellor, his close friend and fellow soccer fan, who was Treasury Chief Secretary. David spoke to Richard Faulkner, who advised Littlewoods, and over a lunch in the Fulham Road they worked out a new scheme whereby the Treasury would reduce the duty on Pools even further if the Pools would put up at least a similar sum to create a £60 million fund not just for football but for other sports and for the Arts as well. The quid pro quo was that the Government would not press ahead with a National Lottery.

Early in 1991 Des Pitcher, the Managing Director of Littlewoods, was summoned to the Treasury to agree this deal. At the meeting, attended by Norman Lamont, David Mellor and the Treasury Permanent Secretary, Terry Burns, Des first asked for the Pools to become a National Lottery, but this was turned down flat. A deal was then done whereby Pools duty was to come down by 5 per cent, although Des had to offer a 10 per cent contribution in order to produce the magic figure of £60 million for the Sports and Arts Foundation.

This apparent benevolence on the part of the Pools was in fact an ingenious proposal designed to protect their trading future. It was a pretty blatant attempt by the Football Pools industry to prevent the Government from bringing in a rival. The Pools sold the idea to the Treasury, and Norman Lamont did not tell me about it before he made the announcement in his Budget. This was a remarkable example of how Budget secrecy does not help the good administration of the country or the cohesion of government policy. David Mellor at that time was sceptical about the idea of a lottery, although he now has all the enthusiasm of a convert. Norman Lamont was 'interested but not very'.

Despite lack of Treasury approval for developing my idea, the Home Office set to work preparing a paper on the National Lottery and we had it ready by 30 April. I persuaded Chris Patten and Douglas Hurd to support our proposals, while Tim Renton, as Arts Minister, and Michael Heseltine were both keen on the idea. Chris said he could see no downside from the point of view of either the Party or the Government, but he realized that the Treasury was in some difficulty because of its private deal with the Pools for the Sports and Arts Foundation. Treasury Ministers were supported by Ken Clarke, who also opposed a National Lottery on the grounds that it would jeopardize the Foundation. The messages coming from the Treasury about a lottery proposal were now distinctly cool.

My shrewd and experienced Private Secretary, Colin Walters, said, 'I do wish you wouldn't take on the Treasury. You won't win.' He was even concerned that if defeated, the Treasury would 'seek revenge' by trying to cut Home Office spending plans. However, I thought it quite absurd that Norman Lamont and the Treasury should have been bought off for as little as £60 million when the revenues flowing from a National Lottery could amount to billions of pounds. The amount of money that a National Lottery could raise would be between ten or twenty times greater than that offered by the Pools. It was not even a question of a bird in the hand being better than two in the bush. It was more a question of half a bird compared with a flock. I was now even more determined to pursue the idea.

In the autumn I encouraged Ivan Lawrence, the MP for Burton, a good friend and the Chairman of the Home Affairs Backbench Committee, who had won a place in the ballot for Private Members Bills, to bring in a Bill to set up a National Lottery. This would bring the whole issue to the fore and compel the Government to make up its mind. The campaign for a National Lottery would be so popular that the Government would have to accept it. I went to see John Major and persuaded him that as the prospects of actually finding a large amount of money from public expenditure for the Arts, Sport and the Heritage, and indeed to celebrate the Millennium, would be well nigh impossible, the answer was a National Lottery. It would provide a substantial amount of money to improve the quality of life throughout our country.

Chris Patten, conscious of the need for popular policies which would actually win some votes, now wanted to commit the Conservative Party to a National Lottery in the Election Manifesto. When I met John Major and Norman Lamont on 14 January 1992 I was given the go-ahead to prepare a White Paper, but there was still doubt about whether the lottery would be left for the Manifesto or be announced before the General Election. In my view it would have a much greater impact if it was announced before the Election, since otherwise it would be lost in all the other Manifesto commitments.

From the work we were doing it was clear that after two or three years, if it was competently run, a National Lottery could produce sums as large as £1 billion for good causes. I wanted to see it up and running by 1994 and so I got the agreement of the Prime Minister to publish a White Paper. It was typical of the Treasury that having lost this particular battle they now wanted to profit from it. I had to insist on a cast-iron assurance, enshrined in the White Paper, that money for the lottery would be additional funding for public sector projects and not a substitute, an option the Treasury wanted to keep open. Furthermore, I resisted the Treasury's demand for too high a tax on lottery tickets. Clearly, some Treasury officials need a stake through the heart before policies are safe from their clutches.

The White Paper was published on 6 March and received a generally favourable welcome. It appeared just in time, because on 11 March John Major decided to call a General Election. The Party was now clearly committed to the National Lottery, and the legislation to estabish it has since been passed by Parliament.

Our work on preparing the National Lottery made me think about the division of responsibilities in the Home Office. I had come to the conclusion that it would be better if there was one Cabinet Minister responsible for the Arts, Sport, Broadcasting, Tourism and the National Heritage. I had been responsible for several of these matters during my ministerial career in the Departments of Trade, Environment, Education, and now at the Home Office. I therefore suggested to Sir Robin Butler, the Cabinet Secretary, that there should be a new Department to cover these areas of national cultural interest. As far as the Arts and Sport were concerned this would be a quite simple matter, because there were already separate Ministers for the Arts and for Sport, although the two responsibilities had been shuttled from one Department to another over the years.

Significantly I recommended that responsibility for broadcasting should be transferred away from the Home Office. I think I was the first Home Secretary prepared to surrender ministerial responsibility for broadcasting policy, but I believed the Home Office was not the right place for this. Television and broadcasting were being driven forward by diversity and technological change, which meant that the regulation of broadcasting would play a less significant role in the future. Moreover television, particularly through Channel Four, had become an important commissioning agent for new films and programmes, and changes at the BBC were moving in the same direction. It therefore seemed to make sense that broadcasting should be in the same Department as that responsible for the film industry and support for the Arts. I also suggested that heritage responsibilities should be moved from the Department of the Environment, as these too were concerned with the historic culture of our society. In addition I proposed that responsibility for the British Council and the World Service should be transferred from the Foreign Office to the new Department.

In the spring of 1992 I asked Robin Butler to submit these proposals to the Prime Minister, and I also put them to John's Policy Unit at Number 10, as they were looking for new ideas on the structure of Government. I was very glad these proposals were accepted by the Prime Minister and put into the Manifesto. In the discussion to finalize the Manifesto, Douglas Hurd, as Foreign Secretary, refused to give up responsibility for the British Council and the World Service. It was initially envisaged that the new ministerial post would not be in the Cabinet, but it seemed to me totally unacceptable to have a Minister answerable for the BBC who did not sit at the Cabinet table by right. I noticed that in the discussion on this point David Mellor strongly supported my view, thereby demonstrating bags of foresight about the 'Ministry of Fun' which he was to be the first to inherit after the 1992 Election.

Racing

One of the unalloyed pleasures of the Home Secretary is to discharge his responsibility for the racing industry. I asked my Private Office to arrange some visits to racecourses to fit in with other duties. As it turned out, a prison in the morning and a race meeting in the afternoon just about filled the bill. The economics of the racing industry were in a mess, with the business being run shambolically and each interest group – owners, trainers, bookies, jockeys and racecourse owners – vying with and blaming the rest. 'Stoker' Hartington, the newly appointed Chairman of the Jockey Club, was sensibly trying to fashion a committee representing the various interests in order to run racing. This was certainly a step forward.

The betting levy was a way of taking some of the bookies' profits from the £6 billion a year of bets they handled, so that finance could be ploughed back into improving racecourses and increasing prize money. The racing industry and the bookies were supposed to agree the levy each year, but when I was Home Secretary they could not agree and it fell to me to determine the amount. I persuaded Norman Lamont to reduce betting duty and this was added to the levy which I announced. The industry was better financed that year than for a very long time, and so Norman and I were popular figures, at least on racecourses.

In early June 1991, at the end of a Cabinet meeting, I thought I heard the Prime Minister say, 'I am going to the Derby.' I said, 'I'm delighted to hear that. I'm going myself and we'll have a good day's racing. It will be very popular for the Prime Minister to be seen at the Derby. You'll enjoy it.' John looked puzzled and then, realizing I had misheard him, said, 'No, I'm not going to the Derby. I'm going to have lunch with Mugabe.' 'That is a pity,' I said, 'because it won't be as enjoyable or as popular.'

Winning a Fourth Term

General Election planning was clearly in Chris Patten's hands, but occasionally John Major asked for my views. In January 1991, just after the Gulf War had started, we discussed a possible date for the General Election. At that time John favoured an early Election in the summer provided the Gulf War was over. Ministers in each Department were asked to prepare Manifesto commitments to be ready by the end of March.

In January, Maurice Saatchi asked me to lunch in order to meet David Owen. Maurice, a close friend of David's, was appalled that his talents were not being used and wanted to try and build a bridge to lead David into the Conservative camp. The difficulty was that David was not a Conservative – indeed I doubt whether he will ever be one. He was still the Leader of the Social Democrat Party, which had two other MPs in the House of Commons, Rosie Barnes and John Cartwright, whom he could not abandon. However, no one believed they would hold their seats, and at that time David Owen had not decided whether he himself would stand for re-election. At our lunch he said, 'The only real issue which still interests me in British politics is constitutional reform. I hope that the Tories will adopt proportional representation for the European Elections.' This was clearly a non-starter as far as the Conservative Party was concerned. As regards Europe, David believed that Margaret Thatcher's interventions had saved the Community from a federal future which he strongly opposed.

Following that lunch, I arranged a dinner at our house in Pimlico for John Major and Chris Patten to meet David Owen. By that time Owen had decided not to stand at the next Election, but Chris still felt that his endorsement would be worth one or two per cent of the votes. David Owen clearly liked John, who was a little reserved, but there was nothing John could really offer as there was no question of Tories standing down in the SDP MPs' seats. I was frankly doubtful whether Owen still had a sufficient following to make any significant difference to the votes at a General Election. Owen did, however, favour an early Election, as did John, although Chris was more circumspect.

In the national opinion polls early in 1991, the Conservatives had moved ahead of Labour after John had become leader, but this was not reflected in by-election results. In March, a by-election took place in Ribble Valley following the elevation of David Waddington to the peerage and to the governorship of Bermuda. Chris thought that we would hold this seat with a majority of 2–4,000 and private opinion polls for Central Office supported this view. In the event there was a Liberal Democrat majority of 4,000, which left Chris looking as wrongfooted as I had been over Eastbourne. It was after this defeat that he gloomily asked me at a Cabinet meeting, 'How can you ever win a by-election?'

By the end of March Labour was once again ahead in the polls. That spelt the end of any chance of a summer Election. However, once Parliament had risen we began to close the gap on Labour, and it looked as if a good time to go to the country would be after the Tory Party Conference in November. On 16 September John Major came to have lunch at Dorneywood. The newspapers were full of speculation about an autumn Election, with which my name was particularly associated. The reason for this was that we had moved ahead of Labour in one poll and I had cheerily said to a doorstepping television crew, 'It's looking good.' This was seized on as evidence that I favoured an early Election.

John and I discussed this privately after lunch and I said, 'I favour November the seventh.' John replied, 'You are in a minority.' I offered to deny the stories appearing in the papers and to disassociate my name from 7 November, but John said, 'Don't do that. I don't want to close any option and it may just be possible. But what I don't want is to win with a small majority. That would be the worst of all possible worlds, and it would leave the likes of Nick Budgen calling the shots.' However, within a week an opinion poll in the *Sunday Times* showed that the Tories had slipped again to four points behind Labour – an autumn Election was not on.

At a post-Cabinet political discussion on 6 November Chris Patten told us that even after he had collated all the ideas from colleagues for a possible autumn Election, the Manifesto still seemed very thin and uninteresting. He said, 'Could we please go back to the drawing-board?' Morale in the Party was low, as the view had now become established that Labour – even under Kinnock – was going to win. At the 6 November meeting John Gummer said that to his certain knowledge four Cabinet Ministers, or their wives, had said at his dinner table that it would not be too bad a thing if we went into Opposition for a short period. John replied, 'I hope that doesn't get out.' I was amazed to hear this news, and surprised that John Gummer had such pessimistic friends.

During the winter there was a short flurry of speculative debate about a spring as opposed to a summer Election. David Mellor was particularly keen on running the full term to July. But John Major, fed up with mounting election fever in the press and sensitive to the charge of dithering, decided we had waited long enough and called the General Election for 9 April. We were behind in the polls and Central Office ran a very unconfident campaign. It did not help that the Party had a Director of Communications who was not notable for either directing or communicating. Brendan Bruce's talents were sorely missed. The Conservative campaign was saved from utter disaster by John Major's determined and unflappable personal leadership and, halfway through, his use of the soapbox to address election crowds.

The Labour Party threw prospective victory away by making two big blunders. First, John Smith's Shadow Budget gave us some wonderful ammunition by advocating tax increases which, it was claimed, were meant to hit only the rich. However, Labour had totally failed to learn the old, old lesson that Opposition Parties do not win elections by promising only selective tax increases. The public simply did not believe that Labour would keep their marauding hands out of all taxpayers' pockets. Second, Labour's Sheffield Rally, held one week before polling day, was far too triumphalist. Neil Kinnock sank his Party's campaign by bawling out three times, 'Well all right? Well all right? Well all right?' The next day in one of my own campaign speeches, I likened this to 'the cry of the holiday rep on the coach, greeting the new batch of beery arrivals. There is a fine line between confidence and cockiness, and on Wednesday night in Sheffield, Mr Kinnock stepped over it.' When the Labour campaign then began to introduce Shadow Cabinet members as Ministers in the Government-in-Waiting, a distinct feeling grew among our campaigners, and commentators, that here was a Party about to get its comeuppance.

Nobody more typified Labour's smug complacency than my Shadow, Roy Hattersley. In the various studio confrontations we had during the Election campaign it was obvious that here was someone convinced that he was about to achieve his destiny as Home Secretary in a Labour Government. His demeanour was that of a man who could taste high office and already feel the soft leather of the ministerial car cushioning his ample frame. In our face-to-face debates his conceit repeatedly got the better of him, as each time he used the phrase, 'When I am Home Secretary . . .' But as I said to the Conservative Party's opening Election rally, 'Mr Hattersley's mind is on his next novel and his next menu. We must ensure that the prospect of ministerial office does not disrupt the literary career of Labour's leading gastronome.'

The Liberals too began to behave cockily as the final opinion polls indicated a hung Parliament. Paddy Ashdown spoke about the terms he would demand for Liberal cooperation with a minority Government, and there was talk of how many Cabinet posts the Liberals might demand. The fact that, in the final days of the campaign, the Conservatives were turning their fire on proportional representation – the Liberals' main demand – was regarded by commentators as proof positive that the Conservatives were running scared. But this issue gave me my best opportunity to enter the campaign. In a German federal election on 5 April, proportional representation had enabled Fascists to enter the State Parliament after winning 11 per cent of the popular vote. Since PR was also one of the demands of the French National Front, this allowed me to claim that, 'Proportional representation has helped the Fascists to march again in Europe. It is a terrible warning to us about what could happen if we threw away our system of first-past-the-post elections. If PR turned out to have the same results in Britain it would be a pact with the devil.' My speech made most of the front pages and helped to knock on the head the idea that PR was an unqualified blessing.

On Wednesday 8 April I went with Tony Kerpel, and fellow senior Ministers, to the final Conservative Election press conference at Central Office. At a depressing pre-meeting everyone had tales of constituency seats they had visited and which, they predicted, we were going to lose. Ken Clarke said that Edwina Currie and Greg Knight were not going to win in Derbyshire. But I was more optimistic. Having just campaigned for Alistair Burt in Bury North, and David Sumberg in Bury South, where we had received a very friendly reception in the huge open-air market, I was convinced we would hold these seats which most other people had written off. Michael Heseltine was also optimistic, but then he had had a good campaign and was a winner either way, since if John lost the Election the Party would almost certainly want to elect as his successor a fighting cock. I had taken a bet with David Dimbleby of the BBC, who was convinced the Conservatives would lose, that we would win with a majority of twenty. I had won a similar bet with him over the 1987 election.

At the debriefing after our press conference, Chris Patten was particularly depressed because by that time he had sensed that whatever happened he would lose his own seat at Bath. The discussion then turned to Election night, and Chris gave the clearest indication of his belief about the likely Election result. He asked all ministerial colleagues not to appear on television in Election programmes late on Thursday night or early on Friday morning. He asked those of us already committed to appearing, as I was, to cancel, which I did. Clearly Chris was expecting that the Government was going to lose its overall majority and that nothing should be said about negotiations or deals with other Parties until he and John Major had analysed the implication of the results. From the very top of the Party the prospect of defeat was being signalled. Fortunately, the electorate had other ideas. The Conservatives were re-elected with 336 seats, an overall majority of 21. Labour won 271 seats and the Liberals 20.

Standing Down

In the autumn of 1991, some six months before the General Election, Mary and I were on holiday abroad. Being away from Britain for a short time allowed us to reflect together in a rather calmer way about my political life and career.

I had been in the House of Commons for twenty-three years, and I still very much enjoyed being a Member of Parliament. I had been a Minister for thirteen years: two years under Ted Heath, nine with Margaret, and just under two with John. I was proud of the innovative changes in technology and the major education and prison reforms which I had introduced, and many other developments which I had furthered. Much had been achieved and I doubted whether the next five years would be as interesting, stimulating and adventurous as the previous ten.

A General Election was on the way, and provided that the Conservatives won a fourth successive term I might be reappointed to a Cabinet post. However, the leadership of the Party had jumped a generation and was an issue in which my name no longer featured. Moreover, unlike my time with Margaret I was not a member of the Prime Minister's inner circle. He did not seek my views on matters apart from those affecting my own Department, and in any event he had his own kitchen Cabinet and his own style. I felt I had played my part in the great Conservative revival of the 1980s and that this fascinating and turbulent chapter of my life was coming to an end. I therefore began to adjust my mind and my outlook to a new pattern for a future life outside Government.

Following his 1992 General Election victory John, as I had expected, did not want me as part of his senior team. The guard was changing. I had no complaint about that, as every Prime Minister must appoint whomsoever they want as part of their inner circle. However, John did ask me to continue serving in the Cabinet as Secretary of State for Wales. When I told him I did not wish to accept the job he urged me to consider it and to come back to him later in the day. I then explained to him that I had decided in my own mind that I wanted to leave the Government, and over the last six months had been planning my future life on that basis. So in spite of his offer I told John that I felt it would be better to make a clean break and to leave the Government.

Over the years, I have seen too many politicians of both Parties clinging to office and enduring a rather humiliating and long-drawn-out twilight where increasing age and public speculation about when they would be dropped from Cabinet diminished their standing. However, I love the House of Commons and certainly wanted to remain as an MP, while doing everything I could to ensure that the Government followed a sensible economic policy of low taxation and restrained expenditure, and the right European policy, which is a non-federalist one. I was also looking forward to the opportunity to write more books and articles, and to re-involve myself in the business activities which I had once so much enjoyed.

I have no regrets about my decision. I have found it stimulating to be involved again in two of my first interests, industry and technology, through advising Hanson, ICL and Cable and Wireless. It has been challenging and enjoyable to write two books – this autobiography, and the anthology, *The Faber Book of Conservatism*, in which I identified the ideas, attitudes and temperament which have characterized Conservatism down the ages.

To serve continuously as a Minister for eleven years is a long commitment, and I noticed that even Margaret towards the end was slowing up. There were days when her red boxes were not completed, and her meetings were sustained by instinct more than anything else. Now that she has had a break – albeit unwilling on her part – her batteries are recharged and the adrenalin is flowing again. Ministers do need periods in their lives away from daily ministerial duty. That has become so onerous that there is little time for reflection about the bigger underlying changes affecting society and Britain's position in the world. Ministers, necessarily preoccupied with the immediate crisis and the issue of the moment, find it difficult to step back and look at the broader scene. Indeed, if they do step back then one of their colleagues will take the opportunity to step ahead of them.

I have always been blessed with excellent good health and stamina, but few people are aware of the long hours that are demanded by ministerial duties, constituency claims, the processes of the House of Commons and above all the continuing and increasing pressure of paper that comes in every night at about 10 p.m. in anything from one to four red boxes which have to be cleared by breakfast-time. I know from observation that many Ministers switch to automatic pilot on a course set by their officials simply to avoid being swamped by this inexorable tide of paper. In the past, periods of Opposition have provided politicians with a natural break and a capacity to regenerate. Parties that remain in office for a long period of time must find other means to rekindle their momentum, and inevitably this means more comings and goings among ministerial ranks.

When I look back on the 1980s I count myself extremely lucky to have played a major role in the changes of that decade. It was a good time to be at the top table of British politics. Education reform was essential, and I decided to follow Milton's advice to 'strike high and adventure dangerously'. The Education Reform Act was based upon the twin principles of raising standards and extending choice. It was bitterly opposed at the time, but I am glad now that it has been largely accepted by both the Labour and Liberal Parties. The reformed education system now needs a period of calm consolidation. Education will never be stripped of controversy, but it should be stripped of Party polemics.

I was one of those in the Thatcher decade who believed in the dispersal of power, and one of the mistakes we made was to leave too much power in Whitehall. I have never believed in the infallibility of central government, and the closer I came to it the more that view was confirmed. As a Conservative, I wanted to see more power given to individuals so that their creativity, commitment and energy were given full play.

The community charge was an attempt, which failed, to give local authorities a tax base that would make them more truly accountable to every adult local elector. Rate-capping and an increasing dependence upon central government grants weakens the independence of local authorities. Over the next ten years we need to develop a new constitutional settlement between local and central government, otherwise the drift towards a more centralized state will continue.

There is much unfinished business from the Thatcher decade. Attitudes were changed, and for a time we really did achieve high levels of economic growth. Britain regained confidence in its national ability, but then we wandered off the path. We are now seeking to return to that path, and we should learn from our mistakes. I do not share the view that Britain is a middle-aged country set upon an inevitable course of economic decline, that many institutions are so discredited that they are at the point of collapse, and that our future is one of genteel impoverishment. What the Thatcher years showed was that it was possible for Britain to regain its confidence, that the British respond to leadership, and that Britain continues to possess large reservoirs of resourcefulness and resilience embodied in its people.

A National Strategy for
Information Technology

Many British industries from textiles to motor cars are facing powerful competition and all forecast fewer jobs, contraction or even closure. This is not a new problem for us. This industrial decline set in many years ago and governments of both parties have been too preoccupied with trying to stop that decline or to lessen its social results. Let us for once look at those areas where we can hope to expand and to create the new wealth to replace the dying industries.

The most successful countries in the future will be those with a strong and inventive electronics industry with close links with downstream consumer industries, particularly the capital and consumer goods industries. Britain must not be left behind in this technological race, we will have to run very hard to keep abreast of our European partners and to keep ahead of the newly industrialized countries of the developing world.

By far the clearest opportunity lies in Information Technology. By that I mean all those hardware and software companies that design, manufacture and supply projects like the vast computer system for PAYE to microprocessors which can program energy saving in the home and like TV signals via satellite to leisure and learning for the family. It is an industry where we already have a wide range of skills; many developments like Prestel that have a world lead, and many well trained and highly skilled people. It is a fiercely competitive industry. Since every developed country has come to the same conclusion, their governments have decided to involve themselves in promoting or protecting their own information technology industry. The Japanese Government for example has injected £1,100 million into the industry to catch up with America.

The British Government remains detached, although it has some direct investments in some small companies, and it does allocate funds to development projects and it is a major public purchaser of information technology products and systems. I wish to argue for the development in a very short space of time of a National Strategy in which the Government has to take the lead. Its role should be that of coordinator and catalyst. I am not arguing for a National Plan type of intervention with vast state intervention and direction of investment. The opportunity for Britain in this industry is immense and we must not let it slip between our fingers. I propose a ten-point programme.

1 *A Minister for Information Technology should be appointed within the Department*

of Industry. He would have responsibility for the whole range of information technology activities within the Department and for British Telecommunications. He would liaise with other departments and act as a spur to them, in such subjects as the training and education in computer skills; their policies of public procurement and their own use of modern techniques. This appointment is not a gimmick. It is essential to have a focal point in Government for this diverse industry which can draw all the leads together. This will not entail a new bureaucracy. The departments involved already exist, but there is a need at the administrative level as well for a central focus.

2 *The Government should prepare and issue a Policy Document 'Information Technology in the UK in the 1980s'*. No such document has ever been issued. It should embody a programme outlining the opportunities that exist and pointing out clearly how they can be maximized. There is an inevitable interface between the public and private sectors and that should be creative and helpful, not hostile and suspicious. Such a document is the essential strategic thinking for this industry. Once it is prepared it should be launched with the personal endorsement of the Prime Minister.

3 *The Departments of Industry and of Trade should initiate a strong programme to sell the products of Britain's information technology abroad*. Increasingly major sales are made by close collaboration between the Government and private industry – radar, telephone exchanges, transnational data networks, and satellites. When Ministers go abroad they must be fully briefed on the opportunities for British information technology in the country they are visiting. Again there is need for a central focus.

4 *The Government should announce a new Procurement Policy replacing the ICL-orientated policy with one concerned with national interest*. Certain European Governments and the USA will continue their covert policies to support their own nation's industry. We can either have no such policy; keep it covert; or declare it openly. I favour the latter, but it can be given a European slant as well. The national interest must be broadly defined to encompass not just hardware, but the terminals, the peripherals, the software and the research which are made or carried out in the UK.

5 *The Government should identify a number of applications for advanced systems within its own activities and procure them from the British information technology industry*. Some examples of these are:
a) The introduction of the electronic office into Whitehall.
b) The use by Government at home and in embassies abroad of Prestel.
c) The wider use of information technology in the Health Service. There is a vast range of applications from diagnostic analysis to patient treatment.
d) Schools should be provided with small and low-cost micro-computers and software systems. To give a boost to our own hardware industry they should be asked to design and supply these quickly.
e) A more concentrated national space and satellite programme.

f) Energy-saving systems in buildings, starting with the Government's own estate.

g) The improvement of telecommunications particularly in the City of London.

6 *Corporation Tax should be changed so that the discrimination against Service industry companies is reduced or eliminated.* The combination of capital allowances and stock relief means that manufacturing companies pay a very low level of Corporation Tax. Computer Service companies pay a much higher proportion of their earnings in tax, which reduces the amount of funds they can generate internally to grow. Service industries in general are going to create many new jobs: we should not have a tax regime which discriminates against them.

7 *The new Minister should take the lead in setting up technology agreements.* An initiative taken now with the unions and employers could facilitate the adoption of information technology in the years to come. The TUC has adopted a policy generally in favour of information technology as they can see the job-creating prospects, but some Trade Unions are actively hostile to the introduction of information technology.

8 *The Government's Research & Development programme in information technology is almost exclusively a preserve of Universities and the Government research establishments and it should be put on a wider basis.* There are real centres of excellence in British research & development – the radar and signals establishment at Malvern; the BBC at Kingswood Warren; the Post Office and the National Physical Laboratory. Industry should be involved with the programmes of such establishments. Research and development should be encouraged in the private sector by the deliberate front loading of certain contracts, as the Americans have done, to allow companies to recover part of their research & development expenditure. By these means IBM in 1972–1974 received from the US Government over $900 million.

9 *The Enterprise Zones should be the subject of a major Government initiative in promoting information technology in the small firm.* Within these zones really advanced systems could be set up to meet the needs of the new firms which could quite literally only have to 'plug in'. One of the zones, possibly in Docklands, could also provide workshops and training facilities in information technology and a working display of the office of the future. This would assist those in declining industries and areas to appreciate and welcome the shape of things to come.

10 *The Government should ensure that more people are trained at all levels in these new skills.* A recent survey on educational computing concludes that: 'Computer education in Britain's schools, colleges and universities is largely out of touch and ill-equipped to meet the needs of the 80s.' Out of the 116 Local Education Authorities only a tiny handful have people employed solely to advise on teaching with computers. After 16, there is a need for more post school vocational training. Our polytechnics and universities are not turning

out sufficient electronic engineers and the bias against computer sciences needs to be rectified.

It would be naïve and misleading to say that such a programme would not cost money. It will, but a lot of this is already being made available in the public sector in many diverse and often unrecognizably associated ways. So the effectiveness of what we spend could be significantly improved. In the case of direct public investment the largest segment will be the capital expenditure of British Telecommunications, and as this is profitable they should be given the go-ahead to raise whatever they need from the market. The cash requirement of British Telecommunications will be reduced to the extent that the private sector is allowed to provide peripheral equipment. It is essential therefore that the telecommunications monopoly should be removed as soon as possible.

I would envisage some new money being made available. At the moment the total annual spend of the Department of Industry on Information Technology is about £17 million, which is roughly equivalent to three weeks' running losses of British Steel. We must get our industrial priorities right. Let us provide more for the wealth creators of the future.

The Blueprint for Education Reform, December 1986

What is wrong?

1 Widespread dissatisfaction with the *standards* of education.
2 The quality of teaching is not what it should be.
3 Too many children in the 4th and 5th year in our towns and cities absent themselves since they are bored.
4 A disciplined framework is all too rare.
5 There is a stark choice between the state sector 93% with private sector 7% – there are not enough halfway houses to allow the effective exercise of parental choice.
6 Too many LEAs are imposing their own political prejudices upon the system in their charge.
7 Their administration at the local level is frequently inefficient, over-bureaucratic and costly.
8 There is too much local variety in what is still regarded as a national system.

A major series of reforms are needed. There will be two major ways forward – one of centralizing the power to influence and determine the curriculum and the second of decentralizing the running and control of schools.

The Centralizing Measure

The Curriculum

1 We must establish a national core curriculum. This will lay down the basic subjects which must be taken up to the age of 16. This will involve a restriction of choice that is now made at 14. This will involve laying down in a much more prescriptive way the time that is devoted during the teaching years to various subjects.
2 We must also lay down within each subject – in both primary and secondary schools – the clear and specific targets of achievement at various ages. We should not shrink from keeping children down for a year in certain subjects to ensure that they acquire the basic skills in reading, writing, speaking and numeracy. Work is already well in hand on the maths curriculum following the Cockcroft report. The English Committee will provide a basis for an English curriculum.

3 Once established the curriculum will have to be inspected on a more regular basis than now. We will need a much enlarged national inspectorate. This will mean taking into Central Government employment the local inspectors and advisers.

4 We cannot just determine the curriculum ourselves as Central Government since that would create a precedent for any future Government. We must devise a series of checks and balances in the method of setting a core curriculum. I will present further ideas on this.

5 This must be done in a way that does not destroy the valuable methods of teaching that have been developed by our better teachers from their own initiative within their schools.

All this will need legislation preferably in the 1st session of the next Parliament. This is a major departure from the 1944 Act and indeed from the Institution of English education before that. We are the only country in the world that has developed in this way and the case for this major reform is evident and will be enforced vigorously.

The Decentralizing Measures

School Autonomy

1 Within 5 years every secondary school and many of the larger primary schools should be given control of their own budget. There are powers in the 1986 Act to allow the Secretary of State by order to require the LEAs to transfer some expenditure on items to the Schools. These should be sufficient to achieve our object.

We will need at least 5 years for this. It has taken Cambridgeshire 4 years to delegate limited budgetary control for 6 out of 48 secondary schools. However, some LEAs will be most reluctant to move down this road.

2 The weak link in this programme is the inadequacy of many Governing Bodies and the lack of financial managerial experience of heads and deputy heads. The new governing bodies with more elected parent governors; with the system of annual parent meetings and annual reports will be operating for the autumn term 1988. It is essential that we get good people to serve as governors since they will have control of a sizeable budget; increased powers over the appointment of the head and increased power of school discipline. We must run more courses for governors. It will be necessary to have some reserve powers for the LEAs and even the Secretary of State to make appointments to Governing Bodies which get into difficulties or which are being subverted by political groups.

3 The training of heads and deputies must be put in hand at once – before the Election. I also want to establish a staff college for the training of Heads and Deputies. Plans are in hand and we could announce this before the Election.

4 The key question is the basis on which the delegated budget should be determined. The LEA could decide as it does at the moment. We should

move away from this to a national formula based upon the cost to educate a child in a primary or secondary school. We should aim to move to the formula in as many secondary schools over the next 5 years. There must be some pilot projects. Legislation will be needed.

The independence of State Schools

1 We will allow the governing bodies of state-maintained schools, particularly secondary ones, to become independent charitable trusts. The school property would be transferred from the LEA to the Trusts. They would be funded on a formula basis by funds from the Secretary of State – they could be channelled via the LEA. Such schools would be obliged to conform to the National Curriculum. This would allow the parents and Governors in areas where the LEA is pursuing policies which are unpopular, to exercise their choice to run an independent school. This will only work if the quality of the governing bodies is improved. The governing bodies would need to get the approval of the parents for such a change. The trusts would have similar powers to voluntary aided schools, though we should consider whether this would extend to the dismissal of staff. The Chairman of the Governors will be a key figure – for he will have to go out and sell the school. In effect this would give such a school the status of a CTC.

2 At the same time we must pursue the establishment of at least 20 CTCs.

3 We must establish a system for the capital requirements of such schools. This could be done on extended formula but I do not want to rule out recourse to private capital markets.

The Extension of Choice in the State Sector

Within the next 5 years the great majority of schools will remain the responsibility of and under the control of the LEAs but this must not discourage us from taking the steps outlined above – indeed they are even more necessary.

In these schools we should move to a system of open enrolment. In this way the popular and well run schools will attract more children. They should be allowed to recruit up to their physical capacity.

The essential drive behind all these changes is to increase parental choice. This is the only way that fundamental reform can be achieved. The alternative would be a dictate from a greatly expanded DES. This could lead to a form of Health Service and we would be no surer of achieving what we want which is better schools.

The technical and vocational content of education

1 We must continue to build on the success of the TVEI for 14–18 year olds. Education for the not academically gifted child must be better and more relevant. This is principally a matter of building on the foundations we have laid. I hope that the CTCs will become beacons which others will seek to emulate.

2 It is important to make it easier and more attractive for such children to continue with education and training after 16. The academically gifted tend to go, the others do not yet they will need more training and more education. We must aim to increase the staying-on rate for 16-year-olds.

Party Leadership Election:
The Baker Rules

We will be taking many telephone calls on this subject and we will all, no doubt, be interrogated by our friends and acquaintances. For guidance on our position you should be aware of the following. You should say as little as possible about the contest, but be guided by these points.

1 I have made it clear that an election for leader is, in my view, both unnecessary and unwanted.
2 It is vital to restore Party unity and to return to the attack on Labour and the pursuit of positive Conservative policies. That will happen immediately after the unwelcome distraction of a leadership contest.
3 The conduct of the election is a matter for the Parliamentary Party with consultations as laid down in the rules. Conservative Central Office has no constitutional role to play.
4 If a caller is a Party member, they should be advised to express their views through their Constituency Association. CCO is *not* a route for this.
5 Under no circumstances will anyone here disparage those opposing the Prime Minister's Leadership. After the contest is over, we must ensure that Conservative colleagues can unite again behind the Party Leader. But we must not create the impression of neutrality; we are the office of the Leader of the Party and support her unreservedly.
6 But it is not appropriate for CCO to seek to interfere in the Parliamentary Party's exercise of its responsibilities; so far as possible, for us it will be 'business as usual'.

Index

Rent Acts, 17
Renton, David, 207
Renton, Tim, 309, 330, 358–9, 388, 393–5,
    397, 398, 400, 401, 463
Republican Party (US), 305–6
Research Machine, 61
Richard II (Shakespeure), 13–14
Richmond, Surrey, 7, 9
Richmond, Mark, 243
Richmond Theatre, Surrey, 7
Ricketts, Ray, 222
Ridley, Nicholas, 36, 142, 303, 330, 371, 379;
    and the Falklands, 65–6, 69; opposes 'Fair
    Fares', 99; and uniform business rate, 124;
    becomes Environment Secretary, 126,
    157–8; and community charge, 128–31, 137;
    character, 158–9; school funding, 220; and
    Thatcher, 258, 259, 415; and Barlow Clowes
    investors, 314; criticism of Germans, 349;
    resigns, 357–60; warns that the pound is
    overvalued, 371
Rifkind, Malcolm, 222, 402–3; becomes
    Scottish Secretary, 127, 304; and community
    charges, 136, 333; and Thatcher leadership
    campaign, 397, 405
Rippon, Geoffrey, 64, 114
Road to Wigan Pier (Orwell), 28
Robbins Report, 233
Rock, Patrick, 131
Roman Catholic Church, 217–18
Rome, Treaty of, 439–40
Rome Summit, 376–7, 378
Ronan Point disaster, 28
Rothschild, Victor, 36, 47–8, 121
Rottweilers, 435
Rowe, Andrew, 17
Royal College of Veterinary Surgeons, 435
Royal Commission on the Criminal Justice
    System, 431
Royal Shakespeare Company, 16–17
Royle, Tony, 69
'RPI minus X' formula, 84
RSPCA (Royal Society for the Prevention of
    Cruelty to Animals), 435
Ruhe, Volker, 348, 351
Rumbold, Angela, 141, 229, 241, 458
Runcie, Robert, Archbishop of Canterbury,
    147
Runciman, Lord, 431
Ryder, Richard, 55, 391–2, 402, 404, 434

Saatchi, Maurice, 467
Saatchi and Saatchi, 52, 181
Sainsbury, John, 147
Sainsbury, Susie, 69
Sainsbury, Tim, 69
St Andrew's University, 94
St James's School, Bolton, 219
St John Stevas, Norman, 58
St Marylebone, 32–3, 95–6
St Marylebone Grammar School, 42, 223, 224
St Paul's School, Hammersmith, London, 7–11

sales tax, 117
Salmon, John, 372
Sargeant, John, 397
satellites, 91–3
Scanlon, Hugh, 39
Schauble, Wolfgang, 446
Schenger Accord, 443
school governing bodies, 170
schools: management of, 211–12; per capita
    funding, 212–13; open enrolment, 213;
    grant-maintained, 214–21; parental ballots,
    215–16
Schools Examination and Assessment Council
    (SEAC), 198, 200
Schreiber, Mark, 34
science, 248–51; *see also under* national
    curriculum
Scotland, 20
Scotti, Signor (Italian Interior Minister), 446,
    447
Scottish Nationalists, 51
Scottish Office, 121, 122
SDP *see* Social Democratic Party
Second World War, 4–7, 15, 70
Securicor, 83
Security Services Bill, 259
Self Help Against Drugs Organization
    (SHADO), 148
Sellafield, 151
sex education, 170
Sexton, Stuart, 166, 224
Shackleton, Lord Edward, 66
SHADO (Self Help Against Drugs
    Organization), 148
Shakespeare, William, 3, 7, 9, 14, 30, 275
Sharp, Eric, 76, 77, 81, 156, 185
Shaw, George Bernard, 7
Sheffield, HMS, 72
Shell UK Ltd, 19
Shelton, Bill, 225
Sheppard, David, Bishop of Liverpool, 106,
    147
Sherbourne, Stephen, 270, 323
Sheridan, Richard Brinsley, 7
Shersby, Michael, 25–6
Shore, Peter, 30, 36, 66, 142
Sieff, Marcus, 38
Single European Act (1986), 283, 439, 441
sixth-form conferences, 46
Skegness Grammar School, Lincolnshire, 219
Skinner, Dennis, 77, 375, 383, 396, 413
small businesses, 47
Smart, Judy, 417
Smith, Dudley, 28
Smith, John, 346, 469
Smith, Rob, 168, 195
Smith, Sydney, 12
Smithies, Fred, 175
Soames, Mary, 287
Soames, Nicholas, 240
Social Democratic Party, (SDP), 50, 58, 71,
    77, 368, 467